Historic Cities: Issues in Urban Conservation

Readings in Conservation

Historic Cities: Issues in Urban Conservation

Edited by Jeff Cody and Francesco Siravo

The Getty Conservation Institute, Los Angeles

The Getty Conservation Institute

Timothy P. Whalen, *John E. and Louise Bryson Director*
Jeanne Marie Teutonico, *Associate Director, Programs*

The Getty Conservation Institute (GCI) works internationally to advance conservation practice in the visual arts—broadly interpreted to include objects, collections, architecture, and sites. The Institute serves the conservation community through scientific research, education and training, field projects, and the dissemination of information. In all its endeavors, the GCI creates and delivers knowledge that contributes to the conservation of the world's cultural heritage.

Published by the Getty Conservation Institute, Los Angeles
Getty Publications
1200 Getty Center Drive, Suite 500
Los Angeles, California 90049-1682
www.getty.edu/publications

Tevvy Ball, *Project Editor*
Sheila Berg, *Manuscript Editor*
Jeffrey Cohen, *Designer*
Amita Molloy, *Production*
Nina Damavandi and Kelly Peyton, *Image and Rights Acquisition*

Distributed in the United States and Canada by the University of Chicago Press
Distributed outside the United States and Canada by Yale University Press, London

Front cover: Beni Isguen, part of Ghardaia, Algeria, 2009. Detail. Photo by George Steinmetz. See p. 131.
Back cover: City Hall extension, Murcia, Spain, 1991–98. Photo by Michael Moran. See p. 406.

Printed in China

Library of Congress Cataloging-in Publication Data
Names: Cody, Jeffrey W., editor. | Siravo, Francesco, editor.
Title: Historic cities : issues in urban conservation / edited by Jeff Cody and Francesco Siravo.
Description: Los Angeles : The Getty Conservation Institute, [2019] | Includes bibliographical references and index.
Identifiers: LCCN 2018042061 | ISBN 9781606065938 (pbk.)
Subjects: LCSH: Historic preservation. | Cities and towns. | City planning.
Classification: LCC CC135 .H469 2019 | DDC 363.6/9—dc23 LC record available at https://lccn.loc.gov/2018042061

Contents

Foreword

We are pleased to publish *Historic Cities: Issues in Urban Conservation*, the eighth volume in the Getty Conservation Institute's Readings in Conservation series, which provides edited selections of significant texts that focus on particular areas of conservation. The initial volume, *Historical and Philosophical Issues in the Conservation of Cultural Heritage*, published in 1996, has been followed by readings on the conservation of paintings, photographs, textiles, archaeological sites, and paper and preventive conservation. We are delighted that these well-curated collections have been useful not only to students and teachers of conservation but also to wider audiences.

Conserving urban settlements is a major global challenge, and we expect that this volume, devoted to such a timely topic, will also find a broad following. Population increases, economic development, climate change, and a range of other factors have contributed to rising concerns about how best to use, rather than abuse, the rich architectural legacy in cities worldwide. At the Habitat-III conference in Quito, Ecuador, in October 2016, UNESCO underscored these concerns when it addressed the importance of culture in the context of sustainable urban development.

The GCI has been actively involved with urban conservation since 1991, when we initiated a six-year collaboration with the city of Quito to help preserve its historic colonial center. Since then, the GCI has worked locally and globally on urban conservation issues. Our major projects have included collaborating with the municipality of Los Angeles to develop and implement a monumental citywide survey of historic resources; assisting the Organization of World Heritage Cities in putting together five World Symposiums and Congresses for mayors of cities on the World Heritage List; organizing an international symposium in 2013, "Minding the Gap: The Role of Contemporary Architecture in the Historic Environment"; and partnering with organizations in Southeast Asia to develop and deliver urban conservation planning courses for planners and architects in the region.

This volume was edited by two colleagues with extensive global experience. In addition to consulting for the GCI, Francesco Siravo has worked for many years with the Historic Cities Programme of the Aga Khan Trust for Culture, primarily in Africa and Asia. Jeff Cody has worked at the GCI since 2004, coordinating several education and training courses, including those related to urban conservation. We are grateful to Francesco and Jeff for their commitment to this project and for bringing their considerable knowledge about historic cities to this stimulating and richly illustrated volume. We hope it will be of interest to those who love cities and of great value to all those involved with protecting historic urban environments.

Timothy P. Whalen, *John E. and Louise Bryson Director*
The Getty Conservation Institute

Preface

Too many cities worldwide are in crisis. When measured by ecological, social, and other criteria, many cities fall far short of delivering healthy conditions in which ever greater numbers of residents are living. As noted in the Rockefeller Foundation's *Century of the City: No Time to Lose* (2008), by 2050 not only will three quarters of the world's population live in cities, but most urban growth will occur in the Global South, placing huge burdens on housing, transportation, and other infrastructural systems.[1] As urban populations mushroom, cities and their leaders often lack effective means of coping with the myriad implications that stem from more people living in "mal-developed" conditions.[2] Some of that "mal-development" is recent—for example, the effects of refugee migration after massive urban destruction in the eastern Mediterranean region since 2003—while some of it arose more incrementally, and globally, from poorly conceived assumptions concerning progress during a carbon-based era when climate change seemed a distant worry and when modernization was sometimes equated with the numbers and heights of structures.[3] There are several crucial dimensions of this seemingly unstoppable trend toward global hyperurbanization, ranging from health and education to shelter and governance. This book focuses on what might be called a cultural dimension associated with urbanization: how to protect or conserve a reasonable amount of significant "historic fabric" in cities so that tangible links to the past can provide foundational bridges into the future.[4]

This book is not intended to be a step-by-step primer, with easy-to-follow recipes. Nor is it a constellation of case studies representing every region, although naturally particular cities are discussed in detail. Instead, our approach has been to achieve several kinds of balance: between theories and practices, between "Eurocentric" historic urbanism and other kinds of global cities, and between older perspectives and newer trends to confront the challenges of urban conservation. We have defined "reading" in two ways: words that can be read in the conventional sense of "reading" (the essays making up the eight parts of the book); and compelling images that can be "read" semiotically, as reflecting crucial urban conservation realities (the visual summaries following each part). The appendix comprises selected charters, declarations, and principles concerning urban conservation that attest to the protracted nature of the challenges associated with this multifaceted kind of conservation endeavor, in many geographic and cultural contexts. We have not included a comprehensive bibliography devoted to urban conservation, in part because such an exhaustive list would consume a huge chunk of budgeted space but also because by the time such a list is published, it is already obsolete.[5] We have instead selected a broad spectrum of perspectives regarding urban conservation—several from authors who, because of either linguistic or cultural obscurity, have remained out of the limelight—that are introduced as catalysts for further learning by conservation professionals, within professional architecture or planning curricula, or in other university and training contexts where urban transformation as a subject of study is being broached. Our hope is that this text will fulfill the simultaneous needs for possessing a breadth of perspectives concerning cities with historic places and a depth of insights about conservation approaches that might be effective within those unique cities.

One of the key rationales underlying this text is that as global urbanization runs rampant, architectural heritage becomes more imperiled, fragile, and expedient. This is true not only for individual buildings but also for a broader scope of urban structures and spaces. Few historic places survive the onslaught of poorly coordinated mal-development, an artifact of harmful planning practices related to so-called urban renewal that have rewarded investors while ignoring less wealthy and less powerful residents from North American cities in the 1960s to Chinese (and other) cities more recently. All too often, insufficiently protected historic places either have been razed due to governmental policies, zoning regulations, and plot ratios or have undergone progressively destructive deterioration triggered by exploding demographics and failing infrastructure. Tourism, as beneficial as it might be for economic and cultural reasons, has contributed to the crass commercialization of historic places (e.g., Venice, Italy, or Lijiang, China). At the level of individual buildings, ill-conceived policies calling for the retention of skin-deep portions of historic buildings have resulted in lamentable "facadomies" in cities worldwide, while at a larger scale mega-events such as the Olympic Games have led to urban evisceration (e.g., Beijing). In the past century, many cities have been razed by warfare: two world wars and the subsequent Cold War in Europe (Dresden, Coventry, and Bucharest); and in the early twenty-first century, this has occurred throughout the Middle East (Aleppo, Damascus, Baghdad, Mosul, Kabul, Herat, Tripoli, Sana'a, etc.).

The architect Marwa Al-Sabouni has written a book, *The Battle for Home: The Memoir of a Syrian Architect* (2016), about the unimaginable challenges confronting Homs, one of those ravaged cities. In an interview with a journalist in July 2016, Al-Sabouni reflected on the role of architecture in Homs: "Architecture should hold the values—the aesthetic values, the moral values—of the place. Architecture should contribute to the life of the people. It should be responsible for their spiritual, social and psychological needs, not only . . . the practical needs."[6] She was asked whether she thought rebuilding a city on "a blank slate" would be "an interesting challenge," to which she replied, "It shouldn't be done from scratch. . . . [T]he place, even if it's destroyed, the place has a memory. And it's not . . . just in the stones, because architecture, if we are talking like cars, . . . is the path for the vehicles to move on. And so as the road takes you to places, also architecture takes you to places[,] . . . not by configuration. It takes you even with the details. Each detail has a value to hold and suggestion to make. So it shouldn't be done from scratch. It should hold the memory of what was important for people in the place."

If a reasonable amount of visual or cultural heritage is to survive as the recipient of value or memory, as Al-Sabouni aptly expressed it, and if we truly hope to leave some historic portions of our cities "inheritable" in a way that doesn't trivialize their significance, then we need to recognize the losses occurring to historic urban places worldwide and reassess how these places are being conserved, restored, reused, and rehabilitated or, conversely, how they are being ignored, mangled, subverted, or demolished. As the architecture critic Edwin Heathcote has suggested, many "contemporary cities are excoriated for their fumbling attempts at creating new forms of urbanity, new ideals of beauty. . . . Perhaps we have lost the knack of creating beautiful cities."[7] However, the implications of the worldwide loss of urban historic places reach well beyond aesthetics or nostalgia, because often when urban places are fundamentally transformed, those who had previously inhabited or used those places become themselves expelled or otherwise displaced. Erasing historic urban architecture and sites is often a harbinger of social inequality and spatial reconfiguration. Finding a "creative synergy between old and new, between change and continuity" is a daunting challenge for those seeking to retain or create viable urban places.[8]

This collection of readings seeks to highlight that challenge and assist those who face it. First, though, we should confront linguistic challenges, because the title and subtitle of this book feature two pairs of words, *historic cities* and *urban conservation,* whose connotations can be confusing. As perceptive scholars of conservation have explained, "The 'historic city' was conceived [in the mid-nineteenth century] in contrast to the modern city ["the transformation of urban space wrought by the industrial revolution"][,] . . . [which was] invented and reinforced through cycles of destruction, as the old core was challenged by modern technologies and lifestyles."[9] Thus, a binary opposition was created between "historic cities" and "modern cities," which, as Michele Lamprakos suggests, "underwrites the myth of progress[,] . . . bifurcates the city into old and new, and [amputates] it from its region."[10] Other scholars and practitioners have taken issue with the word *city* itself, preferring instead (as adopted by UNESCO in 2011) the term "historic urban landscape."[11] In this book, we refer to "historic cities" not because we reject the holistic approach to urban conservation suggested by proponents of "the historic urban landscape" and not because we seek to split the historic from the nonhistoric but instead (a) to reinforce the point that many cities have historic components, buildings, sites, spaces, and "details" that embody memory, as the architect Al-Sabouni suggested; and (b) to emphasize that most historic places need particular kinds of stewardship, attention, and sensitivity in terms of their planning and protection. All cities are not historic, but when historic places within cities are affected by maldevelopment, sensitive stewardship is warranted.

This kind of particularized care for the conservation of historic places in cities is what we refer to as "urban conservation"; these two words should not be construed as advocating either the sole protection of singular monuments or the wholesale freezing of an entire vibrant city, which would be an unrealistic exercise in nostalgic excess that would result in stasis, paralysis, kitsch, and other negative outcomes. However, equally untenable results occur when policy makers allow neoliberal market forces to exclusively determine what occurs within and to historic urban places.[12] Two respected conservation scholars have defined urban conservation "as a process that seeks to coordinate and regulate the process of continuity and change of an urban structure and its values."[13] We concur with the thrust of this definition, because it assumes the need for both particular, technical expertise (when intervening sensitively and professionally on buildings or spaces erected with a range of historic materials and structural systems) and holistic involvement from many kinds of stakeholders in the ongoing urban drama that leads from the present into the future. Urban conservation seeks to protect the significance of historic places in dynamic cities, so that as change inevitably occurs, it is managed carefully and constantly so that urban transformation does not imply an obliteration of the past.

As we probe relevant issues in urban conservation, we are advancing a thesis, the first portion of which suggests that globally during roughly the past two hundred years many cities have been transformed by at least one of three critical ruptures: first, the dramatic effects in the nineteenth century of the Industrial Revolution, urban redevelopment, and colonialism; second, those related to the destructions that took place during World War II; and third, those related to phenomena of globalization, mass tourism, and unparalleled real estate development that in the second decade of the twenty-first century continue to challenge historic urban areas. We devote the first three parts of the book to presenting this portion of our argument. Parts I and II reflect the physical and geographic differences in how and where humans have created cities over time, as well as the historical relationships that have been created between physical historic cities and metaphysical, spiritual, or religious realities. In part III, we outline the reactions to the three pivotal transformations we are emphasizing. In part IV, we explore the implications of the clear divide that emerged in the early twentieth century between those who advocated the idea of continuity in city planning and those who considered the old city a tabula rasa, to be replaced by a new, ready-made concept of the city.[14] In part V, we confront the challenge of how to "read" the historic city, both in terms of its physicality and form and in terms of its less tangible dimensions. Although our emphasis in this book remains largely with physical, or tangible, issues of urban conservation, we are well aware of the importance of culturally mapping and then conserving so-called intangible resources, and some key readings highlight this point. The final three parts of the book (VI, VII, and VIII) explore both historic and contemporary conservation practices that underscore the importance of timely, careful, and strategic urban interventions, the inclusion of ideas and other active participation from all urban stakeholders, the crucial need for honest public governance, and the fundamental importance of seeing urban conservation as a holistic cluster of actions involving the entire city and its hinterland, that is, its historic urban landscape.

This book's genesis occurred during a pivotal time in the early twenty-first century, not only because of global urbanization and its implications, but also because of the new meanings attached to the notion of urban conservation. The terms "historic urban landscape" and "intangible resources" reflect the worthy intention to capture the physical complexity and immaterial attributes that define historic urban areas, but they are often interpreted in ways that are inaccurate or misleading, especially when translated into other languages or called upon to justify doubtful outcomes. Another keyword related to urban conservation is "sustainability," a fundamental concept in the UN's Habitat III conference in Quito, Ecuador, in 2016 and crucial to managing historic areas (see part VII) but a concept that may nonetheless be confusing, especially if used as a buzzword, without a clear definition of its appropriateness and range of applicability. "Sustainability" can thus be invoked either to carry out unjustified retrofitting of historic buildings or to validate questionable transformations that may introduce invasive new materials and technologies.

More recently, a new trend in conceptualizing conservation has emerged—"critical conservation"—offered as a distinct, innovative field of inquiry by several postgraduate architectural conservation training programs worldwide.[15] Some critical conservation adherents suggest that this new approach is justified by the need to overcome the dichotomies past/future, traditional/modern, conservation/development. One of the aims of those advocating for critical conservation is to offer a wider range of critical tools to question traditional conservation approaches and actions while also offering a critique of (without necessarily outright criticizing) potentially outmoded methodologies and well-entrenched international organizations.[16] At this stage it is unclear what contribution critical conservation will eventually bring to the field of urban conservation or how that approach might evolve as challenges related to urban conservation persist.

What seems already evident from the existing literature, however, is that denying the specificity of historic urban areas is antithetical to the fundamental premise of this book. Many of the readings we have selected, starting with Cederna's passionate text at the beginning of part I, underline the fact that our common urban past, far from being the result of an undifferentiated historical continuum, is in reality a historically determined, finite resource, with formative characters that are distinct, unique, and unrepeatable. As such, it requires methods of interpretation, planning, and management that are markedly different from those applicable to the contemporary city. A recognition of the identity, significance, and inherent qualities of each place is the necessary first step to ensure continuity and compatible change in historic urban areas (or "landscapes").

This fundamental premise has helped us navigate through the vast literature on historic cities and the rapidly evolving terms, theories, and practices of urban conservation in the early twenty-first century. Ultimately, our intention has been to assemble a critical mass of practical references and ideas from several global contexts. They are meant to educate, inspire, and motivate the search for continuity in historic urban places, so that they can be inherited, together with their rich heritage and significance, by those who will come after us.

Notes

1. Neil R. Peirce and Curtis W. Johnson, eds., *Century of the City: No Time to Lose* (New York: Rockefeller Foundation, 2008).
2. Ibid., 12.
3. See, e.g., regarding China, Piper Gaubatz, "China's Urban Transformation: Patterns and Processes of Morphological Change in Beijing, Shanghai and Guangzhou," *Urban Studies* 36, no. 9 (1999): 1495–1521.
4. This point mirrors some key conclusions from Habitat III (2016). See, e.g., Nancy Duxbury, Jyoti Hosagrahar, and Jordi Pascual, "Why Must Culture Be at the Heart of Sustainable Urban Development?," United Cities and Local Goverments, 2016, www.agenda21culture.net.
5. This is not to suggest that bibliographies are not helpful. See, e.g., the annotated bibliography, "Contemporary Architecture in the Historic Environment," www.getty.edu/conservation/publications_resources/pdf_publications/cahe_bibliography.html.
6. See www.npr.org/2016/07/20/486785267/the-battle-for-home-traces-syrias-history-through-architecture.
7. Edwin Heathcote, "The Bad and the Beautiful," *Financial Times*, 12 January 2013.
8. Michele Lamprakos, "The Idea of the Historic City," *Change Over Time* 4, no. 1 (Spring 2014): 29.
9. Ibid., 27; and in italics, a phrase defining "the modern city," from Francoise Choay, *The Invention of the Historic Monument*, trans. Lauren M. O'Connell (Cambridge: Cambridge University Press, 2001), 120.
10. Lamprakos, "The Idea of the Historic City," 29.
11. See also Francesco Bandarin and Ron Van Oers, eds., *Reconnecting the City: The Historic Landscape Approach and the Future of Urban Heritage* (Chichester: John Wiley & Sons, 2015).
12. For neoliberalism and the "heritagization" of urban resources, see Chiara De Cesari and Michael Herzfeld, "Urban Heritage and Social Movements," in *Global Heritage: A Reader*, ed. Lynn Meskell (London: Wiley-Blackwell, 2015), 171–96.
13. Silvio Mendes Zancheti and Jukka Jokilehto, "Values and Urban Conservation Planning: Some Reflections on Principles and Definitions," *Journal of Architectural Conservation* 3, no. 1 (1997): 44.
14. In contrast to this approach, see Bryony Roberts, ed., *Tabula Plena: Forms of Urban Preservation* (Zurich: Lars Muller, 2016).
15. See, e.g., Harvard University's Critical Conservation master's program in the Graduate School of Design; the University of Göteborg (Sweden); the Australia National University (Canberra); and the International Institute of Asian Studies (University of Leiden, the Netherlands).
16. See, e.g., Rodney Harrison, *Heritage: Critical Approaches* (London: Routledge, 2013), 8–9, where he laments that "heritage is increasingly officially defined and governed by a common set of philosophies that have their origins in a particular, modern, Euro-American way of thinking."

Acknowledgments

This volume has benefited greatly from the advice and kindness of many colleagues in the fields of architecture, urban planning, and heritage conservation. Eight of these colleagues formed our advisory committee, which steered us and gave us confidence in the face of many challenges. In particular, we would like to thank Françoise Descamps, Claus-Peter Echter, Jukka Jokilehto, Susan Macdonald, Azar Soheil, Christian Ost, and Dennis Rodwell. Sadly, the eighth member of our committee, Ron Van Oers, died unexpectedly in April 2015. His deep interest, knowledge, and commitment to urban conservation will be missed by all who knew him.

This book would not have been possible without strong support from the very beginning from Jeanne Marie Teutonico, Associate Director of Programs for the Getty Conservation Institute (GCI), and Tim Whalen, the John E. and Louise Bryson Director of the GCI. Susan Macdonald, Head of the GCI's Buildings and Sites Department, has also been an ardent supporter of our work from the outset. Cynthia Godlewski, who guided publication of the previous volumes in the *Readings in Conservation* series, has been consistently encouraging, insightful, and patient in guiding the production of this volume. Other GCI colleagues—Anna Duer and Alison Reilly, in particular—have kindly prodded us along as they organized files, triple-checked references, secured copyright permissions, and solved countless other problems.

We also thank the attentive and committed team of Getty Publications staff who shepherded this book through complex editing and production stages. In particular, we are grateful to Tevvy Ball, project editor, for his savvy and willingness to explore a new format for the images; Sheila Berg, for her expert copyediting; Sharon Grevet, David Sánchez, and Aimee Ducey-Gessner, for their precise translations of assorted excerpts; Jeffrey Cohen, for his excellent design; Amita Molloy, for her skillful production coordination; and Nina Damavandi and Kelly Peyton, for their indefatigable persistence in securing permission for reproducing images in the Visual Summaries.

This project is the result of our combined international experience in the field of urban conservation. Francesco Siravo wishes to acknowledge Leonardo Benevolo, who first inspired him to engage in urban conservation and provided early guidance in the development of conservation plans for the historic centers of Anagni, Lucca, Rome, and

Urbino; Richard Leakey, who as director of the National Museums of Kenya entrusted him with the preparation of his first conservation plan for Lamu, Kenya; and Stefano Bianca and Cameron Rashti, the former and present directors of the Historic Cities Programme of the Aga Khan Trust for Culture (AKTC), for the opportunities and conservation experience gained as a longtime consultant for the AKTC in Bosnia-Herzegovina, Egypt, Malaysia, Mali, Pakistan, and Zanzibar.

Jeff Cody's experience, primarily in Asian contexts, stemmed in part from his teaching and professional work at the Chinese University of Hong Kong from 1995 to 2004, where he benefited greatly from working with several city-obsessed colleagues: Tunney Lee, Tom Campanella, Nelson Chen, Puay-peng Ho, and Wallace Chang. At Cornell University as a graduate student, Jeff's urban history interests were nurtured by three mentors: John W. Reps, Michael A. Tomlan, and Sherman G. Cochran. In 2016, Jeff was a fellow at the American Academy in Rome, where for six superlative months he conducted research related to this book and was assisted not only by the exceedingly generous staff of the American Academy but also by kind help from Lorenzo Berna, Giancarlo Cataldi, Allan Ceen, Pier Luigi Cervellati, Piero Garau, Gian Luigi Maffei, Steven Semes, Nicholas Stanley-Price, and Giuseppe Strappa. Jeff also benefited greatly from the insights of instructors and participants in the short, intensive urban conservation courses he coordinated in Malaysia from 2012 to 2015.

As this book progressed, friends and colleagues in France, India, and Italy provided valuable suggestions, particularly Pierre Clément, Françoise Ged, Charles Goldblum, and Nathalie Lancret, as well as Rahul Mehrotra, Azhar Tyabji, and Francesco Scoppola. Jonathan Bell, Theeng Kok, Miquel Ortiz, and Ian Dull also provided very helpful research assistance during the early stages of the work.

Finally, we would like to acknowledge our wives. Francesco's wife, Ann Pulver, has been an engaged colleague in Anagni, Lamu, and Zanzibar. Jeff's wife, Mary Day, now deceased, was someone whose love of historic cities and keen talent for finding clarity in disorder helped Jeff bring this publication to fruition.

As with any work of such scope, especially considering the multifaceted dimensions of historic cities and the thorny conservation challenges they present worldwide, this volume undoubtedly contains imprecisions and errors, despite the wonderful help received to prevent their occurrence. Naturally, we take full responsibility for these.

Note to the Reader

The readings in this volume come from a wide range of historical and contemporary sources and a variety of genres. In preparing these texts for publication here, a number of conventions were observed.

Every attempt has been made to respect the textual integrity of the original material. Capitalization has in most cases been standardized in heads and subheads, and footnotes in the original publication appear here as endnotes. With texts originally written in English, in all other stylistic matters—spelling, punctuation, capitalization—the original style has been retained. Footnotes and references have not been edited or completed with additional information but appear as they did in the original publication.

Editorial additions, restorations, and corrections to the original text appear within brackets. When the original texts have been editorially abridged for publication here, deleted passages within the body of the excerpted text are indicated by ellipses in brackets; cross-references to elided material have been deleted. Elisions of more than one paragraph are indicated by the symbol —w—, placed on a separate line. Ellipses appearing in the original text are indicated by ellipses without brackets. If there are numbered notes, and some notes have been elided, the remaining notes have been renumbered consecutively. Similarly, if there are numbered illustrations, and some have been deleted, the remaining illustrations have been renumbered consecutively. Type garbled in the original has been corrected in brackets. To avoid redundancy, where the original text contains information that has been editorially extracted and used in the chapter title (author name, book or chapter title, etc.), it has been silently deleted from the text itself.

The readings have been dated and, for the most part, arranged thematically in each of the book's eight parts. Dates appear as part of the title of each reading. When a text's date of composition differs significantly from its date of publication, and the date of composition is known, the date of composition is given in the title. With previously published translations, the publication or composition date of the text in its original language, if known, is given. For all readings, the date of publication and the original title of the work, as well as the edition and page numbers from which our selection has been taken, appear in the source note at the bottom of the first page.

For texts originally written in a language other than English and translated for this volume, every effort has been made to produce a translation that is both accurate and, as far as possible, stylistically faithful to the original. Particular attention has been paid to the specific meanings of conservation terminology. Care has been taken to provide translations that are contemporaneous with the texts and reflect the meanings of the historical period in which they were written.

Part I

The Shared Nature of the Historic City

Defining the nature of the historic city is an issue that comes up frequently in the specialized literature[1] and among administrators, professionals, and residents who face the challenging problems posed by its traditional fabric: If there is such a thing as the "historic city," does it have features that are similar across countries and cultures? And is there something specific about the historic character of the city that warrants a special approach to both conservation and city planning?

In many respects, providing an answer to these questions lies at the very core of the readings presented in this book, because if there is no basis for assigning special value or recognizing a distinct character of the historic city, then there is no need to identify criteria and methods for intervening in traditional city contexts that are separate from those that apply to any contemporary city. The same planning methodology could be used indifferently in all urban situations, irrespective of age and geographic location and regardless of the specific problem to be addressed. Planning for a new city, a new expansion area, or a preexisting city sector would only be different facets of an all-encompassing discipline, characterized by homogeneity of principles and practical applications.

Instead, one of the main premises of this book is that the historic city is indeed a distinct urban entity and that few of the conventional planning criteria that apply to the contemporary city can be used or easily adapted to a traditional urban context. The very nature of the historic city demands that we understand the profound disconnect that has occurred in city building since the Industrial Revolution; that we move away from a purely quantitative or mechanical interpretation of urban phenomena to look at the symbolic meanings and the very different physical patterns that underlie the cities of the past; and that we equip ourselves to recognize and appreciate the spirit of places, the subtle clues that set historic places apart from the look-alike sameness of most present-day urban developments.

Part I presents a selection of readings that address and clarify some of these aspects. The first reading, from Antonio Cederna, examines what makes our epoch different from the previous ones and explains why the cities inherited from the past are so

Hubert Sattler, *Panorama of Constantinople from the Suleymaniye Camii*, 1844. Detail. See p. 53.

different from those of today. It rebuts the oft-repeated argument that since cities have always been transformed we should do the same and that in fact we have the right, if not the historical obligation, to leave our mark on the urban landscape. These views are usually accompanied by apodictic statements, such as "Cities should not become museums"; "We do not want to embalm our cities and landscapes"; or "Life cannot be frozen in time."[2] Cederna's passionate analysis argues that what may sound reasonable or superficially true is actually based on a poor understanding of history and on flawed and sometimes dishonest arguments.

The subsequent readings in this part dispel the idea that we can apply present-day criteria to interpret and intervene in the traditional urban fabric. This awareness is important in order to counteract the widespread perception that historic cities have to conform to today's views and demands in order to justify their continued existence and "prove" their sustainability for the future. This is even truer if we consider that contemporary expectations, which at first often seem fundamental requirements, are themselves transient and eventually superseded by different and more sensible views. A good case in point is the obsession with bringing motorized traffic into historic settings, which, at least in Europe and the United States, prevailed throughout the 1960s and part of the 1970s[3] but which was later discarded in favor of greater emphasis on public transportation, bicycling, and pedestrian movement, even outside the old city areas.[4] This was not only the result of a fuller appreciation of the damage inflicted by road widening and traffic-related air pollution in historic city centers, but it was also due to a general trend—fueled in part by so-called New Urbanists—toward more intelligent forms of city growth based on mixed land uses, walkable neighborhoods, a variety of transportation modes, compact design, and the preservation of existing man-made and environmental assets.[5]

In many respects, when thinking about current interpretations of the urban landscape, it is important to remind ourselves that past generations looked at the city in ways that were different from ours. As Joseph Rykwert explains in reading 2, common memories, religious events, natural features, symbols of power, cultural habits, and even emotions were associated in the past with the spaces, streets, memorials, and monuments of the city. That we are no longer able to fully appreciate these associations is no justification for disregarding and obliterating them. It is precisely this stratification of meaning that accounts for the urban qualities and fuller experience often described by travelers and residents who visit and live in historic city areas. These qualities are interconnected and will remain embedded in these special places for as long as we are able to preserve and maintain their presence in the physical settings of our cities.

The spiritual nature of the city of the past is emphasized by Seyyed Hossein Nasr, who, in reading 3, highlights the many parallels found in traditional Chinese, Christian, Hindu, and Islamic sources, in which the city is interpreted as a tangible reflection of spiritual and archetypal symbols that transcend contingent realities. These symbolic meanings persist through time and are deeply rooted in the fabric of old cities, as Paul Wheatley also suggests in his "City as Symbol," in spite of the transformations that have occurred over time. Nasr's contention is that they continue to be essential for "our own identity as human beings . . . [and] our spiritual health." It was the *humanness* of traditional architecture and town settings that Bernard Rudofsky captured in his eye-opening exhibition, *Architecture without Architects*.[6]

It is certainly true, as Wheatley highlights in reading 4, that the physical shells of cities that still exist were designed for very different purposes and have often proved difficult to adapt to the imperatives of modern industrial societies. However, this is more a reflection of our inability or unwillingness to understand the nature of these spaces than any insurmountable obstacle to adapting them in ways that are compatible and respectful. One of the hallmarks of the traditional fabric of old cities has been its responsiveness to change and ability to take on added significance over time. But this is possible today only if change is accompanied by an understanding of the nature of these spaces, based on a recognition of their transformations over time, external constraints, and physical consistency, as well as original meanings and purposes.

All these aspects have an immediate bearing on what Christian Norberg-Schulz in reading 5 defines as the *genius loci*, the sense of place that embodies a "meaningful correspondence between site, settlement and architectural detail," all features that contribute to the strength of a place and can improve its prospects for the future, although only if properly "understood and respected." Norberg-Schulz's analysis includes an explicit condemnation of the prevailing laissez-faire attitude that ignores the identity of places and eventually gives free rein to the blind acceptance of change for change's sake. This attitude is a relatively new and untested phenomenon in societies around the world, often imposed from the top, which goes against a basic human need: the need for identity and stability of place as a precondition for the nurturing of stable and self-confident communities. As Norberg-Schulz states, "We have every reason to believe that the human alienation so common today, to a high extent is due to the scarce possibilities of orientation and identification offered by the modern environment." Laurence Loh (reading 6) relates genius loci to Asian contexts, arguing that "spirit of place conveys the cultural essence of a site," but Loh also links this distinctive, place-rooted spirit to the larger concept "authenticity," as ratified in documents such as the Nara Document on Authenticity (1994) and as reflected in award-winning conservation projects throughout Asia. Loh emphasizes the importance of validating "intangible heritage," expressions of which are "'spiritual assets' that are unquantifiable and impossible to label, but nevertheless are central to the Asian approach to heritage conservation."

Lewis Mumford, in his iconic essay "What Is a City?," emphasizes in reading 7 that "cities are a product of time" but that "by the diversity of its time structures, the city in part escapes the tyranny of a singular present, and the monotony of a future that consists in repeating only a single beat heard in the past." Writing from an American perspective but attempting to be universal in scope, Mumford points to the crucial connections between "the countryside" and the city, between "remote forces and influences" in the city that "intermingle with the local."

The accelerated pace of change we are witnessing today is the result of the dramatic and unprecedented phenomena of rapid population growth, massive migration across continents, social inequality, international conflict, and the predominance of unrestricted diktats of market forces, often associated with contemporary "neoliberal" economics.[7] But when we examine the debate surrounding the transformation of historic cities and urban areas more closely, finding a reasoned assessment of the underlying causes, a recognition of the values and common assets worth protecting, or a dispassionate evaluation of alternative strategies for governance and controlled transformation is rare indeed. Rather the debate is often based on cultural biases and ideological confrontation.[8] The arguments used by the twentieth-century modernist avant-garde, with its iconoclastic approach to the past, are often revived to demand development at any cost. However, this demand seems oblivious to the fact that modernism itself should be seen and interpreted from a historical perspective, as a then-justifiable break with traditional forms and styles that has today run its course.

In the early twenty-first century, as a result of the pervasive and irreversible diffusion of the International style and its later developments, this approach no longer has any justification when dealing with our ever-shrinking urban heritage. Nevertheless, most arguments in favor of unrestricted change in historic areas—such as those that compare conservation to embalming or an immoral act of falsification, or those that see conservation as an undue restraint on private initiative and personal creativity—are intended to justify or condone practices of demolition and reconstruction, whose ultimate purpose is to gain from higher land and rent values, often at the expense of public assets and against the will of the majority of the residents. Very rarely are such simple realities openly recognized for what they are, or their ideological pretenses demystified to achieve a more balanced appreciation of old cities as cultural experiences that must not be lost.

Notes

1. Michele Lamprakos, "The Idea of the Historic City," *Change Over Time* 4, no. 1 (Spring 2014): 8–38.
2. This is a cliché that resurfaces periodically in debates and seminars, such as the one reportedly expressed by Rem Koolhaas during a presentation at the Venice IUAV in June 2014: "Cities change and it is impossible to halt the process as the city is an organism and, as such, inevitably changes over time" (translated from Italian, as reported at www.ediliziaeterritorio.ilsole24ore.com/art/progetti-e-concorsi/2012-06-14/koolhaas-purini-secchi-dialogano-142731.php?uuid=AbHNjCsF). This maxim states the obvious, but it also seems to suggest that since change is inevitable any attempt to manage it is essentially a pointless exercise.
3. A critical review of traffic problems and solutions to facilitate vehicular movement in towns is contained in Colin Buchanan, *Traffic in Towns: A Study of the Long Term Problems of Traffic in Urban Areas* (London: HMSO, 1963).
4. Peter Newman and Jeffrey Kenworthy, *Sustainability and Cities: Overcoming Automobile Dependency* (Washington, DC: Island Press, 1999).
5. Andres Duany and Jeff Speck with Mike Lydon, *The Smart Growth Manual* (New York: McGraw Hill, 2010).
6. Bernard Rudofsky, *Architecture without Architects: A Short Introduction to Non-Pedigreed Architecture* (London: Academy Editions, 1964).
7. Lamprakos, "The Idea of the Historic City," 27.
8. "Isn't history moving forward? Can we oppose its fateful course? Doesn't life have its rights? Don't we already have too many monuments in our country? Can we 'freeze' or 'embalm,' etc., a landscape or a monumental complex?" Quotation from Antonio Cederna, *I vandali in casa* (Vandals at Home), 13, illustrating some of the arguments often used to justify the need for change.

Reading

1

Antonio Cederna

Vandals at Home (1956)

In his passionate introduction to a series of articles denouncing the destruction of Italian monuments and sites, Antonio Cederna, an archaeologist turned journalist and environmentalist, explains why it is wrong to assume that because all epochs have destroyed the artistic heritage of the previous ones, our epoch also has the right to change at will the form and structure of historic cities. He points out that unlike any epochs before, our relationship with the past is the result of more than 150 years of historical criticism as well as archaeological and other scientific studies. This has led to an irreversible critical understanding of history and a fuller appreciation of heritage. Consequently, Cederna advocates a clear distinction between the old and new parts of the city: being truly modern, in his view, means respecting the past for what it is while responding to the needs of contemporary societies.

INTRODUCTION

Italy's destroyers hold dear another more ambitious argument that would like to be defined as "historical." With swelled chests they assert that, seeing as how each epoch has destroyed the monuments of the previous one, then they too have the right to destroy the past to reconstruct the new. And as each epoch has left behind its own lasting imprint, so must ours also leave its own "stamp" on the city, alongside and on top of that of the past. With such declarations, they feel themselves to be a living part of history, indeed (the irony is palpable) of tradition, the interpreters and prophets of contemporary society. The absurdity of this further pretext is apparent if we can shake off the usual laziness.

From Antonio Cederna, *I vandali in casa* (Bari: Editori Laterza, 1956), 6–11, 13–16. (Excerpt translated from the Italian.)

A first consideration teaches us that the "ancients," from the Middle Ages to the nineteenth century, cannot be in any instance masters, and only coarse minds can take inspiration from them as leading by example, the case that interests us. The ancients, in fact, have been responsible over the centuries for wreaking boundless and irreparable havoc, time after time, vehemently deplored and reflected upon by the intelligent people who were in attendance. During the Middle Ages, magnificent classical monuments were destroyed; in the Renaissance, magnificent classical and medieval monuments; in the Baroque era, magnificent medieval and Renaissance monuments; in the Neoclassical period, they destroyed magnificent medieval, Renaissance, and Baroque monuments. From century to century, thousands of Greek and Roman statues were reduced to mortar, mountains of temples, palaces, and tombs were baked in the furnaces, limitless expanses of mosaics and frescoes were turned to dust, gigantic pagan and Christian monuments were annihilated that it had seemed were to persist for all eternity. Can we continue today down this road? Can we ignore the substantial differences that separate, also in this domain, our times from the entirety of the past? To the contrary, we today have conducted ourselves in a diametrically opposed manner, because something new happened that made us different and better.

Today, we (civilized people) do not plaster walls with the dust of ancient statues, we do not build buildings with the travertine of the Colosseum or with bricks from the imperial baths, we no longer rip up the roof tiles of the Pantheon for our own roofs or the columns of the Forum for our churches, we no longer replace the head of an ancient statue with our own portrait, we no longer use sarcophagi as bathtubs, nor *bucchero* goblets as chamber pots. The Parthenon no longer serves as an armory, and we would not transform a nymphaeum into a gas station to adapt it to the new era, or a basilica into a train station. History itself forbids us, which the vandals in vain purport to support by ignoring it. Progress forbids us, and civilization. Among other things, the disciplines that only in recent times we invented forbid it: historical studies, the sciences of antiquity, archaeology, art history, aesthetics, and so on, that have taught us to historically understand the work of art in its tangible and specific values, and at the least to separate artistic appreciation of it from any practical utility, and therefore also to respect it, conserve it, and reintegrate it in its best condition. Countless other providential circumstances contribute to the study, recovery, safeguarding, and material conservation of the work of art: from the museum to the restoration studio, from the specialized seminar to protective measures against bombs and parasites, from legislation dedicated to preservation to projects organized by countless specialists and scholars, and so on: all the things that did not fall from heaven but are rather the fruits of our civilization, and which the preceding epochs only possessed in rough outline and in isolated cases. It is that very history that requires us today to be aware of the advantage gained, that helps us to understand the reason for which so much destruction occurred in the past. History requires of us today, if we want to be truly modern and civilized, to respect its imprint, to do that which was not possible in the past. It compels us to conserve monuments rather than destroy them, to make use of all the new instruments that it has put at our disposition. Today's vandals seek in the past the justification for their deadly projects; they behave like troglodytes, incapable of distinguishing the past from the present. For them, obviously, the fruits of progress, of science, and research have no meaning.

Another fundamental consideration, while justifying the ancients for destruction carried out, opposes the presumption of the vandals to leave their dirty stamp in the historical centers of our cities. Just as today our society has provided us with the instruments to respect the ancient, so modern architecture, inasmuch as it is modern, must respect the character and autonomy of that of the past with which it has nothing more to do, neither materially nor spiritually. From the Pharaohs to Baron Haussmann some things have certainly remained constant and unchanged in the architecture of the past, if through a thousand stylistic solutions: the materials—stone, mortar, brick—and a few basic static relationships between load-bearing and carried elements, walls and roofing, column and arch, pillar and vault, and so on. This could also be the case for monuments born materially from preexisting monuments. The travertine of the Colosseum served splendidly for the construction in the sixteenth century of Saint Peter's in the Vatican; in a similar way, one hundred Italian churches could be rebuilt over the course of centuries, often keeping intact the character of each subsequent style, from Santa Maria Maggiore in Rome—paleo-Christian-Renaissance-Baroque-eighteenth century—to the cathedral of Syracuse—fifth-century Greek through Christian-medieval-eighteenth century. Only the common denominator comprised of the perseverance of the materials and static principles has made possible similar interesting metamorphoses.

The vandals are completely aware of this, who, nonetheless, crude and interested as they are, take care to draw logical conclusions: and while they flaunt proudly their modernity (exactly because they are modern only for appearance's sake), they refuse to understand that it is exactly the specific qualities of modern architecture that prohibits building the new at the expense of the ancient, its character and its centuries-old environment. Modern architecture is the daughter of the Industrial Revolution that led to the discovery of new, revolutionary materials, like iron, steel, and reinforced concrete, from which the skeleton construction derived and the subsequent abolition of the traditional static relationships that held up all architecture of the past, changing in one hundred years the essence of architecture. So much so that no one today would think to complete the Basilica of San Clemente or the Baths of Caracalla in a functional style, or to convert Castel Sant'Angelo into a helicopter landing pad. So much so that modern architecture has been able to develop to the fullest its own possibilities precisely in buildings utilizing that which had never existed in the past: crystal palaces, Palais des machines, railway stations, industrial facilities, skyscrapers, and so on. Change the material, change the dynamics, change the spirit: an architecture that allows itself to substitute the load-bearing wall with a wall of glass is something entirely alien to that which preceded it for a few millennia. Every continuity between Wright's Fallingwater house and the Farnese palace has been broken.

Let's leave aside more general considerations, which the vandals and their supporters would not be able to understand, and conclude that recognition of the authentic needs and characteristics of modern building makes evident the definitive break that occurred in the past century between all of past architecture and contemporary architecture: every simplistic addition of modern buildings in the context of the ancient city is an operation destined to fail and to end up in reciprocal contamination. If then we consider the reality of things, that is, the multitude of anonymous, indefinable eyesores in which a countless gang of speculators and money-grubbers are submerging Italy, and realize what kind of "stamp"—which the vandals claim as modern—they want to leave, we realize with horror the mortal risk that the artistic and monumental heritage of our country is facing.

A consequence of the premises is another absurd pretense of the vandals that would reinvent itself as wise, yet instead is born from total ignorance of the problems of a modern city. The vandals say that it is also necessary "to adapt our old cities to the needs (unavoidable, inevitable, unstoppable, imprescriptible, etc.) of new times," and that historic city centers do not have to be "cold museums" but rather liberally overrun with the enlivening flux of means of transportation, that is, by "modern life" (as ignorant as they are, they happily identify modern life with the internal combustion engine and museums with refrigerators). This exists not in heaven or on earth. Indeed, it is well known that mankind, from Adam to Garibaldi, always moved from one place to another by foot, in a wagon, or on the back of a quadruped, whether horse or donkey. Similarly, it is well known that modern means of transportation and locomotion are rather recent inventions, an outcome of the aforementioned major phenomenon known as the Industrial Revolution, which in one and a half centuries changed the face of the world. Every child knows that motorized traffic has created in the city in this century problems completely foreign to all eras that came before. The chipped stone of the Simplon tunnel, whose arrival, together with the discovery of new building materials and the assimilated historical awareness of the past, strengthened as a result the definitive break with the history of the city. In this way, as with architecture, serious modern city planning has nothing to do with that which preceded it for millennia: to insist today on "adapting" a network of city streets originating in the Middle Ages or Baroque era, Siena or Rome neighborhoods, to the "needs" of thousands of motor vehicles is like purporting to transform, with some touch-ups, a litter into an automobile, a crossbow into a machine gun, or a drum into a radio-phonograph. In addition to being bad intentioned, our vandals are stupid: in order to "adapt the ancient to the modern" they resort to the inglorious method of evisceration.

Evisceration for the sake of traffic circulation is called, by the vandals and their buglers, a "surgical procedure." While a surgical intervention supposedly is practiced with the goal of saving the ill, evisceration brings about the immediate death of the affected historic center, in addition to being the premise with the most vast and lethal outcomes for the entire city, producing effects exactly opposite those desired. Aiming to widen an old road, puncture a public square, "isolate" a monument or simply "break off" a corner, evisceration does nothing else than beckon new traffic into the historic center of the city: the resulting highly profitable construction of new buildings in place of old demolished ones aggravates congestion exactly where it wanted to ease it. Destruction of the unity of an old neighborhood, destruction of houses, churches, gardens, apartment buildings, degradation of the environment around monuments, ignominious counterfeiting of the ancient and modern (with the vain pretext of invoking this or that), thickening in the historic center of all those modern functions that need to be organized in modern centers to the grave detriment of future, functional development of the city: these and no others are the benefits of any evisceration (gash, cut, gap, alteration, touch-up, removal, whatever it may be). With the passage of time, the situation in the devastated area becomes unsustainable: another evisceration will seem to be necessary, and yet another, and so on up until complete destruction of the ancient and illustrious historic city center. [. . .]

The vandals' genius lies in half truths, approximation, generic and summary argumentation, limp wisdom. Perhaps history does not go on? Is it possible to oppose its inevitable passing away? Doesn't life have its own laws? Have we not perhaps too many monuments in our country? Is it possible to "crystallize," "embalm," etc., a landscape or a group of monuments? And in the general vulgarity of taste, in the lack of preparation of public opinion, this half-baked historicism (where "everything changes," "everything is relative," etc.) foments and spreads quickly. By now we live in a paradoxical situation: the merciless destruction of our cities, the vulgar degradation of the most extraordinary monumental and natural settings, and the boundless invasion of the ugly—outcomes of the spirit of violence of the speculating vandals, the abject conformism of the responsible agencies, and the mental laziness of the cultured classes. Skeptical current opinion considers this by now a "reality" to which we must stoop. Every step on the way to ruin becomes a pretext and justification and incentive for a greater ruin: the illegality, stupidity, negligence, and anarchy become considered de facto conditions which "it is not possible not to be aware of." The triumphant behemoths consider the testaments to art and history in our cities to be nostalgic obstructions, and they find negligible the motives of intelligence, culture, and civilization. "That which is real is rational," they voluntarily babble, and whoever should oppose them presumes, insanely, to repeat the gesture of Joshua.

The exact opposite of what the vandals purport is true. The true and rational reality of our time is respect for the ancient; it is the new development in the life of the city for which every continuity with the past is forever interrupted. The vertiginous increase in population and its concentration in large urban centers, the exploitation of new sources of energy and production, industrialization, specialization, the multiplication of public structures and essential services, the weight and concentration of business, markets, administration and commerce, the standardization of architectural systems, the upheaval in human relations created by new means of transportation, traffic, and communication, and so on and so on, have made the modern city in its structure, dimensions, and purpose, a completely new phenomenon with respect to the city of the past, from antiquity to the nineteenth century. To claim to "adapt" an old city to the demands of modern life leads, let us repeat, to a deformed compromise, to a work of incivility and atavism: destruction with no return (as opposed to what occurred in previous epochs) of priceless artistic and cultural heritage while creating an ambiguous and irrational forgery of modernity. It has been proven by the state of paralysis of our cities: after decades of eviscerations and contamination between ancient and modern, they are expanding through successive additions, filling all of the free or green spaces in the center and on the periphery, with traffic filling the historic centers ever more densely. Evisceration, annihilation of monument zones, traffic congestion, difficult connections, wasting of time and physical exhaustion, small towns and working-class neighborhoods, lack of air, light, and reprieve, overcrowding, promiscuity, impossible hygienic conditions, chaos at the disparate levels of public interest: such are some of the characteristics of our anti-cities, led by Rome. The structure of our cities is decades behind the needs of the times: having lost their ancient physiognomy, they did not know how to take on a new one in keeping with the new state of the world in which we live. Their growth has created a monstrous hypertrophy.

A half century of self-absorbed incomprehension of the laws of the ancient and modern has resulted in a false architectonic modernity, a useless destruction of great swaths of artistic heritage, and totally irrational urban planning. In the last interminable postwar period, there has been no practical cultural progress corresponding to the raging anarchy in the building industry, which faces today a decisive dilemma: renewal of the city or its end, salvation of an immense artistic heritage or its destruction, construction or a genuine definitive rejection of the modern. A basic consideration is obvious: only by conserving the character and environmental unity of ancient urban centers can the general conditions be established for real modern and efficient development of our cities.

Only stubborn people can think—only the destroyers of Italy—can be interested in making us believe that preservation of the ancient is a purely passive task of conservation. Only retrograde minds can believe that they can arrogate ancient nuclei, tearing away the fabric, capacity and functions belonging to modern urban planning. Only vandals can claim that the modern city is born from the rubble of the ancient one. We must fix in our minds the conviction that integral preservation of the old and creation of the new in cities are complementary tasks, two indissoluble moments in the same procedure, that ancient and modern have distinct material and spiritual prerogatives and are mutually necessary. Only by acknowledging the full autonomy of the two terms is it possible to resolve and position the seeming conflict, which is to progressively develop an old city without destroying the evidence of its history. In conclusion, only those who are modern respect the ancient, and only those who respect the ancient are fit to understand the necessity of modern civilization.

Reading

2

Joseph Rykwert

The Idea of a Town: The Anthropology of Urban Form in Rome, Italy and the Ancient World (1976)

Joseph Rykwert, an influential architectural historian and critic, in this book on the interpretation and genesis of urban form, provides an inspiring overview of the underlying principles governing urban establishment and change in traditional societies. These include ancient Rome, India, Mande towns in West Africa, Bororo towns in Brazil, and other urban foundations in China, Africa, and precolonial North America. He interprets the city of the past "as a total mnemonic symbol, or at any rate a structured complex of symbols; in which the citizen, through a number of bodily exercises, such as processions, seasonal festivals, sacrifices, identifies himself with his town, with its past and its founders." Rykwert notes similarities and recurrence of symbols in distant urban cultures but cautions against interpreting them as evidence of reciprocal influences. He favors instead the notion of a deep-rooted urban construct, which is profoundly ingrained in the universal human experience of past societies.

Preface

We think of the town as a tissue of buildings which grows more or less unpredictably and is traversed by roads, pierced by squares, or else as a mesh of roadways fringed by buildings at the outskirts and webbed by them at the centre. Although we regard them as natural phenomena, governed by an independent, uncontrollable and sometimes unpredictable law of growth or expansion, like that of natural organisms, the truth is that towns do not grow by interior and inscrutable instincts. They are built, piece-meal by individual inhabitants, in larger tracts by speculators or authority. Now and then, particularly when a new town is founded, the authorities, whether local or national, on the advice of their experts treat the public to a display of embarrassment. It appears that civic authorities, or even the planners themselves, are not able to think of the new

---

From Joseph Rykwert, *The Idea of a Town: The Anthropology of Urban Form in Rome, Italy and the Ancient World* (London: Faber and Faber, 1976), 23–26, 190, 202.

town as a totality, as a pattern which might carry other meanings than the common-places of zoning (industry, habitat, leisure, etc.) or circulation. To consider the town or city a symbolic pattern, as the ancients did, seems utterly alien and pointless. Nowadays if we think of anything as 'symbolic' it is practically always an object or action which can be taken at a single view.

The conceptual poverty of our city discourse is exposed even when we look at the recent past. In the nineteenth century the criteria for establishing its terminology were perhaps still more directly 'positive' than they are now. The distinction between town or city would be made, for instance, in terms of the paving of streets.

Going further back, however, the tone of the discourse changes, as might have been expected. Charles Daviler, a French seventeenth-century theorist, defines a town in his dictionary of architectural terms as 'an ordering of blocks and quarters disposed with symmetry and decorum, of streets and public squares opening in straight lines with a fine and healthy orientation and adequate slopes for the draining of water. . . .'[1] But his description stands at the end of a tradition. 'The city', proposes a recent writer, 'is first of all a physical reality: a more or less sizeable group of buildings, of habitations and public buildings. . . . The city begins only when paths are transformed into roads. . . .'[2] He follows his nineteenth-century predecessors. This definition is a long way from Nicias's rousing words to the Athenian soldiers on the beach at Syracuse: 'You are yourselves the town, wherever you choose to settle . . . it is men that make the city, not the walls and ships without them. . . .'[3]

Traffic in cities has today become so thick and clotted that it is hardly surprising to find this concentration on the road pattern among our contemporaries. Traffic engineering is regarded as having superseded town planning; the street pattern, the railway or underground, are superimposed on each other, and together become that aspect of the city which has the greatest notional and conceptual validity. As traffic congestion and the attendant problems mount, so traffic surgery assumes an increasing importance in the public mind. Nor is this the only aspect of city planning which has turned into a craft of keeping one step only behind current development. Economists have for nearly two hundred years encouraged us to think that the rate of growth of urban population is to be equated with the growth of the gross national product (which they seem to consider good in itself, however it affects the individual). In spite, therefore, of the complaints about crises in traffic or about the shortage of city space, complaints which planners utter ritually whenever these problems are under discussion, when a town fails to expand at an even rate (as has been the case of the Rhine Randstadt), the same planners confess themselves dismayed by such a symptom of economic crisis.

It is commonly assumed, not only by planners, but by public authorities and even by the general public, that future expansion will go on at the present rate, forecasting the future by simple statistical inference. The possibility of new developments is elided from the argument by silence. The conceptual framework within which planners work has been designed to evade the issue of imposing any order of an extra-economic nature on the city. Fear of restriction often appears in the form of a fear of cramping an autonomous growth. That is why town planners, when talking about the way towns live and grow, invoke images drawn from nature when they consider town plans: a tree, a leaf, a piece of skin tissue, a hand and so on, with excursions into pathology when pointing to crises. But the town is not really like a natural phenomenon. It is an artefact—an artefact of a curious kind, compounded of willed and random elements, imperfectly controlled. If it is related to physiology at all, it is more like a dream than anything else.

Although the last half century has accustomed us to regard dreams as objects susceptible of serious, even scientific, study, yet the suggestion of fantasy which the word implies is regarded as offensive in the context of urban planning. This is partly because it is a matter where capital investment is huge, and partly because the well-being of masses, a well-being equated with physical amenity, is at stake.

Here again we are up against the poverty of much urbanistic discourse. The way in which space is occupied is much studied, but exclusively in physical terms of occupation and amenity. The psychological space, the cultural, the juridical, the religious, are not treated as aspects of the ecological space with whose economy the urbanist is concerned. His attention is focused on the more immediate physical problems, the resolution of which seems most urgent. But the solutions proposed, because of their physical presence, impinge on the symbolic world of the citizens; and often the arbitrary forms thrown up by harassed planners and architects are evolved on an irrational residue, motivated by unstated spiritual as well as aesthetic prejudice whose very irrationality contributes further to the instability of the community, and may set up a pattern of interaction between the community and its outward shell which will be disastrous for both.

Such procedures have been criticized by a number of sociologists.[4] It seems to me that they are right: that some consideration must be given to the model, to the conceptual prototype of the town which its inhabitants construct mentally, and which is often exemplified in their homes. So often the home is felt to be a miniature of the city: not as it is, but as we want it. Patterns of behaviour, even of movement may sometimes be explained as being attempts to reconcile such a conceptual model with the actual, with the physical structure of the city, of which the inhabitants may be aware only in the form of diagrams as of underground trains or bus routes.

The conceptual model I spoke of is rarely derived from such diagrams. More commonly it is related to views we hold about the space and the time we inhabit. And it is intended to anchor our views to a specific place: a particular home, a particular town.

The very statement of the problem suggests that there is no immediate solution to hand. I therefore propose to examine a closed (because past) situation, which is apparently familiar, and yet full of implications for anyone thinking about the way in which we take possession of our homes. The rectilineal patterns of the Roman towns, which survive in the street patterns and even the country lanes of old imperial lands, from Scotland to Sudan, are often thought to be the by-product of a utilitarian surveying technique. This is not how the Romans themselves saw it: the city was organized according to divine laws. The home was governed by the father of the family as the city was by the magistrates; and the paterfamilias performed in his home the complex rituals of the state religion which the colleges of priests performed for the state. The analogy between city and home, and city and land, was familiar to the Romans as it probably was to the Etruscans before them.

Before the Roman cities assumed the gridiron pattern familiar to us now, the idea of a regular city plan had to be formed in their minds. The rectilineal city was not something at which they arrived by hit-or-miss experimentation, and explained afterwards. On the contrary, it seems to me that such a device would have to have arisen from just such a model as I have mentioned. Its origins are therefore primarily interesting to me because they show the elaborate geometrical and topological structure of the Roman town growing out of and growing round a system of custom and belief which made it a perfect vehicle for a culture and for a way of life.

Over the millennium of Roman imperial rise and decline, the city underwent many changes, interpretations became increasingly elaborate and even conflicting, the rites whose meaning was sometimes forgotten were re-interpreted anachronistically. I will not be concerned with Roman and Etruscan history, except incidentally, as they bear on the development of the model and its transformation in time, which is much slower, much more gradual (as is always the case of ritualized art, ritualized procedure) than the changes in political and sometimes also religious ideas. I have chosen to deal primarily with Roman towns because theirs was an assertively urban civilization, entirely different from the one which we inhabit, and yet very amply, very accessibly documented. But I do not think the Romans' customs and ideas can be understood without comparing them with those of other peoples, usually weaker and sometimes of the most primitive savagery or so they would have seemed to the Romans. The Romans were not alone among ancient peoples in practising a form of rectilineal planning and orientation. All the great civilizations practise it, all have mythical accounts of its origins, and rituals which guide the planner and the builder. [. . .]

The City as a Curable Disease: Ritual and Hysteria

The parallels—to begin with them—were deliberately widely chosen, but the choice was made from an overwhelming mass of material. The Indian and the Chinese parallels present a highly complex cosmology and social condition embodied in urban form; the Mande have a highly dramatic pantomime of this same kind of belief; so do the Sioux. They and the Bororo show most intimately man's dependence on the immediate shape of his home, his tangible environment. These instances belong to different continents and highly diverse cultures. No doubt, some readers will want to explain certain similarities (as for instance the striking parallels between the Mande custom and the Roman) by a simple act of diffusion; but the parallels extend across the ancient world to China,[5] and further into Mesoamerica and even the Amazon forests: and I dare say, if total coverage was wanted, it would be possible to find adequate instances from the Bantus of South Africa to the Canadian North-West Territories. In time, too, the stretch seems inconceivable. From Paleolithic times the concepts of orthogonality and of orientation persist extraordinarily.

—w—

It is difficult to imagine a situation when the formal order of the universe could be reduced to a diagram of two intersecting co-ordinates in one plane. Yet this is exactly what did happen in antiquity: the Roman who walked along the *cardo* knew that his walk was the axis round which the sun turned, and that if he followed the *decumanus,* he was following the sun's course. The whole universe and its meaning could be spelt out of his civic institutions—so he was at home in it. We have lost all the beautiful certainty about the way the world works—we are not even sure if it is expanding or contracting, whether it was produced by a catastrophe or is continuously renewing itself. This does not absolve us from looking for some ground of certainty in our attempts to give form to human environment. It is no longer likely that we shall find this ground in the world which the cosmologists are continuously reshaping round us and so we must look for it inside ourselves: in the constitution and structure of the human person.

Notes

1. C. A. Daviler, 'Explication des Termes d'Architecture,' *Cours d'Architecture*, II, Paris, 1691, s.v. *Ville*, p. 336: 'C'est par rapport à l'Architecture civile un compartiment d'Isles et de Quartiers disposés avec symétrie et décoration, des Rues et Places publiques percées d'alignement en belle et saine exposition avec pentes nécessaires pour l'écoulement des eaux. Voyez Vitruve, *liv.* I, chap. 6.'
2. Pierre Leliévre, *La Vie des Cités de l'Antiquité à nos Jours*, Paris, 1950, p. 11.
3. *Thucydides*, trans. Thomas Hobbes, VII, 63, pp. 308–9.
4. P.-H. Chambart de Lauwe, with S. Antoine, L. Couvreur, and J. Gauthier, *Paris et l'Agglomération Parisienne*, Paris, 1952, I, pp. 247 ff.
5. On the rise of urban societies, see Robert McC. Adams, *The Evolution of Urban Society*, Chicago, 1966.

Reading

3

Seyyed Hossein Nasr

The Spirit of the Cities (2001)

Seyyed Hossein Nasr is an Iranian philosopher and professor of Islamic Studies who has written on philosophy, religion, music, art, architecture, science, literature, and intercultural dialogue. In this essay, he discusses the deeper significance of traditional cities as a symbolic manifestation of the human body and transcendent realities. These, in the author's opinion, are recurrent interpretations, common to many traditional societies. In the essay's concluding remarks, Nasr underlines that historic cities are not just relevant for national identities or cultural reasons but also, and even more, for the continuity and meaning they give to our existence as human beings.

When we speak about historic and sacred sites, it is of utmost importance to understand why they are significant. Even if we are not philosophers or architects, while walking through the narrow streets of [Carcassonne] in France, Fez in Morocco, Isfahan in Persia, or Benares in India, we feel that we are in an ambience that touches us very deeply. It is another space, another place. But our present-day worldview prevents us from taking such an experience seriously. It is a worldview that reduces the human being to molecules banging against each other and the cosmos to dust that has evolved over billions of years into its present structures. It is a worldview therefore, that makes the word "spirit" ultimately meaningless, simply a poetic metaphor with no correspondence to objective reality as far as the accepted, legitimized structure of knowledge in our world is concerned.

From Seyyed Hossein Nasr, "The Spirit of the Cities," in *Historic Cities and Sacred Sites: Cultural Roots for Urban Futures,* edited by Ismail Serageldin, Ephim Shluger, and Joan Martin-Brown (Washington, DC: World Bank, 2001), 3–10. Reproduced courtesy of the World Bank.

City as Reflection of the Human Body

In many traditional sources—Islam, Hinduism, the Chinese tradition and Christianity, and many other religions—the human body itself is oftentimes compared to a city or kingdom, with all its political and social functions. There is a famous book by Ibn 'Arabi, the celebrated Andalusian mystic, whose very title, *al-Tadbirat al-ilahiyyah fi islah al-mamlakat al-insaniyyah* ("Divine Governance of the Human Kingdom"), indicates its content. The content concerns how to govern the city or kingdom of the human state whose various functions are compared to that of a polis, which is comparable to the body. The famous *Rasa'il* ("Treatises"), written a thousand years ago in the cities of Basra and Baghdad by "The Brethren of Purity," contains a whole section on how the body is like a city.

The body as envisaged in such sources is not the same body whose anatomy is studied in modern medical schools. It is the body as understood traditionally, which means the locus of the confluence of the physical, the psychological, the emotive, the intellectual, and the spiritual, which is not to be confused in any way with the psychological. The city was not only compared to the body and the body to the city, but the city was the body expanded macrocosmically, providing the loci for all these elements. The heart corresponded to the center, and the various parts of the body corresponded to various functions in the city, as we shall see in a moment.

It is amazing how universal this concept is. One can think immediately of the examples of sacred cities of Islam, especially the City of Mecca, the supreme spiritual center of Islam. According to numerous treatises written on the subject, the *Ka'bah* at the very heart of the city corresponds to the human heart. Much of the beautiful City of Mecca has now been destroyed through modern urban design. Nevertheless, the center survives, which demonstrates the direct relationship between the inner heart, the heart of the city, the heart of the universe, or at least the Islamic universe, and the human heart.

There is the example of the Ming Tang in classical China, in which a three-dimensional magic square dominated the numerical symbolism of the 12 chambers of the Ming Tang, which always added vertically to the number 11. This number symbolized the wedding between Heaven and Earth. It was here that the emperor resided, he being the bridge between Heaven and Earth and representing precisely the function of man in his universal aspect.

The space of the cathedral symbolizes the form of the Body of Christ, as represented by the cross. It was in consideration of this space that the old European cities, which retain their beauty for people today, were planned always having a cathedral in the middle.

To come back to the question of the body and the city, all of our limbs are organically tied to the function of the heart. We are an overly cerebral civilization and always identify thinking with the head. We must recall that there is also "heart knowledge." The heart as the seat of the intellect and organ of intuitive knowing is mentioned in the Bible, the Upanishads, Chinese classical texts, the Quran, and so many other sacred writings of the world. The heart is the seat of intelligence, not the discursive and divisive intelligence that is associated with the brain and the mind, but unitive, integrated intelligence that knows by immediacy and in a synthetic manner.

This heart-center is, therefore, at once the center of life and the center of intelligence that emanates from the center to all the parts of the body. In the traditional and sacred city the heart always corresponds to the place of worship. It is from that center that all of the other parts of the city grow and to which they are organically related.

What are the powers and functions that we have within ourselves? We possess an intellective and religious power and function. We have an active aspect associated with our will. We make and produce things, and we live a life that must be lived according to certain laws.

All of these powers and functions of the human being associated with parts of the body and the mind are reflected in the traditional city. It always had spaces and sites for the following functions:

1. The intellective and religious function. Why do I put these together? Because through most of human history, among those very people who created the cities that we call historic cities, the religious and intellectual functions were united—whether in the Egyptian and Babylonian priesthood, the Brahmins, the Mandarin class, the Islamic *'uloma,'* or the medieval Christian priesthood. In traditional societies the functions of the theologian, priest, and scientist were united in a single organ that was conceived as the heart of society, while from another point of view it corresponds to the head, as one can see mentioned in certain classic Hindu texts.
2. The active element. It includes on the one hand the political and military functions of the city, and on the other the mercantile functions.
3. The production element. It includes farming and arts and crafts.

All of these are functions for which the living city had to provide architectural space as organically unified as are the heart, the head, the arms, and the feet of the human body. Furthermore, in the traditional ambience these spaces were always related to the heart-center, as are parts of the human body to the human heart.

Wonderful examples of this principle exist in the classical cities of the world. Since I know a little bit more about the Islamic world than other places, my examples come from that world. In what remains of the traditional cities of the Islamic world, such as Fez or Isfahan, one always sees this organic interrelationship between the mosque or religious center and the various spaces associated with functions that are always related to the center. In this pattern there is an unbelievable unity that comes from the integration of the various functions of the city with the heart-center.

Without the heart-center, which is always related to the Sacred, as in the case of the microcosm, in which the heart of human beings is the seat of Divine Presence, there can be no veritably human city. We have forgotten the heart-center of ourselves as well as of the world around us. This is the reason that we feel in such inhuman ambiences in modern cities that we build based on planning that does not have a heart.

This is why the historic cities always give us a sense of intimacy, of belonging, of being at the center. In these sacred and historic cities there is always a center, which reflects our own center. This point is what really distinguishes the traditional city from much that has been built in the last two or three centuries, especially the last century. The distinction is between the possession of a center or lack thereof. We have lost our own center, so we build cities without centers.

City as Archetypal Reality

Another important philosophical point has been discussed in many different traditions, yet appears strange to us because it lies outside of our worldview and does not make any sense within the paradigm that dominates our minds. It is that traditional cities have a kind of archetypal reality. They are not just physical conglomerates that were built as an ensemble. They reflect a reality from the spiritual world in the same way that, according to all traditions, what is below is a reflection of what is above. In the Western tradition, this concept is identified with Plato and the Platonic ideas and is well known in the West, even if not accepted in the prevailing Western *Weltanschauung*. There are other examples of this concept such as *menok* and *getik* in the Zoroastrian religion, and *nama* and *rupa* in Hinduism. The city itself was conceived to be a kind of reflection on Earth of a celestial, archetypal reality.

—~—

The idea of qualitative space, of sacred geography, of certain sites that attract the sacred, are universal among traditional people. China has developed the extensive science of *feng shui* concerning this qualitative and sacred geography. Other civilizations have not elaborated it so systematically but have nevertheless spoken about it in different ways.

Some historians have written that as soon as Christianity and Islam appeared, they simply took over the cemeteries of religions that existed before and converted them to Christian and Muslim cemeteries because this was the easiest thing to do. Or it is said that Christians and Muslims simply took over the various temples of the Greeks or the Zoroastrians and built churches or mosques in their place.

There was no shortage of space at that time, as in today's modern cities. Why is it then that so many Byzantine churches are built on top of Greek temples? Why is it that the most extensive and beautiful mosque in Persia, in my view, the Jamiy' Mosque of Isfahan, began to be built at the site of an old Zoroastrian fire temple and only later expanded in the area next to it? In India this occurred over and over again. In Europe one can see many Bogomil funerary sites in Yugoslavia. When those poor Muslims of the Balkans who are being massacred every other day became Muslims, they built their cemeteries there. All of these examples point to the idea that there are certain sacred sites and places on earth.

The fact that many have lost the sense of the sacred does not change the character of that reality. Even those of us who have lost the sense of the sacred, however, feel something of the presence of the sacred when we go to those places. That is why they are so precious and that is why preserving them is so important.

A center becomes sacred for many different reasons. One is sacred geography, the nature of the topography, the subtle forces involved, and all that goes with those types of traditional sciences, especially sacred geometry. Another has to do with certain events, either mythical or historical, but pertaining to sacred history. Babylon, Athens, Rome all had mythical or religious beginnings. The same is true for Benares; Madura, the birthplace of Krishna; Kyoto; the Isle of Ise in Japan; many places in China; many sites in the New World—the Hopi reservation. In the reservation in which the Navajos settled after being nomadic people, their pattern of settlement began with a vision that identified the sacred centers. These then determined where the settlements in New Mexico and Arizona were located.

Examples of these principles are legion. I will just draw one example, which also touches us very deeply politically and historically today. That is the City of Mecca, the center of the Islamic world. It is called in Arabic *Umm al-qura*, that is, "Mother of all cities." Of course, in days of old, for each civilization its world was *the* world, because it was a sacred world.

Today the sacred quality is lost, but, strangely enough, the idea in its secularized form has manifested itself in another way. Eurocentrism also sees its view of the world as the only worldview. In the old days people were at least more honest about it. Therefore, *Umm al-qura* does not mean "Mother of all cities" on earth, but "Mother of all cities" in the Islamic world, that is, the source or principle of all legitimate cities. There are many mystical treatises in Islamic languages about the interrelationships among various cities, such as Mashhad in my own home country of Iran, in the province of Khorasan, and their inward relation to Mecca.

According to Islamic eschatological sources, when the Mahdi comes at the end of the world, he will put his back to the wall of the *Ka'bah*, call out to those destined to aid him, and those in Khorasan and elsewhere destined for the call will hear his appeal. This, many will claim, is merely folklore. But it is not important how modern people judge such assertions. The important thing is the significance of this way of looking at things for the understanding of the creation of sacred space and sacred cities.

Another interesting case is one in which the archetypal city of three different religions meets in one, single reality on earth, Jerusalem. This is the reason that the problem of Jerusalem is so intractable politically. It is not simply one city among others. For 2,000 years the Jews said "Next year in Jerusalem," and finally, after 2,000 years, they have come back to that holy city. The Muslims have been there for 1,400 years, and nothing in the world is going to change the sacred character and significance of Jerusalem for them. The Christians have been there for 2,000 years. The Church of the Holy Sepulchre, and all the events of the end of the life of Christ, are related to the city.

Therefore, in a sense, the city is a meeting of archetypal realities that determined its earthly urban reality, some of which has been destroyed by the creation of profane architecture in recent years. However, no matter how much Jerusalem has been vilified by high-rises at the very place where Christ is supposed to descend at the end of the world, it does not change the ultimate nature of the sacred city. It will retain its sacred character as long as those religions that hold this city as sacred remain alive and their sacred sites remain protected in that holy ambience.

—∿∿—

But ultimately, as long as we live as human beings on earth, the truth is always present. Sacred cultures will not disappear completely. At this moment we are destroying both our historical heritage and our natural heritage with a rapidity never seen in human history. Not even Genghis Khan could do things like what we are doing through "development." At this time I believe there is nothing more important than to realize that what remains of our historic cities, of our sacred sites and sacred places, is significant not only for national identity or archaeological records but also for our own identity as human beings. It is through these sites that we remember who we really are, where we come from, and where we shall go at the end of our earthly journey. Thus, the significance of such cities and sites is far greater than any immediate economic, political, or even cultural factors that we might consider. Such places are necessary for our spiritual health. They are necessary for our continuation as human beings. The preservation of our sacred sites and historic cities is not only an investment in culture. It is also an investment in the continuity of our existence here on earth and in the meaning of our lives as human beings.

Reading

4

Paul Wheatley

City as Symbol (1969)

Paul Wheatley was a historical geographer who specialized in Southeast Asia and China but always maintained a broad interest in the history of places, cities in particular. His best-known works include The Pivot of the Four Quarters, *on Chinese urbanism;* Nagara and Commandery, *on Southeast Asian urban origins; and* The Places Where Men Pray Together: Cities in Islamic Lands, Seventh through the Tenth Centuries, *published in 2000, a year after his death. In this little-known but brilliant lecture, Wheatley demonstrates how cities in several traditional contexts, not necessarily related to each other, share a connection to cosmological principles in the establishment of "sacred enclaves."*

We are living at a culminating period in the history of the city, at a time in fact when we can confidently anticipate the conclusion of two cycles in the process of urbanization. The first is that which took its origin some five thousand years ago with the so-called (but somewhat inappropriately named) Urban Revolution; the second constitutes an epicycle on this secular process which was initiated as recently as the eighteenth century, when the emergence of modem industrial technology began to exacerbate inequalities in the incidence of urbanism among the world's populations. Now, when the rate of urbanization in industrial communities is tending to decline at the same time as it is accelerating in most underdeveloped countries, we are approaching the time when not only will all men live in terms of the city, but urban dwellers will again be distributed more or less in accordance with regional population densities. It seems inevitable that by the end of the twenty-first century a universal city, Ecumenopolis, will have come to comprise a world-wide network of hierarchically ordered urban forms enclosing only such tracts of rural landscape as may be judged necessary for man's survival.[1]

From Paul Wheatley, *City as Symbol: An Inaugural Lecture Delivered at University College, London, 20 November 1967* (London: Published for the College by H. K. Lewis, 1969), 3–12, 15–18, 24–26.

At this climacteric juncture it is not unnatural that the advancing frontiers of urbanism and of urbanization in recent and contemporary times should have been the subject of more intensive study than has been accorded the long preceding periods of traditional city life. And it was to be expected that investigation of contemporary urbanism would focus on its most impressive manifestations, namely the cities of Western Europe and North America, and, to a lesser extent, those of Japan. The result is that the study of urban phenomena has been confined very largely to these realms, with only occasional tentative forays into peripheral territories—which more often than not have been regions of exported European culture. It follows that most of the formulations and hypotheses current in urban studies are based on the Euro-American experience, and have comparatively seldom been tested in the conditions of the traditional world.

This lack of attention to cities outside the cultural sphere of the West becomes all the more important when we remember that two out of every three people in the world today are living in so-called under-developed territories, territories which have as many large cities and as many dwellers in large cities as do the industrialized nations. In other words, urbanism (though not at present urbanization) is as significant a phenomenon in the under-developed as in the industrialized sectors of the world. Of course, by no means all cities in the under-developed world are "traditional" in the sense in which I am using the term. Many constitute islands of Westernization in a sea of traditional society, and not infrequently all or a proportion of their inhabitants have closer affinities with the industrial mores of the West than with the disintegrating traditions of their own cultures. Yet the fact remains that the urbanist who ignores the traditional city is rejecting something like half the data potentially available for even a synoptic study; and it is self-evident that in the perspective of history by far the greater proportion of urban dwellers have lived in traditional-style cities, among them some of the most impressive examples of urban form ever to have been constructed. [. . .]

[. . .] [W]e are so poorly informed about the traditional city that it is often difficult to say which elements of current urban theory are applicable to it and which are not. At the most elementary level of investigation, for example, there have been few studies of the functions of such fundamental units of urban structure as the ethnic quarter and the ward, of the way in which they articulate with municipal government, and of the instruments employed in the resolution of conflicts between them. An awareness of a general absence of autonomous self-governing associations in the cities of Asia and pre-conquest America, as opposed to the prevalence of commune organization in Europe, is only now beginning to inform the literature of urban studies.[2] Neither do we know as much as we would like about the various roles, social, political, and economic, of the extended family in urban life, and of the manner in which its divers activities are integrated with those of the quarter and of the city in general; nor has the functional and morphological significance of the powerful gentile institutions that commonly occur in traditional cities been elucidated to our complete satisfaction. [. . .] [O]ur knowledge of the traditional city is miniscule compared with that available to the student of Western urbanism. In these circumstances it is not surprising that the more sophisticated quantified techniques that have been employed in the analysis of the internal structure and external relationships of Western cities have seldom, if ever, been applied to the pre-industrial city.

The reasons for this neglect of non-Western urban patterns are complex. [. . .] Generally speaking, while sociologists directed their efforts towards an understanding of Western-style urbanism, the traditional city was the preserve of anthropology and, to a lesser extent, of geography, both disciplines in which structural-functional theory constituted the prevailing ideology during the formative period of urban studies. But structural-functionalism was better adapted to the evaluation of equilibrium, stability, and integration than to the study of conflict and change, and I suspect that the interests of some students of the traditional world may have been diverted away from the city by the inadequacies of the conceptual tools available to them. Particularly was this likely to have been true at the time when, under the pervasive influence of the Chicago school of the nineteen-twenties and -thirties, the urban environment was regarded as primarily disruptive of the bonds of kinship, of family life, and of neighbourliness at the same time as it was held to promote impersonality, anonymity, and transitoriness in personal relationships.[3] Equally important in the case of geography, I think, has been the predominantly anti-urban sentiment of the British and American intellectual tradition, which seems to have exerted a wholly disproportionate influence on students of the traditional world. [. . .] It is the city which has been, and to a large extent still is, the style centre in the traditional world, disseminating social, political, technical, religious, and aesthetic values, and functioning as an organizing principle conditioning the manner and quality of life in the countryside. [. . .]

On the comparatively rare occasions when urbanists have investigated the pre-industrial city they have almost invariably done so in terms of the values and mores of Western civilization, and paid little or no attention to the logical structure of the culture concerned. [. . .] Perhaps the most influential of all such ethnocentric approaches to urban study in recent times has been that propounded by Max Weber nearly fifty years ago. By insisting on an essentially European (or at least Western) functional basis for city status he excluded those urban forms characteristic of most of the rest of the world. Those communities which failed to incorporate the salient features of the European city failed in greater or lesser measure to qualify as urban. [. . .] [I]n the perspective of world urbanism the European experience has been decidedly aberrant. In that diminutive peninsula projecting from the western marches of Asia there has evolved in comparatively recent times a mode of urbanism that differs in many important respects from that of the rest of the world in earlier ages. It has been this genre of city which, in its modern industrialized form in Europe, America, and Japan, and in somewhat diminished export versions in a few other territories, has become the ideal-type city, the norm of contemporary urban life. It is this mode of urbanism with which modern urban theory is almost exclusively concerned, and which, although exceptional in the perspective of both time and space, afforded a focus of enquiry for the formative theoretical work of the giants among urbanists, Louis Wirth, Georg Simmel, Pitirim A. Sorokin, Carle Zimmerman, Robert E. Park, N. J. Spykman, and so forth. [. . .]

[. . .]

[C]ertain aspects of the pre-industrial city have been even more than usually neglected. First, from the innumerable topics which offer themselves for discussion, I have selected one which has been ignored by virtually all students of urbanism, yet which is of fundamental importance because it pervades the whole range of activities focused in the traditional city. I am referring to the cosmo-magical symbolism which informed the ideal-type traditional city in both the Old and New Worlds, which brought it into being, sustained it, and was imprinted on its physiognomy. [. . .] [F]or the ancients the 'real' world transcended the pragmatic realm of textures and geometrical space, and was perceived schematically in terms of an extra-mundane, sacred experience. Only the sacred was 'real', and the purely secular—if it could be said to exist at all—could never be more than trivial. For those faiths which derived the meaning of human existence from revelation no site was, apart from a possible incidental soteriological sanctity, intrinsically more holy than another; but in those religions which held that human order was brought into being at the creation of the world there was a pervasive tendency to dramatize the cosmogony by constructing on earth a reduced version of the cosmos, usually in the form of a state capital.[4] In other words, Reality was achieved through the imitation of a celestial archetype, by giving material expression to that parallelism between macrocosmos and microcosmos without which there could be no prosperity in the world of men. Some of the most dramatic examples of such plastic representations of heavenly prototypes are to be found in the great cult cities of ancient Cambodia. There successive national capitals, and particularly that now known as Aṅkor Thom, were nothing less than translations into stone of the cosmological myths of India. They were, as one French scholar has phrased it, "diagrammes magiques tracés sur le parchemin de la plaine,"[5] in the construction of which art was not an aesthetic adventure, but a technique in the service of the liturgy. Although—or rather because—the whole city, indeed the whole kingdom, was dependent on the produce of its irrigated padi fields, the Khmers did not hesitate to undertake the colossal expenditure of labour, and to devise the costly solutions to engineering problems, necessary to render their city a worthy likeness of Indra's capital on Mount Meru. In the eyes of a Khmer monarch a benign environment combined with careful husbandry within the framework of an irrigation-based ecotype alone were incapable of ensuring the prosperity of the capital and of the kingdom. Only those factors operating in the context of a perfect correspondence and harmony between the planes of existence could achieve that goal.

The remarkable extent to which the Khmers subordinated their technology to their symbolism has been the subject of numerous studies, mainly by the scholars of the École Française d'Extrême-Orient. The symbolism of the central temple-mountains modelled on canonical descriptions of Mount Meru and laid out as chronograms symbolizing a sacred cosmography, the myth of the Churning of the Ocean laid out in stone over an area of six square miles,[6] the towers of the Bayon each bearing four faces of Jayavarman VII in the likeness of Vajradhara and so arranged as to simulate the miracle of Śrāvasti,[7] the outer wall of the city and its moat representing the Cakravāla mountains and the Ocean bordering the Buddhist universe[8]—all this and much else besides has been elicited and amply documented, primarily by members of the École. But, although the material expression of this symbolism is perhaps better preserved in Cambodia than in most other realms of nuclear urbanism, and interpretations there more readily endorsed by epigraphic prescription, analogous modes of symbolism are clearly apparent in cities throughout much of the rest of Asia, though naturally they are mediated through a variety of cultural traditions. I need only draw attention to certain traditional Indian urban forms which were modelled on that city where in the age of gold the Universal Sovereign had dwelt,[9] to Arthur Pope's expositions of the architectural symbolism of Persepolis, to the magistral papers of Roscher[10] and Wensinck[11] on the concept of the *omphalos* among the Western Semites, as well as to the works of Walter Krickeberg,[12] Paul Westheim,[13] and Michael Coe[14] on the cosmological symbolism of ancient Mexican cities.

[. . .]

The establishment of a capital as an imitation of a celestial archetype in the way that has been described also required its delimitation and orientation as a sacred territory within the continuum of profane space. This was customarily effected in relation to that point, the holy of holies, whence the sacred *habitabilis* had taken its birth, and whence it had spread out in all directions. This central point, the focus of creative force, was the place where communication was achieved most easily between cosmic planes, between earth and heaven on the one hand, and between earth and the underworld on the other. It was through this point of ontological transition that there passed the axis of the world, represented in most instances by the capital city. In Eliade's phrasing, Reality had been achieved through participation in the Symbolism of the Centre. [. . .]

In the cities of the ancient Middle East, south India, Ceylon, and in those of Hindu and Mahayana South-East Asia, it was a temple which occupied this most sacred site at the axis of the kingdom. [. . .]

—ʌʌ—

In the ancient Semitic world there were numerous places which at one time or another in various traditions were regarded as *axes mundi*. One of these was Golgotha, in the folklore of the Eastern Christians conceived as the summit of the cosmic mountain upon which Adam had been both created and buried.[15] [. . .] But the really great cosmological centre of the Semitic world in later times was Jerusalem, the very *omphalos* of the world, and it was this symbolism which was subsequently transferred by Muslim *ḥadīth* to Mecca, a point which had been in existence—according to a tradition preserved by Azraqī on the authority of one of Muḥammad's contemporaries, the converted Jew K'ab al-Akhbār, for 'forty years before Allāh created the heavens and the earth.'[16] Another *ḥadīth* accords the Ka'bah a priority of two thousand years over the rest of creation, but the discrepancy is of little consequence. The important thing is that Mecca, or strictly speaking the Ka'bah, was held to represent the navel of the earth (*ṣurrat al-arḍ*), the spot from which the creation of the world had begun. [. . .]

There is still another aspect of this notion of centrality which deserves mention. The capital, the *axis mundi*, also the point at which divine power entered the world and diffused outwards through the kingdom. When Jayavarman VII of Cambodia had his own face, in the likeness of Vajradhara,[17] carved on the four sides of each of the fifty-four towers of the Bayon, he was ensuring the projection of the divine power channelled through his temple-mountain to the four quarters of his kingdom. The city gates, where power generated at the *axis mundi* flowed out from the ceremonial complex towards the cardinal points of the compass, possessed a heightened symbolic significance which, in virtually all Asian urban traditions, was expressed in massive constructions whose size far exceeded that necessary for the performance of their mundane functions of access and defence. Most frequently, gate towers of this character were patterned on those architectural features which denoted the axis of the kingdom. Whereas, for example, in the temple-city of South and South-East Asia the *gopura* often reproduced the temple or temple-mountain at the centre of the city, the Chinese gate-tower conformed to the same general architectural principles as did the imperial palace. Like so many other aspects of urban design, in the Chinese culture realm this feature is well illustrated by Peiching, where the Gate of Heavenly Peace at the entrance to the Imperial City overtops all buildings within the walls, and the Meridian Gate all those within the Forbidden City.[18] But the architectural prominence of gate-towers, instruments for the projection of authority in the four cardinal directions, is a characteristic feature of the urban hierarchy in almost all realms of Asia.

The third aspect of cosmo-magical urban symbolism which I shall mention was the emphasis on the cardinal compass directions resulting from the techniques of orientation involved in the delimitation of sacred (that is, habitable) territory within the continuum of profane space. The sacred enclave defined in this manner provided the theatre within which could be conducted the seasonal rituals and ceremonies necessary to maintain that harmony between the macrocosmos and the microcosmos on which depended the fortunes of the kingdom. The resulting cardinal orientation and axiality which characterized a high proportion of the cities of the traditional world has often been discussed at length, so I shall mention one point only. Despite the fact that Chinese and Indian cities were expressions of affinal attitudes towards the cosmological ordering of space, there was a difference of emphasis in one important feature: in the Chinese city the main processional axis running from south to north, 'the celestial meridian writ small' was—as befitted a culture permeated with the symbolism of an ominous, threatening north opposed to a benign, auspicious south—of greater significance than any avenue running from east to west. And on this longitudinal axis were ranged the more important official buildings, which themselves faced south towards the Red Phoenix of Summer. It should, incidentally, be noted that the function of the master north-south axis of the Chinese city was quite different from that of the vista avenue in the Baroque city of Europe. Whereas the latter was designed to impress by the prospect it afforded of a distant architectural feature of central importance, the

Chinese processional way was of symbolic rather than visual significance. In fact, its full sweep was never revealed at one time or from one place. It afforded not so much a vista as a succession of varied spaces integrated into an axial whole in a manner inevitably reminiscent of the Chinese scroll painting. This axial design also is superbly executed in Peiching, where the official visitor was formerly confronted in his progress along the processional way by a seemingly interminable succession of gates, towers, and walls, the passing of each of which brought him nearer not only to the centre of the city but also to the *omphalos* of the kingdom, of the world, and of the universe, the point where the Son of Heaven, in the words of Mencius (VIIIA, xxi, 2), 'stood in the centre of earth and [thereby] stabilized the people within the four seas.'

These Asian capitals were not, as is sometimes supposed, solely—or even primarily—expressions of pomp and glory, though these considerations did enter into their construction. Rather they were the material instruments of a particular political theory, and the symbolism inseparable from that role was not a mere decorative veneer but one of a functionally interrelated core of urban institutions. Not only is the cosmomagical basis of this theory evident in the design of such cities as well as in textual and epigraphic prescriptions, but a re-reading of the classical literatures of the several Great Traditions of Asia sometimes reveals evidence of this symbolism in somewhat unexpected contexts. [. . .]

Meagre though our knowledge of traditional cities has proved to be when considered in ecumenical perspective, it is nevertheless apparent that in many respects they did not conform to the models devised by students of contemporary Western urbanism. In the first place they were not all characterized by compact groupings of population. Among the Maya, in pre-Chimú Peru, in the Nile valley prior to the advent of the New Kingdom, in China of the Shang and Western Chou dynasties, and through most of western South-East Asia in pre-colonial times the prevailing urban form was that which Professor S. W. Miles has categorized as the 'extended boundary city,' namely, a focally situated ceremonial complex serving a population scattered through the surrounding countryside. Moreover, early cities, whether of dispersed or compact form, showed little tendency to absorb excess rural population: in fact the peasantry was seldom free to migrate to the city. Nor did the oft-cited negative relationship between degree of urbanization and density of agricultural population invariably obtain in the traditional world. More generally, it can be confidently asserted that not all types of pre-industrial city equally generated social and economic change or mediated it in the same manner as does the contemporary city, and nor did the opportunist practices of the market place always determine the prevailing urban ethic. Finally, [. . .] although the pre-eminence of the central tract over the periphery is characteristic of both modern and traditional urban forms, whereas in the former it derives primarily from economic and technological considerations, in at least a substantial proportion of pre-industrial cities it was induced by a principle that may conveniently be termed proximity to the sacred. [. . .]

In short, the representative capitals of the traditional world were *axes mundi* where it was possible to effect an ontological transition between the worlds, quintessentially sacred enclaves within which man could proclaim the knowledge that he shared with the gods and dramatize the cosmic truth that had been revealed to him. As such they were more often than not constructed as *imagines mundi* with the cosmogony as paradigmatic model, islands of sacred symbolism in the intrinsically hostile continuum of profane space. They were theatres for the performance of the rituals and ceremonies which guaranteed man's liberation from the terrors of the natural world. [. . .]

Generalizations of this nature are too gross to do more than indicate the sort of problems involved in the study of traditional urbanism. They also rely too heavily on stylistic rather than analytical conceptions, so that they are perhaps not potentially expressive of genuine structural regularities. They certainly possess no explanatory power. Almost the only thing of which we can be sure is that a much more intensive study of traditional urbanism will be a prerequisite for a full understanding of the uniqueness of the contemporary Western-style city. But this investigation will have to be undertaken in terms of the norms and values of traditional cultures; otherwise it is unlikely that its categories, devised solely on the basis of form, imposed rather than educed, will be truly homologous: and, instead of explaining the functioning of these cities, we shall merely be defining accidental intersections of essentially non-congruent systems. A general, as opposed to a Western, theory of urbanism is still some way in the future.

Notes

1. This view of man's urban future has been substantially influenced by the writings of Konstantinos A. Doxiadis, *Ecumenopolis: Towards the Universal City* (Athens, 1961); *On the Measure of Man* (Athens, 1964); and *The New World of Urban Man* (Athens, 1965); and to a lesser extent by Lowdon Wingo, Jr. (ed.), *Cities and Space: The Future Use of Urban Land* (Baltimore, 1963); Richard L. Meier, *A Communications Theory of Urban Growth* (Cambridge, Mass., 1962).
2. The best discussion of this distinction on an ecumenical, though selective, basis is that incorporated in *La Ville. Recueils de la Société Jean Bodin*, 6 (Bruxelles, 1954).
3. The classic statement of this point of view was enunciated by Louis Wirth in "Urbanism as a Way of Life," *American Journal of Sociology*, 44 (1938), 1–24.
4. For a discussion of this polarity in the power of religions to transform secular into sacred landscapes see Erich Isaac, 'The Act and the Covenant: The Impact of Religion on the Landscape,' *Landscape*, 11 (1961–62), 12–17.
5. Bernard-Philippe Groslier, *Angkor. Hommes et Pierres* (Paris, 1956), p. 11.
6. *Vide* Coedès, *Pour Mieux Comprendre Angkor*, p. 101.
7. Bernard-Philippe Groslier, *The Art of Indochina* (New York, 1962), p. 183.
8. Robert von Heine-Geldern, 'Weltbild und Bauform in Süostasien,' *Wiener Beiträge zur Kunst- und Kulturgeschichte Asiens*, 4 (1930), 28–78.
9. *Vide*, for example, Prasanna Kumar Acharya, *Indian Architecture* (Oxford, 1928); Binode Behari Dutt, *Town Planning in Ancient India* (Calcutta and Simla, 1925).
10. W. H. Roscher, 'Neue Omphalosstudien,' *Abhandlungen der Königlich Sächsischen Gesellschaft der Wissenschaft, Phil-hist. Klasse*, 31 (Leipzig, 1915).
11. A. J. Wensinck, ,'The Ideas of the Western Semites Concerning the Navel of the Earth,' *Verhandelingen der Koninklijke Akademie van Wetenschappen te Amsterdam*, Afdeeling Letterkunde, n.s., 17 (1916).

12. Walter Krickeberg, 'Bauform und Weltbild im alten Mexico,' in *Mythe, Mensch and Umwelt*. Beiträge zur Religion, Mythologie und Kulturgeschichte (Bamberg, 1950).
13. Paul Westheim, *Arte Antiguo de México* (México, 1950).
14. Michael D. Coe, 'A model of ancient community structure in the Maya lowlands,' *Southwestern Journal of Anthropology*, 21 (1965), pp. 97–114.
15. *Vide* Holmberg-Harva, 'Der Baum des Lebens,' p. 72, citing Mansikka on traditions of the Little Russians.
16. Azraqi (d. ca. 858), *Akhbār Makkah*. Wüstenfeld's edition (Leipzig, 1858), p. 1; cf. also Wensinck, "The Ideas of the Western Semites," p. 18.
17. The aspect of Vajrapāṇi assumed by Lokeśvara when expounding the Law. *Vide* Coedès, *Pour Mieux Comprendre Angkor*, Ch. 6, and Jean Boisselier, 'Vajrapāṇi dans l'art du Bàyon,' *Proceedings of the Twenty-second Congress of Orientalists*, 2 (Leiden, 1957), 324–32.
18. Osvald Sirén, *The Walls and Gates of Peking* (London, 1924); Andrew Boyd, *Chinese Architecture and Town Planning 1500 B.C.–A.D. 1911* (Chicago, 1962), pp. 60–72.

Reading

5

Christian Norberg-Schulz

Genius Loci: Towards a Phenomenology of Architecture (1979)

Christian Norberg-Schulz was a Norwegian architectural historian and critic who exerted considerable influence on the theory and understanding of architecture and urbanism in the second half of the twentieth century. In his seminal and best-known publication, Genius Loci, *Norberg-Schulz invites us to consider the loss of natural and man-made places as well as the rapid and increasing homogeneity of cities and urban spaces worldwide. He reminds us of the significance of place and its psychological implications for human life and development. In his view, an understanding of "loci," and the spirit and relationships that animate them, is the precondition for planning that aspires to preserve and reinforce a sense of place, as opposed to the prevailing planning practice of allocating land for different uses and densities independent of the quality and character of the context.*

VII PLACE

1. Meaning

To arrive at an understanding of the *genius loci*, we have introduced the concepts of "meaning" and "structure." The "meaning" of any object consists in its relationships to other objects, that is, it consists in what the object "gathers." A thing is a thing by virtue of its gathering. "Structure," instead, denotes the formal properties of a system of relationships. Structure and meaning are hence aspects of the same totality.[1] Both are abstractions from the flux of phenomena; not in the sense of scientific classification, but as a direct recognition of "constancies," that is, stable relationships which stand out from the more transitory happenings. [. . .]

From Christian Norberg-Schulz, *Genius Loci: Towards a Phenomenology of Architecture* (New York: Rizzoli, 1980), 166, 168–73, 175–76, 179–80, 182, 185, 189–91, 194–95, 198, 200–202. Originally published in Italian as *Genius loci—paesaggio, ambiente, architettura* (Milan: Grupo Editoriale Electa, 1979). Reproduced with permission of Christian Emanuel Norberg-Schulz on behalf of the Estate of Christian Norberg-Schulz.

When discussing the natural and man-made place, we gave a general survey of their basic meanings and structural properties. The natural meanings were grouped in five categories, which sum up man's understanding of nature. Evidently man interacts with these meanings. He is a "thing" among "things": he lives among mountains and rocks, rivers and trees; he "uses" them and has to know them. He also lives with the "cosmic order": with the course of the sun and the cardinal points. The directions of the compass are not mere geometry, but qualitative realities which follow man everywhere. In particular, man is related to the "character" of things. From the initial animistic stage he gradually develops a conscious or unconscious understanding that there exists an *Übereinstimmung*, a correspondence, between his own psychic states and the "forces" of nature. Only thus he may obtain a personal "friendship" with things, and experience the environment as meaningful. He cannot be friends with scientific "data," but only with qualities. Man also lives with "light" and is tuned by light. Personal and collective attitudes ("mentalities") are in fact influenced by the environmental "climate."[2] Finally man lives in "time," which means that he lives with the changes of the other four dimensions. He lives with the rhythms of day and night, with the seasons and in history.

—∾—

[. . .] The Greek *polis* was based on a creative transposition of meanings. The meanings which are revealed in certain natural places, were translated into buildings and moved to the city, through the erection of similar buildings there. It is a grand conception, indeed, to visualize the qualities of a landscape by means of a man-made structure, and then to gather several landscapes symbolically in one place! We have seen that the *genius loci* of Rome stems from such a gathering.

[. . .]

The making of places we call architecture. Through building man gives meanings concrete presence, and he gathers buildings to visualize and symbolize his form of life as a totality. Thus his everyday lifeworld becomes a meaningful home where he can dwell. There are many kinds of buildings and settlements. What they gather varies according to the building task and the situation. Vernacular architecture, that is, farms and villages, brings the immediate meanings of the local earth and sky into presence. Hence it is "circumstantial" and intimately connected with a particular situation. Urban architecture, instead, has a more general value, as it is based on symbolization and transposition.[3] Urban architecture therefore presupposes a formal language, a "style." In town, "foreign" meanings meet the local *genius*, and create a more complex system of meanings. The urban *genius* is never merely local; although the examples of Prague, Khartoum and Rome have taught us that the local character plays a decisive role in giving the settlement its particular identity. Urban gathering may be understood as an *interpretation* of the local *genius*, in accordance with the values and need of the actual society. In general we may say that *the meanings which are gathered by a place constitute its genius loci*.

Architecture is born from the dialectic of departure and return. Man, the wanderer, is on his way. His task is to penetrate the world and to set its meanings into work. This is the meaning of the word *settle*. A settlement sets truth into a work of architecture. To set-into-work here means to build the boundary or "threshold" from which the settlement begins its presencing. The threshold is the meeting of "outside" and "inside," and architecture is hence the incarnation of the meeting. "The place-searching and place-forming characters of plastic incarnation"[4] here find their "look" and at the same time man finds his "outlook."[5] Thus the threshold is the "gathering middle,"[6] where things appear in "limpid brightness."

2. Identity

Places where natural and man-made elements form a synthesis are the subject-matter of a phenomenology of architecture. The primary relationship between the two kinds of elements is denoted by the world location. Where does man locate his settlements? Where does nature form places which "invite" man to settle? The question has to be answered both in terms of space and character. From the spatial point of view man needs an enclosure, and accordingly tends to settle where nature offers a defined space. From the point of view of character, a natural place which comprises several meaningful things, such as rocks, trees and water, would represent an "invitation." We have in fact seen that Rome was founded in a place where these elements were present. Sometimes the conditions may be favourable both with regard to space and character, other times only one of the two needs is naturally satisfied (or even none). Where the actual conditions are favourable, visualization becomes the most important means of place concretization, whereas a location where nature offers less, has to be "improved" by complementation and symbolization.[7]

In a very general sense, the surface relief of the earth slopes down towards the sea. Except for a few isolated internal basins (possibly of volcanic origin), a "normal" country is always directed towards the sea.[8] On an extended plain this direction is obviously less strongly felt than in a valley. In general, the movement of the land corresponds to a system of rivers (and lakes) which visualize the spatial pattern. When the river approaches the sea, the valley usually opens up and becomes an amphitheatrical bay. The location of human settlements are to a high extent determined by these conditions. Spaces such as plains, valleys and bays have given rise to characteristic types of settlements, and mostly a river, a confluence, or a shore have been used for spatial fixation. The endings of numerous place names express this state of affairs: "ford," "port," "mouth," "gate," "haven," "bridge." When the surface relief of a hill landscape gets accentuated, however, the natural places are found on the tops and crests of the hills rather than in the bottom of the valleys. We see thus that the scale of the surface relief may influence location. A top is obviously also often chosen because it forms a natural centre to the surrounding landscape. Another general factor which influences location is the direction of the sun. A slope exposed to the south is evidently more favourable than a northern one, and in many parts of Europe it is therefore common that farms and villages are situated on the north side of the valleys. Sometimes exposure and natural space collaborate to create very favourable conditions for settlement, other times they are contradictory and some kind of compromise becomes necessary.

If man-made places are at all related to their environment, there ought to exist a meaningful correspondence between natural conditions and *settlement morphology*. The basic problem to be solved by a settlement is how to gather the surrounding landscape. How do we, in terms of space, gather a plain, a valley, an undulating series of hills, or a bay? Evidently, each of these situations are open to different interpretations.[9] The simplest, *vernacular*, solution consists in a direct adaptation to the natural space. In a defined valley this would mean to form a row parallel to the direction of the land, that is, along the natural path of communication. This pattern is found in many countries, for instance in the narrow valleys of Telemark and Setesdal in Norway, where the row-*tun* is the dominant type of rural settlement.[10] An *urban* valley-settlement, instead, represents a centre which gathers the surrounding space. This is achieved by introducing an axis across the valley, mostly in connection with a ford or a bridge-point. The centre thus formed is still a function of local circumstances without "cosmic" implications. When the Romans used a site of this kind, however, they usually placed their *cardo-decumanus* axes on one side of the river, reducing thus the importance of

Fig. 1. Place: enclosure and gathering. Monteriggioni, Tuscany.

the local space (London, Paris, Cologne, Ratisbon, Turin, etc.). The Roman colonial settlement therefore represented an absolute system, albeit of natural derivation, rather than a gathering of the local landscape. This is particularly evident in Florence where the Roman axes were turned at an angle to the river and the valley. During the Middle Ages the boundary of the urban enclosure was turned back to correspond with the river. Another example of "place-free," "cosmic" orientation is the traditional east-west axis of the Christian church, which in many Mediaeval towns contradicts the dominant directions of the urban tissue.

Settlements on a plain have analogous possibilities of interpretation. Here the basic vernacular form is not the row, but the dense cluster or enclosure (*Rundling, Vierkanthof*). These forms express the general, directionless extension of the surrounding land. The development of an urban centre is usually combined with geometrization, such as the building or a regular, square or rectangular enclosure (Montagnana etc.), or, less frequently, a ring. When a river is present, interesting combinations of enclosure and longitudinal-transversal directions are formed. A good example is furnished by Moscow, where the triangular shape of the Kremlin is due to the interpenetration of ring, river and transverse axis. On a plain, the Roman scheme is congenial, but evidently it still represents an abstraction, as is shown by Lucca, where the system was filled in by a dense cluster of houses during the Middle Ages.

Building in an extended hilly landscape poses different problems. Here directions are neither in fact nor potentially present, and the only possible structuration consists in visualizing the tops and crests by means of concentrated or longitudinal clusters. The result is well known from Italy, where "hill-towns" are legion. In general they belong to the vernacular category, but sometimes they gain the importance of a centre, mainly due to an isolated, dominant location (Orvieto) or through vertical accentuation (Palombara). A centre is also formed when several crests meet, as is the case in Siena, where the town integrates three significant directions: north (Florence), south (Rome) and west (Grosseto, coast). When the scale increases and the hills become mountains, the settlements are usually located in the sloping mountain-side, forming a series of terraces. Good examples are furnished by Gubbio and Assisi. Terraces also represent a natural solution when an amphitheatrical bay has to be built, which moreover demands a continuous engirdling disposition of the houses. Islands and promontories are somewhat related to the tops and crests of the inland. Sperlonga is thus clustered along the crest of a promontory, whereas the Castello on the Island of Giglio rests on an isolated hillock near the top of the island. On the same island an archetypal bay-settlement is also found (Giglio Porto).

Our few remarks on the location and spatial morphology of settlements might seem trivial. Today, however, these simple structural relationships are hardly understood and still less respected. As the general identity of our places depends on such structures, they form an important part of the phenomenology of architecture. In general, all the types of settlement mentioned, represent variations on the *figure-ground* theme. We understand that "figure" here does not mean a "foreign" element which appears on a "neutral" ground, but a visualization of potentially present foci.

So far, we have mainly treated the external structure of settlements, that is, their "direct" relation to the environment. The *internal* structure is necessarily coordinated with the external relations. The urban spaces do not form an independent interior world. To allow for man's orientation and identification they have to concretize the general situation of the settlement. Obviously this cannot be done by means of visualization, and symbolization comes to play a decisive role. This implies that the aspect of character gains in importance, but a few spatial problems also have to be mentioned. Whereas the interior spaces of vernacular settlements form a continuation of the surroundings, or a simple "space within space" relationship,[11] urban settlements are distinguished by a definition of spatial foci which make the citizen experience the general role of the place as a local or regional centre. To fullfil their function, these spaces ought to contain all those "things" (buildings, monuments, etc.) which make manifest the meanings gathered by the place. Thus Heidegger says: ". . . the things themselves *are* the places, and do not only 'belong' to a place."[12] In European towns the path structure is usually centred on the foci, making thus the whole settlement appear as a meaningful organism, where the meanings present at the centre determine the form, in interaction with the external situation. The paths so to speak illustrate how the meanings were brought inside from the "threshold" of the city gate.

Examples which illustrate the role of urban foci as gathering centres are legion. We have already mentioned the Greek *agora* and the Roman *forum*, and may add the Mediaeval markets and cathedral squares.[13] On the European continent the cathedral is preceded by an urban space which serves to unite the symbolic interior of the building with the town as a whole. The integration of outside and inside is furthermore expressed by deep embrasured portals. In England, instead, the cathedral is located within a precinct; a more conservative solution which divides space in two qualitatively different domains. The formal solution of the urban foci is particularly beautiful in Siena, where the squares of cathedral and town hall are placed on either side of the meeting point of the three paths mentioned above. A splendid answer to the problem of urban gathering is also offered by St. Mark's Square in Venice, where the large piazza forms a meaningful transition between the dense labyrinth of the city and glittering expanse of the sea.

The *identity* of a place is determined by location, general spatial configuration and characterizing articulation. As a totality we experience for instance a place as "a dense cluster of enclosed stone houses in a hill side," or as "a continuous row of brightly coloured veranda houses around a small bay," or as "an ordered group of half-timbered gable houses in a valley." Location, configuration and articulation do not always contribute in the same measure to the final result. Some places get their identity from a particularly interesting location, whereas the man-made components are rather insignificant. Others, instead, may be situated in a dull landscape, but possess a well-defined configuration and a distinct character. When *all* the components seem to embody basic existential meanings we may talk about a "strong" place.[14] The three cities analyzed above, are such strong places, although Khartoum leaves something to be desired as regards characterizing articulation. The elements, however, are there, and the "strength" of the place could easily be improved if the *genius loci* is understood and respected.

In any case a strong place presupposes that there exists a meaningful correspondence between site, settlement and architectural detail. The man-made place has to know "what it wants to be" relative to the natural environment. Such a correspondence can be achieved in many different ways. We have already mentioned the vernacular "adaptation" and the urban "interpretation." The possibilities of interpretation are evidently determined by the site itself and by the historical circumstances which may both favour a certain approach of the "romantic," "cosmic" or "classical" type. Moreover an interpretation is always open to individual variations. In general settlements are therefore characterized by basic motifs which are varied according to the circumstances. *Theme and variation* is in fact a basic means of artistic concretization. The "theme" represents a general complex of meanings, and the "variations" its circumstantial realization. Such themes may be a particular type of building as well as motifs of "critical" importance. Well-known examples are the Italian *palazzo*, the French *hôtel* of the *cour d'honneur* type, and the Central European *Bürgerhaus*.[15] The *entrance* is also in most settlements a characteristic motif of "thematic" importance. American towns are thus distinguished by the varied repetition of conspicuous porches. In general "theme and variation" allows for the expression of individual identity within a system of manifest common meanings. Thus it conserves the "spirit" of the place without making it become a life-less straightjacket.

3. History

Our discussion of the identity of a place has already brought us close to the problem of constancy and change. How does a place preserve its identity under the pressure of historical forces? How can a place adapt to the changing needs of public and private life? The common *laissez faire* attitude of today implies a rejection of the first question and a blind acceptance of adaptation to change. We have tried to show, however, that human identity presupposes the identity of place, and that *stabilitas loci* therefore is a basic human need. The development of individual and social identity is a slow process, which cannot take place in a continuously changing environment. We have every reason to believe that the human alienation so common today, to a high extent is due to the scarce possibilities of orientation and identification offered by the modern environment. Piaget's researches in fact show that a mobile world would tie man to an egocentric stage of development, while a stabile and structured world frees his mental powers.[16] Our analysis of the cities of Prague, Khartoum and Rome have moreover shown that it *is* possible to preserve the *genius loci* over considerable periods of time without interfering with the needs of successive historical situations.

Let us sum up *what* ought to be preserved, before we embark upon a discussion of the problem of change. The *genius loci* becomes manifest as location, spatial configuration and characterizing articulation. All these aspects to some extent have to be preserved, as they are the objects of man's orientation and identification. What has to be respected are obviously their *primary* structural properties, such as the type of settlement and way of building ("massive," "skeletal," etc.) as well as characteristic motifs. Such properties are always capable of various interpretations if they are properly understood, and therefore do not hamper stylistic changes and individual creativity. If the primary structural properties are respected, the general atmosphere or *Stimmung* will not get lost. It is this *Stimmung* which first of all ties man to "his" place and strikes the visitor as a particular local quality.[17] The idea of preservation, however, also has another purpose. It implies that architectural history is understood as a collection of cultural experiences, which should not get lost but remain present as *possibilities* for human "use."

What kind of changes does history ask for? In general they may be grouped in three categories: practical changes, social changes and cultural changes. All these changes have physical (environmental) implications. As the cultural and social changes become manifest through their physical implications, we may consider the problem of change in "functional" terms, and ask: How can the *genius loci* be preserved under the pressure of new functional demands? What happens for instance when new or larger streets become necessary? The example of Prague has taught us that a system of paths may develop during history in conformity with the structure of the natural place. We may also remind of Rome, where the breaking through of Corso Vittorio Emanuele (after 1886) fairly well respected the continuity and scale of the traditional Roman street, whereas the *sventramenti* carried out under Fascism introduced a new and "foreign" urban pattern, although the aim was to restore the "greatness" of the Imperial capital.[18] We understand, thus, that it makes sense to talk about "good" and "bad" changes.

One might object, however, that our three main examples are not suitable for illustrating the problem of change. When Prague and Rome started to feel the full impact of modern life, their old centres were already under protection, and Khartoum is still waiting to become a modern metropolis. But the problem of change is not basically different if we consider a great and truly modern city such as Chicago. Even here the *genius loci* is of decisive importance, and changes have to obey to certain "rules." The infinite extension of the Great Plains and Lake Michigan is thus reflected in an "open," orthogonal urban structure, which is concretized in each single building. Enclosed, round or "freely" shaped buildings are "meaningless" in Chicago; the place demands a regular grid. The *genius loci* was understood by the early pioneers, and was set-into-work in the famous "Chicago-construction" which was invented by Jenney about 1880. The local tradition was carried on after 1937 by Mies van der Rohe, whose personal idiom fitted Chicago perfectly. The last and most impressive interpretation of the spirit of Chicago has been given in the 420 metres tall Sears Tower by SOM.[19] Today there is hardly any place where architects are so conscious of the need for adapting to the given environment, and this happens in a city which is among the most dynamic in the world! It would of course have been possible to interpret Chicago differently. The interpretation chosen, however, evidently suited the economic, social, political and cultural intentions of the pioneers. They wanted to concretize the image of an open and dynamic world of opportunities, and chose an appropriate spatial system.

[...]

Our examples show that economic, social, political and cultural intentions have to be concretized in a way which respects the *genus loci*. If not, the place loses its identity. In Boston the *genius loci* was for a long time understood; recently, however, a way of building has been introduced which is foreign to the place, and which deprives man of the satisfaction of one of his most fundamental needs: a meaningful environment. Whereas Chicago possesses the capacity for absorbing this kind of buildings, Boston does not. Thus we learn that cities have to be treated as *individual places*, rather than abstract spaces where the "blind" forces of economy and politics may have free play.[20] To respect the *genius loci* does not mean to copy old models. It means to determine the identity of the place and to interpret it in ever new ways. Only then we may talk about a *living tradition* which makes change meaningful by relating it to a set of locally founded parametres. We may again remind of Alfred North Whitehead's dictum: "The art of progress is to preserve order amid change, and change amid order."[21] A living tradition serves life because it satisfies these words. It does not understand "freedom" as an arbitrary play, but as creative participation.

—~—

As one gets to know different countries; talking with people, eating with people, feeling with people, reading their literature, listening to their music and using their places, one begins to realize that the correspondence of man and place has not changed much throughout history.[22] [. . .]

Creative participation means to concretize the basic meanings under ever new historical circumstances. Participation, however, can only be obtained "by great labor."[23] The "threshold" which is the symbol of participation, is in fact "turned to stone" by "pain." Participation presupposes *sympathy* with things, to repeat the word of Goethe, and sympathy necessarily implies sufferings. In our context sympathy with things means that we *learn to see*. We have to be able to "see" the meanings of the things that surround us; be they natural or man-made. [. . .]

VIII PLACE TODAY

1. The Loss of Place

After the second world war most places have been subjected to profound changes. The qualities which traditionally distinguished human settlements have been corrupted or have got irreparably lost. Reconstructed or new towns also look very different from the places of the past. Before we consider the reasons for this fundamental change, it is necessary to give it a more precise definition in structural terms. Again it is useful to employ our concepts of "space" and "character," and relate them to the more general categories of natural and man-made place.

Spatially the new settlements do not anymore possess enclosure and density. They usually consist of buildings "freely" placed within a park-like space. Streets and squares in the traditional sense are no longer found, and the general result is a scattered assembly of units. This implies that a distinct figure-ground relationship no more exists; the continuity of the landscape is interrupted and the buildings do not form clusters or groups. Although a general order may be present, particularly when the settlement is seen from an airplane, it usually does not bring about any sense of place. The changes done to already existing towns have analogous effects. The urban tissue is "opened up," the continuity of the urban "walls" is interrupted, and the coherence of the urban spaces damaged. As a consequence, nodes, paths and districts lose their identity, and the town as a whole its imageability. Together with the loss of the traditional urban structure, the landscape is deprived of its meaning as comprehensive extension, and reduced to rests within the complex network of man-made elements.

The *character* of the present day environment is usually distinguished by monotony. If any variety is found, it is usually due to elements left over from the past. The "presence" of the majority of new buildings is very weak. Very often "curtain-walls" are used which have an unsubstantial and abstract character, or rather, a lack of character. Lack of character implies poverty of stimuli. The modern environment in fact offers very little of the surprises and discoveries which make the experience of old towns so fascinating. When attempts to break the general monotony are made, they mostly appear as arbitrary fancies.

In general, the symptoms indicate a *loss of place*. Lost is the settlement as a place in nature, lost are the urban foci as places for common living, lost is the building as a meaningful sub-place where man may simultaneously experience individuality and belonging. Lost is also the relationship to earth and sky. Most modern buildings exist in a "nowhere"; they are not related to a landscape and not to a coherent, urban whole, but live their abstract life in a kind of mathematical-technological space which hardly distinguishes between up and down. The same feeling of "nowhere" is also encountered in the interiors of the dwellings. A neutral, flat surface has substituted the articulate ceilings of the past, and the window is reduced to a standard device which lets in a measurable quantity of air and light. In most modern rooms it is meaningless to ask: "What slice of sun does your building have?", that is: "what range of moods does the light offer from morning to night, from day to day, from season to season, and all through the years?"[24] In general, all *qualities* are lost, and we may indeed talk about an "environmental crisis."

It has often been pointed out that the modern environment makes human orientation difficult. The work of Kevin Lynch evidently took this deficiency as its point of departure, and he implies that poor imageability may cause emotional insecurity and fear.[25] The effects of scarce possibilities of identification, however, have hardly been the subject of direct study. From psychological literature we know that a general poverty of stimuli may cause passivity and reduced intellectual capacity,[26] and we may also infer that human identity in general depends on growing up in a "characteristic" environment. The environmental crisis therefore implies a human crisis. Evidently the environmental problem has to be met with intelligence and efficiency. In our opinion this can only be done on the basis of an understanding of the concept of place. "Planning" does not help much as long as the concrete, qualitative nature of places is ignored. How, then, may a theory of place help us to solve our actual problems? Before we give some suggestions for the answers to this question, we have, however, to say a few words about the reasons for the environmental crisis.

Paradoxically, the present situation is a result of a wish for making man's environment better. The open, "green city" thus represented a reaction against the inhuman conditions in the industrial cities of nineteenth century Europe, and modern architecture in general took the need for better dwellings as its point of departure.[27] [. . .]

Why, then, did the modern movement lead to the loss of place rather than a reconquest? As far as we can see, the main reasons are two, and both imply an insufficient understanding of the concept of place. They are moreover related to the dimensions of "space" and "character' and thus confirm the validity of our approach. The first reason has to do with the crisis as an *urban* problem. The loss of place is first of all felt on the urban level, and is, as we have seen, connected with a loss of the spatial structures which secure the identity of a settlement. Instead of being an urban place, the modern settlement is conceived as a "blown-up house," of the type developed by the pioneers of modern architecture: Frank Lloyd Wright, Le Corbusier, and Mies van der Rohe. The plan of the modern house was defined as "open," and the space as a "flowing" continuum which hardly distinguished between outside and inside. Such a space may be appropriate for a sub-urban one-family house (as was the ideal of Wright), but it is questionable whether it suits an urban situation. In the city a clear distinction between private and public domains is necessary, and space cannot "flow" freely. This problem was, however, partly understood by the pioneers; the urban houses of Le Corbusier constitute true "insides" and Mies van der Rohe already in 1934 suggested the use of enclosed "court houses" for the city.[28] When we talk about the modern settlement as a "blown-up house," we rather have in mind the fact that *quarters* and *cities* are conceived as large open plans. In the urban projects of the 'twenties and 'thirties, and in many neighbourhoods which are built today, true urban "insides" are lacking; the space is freely flowing between slab-like buildings which resemble the freestanding walls of an "open" plan, such as the plan of the Barcelona-pavilion by Mies van der Rohe (1929). Spatially, the modern city is therefore based on a *confusion of scales*; a pattern which might be valid on one level is blindly transferred to another. This unfortunate "solution" to the problem of the settlement became possible because the concept of "milieu" was at the outset of the modern movement only understood in physical terms, that is, as a mere need for "air, light and green."[29]

The second reason has to do with the idea of an *international style*.[30] In the 'twenties it was maintained that modern architecture should not be local or regional, but follow the same principles everywhere. It is characteristic that the first volume in the series of *Bauhaus-bücher* was called *Internationale Architektur*. Although Gropius reacted against the world "style," he thus embraced the idea of internationalism. Thus he said: . . . "The forms of the New Architecture differ fundamentally . . . from those of the old, they are . . . simply the inevitable, logical product of the intellectual, social and technical conditions of our age."[31] This does not mean, however, that modern architecture was conceived as a mere practical product; it also ought to give "aesthetic satisfaction to the human soul."[32] This satisfaction ought to be achieved by substituting a "welter of ornament" with simple, mass-produced forms. The result was what Venturi appropriately has called an "architecture of exclusion." This does not mean, however, that the buildings of the European pioneers were aesthetically poor, or "characterless," in an absolute sense. [. . .] But something strange happens when the ascetic character of early modernism is transferred to the *urban* level. What was a subtle interplay of forms, which (almost) confirms Mies' thesis that "less is more," becomes sterile monotony.[33] The essence of settlement consists in *gathering*, and gathering means that different meanings are brought together. The architecture of exclusion mainly told us that the modern world is "open"; a statement which in a certain sense is anti-urban. Openness cannot be gathered. Openness means departure, gathering means return.

It is somewhat unfair, however, to blame the modern movement for shortcomings which only belonged to a certain phase of its development. The modern movement did not come to an end with the images of a green city and an international architecture. Already in 1944 the spokesman of the movement, S. Giedion, put forward the demand for a "new monumentality" and said: "Monumentality springs from the eternal need of people to create symbols for their activities and for their fate or destiny, for their religious belief and for their social convictions."[34] And in 1951 a CIAM conference discussed the *Core of the City*, that is, the problem of introducing in the open tissue of the modern settlement a gathering focus. Again we may refer to Giedion: "Contemporary interest in the core is part of a general humanizing process; of a return to the human scale and the assertion of the rights of the individual . . . "[35] Finally, in 1954, Giedion wrote an essay with the title "On the New Regionalism" where he asked for a new respect for the "way of life," which ought to be studied with "reverence" before designing a project. "The new regionalism has as its motivating force a respect for individuality and a desire to satisfy the emotional and material needs of each area."[36] We understand thus, that the leaders of the modern movement already 20–30 years ago foresaw some of the most important problems we are facing now. Those who got stuck with the early images of a green city and standardized form, were the epigones and vulgarizers of modern architecture.

2. The Recovery of Place

The critics of the modern movement usually take the general discontent with our present environment as their point of departure, and maintain that modern architecture has not been able to solve the problem. Furthermore they often criticize the architects for carrying out any commission without taking into consideration the consequences of their actions for society and the anonymous "user." Thus the social psychologist Alfred

Lorenzer writes: "The architect as a mere technical aid to the dominant powers, corresponds to the ideal of consequent functionalists. The *sacrificium intellectus* of these architects is architecture."[37] Whereas we have taken the general criticism very seriously, and asked whether the modern movement really failed in giving man a new dwelling, the statement of Lorenzer sounds rather surprising to those who have participated actively in the propagation of modern architecture. It is certainly possible to find cases when protagonists of the modern movement served as "aids" to the dominant powers, but the fact that many of them had to leave their countries or withdraw from active professional life because of their artistic creed, is certainly more significant. Thus Giedion could write: "Architecture has long ceased to be the concern of passive and businesslike specialists who built precisely what their clients demanded. It has gained the courage to deal with life. . . . "[38] The criticism of Lorenzer therefore only holds true for the work of certain imitators who did not really understand the aims of the modern movement, and his criticism obviously stems from an insufficient comprehension of the concept of "functionalism." We have demonstrated that the point of departure of the modern movement was profoundly meaningful and that its development showed an ever more complete understanding of the environmental problem. A *constructive* criticism on this basis is given by Robert Venturi in his remarkable book *Complexity and Contradiction in Architecture*, which advocates a "both-and" rather than an "either-or" approach.[39]

The basic aim of the second phase of modern architecture is to give buildings and places individuality, with regard to space and character. This means to take the circumstantial conditions of locality and building task into consideration, rather than basing the design upon general types and principles. [. . .]

Where then, do we find a creative interpretation of the actual situation? Where do we find an architecture which avoids the dangers mentioned above, and represents a true contribution to the solution of the environmental crisis?

Our brief survey of the aims of Aalto, Kahn, the later Le Corbusier, and some exponents of the third generation, shows that the means for a solution of the environmental crisis exist. It has already been demonstrated, and in most convincing ways, how we may create places which serve the complexities and contradictions of contemporary life. When the examples still remain scattered and quantitatively scarce, it is both because of a general social inertia and because of vested interests which do not accept improvements before they "sell." A reason is also, however, the lack of a clear understanding of the environmental problem. It is our conviction that such an understanding only is possible on the basis of a *theory of place*. As particularly valuable contributions to the development of such a theory, we have mentioned the writings of Lynch and Venturi. A theory of place does not only integrate the different contributions, offering a comprehensive conception of the relationship between man and his environment, but it also shows that the history of modern architecture has a direction and a goal: architecture as the recovery of place. Thus the "new tradition" advocated by Giedion becomes meaningful. Moreover the concept of place unites modern architecture with the past. "Both above and below the surface of this century there is a new demand for continuity. It has again become apparent that human life is not limited to the period of a single life-span."[40]

When we see architecture from this point of view, we gain understanding and a direction for our work. This direction is not dictated by politics or science, but is existentially rooted in our everyday lifeworld. Its aim is to free us from abstractions and alienation, and bring us back to things. But theory is not enough to gain this end. It also presupposes that our senses and our imagination are educated. This was also understood by Giedion who concluded his book *Architecture, you and me*, with a chapter on "The demand for Imagination."[41] Today man is mainly educated in pseudo-analytic thinking, and his knowledge consists of so-called "facts." His life, however, is becoming ever more meaningless, and ever more he understands that his "merits" do not count if he is not able to "dwell poetically." "Education through Art" is therefore more needed than ever before, and the work of art which above all ought to serve as the basis for our education, is the place which gives us our identity. Only when understanding our place, we may be able to participate creatively and contribute to its history.

Notes

1. We may in this context remind of concepts such as "form" and "content."
2. Hellpach, *Geopsyche*.
3. A. Rapoport, *House Form and Culture*, Englewood Cliffs 1969, turns these facts upside-down maintaining that the buildings of "the grand design tradition" are unusual and are built to "impress the populace"!
4. Heidegger, *Die Kunst und der Raum*, p. 13.
5. Heidegger, *Poetry . . .*, p. 43.
6. Heidegger, op. cit., p. 204.
7. Thus the Egyptians only built pyramids in the North. In the South, at Luxor-Thebes, they used the mountain itself.
8. The only large-scale exception is the desert, whose "cosmic" character in fact depends on the lack of particular directions. It is "isolated" and simultaneously "infinite."
9. See J. M. Houston, *A Social Geography of Europe*. London 1963. Chapter 8, pp. 157 ff.
10. G. Bugge, C. Norberg-Schulz, *Early Wooden Architecture in Norway*. Oslo 1968.
11. For instance in the *Vierkanthof* or *Rundling*.
12. Heidegger, *Die Kunst und der Raum*, p. 11. My italics and quotation marks.
13. Giedion, *Architecture, you and me*. Cambridge, Mass. 1958, pp. 130 ff.
14. Cf. the concept "strong Gestalt."
15. For variations on the *palazzo* and *hôtel* themes, see Norberg-Schulz, *Baroque Architecture*.
16. Norberg-Schulz, *Existence . . .*, p. 35. For a general discussion of alienation see R. Schacht, *Alienation*. New York 1970.
17. We ought to emphasize again that the atmosphere to a high extent depends on the conditions of *light*.
18. S. Kostof, *The Third Rome*. Berkeley 1973.
19. Designers Fazlur Kahn and Bruce Graham.
20. This has also been forgotten in a city such as Moscow.

21. A. N. Whitehead, *Process and Reality*. New York 1929, p. 515.
22. Already Vitruvius wrote: "Southern peoples have the keenest wits, but lack valour, northern peoples have great courage but are slow-witted." VI, i, ii.
23. Giedion, *Constancy, Change and Architecture*. Harvard Univ. 1961.
24. Kahn, *Credo*, p. 280.
25. Lynch, "The Image . . . ," pp. 4–5.
26. A. Rapoport, R. E. Kantor, "Complexity and Ambiguity in Environmental Design," in *American Institute of Planners Journal*, July 1967.
27. Norberg-Schulz, "The Dwelling and the Modern Movement," in *LOTUS International*, no. 9, Milan 1975.
28. P. Johnson, *Mies van der Rohe*. New York 1947.
29. Which, according to Le Corbusier, are the *joies essentielles*.
30. H. R. Hitchcock, P. Johnson, *The International Style*. New York 1932.
31. W. Gropius, *The New Architecture and the Bauhaus*. London 1935, p. 18.
32. Gropius, op. cit. p. 20.
33. See for instance Lafayette Park in Detroit by Mies van der Rohe, 1955–63.
34. In P. Zucker, *New Architecture and City Planning*. New York 1944. Also in Giedion, *Architecture, you and me*, p. 28.
35. Giedion, op. cit. p. 127.
36. In *Architectural Record*, January 1954, "The State of Contemporary Architecture, the Regional Approach." Also in Giedion, op. cit. p. 145.
37. H. Berndt, A. Lorenzer, K. Horn, *Architektur als Ideologie*. Frankfurt a.M. 1968, p. 51.
38. Giedion, *Space, Time and Architecture*, p. 708.
39. Venturi, *Complexity and Contradiction in Architecture*. New York, 1966.
40. Giedion, *Constancy . . .* , p. 7.
41. Giedion, *Architecture, you and me*. Cambridge, Mass., 1958.

Reading

6

LAURENCE LOH

Conveying the Spirit of Place (2007)

Laurence Loh, a practicing architect in Penang, Malaysia, is recognized as one of the foremost conservation specialists in the region. He is also active as a teacher in various Asian universities and UNESCO-related training programs. In the brief excerpt below, Loh expands on Norberg-Schulz's definition of place to introduce the concept of authenticity, defined in the Nara Document *(1994) as the determining factor in recognizing the value of heritage properties. But assessing the relevance of formal, spiritual, and environmental values must be related to the cultural and social context to which they belong. From this premise, Loh highlights the difference between Western and Eastern notions of value and authenticity and the importance of the intangible to giving a place its distinctive character. "The spirit of place," he concludes, "comes alive not just in the ways a site is conserved and presented, but in the ways it is used and valued by people."*

Spirit of place conveys the cultural essence of a site. In historic sites it encompasses the meanings of a place accrued through time and through its past and present uses. Expressed through the tangible built heritage, these intangible heritage values give the place its distinctive character, an aura that draws people to the place, speaks to them, engages their emotions and, often, gives them a sublime experience of their surroundings.

The concept may be better understood if one alludes to the notion of "body and soul." The body is the physical fabric of the heritage site in its original state and setting. The soul, the spirit of place, is the sum of the site's history, traditions, memories, myths, associations and continuity of meanings connected with people and use over time. Collectively, these tell the story of the place, generate its identity and give it emotional impact.

From LAURENCE LOH, "Conveying the Spirit of Place," in *Asia Conserved: Lessons Learned from the UNESCO Asia-Pacific Heritage Awards for Culture Heritage Conservation* (2000–2004), edited by Richard A. Engelhardt and Montira Horayangur Uanakul (Bangkok: UNESCO, 2007), 9–10, 12. Reproduced courtesy of UNESCO.

How does conservation of a physical structure articulate its spirit of place? Primarily, the place has to be true to its history. This truth must be conveyed in the very process of conservation itself, in a heritage site's physical form, in its contemporary use, and in its interpretation and presentation.

Authenticity, East and West

Most fundamentally, the spirit of a place resides in its authenticity, retention of which is an essential condition of heritage conservation, as reflected in many international charters, especially the Nara Document on Authenticity. The challenge, therefore, is first to identify the authentic elements that define the character of a place and convey its spirit, and, secondly, to ensure that through the conservation process these elements are maintained, safeguarded and celebrated.

[. . .]

But renewal in the conservation of traditional Asian architecture raises the question of authenticity. To Western eyes, accustomed to the preservation of frescoes in their found fragmentary form, not only would the new painting look too bright, fresh and intact, but also it would be deemed poor conservation practice, resulting in the loss of material authenticity. From the Chinese viewpoint, however, renewal of the frescoes conforms to traditional religious beliefs and promotes continuity through artisanship and apprenticeship. There is authenticity in form and function as well as meaning, helping to preserve the temple's cultural essence, enhancing its spirit of place.

Histories Revealed

Since heritage is by definition a legacy of the past, revealing the history of a heritage site is vital to manifesting its spirit of place. Visual evidence of the march of time, and clear interpretation of that evidence, makes people feel they have direct access to the history of the place. This can be achieved by displaying a site's accretions over its lifetime, rather than restoring it to a state at a chosen moment in time. Exhibiting a site's historical timeline often enlarges its significance and amplifies its spirit of place.

[. . .]

Traditions revived, meanings recovered

Spirit of place comes alive not just in the ways a site is conserved and presented, but in the ways it is used and valued by people. How a place is animated by its community gives it meaning, just as a place has meaning for its community, be it historic, social, spiritual or aesthetic. The best conservation brings out the values implicit in the heritage site and integrates them into the life of the community. By taking part in the conservation work, and then using and maintaining the building after it is conserved, the community breathes life into the site, invigorating its spirit of place.

—~~—

Life enhancing architecture

[. . .] [R]egional examples carry within them abstract and metaphysical concepts that are as important as the authentic, physical substance of the sites. Expressions of intangible heritage are "spiritual assets" that are unquantifiable and impossible to label, but nevertheless are central to the Asian approach to heritage conservation—both in how heritage is perceived and how it is conserved.

It is the totality of these tangible and intangible values, recognized and recovered, or created in addition to original themes, which reveal the spirit of place within the architecture. It is an architecture that is life enhancing, that forces us to engage with the site through the use of all our senses, and that allows us to be touched by a place where our sense of self and well being is strengthened and revitalised.

The message that buildings with a strong spirit of place convey is that the answers are not to be found in a purely rigorous analytical approach. A system of evaluation is only a starting point for conservation practice. Looking beyond, it is about allowing what is living to stay alive and true to the place. It is about letting the architecture, the traditions and the cultural essence live on with minimal intervention. Often it is also about the recovery of meaning that has been lost through attrition. If change is necessary, the change must be so seamless that very quickly it becomes absorbed into the original value system. Before long, it attains its own meaning and becomes part of the collective memory, as if it has always been there as part of the place.

Reading

7

LEWIS MUMFORD

What Is a City? (1938)

This reading is from Lewis Mumford's (1895–1990) introduction to the Culture of Cities *(1938), a text that, as the first comprehensive treatment of the nature of the city, would be enormously influential for countless sociologists and urban planners in the years to come. Mumford's general observations about the city remain valid today in spite of the distinction he makes between urban and rural space, which seems less relevant in our time of unprecedented city development. But, as noted by Mumford, cities remain the points of maximum concentration of power and culture, represent "man's greatest work of art," and continue to dominate both materially and spiritually the lives of our communities. As a product of time, they also embody our collective history and, through the act of preservation, "escape the tyranny of a single present" and give "lasting shape . . . to moments that would otherwise vanish with the living."*

The city, as one finds it in history, is the point of maximum concentration for the power and culture of a community. It is the place where the diffused rays of many separate beams of life fall into focus, with gains in both social effectiveness and significance. The city is the form and symbol of an integrated social relationship: it is the seat of the temple, the market, the hall of justice, the academy of learning. Here in the city the goods of civilization are multiplied and manifolded; here is where human experience is transformed into viable signs, symbols, patterns of conduct, systems of order. Here is where the issues of civilization are focused: here, too, ritual passes on occasion into the active drama of a fully differentiated and self-conscious society.

Cities are a product of the earth. They reflect the peasant's cunning in dominating the earth; technically they but carry further his skill in turning the soil to productive uses, in enfolding his cattle for safety, in regulating the waters that moisten his fields,

Excerpt from *The Culture of Cities* in *The Lewis Mumford Reader,* edited by Donald L. Miller (New York: Pantheon Books, 1986), 104–7.

in providing storage bins and barns for his crops. Cities are emblems of that settled life which began with permanent agriculture: a life conducted with the aid of permanent shelters, permanent utilities like orchards, vineyards, and irrigation works, and permanent buildings for protection and storage.

Every phase of life in the countryside contributes to the existence of cities. What the shepherd, the woodman, and the miner know becomes transformed and "etherealized" through the city into durable elements in the human heritage: the textiles and butter of one, the moats and dams and wooden pipes and lathes of another, the metals and jewels of the third, are finally converted into instruments of urban living: underpinning the city's economic existence, contributing art and wisdom to its daily routine. Within the city the essence of each type of soil and labor and economic goal is concentrated: thus arise greater possibilities for interchange and for new combinations not given in the isolation of their original habitats.

Cities are a product of time. They are the molds in which men's lifetimes have cooled and congealed, giving lasting shape, by way of art, to moments that would otherwise vanish with the living and leave no means of renewal or wider participation behind them. In the city, time becomes visible: buildings and monuments and public ways, more open than the written record, more subject to the gaze of many men than the scattered artifacts of the countryside, leave an imprint upon the minds even of the ignorant or the indifferent. Through the material fact of preservation, time challenges time, time clashes with time: habits and values carry over beyond the living group, streaking with different strata of time the character of any single generation. Layer upon layer, past times preserve themselves in the city until life itself is finally threatened with suffocation: then, in sheer defense, modern man invents the museum.

By the diversity of its time structures, the city in part escapes the tyranny of a single present, and the monotony of a future that consists in repeating only a single beat heard in the past. Through its complex orchestration of time and space, no less than through the social division of labor, life in the city takes on the character of a symphony: specialized human aptitudes, specialized instruments, give rise to sonorous results which, neither in volume nor in quality, could be achieved by any single piece.

Cities arise out of man's social needs and multiply both their modes and their methods of expression. In the city remote forces and influences intermingle with the local: their conflicts are no less significant than their harmonies. And here, through the concentration of the means of intercourse in the market and the meeting place, alternative modes of living present themselves: the deeply rutted ways of the village cease to be coercive and the ancestral goals cease to be all sufficient: strange men and women, strange interests, and stranger gods loosen the traditional ties of blood and neighborhood. A sailing ship, a caravan, stopping at the city, may bring a new dye for wool, a new glaze for the potter's dish, a new system of signs for long-distance communication, or a new thought about human destiny.

In the urban milieu, mechanical shocks produce social results; and social needs may take shape in contrivances and inventions which will lead industries and governments into new channels of experiment. Now the need for a common fortified spot for shelter against predatory attack draws the inhabitants of the indigenous village into a hillside fortification: through the compulsive mingling for defense, the possibilities for more regular intercourse and wider cooperation arise. That fact helps transform the nest of villages into a unified city, with its higher ceiling of achievement and its wider horizons. Now the collective sharing of experience, and the stimulus of rational criticism, turn the rites of the village festival into the more powerful imaginative forms of the tragic drama: experience is deepened, as well as more widely circulated, through this process. Or again, on another plane, the goldsmith's passive repository for valuables becomes, through the pressure of urban needs and the opportunities of the market, the dynamic agent of capitalism, the bank, lending money as well as keeping it, putting capital into circulation, finally dominating the processes of trade and production.

The city is a fact in nature, like a cave, a run of mackerel, or an ant heap. But it is also a conscious work of art, and it holds within its communal framework many simpler and more personal forms of art. Mind takes form in the city; and in turn, urban forms condition mind. For space, no less than time, is artfully reorganized in cities: in boundary lines and silhouettes, in the fixing of horizontal planes and vertical peaks, in utilizing or denying the natural site, the city records the attitude of a culture and an epoch to the fundamental facts of its existence. The dome and the spire, the open avenue and the closed court, tell the story, not merely of different physical accommodations, but of essentially different conceptions of man's destiny. The city is both a physical utility for collective living and a symbol of those collective purposes and unanimities that arise under such favoring circumstance. With language itself, it remains man's greatest work of art.

Through its concrete, visible command over space the city lends itself, not only to the practical offices of production, but to the daily communion of its citizens: this constant effect of the city, as a collective work of art, was expressed in a classic manner by Thomas Mann in his address to his fellow townsmen of Lübeck on the celebration of the anniversary of Lübeck's foundation. When the city ceases to be a symbol of art and order, it acts in a negative fashion: it expresses and helps to make more universal the fact of disintegration. In the close quarters of the city, perversities and evils spread more quickly; and in the stones of the city, these antisocial facts become embedded: it is not the triumphs of urban living that awaken the prophetic wrath of a Jeremiah, a Savonarola, a Rousseau, or a Ruskin.

What transforms the passive agricultural regime of the village into the active institutions of the city? The difference is not merely one of magnitude, density of population, or economic resources. For the active agent is any factor that extends the area of local intercourse, that engenders the need for combination and cooperation, communication and communion; and that so creates a common underlying pattern of conduct, and a common set of physical structures, for the different family and occupational groups that constitute a city. . . .

Historically, the increase of population, through the change from hunting to agriculture, may have abetted this change; the widening of trade routes and the diversification of occupations likewise helped. But the nature of the city is not to be found simply in its economic base: the city is primarily a social emergent. The mark of the city is its purposive social complexity. It represents the maximum possibility of humanizing the natural environment and of naturalizing the human heritage: it gives a cultural shape to the first, and it externalizes, in permanent collective forms, the second. "The central and significant fact about the city," as [Patrick] Geddes and [Victor] Branford pointed out, "is that the city . . . functions as the specialized organ of social transmission. It accumulates and embodies the heritage of a region, and combines in some measure and kind with the cultural heritage of larger units, national, racial, religious, human. On one side is the individuality of the city—the sign manual of its regional life and record. On the other are the marks of the civilization, in which each particular city is a constituent element." . . .

Part I

Visual Summary: The Shared Nature of the Historic City

Hubert Sattler, *Panorama of Constantinople from the Suleymaniye Camii*, 1844.

The Austrian painter Hubert Sattler (1817–1904) traveled widely as he created "cosmoramas," or perspective views, of world cities and landmarks. This enticing view, painted for a growing market of European armchair travelers, depicts pre-industrial Istanbul under the Ottoman Empire, prior to the widespread demolition of its vernacular buildings and other historic places that occurred after the 1950s. Post-Ottoman Istanbul has continued to face formidable conservation challenges throughout the past and present centuries.

Church of Santa Maria delle Lauretane, via San Giovanni in Laterano, Rome, during demolition, 1959.

PLATES I.1A, I.1B, AND I.2

These images of "evisceration" from post–World War II Italy were included in Antonio Cederna's *Vandals at Home* (reading 1), a passionate plea to avoid "anonymous, indefinable eyesores." Cederna, a keen photographer, captured the church of S. Maria delle Lauretane in Rome during demolition and a fragment of S. Giovanni in Conca in Milan after demolition. Trivialized to the point of absurdity, the latter church has become a traffic island dominated by the high-rise structures of postwar Milan. This patent reductio ad absurdum testifies to a trend increasingly seen worldwide after Cederna's plea was published.

Part I

VISUAL SUMMARY

Church of Santa Maria delle Lauretane, via San Giovanni in Laterano, Rome, during demolition, 1959.

Fragments of the Church of San Giovanni in Conca, Milan, circa 1950s.

Part I

VISUAL SUMMARY

Procession in the old city of Madurai, India. Drawing by Manohar Devadoss, 1985.

PLATE I.3

Joseph Rykwert (reading 2) reminds us that "the town is an artefact . . . imperfectly controlled[,] . . . more like a dream than anything else." He explains that historically, residents living within this "dream" often mentally "constructed the conceptual prototype of the town," a "psychological space," as well as an ecological or economic one, which reflected the "symbolic world of the citizens." In this sketch of Madurai (Tamil Nadu), India, a local artist captures how urban, physical spaces were (and still are) often conceptualized as venues for religious and spiritual activities.

"Christos Pantokrator" from the thirteenth-century manuscript *Bible moralisée*.

PLATES I.4 AND I.5

In this figure of Christ Pantocrator, we confront God as the supreme architect of the universe, circumscribed within a circle. God endows his creation with geometric principles and symbolic meanings, reflected in all scales, from microcosm to macrocosm, from spiritual to material manifestations, including the human city, an "archetypal reality" as explained by Seyyed Hossein Nasr (reading 3). Thomas Aquinas expressed it this way: "God, Who is the first principle of all things, may be compared to things created, as the architect is to things designed [*ut artifex ad artificiata*]" (*Summa Theologica* I. 27, 1, r.o. 3).

Even more direct connections between human bodies and urban design are seen in this 9-square grid, or *parama-shayika,* a template or "shastric paradigm" for city-building recommended in the *Rajavallabha,* one of several ancient Indian *Vastu Shastra* texts that traditionally served as architectural treatises. Several authors in part I reflect on the significant connections between earthly, physical cities and cosmic, spiritual realities.

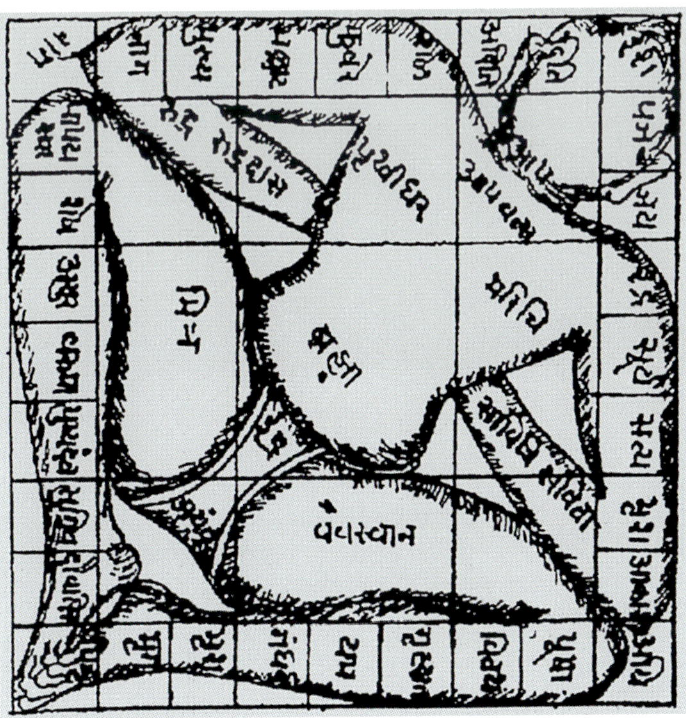

Reproduction of a Paramashayika (template) for city building from an ancient Indian text.

Arulmigu Arunachaleswarar Temple, Tiruvannamalai, Tamil Nadu, India, 2010. Photo by Dmitry Rukhlenko.

The temple of Angkor Wat, Cambodia, 2005. Photo by Charles J. Sharp.

PLATES I.6 AND I.7

Seyyed Hossein Nasr, Paul Wheatley, and Christian Norberg-Schulz (readings 3, 4, and 5) underline the significance of linkages between humankind's cosmic interpretations and certain cities that served as lenses through which humans might get closer to the cosmos. Two examples are Tiruvannamalai (Tamil Nadu), India, and Angkor, Cambodia. The temple-city of Tiruvannamalai has *gopurams*—monumental, ornate gatehouse towers—that define the sacred precincts of the Shiva-inspired Annamalaiyar Temple (ninth century and later additions). Angkor Wat, here seen commanding its moat-protected site, was a Vishnu-venerated temple-mountain (early twelfth century) that simulated the sacred Mount Meru in the Himalayas. It is one of a network of sacred temples associated with the city of Angkor Thom and the vast cultural landscape of early Khmer culture.

The Ise Grand Shrine, Mie Prefecture, Japan, 1953. Photo by the Asahi Shimbun Company.

Itsukushima Shrine, Miyajima Island near Hiroshima, Japan, 2006. Photo by Jeff Cody.

PLATES I.8 AND 1.9

The Ise Grand Shrine is a Shinto shrine (known as Jingū) dedicated to the sun goddess Amaterasu. Although established about two thousand years ago, the first shrine building was erected in the late seventh century. The first ceremonial rebuilding was done in 692. Since then, every twenty years older shrines are dismantled and replaced by replicas erected adjacent to the site of the former structures. The present buildings, dating from 2013, are the sixty-second iteration and will be dismantled and rebuilt again in 2033. The Itsukushima Shrine on Miyajima Island, near Hiroshima, is not rebuilt systematically, but its wooden members are regularly inspected for repairs or replacement. The current shrine, shown here, thus appears much newer than the original one, erected in the sixth century. These sacred places, although often rebuilt, exemplify the respect for the spirit of place highlighted by Laurence Loh (reading 6).

The Grand-Place, Brussels, 2013. Photo by Framepool RS.

Lonely Vista, pencil and paper drawing by Nancy Wolf, 1979.

PLATES I.10 AND I.11

The Grand-Place (Grote Markt) in Brussels has been the city's focal point since the thirteenth century, and the City Hall, with its commanding spire, has been the seat of municipal power since the early fifteenth century. This place exemplifies Lewis Mumford's definition of the city (reading 7) as "the form and symbol of an integrated social relationship," even if this relationship has changed greatly since this square was originally conceived as the "seat of the hall of justice" (Mumford). Conversely, this "Lonely Vista" by the artist Nancy Wolf is a "product of time" (Mumford), where demolition, neglect, and evisceration are in striking contrast to the notion of the city as a "work of art," a definition Mumford applied to the world's most vibrant cities.

PLATE I.12

Jörg Müller's posters vividly illustrate the impact of the automobile on traditional urban settings, in this case an imaginary European city observed in its transformations from 1953 to 1976. This imaginary city is incrementally reconfigured, from being a "specialized organ of social transformation" (Mumford) to a place where new traffic is "beckoned into the historic center . . . [and where] the highly profitable construction of new buildings" (Cederna, reading 1) has erased the memory and meaning of earlier urban places and settings.

The Changing City, from a series of drawings depicting a European city evolving over time. Illustrations by Jörg Müller, 1977.

Part II

Geographic Diversity of Historic Cities

The texts in part I highlight the differences that separate historic cities from contemporary ones, but of course historic cities are themselves different from one another. These differences are most apparent if one compares the urban structures belonging to diverse cultural and geographic traditions. Only a partial survey of these differences is possible in a book of this nature, but we have attempted to select texts that distinguish the characteristics of historic cities that arose in "Western" (Europe and the Americas) and "non-Western" contexts (Africa, China, India, Japan, Middle East). The readings attend to significant urban traditions either as stand-alone settlements or as part of larger city agglomerations, and special consideration is given to differences in physical structure and patterns of use since these are easier to characterize and compare across urban cultures.

Here we confront another series of challenges associated with understanding the nature of the historic city: how to overcome Eurocentric approaches, how to move beyond a preponderance of and overreliance on "Western" scholarship and examples, and how to grasp the often obscured but fundamental internal dynamics of historic cities derived from "non-Western" cultural traditions. As insightful urban specialists have pointed out, trying to explain complex urban dynamics in broad terms—Western/non-Western, traditional/modern, globalized/localized—is fraught with danger.[1] However, the intention here is to suggest the richness and stimulating diversity of the world's urban heritage, not to pigeonhole cities into abstract, confusing, or artificial categories.

In reading 8, Leonardo Benevolo provides a synthesis of the diverse character of European historic cities, which underlies the very multiplicity of urban expressions as a distinguishing feature that can be observed across the continent and throughout an urban history that spans more than fifteen centuries. He recognizes the trademarks of the medieval and postmedieval European city (up to the advent of the Industrial Revolution) in the interplay between regularity and irregularity, in the dynamic—and sometimes the conflict—between the private and public realms, in the limits to growth

Leonardo da Vinci, *Map of Imola*, 1502. Detail. See p. 126.

imposed by defensive circuits and economic self-sufficiency, and in the consequent visual completeness of urban representations where past and present are harmonized in a single and strongly characterized city view. An understanding of these traits is also the key to approaching and resolving the conflicts and planning requirements of the European historic city in the postindustrial age. This is a task that must be tackled with careful forethought and full awareness of the issues and implications at stake. Today, in the absence of the self-regulating mechanisms of gradual city growth and adjustment that prevailed in the past, only a full understanding of the historic urban context can curb irreversible transformations and the use of ill-suited planning practices in old city areas, such as hastily conceived beautification projects, traffic congestion easements, or "functional adaptations" based on incompatible contemporary standards.

The birth and early development of the North American city is discussed by Thomas Bender in reading 9. He sees in the structure of port cities derived from European models the common spatial model for all major cities up to the time of the American Revolution. This was followed by the introduction of the gridiron plan, which became the norm during the nineteenth century and constituted the organizing principle whereby city expansion and the gradual diversification of land uses took place. However, it was only after the 1870s, with new technological developments and the invention of the elevator, electric streetcars, rail networks, and eventually the automobile, that the American city took on its distinct and unmistakable shape: a financial and administrative high-rise core, commercial downtown areas, inner-city working-class neighborhoods and manufacturing districts, and outlying upper-class neighborhoods distributed throughout a larger metropolitan area. This model has been adopted and propagated up to this day in countless cities around the world as one of the paradigms for contemporary urban design and expansion, often done in uncritical and mechanical ways, with little attention paid by decision makers to urban historical roots and formation.[2]

In Latin America, the historic organization of urban space stemmed primarily from colonialism, even if several vast urban centers predated the domination of the continent by colonizers from the late fifteenth to the early nineteenth century.[3] Alfonso Ortiz Crespo (reading 10) summarizes key elements of Spanish colonial urbanism, emphasizing that the grid was the dominant but highly variable model for creating and expanding cities in Latin America. Citing other authorities such as Ramón Gutiérrez and Jorge Hardoy, Ortiz explains that although the Ordinances for New Settlement (Ordenanzas de Nueva Población) were often used as a guide for urban design, there were already 180 cities existing on the continent by 1573 when the Ordinances were promulgated from Spain. Ortiz suggests that in general terms, Latin American cities can be understood as having derived from a common model but with variations according to site, dates of foundation, form, and the imprint of preexisting indigenous settlements.

The basic principles of traditional Muslim cities are analyzed by Stefano Bianca in reading 11. He highlights the homogeneous and yet differentiated structure of the historic urban fabric in cities such as Cairo, Fez, and Tunis, to name but a few. The apparent lack of public open spaces and the absence of freestanding monuments in Muslim cities are often disconcerting to non-Muslim observers, until the nature of the continuous architectural fabric of these cities and their internal workings are perceived and understood. A multifunctional city core, with an interconnected system of covered bazaars, *hammams,* and madrasas, surrounds the principal mosque, whose multiple access points, pillared hall, and interior courtyard act as the city's main public space and concourse area. A complex and highly articulated system of pedestrian spines and alleyways connects this central core to the residential quarters through a system of gates, internal passages, and cul-de-sacs designed to filter the flow of people and manage the transition from public spaces to the private sphere of the individual residential units. Public spaces are organized to protect and avoid any infringement on the privacy of the family. This consistent "cellular" composition of interconnected but clearly diversified precincts explains the "extraordinary sense of inner unity and homogeneity" of traditional Muslim cities. It also explains the devastating impact modern developments have had on their traditional fabric, based as they are on the very opposite: rigid separation of functions, sweeping vehicular movement, and the fragmented and unrelated development of detached architectural structures.

In the early twenty-first century, in terms of infrastructural development and urbanization, Asia is the world's most frenzied continent.[4] China and India, in particular, are luring their residents into historic areas of older cities, newly designed cities rooted in formerly rural landscapes, or newly developed areas of preexisting cities. This seemingly unstoppable urbanizing trend can also be seen in other Asian countries and regions experiencing newfound economic prosperity, such as Japan, Malaysia, Indonesia, and countries bordering the Mekong River. As new cities are created and as older ones face the myriad challenges associated with their need to adapt to activities and densities that outstrip original functions and scales, much loss of historic urban fabric has occurred.[5] Indeed, these losses continue apace.

In light of these cataclysmic urban changes in Asia, how should we understand the basic underlying principles that governed traditional cities in cultures touched by either China's or India's influences? Yinong Xu in reading 13 articulates some of these principles as they relate to China. He notes that the "Chinese city [was not a corporate entity on its own but instead] an instrument of the imperial government." It was "given form not only by the practices and ideas that derived from its particular . . . circumstances, but also by a set of changing values and benefits that were an integral part of a widely shared worldview of the traditional Chinese as a whole"; and it responded to the city-making principles embedded in the "Kaogong-ji" section of the *Zhou li,* with its "cardinal orientation, cardinal axiality, and a more or less square perimeter delimited by a massive wall."[6]

Turning to premodern India, Vibhuti Sachdev and Giles Tillotson (reading 12) explain that "indigenous architectural design was governed by a broad but distinctive body of theory known by the Sanskrit term *vastu vidya* ('architectural knowledge'). It was never static or uncompromising[,] . . . but as it developed over time it provided a consistent logical structure within which to conceptualize design. As architecture has evolved in India over the past 150 years, in response to British colonial and post-colonial policies, *vastu vidya* has become increasingly marginalized and fragmented, decreasingly practised and understood."[7]

This "hidden order" can also be recognized in Japanese traditional cities, some of which reflected Chinese assumptions of urban space, especially during the Tang dynasty (e.g., Kyoto and Nara, eighth and ninth centuries C.E.). However, Barrie Shelton (reading 14) is less interested in precise parallels with Chinese urbanism; instead, he is intrigued with respecting the ways that Japanese urban fabric and form is often simultaneously traditional and contemporary. Shelton points to perceptive comments on distinctive Japanese urban by scholars such as Botond Bognar, who explains that the spatial structure of Western cities "is primarily centrifugal in character," whereas that of Japan "moves, centripetally from outside in."[8] Bognar asserts that "the Japanese city is created, perceived and understood as an additive texture of its parts or places and thus is denoted by the external distribution of signs and symbols rather than by the physical entity of its objects and enclosures."[9] Japanese scholars of their country's urban traditions have likewise explained that Japanese cities reflect an inherent historical layering.[10]

The two readings on African urbanism included in part II, from Suzanne Preston Blier and David Adjaye (readings 15 and 16), also attempt to categorize cities using both geographic and cultural parameters. Blier's synthesis suggests that "three historic patterns of urban settlement are found in Africa": monumental urbanism (with substantial stone structures); satellite urbanism (a result of collaborations "between interlinked community clusters"); and migratory urban settlements (prevailing in central Africa) that share "a relatively nomadic identity." Blier concludes that "taken together, these diverse African settlements convey the early and enduring importance of ancient cities in Africa as focal points of political and artistic engagement, complex administrative organization, and trade affiliations with centres near and far." These older characteristics often persist as determining factors in the organization of some contemporary African cities, such as in the case of Ibadan, Nigeria, and Kampala, the ancient capital of the Buganda Kingdom near Lake Victoria Nyanza, which are often considered superficially the exclusive result of colonial and postcolonial urban developments.

David Adjaye's summary looks at more recent city developments, based on a pilgrimage he undertook to capital cities throughout his native Africa intermittently between 2000 and 2010. In his attempts to understand the nature of urban Africa, he adopts a geographic perspective that divides the continent into six regions: the Maghreb, Desert, the Sahel, Savanna and Grassland, Forest, and Mountain and Highveld. Adjaye points out that each region's unique conditions have influenced its architecture and urbanism.

The readings in part II are salient reminders of how historic cities hold deep (and sometimes deeply hidden) clues that relate to a layering of time, space, and form. Historic cities are palimpsests, where new additions arise over time on the remains of previous buildings and urban places in ways that can be understood by patient, perceptive observers. This has occurred historically in most parts of the world, regardless of geographic location or cultural particularity. However, all too often today this layering is being obliterated—by warfare or insensitive, profit-driven actions—in ways that obscure the connections between present and past, between what Lewis Mumford called at the end of his essay in Part I, "the individuality of the city" and "civilization, in which each particular city is a constituent element." What follows, then, is an implicit, collective plea for a more sensitive understanding of each city's individual character, as reflected in what some call today its "built environment," or what others term its "cultural landscape." Without an understanding of the nature of the historic city (where "nature" connotes a multiplicity of meanings), its future is more imperiled than ever before.

Notes

1. See, e.g., William S. Logan, ed., *The Disappearing "Asian" City: Protecting Asia's Urban Heritage in a Globalizing World* (Oxford: Oxford University Press, 2002).
2. Jeffrey W. Cody, *Exporting American Architecture, 1870–2000* (London: Routledge, 2003).
3. Michael J. Heckenberger et al., "Pre-Columbian Urbanism, Anthropogenic Landscapes, and the Future of the Amazon," *Science* 321 (29 August 2008): 1214–17.
4. Neal R. Peirce and Curtis W. Johnson, eds., *Century of the City: No Time to Lose* (New York: Rockefeller Foundation, 2008); Thomas J. Campanella, *Concrete Dragon: China's Urban Revolution and What It Means for the World* (New York: Princeton Architectural Press, 2008); and Robin Visser, *Cities Surround the Countryside: Urban Aesthetics in Postsocialist China* (Durham, NC: Duke University Press, 2010). Regarding "Asia" as a cultural construct, see especially Vimalin Rujivacharakul, H. Hazel Hahn, Ken Oshima, and Peter Cristensen, eds., *Architecturalized Asia: Mapping a Continent through History* (Hong Kong and Honolulu: Hong Kong University Press and University of Hawai'i Press, 2013).
5. Brenda Yeoh and Shirlena Huang, "Singapore: The Case of the Kampong Glam Historic District," *Cities* 13, no. 6 (1996): 411–22; Elizabeth Vines, *Streetwise Asia: A Practical Guide for the Conservation and Revitalisation of Heritage Cities and Towns in Asia* (Bangkok: UNESCO Bangkok, 2005); Florian Steinberg, *Revitalization of Historic Inner-City Areas in Asia: The Potential for Urban Renewal in Ha Noi, Jakarta, and Manila* (Manila: Asian Development Bank, 2008); and Mike Ives, "Colonial Architecture Fades from Ho Chi Minh City, and Residents Mourn," *New York Times*, 25 February 2016.
6. Yinong Xu, *The Chinese City in Space and Time: The Development of Urban Form in Suzhou* (Honolulu: University of Hawaii Press, 2000), 3, 33.
7. Vibhuti Sachdev and Giles Tillotson, *Building Jaipur: The Making of an Indian City* (London: Reaktion Books, 2002), 7. Not included in the reading in this part.
8. Botond Bognar, *Contemporary Japanese Architecture* (New York: Van Nostrand Reinhold, 1985), 67, quoted in Barrie Shelton, *Learning from the Japanese City: West Meets East in Urban Design* (London: E & FN Spon, 1999), 11–12.
9. Ibid.
10. E.g., Hidenobu Jinnai, "Tokyo Then and Now: Keys to Japanese Urban Design," *Japan Echo* 14 (1987): 20–29; quoted in Shelton, *Learning from the Japanese City*, 14.

Reading

8

LEONARDO BENEVOLO

The Physical Landscape of Cities (1993)

As a practicing city planner, teacher, and architectural and urban historian, Leonardo Benevolo has been enormously influential in shaping the course of global urban studies as well as Italian practices and theories of urban conservation in the post–World War II years. His books on cities and architecture have been translated into numerous languages and, as in the case of The Origins of Modern Town Planning *and the* History of Modern Architecture, *have offered an original vision that goes beyond formal analyses to explain the social and political roots of contemporary architecture and town planning. In this lesser-known essay, Benevolo examines the principles and forms of the European city and provides a stimulating summary of its constituent and lasting character beyond general periodization and geographic diversity.*

How does one approach the multiplicity and richness of the urban landscape in Europe? It seems natural to study each city on its own, or to gather a set of examples, defined by conventional boundaries of place and time: Erwin Gutkind's geographic encyclopedia, organized by nation, or discourses focused on key historic periods: the Middle Ages, the Renaissance, and so on.

To attempt an overarching summary that examines the attribute "European" throughout the entire span of history is much more perilous, and therefore must be brief. In the short book that I wrote for the series "The Making of Europe," I tried to recount sequentially, and succinctly, the stages of historical development. In an even shorter essay such as this one, it is necessary to abandon the anchor of chronology and hazard a general description that illustrates the lasting character glimpsed beneath periodization.

From LEONARDO BENEVOLO, "Lo scenario fisico delle città," in *Principii e forme delle città,* by Leonardo Benevolo et al. (Milan: Credito Italiano-Libri Scheiwiller, 1993), 47–53. Reproduced courtesy of Studio Architetti Benevolo.

The signature paradox of the European city is inescapable: multiplicity constituting the very essence of specificity. In the interests of expediency, I have condensed the general discourse to only a few pages, and return to a few provocative points, arranging them in twenty or so examples chosen randomly among cities, not too big or too small, that are well suited to embody the diversity of circumstances and outcomes that the last fifteen centuries of history and the two and half million square kilometers of European territory manifest. The reader can easily substitute other more familiar examples, recomposing the array of diversity for himself.

A good dose of the arbitrary and subjective resides in the general considerations and examples, which I could not eliminate and which seems to me coherent with our subject. European reality—in this and other disciplines—allows for a great number of viewpoints, angled according to the inclinations of the writer. I let my own guide me, without trying to correct them, and perhaps this is a way to stay inside the complicated and paradoxical history of our subject.

In reality—and not in the written word—homogenization of European differences is quite probable, due to the pressures of the common market and the mass media of our time. Defense of these differences is an important task but has been rehashed enough: the most refined syntheses are exposed to the risk of banality, just as the discourse slides from the world of daily life into that of entertainment and leisure time. Remaining engaged with reality, which means being precariously poised between the perfection and imperfection of discourses, is for the moment inevitable. Historical research can offer itself as a reproduction of the complications and convolutions of its own subject, sacrificing somewhat the coherence of the larger picture.

The fundamental character of European cities engages oscillations between select pairings of polarities, which can be described as follows.

I. Regularity and Irregularity

The tension between these two terms is introduced at the outset by the ambivalent relationship—that of origin and separation—with the ancient Greco-Roman city.

Beginning with the first urban experiments of three thousand years ago, the city is an elaboration of the enclosed space, excluding the boundless surrounding environment and isolating a bounded environment, perfected in its architectonic scope. Each environment sees itself from within, and only a few elevated structures—the *ziggurat*, or pyramids—emerge for a moment in time and are visible from the outside, recalling the neolithic custom of arranging human artifacts directly in the natural landscape.

In the Greco-Roman city, some enclosed areas—the columns that encircle the periptery temple and some other public buildings—are seen from without and define the overall space of the city. This contrasts with citizens and their homes, and expresses the dominant character attributed to the communal homeland and its emblems. The architecture inside the urban area characterizes the city in its entirety. Since the time of Hippodamus, the extension of a systematic design for the city plan derives from this same concern. In the Roman era, uniform arrangement of monumental buildings, the urban terrain, and rural plottages becomes a sign of civilization, which makes Roman settlements, among the inarticulated landscapes and preexisting communities, recognizable in all regions of the empire.

The Greco-Roman urban and public building framework disintegrates after the collapse of the empire; European cities born from its vestiges, or, in the northern realms beyond the borders of antiquity, shed its sacral and hierarchical character (as we shall see) but are still pressed to compare themselves with this past, different yet a nevertheless obligatory contrast. There is the grandiose body of Rome, ravaged by the Gothic War of 535–553 and more deeply by the Norman conquest in 1085. There is the mirage of the new imperial capital, Constantinople, that survives, impregnable, beyond the Dardanelles. There are the ruins of cities, small and medium in size, the aqueducts, roads, bridges, gateways, reservoirs, city walls, and border fortifications, that through their survival delineate the ancient imperial territory. Even for the cities born *ex novo* during the Middle Ages in regions where Roman colonization did not arrive, the psychological reference point of an antiquity made mythic by distance remains valid: Aachen, which looks to Ravenna, Moscow, which is called the third Rome. Cohabitation, physical or mental, with ruins that signify a lost level of civilization, in part forgotten, remains a constant companion of European cities: during the enigmatic Middle Ages, from the Renaissance and beyond, recognized as a legitimate source of "modern" culture, and also as a general meditation on the ultimate causes of human actions: the envy of time and fortune's capriciousness. The example of medieval and modern Rome—contrasted with the looming bastions of the ancient metropolis at every step—demonstrates this best of all [. . .] .

The specific challenge that ancient cities present is precisely the intellectual regularity of their design and their normalizing architectonic framework. The distinct characteristic of European cities, from the Middle Ages on, is instead acceptance, and at times, systematization of irregularity, which allows for complete consonance between place and function. Between regularity and irregularity, a tension is established that is never fully resolved in one sense or the other. In the Gothic era, Western Europe reinvents a continuous three-dimensional grid, capable of accommodating every kind of architectural object in the city plan. During the Renaissance, this grid is rationalized, arranging in its intersections architectonic orders gathered from antiquity, and presumes, in the pages of its treatises, to impose a predetermined geometric form on entire cities. The Enlightenment attempts to exhume and scientifically verify the controversial architectonics inherited from antiquity and to adopt them as an unchanging rule for the design of modern structures. Sooner or later each of these initiatives, however, cannot grasp a world irreversibly changed.

Perfection assumed to be a paradigm of the Greco-Roman city, materialized in the dominance of grandiose public structures, collapses intellectually. It is supplanted by an accepted imperfection that opens, nevertheless, the field to outcomes of great qualitative value: Venice, Pisa, Florence, Bruges, Nuremberg, Urbino, Bath. European cities realize the thousand variations of a non-paradigmatic excellence, founded in the specificity of a local situation, not reproducible, and mysteriously sublimated to a universal plane. This secondary road to qualitative perfection, paradoxically gained from a sum of balanced defects, is the distinct contribution of European tradition to the present era, where it is the only viable model in a society as pluralist and incomplete as ours.

The infinity of instances where regularity and irregularity intersect is a concrete feature distinguishing European urban spaces. The layouts of medieval urban areas that remain dominant in most European cities are, in succeeding epochs, systematized, reinterpreted, and enriched through the application of elementary geometry, projective geometry, and finally by Hogarth's line, freely curving, which becomes the rule for planning parks from the mid-eighteenth century onward, yet persists just enough to impede the homogenization of the urban landscape to a single visual norm. Exactly this contamination, from thousands of sources, becomes the guarantee of historical authenticity in urban development, the recognizable sign of European space in contrast to the arrhythmic convolutions of Islamic and foreign urban designs, or the uniform regularity of colonial grids, which Europeans laid out on five continents. This establishes a subtle yet insuperable distinction between architecture and urban design, between planning a building and planning an urban organism. The city is not just a large building, but rather the place where many buildings cohabitate and displace each other; architecture manifests itself and discovers its limitations when confronted with other buildings.

II. Public and Private

The second aspect of the European city's detachment from the ancient city is the desecration of public structures, introducing a new homogeneity among all monuments. The idea of the city as a supreme manifestation of human coexistence, theorized in Aristotle's *Politics* and realized to some degree in the Greco-Roman experience, is definitively dismissed by Saint Augustine, who in *City of God* situates the city in heaven, making it a metaphor for saints living in the presence of God. The reality of the sublunary world becomes, from the Christian perspective, contingent, perishable, that is, materially incomplete.

From the outset, Christian churches do not resemble pagan temples, nor the buildings that demonstrate the eminence of secular public functions, like the baths and theaters. The latter are monuments intentionally heterogeneous from the rest of the city, even in the technological sense: they are constructed by different processes and with different materials in order to endure longer. The first Christian basilicas of the 4th century A.D., on the other hand, even when grandiose and richly decorated, are technically ordinary structures, destined for an average life span.

The relevant consequence, in our field, is a new distribution of the tasks that control urban design. The authorities, whether civil or religious, are tasked with coordination that nevertheless does not absolutely prevail over the inhabitants' initiatives, a precariously balanced confrontation. On occasion, antagonism arises between them, open to a range of demands that exclude either the absolute dominance of the public planners or the absolute freedom of private persons. Only during a short period of time, in the first half of the 19th century, political theory hypothesized each of these extremes in response to new problems raised by the Industrial Revolution. Yet immediately afterward both were rejected, and specific experiments are collocated, as always, in an intermediate zone.

This allows for the direct comparison of all urban monuments, and grounds fragmentary land parcels in a spatial continuity extending to the entire urban organism. Some buildings possess their own inner balance between their physical volume and adjuvant spaces (courtyard, lawns, garden), but all face the public space by means of a two-sided wall—the facade—that simultaneously serves the building (it provides light, gives access, introduces it) and qualifies the surrounding urban environment.

In particular, the illumination of internal spaces provides many suggestive solutions that together characterize the buildings and the urban fabric. It is enough to recall two: the transformation of the facade into a perforated screen, which Venice extrapolated from Constantinople, and entails the transversal arrangement of walls studded with pillars lining deep passageways. Then the opposite solution, which was adopted in Bruges, Lübeck, and in many other northern cities, which frames the building with gabled, load-bearing walls parallel to the facade, entrusting illumination of the interior to the steeply pitched roof, onto which open various orders of dormer windows. In the first example, a horizontal curtain of loggias faces the canals in continuous procession. In the second, a serrated curtain that denounces the individuality of every building, even if the voids remain small and uniform. Both devices can be selectively curved, to adapt to the very sinuosity of the walls.

The specifically European invention of the facade facilitates cooperation between civic authorities and particular subjects. Public space is enriched to the detriment of the private spaces they face. City regulations are carried out above all at this interface, standardizing it in various ways: in the Middle Ages with detailed rules regarding planimetric positioning, layout, overhangs, and materials; also in the Renaissance imposing a uniform design on the architectonic apparatus.

Public space, in turn, is not a limited enclosure, or series of enclosures: it becomes a continuous environment in the body of the city, including the streets and squares, organizing them in a hierarchy referring to the organism as a whole. In this environment, the facades of public and private objects coexist, and the abrupt passages between their architectonic character remain in plain sight. The continuity of the urban landscape becomes a narrative: open, unfinished. Ruptures, conflicts of dimensionality and form, are absorbed in the urban spectacle, amending and balancing the one-sidedness of architectonic choices at the building level, allowing the fringes to remain free for other amendments and developments with the passing of time.

III. Autonomy and Environmental Integration

The character of extensive urban organisms depends in the first place on the nature of public authority, which is in general complex, and originates from, in diverse ways, the very population of the city.

Political autonomy, which European cities share with the most ancient Sumerian cities and the Greek *polis,* determines the principal characteristics of the built environment. Most important, its physical dimension. European cities, even if open to the world economy on the horizon, do not have the resources of a large territory, and do not grow beyond a limited size, which during the Middle Ages was around 500 hectares and 150,000 to 200,000 inhabitants, its constancy due to a series of "normal" technical conditions: pedestrian mobility over distances not greater than two or three kilometers, coverable in not more than half an hour; access to water and food without organization and exceptional effort (unlike in the ancient world, Islamic and Eastern, where large despotic states were able to support—found, destroy, transport—much bigger cities, some thousands of hectares with a million or more inhabitants). After the 16th century, some cities that will become the stable capitals of nations—Madrid, Paris, London, Vienna, Naples—slowly grow to a half million inhabitants until the Industrial Revolution makes larger quantities possible. First London reaches a million inhabitants at the end of the 18th century. But even today, while elsewhere in the world a few cities reach ten or twenty million, Europe has succeeded in controlling the size of London and Paris to around six to seven million. Autonomy has a qualitative effect: it means relationships of two kinds between governments and the governed, invention and preservation of the collective identity, and the ability to share cultural heritage, using differences as an opportunity for debate. Each city has a distinct character, even an excess of character, which becomes capable of orienting modern development much more prominently, and behaves in turn like a psychological brake that impedes the arrival of quantitative growth and its cancellation of qualitative identity.

Since the Middle Ages, the overall view of the city from without has been carefully curated. The horizontal dimension, subject to the limitations described above, is balanced somewhat by the vertical structures—towers, belfries, domes—that signify the principal public and private buildings and audaciously approach technical limitations. Often one of these buildings—the cathedral, town hall, or noble residence—is treated as the central object of the visual picture, while the surrounding outer city wall dotted with towers delineates the external boundary. Perspective views of the entire city that were disseminated from the late 15th century onward express and emphasize this investigation of visual completion. Remember the "chain" view (ca. 1490), in which Florence resembles a flower, where Brunelleschi's dome is the central stamen, and the city wall, simplified to appear circular, is the surrounding corolla. The natural background is sometimes distanced, sometimes fused with the selfsame urban image, encompassing the most recognizable element (Mount Etna in Catania) in the representation. For some cities located in the hills, the distinction between artificial and natural landscapes is impossible, and the city becomes an inhabited three-dimensional hill (Orvieto, Siena, Urbino). The alliance between architecture and the natural tableau, very tight in the Middle Ages, remains for a long time a characterizing element of European cities. Openings between the constructed landscape and the open landscape—cultivated countryside, the sea, rivers, forests, hills—are integrating parts of the traditional image: it is enough to recall Siena, Urbino, Prague, Avignon, Genoa, Naples, Toledo.

Nature and history reflect one another directly in these cities; they exchange qualities and offer up a compelling foundation for human presence and settlements in the earthly landscape.

IV. Continuity through Time: Permanence and Innovation

The characteristics listed up until now—irregularity, imperfection, autonomous characterization, with their formal consequences—cooperate and ingrain temporal events in the urban landscape with particular clarity. The city is by nature an engine of time that conserves the past and prepares the future. The European city fulfills this function so pliably that it transforms itself into a kind of chronological diagram. From the diachronic continuity of history a synchronic image is extracted, immediately understood, which plays a fundamental role in daily life and acts as a stabilizing element for cultural balance, epoch after epoch.

From the 16th to the 18th century, European culture feels the need to recapitulate this patrimony, with the tools of literature and painting. . . . [T]he most refined means of visual culture are busied with representation of the shape of the city, where all contributions from the preceding historical eras are assembled and reconciled.

From the late 18th century onward the Industrial Revolution mobilizes European cityscapes and countrysides, fracturing the balance maintained over many centuries: the number of buildings increases, new kinds of settlements appear—industrial factories, workers' housing projects, new public services (hospitals, markets, schools, cemeteries, etc.), new modes of travel (canals in the late 18th century, the railways of the mid-19th century, roads for automobiles, airports and electrical wires at the onset of the 20th century)—and reduce dramatically the time available to calculate the effects of these hurried changes.

The continuity of the cycle of experience that we have attempted to describe is endangered. But the framework of the city realized over the preceding thousand years and the universe of habits, thoughts, and desires accumulated over such a long time within it resists in its own way, and is still valid as a primary reference for culture and the daily life of the present.

Assessment of the balancing act between permanence and transformation, between values—those saved, lost, and added—is on the one hand the necessary conclusion of the discourse under consideration up until now; on the other hand, the point of departure of today's key tasks. [. . .]

Reading

9

Thomas Bender

The American City: What Shaped Its Development? (1982)

An American historian specializing in urban history and the humanities, Thomas Bender has written extensively on the intellectual fabric and social identity of North American cities. In this essay, he follows the development of the American city from the beginning of the nation through its gradual transformation in the mid-nineteenth century and the momentous upward and outward changes that, after the 1870s, followed the introduction of the elevator, the electric streetcar, and the elevated railway. The diffusion of skyscrapers and the enormous city expansions that have resulted in the conurbations of the East and West Coasts can be traced back to these earlier developments, which became one of the models for contemporary megalopolises worldwide.

Cities, like people, have individual "personalities." The particular character of a city—its physical form and its social organization—is the product of its singular geography and history. It is difficult, therefore, to write a history of the American city. Yet in reflecting upon the past two centuries of American urban development, it is immediately apparent that whatever the particular variations one finds in New York, Boston, Philadelphia, Chicago, St. Louis, New Orleans, and Los Angeles, all of these cities and others have participated in a general process of urbanization. And it is possible, if these variations are kept in mind, to describe the general historical trends and benchmarks in the history of the physical development of the American city.

At the time of the American Revolution, all major American cities were port cities. The port provided the basis of the urban economy, and it supplied a principle of order for the social and physical organization of the city. The image of the port identified the city, and it is for this reason that nearly all views of New York, Boston, and Philadelphia during this period place the harbor, with its ships and wharves, in the foreground. This idea of the city as a port continued to dominate urban perception until the middle of

From Thomas Bender, "The American City: What Shaped Its Development?" in *Cities: The Forces That Shape Them,* edited by Lisa Taylor (New York: Rizzoli International, 1982), 50–52.

the nineteenth century. The opening passage of *Moby Dick* (1851) captures the physical and the psychological centrality of the port in New York City on the eve—as Melville's last sentence suggests—of that city's transformation into an industrial and administrative center:

> There is now your insular city of the Manhattoes, belted round by wharves. . . . Right and left, the streets take you waterward. . . . Circumambulate the city of a dreamy Sabbath afternoon. Go from Corlears Hook to Coenties Slip, and from thence, by Whitehall northward. What do you see? Posted like silent sentinels all around the town, stand thousands upon thousands of mortal men fixed in ocean reveries. Some leaning against the spiles; some seated upon the pier heads; some looking over the bulwarks of ships from China. . . . But these are all landsmen; of week days pent up in lath and plaster—tied to counters, nailed to benches, clinched to desks.

Although the sea and the port remained dominating facts of urban life during the first century of American national existence, the city by 1850 differed in important respects from its late-eighteenth-century predecessor. It is common and appropriate to call the late-eighteenth-century city a walking city. A comfortable walk represented the limits of human movement and, by implication, urban culture. In our age of telephones and television, we are inclined to forget that until the second half of the nineteenth century people and messages moved at the same speed; messages, whether spoken or written, could be communicated only through direct human contact. With such limits on movement and communication, urban life could not be managed over a territory with more than a one- or two-mile radius from the center.

Within the compact bounds of the walking city, various urban activities and social classes were situated cheek by jowl. In the wharf area of the city there was some clustering of special functions, but for the most part, functional specialization of land use was very weakly developed. There was an identifiable cluster of counting houses, warehouses, and shipping-related artisans around the wharves; nearby there was a group of homes for rich merchants. But that was the extent of differentiation. There was no strictly residential district, nor was there a district exclusively devoted to business. Residential segregation by class and ethnicity was quite limited. In fact, given the character of the social and economic system, employees often lived in the same houses as their employers. Businesses were small; the only employees were one or two apprentices or young clerks in training. Work was often conducted in the home of the master or merchant, and the young employees lived with their employer as one of the family. The architecture of the city reflected this absence of sharp distinction among functions. Business and residential architecture were of similar style and scale.

Urban development in the decades following the Declaration of Independence proceeded slowly; but after 1820, changes in the Atlantic economy and the development of internal transportation and a national market within the United States stimulated unprecedented urban growth. In 1800, no American city had a population of one hundred thousand; only 6 places had ten thousand or more people. By 1870, however, 168 places had populations over ten thousand, and 15 cities had populations over one hundred thousand. New York, with its population edging toward one million, was for the first time entering the same league as Paris and London. It is not, however, simply a matter of noting that there were now large cities; it is also important that during the first three-quarters of the nineteenth century, a dense national system of cities was developed in the United States.

This period of prolific city founding and building made the gridiron plan the basic urban form in America. Although there had been earlier gridiron plans (Philadelphia in the seventeenth century, Savannah and Los Angeles in the eighteenth century), the gridiron was now the norm. The Illinois Central Railroad even developed a standard form for platting cities along its route; one had only to write in the name of the town. The future growth of some older cities also came to be based on the gridiron. New York, for example, approved in 1811 a gridiron plan to govern the northward development of Manhattan Island above Houston Street. Of major American cities, only central Boston and Lower Manhattan exemplify the earlier European sense of enclosed space and of streets as milieus rather than as arteries. The feeling of openness and movement that is characteristic of the American city is a legacy of the adoption of the gridiron as the basic American urban form. This distinctive quality struck Jean-Paul Sartre when he visited New York in 1945: "These long, perfectly straight lines suddenly gave me the feeling of space. Our cities are constructed to protect us against it; the houses cluster like sheep. But space crosses through New York, quickening and expanding it."

Changes in the economy and in the scale of cities altered the organization of social life and space within individual cities. Although the port remained an important image and fact at mid-century, the city no longer clustered so tightly about the harbor. Cities were becoming more extensive, partially aided by the development of omnibuses and horse-drawn street railways. The separation of work and residence, dating from this period, marks a fundamental watershed in the business and social history of urban life. With the breakdown of the traditional apprenticeship system for artisans, work groups increased in size and most employees remained wage-earners for life. Hence they sought out cheap housing of their own, while the master, now a "boss" or "merchant capitalist," also moved away from the workplace to an exclusively residential area. Although a full specialization of urban space would occur only after 1870, the future had become apparent by mid-century: the places of work and residence had become distinguished in terms of location, architecture, and social experience.

To contemporaries, the mid-nineteenth-century city most resembled chaos. It was a crowded jumble of small buildings. The vast increase in population occurred within tight constraints. Construction technology, as well as the lack of a safe passenger elevator, kept the upward limit of buildings at five stories, and adequate urban transit had to await the electric streetcar in the late 1880s. Even though the city's territory had been extended somewhat by mid-century. the increase in population was accommodated primarily by unprecedented crowding.

If the eighteenth-century city had been compact and orderly enough to be grasped as a whole, for the urban dweller after 1850 the city was a multiplicity of environments that were not known. Bird's-eye views of the city, models, and observation points, such as church steeples, were popular ways of trying to get an image of the whole.

In retrospect, the mid-century city was not so lacking in rhyme and reason as contemporaries feared. By 1870, there were strictly commercial areas along the waterfront; nearby were the sorts of manufacturing enterprises associated with shipping or likely to be organized by merchant capitalists. In a distinct area, as on State Street in Boston or Wall Street in New York, were clusters of financial institutions. Not far away were slum neighborhoods (as New York's Five Points and the Lower East Side generally) and an upper class neighborhood (as Washington Square in New York or Beacon Hill in Boston). Beyond this center-city cluster of commercial and residential space, the bulk of the city extended perhaps three or four miles into a kind of ragged and mixed-use cityscape marked by pockets of commercial, industrial, and residential uses. While one could call this fringe area confused, it is more precise to call it ill-defined and literally undistinguished urban space.

After 1870, technology facilitating both vertical and horizontal movement provided the basis for a dramatic reorganization of urban form in America. The first use of an elevator in an office building was in New York's Equitable Life Assurance Building in 1871. The elevator equalized the rental value of all floors. This raised land values in the center of the city and drove less intensive land users out. Between 1870 and 1920 the tall central-city office building eclipsed the old five-story city and created a skyline, the icon of the modern American city. For some, the skyscraper symbolized possibilities of modernity; for others, these fruits of technology were more problematic. When T. H. Huxley entered New York Harbor in 1875, he rejoiced in the sight of the Tribune and Western Union Buildings, symbols of modern communications, battling a traditional urban icon, the spire of Trinity Church, for command of the skyline. But when Henry James returned to New York in 1904, after a thirty-year absence, he was grieved to see Trinity "so cruelly over topped."

However one interprets the tall office building as a symbol, it represented in fact a new era in the history of the urban economy. During the age of trusts, large cities, especially New York City, became financial and administrative centers, directing national corporations with plants in a myriad of smaller cities and towns. These changes in the economy, as much as building techniques, brought the skyscraper to the city.

While the city was soaring upward, it was also extending outward, producing the well-known American pattern of central business core, close-in slum and working class residential areas, and a series of prosperous suburban residential rings. The advent of electric streetcars and elevated railways extended the bounds of the city to a radius of ten miles or more. The effect of the streetcars, which typically converged at the center, was to create a funnel that exalted the central business district as the locale for offices, entertainment, government, department stores, and specialty shops. The downtown became the symbol of civic unity and achievement, and during this period a variety of City Beautiful plans were proposed; those adopted left a legacy of Beaux-Arts civic centers.

The creation of purely residential neighborhoods, having only local consumer businesses like grocery stores, candy stores, flower shops, and, later, neighborhood movies, was another product of this expansion of the city. Neighborhoods, defined by class and ethnicity, arrayed themselves along the streetcar lines radiating from the center. Manufacturing, which had once shared central city sites with other mixed uses, now demanded more and different space. Factories were built along industrial corridors well served by water and rail transportation. These areas were not so far out as the upper-class suburban rings, and, as one might expect, they were usually near the inner ring of residential neighborhoods populated by the working classes.

The years from 1890 to 1945 were the classic years of the big city and its "downtown." After World War II, the streetcar no longer funneled all urban activity toward the center. The automobile and the freeway offered a more extensive and flexible pattern of urban movement; concurrently, the FHA, the G.I. Bill, and the tax system made suburban living possible for the greater part of the urban population. The central city (with an increasingly black population) lost importance relative to a variety of other (overwhelmingly white) sub-centers in the metropolitan region. The cityscape became flattened out into one of two forms: a multicentered grid on the model of Los Angeles or a center city with a circumferential series of sub-centers of residence and business, as in the case of Boston. The majority of jobs and homes in most metropolitan areas had shifted from the city to the suburbs by the 1970s. The icons of the metropolitan area became the suburban home, the shopping center, the industrial park, the office building in a "campus" setting, and the desolated and impoverished inner city.

In a sense we have today returned to the mixed urbanscape with the multidirectional movement that was characteristic of the old walking city, but life in modern metropolitan areas is lived on a stage that would have been unimaginably vast to our urban forebears. Indeed, some commentators are inclined to refer to the populated areas between Washington and Boston on the East Coast, around the Great Lakes, and between Los Angeles and San Francisco on the West Coast as megalopolises. The walking city was a world unto itself; now, it seems, all the world is a city.

Reading

10

Alfonso Ortiz Crespo

The Grid: Classical Model (2007)

Alfonso Ortiz Crespo is an architect from Quito, Ecuador, specializing in architectural conservation. He has been engaged directly in the restoration of various historic buildings in Quito and has published on the urban history of the city and its monuments. In the book Damero *(Grid), coedited with Matthias Abram and José Segovia Nájera, Ortiz offers an overview of traditional Latin American cities, whose early development was largely based on the regular gridiron plan codified by the Spanish colonizers in the Ordenanzas de Nueva Población, promulgated by King Felipe II in 1573. The reading provides a succinct account of traditional Latin American cities categorized by form and period of founding. In addition to the gridiron model, Ortiz considers the spontaneous foundations and the settlements that originated from or were superimposed on older indigenous layouts.*

Jorge Enrique Hardoy, one of the most important scholars of the urban history of Latin America, writes:

> The origin of urban centers, whether planned or spontaneous, and the functions they fulfilled were both intimately linked to their location. These were the factors that most influenced the divergence of colonial cities from legislation that endeavored, by means of certain urban development principles, to determine their internal structure. Nevertheless, the traditional model was not an idea elaborated in Spain or Europe and then transplanted to the Americas. It was a product of the progressive perfection of certain distinct concepts that were employed in the Americas comprehensively for the first time. Legislation supported this process but did not precede it.[1]

From Alfonso Ortiz Crespo, "El damero: Modelo clásico," in *Damero*, edited by Alfonso Ortiz Crespo, Matthias Abram, and José Segovia Nájera (Quito: FONSAL, 2007), 79–82. Edited and published by the Fondo de Salvamento del Patrimonio Cultural (Fonsal), currently Instituto Metropolitano de Patrimonio - Municipio de Quito.

For his part, Ramón Gutiérrez explains the different processes of occupation of the American territory. The kingdom of Portugal, more intent on creating enclaves, developed a city that "accumulated the colonizing knowledge of the Portuguese: It respected topographies, adapted to the conditions of the setting, and sought solutions particular to each circumstance. The Spaniards, more intent on multiplying their foundations in the immense territory, required the rapid formulation of a model,"[2] in order to create nodes for a network that combined navigation with the penetration of a very ample territory.

J. E. Hardoy reminds us that since the most important and most populated cities used the grid, **the idea that all colonial cities employed the regular model has become widespread,** with the orthogonal grid forming square blocks, which identifies it as the traditional model of the Spanish-American city. He also notes that **secondary cities not adhering to this regularity are much more numerous.** In fact, the existence of legislation does not necessarily mean that all the cities were founded following the established model. First of all, one must remember that **by the time of the enactment of the Ordinances in 1573 more than 180 cities had already been founded on the continent and, second, although there was a will to use the grid, not all colonial Spanish cities in the Americas followed it.** In any case, it is necessary to emphasize the desire to employ a geometric urban structure, *characterized by order, rationality, and the amplitude of its basic organization.*

The reasons that some of the new cities did not follow the traditional model differ widely. As mentioned above, the Ordenanzas de Nueva Población, the body of law that precisely fixed the model, were not issued until 1573. Consequently, many of the cities that had been founded in the preceding seven decades were the result of experiences that gradually perfected a model that subsequently was transformed into law. In addition, as we shall see below, many cities arose from spontaneous settlements; others were mining centers situated in rough terrain near the deposits; certain foundations sought safety in their location, so that the topographic conditions (hills or valleys) or the presence of geographic accidents (rivers or ravines) imposed themselves on the comfort of flat terrain on which to lay out a regular grid; port cities were established near the best anchorages and in easily defended sites; in effect, territorial context took precedence over any other criteria.

Typology of Cities

These cities formed nodes in a very extensive network that served to control, administer, exploit, maintain, and defend the territory. Hardoy stresses that their **functions were intimately linked to their location;** a maritime city, for example, had different functions from a city in the interior. Several years ago a worthwhile effort was made to systematize certain functional, formal, and situational characteristics, as well as relationship and development, of Spanish-American cities in order to understand them better; this study continues to be valid and is well worth reconsidering.[3]

> In the face of the complexity of the phenomenon, in its temporal as much as in its spatial aspect, the "type" seems a valid instrument, capable of communicating and generalizing an urban reality. Understanding "type"—within a theory of approximate knowledge—as the ordered combination of different classifications that, in fact, allow one to take inventory of a great variety of elements, in this case cities, based on various groups.[4]

Thus this study developed a **classification by date of foundation:** *first epoch* (1492–1570), from the *discovery, new settlement, to pacification*, until the city acquired its determining characteristics; *second epoch* (1570–1700), when the urban model was consolidated and colonial society, just as much as production and commerce, was firmly structured; *third epoch* (1700–1810), during which the autonomy of the colonies progressed to complete independence, generating their own structures.

In terms of **form** the cities were classified as *regular,* by its grid layout, for example, Guatemala City (Guatemala). This resource of the grid is easily manageable in the territory, because it can expand indefinitely as long as significant physical obstacles do not prevent it. This is what occurred in cities as large as Buenos Aires, in which the original grid utilized at its founding continuously expanded with the passage of time and was transformed into an immense grid that today occupies all of the territory. The grid experienced several transformations on account of a series of urban innovations that became

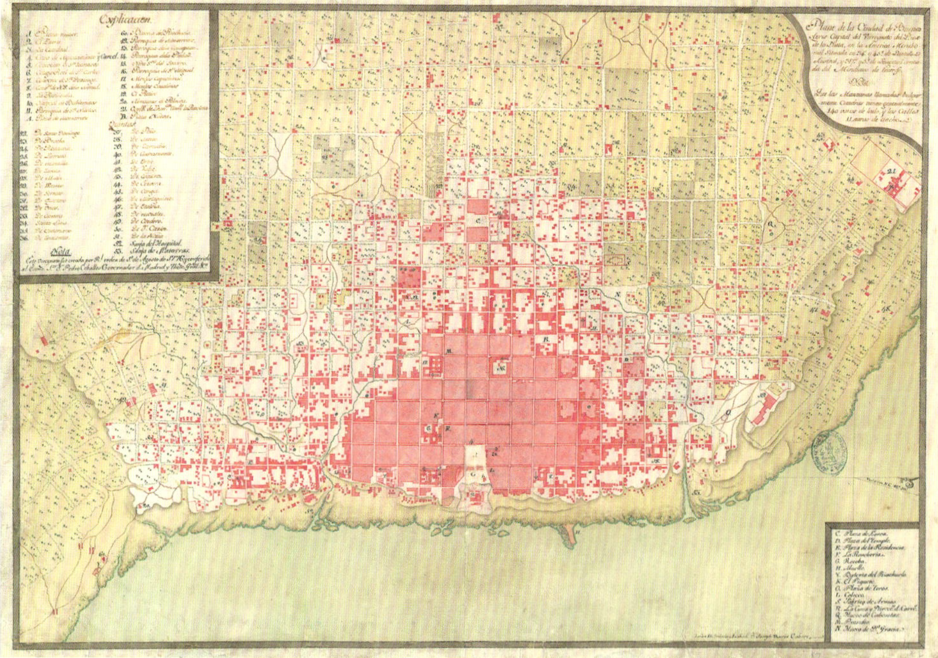

Fig. 1. Buenos Aires, Argentina, from *Urbanismo español en América* [1776].

fashionable at the end of the nineteenth century, such as inserting diagonal avenues or significantly enlarging other arteries.

Those with a *semi-regular* layout flexibly adapted to the conditions of the site, such as Havana (Cuba). *Irregular,* those where no norms were applied, generally arose spontaneously, for example, Guanajuato (Mexico).

Some cities—in particular, mining cities—were not formally founded but rather were established and grew spontaneously. Such settlements continued to grow while the mineral was extracted and declined when production or the relative value of the minerals sank.

The historian Ramón Gutiérrez distinguishes additional urban forms: **superimposed** cities, organized over the older structure of an indigenous settlement that conditioned its urban layout (Cusco or Mexico City). The **Indian pueblos** that arose from the policy of reduction, that is, from the process of concentrating the dispersed indigenous population in settlements, in which *elements of the Spanish city can be recognized but which also respond to the uses and traditions of the pre-Hispanic cultures;* this typology also includes the neighborhoods of indigenous peoples in the Spanish settlements.

The **alternative model,** a particularity of the indigenous settlements established by the Jesuit missions in Paraguay, Moxas, and Chiquitos. The settlements of **spontaneous foundation,** which are urban structures born out of a generative element such as the intersection of routes, the presence of inns, of rural chapels or shrines, of ranches or plantations, which after their consolidation were "relaid out" to transform them into grids.[5]

[. . .]

Notes

1. Jorge Enrique Hardoy, "La forma de las ciudades coloniales en Hispanoamérica," Psicon 5: America Latina: *Le città coloniali* (Florence, 1975), 30.
2. Ramón Gutiérrez, "Cultura urbana hispanoamericana y sus contactos con la experiencia portuguesa en Brasil: Modelo y heterodoxias," in *A Construção do Brasil urbano* (Convento da Arrábida Lisboa, 2000).
3. The study was published in *Urbanismo español en América* (Madrid: Editora Nacional, 1973), 19-23, and was compiled by the architects Javier Aguilera Rojas, Joaquín lbáñez Montoya, and Luis J. Moreno Rexach. It served as the basis for the classification of 38 sites in the Americas whose historical plans were reproduced from documents in the Archivo General de Indias (Seville) and in the Archivo del Servicio Histórico Militar and included in the same publication.
4. Ibid, 19.
5. Ramón Gutiérrez, "Cultura urbana hispanoamericana y sus contactos con la experiencia portuguesa en Brasil: Modelo y heterodoxias."

Reading

11

Stefano Bianca

Urban Form in the Arab World: Past and Present (2000)

In this excerpt, Stefano Bianca, a Swiss architect, planner, and architectural historian whose major focus has been the architecture of the Muslim world, takes the reader through a synthetic review of the formative principles of the Islamic city. The interpretation of the "sacred," the nature of public and private realms, the notion of exterior and interior space, and the multipolarity and gradation of the urban fabric are among the features that characterize, albeit with geographic and cultural variations, the galaxy of North African, Middle Eastern, and Asian Muslim cities. The overview shows clearly the considerable differences that distinguish these cities from the European townscape tradition and that explain the unresolved conflicts and acute disruption generated by the imposition of Western planning methods on the preexisting Islamic urban context.

CHAPTER 2 BASIC PRINCIPLES

[. . .]

The Islamic approach to religious and social institutions, combined with its high appreciation of tribal structures and the family clan [. . .] gave rise to a particular concept of sacred space. On the one hand, the religious building of the mosque is fully integrated into the social life and the architectural fabric of the town and fulfills comprehensive civic functions. On the other hand, the private home has acquired a degree of sacredness which is probably unique in comparison with other civilizations. Accordingly, it can be said that the sacred within the Islamic city does not stand out in concentrated and isolated form but spreads over the urban fabric as a whole—not unlike the multitude of fountains which give life to the many houses and mosques of the city. Totally immersed in the cellular structure of the town, it imbues man's built environment with a continuous remembrance of the divine, without ever confusing the timeless and the mundane.

From Stefano Bianca, *Urban Form in the Arab World: Past and Present* (London: Thames & Hudson, 2000), 36–40, 156–58. Reproduced courtesy of the author.

Fig. 1. Aerial view showing the Qairawiyin Mosque in Fez embedded in the urban fabric.

The physical effects of this attitude are visible in the homogeneous and yet highly differentiated structure of traditional Muslim cities. While the architectural fabric tends to be continuous, i.e., undisrupted by massive freestanding religious or public buildings or by major open spaces highlighting individual monuments, it also shows a clear internal differentiation into a series of self-contained cellular compartments, which allow the private or sacred character of individual spaces to be protected where and when needed. As a rule, the public spaces lack the rigid layout which is imposed by highly formalized institutions, allowing for a high degree of interaction between various social activities, including religious functions. The mosque, as the main public core, is usually embraced by markets, and together they form a coherent architectural complex. As the prayer space has to meet special requirements of cleanliness, it is always neatly defined, and marked by gates and thresholds where visitors take off their shoes. The transition from the secular to the sacred spheres, both contained within the same public section of the urban fabric, is accomplished by a few steps, which allows for easy interaction between the mosque and the market.

Meanwhile, the residential districts are shielded off from the main streams of public life. The houses, often closely knit together, or built wall to wall in the case of courtyard structures, form inward-oriented autonomous units which are protected against visual intrusion from the street or from neighbouring buildings. The access from the public areas to residential quarters is usually tortuous and broken into successive hierarchical sections which herald increasing degrees of privacy. Dense residential quarters tend to swallow the street space and to convert it into private access corridors. Thus, the sanctuary of the house is not directly exposed to alien influences:

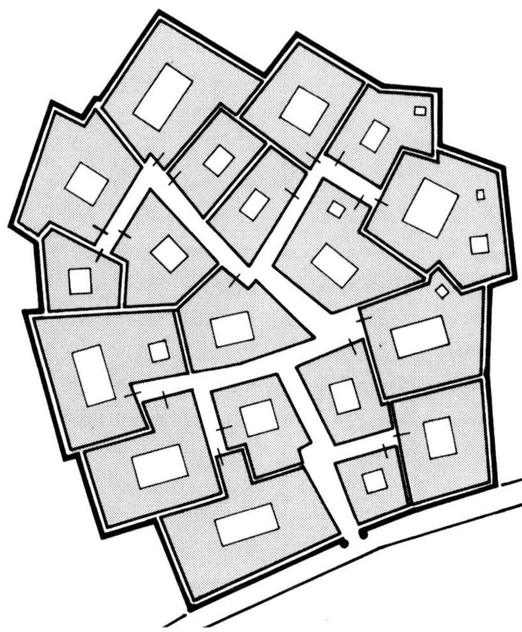

Fig. 2. Typical structure of a cluster of courtyard houses around a ramified dead-end alleyway.

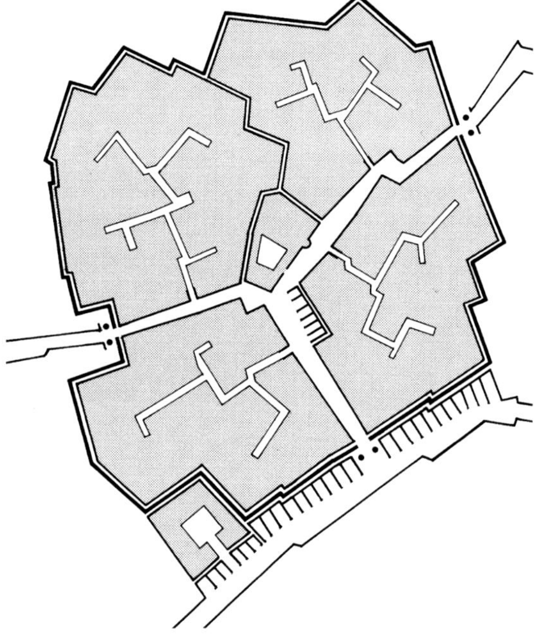

Fig. 3. Typical structure of a residential district in North African cities, composed of individually accessible cluster-units.

it can assimilate the external world after the circulation has been gradually filtered by various intermediate sections of the street network. Dead-end alleyways and a progressive sequence of gates and thresholds are the preferred tools for achieving this protection, which preserves the "aura" of the family sphere and prevents frictions with the public realm.

In accordance with this spatial logic, the public street network of traditional Islamic cities was reduced to the sheer minimum required to provide connections between the main city gates and the central markets and to ensure the selective accessibility to private quarters. The major circulation streams were deliberately channelled around the "islands" of ritually pure space and protected private domains, so as to avoid an inappropriate mix of activities. Public open space was detached from the main arteries in order to differentiate it according to specific uses and to integrate it into corresponding public buildings, such as mosques, madrasas and caravanserais. Available open spaces in the residential areas were absorbed by the housing clusters, where they emerged in the form of enclosed courtyards which often became the core of individual dwelling units, allocated to well-defined social purposes.

The clear attribution of open space to specific social and architectural entities meant that there was no "anonymous" ground to be managed by public institutions. Since Islam conceded a large amount of autonomy and responsibility to various social groups within the society, city planning in the modern institutional sense was practically absent. The groups, whether family clans, foreign ethnic communities or professional corporations, were always allowed to take charge of the respective sections of public open space running through their "territory," in both residential districts and market areas. Former thoroughfares were often deliberately interrupted to cut direct access and privatize the street space. Since the definition of private territorial identities was so dominant, this led to the absence of representative civic space in the Western sense, and also to the lack of undefined public open space which, if it ever existed, tended to be neglected or rapidly appropriated for other uses.

These religiously sanctioned ways of dealing with public and private space resulted in townscape principles very different from those of the classical European tradition. Except in palatial cities, there was little or no intent to impose formal planning principles through the street layout by creating large avenues, representative public spaces and rational land subdivisions. The prevailing attitude was to transform anonymous (quantitative) space into personalized (qualitative) space by defining and enclosing a multitude of self-contained individual volumes and developing them from within, in ways which made them virtually autonomous. The coordination between single units occurred implicitly through the inner affinity of their structuring principles, and not through outer geometric arrangements. Buildings thus tended to become architecturally self-sufficient, imposing their law on the street system rather than depending on a predetermined circulation layout. With the composite growth of such individual nuclei, public space was often constricted or reduced to a kind of interior corridor system, framed by adjacent buildings and leaving no loose residual spaces. The internal structuring system of residential units followed similar principles: rooms were not created by mechanical subdivision of the available space but by a cellular aggregation process, which allowed the main reception rooms to become almost autonomous, self-centred shells and create "houses" within the house, so to speak. The internal circulation system of the whole housing unit was subservient to this principle and had to adjust to the access requirements or restrictions imposed by the shapes and functions of the main rooms.

The structuring laws of both the house and the city were thus based on progressive differentiation of "interior" niches from "exterior" spaces, the notion of "interior" and "exterior" being relative values within a large spatial spectrum which ranged from the small private room to the complete urban structure. The resulting cellular structure of the house and the city was predicated on the "wholeness" of each self-contained unit, regardless of its relative position in the urban system. The outcome was the typical multi-focal pattern defined by the countless "centres" of individual buildings rather than by a rational grid of streets and squares. Yet the morphological homogeneity of that pattern allowed the multiple individual forms to merge into a lively and highly differentiated architectural unity.

CHAPTER 7 TRADITIONAL URBAN FABRIC

[. . .]

Thus the typical urban form of historic Arab cities grew as a compact aggregation of smaller and larger precincts, each one equipped with the appropriate cellular infill, as well as inbuilt open spaces, access systems and shared facilities allocated to the respective groups of collective and individual users. The fact that all these micro-elements of urban form shared the same structural principles, in spite of different functions, made them fully compatible. Their largely self-centred and self-contained character, due to the vertical orientation of interior courtyards and air shafts, facilitated horizontal cohesion, favouring their integration into larger urban components which were complete in themselves at each stage of development, in space and in time.

By a series of centring, enclosing and incorporating processes through ascending hierarchic levels of the urban structure, this remarkable system of space management produced a differentiated and yet totally homogeneous type of urban form, where the divisions provoked by isolated public open spaces and an incisive street network were avoided or overcome. Since the adopted circulation system made it possible to select and regulate the desired degree of seclusion within a continuous and extremely dense urban fabric, it was the ideal tool for neutralizing the antagonism between open and closed spaces, public and private zones, and male and female realms. The polarity between opposite qualities, while balanced and resolved within the overall structural pattern, remained the spring of the urban system, producing the pulsations which kept the organism of the city alive.

In his perceptive morphological studies, Johann Wolfgang van Goethe wrote that the main driving forces of growth and metamorphosis in nature are polarity and gradation ("Polaritat und Steigerung"), through their mutual interaction. Looking at our analysis of traditional Arab urban form, we realize that it is precisely the combination of these two forces which bestows life, unity and an "organic" quality on its vernacular urban patterns. It is indeed striking to observe how the polarizing force implied in the nuclear cellular structures (i.e., their articulation by division of space into "included" and "excluded" portions) provides clear separation between neighbouring buildings, while simultaneously exerting a strong contraction at the next structural plane of urban form. The "push-forces" at a lower level are so to speak transformed into "pull-forces" at an upper level, allowing the existing dualities to be absorbed by progressive integration into a higher order. This hierarchy occurs on virtually every plane of the urban structure, from the single room to the house, to the residential cluster, the market compounds, the enclosed street sections and the walled city as a whole. Potentially conflicting units can therefore be placed side by side and integrated into a highly articulate and cohesive overall system of urban form.

The result is a breathing and "animated" urban structure, projecting a radiant inner unity which is fundamentally different from the sterile uniformity produced by more mechanical modes of addition or subdivision. It is indicative of the higher (one could even say spiritual) nature of such a type of unity that it is capable of spreading and multiplying itself without ever losing its essential qualities. As it is present in every single "seed" of the complex cellular urban structure, the entire urban fabric down to its smallest particles is so to speak impregnated with the attributes of wholeness and unity. The city turns into a vibrant multi-focal pattern, embracing scores of self-contained sub-centres, which all share the "wholeness" of the overarching system. This structural order translates into a paradoxical physical experience which is characteristic of most traditional Arab cities: one always has the feeling of being at the centre of things, in whatever sub-unit of the composite urban structure it may be.

It can be concluded that the inner unity of the urban fabric is predicated on the capacity to express and articulate different needs in a consistent language of affiliated forms, based on the variation of cellular patterns at different hierarchic planes. The integration of individual components is sustained by multiple structural analogies and by ascending correspondences within the deep structure of the city. Thus the urban fabric gains access to a symbolic dimension, since small elements can reflect the structure of the whole in the same way that the human microcosm can mirror the universe. It is this hidden vertical reference system which gives depth and unity to the urban fabric, instills spatial quality to its individual components, and grounds man in his environment by inscribing his temporal urban existence within a timeless order.

Reading

12

VIBHUTI SACHDEV AND GILES TILLOTSON

Building Jaipur: The Making of an Indian City (2002)

Vibhuti Sachdev and Giles Tillotson have written extensively on the history and traditional architecture of India. In this excerpt focusing on the case of Jaipur, they elucidate the kingship and city concepts that informed traditional planning in precolonial India. Their point of departure is the analysis of the canonical texts (shastras) *that regulate the conduct of the king and the order of human affairs, including architecture, planning, and the establishment of distinct types of cities, towns, and fortified forts on the basis of their purpose and location. An aspect that appears common to the selection of sites for the establishment of a settlement is its association with a sacred event or godly action, a consideration that confirms, also in the case of India, the reference to archetypal symbols and transcendent realities discussed in part I.*

1 CONCEPTUAL CITIES

[. . .]

We have here chosen to focus on a few salient elements that were consistently present in definitions of kingship and of cities up until the eighteenth century. We have drawn chiefly on two related genres of literature. The first is *niti shastra*, or treatises on politics and statecraft. Here we have used in particular the ancient classic of the genre, the *Arthashastra*, composed during the Mauryan period (fourth to third centuries B.C.) and well known ever since, and—to give a more contemporary perspective—the late derivative work the *Sukraniti*. The second genre is *vastu shastra*, treatises that deal with architecture, planning and all other aspects of design. Here again our sources include two early classics, the *Manasara* and the *Mayamata*, and also two later works—the *Samrangana Sutradhara*, written in the eleventh century for Raja Bhoja of Dhar, and

From VIBHUTI SACHDEV and GILES TILLOTSON, *Building Jaipur: The Making of an Indian City* (London: Reaktion Books, 2002), 10–17, 26, 29. Reproduced by permission of Reaktion Books.

Mandan's *Rajavallabha*, written in the fifteenth century for Rana Kumbha of Mewar. [. . .]

The Shastric King

[. . .]

[. . .] [S]ince it is the king who makes the rules and establishes customs, both by imposing them on his subjects and by following them himself, it is the king who is responsible for guiding men's conduct. The king is therefore the cause or maker of time.[1]

Following the customary preamble and insistence on the importance of his theme, this is the first point of substance made by the author of the *Sukraniti*, a Sanskrit treatise on polity, of uncertain date.[2] In linking the king to the cosmic order, and attributing to him a power comparable to that of the planets, the author is assuming familiarity with the more general idea of the king as a representative, even an embodiment, of god.[3] A little later he lists the eight functions of the king as punishing the wicked, dispensing charity, protecting his subjects, performing rites and sacrifices, acquiring revenue, converting independent princes into tributary chiefs, conquering enemies and generating wealth from the land.[4] The king must keep himself informed on the well-being of his subjects, as dispraise can do him much harm—after all, it was the criticism of a mere washerman that led Rama to forsake Sita.[5]

The king who is most praised is one who is educated in the arts and sciences, because if he is trained in all branches of learning he will not incline to wrong deeds and will earn the respect of the good. The logic of this idea implies a contract: the identification of the king as a god confers upon him not only privileges but also duties to behave in certain ways and to acquire certain qualities. Each and every one of his actions—including his engagement in *puja* (prayer and ritual) and his patronage of learning—is measured against what is expected of a king. Therefore the king should revere his *guru* (or personal preceptor) and through association with him acquire knowledge of the *shastras* (the canonical treatises). More than this, he should take steps to advance the arts and sciences amongst his people, by regularly honouring those who are well versed in all sacred texts such as *vedas* and *puranas*, and those who understand astrology, medicine and sacred rites, including *tantra*.[6]

The Shastric City

No fewer than eight distinct types of city and town (and a further eight types of fort) are defined by the *Manasara* and another major *vastu shastra* text, the *Mayamata*. In this instance we are confronted not with a hierarchy but with specialisms, and the first on the list, far from being way off any realizable register, is in fact a basic or standard type whose very name, *kevala nagara*, means "only" or "ordinary." A densely populated mercantile town, the *kevala nagara* is protected by a wall with a gate at each of the

Fig. 1. Vishvakarma, the divine architect.

four cardinal points. It is the second on the list that is the *rajadhani* or *rajadhaniya nagara*, the royal capital. This is defined as a city, impregnable on the north and east sides, with the royal palace near the centre and a guard facing towards the east and the south, and around the palace the houses of people of all classes, including the most wealthy and meritorious citizens of the state. A *pura*, by contrast, lacks the palace and the emphasis is on trade. A *kheta* is a town situated close to a river or a mountain, and is exclusively inhabited by members of the Shudra caste; a *kharvata* is a town within the hills; and a *kubjaka* is an unprotected town located between a *kheta* and a *kharvata*. A *pattana* is a trading town situated by the coast or a waterway, and a *shibira* is a fortified town, protecting the kingdom's border. The eight forts have similarly specialist functions and are distinguished by location, population and the presence or absence of the king.[7]

The location of some of these forts and cities is already implied in their definitions, but beyond this is the idea that the best site is one to which can be attributed some sacred association—a site that may be identified with a legend, or as the scene of some action of a god. All associations of the site will be borne by the city and will influence its fortunes. Before building can commence, offering must be made to propitiate the gods and demons.[8]

Once the site is selected and purified, the laying out of the plan involves referring to a set of diagrams. The chapters on planning in the *vastu shastras* describe a sequence of 32 *mandalas*, a set of grids of increasing complexity. The first and simplest is a single square—notionally a 1 × 1 grid. The second is a square subdivided into four equal parts—a 2 × 2 grid. The third has nine parts, the fourth sixteen, and so on, until the

Fig. 2. The palace of Amber, from above.

last, 32 × 32, or 1,024-square grid. These are the *vastu purusha mandalas*, the elementary principles for any division of space.[9] All of the subsequent chapters on specific constructions—whether single houses or temples, palaces, villages or towns—refer back to the types thus defined. No fixed dimension is attached to any *mandala*, and we should not suppose that the more complex versions are necessarily intended for larger works. They are primary planning forms that can be used in any context.

The *Mayamata* says that for any town it is appropriate to use the four-square mandala (called *pechaka*) or the 100-square mandala (called *asana*) or any of those in between; that is to say, anything from a 2 × 2 to a 10 × 10 grid, thus excluding the first in the sequence as too simple, and all of the more complex forms.[10] The *Manasara* roughly agrees: identifying the lines of the grid with the city's main streets, it says that the number of streets running from west to east and from north to south may be anything between one and twelve.[11] Two later *vastu shastra* texts are much more specific. The *Samrangana Sutradhara* says that the 64-square *mandala* (called *chandita*) is appropriate for all towns; and the *Rajavallabha* recommends the same model for use in cities, palaces and villages.[12]

The widths of the streets within a town, and one town compared with another, vary according to a strict hierarchy. It is not appropriate for a small town to have streets of the greatest width. An ordinary town, according to the *Mayamata*, can have as many as 13 separate street widths, increasing in increments of half a *danda*, from 1 to 7 *danda*.[13] Almost all the texts speak of a principal street or group of streets called *rajmarg* (or royal highway), which runs through the centre of the town and connects with the palace. [. . .]

The construction of temples within the town is also a responsibility of the king. Whatever his own personal affiliation, he must build and maintain temples to all of the gods and join with the people in the celebration of their festivals.[14] The *Manasara* goes so far as to specify particular districts within the town for each of the principal deities; but it is consistent with the other *vastu shastras* in insisting that a royal capital must have a Vishnu temple at its centre.[15] All the temples face east or west, or towards the town centre, and a temple outside the town must not have its back towards it.[16]

In a town or city intended for a general population including all four castes, the distribution of the people is systematic. The district where each citizen resides and works is determined by his caste and occupation. The standard pattern is the one described in the *Samrangana Sutradhara*, which places Brahmins in the north, Kshatriyas in the east, Vaishyas in the south and Shudras in the west.[17] Detail is added to this broad distribution by reference to the associations of the deities who govern each of the subdivisions of the *mandala*. For example, the south-eastern corner of the *mandala* is attributed to Agni, the god of fire; and accordingly the south-eastern corner of the city is reserved for those who work with fire, such as blacksmiths and cooks. The north-western corner, by contrast, is assigned to Vayu, the god of wind; and this direction is accordingly preferred for trades which involve movement, such as keeping carriages or being a shepherd.[18] Each of the bazaars is allocated to a particular plot of the *mandala* according to the type of produce sold.[19] The system is elegant but not so rigidly drawn as to defy utility, and the texts are equally insistent that all costly goods such as gems, gold and fine textiles should be sold on the central streets leading to the palace, and that flowers and incense should be sold in shops located outside the temples.[20]

Shastra and Archaeology

The process of rendering shastric ideas diagrammatically is hazardous, if one visual realization is presumed to exclude others, since in practice many are possible. But taking the definitions of city and palace given above, one possible rendering of a paradigmatic capital city would be as in figure 3. If the texts define paradigms, it might reasonably be asked why in the archaeological record there are few, if any, actual towns that closely correspond to them. The apparent discrepancy between the shastric idea of a town and those that have been built has led many to question the role of *vastu shastra* in the history of Indian architecture as a whole. [. . .]

However, it is important to bear in mind that a diagram such as figure 3 represents a concept; it is not a plan. It functions in the mind of the architect like a mnemonic—as a shorthand depiction of the ideas outlined above and elaborated only verbally in the texts—it is not a blueprint. For a town to be built in exact visual accordance with such a diagram would only be possible if it were built in a single process, on a previously clear site. And in reality that never occurs. The great majority of towns and cities in India (as elsewhere) have grown incrementally over long periods, not from one preordained plan.

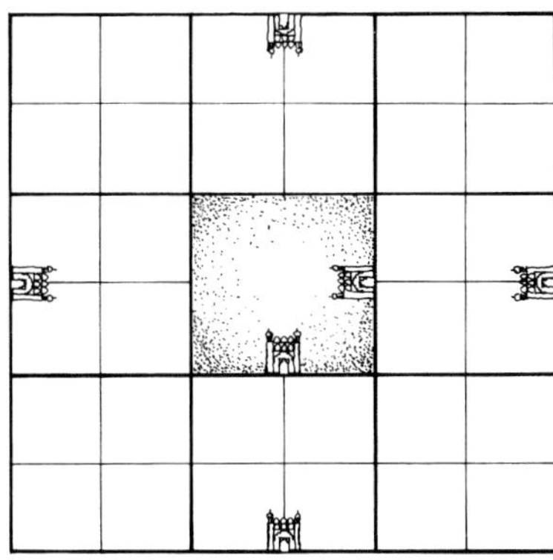

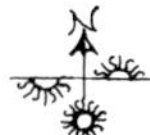

Fig. 3. A paradigmatic capital city, drawn according to general shastric definition.

The opportunities for new, planned cities are comparatively rare, and even then no site is wholly without features.

Moreover, in spite of this limitation, the archaeological record does in fact contain some instructive examples, most of which are perfectly well known. In the south of India there are a number of cities where the sacred association of the site is crucial. The city of Madurai, though of earlier foundation, was redeveloped under Nayaka patronage in the seventeenth century, and is centred on the ancient shrine of Minakshi-Sundareshvara. Minakshi was born a Pandyan princess but became a goddess through her marriage with the pan-Indian god Shiva (known as Sundareshvara, the beautiful Lord). The site is therefore one that connects local royal power with the Hindu pantheon. In a similar way, Vijayanagara, the capital of the most powerful southern empire between the thirteenth century and the sixteenth, was founded on ground identified as Kishkinda, the scene of a decisive episode in the pan-Indian epic the *Ramayana*. Incidents of the story are marked on the landscape. And, as if this were not enough, here too stands the shrine of a local goddess, Pampa, who became a consort of Shiva.

The town plan of Madurai, as developed by the Nayakas, involves a grid of streets surrounding the temple, which is thereby fixed in the *brahmasthana* of a *mandala*. An even clearer example of the fulfilment of this same model is the celebrated temple-city of Srirangam (built between the thirteenth century and the eighteenth). Here we find the optimum seven concentric enclosures, with the temple at the centre, surrounded first by its lesser shrines and offices, and further out by the houses of the citizens. The geometrical irregularities of both Madurai and Srirangam when they are rendered as modern plans are something to which we shall return. For the moment we may note that if the mandalic conception of these places sometimes escapes the attention of modern archaeologists, it is nevertheless made abundantly clear by indigenous, conceptual representations of them.

Notes

1. *Sukraniti* I. 41–4 (B. K. Sarkar, trans., *The Sukraniti*, repr. New Delhi, 1975, pp. 5–6).
2. Although at least one authority (Lallanji Gopal, *The Sukraniti: A Nineteenth-Century Text*,

Benares, 1978, places the *Sukraniti* as late as the nineteenth century, others have offered various dates, mostly from AD 700 onwards. In the present context this dispute is of little importance, since a part of the case being made is that all such treatises draw on an inherited body of knowledge.

3. See, for example, *Manusmriti* VII. 5–8 (Wendy Doniger, trans., *The Laws of Manu*, London, 1991, p. 128).
4. *Sukraniti* I. 245–8 (Sarkar, 1975, pp. 18–19).
5. *Sukraniti* I. 260–9 (Sarkar, 1975, p. 19).
6. *Sukraniti* I. 295–7, 740–1, II. 246–50 (Sarkar, 1975, pp. 21, 50, 76).
7. *Manasara* X. 39–87 (Acharya, 1934, pp. 95–7); *Mayamata* X. 5–36 (Bruno Dagens, trans., *Mayamatam: Treatise of Housing, Architecture and Iconography*, 2 vols, New Delhi, 1994, vol. 1, pp. 89–97). A different list is given by *Samrangana Sutradhara* XXII. 2–7 (D. N. Shukla, trans., *Samrangana Sutradhara*, Delhi, 1994, p. 99).
8. *Manasara* IV, VIII (Acharya, 1934, pp. 13–14, 59–62); *Mayamata* IV, VIII (Dagens, 1994, vol. 1, pp. 17–21, 51–5); *Samrangana Sutradhara* XVIII. 1–28 (Shukla, 1994, pp. 81–3); *Rajavallabha* II. 2 (Ojha, 1934, p. 17); *Vishvakarma Prakash* V. 1–183 (Pandit Mihirchand, trans., *Vishvakarma Prakash*, Bombay, 1988, pp. 33–46).
9. E.g. *Manasara* VII (Acharya, 1934, pp. 33–57); *Mayamata* VII (Dagens, 1994, vol. 1, pp. 37–49).
10. *Mayamata* X. 16–17 (Dagens, 1994, vol. 1, p. 93).
11. *Manasara* X. 110–14 (Acharya, 1934, p. 98).
12. *Samrangana Sutradhara* XXIII. 2–4 (Shukla, 1994, p. 103); *Rajavallabha* II. 4 (Ojha, 1934, p. 18).
13. *Mayamata* X. 18 (Dagens, 1994, vol. 1, p. 93). A *danda* (rod) is a unit of measurement roughly equivalent to 2 m.
14. *Arthashastra* II. 4.17 (Kangle, 1972, p. 70); *Sukraniti* IV. 4.132–3, 405–12 (Sarkar, 1975, pp. 166, 182).
15. *Manasara* IX. 383–98, X. 44–7 (Acharya, 1934, pp. 84, 95).
16. *Rajavallabha* IV. 12 (Ojha, 1934, p.41; *Samrangana Sutradhara* XXIII. 124–5 (Shukla, 1994, p. 111) suggests, however, that the last problem can be overcome by painting an image of the deity on the temple's rear wall.
17. *Samrangana Sutradhara* XXIII. 88–103 (Shukla, 1994, pp. 108–9). The same distribution is given by *Arthashastra* II. 4.8–15 (Kangle, 1972, pp. 68–9). An alternative pattern follows the same sequence of castes but starts with the east (for Brahmins) and ends with the north; see, for example, *Rajavallabha* IV. 18–20 (Ojha, 1934, p. 42–3).
18. *Samrangana Sutradhara* XXIII. 88–103 (Shukla, 1994, pp. 108–9); *Arthashastra* II. 4, 8 and 12 (Kangle, 1972, pp. 68–9); *Rajavallabha* IV. 18–20 (Ojha, 1934, pp. 42–3).
19. E.g. *Mayamata* X. 77–87 (Dagens, 1994, vol. 1, pp. 107–9).
20. E.g. *Mayamata* X. 86–7 (Dagens, 1994, vol. 1, p. 109).

References

Acharya, P. K., *Architecture of Manasara*, Manasara series, vol. IV (1934; repr. Delhi, 1980).

Dagens, Bruno, trans., *Mayamatam: Treatise of Housing, Architecture and Iconography*, 2 vols (New Delhi, 1994).

Doniger, Wendy, trans., *The Laws of Manu* (London, 1991).

Gopal, Lallanji, *The Sukraniti: A Nineteenth-century Text*, Bharati Prakashan (Varanasi, 1978).

Kangle, R. P., trans., *The Kautiliya Arthasastra*, part 2 (repr. Delhi, 1972).

Mihirchand, Pandit, trans., *Vishvakarma Prakash*, Khemraj Shrikrishnadas (Bombay, 1988).

Ojha, Rarnyatna, trans., and Madhavaprasada Vyasa, rev., *Vasturajavallabha of Mandana Sutradhara*, 2nd edn (Benares, 1934).

Sarkar, B. K., trans., *The Sukraniti* (1st edn, 1914; repr. New Delhi, 1975).

Shukla, D. N., trans., *Samrangana Sutradhara* (Delhi, 1994).

Reading

13

Yinong Xu

The Chinese City in Space and Time: The Development of Urban Form in Suzhou (2000)

Yinong Xu, an architectural and urban historian originally from Beijing, now teaches at London's South Bank University. He received his PhD from Edinburgh University, where he studied the city of Suzhou (Jiangsu), which flourished under the Ming and Qing periods (1368–1911) and is famous for its traditional gardens. In this reading he discusses the principal characteristics of the traditional Chinese city. A central aspect of Xu's interpretation is that the Chinese city was first and foremost an instrument of the imperial government and that its social and formal characteristics are closely interrelated. His work exemplifies the high-quality scholarship on Chinese architecture by a younger generation of Chinese scholars, who are also providing new insights into the rich history of Chinese urbanism.

INTRODUCTION

[. . .] [T]he importance of studies of Chinese urban history lies not only in its distinctiveness from that of the West but in the fact that the range and variety of Chinese experience in building, adjusting, governing, and inhabiting cities, as well as in relating cities to the rest of society, is by far the largest block of such human urban experience. It therefore constitutes an indispensable parameter of comparison for urbanism in other cultural spheres and is a rich source of suggestion and of inspiration.

To illustrate this, an obvious and revealing example can briefly be cited here. One standard view of preindustrial European cities is that they usually possessed separate legal and political status as organized entities, which set them apart from the countryside. In the introduction to his masterly survey of a thousand years of urban architecture in western Europe, Wolfgang Braunfels has gone so far as to argue that the reasons

From Yinong Xu, *The Chinese City in Space and Time: The Development of Urban Form in Suzhou* (Honolulu: University of Hawai'i Press, 2000), 2–4, 31–36, 39, 91–92.

for the urban failure and disorder in the modern era, for which architects and urban designers have partly been responsible, must be sought in changes in the general political function of cities:

> Cities no longer form unities but serve both the interests of the individual and those of the state with its manifold business, the new "one world." They represent only to the most limited extent an independent body corporate, for their areas of existence are interwoven in different ways, with the states to which they are subordinated and with the rural areas that surround them.[1]

Interestingly, no Chinese city in the imperial era was ever a corporate entity of its own; nor did any of them have the organizational features that set European cities apart in legal and political ways. The Chinese city was an instrument of the imperial government and thus an integral part of the "one world"; its area of existence was more than interwoven with the state to which it was subordinated and with the rural areas that surrounded it. Yet one can hardly deny that such a city captured "the imagination with its order" as much as any preindustrial European city is believed by Braunfels[2] to have done. Paradoxically, it is the cities of modern China that have evinced a kind of urban-rural dichotomy and at the same time show marked disorder in urban architecture. Whether the reasons for the modern failure on both sides of the world lie more in the process of rapid change itself than in the direction of change falls beyond the scope of the present study. Suffice it to say that Chinese urban history deserves much more attention than it is presently given in the academic field of architecture.[3]

—w—

Although works of Western scholarship on urban development in traditional China have markedly increased in the past few decades, there seem to exist at least two biases apparent in them. One appears to be either that sociological interests override careful examinations of the formation and transformation of the spatial and physical features of the cities or that an overemphasis of the cities' formal and technological aspects detaches them from social contexts. Can urban phenomena be sufficiently explained solely in either social or formal terms? On this issue, Bill Hillier and Julienne Hanson's work throws important light. Any architectural structure, they argue, "is an object whose spatial form is a form of social ordering."[4] The social and the spatial cannot be treated as distinct, separate entities, because human societies are spatial phenomena. Thus not only does society have a certain spatial logic, but space has a certain social logic to it.[5] If this line of argument is valid, a sensible understanding and discussion about cities should therefore employ a two-way approach: to study the social contexts that create and order the spatial and formal elements into patterns as a part of society *and* to study the spatial and formal features that not only reflect the social phenomena but are themselves characters of social ordering. The other bias is that attention is more often paid to the imperial capitals than to local cities. A noticeable deficiency in this scholastic imbalance is that the imperial capitals, important as they are to our understanding of the history of Chinese city planning, do not constitute the whole picture of China's urban experience. There are two basic reasons for this understanding. The first is the plain fact that the vast majority of urban centers in the premodern era were not imperial capitals. The second reason lies in the realization that [. . .] the idea of building the imperial capitals, especially in its cosmological aspects, is profoundly different from that of building, maintaining, and governing local cities. [. . .]

CHAPTER 2 THE CITY IN ITS BEGINNING

[. . .] [T]he following section examines the canonic principles of city planning recorded in the *Zhou li* and, in particular, its last section, "Kaogong ji." They not only reveal a considerable body of lore, practices, and ideas connected with city building accumulated by the end of the Warring States but are strongly characteristic of the Han synthesis. [. . .]

The *Locus Classicus*

[. . .] [T]he basic structure of the *Zhou li*, and the numerical-symbolic references in particular, date from about the time of Han Wudi (156–87 B.C.). [. . .] The *locus classicus*[6] for the ideal layout of the Zhou capital city is the "Kaogong ji" section. [. . .] For convenience, I have grouped the characteristic features of the principles of city building prescribed in the "Kaogong ji" into four categories: choice and preparation of the site, cardinal orientation, city layout, and disposition of principal structures.

Choice and Preparation of the Site

Ideally, the city has to be at the center of the land. The precise position of this cosmic pivot should be calculated, as explained in the *Zhou li*, by the official known as the Da Situ, with the gnomon shadow template (*tugui*), the length of the gnomon being one *chi* five *cun*. [. . .]

Cardinal Orientation

The orientation of the city to the four cardinal points is omnipresent in the construction of almost all the Chinese capitals. [. . .] Wheatley observes that prominent among the morphological features that the ideal type Chinese city shared with a majority of the great capitals of Asia were cardinal orientation, cardinal axiality, and a more or less square perimeter delimited by a massive wall. There was, however, a difference of emphasis in one important feature of their plans: much greater significance was given to the main processional axis running from south to north, "the celestial meridian writ small," as Wheatley calls it, than to any average running from east to west."[7]

The preference of the south-north axiality may, on the one hand, come from the basic pragmatic requirement of buildings' southern exposure for biological reasons, which later gave rise to the general conceptual partiality of the Chinese for facing the south. On the other hand, this preference may come from the equatorial character of Chinese astronomy, which concentrates attention on the Pole and circumpolar stars, as opposed to the ecliptic-emphasizing nature of Greek and medieval European astronomy and to astronomy based on azimuth and altitude as practiced by the Arabs.[8] [. . .]

City Layout

The ideal layout of the city is summarized in the following passage of the "Kaogong ji":

> The artificers, as they built the capital, demarcated it as a square with sides of nine *li*, each side having three gateways. Within the capital there were nine meridional and nine latitudinal avenues, each of the former being nine chariot tracks wide.[9]

Figures 2.1, 2.2, and 2.3 show three drawings of the ideal royal Zhou city, produced in the mid-tenth century. [Figs. 2.2 and 2.3 not included here; fig. 2.1 is here fig. 1.—Ed.] Whereas the problem of layout concerning the proportion of subdivision has evoked controversial speculations,[10] there is no question that this idealized urban plan relied on the same principle of subdivision as the old well-field (*jingtian*) system of land settlement and cultivation, as Granet has noted.[11] In cosmological terms, this aspect might turn out to have been more significant in the city as a microcosm and the very center of the earth than in the methodological application of the well-field system in city layout, in that the ruler of all-under-Heaven was expected to reside in a structure that was a symbol of the earth. First, since the ancient Chinese perceived the earth as a square checkerboard, the form of a square was obviously taken to be a prerequisite for the general morphology of an ideal capital that would be a replica of the earth.[12] Second, and perhaps more profoundly, the layout of the city was analogous to the administrative subdivision of the royal territory and further to the conceptual subdivision of the whole world. According to the "Yu gong" section of the *Shang shu*, Yu, a legendary hero-emperor, divided the land of China into nine regions, or nine provinces (*jiuzhou*), after having mastered the waters.[13] Furthermore, the Middle Kingdom (Zhongguo, also denoting present-day China) was thought to hold a central place among the nine greater regions of the whole world.[14] It is therefore reasonable to think of the city that was subdivided into nine units, with the royal palace in the center, as a microcosm embedded in a concentric system, from the Chinese empire up to the scale of the whole world, on the pivot of which resided the Son of Heaven. The third significance lies in the network of the well-field system into which the capital city is embedded. The capital (*guo*) was constructed in such a symbolic way that the grid scheme of its subdivision and the units of its measurement were identical with those of the country field (*ye*),[15] and the perspec-

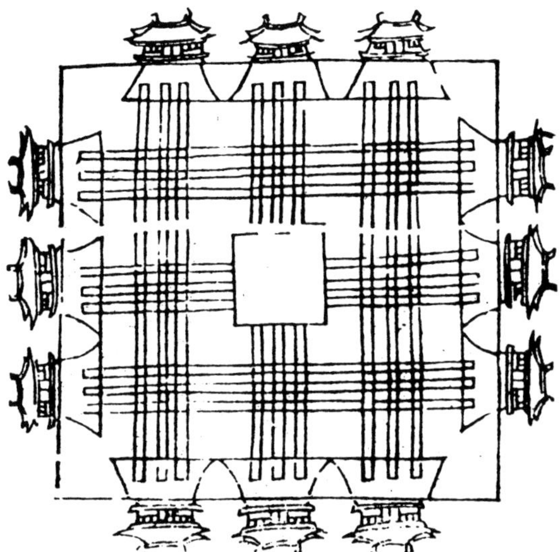

Fig. 1. Canonical plan of the royal Zhou capital (Wangcheng) in the *Sanli tu jizhu* (*juan* 4.3b), produced in the mid-tenth century.

tive of this checkerboard pattern radiated from the capital outward, ideally in all directions to the frontiers of the world.

[. . .]

[I]t seems worth emphasizing the exclusive application of the number nine for the capital and the decreasing arithmetical progression for other cities in the hierarchical range. Odd numbers were regarded as of *yang*, and nine, the largest of odd numbers, was the supreme *yang* number denoting Heaven and was thus associated with the Son of Heaven. As in other civilizations, the larger and higher the construction is, the higher the number employed in it and the more noble and majestic it is considered to be rendered. In China, this hierarchy was constitutionalized in detail as formal rituals (*li*) as early as the late Zhou.[16] In the case of city construction, for instance, a passage in the *Zuo zhuan* explains:

> The walls of any state capital which exceed a hundred *zhi*[17] [in circumference] constitute a danger to the state. According to the institutions of the former kings, the walls of a city of the first order must not exceed one-third the length of that of the capital, that of a second-order city one-fifth, and that of third-order city one-ninth.[18]

By the Han period, the basic formula of this matter became fairly standardized, and, as recorded in the *Han shu*, "it is a matter of the *li* that from the higher to the lower [the number employed in any event] descends with a difference of two."[19] This ritually classified order was also expressed in many other aspects of city construction, with the city where the Son of Heaven resided on the top of the hierarchy.

One of the most notable and important features in the mode of the canonical disposition of these principal urban structures, and, indeed, in the whole set of city planning principles prescribed in the *Zhou li,* ideal as they were,[20] is the proper, symbolic positioning of every physical element of the city by reference to cardinal orientation, with an emphasis on the south. It formed an order that was seen as durable because it was not arbitrary but based on an understanding of Nature, the eternal standard. As the *Zhou Yi qianzaodu,* possibly written in the first century B.C., expounds,

> What does not change [in the universe] is the proper position [of each of the myriad things]. Heaven is above; Earth is below. The monarch faces south; the subjects face north. The father sits and the son prostrates himself. These are what do not change.[21]

The canonized principles of city planning, as many other institutions of the state, were defined by defining the order of Heaven and Earth, to paraphrase Sivin, who concisely interprets one of the passages on this point by Dong Zhongshu (179–104 B.C.).[22]

—∞—

Conclusion

[. . .] [A]ny sweeping generalization about Chinese cities in space and time may lead to oversimplification of their remarkably continuous, and yet highly complex, urban history. They constitute the wider context of that distinctive history [. . .]. In order for the reader to keep in mind these general characteristics as the study proceeds, a brief summary of them is necessary.

It is important to reiterate first that it proves to be illusive and misleading to talk about *the* Chinese city either as a constructed ideal type that seemingly provides a set of conclusions in the form of generalizations or as one of the actual cities that symbolizes Chinese culture as a whole. China's cities and the process of their development were highly differentiated in their administrative status, geographical locations, conditions of local economic development, and process of urban construction and transformation. This range of significant width in time and space has led to the realization that, in the words of Samuels, "no one ideal construct can suffice to explain the varied and complex history of urban China."[23] Also, there has not been a single city ever standing as the hub and the symbol of the history and cultural achievements of Chinese civilization. This distinctive phenomenon of urbanization in imperial China has been asserted by Mote in a sweeping comprehensive manner.[24] He also suggests, as I believe was the case, that the concept of the "provincial" as opposed to the "metropolitan" did not exist in China, especially from Tang times onward, as it did in the cultural life of Europe.[25] Indeed, the cultural and material life of some of the Yangzi Valley provinces was recognized as being superior to that of the capitals and the provinces adjacent to them in the North.

Arguments in this direction are not meant to deny that premodern Chinese cities are in comparative perspective a distinct cultural type nor to neglect the fact that in the national capital, careers were different in character and prestige from those in the provinces and architectural features were often more splendid and imposing. Instead, they stress the necessity that any single city is to be considered as part of a continuous tradition of city building. [. . .]

The process of formation and transformation of urban space in China varied across sociogeographical regions. In overall perspective, many local cities on the North China Plain were older, with their rational fortified patterns imposed from above and other urban structures later gradually filling in, than most of the cities in the South, which were later and closer to their unplanned origins, on which some degree of planning was superimposed.

Notes

1. Braunfels 1988, p. 1.
2. Ibid.
3. The paucity of knowledge about China's urban history, and the insufficient awareness of its importance to the studies of the urban history of the world, are partly reflected, for instance, in the place of the description of Chinese cities in A. E. J. Morris' *History of Urban Form: Before the Industrial Revolutions*. [. . .] In terms of the entire urban history of the world, the proportion of attention given to the Chinese experience seems regrettable.
4. Hillier and Hanson 1984, p. 9. [. . .]
5. Ibid., p. 22.
6. I borrow this word from Wheatley 1971, p. 411.
7. Wheatley 1971, pp. 433–42.
8. Needham 1959, pp. 266–267.
9. *Zhou li, juan* 41, p. 289. Translation by Wheatley (1971, p. 411) with minor modification. For a different rendering, see Steinhardt 1990, p. 33. For a French translation, see Biot 1851, vol. 2, p. 6.
10. Wheatley (1971, pp. 411, 414) suggests that the text of the "Kaogong ji" might have incorporated a confusion between the postulated nine meridional and nine latitudinal avenues of the city and the nine units of the well-field system. [. . .]
11. Granet 1930, pp. 243–244. Balazs (1964, p. 68) explicitly speaks of the "rural origin" of such spatial organization. [. . .]
12. The assumption of "heaven round, earth square" (*tianyuan difang*) is of great antiquity. It was, for example, expounded in the *Huainanzi* and some other writings and incorporated in one of the ancient astronomical theories, that of the Gai Tian school. For an introduction to and discussion of the school, see Needham 1959, pp. 212–213.
13. *Shang shu, juan* 6, pp. 34ff. Needham (1959, p. 500) regards this section as the oldest Chinese geographical document.
14. *Shi ji, juan* 74, p. 2344. Zou Yan (ca. 305–240 B.C.) refers to the Middle Kingdom by the name the "Spiritual Region of the Red Continent" (Chixian Shenzhou). Thus, the area of China was also named the "Central Region" (Zhengzhou) or the "Central Earth" (Zhongtu). For a discussion of the cosmological significance of the idea of the Nine Provinces, see Henderson 1984, pp. 66–68.
15. In the "Kaogong ji" we read, for example, that "the market and the royal court of audience each occupies an area of one *fu*," with Zheng Xuan and Jia Gongyan explaining that "each occupied

one hundred square *bu*." This measurement is identical with that of the well-field system. Cf. *Zhou li, juan* 11, pp. 73ff., and *juan* 15, pp. 102–103.
16. Cf. *Li ji, juan* 23, pp. 203–205; *Zuo zhuan, juan* 9: "Zhuang 18th year [676 B.C.]," p. 71.
17. *Zhi* was an area unit for the measurement of city walls. One *zhi* equaled three *zhang* in length by one *zhang* in height.
18. *Zuo zhuan, juan* 2: "Yin 1st year [722 B.C.]," p. 14. Cf. Legge 1960, vol 5, p. 5.
19. *Han shu, juan* 73, p. 3127.
20. Pragmatic theories of city planning had been developed by the end of the Warring States period, among which the most representative is found in the *Guanzi*. [. . .]
21. *Zhou Yi qianzaodu, juan* A.2.
22. Sivin 1995.
23. Samuels 1978, p. 713; cf. Skinner 1977a.
24. Mote 1977, pp. 101–102. [. . .]
25. Mote 1977, p. 118.

References

Chinese References

Guanzi 管子 (The Book of Master Guan). Compilers unknown; attributed to Guan Zhong 管仲. Zhou and Western Han. Commented on in Qing by Dai Wang 戴望 in the edition *Guanzi jiaozheng* 管子校正 (Rectification of the *Guanzi*). *Zj* ed. Beijing: Zhonghua shuju, 1954.

Han shu 漢書 (History of the Western Han Dynasty [206 B.C. – A.D. 9]). Ban Gu 班固 (A.D. 32–92). Eastern Han. Commented on in Tang by Yan Shigu 顏師古 (A.D. 581–645). Beijing: Zhonghua shuju, 1962.

He Yeju 賀業鉅 (1986). *Zhongguo gudai chengshi guihua shi luncong* 中國古代城市規劃史論叢 (Collective Discourses on the History of Ancient Chinese City Planning). Beijing: Zhongguo jianzhu gongye chubanshe.

Li ji 禮記 (Record of Rites). Ed. Dai Sheng 戴聖. Western Han, ca. 50 B.C. *Sz* ed. Beijing: Zhonghua shuju, 1980.

Shang shu 尚書 (Book of Documents). Writers unknown. Tenth century B.C. to ca. A.D. 320. *Sz* ed. Beijing: Zhonghua shuju, 1980.

Shi ji 史記 (Historian's Record). Sima Qian 司馬遷 (ca. 145 or 135–? B.C.). Western Han, ca. 104–91 B.C. Beijing: Zhonghua shuju, 1959.

Zhou li 周禮 (Record of the Rites of Zhou). Compilers unknown. Western Han, perhaps containing some material from Late Zhou. *Sz* ed. Beijing: Zhonghua shuju, 1980.

Zhou Yi qianzaodu 周易乾鑿度 (Penetration of Qian of the *Zhou Yi*). Writers unknown. Han, ca. first century B.C. *Sq* ed. Shanghai: Shanghai guji chubanshe, 1987.

Zuo zhuan 左傳 (Zuo's Commentary). Zuo Qiuming 左丘明. Zhou, compiled between 430 and 250 B.C., with additions and changes by Confucian scholars of the Qin and Han. *Sz* ed. Beijing: Zhonghua shuju, 1980.

Western Language References

Balazs, Etienne (1964). *Chinese Civilization and Bureaucracy: Variations on a Theme*. Trans. by H. M. Wright and ed. by Arthur F. Wright. New Haven and London: Yale University Press.

Biot, Edouard (1851). *Le Tcheou-li*. 2 vols. Paris: Imprimerie nationale.

Braunfels, Wolfgang (1988). *Urban Design in Western Europe: Regime and Architecture, 900–1900*. Trans. by Kenneth J. Northcott from the 1976 edition under the title *Abendländisch Staadtbaukunst: Herrschaftsform und Baugestalt*. Chicago: University of Chicago Press.

Graham, A. C. (1989). *Disputers of the Tao: Philosophical Argument in Ancient China*. La Salle, IL: Open Court Publishing Co.

Granet, Marcel (1930). *Chinese Civilization*. Translated by Kathleen E. Innes and Mabel R. Brailsford. London: Kegan Paul, Trench, Trubner & Co., Ltd.

Henderson, John B. (1984). *The Development and Decline of Chinese Cosmology*. New York: Columbia University Press.

Hillier, Bill, and Julienne Hanson (1984). *The Social Logic of Space*. Cambridge: Cambridge University Press.

Legge, James (1960). *The Chinese Classics*. 5 vols. Hong Kong: Hong Kong University Press.

Morris, A. E. J. (1994). *History of Urban Form: Before the Industrial Revolutions*. 3rd ed. Essex: Longman Scientific & Technical.

Mote, F. W. (1977). "The Transformation of Nanking, 1350–1400." In Skinner, ed. 1977 (see citation), pp. 101–153.

Needham, Joseph (1959). *Science and Civilization in China*, Vol. 3. Cambridge: Cambridge University Press.

Rickett, W. Allyn (1985). *Guanzi*, Vol. 1. Princeton, NJ: Princeton University Press.

Samuels, Marwyn S. (1978). "Review Article: The City in Late Imperial China." *Journal of Asian Studies* XXXVII, no. 4 (August 1978): 713–723.

Sivin, Nathan (1995). "State, Cosmos, and Body in the Last Three Centuries B.C." *Harvard Journal of Asiatic Studies* 55, no. 1 (June 1995): 5–37.

Skinner, G. William, ed. (1977). *The City in Late Imperial China*. Stanford, CA: Stanford University Press.

Skinner, G. William (1977a). "Introduction: Urban Development in Imperial China." In Skinner, ed. 1977, pp. 3–31.

Steinhardt, Nancy Shatzman (1990). *Chinese Imperial City Planning*. Honolulu: University of Hawai'i Press.

Wheatley, Paul (1971). *The Pivot of the Four Quarters: A Preliminary Enquiry into the Origins and Character of the Ancient Chinese City*. Edinburgh: Edinburgh University Press.

Reading

14

Barrie Shelton

Learning from the Japanese City: Looking East in Urban Design (2012)

Barrie Shelton is an Australian urban designer and urban historian with a personal interest in Japanese cities. His remarks about the patterns and forms of the Japanese city highlight the diverging notions of space in Japanese urban contexts and the Western cityscape. Although Shelton's observations often apply more directly to the contemporary Japanese city, he sees in the organization of the contemporary urban fabric traces of earlier, traditional urban forms. He quotes in this respect Jinnai Hidenobu's studies on Tokyo, whose underlying organization mirrors the vanished structure of Edo. (See also Jinnai, reading 33, part IV.) Shelton's text is interspersed with references and observations from Western and Japanese scholars who offer stimulating and often complementary points of view about their respective urban cultures.

Japanese cities may have different (in some instances almost opposite) patterns and forms to those of the West, but to suggest that these are somehow less valid or that there is no convincing archetype or that the rural origins of some urban patterns devalues them is, I think, misleading. Like many views of cultural artefacts the world over, such misgivings seem to be somewhat Eurocentric in their viewpoint.

However, there is much to suggest that Western visitors' responses, including those of urban professionals, have been growing more appreciative and respectful over recent decades. And in Japan itself, discussion and presentation of Japanese cities by designers and urban scholars has been changing from embarrassment and apology to more purposeful and confident exploration and promotion. There has been a steady process of discovery and acceptance of forms previously put aside as unworthy of serious investigation. The processes leading to greater appreciation may well resemble those that led to the earlier admiration of Japanese architecture: namely that of outsid-

From Barrie Shelton, *Learning from the Japanese City: Looking East in Urban Design*, 2nd ed. (London: Routledge, 2012), 7–11, 31–33, 40–42.

ers developing their own conceptual pursuits and theories that allow them 'to see' merit in the unfamiliar. Cities are, after all, far more complex assemblages than buildings: and therefore changes in attitudes towards them more convoluted, fragmented and slow; although in the end, these may well be more profound? [. . .]

Drawing on the pioneering 1960s work of Teiji Itoh, Arata Isozaki and colleagues (Toshi Design Kenkyutai, 1968), one of the first Western writers to attempt to understand the Japanese city on its own terms was Gunther Nitschke (1966). He admonished those Europeans who had earlier seen only the superficialities of traditional Japanese architecture while in pursuit of their Modernist ends, namely transparency, flexibility and lightness. Specifically, he tried to get closer to the Japanese idea of space, including city space, and made a number of important observations. He recognized that the Japanese sense of space is not something created by compositional elements. In other words, a city in Japan was not something 'enclosed' by buildings and walls. Its shape was forever 'vague'. A space or 'place' was an area defined by 'certain human activities'; consequently, it would move with the activity that gave it definition. He stressed this point by way of reference to the grand European parade or gathering where spatial setting (e.g. Paris' Champs-Elysees, Rome's St Peter's Square or London's Mall) is more important than the activity in the process of place-making; whereas in Japan, it is the procession or other event independent of spatial setting that makes a place (Nitschke, 1966, p. 126). Consequently, a Westerner must put aside his precious notions of enclosure and physical definition to appreciate Japanese space. Nitschke also noted that communal facilities in Japanese cities tend not to be centralized as in the West but scattered. [. . .]

Nitschke still had in mind traditional Japan. More recently, some observers have tried to see merit in Japan's rather maligned modern cities. One observation (consistent with that of a 'scattered' centre) is that city form constantly thickens and thins, and rises and falls over a wide area. Within this pattern, Westerners are surprised by the cheek-by-jowl proximity of the big concrete-and-neon networks of roads to the labyrinths of little lanes enmeshed within the big networks.

On this point, the Tokyo-based English writer Peter Popham has likened the urban fabric of Tokyo to a spread of areas, each with a high hard concrete commercial 'shell' containing a pliable retail and service 'white' and a positively soft residential 'yolk' (Popham, 1985, p. 48). This means the general profile of the city is one of alternating ridges (higher buildings) and depressions (lower buildings). Unlike in Western cities, he notes that the quieter streets and places of relative tranquility are not necessarily that way because they are peripheral but because they exist within the shell-protected depressions. Popham is one who has looked at Japanese cities with a critical but compassionate eye that is rewarded with insight.

Botond Bognar is another author who has recognized the outsiders' difficulties in overcoming their perplexing first impressions of Japan's cities and made a more scholarly probe into the country's cultural, architectural and urban traditions. As backcloth to his informative survey of Japanese architecture and urbanism, Bognar (1985) also expanded upon the kinds of observations made by Nitschke: the traditional absence of

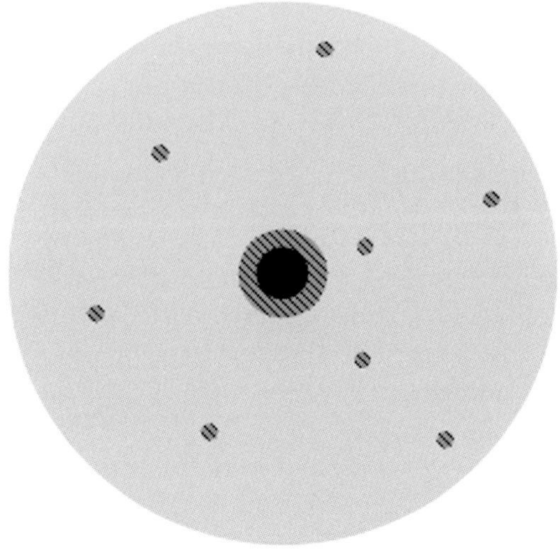

Fig. 1. Hard Shells and Soft Yolks. Although usually higher density, the Japanese city is generally less centralized than its Western counterpart with a series of 'hard shells' and 'soft yolks' over a wide area (above), while that of the Western city tends to rise to a more restricted and visually dominant centre (right).

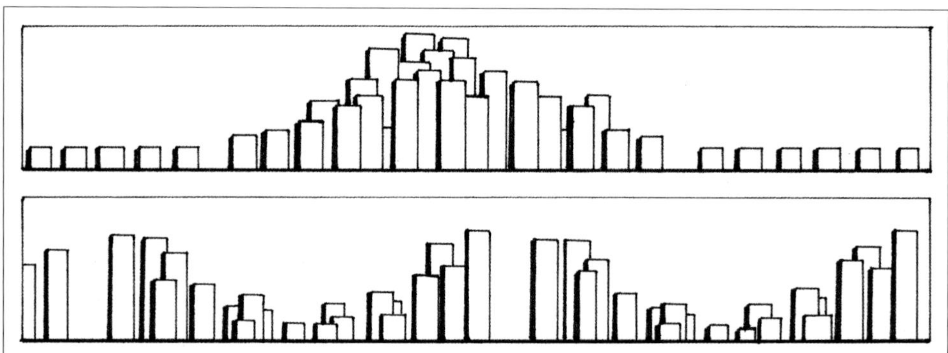

Fig. 2. Hard Shells and Soft Yolks – City Section. In the Japanese city, lower buildings and relatively quiet streets (or 'soft yolks') commonly lie between bands of higher buildings that follow busy thoroughfares (bottom). In the Western city, however, the built skyline is more likely to stand as a concentrated and distinct 'peak' at a primary centre (top).

well-defined centres, the absence of towers and squares, the dependence of 'spatiality . . . on the current happening', and so on. He concluded that the spatial structure of Western cities 'is primarily centrifugal in character' whereas that of Japan 'moves, centripetally from outside in.' Further, he saw a consistency with architecture for he likened the city to the traditional house which was laid out horizontally and had no central space (Bognar, 1985, p. 67).

Writing some twenty years later than Nitschke, Bognar places rather more emphasis upon the experience of the city and on the present, constantly making connections between traditional and contemporary form. He refers (by way of Kazuhiro Ishii) to the structural clarity of the Western city in contrast to Japanese irregularity and adds his own insights. 'The Japanese city', says Bognar, 'is created, perceived and understood as an additive texture of its parts or places and thus is denoted by the external distribution of signs and symbols rather than by the physical entity of its objects and enclosures' (*Ibid.*). Consequently, activity, signs and symbols are collectively Japan's urban place-makers rather than buildings, monuments and spaces. He concludes that the Westerner has 'A predominant reliance on visual perception [which] . . . tends to objectify and to instil feelings of mastery over the environment, since the eye sets everything at a distance and maintains order. In the Japanese environment only fragments signified by scattered signs and symbols are encountered. These fail to provide an objective perspective of a definite overall spatial pattern' (*Ibid.*).

This is the root of the failure of even the perceptive Jan Morris (and most visitors before or since) to respond to and make sense of even the relatively ordered Kyoto—although Morris, as earlier acknowledged, had the wit and experience to realize that her interpretive machinery may have been culturally too defective to allow for reasonable understanding. While some Westerners have shown less antipathy towards Japanese cities in recent years, many leading Japanese designers and scholars have themselves studied them more seriously than ever before and speculated on their formal traditions and character. Indeed, it is this writing that has informed much Western writing: practitioner-theorists such as Ashihara and Maki and scholars such as Jinnai have written extensively on the Japanese city (past and present) and on the design implications (future) of their conclusions. Hidenobu Jinnai, in his extensive studies of Tokyo, has revealed just how much of the pattern of the present-day city (roads, activities, lot sizes, etc.) bears powerfully the imprint of previous forms. He shows how 'the structure of old Edo survives in the substructure of modern Tokyo' (Jinnai 1987, p. 24). For instance, new luxury hotels, almost all of Tokyo's college campuses and many of the city's parks all occupy former *daimyo* (i.e. lords') estates in the more elevated parts of the city and are served by old route networks. While, unlike in many Western cities, old buildings have been obliterated, links with the past are nevertheless strong, especially in the 'organization of space.'

More important, from the standpoint of this book, are his particular insights into the character of Japanese city space. For example, he contrasts the main central places of traditional Japanese and European cities: in Japan 'it was the bridges and their environs, which offered sweeping vistas and an exhilarating sense of openness' and were the equivalents of European squares with their contrasting heavy masonry enclosure (*Ibid.*). Thus, Edobashi (bridge) as an open functional node was to Tokyo as the Piazza San Marco was to Venice as a closed formal space.

The late Yoshinobu Ashihara was one of Japan's leading architects and a member of the country's elite Japanese Academy. He likewise contrasted European city form with that of Japan. He not only showed them to be different but proffered the superiority of the chaotic Japanese forms over their more ordered European counterparts. Ashihara conceded that Japanese cities do appear to be very messy but also observed that they work remarkably well, contending that behind the visual chaos (which so many writers have been quick to condemn or cheaply glamorize) there is a 'hidden order', rooted in Japanese geography, history and culture (Ashihara, 1989).

Cities

[. . .]
I shall imagine for a moment that I have been whisked in the dead of night from an airport or station to a house in an unfamiliar city. At morning light, I am cast out into the street and have the task of placing myself. I have a map and my eyes to fathom my location.

In a Western city, I must first look for the street name and the number of the house. [. . .]

In a Japanese city, however, I look not for a horizontal street sign but for a vertical signboard which is usually attached to the very corner of one or other side of the corner-turning building or wall "rounding" two anonymous streets. If the corner is chamfered it may appear on the diagonal cut across the corner. Whichever, the board will give the number of the *chome* which is an aerial unit, and the name of the *machi* which is a larger areal unit in which a collection of *chome* nest. The *chome* approximates to a Western street block or collections of small blocks and may be of a regular or irregular shape. It is, however, in contrast to the street, an aerial unit. The placement of the sign on a chamfered corner is significant in that the diagonal enables the sign to signify more accurately the area. It is not unusual in Japan for a street corner property to have its boundary fence or building wall cut at an angle to allow for better viewing and turning in the characteristically narrow streets and this is especially common in newer suburbs.

Within these areas, property numbers may not occur sequentially but be dotted seemingly haphazardly (often in order of subdivision or building) over the land's surface. In this situation, anonymous streets may either occur within these areas or as dividing lines between them: in other words they are not the lines of unifying identity as in the West. Thus the *chome* nest within the *machi*, and together form part of a layered patchwork or mosaic, which forms the city's organizational framework.

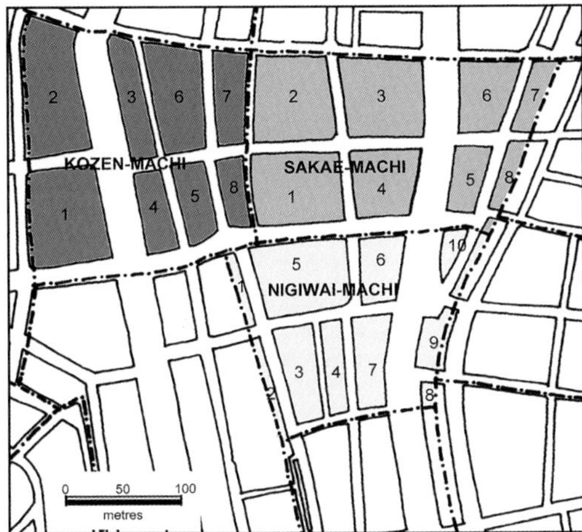

Fig. 3. Patchwork of areas, Nagasaki, Japan. In Japan, the streets are mostly subsidiary to a patchwork of areas—*machi, cho, chome*.

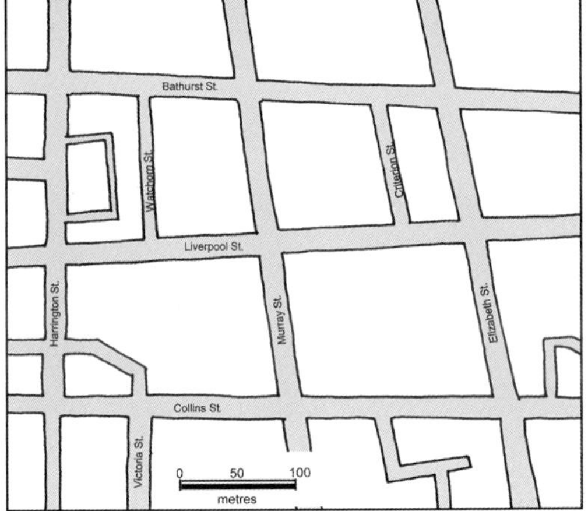

Fig. 4. Network of streets, Hobart, Australia. Streets combine to form a network of formed and named linear spaces in most Western cities.

[. . .] Order in the Western city is underpinned by the notion of street, or even highway as the key visual ordering device.

From Antiquity to Modern times, there has been a pre-occupation in Western city planning with axes, symmetry, gateways, grand vistas and monuments and it is the network of streets and squares to which these concepts have been applied. Such ideas are strongly deterministic of the placement and execution of buildings and spaces in relation to each other. These are long and established practices of intervention and control of city form although more informal (irregular and organic) ideas have also existed. Nevertheless, the essential element about which modern townscape planning has evolved is the street or at least the linear spatial experience. [. . .]

[. . .] In conservation planning, the keeping of an individual building was seen to lose part of its worth if it was to be kept independent of its (usually street) context. Indeed, in design, 'urban contextualism' is an approach whereby the form of a building is derived from the analysis or at least observation of its surrounding (again mainly street) context and this became very strong in the 1980s: Brent Brolin's book, *Architecture in Context* (1980), reflected well those sentiments. (Significantly, it is a term borrowed from linguistics where the meaning of a word is interpreted according to its relationship with the wider text.)

Some cities have gone to extraordinary lengths to ensure that contextual criteria, with an emphasis on the continuity of street lines (alignments, heights, patterns), are followed in new design, often with dubious results. Even in the relatively mixed form city environments of Australia (compared to the more consistent European ones), design guidelines have been attached to city plans to cover (in addition to the above) such items as roof form, materials, building details, retention of old street façades, etc. The chief concern in such cases is for a consistent visual language, which has at its heart the linear street and, in turn the network and hierarchy of linear streets, as the primary formal element about which urban design must revolve.

[. . .] [T]he Japanese notion of the city [is] as a patchwork of relatively autonomous plots. In a patchwork model, the street primarily forms a kind of leftover space that serves as the route or service conduit between plots and is born of the necessity to move people and things from one plot to another, although there are other roles. There are those of accommodating local activity (mostly in the form of spill-over activity from the buildings themselves) and as a communication channel (in the sense of transmitting information) [. . .]. In the network model, the streets are more the public spaces which command a collective respect and stage-set response from the individual developments that line them. In the former, the emphasis is on essentials. In the latter, while no one would deny a practical role, there is also the very important dimensions of visual and sequential address (façade and numbering). Such a model is rather more deterministic of pattern and form with the Japanese model offering greater flexibility. Thus, we are again comparing a way of thinking that is linked to line (or, collectively, a network of lines) with one that revolves about areas (or, collectively, a mosaic of patches).

References

Ashihara, Yoshinobu (1989) *The Hidden Order: Tokyo through the Twentieth Century*. Tokyo: Kodansha International (Originally published as *Kakureta chitsujo*. Tokyo: Chuokoron-sha, 1986).

Bognar, Botond (1985) *Contemporary Japanese Architecture*. New York: Van Nostrand Reinhold.

Brolin, Brent (1980) *Architecture in Context*. New York: Van Nostrand Reinhold.

Jinnai, Hidenobu (1987) Tokyo then and now: Keys to Japanese urban design. *Japan Echo*, 14: pp. 20–29.

Nitschke, Gunter (1966) "'Ma': The Japanese sense of 'place' in old and new architecture and planning." *Architectural Design*, March, pp. 117–130.

Popham, Peter (1985) *Tokyo: The City at the End of the World*. Tokyo: Kodansha International.

Toshi Design Kenkyutai (1968) *Nihon no Toshi Kukan (Japanese Urban Space)*. Tokyo: Shokokusha.

Reading

15

Suzanne Preston Blier

The African Urban Past: Historical Perspectives on the Metropolis (2011)

Suzanne Preston Blier is a distinguished scholar of African art and architecture currently teaching at Harvard University. In this reading from her contribution to African Metropolitan Architecture, *she explores the urban past of the continent, remarking at the outset that the notion that Africa never had an urban culture is entirely false. Urbanism has indeed figured prominently in the African past. Its various incarnations have spanned the entire continent, encompassing the stone centers of northern, eastern, and southern Africa, the earthen cities of West Africa, and the impermanent, migratory settlements of the central regions of the continent. Certainly less durable than their European and Asian counterparts, traditional African cities have been more flexible and adaptable to changing circumstances, and, in Blier's view, more egalitarian and innovative.*

[. . .] There are many definitions of what constitutes a city, but normally the label refers to a well-populated centre inhabited by a relatively heterogeneous population, marked by complex sociopolitical institutions and distinctive forms of planning and architecture.[1] In the West, urbanism has historically been viewed as a mark of civilization, an attribute that, falsely, precolonial Africa was once seen to lack. In Africa, urbanism has long figured prominently. [. . . .]

Patterns of Urban Development

Three historic patterns of urban settlement are found in Africa. Monumental urbanism is characterized by substantial permanent structures in stone, and was especially prominent in north, eastern, and southern Africa, from Egypt and Eritrea to Zimbabwe. Satellite urbanism is characterized, in both early and later contexts, by collaboration between

From Suzanne Preston Blier, "The African Urban Past: Historical Perspectives on the Metropolis," in *African Metropolitan Architecture,* vol. 1, by David Adjaye, edited by Peter Allison (New York and London: Rizzoli and Thames & Hudson, 2011), 15–19. Reproduced courtesy of Suzanne Preston Blier and Adjaye Associates.

interlinked community clusters that together create an urban settlement structure. This type of settlement, which is normally identified with earthen structures, is found especially in West Africa, from Mali to northern and southern areas of Nigeria. Migratory or peripatetic urban settlements characteristically prevailed in central Africa, these cities sharing a relatively nomadic identity. Related cities were often reestablished on a new site following the death of a ruler or a sequence of traumatic events. Many peripatetic cities were built of more ephemeral materials, such as raffia and bamboo, but were also associated with more permanent ritual sites, such as cemeteries. In some African urban contexts, several of these design attributes were at play, with local building materials providing unique possibilities for creativity.

Monumental Urbanism: North, Eastern, and Southern Africa

Metropolitan centres in Egypt were among the largest and most durable in urban global history. These cities featured an array of monumental building forms serving multiple functions, some dating back to the predynastic and early dynastic period.[2] [. . .]

Aksum (400 BCE to CE 619), situated in modern Eritrea, was also an important early urban centre, known for its grouping of seven large-scale stone menhirs, a broken one now weighing 500 tons.[3] Similar in style, these monuments include images of windows and portals, as if to suggest the portals found in this area. Aksum is thought to have been a compact city inhabited by political and trade elites, with producers at the centre's outskirts. Its rulers also controlled several Red Sea ports, as well as nearby lands in Yemen, and its population was diverse, in keeping with its role in a trading empire that circulated goods from India to the Mediterranean. Aksum's conversion to Christianity was among the earliest in Africa, and it was eventually taken over by Ethiopian rulers.

To the south, the stone remains of the elaborate Shona capital of Great Zimbabwe, which flourished in the 11th–14th centuries CE, covered some 722 hectares and as many as 18,000 people may have lived here. Similar stone walls are found at distances several hundred kilometres away. An oracle site and trading depot were among this centre's possible draws, the latter dealing with goods from as far away as China. Other cities rose along the East African coast from the 8th to the 19th centuries CE, some with richly decorated, stone-like, coral edifices. These Swahili coastal sites, such as Kilwa and Mombasa, also benefited from the Indian Ocean trade in gold, ivory, slaves, and other goods. Like the new trade language, ki-Swahili, that became the lingua franca along this 1,500 km coastal region, Swahili cities are noted for their ethnic diversity—local African, Arabic, and Persian attributes being among those found.

Satellite Urbanism: West Africa

Numerous metropolitan centres emerged in West Africa in regions south of the Sahara. One of the most important of these was Jenne-Jeno, a grouping of urban settlements established along the inner Niger River floodplain of Mali, within a few kilometres of Jenne (Djenne). [. . .]

[. . .]

The Tellem (11th–16th century CE), and the Dogon populations that merged with and replaced them (14th century onwards) in Mali's Bandiagara Escarpment, created a number of urban settlements as well. These densely populated centres were ethnically diverse: the Dogon arrived in waves as they escaped from the reach of Islam, dynastic expansion, and slavery. They created a new culture here based on agricultural innovation (irrigated onion farming), technological and ritual specialization (iron working and so on), and various forms of external trade. Related architecture suggests not only Mande architectural sources, but forms of symbolic organization consistent with utopian idioms, defined by flexible anthropomorphic design referents, which is a feature of other populations in the West African savanna area.[4]

Clustered or satellite cities also appear to have distinguished the densely populated Igbo communities in southeast Nigeria. By the end of the first millennium CE the Igbo area was in trade contact with regions as far away as southwest Asia, creating works of extraordinary complexity in bronze and elaborate burial forms at Igbo Ukwu sites. [. . .]

In Yoruba oral traditions, a complementary satellite-style urbanism is said to have characterized the city-state of Ife (Ile-Ife), a polity rising to power in southwest Nigeria by the end of the first millennium.[5] [. . .]

During Ife's florescence in the 12th–15th centuries this metropolitan area may have covered 30 square kilometres, with a population of about 130,000. [. . .] Yoruba metropolitan centres grew to enormous scale and featured unique craft specialization (from metal- and glassworking to weaving and dyeing), marked population diversity (through trade and war), and major population shifts throughout the year (many inhabitants moving to distant agricultural fields for part of the rainy season).

[. . .] Frequently sited on hills, where the palaces are the most prominent architectural feature, Yoruba cities incorporated striking axes and sightlines, along with a grid-style radial form, in keeping with urban planning in the grand manner. Characteristically, the palace was the largest, tallest, most ornate structure in city, with surrounding walls that were exceptionally high. [. . .] In both mythic and spatial terms the city of Ile-Ife complements at once the mounded pregnant body of the mother goddess Yemoja, the watery surround where the culture hero Odudua is said to have first sprinkled sand to create earth, and the image of a tortoise in reference to Obatala, the head of the opposing deity's pantheon. The city is also divided ritually into quadrants, which are traversed yearly by ceremonial paths that crisscross the city (and the year), dividing the centre between competing families and deities.

In the Edo royal capital, Benin City, southwest of Ife, European travellers who began reaching this area in the middle of the 15th century describe an impressive urban centre distinguished by broad avenues and well-constructed residences. [. . .]

To the west, in the Fon Kingdom of Benin Republic, early urban centres were planned with a centralized palace, market, temple complex, and circumscribing moat-wall system, similar to Yoruba examples. The plan for Abomey, the Fon capital, is said in local oral traditions to have been established by King Agaja (1708–40), the son of Abomey's first king, Hwegbaja. The city was also defined, in important ways, by the strategic positioning of palaces for the crown princes. Placed in a spiral pattern that extended outwards from the central palace, they provided a basis for urban growth and renewal over time. Each crown prince built his own palace in an area of the city along the outward spiral, appropriating adjacent lands from earlier residents to create structures for family members and retainers. In this way, early planners seem to have anticipated new building needs as part of both spatial planning and political strategy. The spiralling design of this urban renewal idiom is said to reference the powerful local rainbow python god, identified with life, wealth, and well-being.[6] The first mosque also is said to have been built in the city during Agaja's reign. The square, rather than circular, shape of Abomey's circumscribing wall suggests complements with early Hausa cities to the northwest, centres that were Islamicized in the 16th century.

Hausa cities, in northern Nigeria and adjacent regions of Niger and Cameroon, have their precursors in the pre-Islamic, Kanem (Bornu) urban centres of the late 8th to 10th centuries that developed in the Lake Chad area around the time of Jenne-Jeno and Igbo Ukwu. Like these other polities, Kanem figured prominently in short- and long-distance trade. In the 11th or 12th century, Kanem's ruler converted to Islam and, in the 14th century, the capital was moved westward into Bornu. [. . .]

Hausa cities emerged in locations close to the intersections of major trade routes, valued resources, especially iron, and powerful spirit locales. Many developed, in part, around the need for protected cattle corrals of Fulani pastoralists who were seeking more settled lives, a feature that Hausa cities share with Timbuktu, which also had a well at its centre. The Kano chronicle dates the first permanent market in Kano to the 15th century, crediting Bornu refugees with this institution. Later that century, the Hausa ruler Muhammad Rumfa constructed, or extended, the Kano city walls and built a centralized palace and a new market, and introduced new forms of pomp and a state council. The Hausa walled city, like other walled cities in this area, also served the protective needs of refugees from neighbouring communities. As with Yoruba, Fon, and other African city wall systems, it also played a role in the control of merchants and goods for purposes of taxes, tolls, and the reduction of smuggling.

Hausa cities were also linked to a system of satellite urban settlements, the six main Hausa cities furnishing key goods or services within the larger network: textiles from Kano, markets in Katsina and Daura, militias from Gobir, and slaves from Zaria, the most southern Hausa city. While certain technical developments, such as the use of domes, distinguished Hausa urban architecture, decorative features varied from one urban locale to another, with palaces, merchant residences, and mosques being particularly ornamental. In symbolic terms, Hausa urban settings carried varied cosmological significance, based in part on orientation toward the cardinal directions and the positioning of special gates.

Central African Migratory Cities

Congo, Angola, Cameroon, Rwanda and other countries in Central Africa also saw the development of urban settlements. These were often characterized by historic patterns of migratory or peripatetic identity. Characteristically, moving capitals of this sort were created at the beginning of each king's reign, or after difficult circumstance. Some migratory cities reached populations of 15,000–20,000 inhabitants and were identified, like early West African cities, by cluster-like relationships with nearby communities. [. . .]

In the Angola-Congo border area near the Luezi River, M'banza Kongo, the capital of the Kingdom of Kongo (1400–1914), was established prior to the Portuguese arrival in 1483. Sited on high ground, it was already a sizable city, comparable in scale to Evora, the then thriving Avis dynastic seat in Portugal. The Kongo practice of assimilating the conquered inhabitants of other regions meant that this urban centre had a diverse population, and it was an important location for royal rituals that continued here over the centuries. While Kongo rulers rebuilt their capital cities on coming to the throne, taking up a previously inhabited site in many cases, the existence of the royal cemeteries gave spiritual vitality when a site was reoccupied.

—∿∿—

The migratory urban centres of Kongo, Kuba and Luba, as well as those of the Lunda Kingdom (c. 1600–1887)—and of the Cameroon grasslands—take an array of symbolic forms. These are linked to internal positioning in relation to nearby rivers or mountains, central axis plans with bilateral siting of key structures (suggesting in some cases spiders or tortoises), and maze-like spatial confirmation within some palace complexes. Other important urban forms associated with migratory settlements include Ethiopian royal capitals and Buganda dynastic capitals, as well as Zulu war centres, the latter evoking Assyrian and Roman war cities.[7]

Taken together, these diverse African settlements convey the early and enduring importance of ancient cities in Africa as focal points of political and artistic engagement, complex administrative organization, and trade affiliations with centres near and far. The communal need to address larger issues (floods, the hunt, protection, manufacturing, trade control) seems to have been important to their success. Whatever the reasons for their development, Africa's urban centres show broad appreciation of the benefits of social aggregation. The more ephemeral materials that distinguish many African cities and towns offer unique advantages to growth and change over time, providing ready flexibility in response to changing needs. If architectural durability is less important in many historic African cities than in the West or Asia, this feature is often replaced by a concomitant interest in creativity and innovation on the part of local leaders, as well as a larger interest in more egalitarian political approaches: perspectives that, even within royal contexts, preclude the descendants of a single ruling line from assuming political and resource control through many generations. African cities are also creative, in many different ways, in providing new opportunities for their residents.

Notes

1. The differences between towns and cities are in truth little defined, with many cultures using the same term for both.
2. This also reflects the frequent association of cities (and societies associated with them) as "civilizations," and those regions lacking such centres as "uncivilized."
3. Other early African trading centres include Tripoli in Libya and Carthage in Tunisia, which were both founded by Phoenician traders and became popular merchant destinations and early European rivals for east-west Mediterranean trade. With the fall of Carthage to Rome in 146 BCE, Tripoli became a protectorate of Kush (Nubia).
4. On Tellem and Dogon architecture, see also Rita Bolland, *Tellem textiles; Archaeological finds from burial caves in Mali's Bandiagara Cliff*, Amsterdam: Royal Tropical Institute; Leiden, Rijksmuseum voor Volkenkunde; Bamako: Institut des Sciences Humaines; Bamako: Musée National, 1991; Jean-Christophe Huet, *Villages perchés des Dogon du Mali: Habitat, espace et société*, Paris: L'Harmattan, 1994. On architectural anthropomorphism, see among others, Suzanne Preston Blier, *The anatomy of architecture: Ontology and metaphor in Batammaliba architectural expression*, Chicago: University of Chicago Press, 1994.
5. Early Yoruba cities were sometimes discounted by Western theorists because they were assumed to be lineage-based (rather than heterogeneous). In Yoruba urban centres, however, "lineage" is used to define a wide array of non-kin social relationships as well, among these prisoners of war and strangers who were integrated into lineage-like units for socio-political-religious reasons.
6. On Fon, Savi and Ouidah architecture, see Michael Houseman, Blandine Legonou, Christiane Massy and Xavier Crepin, "Note sur la structure évolutive d'une ville historique: L'exemple d'Abomey (République populaire du Bénin)," *Cahiers d'Études Africaines*, vol. 26, no. 104 (1986), pp. 527–46; Robin Law, "Ouidah: A pre-colonial urban centre in coastal Africa, 1727–1892," in Anderson and Rathbone, eds., *Africa's urban past*, pp. 85–96; Neil L. Norman and Kenneth G. Kelly, "Landscape politics: The serpent ditch and the rainbow in West Africa," *American Anthropologist*, vol. 106, no.1 (2004), pp. 98–110; Suzanne Preston Blier, "Razing the roof: The architecture of destruction in Dahomey," in Tony Atkin, ed., *Structure and Meaning in Human Settlements*, Philadelphia: University of Pennsylvania, 2005.
7. Beginning in the latter half of the 15th century, Europeans created trading and replenishment centres and, later, forts along the African coast that grew in time into important cities, among them Dakar (Senegal), Accra (Ghana) and Luanda (Angola). By the late 19th century Europeans were also creating inland cities to serve as new colonial capitals, among these Niamey (Niger), Nairobi (Kenya), Harare (Zimbabwe) and Johannesburg (South Africa). Each had its own colonial importance, Nairobi as an East African railway midpoint, Harare as a military protected settler town (organized by Cecil Rhodes), and Johannesburg as a gold-rush town.

Reading

16

Sir David Adjaye

African Metropolitan Architecture (2011)

David Adjaye, a Ghanaian British architect, named among Time *magazine's 100 most influential people in 2017, offers in this reading his impressions of the latest developments of the African city during the colonial and postindependence years. Cities are considered in their varied geographic contexts, a factor that has determined and explains, in Adjaye's view, their diversified outlook and character. Contrary to superficial and cursory understandings, natural features and precolonial elements still persist in many cities of older foundation, determining major locations and urban connections. These were reinterpreted and reshaped during the colonial period, with the creation of new public central areas and main commercial streets, whose underlying structure contains to this day the representative and ever-changing core of major African cities.*

It is over fifty years since the first African countries gained independence—and South Africa has recently emerged as the continent's superpower. Since then nations have been built, and we are now in a position to reflect on the significance of these changes for communities that, prior to colonization, were essentially rural. The colonial city existed primarily for purposes of trade and administration but, after independence, the same cities have become symbols of modernity, nationhood and emancipation. For Africans, this involves a complex negotiation as the identity of place is transferred from local to national significance, and becomes a more artificial construct in the process. Quiet colonial cities have been transformed into metropolitan capitals, and the speed with which this has happened is fundamental to understanding how the African perceives the city.

—~—

From Sir David Adjaye, "African Metropolitan Architecture," in *Adjaye Africa Architecture: A Photographic Survey of Metropolitan Architecture,* compact ed., edited by Peter Allison (New York: Thames & Hudson, 2016), 376–77, 14, 16, 44, 46, 74, 76, 104, 106, 270, 310, 312.

The idea of the metropolitan in Africa is not just about the density of people coming together but includes the parallel layering of many conditions: from the modernity of the city, and its embrace of development and commerce, back to its function as a heroic symbol of emancipation from a colonial past. And [. . .] it may include an imperial past that goes back through the centuries. This complex notion of the metropolitan is further conditioned by the geography of the continent because, although their histories have much in common, the character of each city is unique to its location. My purpose was to understand the interplay between shared themes and special circumstances and, in order to do this, I needed to look at each city on a similar basis.

The continent encompasses a range of climatic zones (the Maghreb, desert, the Sahel, forest, savanna and grassland, mountain and highveld) which, with the rural culture of the hinterland, inflect the identity of each city.

Architecture

When I talk about architecture in Africa, I am not referring to the traditional role of architecture: the creation of symbolic objects—or icons—that are the synthesis of a culture going back over several centuries. I am looking at the architecture of habitation, of humanity in general: the city as an inclusive conglomerate. It is a way of looking at architecture in terms of its collective identity not as a series of freestanding icons.

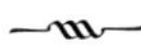

The Maghreb

Due to its Mediterranean coastline, the Maghreb is quite different from Africa's other geographic regions. It includes four major capitals, each with its own relationship to the Mediterranean or the Atlantic and a unique tradition in terms of city-building and architecture. These are complex cities with layers of history, both distant and recent, that give you a sense of a vast trajectory through different kingdoms and different times. But they also have a strong sense of modernity, a modernity that is still evolving. The origins of these cities lie in their walled medinas: the dense, human-scale environments, with very narrow passageways, whose earliest buildings date back to the Middle Ages. Apart from Algiers, where the geography has had dramatic consequences for construction, the buildings of the medina are never more than two or three storeys high. They are agglomerative organizations that provide an infrastructure for the daily life of the city, where rich and poor occupy similar houses located in different quarters. The Maghreb is the one region in Africa where in the medinas you have a sense of an indigenous typology that has survived the modernization of the cities.

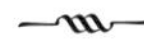

The cities of the Maghreb retain a more complete record of their history than most other African cities. They are cities where you can drive in and immediately understand where you are and where you can go, and I think they have a strong sense of their collective identity. The Maghreb has a long tradition of urbanism that is based on the indigenous precedent of the medina. [. . .] Due to their historic role as centres of trade, they offer a sense of protection—like citadels—and this seems to have been their overriding inspiration. They are an important reference points for people leading a contemporary life in cities, which is very different from places where the indigenous habitat is rural.

—~—

Desert

These four capitals are in locations that distort what you might expect from desert cities; two are on rivers and two on the coast. In many respects the cities of the Sahel, where water is scarce, are closer to what I would otherwise expect in the desert. Nouakchott on the Atlantic coast, Cairo and Khartoum on the Nile, and Djibouti on the Gulf of Aden, are highly developed cities. They represent sophisticated ideas of urbanism and they all have a vibrant civic and communal life, which gives a specific quality to each city. They have precise bucolic aspects, with either the sea or a river for their main respite.

Cairo [. . .] is a city of hybrid styles organized around the old fortified area at its heart. One of the first extensions, the neoclassical city, anticipates the megadensity that occurs in the modernist suburbs as they pull away from the central area, where the residential architecture creates a cooler ground plane that allows the life of the city to extend in all directions without interruption. [. . .]

Comparing Cairo to the other desert city located on a river, Khartoum has a civic quarter that looks across the Blue Nile, just before it joins the White Nile. The university and the administrative departments are also based here, so the public face of the city addresses the river and the commercial and residential areas spread outwards from it. The business area has recently begun to attract glazed towers that depend on technology to make them habitable. [. . .]

[. . .]

[. . .] Nouakchott is the one city in this group that most expresses the desert, even though it is located close to the sea. It is more temperate than if it were in the interior but it nevertheless embodies a strong sense of an abstract and simple geometry that pervades the local culture. [. . .]

[. . .] The mosque in Nouakchott, with multiple domes, celebrates this with great elegance; it represents an architecture of domes, cubes and half-rounds—all very simple but powerful when repeated. Similar shapes can be seen in the city's housing, whose simple volumes are punctuated by apertures, balconies and niches. [. . .]

Djibouti is an intriguing city on the northeast coast of Africa that faces Yemen. It is an important port, which serves Ethiopia and has always been a relatively wealthy trading city. It has absorbed many influences from the Middle East but the old city is organized on a neoclassical grid, with major and minor street, squares and open spaces. [. . .] One side of the street is basically always in the shade. The city has a mixed population that occupies different quarters, though they are no longer as clear-cut as they were in the past. In this respect, this is an unusually accommodating form of urbanism, a low city that is also very public. In some ways, it is like an oasis: in a harsh environment, it offers protection to all who go there.

Beyond the grid of the old town, the new developments adopt a form of coastal architecture—with architecture with terraces and balconies that look towards the view. [. . .]

—w—

The Sahel

[. . .] [I]n the four cities of the Sahel, [. . .] [t]here is a very clear layering of the relationship with the countryside and of how the city engages with its hinterland. Because the landscape is flat and is on the threshold between vegetation and desert, the domestic architecture is generally horizontal—a cellular, atria-like architecture—while civic buildings are more concerned with emphatic vertical symbols. The architecture of Islam, with its domes and minarets, plays a significant role here but there is a more general symbolism that relates to a tradition of marking the distinction between desert and built environment. The sense of materiality in these cities is based on the sand and stone and where there is vegetation, it is encouraged as a way of providing shade and moderating the climate. It can also take on ornamental qualities—framing certain buildings, for instance—but that is not its primary function.
[. . .]

Like fragments from a previous era, the Sahel cities contain some strong colonial buildings that continue to make an important contribution to the larger environment. These buildings started to develop a dry, tropical architecture that could take its place between the forest and the desert. It is an architecture of colonnades and porticoes, rather than interior space; one that starts to talk about moderating the harshness of the heat and giving some respite from the humidity. This is especially clear in the civic buildings of Bamako, and in the shopping buildings where the goods are displayed in a shaded area in front of an enclosed storage space. There is a very interesting mercantile component to the Sahel cities: the way in which produce and goods are thrust into the public realm. [. . .]

—w—

In the Sahel it is the architecture of the poor that most expresses the horizontality of the landscape. This architecture is about walls that enclose individual spaces—

cells—and define perimeters. The thresholds are never experienced visually, except as simple apertures. When you are welcomed through the outer wall, you start to realize that the building is made up of a series of volumes that form deeper and more private spaces, depending on the size of the house. Residences in the Sahel do not normally articulate themselves as singular dwellings but as clusters or groups; this seems to be the operating standard. [. . .] When you travel through the Sahel, this wall and volumetric architecture is the vernacular architecture of the landscape.

—∾—

Forest

[. . .]
Forest is where the wetlands are, where the tropical rains dominate the climate. There is an architecture of fertility in this area, an architecture that has to deal with the climate and at the same time is responsive to the specific conditions in different places. The roof architecture of Freetown is a good example of the language of form that is necessary to deal with the heavy rains. You can also see it in the architecture of Monrovia where you have overhanging roofs everywhere; if you go there in the rain, you understand why certain forms and details are used in such a consistent way. Because of the incredible rains, the architecture of Accra is dominated by big roofs that protect the other building elements from the worst of the weather. [. . .] This readiness to respond to the constant risk of inundation is what I mean about the fertility of the architecture.

—∾—

Colonialism is a defining characteristic in all the Forest cities. You sense a different colonial presence in each of the geographic regions, and their influences define the civic architecture in the majority of capitals. African cities work through the colonial to their current identity, and every one of the cities that I visited included this experience. There were expressions of Frenchness, Belgianness or Portugueseness as integral parts of the current identity. The culture of the African city is basically hybridized and the African citizen sees himself—reads himself—through his local condition, his ethnic group, which is his history, and through his colonial experience, which is his modernity. [. . .]

Bissau's architecture has exactly this type of multiple identity, where you can see both the colonial expression and specific references to the local cultural heritage. In Bissau there is a classical Portuguese influence—it sets up emphatic vistas and avenues—but the residential architecture, sitting within the Portuguese plan, is primarily a response to the climate, making shade from the sun and being able to get rid of water as fast as possible. [. . .] The humidity is articulated by the indoor–outdoor zones that are a prominent part of the residential. These threshold spaces, porches and balconies, are the places where you live.

Kampala is an inland city and the architecture and planning respond to the garden-like nature of the site and the low hills that define different parts of the city. The sense of orientation in Kampala is unique in that the hills always give you an idea where you are. The articulation of the city is understood through the way in which you look at the different hills, so they provide the plan for constructing moments. You have really long views and the key image shows the mosque on top of a hill. The cathedral, with its twin towers and Victorian brick details, is also very prominent, as is the Sikh temple, standing in its own neighbourhood. What is so lovely about Kampala is that you find streets with impressive public buildings and residential streets where you scarcely see any buildings, just a lush landscape with the buildings in retreat. There are very few vertical emphases and those are either religious buildings or office buildings that have recently appeared. The architecture strives to deal with the horizontality of the land, the way in which you create shade, and extension and a relationship to the next site by layering things. You can see this in some of the commercial areas and the way in which the architecture makes things continuous. All the buildings on the main commercial avenue, and on most of the other streets, have projecting balconies and overhangs that define the public zone on the ground plane. In the residential areas there are many places where you could be in an agrarian community, rather than a relatively dense city.

Savanna & Grassland

The rolling out of the landscape, like a carpet, is one of the things that influence the shape of all the cities in this region, and despite the distances between them they have many similarities. In this setting there is a field of architecture that articulates itself to the twists and curves of the topography in Antananarivo and to the soft contours of Gaborone. In Abuja there is an undulating plane with the building pixellated into the landscape, and in Dakar the form of the city addresses the drama of its coastal location. Apart from Antananarivo, with its hills, these cities are short of vantage points and, because of their horizontality, it is difficult to see the edge of them—they just disappear into the wider context. Of the interior cities, two are explicitly colonial—Pretoria and Antananarivo—and two are more recent—Abuja and Gaborone—and represent African modernity. Although the climate is more temperate in this region than others, it is still quite harsh and the architecture has had to come to terms with the strength of the light and the need for shade. This explains the brise-soleil architecture, with its strong horizontals, which articulates Dakar and Pretoria. Abuja uses the technology of tinted glass and in Antananarivo the vernacular roofs and deeply recessed arcades provide a means of controlling the light.

In contrast to some of the other terrains, these cities demonstrate a commitment to public space. This is partly to do with European colonialism—in Dakar, Mogadishu, Pretoria and Antananarivo—but it also figures quite explicitly in the new city of Gaborone, which appears to have accepted the European model for the creation of a forward-looking African city. The fabric of these cities is predominantly horizontal, providing an ideal lining for their civic spaces, and they make use of axes, vistas, imposing facades and formal planting, at a scale that influences their overall organization and development. Towers are more scarce, the most common vertical elements being the minarets and the mid-rise towers of the type you find in Gaborone. The major exception, in terms of architectural space, is Abuja, where the natural landscape continues through the city, due to its relatively low density, and is the primary setting for the country's major institutions.

The original architecture of the colonial cities was very much designed for each place, despite being imposed by foreign powers. Dakar and Antananarivo are genuine experiments in place-making and were organized not just for European settlers, but also to make a relationship with the indigenous communities. I refer to later versions of this architecture as 'tropical modernism'. It is sensitive to climate and terrain and is carefully articulated to reflect a relationship to place, giving each city its own character. At the urban scale, despite the formality of certain elements, the layout of these cities is not something that you would ever find in France. [. . .]

Mountain & Highveld

This terrain includes ten cities, from Asmara in the north to the mountain cities of Mbabane and Maseru in the south. The general environment of the region is comparatively permissive, in the sense that the architecture does not need to take account of the extreme climatic conditions found in other parts of Africa. Because of the elevation, precipitation is high, the vegetation is lush, and the landscape is often bucolic. This is reflected in the picturesque, suburb-like quality that you find in most of these cities, with the exception of Asmara, Harare and Nairobi, the last being the most metropolitan city in the group. I have known about Nairobi since I was a child and heard my parents discussing its high buildings and their contribution to 'the skyline of Africa'. [. . .]

In each of the cities in this region, the landscape is significant for the way in which it allows different types of architectural expression to sit comfortably side by side. In Nairobi, for instance, there are examples of Victorian, Sikh and Hindu architecture, and you have the modernism of different periods, as well as the postmodernism of the circular towers. These cities all have the capacity to absorb many different expressions without any sense of conflict. This is significant in view of their relative isolation, especially compared with West Africa where the capitals are not that far apart. Travelling to Addis Ababa, you fly across a vast landscape with very little physical development, before you rise up to the plateau where Addis stands and realize just how unique its location is. So the distances people may have travelled to reach these cities, and the baggage they bring, is part of their culture and is reflected in the architecture. [. . .]

Part II

Visual Summary: Geographic Diversity of Historic Cities

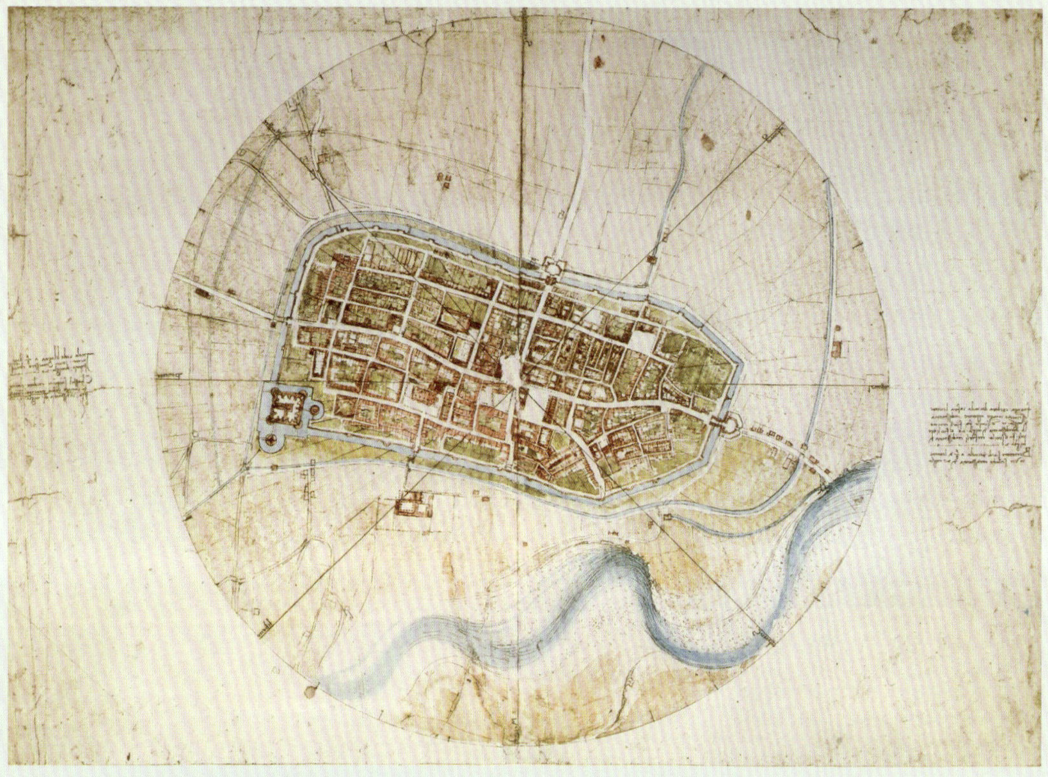

Leonardo da Vinci, *Map of Imola*, 1502.

This view of Imola, a small city about 30 kilometers southeast of Bologna, Italy, was drafted by Leonardo da Vinci for Cesare Borgia, who had taken possession of the city in 1499. The ground plan (an ichnographic view that corrects for oblique vantage points) is oriented to the cardinal compass points via the eight reference lines that Leonardo had also included in his earlier, more famous drawing *The Vitruvian Man* (ca. 1487).

Detail of a fourteenth-century fresco in the Hall of Peace, Siena, Italy, *Allegory and Effects of Good and Bad Government in Town and Country,* Ambrogio Lorenzetti (active 1285–1348).

Woodcut of Nuremberg, Germany, circa 1493.

PLATES II.1 AND II.2

In both these views of Western preindustrial cities, fortifications reinforce the hard institutional boundary between the city and its hinterland (reading 8). In these and other early representations of European cities, the manifestations of preceding historical phases are composed and harmonized into all-embracing iconic city views. This equilibrium was gradually lost with the advent of the Industrial Revolution in the nineteenth century.

Lithograph, *View of Pittsburgh & Allegheny*, 1874. Otto Krebs, lithographer.

Postcard of the Union Loop, downtown Chicago, circa 1913.

PLATES II.3 AND II.4

These views illustrate Thomas Bender's crucial point (reading 9) that U.S. cities became larger, denser, and more industrialized after the Civil War (1865). Note the smoking stacks of Pittsburgh in this 1874 bird's-eye view, as well as the dominant role of intraurban rail transport in Chicago, a development that facilitated the geographic enlargement of many U.S. cities in the late nineteenth century.

Plan of the city of San Francisco de Quito (Ecuador), 1810.

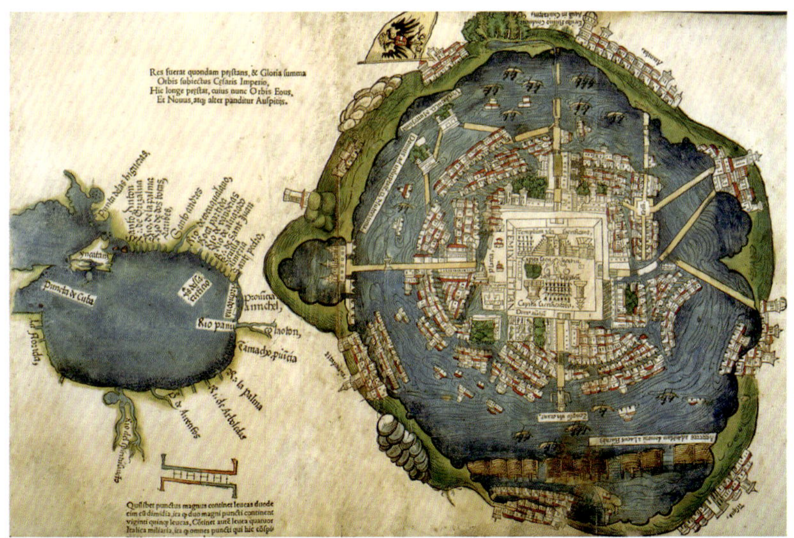

Mexico City, 1524. Woodcut by Hernán Cortés.

PLATES II.5 AND II.6

This early nineteenth-century view of Quito, Ecuador, reflects some of the key principles of city building employed by the Spanish colonizers of South America. As summarized by Alfonso Ortiz Crespo (reading 10), these principles embody the order, rationality, and amplitude of the city's basic organization. This image also shows Quito's mountainous environment and the resulting tension between the man-made grid and the landscape, which was far from being a tabula rasa. The pre-Colombian city of Tenochtitlán (present-day Mexico City), here shown in a 1524 image based on Hernán Cortés's memory of what he had destroyed, was established by the Aztecs in about 1325 on an island in Lake Texcoco. It not only demonstrates a fundamentally different concept of city layout but also suggests that in many cases, including Cusco, Peru, the Spanish built directly on the ruins of older settlements.

Part II

VISUAL SUMMARY

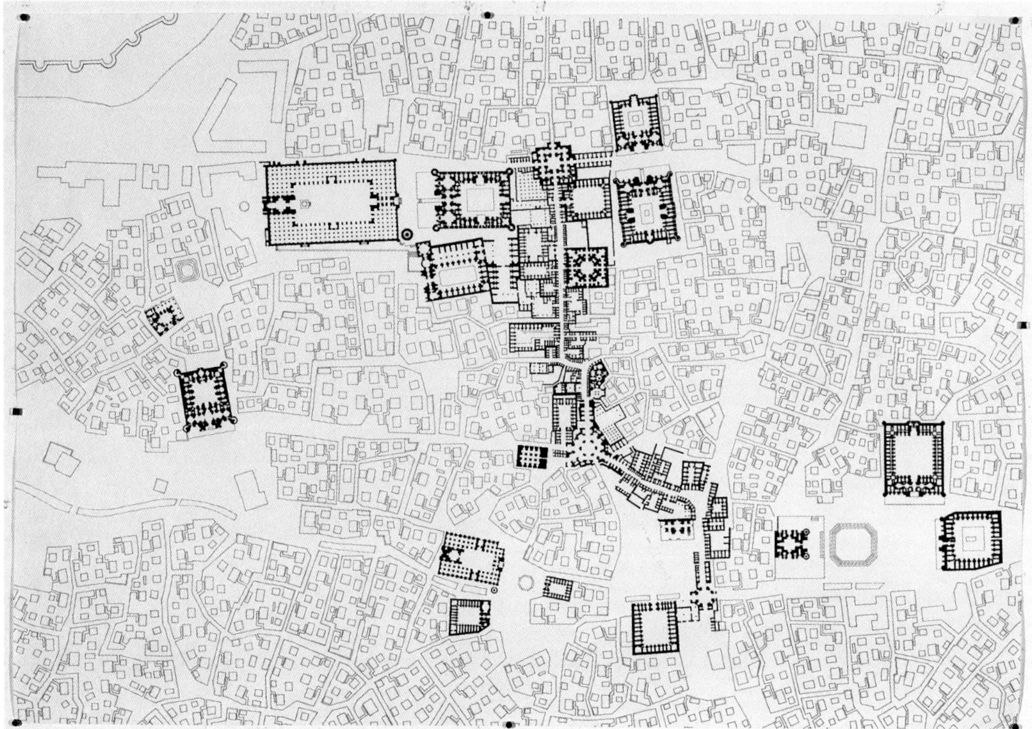

Map of the Bukhara Bazaar, Uzbekistan. Drawing by Klaus Herdeg, 1995.

PLATES II.7, II.8, AND II.9

These three images show the spatial and formal characteristics of Islamic cities discussed by Stefano Bianca (reading 11): a virtually "continuous architectural fabric,"with "clear internal differentiation into a series of self-contained, cellular compartments" and "inward-oriented autonomous units" interspersed with mosques that served as "islands of ritually pure space."

The tomb of Sa'di in Shiraz, Fars Province, Iran, 1976. Photo by Georg Gerster.

Beni Isguen, a part of Ghardaia, Algeria, 2009. Photo by George Steinmetz.

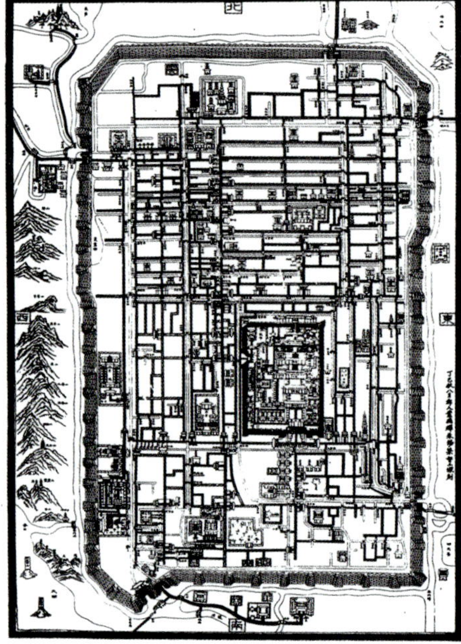

Left: Map of Suzhou, China, adapted from a rubbing of a 1229 map.
Right: City of Nanking (Nanjing), China, circa 1936, showing "Bird's-Eye View of the South Gate."

General view of Woo-Chow City, Guangdong Province, China, 1860s. Photo by Lai Afong (ca. 1839–90) (detail).

PLATES II.10, II.11, AND II.12

These figures convey three of the underlying concepts of city-building in preindustrial China. (1): Mountains behind the city and water in front can be noted to the left and right, respectively, of this 1229 map of Suzhou, originally engraved in stone (Plate II.10). (2) City walls and gates define boundaries and provide access, as seen in this 1936 aerial photograph of Nanjing (Plate II.11). (3): In this mid-nineteenth-century view of Wuzhou (Guangdong), variations of urban forms and materials can be observed that nonetheless conform to Chinese hierarchical notions of space and form (Plate II.12).

PLATES II.13 AND II.14

These two views of imperial Edo depict some of the salient aspects of Japanese urbanism, summarized by Barrie Shelton (reading 14). Plate II.13 reflects the importance of "activity, signs and symbols," which also imply an "objective perspective of a definite overall spatial pattern." In the Edo plan, although this same pattern is manifest, it also reflects the "Japanese notion of the city as a patchwork of relatively autonomous units."

Woodblock print of Nakano-chō Street in the Shin Yoshiwara Entertainment Quarter, Edo (Tokyo) Japan, by Utagawa Toyoharu, circa 1770.

Plan of Edo (Tokyo), Japan, circa 1844–48.

Part II

VISUAL SUMMARY

Roofscape view of Djenne, Mali. Photo by Gisele Taxil, 2016.

Thatched huts, Mursi, Ethiopia. Photo by Gordon Clarke.

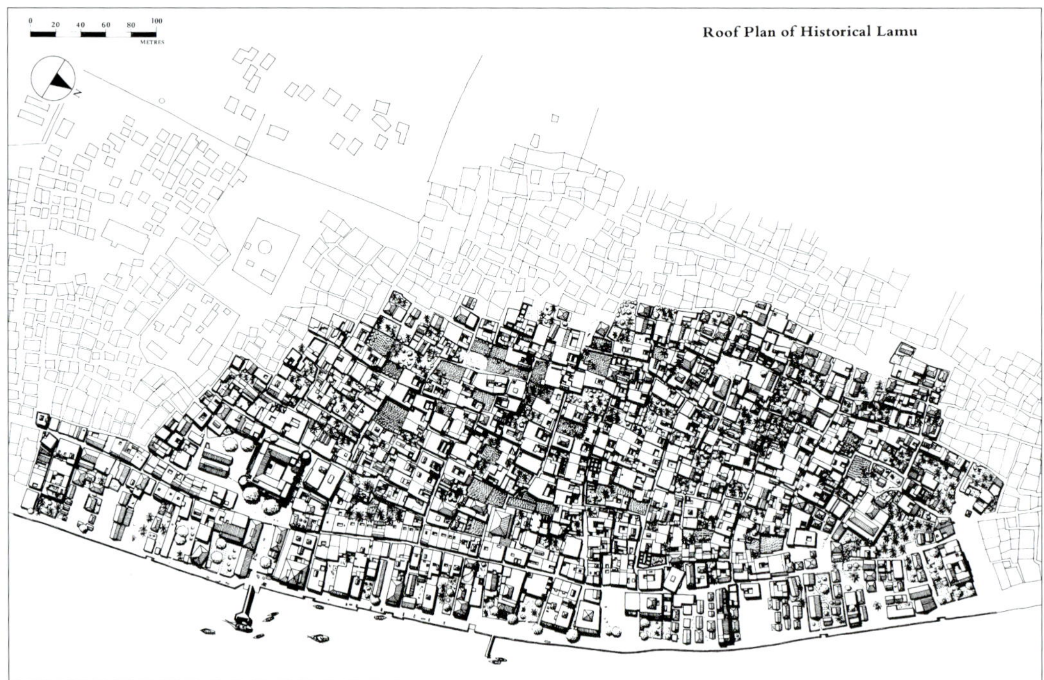

Roof plan of historical Lamu, Kenya. Drawing by Francesco Siravo, 1986.

PLATES II.15, II.16, AND II.17

Suzanne Preston Blier (reading 15) organizes her summary of African urbanism around "three historic patterns": monumental urbanism (with substantial stone structures), satellite urbanism (defined as a "collaboration between interlinked community structures"), and migratory settlements (found primarily in central Africa, as a reflection of nomadic identities). The three examples presented here are the "satellite settlement" of Djenné, Mali, with its earthen structures and remarkable early twentieth-century mosque; a nomadic settlement from Mursi, Ethiopia; and the coastal town of Lamu, Kenya, associated with maritime trade since its establishment in the fifteenth century. Lamu's roof plan illustrates the coexistence of early Swahili stone structures in the inner parts of the town with Anglo-Indian commercial structures along the seafront. The latter were built as a result of colonial influence in the late nineteenth and early twentieth century.

Drone photography captures the dramatic inequality of Nairobi, Kenya. Photo by Johnny Miller/Thomson Reuters Foundation.

Government Road, Nairobi, Kenya, 1927.

PLATES II.18 AND II.19

Sir David Adjaye's review (reading 16) of the urban architecture of Africa is based on an ecological understanding of city growth and diversity. It also emphasizes the "parallel layering of many conditions." This layering is evident in the aerial view of a portion of Nairobi, Kenya, where vernacular, makeshift structures testify to stark inequalities and offer a dramatic contrast with Western European–inspired commercial and institutional architecture. In other African cities, colonial developments were superimposed over pre-colonial settlement patterns.

VISION
SEAS
PHOTO

Part III

Reactions to the Transformation of Traditional Cities: Three Critical Ruptures

To understand the particular problems posed today by the historic city, one must examine the writings of authors who witnessed and reacted to the unprecedented changes and destruction that, at different times over roughly the past two hundred years, traditional cityscapes worldwide have undergone. These reactions can be grouped in relation to at least three different waves of transformation: the dramatic effects in the nineteenth century of the Industrial Revolution, urban redevelopment, and colonialism; the destruction that took place during World War II; and the phenomena of globalization, mass tourism, and unparalleled real estate development that in the second decade of the twenty-first century continue to challenge historic urban areas.

The first wave of transformation is well documented in the writings of exceptionally sensitive figures, such as Victor Hugo in France and John Ruskin in England (readings 17 and 18), who understood and reacted with extraordinary foresight to the demolitions and alterations that characterized city interventions starting from approximately the 1830s. In many respects, it can be said that urban conservation was born out of disorientation and dismay: the shock of having to face the irreversible loss of familiar and cherished monuments led Victor Hugo, in his "Guerre aux démolisseurs" (1832), to argue with great passion about the destruction of Paris's medieval monuments.[1] He had no doubt about what was responsible: collusion between public officials and speculators was the principal cause. Although Hugo lamented exclusively the destruction of historic monuments, he also noted the introduction of sweeping, straight avenues into the organic fabric of the medieval city.[2] A few years later, Baudelaire, in a poem dedicated to Victor Hugo, lamented in a succinct epitaph the swift disappearance of the old city: "Le vieux Paris n'est plus (la forme d'une ville / Change plus vite, hélas! que le coeur d'un mortel)."

Hugo's position was echoed in England by Ruskin, who spoke of the momentous changes occurring in cities across Europe. It was clear to him that these transformations were unprecedented and that they would have a long-lasting effect on cities

Marco Secchi, *Cruise Ships in Venice*, 2017. Detail. See p. 196.

everywhere. He foresaw their nature and the irreversible impact they would have: "The peculiar character of the evil which is being wrought by this age is its utter irreparableness."[3] Ruskin was in fact the first to recognize that these interventions would alter the very structure of preindustrial cities and fought for their survival as intangible monuments frozen in time.[4] The same sudden and irrevocable damage to cherished cities was decried by many who witnessed unprecedented urban developments in the mid- to late nineteenth century—not only in Paris but also in London, Vienna, and Rome.[5]

These radical transformations heralded an entirely new type of city. The latter was not always lamented but embraced enthusiastically: particularly vocal was the unconditional endorsement of avant-garde movements of the early twentieth century. The founder of the Futurist movement, Filippo Tommaso Marinetti, in a speech delivered at the Fenice in 1910 (reading 19), proposed the total rejection of old Venice, the filling of its canals and introduction of motorized traffic into the city. He portrayed Venice's inhabitants as slaves and parasites feeding on the questionable glories of a rotten past who, he said, should be turned instead into the actors of the industrial and military rescue of the city.

Marinetti saw with excitement the development of the modern city. Its defining characteristics were unprecedented demographic growth and social mobility, the presence of specialized functions, large-scale developments, massive infrastructure, faster means of transportation, the assumption of primary planning responsibility by central and local governments, and, increasingly, the commercialization of land and resulting speculation on the value of urban areas, an aspect that makes its appearance for the first time and that would play a crucial role in all subsequent urban developments.[6] All these aspects represented a clear rupture, distinguishing the city of the late nineteenth century and first half of the twentieth from that of the more distant past. The new city, now truly and unequivocally "modern," began in Europe and the United States and, with the global expansion of European colonial powers, spread rapidly and relentlessly to other regions of the world.

There will be no return. The modern city, in its different manifestations, has become the dominant global paradigm, relegating traditional settlements to a secondary, often marginal role. This new urban model exemplifies the prevailing form the city would take throughout and beyond the twentieth century. It also inspired Le Corbusier's famous remark about the demise of the city of the past: "The [old] city is crumbling, it cannot last much longer; its time is past. It is too old. The torrent can no longer keep to its bed."[7]

Le Corbusier's remark was both an ideological stance and a prediction of things to come. In the span of a few years, a devastating wave of urban destruction ravaged Western European, Russian, and Asian cities with unprecedented brutality. The Austrian novelist Stefan Zweig witnessed the global upheaval of World War II, about which he wrote, referring to earlier generations, "In their time some war happened somewhere, but, measured by the dimension of today, it was only a little war"; and, with reference to his own generation, "But in our lives there was no repetition; nothing of the past survived, nothing came back."[8]

As outlined in reading 20 from Robert Bevan's *The Destruction of Memory,* the scale of damage produced by aerial bombing and the wanton devastation of cities on the ground had no precedents. The effect of this destruction on the future of the cities affected by the last world war should not be underestimated, both in quantitative terms and in its role in their subsequent urban development. The serious moral implications of wartime destruction should also be underlined. As Bevan argues, World War II reveals, in its most extreme form, that the physical annihilation of a country's heritage often has no real strategic significance but is primarily aimed at destroying the memory and soul of a nation. Human and cultural genocide are thus two sides of the same coin, whereby the deliberate "destruction of the cultural artefacts of an enemy people or nation is a means of dominating, terrorising, dividing or eradicating it altogether."[9] Tragically, cultural genocide is still with us, as seen during the 1990s war in the former Yugoslavia and today in the intentional destruction perpetrated by the Islamic State of Iraq and the Levant (ISIL) in Iraq, Syria, Libya, and elsewhere.

But the destruction of historic urban places caused by war is only part of the story. A third wave of massive transformations followed World War II, a trail that, in various forms and disguises, can be followed up to the present day. It includes redevelopments carried out in the name of progress, ideology, commercial development, tourism, and mega-events. Considerable decay and transformation have also occurred in the wake of neglect and small-scale development. Four separate readings illustrate these various occurrences, underlining the fact that the urban heritage remains at risk and that its relentless destruction continues apace.[10]

Reading 21 is from Jane Jacobs's *Death and Life of Great American Cities* (1961), in which she strongly criticizes many of the conventional planning methods employed by social and transportation engineers of the twentieth century that led to a considerable loss of historic fabric. Improving social conditions and easing motorized traffic were the preferred justifications for the massive renewal projects implemented in North America from the 1930s to the 1960s, such as the redevelopment of large sections of New York City by Commissioner Robert Moses. Jacobs, through her social activism and influential writing, vehemently opposed the displacement of residents,[11] the clearance of old tenements, and the construction of motorways meant to cut through the center of lower Manhattan like a "meat axe."[12] Jacobs's arguments confront one of the major, recurrent misconceptions of city planners and administrators: the belief that the existing city fabric—the result of a long and complex historical process—can be erased with a single stroke and replaced with "distinguished architecture and imaginative design." The replacement is almost always a disappointment, and it leaves people wondering whether "the new is in fact better than the old."[13]

The destruction of urban heritage motivated by nationalistic pride and propaganda should also be mentioned. Paramount among such acts of destruction, as discussed by Dinu C. Giurescu in reading 22, is the case of Bucharest, capital of Romania, whose center was razed to the ground by Nicolae Ceaušescu and replaced with questionable modernist phalansteries only thirty-six years ago. Bulldozers flattened more than 250 historically significant hectares of a total of 500 within a span of five short years. As noted by Ioana Iosa, this must have been the swiftest and one of the "largest peacetime [events of] urban destruction . . . in recorded history."[14] According to Marcus Binney, a British architectural historian known for his active engagement in conservation, the demolition of Bucharest was "the most dramatic and serious blow to Europe's architectural heritage that has taken place since World War II."[15] Giurescu documents the uprooting of the Romanian nation "from its own urban and rural heritage, from its own history and identity" furthered by "state authority and decrees" in "a social engineering feat never before accomplished in European history."

The loss of historic fabric in recent years is not only the result of willful interventions. Particularly in developing and rapidly emerging countries, the so-called slums often coincide with the historic parts of centuries-old cities, with names that continue to resonate, such as Lahore, Cairo, Lhasa, Mumbai, and Zanzibar, to cite just a few. Here, limited public investment has taken place, and much historic fabric has disappeared as a result of a debilitating and highly destructive process of deterioration, triggered by exploding demographics and failing infrastructure.[16] The downward spiral of decay has transformed these historic areas into marginal, increasingly neglected and dysfunctional sectors of the city. This process of deterioration has been accompanied by unregulated transformations of historic structures, expulsion of residents, and the outright replacement of valuable historic properties with ad hoc, new commercial buildings by businessmen and small-time developers. In reading 23, Mona Serageldin analyzes the underlying causes and mechanisms that lead to these irreplaceable losses and discusses the prevailing attitudes that, in developing and fast-paced economies, lead to the devaluation of the old urban fabric.

Since the 1980s, against this already worrisome scenario of deterioration and uncontrolled change, tourism has spearheaded a new wave of transformations, often justified by the mistaken need to upgrade and "beautify" historic places to respond to the alleged expectations of foreign visitors. Tourism is often seen as the miracle solution that will underwrite the revitalization of historic areas.[17] The advantages for the local administrations and private businessmen are undeniable, but the corresponding negative repercussions on buildings and on the quality of life of residents are rarely considered or quantified.

In social terms, the case of Venice, an international tourist destination par excellence, is perhaps the most illustrative. As pointed out dramatically by Salvatore Settis in reading 24, Venice exemplifies the risk many historic cities face today of becoming both museum and theme park, deserted by their residents and besieged by hordes of visitors. It is a chilling prospect: a city bereft of its social base, its historical significance and image trivialized.

Most recently, increasing pressure has been exerted on historic urban areas by the proliferation of mega-events, which have managed to combine into a single, highly transformative occurrence tourism, commercial development, gentrification, staged happening, universal fair, and international celebration. These short-term events can have long-term impact on the cities concerned.[18] They often leave behind a trail of social disruption and displacement, economic failure,[19] half-baked and unsustainable initiatives, and hurried "beautification" projects, as well as questionable attempts at instant and often disappointing "modernization." All these negative effects have an impact on the urban heritage.

The Beijing Olympic Games of 2008 are a perfect illustration of the nefarious effects that mega-events can have on the historic urban heritage and the city as a whole. The outcome is well presented in Michael Meyer's *The Last Days of Old Beijing*,[20] documenting the passing of the traditional way of life embodied in the city's old neighborhoods to make room for high-rises and oversized commercial malls. The forced evictions and demolitions were meant to transform completely the traditional areas of Old Beijing, considered by the authorities a source of shame and embarrassment and seen by the developers as an extraordinary opportunity for economic gain.

Sze Tsung Nicolás Leong in reading 25 puts the Beijing case in the wider perspective of the willful "erasing of the past" that resurfaces periodically in the history of China, "from imperial rule to communism, from communism to the market economy." The Cultural Revolution of 1966–76 was certainly the most explicit and extreme manifestation of this attitude in the twentieth century, but its long-term effects were mitigated by the limited economic means available at the time. Far more profound and irreversible are the consequences of the new market economy on the traditional urban fabric of China: "when an area is developed, it is almost always cleared of all traces of the past: buildings, streets, residents." As Leong aptly notes, "Ironically, China's current economic revolution is completing the physical destruction of history that was called for during the Cultural Revolution."

Where attempts have been made in Beijing to "preserve" the past, the results have been sorely disappointing, more "fake movie sets"[21] than rehabilitation of authentic, lived-in places. The Beijing case introduces a new paradoxical claim—that the destruction of the centuries-old historic districts of China's capital is a shining example of urban conservation.[22] This and similar claims anticipate, in their most extreme form, the fate of historic cities in the era of neoliberalism. As Michele Lamprakos has remarked, "The historic center has been cleaned up and over-restored" and has become "a kind of stage set for high-end retail, tourism and cultural events."[23] Increasingly, historic areas are being assimilated everywhere in a homologation process that is akin to the transformation of the present-day city into anonymous and shapeless look-alike megalopolises.

Notes

1. Victor Hugo, *Œuvres complètes,* vol. 2 (Brussels, 1837), 641–43: "Le vandalisme fleurit et prospère sous nos yeux. Le vandalisme est architecte. . . . [L]e vandalisme est applaudi, encouragé, admiré, protégé, consulté, subventionné, défrayé, naturalisé." "Guerre aux démolisseurs" was originally written in 1825 and later expanded in the *Revue des Deux Mondes* (1835).)
2. Baron Haussmann, prefect of the Seine from 1853 to 1869, was in charge of implementing the major public works that transformed the city of Paris. Twenty years before Haussmann's massive transformation program, Hugo wrote, "Il veut faire tout à travers Paris une grande, grande, grande

rue. Une rue d'une lieue ! Que de magnifiques dévastations chemin faisant! Saint-Germain-l'Auxerrois y passera, l'admirable tour de Saint-Jacques-de-la-Boucherie y passera peut-être aussi. Mais qu'importe! une rue d'une lieue! Comprenez-vous comme cela sera beau! une ligne droite tirée du Louvre à la barrière du Trône! . . . O merveilleuse perspective!"

3. John Ruskin, Opening Speech delivered at the Crystal Palace in 1851. The last sentence reads, "But the power neither of emperors, nor queens, nor kingdoms, can ever print again upon the sands of time the effaced footsteps of departed generations, or gather together from the dust the stones which had been stamped with the spirit of our ancestors." See also Jukka Jokiletho, *A History of Architectural Conservation* (London: Butterworth Heinemann, 1999).
4. Françoise Choay, *The Invention of the Historic Monument* (Cambridge: Cambridge University Press, 2001), 121–22.
5. Federico Hermanin (1868–1953), an Italian art historian and inspector of antiquities, wrote, "Destroying is easy and a few blows of the pickaxe often wipe out a historical memory forever." He was referring to the transformations of Rome after the unification of Italy in 1861 and to the work of his friend Ettore Roesler Franz, the artist who documented in a famous series of watercolors the vanishing places and customs of the city.
6. Jürgen Oterhammel, *A Global History of the Nineteenth Century* (Princeton, NJ: Princeton University Press, 2014), 226–48; Wolfgang Schivelbusch, *The Railway Journey: The Industrialization of Space and Time in the Nineteenth Century* (Berkeley: University of California Press, 1987).
7. Le Corbusier, *The City of Tomorrow* (New York: Payson and Clarke, 1929).
8. Stefan Zweig, *The World of Yesterday* (London: Cassell, 1987), 7.
9. Robert Bevan, *The Destruction of Memory: Architecture at War* (London: Reaktion Books, 2006), 8.
10. "Half a century after World War II numerous planners throughout Europe, including Germany, have concluded that far more architectural history was destroyed in the urban redevelopment that followed the fighting than by the tens of millions of bombs themselves." Anthony M. Tung, *Preserving the World's Great Cities: The Destruction and Renewal of the Historic Metropolis* (New York: Clarkson Potter, 2001), 17. According to Leon Krier, less than 15 percent of the German buildings spared by the bombing of World War II survive today. See "Architectura Patriae; or The Destruction of Germany's Architectural Heritage,"*Architectural Design* 54 (July–August 1984): 101–2.
11. Estimated to be around 170,000 people for New York City.
12. "When you operate in an overbuilt metropolis you have to hack your way with a meat axe." Robert Moses, quoted in Robert Cowan, *The Dictionary of Urbanism* (Tisbury, U.K.: Streetwise Press, 2005), 250.
13. Edward J. Logue, quoted in Walter Muir Whitehill, *Boston: A Topographical History* (Cambridge, MA: Belknap Press of Harvard University Press, 1979), 204.
14. Ioana Iosa, *L'Héritage urbain de Ceausescu: Fardeau ou saut en avant? Le centre civique de Bucarest* (Paris: L'Harmattan, 2006).
15. Quoted in M. Leary (staff writer), "Romania Demolishes Priceless Architecture in Name of Rebuilding," *Enquirer,* May 15, 1988.
16. In the case of Zanzibar, for example, approximately 85 percent of the buildings in the historic area were in deteriorating or poor condition. In addition, between 1982 and 1992, Zanzibar lost or saw substantially altered 670, or 46 percent, of its 1,450 historic structures. In Islamic Cairo, more than half of the registered buildings were lost during the second half of the twentieth century in the wake of uncontrolled urban development. Often, change occurs as a result of the unregulated expansion of commercial activities and the subsequent large-scale exodus of residents. This is the case in Lahore, whose historic area lost over 60 percent of its residents since 1947.
17. The tourism-based approach as a means to regenerate historic urban areas is well exemplified, with reference to Malta and Gozo, in John Ebejer's article, "Regeneration of Historic Urban

Cores—The Tourism Perspective," *Times of Malta,* 9 March 2003, www.timesofmalta.com/articles/view/20030309/business/regeneration-of-historic-urban-cores-the-tourism-perspective.154895.

18. Here we are paraphrasing the opinion expressed by the British sociologist Maurice Roche, "Mega-events and Urban Policy," *Annals of Tourism Research* 21 (1994): 1–2.
19. In fact the positive economic impact and profitability for the host cities over the long term remains to be proven and is often explicitly questioned. This is what two economists, discussing the likely impact of the UEFA Championship of 2012, have to say: "Although the event will attract a large number of spectators and television viewers, a simple cost-benefit analysis indicates that the costs of hosting the event will exceed the direct economic impact related to increased tourist spending by a wide margin. . . . Sports mega-events may not be effective regional economic development vehicles in transition economies." Brad R. Humphreys and Szymon Prokopowicz, "Assessing the Impact of Sports Mega-Events in Transition Economies: EURO 2012 in Poland and Ukraine," *International Journal of Sport Management and Marketing* 2, no. 5–6 (2007): 496–509.
20. Michael Meyer, *The Last Days of Old Beijing* (New York: Walker & Co., 2008), 38–50.
21. Ibid., 319.
22. According to Liu Qi, senior Olympics organizer, "This area is being protected. When it is complete, these will be Beijing streets from the late Ming or early Qing Dynasties that also have modern content." Quoted in Mure Dickie, "Ancient Quarter Makes Way for Modern Antiquity," *Financial Times,* 17 June 2008.
23. Michele Lamprakos, "The Idea of the Historic City," *Change Over Time* 4, no. 1 (Spring 2014): 28.

Reading

17

Victor Hugo

War on the Demolishers (1832)

In addition to being the most celebrated French novelist, poet, and playwright of his generation, Victor Hugo (1802–1885) was a politician and an essayist who wrote passionately on various subjects, including human rights, the arts, and architectural heritage. His position was echoed in many quarters by such illustrious contemporaries as Charles Baudelaire, Charles Comte de Montalembert, and Prosper Mérimée, who in 1840 would prepare the first list of monuments of national importance. Hugo's campaign against the destruction of France's monuments, at a time of major urban transformation and industrial development, was relentless and profoundly influential. It targeted developers, speculators, and politicians, who in his view were responsible for the obliteration of France's noble heritage. Its beauty, he said, belongs "to everyone, to you, to me, to all of us."

—∿—

In Paris, vandalism flourishes and prospers before our eyes. Vandalism is architect. [. . .] Vandalism is celebrated, applauded, encouraged, admired, caressed, protected, consulted, subsidized, defrayed, naturalized. Vandalism is an entrepreneur working for the government. It sneaks into the budget, and it gnaws away like a rat at cheese.

—∿—

[. . .] It wants to make a big, big, big street all the way across Paris. A street of one league! What magnificent devastations along the way! Saint-Germain-l'Auxerrois will go, the admirable tower of Saint-Jacques-de-la-Boucherie might go as well. But so what! A street of one league! Understand how beautiful it will be! A straight line drawn from the Louvre to the Barrière du Trône! From one end of the street, from the Barrière, we'll contemplate the Louvre's façade. It's true that all the merit of the Perrault colonnade is in its proportions, and this will fade into the distance; but what of it? We'll have

From Victor Hugo, "Guerre aux démolisseurs," *Revue des Deux Mondes* 5 (1832): 614, 616, 621.

a street of one league! From the other end, from the Louvre, we'll see the Barrière du Trône, its two proverbial columns that you know, slender, slight, and risible like the legs of Potier. Oh, marvelous perspective! Let us hope that this farcical project never happens.

—ꟿ—

Have these beautiful and grave buildings repaired. Have them repaired carefully, intelligently, soberly. You have around you men of learning and taste who will enlighten you in this work. And especially, let the architect-restorer be frugal with his own imaginings; let him study the character of each building with curiosity, according to each century and each climate. Let him take in both the general line and particular line of the monument that is placed in his hands; and let him be able to skillfully weld his genius to the genius of the earlier architect.

[. . .]

Let us transcribe here what we've already said on this subject in our first *Note on the Destruction of Monuments* [1825]: "The hammer that is mutilating the face of the country must be stopped. One law would suffice. Let it be done. Whatever the property rights, these ignoble speculators—blinded to their honor by their interests; these wretched men, so imbecilic they didn't even understand that they're barbarians—must not be allowed to destroy a historic, monumental building. There are two things in a building: its use and its beauty. Its use belongs to the owner, its beauty to everyone, to you, to me, to all of us. To destroy it, therefore, is to go beyond one's rights."

Reading

18

John Ruskin

The Opening of the Crystal Palace (1854)

John Ruskin (1819–1900) was the foremost art critic and architectural theorist of nineteenth-century England. He may be considered the father of the modern notion of conservation, as opposed to the stylistic restorations of his era, which he considered akin to destroying a building. In "The Seven Lamps of Architecture," an essay he wrote in 1849, Ruskin advocated the need to be true to the original materials and construction methods of a building and to respect the history and culture of the age in which it was created, all ideas that contributed to the subsequent establishment of a theory of conservation. In this speech delivered on the occasion of the opening of the Crystal Palace in 1854, Ruskin denounced the destruction of old buildings throughout Europe to make room for new squares and boulevards devoid of character and identity and lamented the "utter irreparableness" of this destruction.

[. . .] I have given many years, in many cities, to the study of Gothic architecture; and of all that I know, or knew, the entrance to the north transept of Rouen Cathedral was, on the whole, the most beautiful—beautiful, not only as an elaborate and faultless work of the finest time of Gothic art, but yet more beautiful in the partial, though not dangerous, decay which had touched its pinnacles with pensive colouring, and softened its severer lines with unexpected change and delicate fracture, like sweet breaks in a distant music. The upper part of it has been already restored to the white accuracies of novelty; the lower pinnacles, which flanked its approach, far more exquisite in their partial ruin than the loveliest remains of our English abbeys, have been entirely destroyed, and rebuilt in rough blocks, now in process of sculpture. This restoration, so far as it

From John Ruskin, "The Opening of the Crystal Palace," in *On the Old Road: A Collection of Miscellaneous Essays, Pamphlets, Etc., Etc, Published 1834–1885*, vol. 1: *Art* (Sunnyside, Kent: George Allen, 1885), 360–66. Originally published as a pamphlet titled "The Opening of the Crystal Palace Considered in some of its Relations to the Progress of Art" (London: Smith, Elder & Co., 1854).

has gone, has been executed by peculiarly skilful workmen; it is an unusually favourable example of restoration, especially in the care which has been taken to preserve intact the exquisite, and hitherto almost uninjured sculptures which fill the quatrefoils of the tracery above the arch. But I happened myself to have made, five years ago, detailed drawings of the buttress decorations on the right and left of this tracery, which are part of the work that has been completely restored. And I found the restorations as inaccurate as they were unnecessary.

265. If this is the case in a most favourable instance, in that of a well-known monument, highly esteemed by every antiquary in France, what, during the progress of the now almost universal repair, is likely to become of architecture which is unwatched and despised?

Despised ! and more than despised—even hated ! It is a sad truth, that there is something in the solemn aspect of ancient architecture which, in rebuking frivolity and chastening gaiety, has become at this time literally *repulsive* to a large majority of the population of Europe. Examine the direction which is taken by all the influences of fortune and of fancy, wherever they concern themselves with art, and it will be found that the real, earnest effort of the upper classes of European society is to make every place in the world as much like the Champs Elysées of Paris as possible. Wherever the influence of that educated society is felt, the old buildings are relentlessly destroyed ; vast hotels, like barracks, and rows of high, square-windowed dwelling-houses, thrust themselves forward to conceal the hated antiquities of the great cities of France and Italy. Gay promenades, with fountains and statues, prolong themselves along the quays once dedicated to commerce ; ball-rooms and theatres rise upon the dust of desecrated chapels, and thrust into darkness the humility of domestic life. And when the formal street, in all its pride of perfumery and confectionery, has successfully consumed its way through wrecks of historical monuments, and consummated its symmetry in the ruin of all that once prompted a reflection, or pleaded for regard, the whitened city is praised for its splendour, and the exulting inhabitants for their patriotism—patriotism which consists in insulting their fathers with forgetfulness, and surrounding their children with temptation.

266. I am far from intending my words to involve any disrespectful allusion to the very noble improvements in the city of Paris itself, lately carried out under the encouragement of the Emperor. Paris, in its own peculiar character of bright magnificence, has nothing to fear, and everything to gain, from the gorgeous prolongation of the Rue Rivoli. But I speak of the general influence of the rich travellers and proprietors of Europe on the cities which they pretend to admire, or endeavour to improve. I speak of the changes wrought during my own lifetime on the cities of Venice, Florence, Geneva, Lucerne, and chief of all on Rouen, a city altogether inestimable for its retention of medieval character in the infinitely varied streets in which one half of the existing and inhabited houses date from the 15th or early 16th century, and the only town left in France in which the effect of old French domestic architecture can yet be seen in its collective groups. But when I was there, this last spring, I heard that these noble old Norman houses are all, as speedily as may be, to be stripped of the dark slates which

protected their timbers, and deliberately whitewashed over all their sculptures and ornaments, in order to bring the interior of the town into some conformity with the "handsome fronts" of the hotels and offices on the quay.

Hotels and offices, and "handsome fronts" in general—they can be built in America or Australia—built at any moment, and in any height of splendour. But who shall give us back, when once destroyed, the habitations of the French chivalry and bourgeoisie in the days of the Field of the Cloth of Gold ?

267. It is strange that no one seems to think of this ! What do men travel for, in this Europe of ours ? Is it only to gamble with French dies—to drink coffee out of French porcelain—to dance to the beat of German drums, and sleep in the soft air of Italy ? Are the ball-room, the billiard-room, and the Boulevard, the only attractions that win us into wandering, or tempt us to repose ? And when the time is come, as come it will, and that shortly, when the parsimony—or lassitude—which, for the most part, are the only protectors of the remnants of elder time, shall be scattered by the advance of civilization—when all the monuments, preserved only because it was too costly to destroy them, shall have been crushed by the energies of the new world, will the proud nations of the twentieth century, looking round on the plains of Europe, disencumbered of their memorial marbles,—will those nations indeed stand up with no other feeling than one of triumph, freed from the paralysis of precedent and the entanglement of memory, to thank us, the fathers of progress, that no saddening shadows can any more trouble the enjoyments of the future,—no moments of reflection retard its activities; and that the new-born population of a world without a record and without a ruin may, in the fulness of ephemeral felicity, dispose itself to eat, and to drink, and to die ?

268. Is this verily the end at which we aim, and will the mission of the age have been then only accomplished, when the last castle has fallen from our rocks, the last cloisters faded from our valleys, the last streets, in which the dead have dwelt, been effaced from our cities, and regenerated society is left in luxurious possession of towns composed only of bright saloons, overlooking gay parterres ? If this indeed be our end, yet why must it be so laboriously accomplished ? Are there no new countries on the earth, as yet uncrowned by thorns of cathedral spires, untenanted by the consciousness of a past ? Must this little Europe—this corner of our globe, gilded with the blood of old battles, and grey with the temples of old pieties—this narrow piece of the world's pavement, worn down by so many pilgrims' feet, be utterly swept and garnished for the masque of the Future ? Is America not wide enough for the elasticities of our humanity ? Asia not rich enough for its pride ? or among the quiet meadow-lands and solitary hills of the old land, is there not yet room enough for the spreadings of power, or the indulgences of magnificence, without founding all glory upon ruin, and prefacing all progress with obliteration ?

269. We must answer these questions speedily, or we answer them in vain. The peculiar character of the evil which is being wrought by this age is its utter irreparableness. Its newly formed schools of art, its extending galleries, and well-ordered museums will assuredly bear some fruit in time, and give once more to the popular mind the power to discern what is great, and the disposition to protect what is precious. But it

will be too late. We shall wander through our palaces of crystal, gazing sadly on copies of pictures torn by cannon-shot, and on casts of sculpture dashed to pieces long ago. We shall gradually learn to distinguish originality and sincerity from the decrepitudes of imitation and palsies of repetition; but it will be only in hopelessness to recognize the truth, that architecture and painting can be "restored" when the dead can be raised,—and not till then.

Reading

19

Filippo Tommaso Marinetti

Futurist Discourse by Marinetti to the Venetians (1910)

Filippo Tommaso Marinetti (1876–1944) was an Italian poet and writer, best known as the founder and apologist of Futurism, an art and social movement that developed in Italy in the early part of the twentieth century. The movement celebrated the new in its most extreme manifestations and rejected unconditionally the old, which it considered evil, decadent, and worthy of total obliteration. These views are forcefully expressed in the improvised speech Marinetti delivered at Venice's Fenice Theater on 1 August 1910. Venice, historic city par excellence, is in fact depicted as a diseased and hopelessly romantic place, inhabited by servile middlemen enslaved to the past and tourism. Venice's picturesque canals—Marinetti claimed—would soon be filled and replaced by great roads and fast-moving trains, trams, and automobiles, heralding the advent of a new, modern age. Marinetti's position, albeit intentionally provocative, anticipates the idea of unrestrained urban development, a position that would become increasingly common in subsequent years.

People of Venice! When we cried out: "Slay the light of the moon!" we thought of you, old Venice, sodden with Romanticism!

But now our voice grows louder, and we add to that, in clearer tones, "Liberate the world from the tyranny of love! We are satiated with erotic adventures, lust, sentimentalism, and nostalgia!"

Wherefore do you persist, Venice, in offering up veiled women at each twilight's unfurling upon your canals?

Enough is enough! Cease to whisper obscene invitations to all who cross your path, oh Venice, old panderer, under your heavy, laced, mosaic mantilla, you persist in preparing nights, exhausting and amorous, querulous serenades and fearsome snares!

F. T. Marinetti, "Futurist Discourse by Marinetti to the Venetians" (1910), in *Teoria e invenzione futurista*, edited by Luciano De Maria (Milan: Arnoldo Mondadori, [1968] 1996), 31–33.

Even I, oh Venice, loved the sumptuous penumbra of your great canal, saturated with rare passions, and the feverish pallor of your beauties, who far above, slip away from balconies by stairways woven with flashing lights, threads of rain, and the moon's rays, amidst the clink of crossed swords . . .

Enough! All this absurdity, abominable and vexing, sickens us! By now we want electric lamps, whose thousand points of light cut and rip apart brutally your mysterious darkness, bewitching and compelling!

Your great canal, wide and deep, is destined to become a great mercantile port. Trains and streetcars hurled upon the great roads built on your canals finally filled, will carry stacks of wares among a shrewd crowd, rich and hustling, of industrialists and merchants!

Do not shout out against the alleged ugliness of the locomotives, streetcars, automobiles, and bicycles in which we find the first lines of the great futurist aesthetic. They can always serve to crush those lurid and grotesque professors of the north in their Tyrolean hats.

But you wish to prostrate yourselves before all foreigners and your servility is repugnant!

People of Venice! Why do you still and always want to be faithful slaves of the past, filthy custodians of the greatest brothel in history, nurses in the most dismal hospital in the world, where souls languish, mortally corrupted by the pestilence of sentimentalism?

Oh! Images do I not lack, if I wish to compare your vain and foolish inertia to that of a great man's son or the spouse of a celebrated singer! Your gondoliers, could I not compare them to gravediggers intent on rhythmically digging the sepulchers of a flooded cemetery?

But nothing can offend you, as your humility is infinite!

One knows, after all, that you are prudently preoccupied with enriching the league of great hotels, and indeed, for this reason you persist in your own putrefaction, not lifting a finger!

And yet, you were once upon a time invincible warriors and gifted artists, audacious navigators, ingenious industrialists, and tireless merchants. . . And you have turned into hotel waiters, tour guides, panderers, antiquarians, swindlers, fakers of old pictures, plagiarist painters, and copyists. In the end you have forgotten above all to be Italians, and that this word, in history's parlance, means: *builders of the future*?

Oh! Do not defend yourselves, blaming the discouraging effects of the sirocco! It was indeed that torrid and bellicose wind that filled the sails of the heroes of Lepanto! This same African wind will suddenly grow stronger one infernal afternoon, the silent work of the corrosive waters that weaken your venerable city.

Oh, how we shall dance on that day! Oh! We will egg the waters on, inciting them to destruction! What an immense round we will dance, encircling the illustrious ruin! We will be insanely happy, we, the last rebellious students of this world, too wise!

This is how we sang, Venetians, danced, and laughed before the agony of the isle of serpents, which died like a decrepit mouse behind the dams of Aswan, an immense trap door, automatic, in which England's brilliant futurists imprison the fleeing, sacred waters of the Nile!

Shrug your shoulders and denounce me as a barbarian, incapable of savoring the divine poetry that ripples at the shores of your enchanting islands!

Off with you! You have no cause to be so proud! . . .

Liberate Torcello, Burano, the Isle of the Dead, from all the diseased literature and the colossal romanticist phantasmagoria in which the poets, poisoned by the Venetian fever, have shrouded them, and you may, laughing with me, consider those islands as heaps of excrement left here and there by mammoths when wading through your prehistoric pond!

But you foolishly admire those isles, happy to rot in your dirty water, in order to limitlessly enrich your league of hoteliers, that prepare with care elegant nights for all the great men of the earth!

Certainly, it is no small task, to excite them to love. Say your guest were an emperor, he must slowly navigate through the filth of the great washbasin full of historiated shards, the oars of his gondoliers must plow through several kilometers of liquefied excrement, in a divine odor of piss, passing by barges bulging with beautiful rubbish, among floating refuse of ambiguous origin, in order to arrive, true emperor, at his destination, content with himself and his imperial scepter!

It is clear, oh people of Venice, that which was your glory until today!

Are you not ashamed of this? Shame on you! Throw yourselves down, supine, one upon the other, like sacks of sand to build a bastion at the border, while we prepare a great and strong Venice, with industry, commerce, and military might, in the Adriatic, the great Italian sea!

Reading

20

ROBERT BEVAN

Destruction of Memory: Architecture at War (2006)

Robert Bevan is a British architecture critic, journalist, and heritage consultant who has written passionately about heritage places and their fateful disappearance. This reading focuses on the extensive destruction of heritage cities and sites throughout the twentieth century as a result of world wars and regional hostilities. Suffice it to say that German cities, whose historical legacy was largely unimpaired, lost an average of 40 to 50 percent of their urban heritage during World War II. Bevan's most striking point, however, is that this devastation is most often not the result of accidental or "collateral damage" but the outcome of intentional actions designed to destroy the memory, history, and identity of entire communities. A single unspeakable thread connects the Nazis' Kristallnacht frenzy, the Croatian guns aimed at the Mostar Bridge, al-Qaeda's annihilation of the Twin Towers, and the Bamiyan Buddhas blown up by the Taliban. And the list continues into the twenty-first century. Bevan cautions ominously that "the intentional collapse of buildings is intimately related to social collapse and upheavals," a trend that, far from disappearing, seems poised to continue unabated in the years to come.

INTRODUCTION: THE ENEMIES OF ARCHITECTURE AND MEMORY

[. . .] There is both a horror and a fascination at something so apparently permanent as a building, something that one expects to outlast many a human span, meeting an untimely end. As an architecturally obsessed child I was often absorbed in film footage of the destruction wreaked on Europe's built heritage by the Second World War, or I could be found in the local branch library dragging volumes, half my height, about vanquished treasure houses over to the carpet tiles of the junior section. At the same time it felt wrong even to be considering the fate of inanimate art objects and architecture in the face of the contemporaneous footage demonstrating the perverse suffering inflicted on people in the Holocaust. The latter was by far the greater evil and infinitely

From ROBERT BEVAN, *Destruction of Memory: Architecture at War* (London: Reaktion Books, 2006), 7–17, 23–24. Reproduced by permission of Reaktion Books.

more moving. Dwelling even for a moment on the shattered remains of museums and churches felt, at best, self-indulgent and, at worst, an indication of warped priorities, especially as the Holocaust had touched the lives of family friends terribly.

The levelling of buildings and cities has always been an inevitable part of conducting hostilities and has worsened as weaponry has become heavier and more destructive, from the slings and arrows of the past to the daisy-cutters of today. Continents rather than cities can be devastated. This damage may be the direct result of military manoeuvres to gain territory or root out a foe, or a desire to wipe out the enemy's capacity to fight. The division of the spoils also plays a part. But there has always been another war against architecture going on—the destruction of the cultural artefacts of an enemy people or nation as a means of dominating, terrorizing, dividing or eradicating it altogether. The aim here is not the rout of an opposing army—it is a tactic often conducted well away from any front line—but the pursuit of ethnic cleansing or genocide by other means, or the rewriting of history in the interests of a victor reinforcing his conquests. Here architecture takes on a totemic quality: a mosque, for example, is not simply a mosque; it represents to its enemies the presence of a community marked for erasure. A library or art gallery is a cache of historical memory, evidence that a given community's presence extends into the past and legitimizing it in the present and on into the future. In these circumstances structures and places with certain meanings are selected for oblivion with deliberate intent. This is not 'collateral damage'. This is the *active* and often systematic destruction of particular building types or architectural traditions that happens in conflicts where the erasure of the memories, history and identity attached to architecture and place—enforced forgetting—is the goal itself. These buildings are attacked not because they are in the path of a military objective: to their destroyers they *are* the objective.

Such was the purpose of the Nazi destruction of German synagogues on Kristallnacht in 1938: to deny a people its past as well as a future. More than this, Kristallnacht [. . .] can be seen as a proto-genocidal episode—an act of dehumanization and segregation and a further step down towards the limitless dark cellars of barbarism. The erasure of architecture is a crazed and dusty reflection of the fortunes of people at the hands of destroyers. During the 1990s the wars in the former Yugoslavia, with the torture, mass murders and concentration camps of Bosnia on the one hand and the razing of mosques, the burning of libraries and the sundering of bridges on the other, made me realize that my childhood guilt at considering the fate of material culture was misplaced. The link between erasing any physical reminder of a people and its collective memory and the killing of the people themselves is ineluctable. The continuing fragility of civilized society and decency is echoed in the fragility of its monuments. This cultural cleansing, with architecture as its medium, is a phenomenon that has been barely understood. [. . .]

Much has been written about the deliberate repression of minority cultures—their language, literature, art and customs—but little about the repression of their architecture. [. . .] Numerologists could have a field day with this *matériel*: Kristallnacht began just before midnight on 9 November, the 9/11 of 1938. On the same date in 1989, the first sections of the Berlin Wall began to tumble. Four years later on 9/11, Stari Most, Mostar's historic bridge, was finally brought down into the Neretva river by Croat gunners. Then, of course, came 9/11 in New York—a different day, of course, given the date sequencing used in North America—but the numerals do seem to mark a day for destruction. This is not to make the case for some sort of cosmic agency at work—other dates could equally be matched up for their destructive significance. Such coincidences are possible because of the ubiquity of the deliberate and meaningful destruction of architecture and monuments.

[. . .] There is a bestial carousel quality to the past century's destructive activity: ethnic cleansing can be part of conquest; conquest can be ideological as well as territorial; territorial acquisitiveness can be genocidal and end up in partition. The coverage is thematic rather than geographical or chronological in order to bring connections to bear more readily. Such themes inevitably overlap; the fate of Jerusalem's buildings since the creation of Israel, for instance, could equally be looked at as an example of ethnic cleansing, partition or conquest (where it appears in this book). It aims to weave together some of these threads (it is too widespread an experience to hope for comprehensive coverage) to show the forces at work leading to the *targeted* destruction of architecture beyond that caused by purely military considerations. It looks at the political forces at work in order to make plain the politicized nature of what is happening when China demolishes Tibet's monasteries or Berlin struggles with its National Socialist and Stalinist past. Why did al-Qaeda decide that the World Trade Center was a suitable target and why did the Taliban defy world opinion and reduce the Bamiyan Buddhas to dust? Clausewitz's well-known dictum, 'War is not an independent phenomenon, but the continuation of politics by different means', is the thinking behind the architectural dismemberment under examination.

The violent destruction of buildings for other than pragmatic reasons also happens in peacetime, of course, and it is impossible to separate out fully the depredations of 'progress'—modernity and industrialization, with all their implicit ideological content—from conflicts between classes and other groups within societies that are all part of the continuous remaking of our environments; as cities evolve and change, structures become redundant or more valuable uses for a site are found.[1] Demolition has often been deployed to break up concentrations of resistance among the populace; the Haussmannization of Paris is the most obvious case (although this too was in the wake of violent revolutionary upheavals). Benign or culpable neglect is the more common phenomenon. This may include the bastardization or demolition of a building that no longer has a community to serve it or where its builders lack the economic or political power to resist threatening 'regeneration' or 'improvement plans'.

It accompanies the decline in the power or presence of a community, ethnic or religious group, or class in a locale, or, conversely, can reflect hostility to a group's rise (every time a Bangladeshi family in London's East End gets petrol-soaked rags pushed through its letterbox, this is ethnic cleansing in miniature). That which is valued by a dominant culture or cultures in society is preserved and cared for: the rest can be mindlessly or purposefully destroyed, or just left to rot. These issues are touched upon where the legacy of conflict still determines a country's demolition and rebuilding decisions, or where a country is fragmenting as war approaches. The wars and revolutions of the twentieth and twenty-first centuries, however, where these processes are at their most explicit and brutal, and are pursued with a brutality that escalates with the conflict, are the focus of this book. The intentional collapse of buildings is intimately related to social collapse and upheavals.

—~—

The loss felt by those whose architectural patrimony has been reduced to rubble is not simply dismay at the material cost involved or sorrow over the mutilation of the aesthetic worth with which the structures are regarded. Rather, as Hannah Arendt has argued: 'The reality and reliability of the human world rests primarily on the fact that we are surrounded by things more permanent than the activity by which they were produced'.[2] To lose all that is familiar—the destruction of one's environment—can mean a disorientating exile from the memories they have invoked. It is the threat of a loss to one's collective identity and the secure continuity of those identities (even if, in reality, identity is always shifting over time). [. . .]

External threats can rally even heterogeneous groups together in defence of a national cause and the architectural representations of statehood. By contrast, in wars between ethnic or religious groups, either within a country or across its borders, there is an atomization, a rallying not to the national flag but to their sub-national communities. Here personal identity—the individual self grounded within the collective self—is in danger. In these circumstances there is an intensification of allegiance to the group reflecting a desire for preservation. Ethnicity or religious identification, for instance, can become more important than identifying with a neighbourhood, city or nation-state. It is, in part, this fear of oblivion and defence against it that can make these conflicts so brutal and the destiny of architectural representations of group identity so vital. Nietzsche, identifying in monuments 'the stamp of the will to power', could easily have written the same regarding their demolition as their building. A particular barbarism is fostered in wars between such groups, even if their manifestations sometimes disguise essentially political, economic or territorial concerns, because the consequence of the intensification of identification with a community also results in its corollary—the definition of those outside the group as 'the other', whose 'otherness' is commensurately deepened by this intensification. All conflicts, whether clearly ethnic or economic and expansionist, invoke the notion of the other, whether the other's nationality, race, class, religion, ideology or values. It is the emphasis on the differences between those within and those outside the group that leads to the devaluation of outsiders and their material patrimony.[3] This dehumanization is an essential step towards making it acceptable to dismantle an enemy's heritage, to maltreat and eventually kill them; sometimes these actions are telescoped into one event, such as the burning alive of congregations in their places of worship. The importance of architecture in such conflicts is heightened, especially in the case of commemorative monuments or sacred buildings belonging to the other. Sometimes it is as if the very bricks and stones are guilty of being the other as well as being representative of the other's presence. Their very form can reflect an alien mode of thinking and being; a different cultural genesis—mosque, onion dome, star or steeple.

It is not just the grandest, oldest or most architectonic of monuments that are targeted. Housing, too, especially vernacular housing, can be monumental in the sense of acting as a stimulus to the memories that evoke group identity. The term monument is used here in its broadest sense. These chapters are looking at both 'intentional' and 'unintentional' monuments—those that are directly commemorative and the many more buildings that, by virtue of their history and the identification their builders and users have with them, have had meaning thrust upon them.[4] More figurative works, such as statues, are touched upon but direct iconoclasm has been debated at length elsewhere.[5] Similarly the consequences of war for other artworks, such as looting, have also been well rehearsed (although it is interesting to note that in ethnic conflicts destruction and burning is far more common than seizure of property—the pecuniary advantages are subordinated to the desire to eradicate).[6] [. . .] [B]uildings gather meaning to them by their everyday function, by their presence in the townscape and by their form. They can have meaning attached to them as structures or, sometimes, simply act as containers of meaning and history. Each role invokes memories. We are not talking a Proustian subtlety of scent, taste and texture here, although architecture can certainly have these evocative subtleties. But it remains true that the mere sight of a building—a former home, an old trysting spot, or a hated workplace—can be an instant memory-jerker. Equally, the sheer familiarity of a street, an unconscious sense of a particular degree of enclosure, its sunny side, a familiar turn, can create rootedness in a place and an affiliation with the locale and its community.[7]

Both individual memories and collective memories are in play. Here, collective memory is considered as a bundle of individual memories that coalesce by means of exchanges between people and develop into a communal narrative about its architectural record. This is not a narrative independent of the generations of people who create and re-create the memories but it is independent of any individual within that group. In part, we recognize our place in the world by an interaction with the built environment and remembering these experiences and by being informed of the experiences of others: the creation of social identity located in time and place.

[. . .]

[. . .] These memories are, of course, contested and they change over time. It is a process that is always unfolding and remains ever unfinished. [. . .]

However, a continuity of successive experiences, setting down layers of meaning, can, I suggest, result in an especially strong power of place—a psycho-geography, an 'awareness' of the past (rather than an architectural avatar of a petrified spirit) that is dynamic, handed down by people rather than recorded on the very stones, and is specific to a particular historic and political context. The worth of such places increases where efforts to destroy them remind communities of this value. If the touchstones of identity are no longer there to be touched, memories fragment and dislocate—their hostile destruction is an amnesia forced upon the group as a group and on its individual constituent members. Out of sight can become, literally, out of mind both for those whose patrimony has been destroyed and for the destroyers. The 'how' of the precise psychoanalytic mechanisms at work—whether things are truly forgotten or still present and repressed and therefore unavailable to conscious thought—is best left to physiologists and psychologists.

—ɯ—

Gathering these facts is important because the destiny of buildings in war is often evidence of crimes against humanity, including ethnic cleansing and genocide, and is slowly being recognized as such. The trials being held at the International Criminal Tribunal for the former Yugoslavia at The Hague are crucial in this respect. The levelling of architecture has real-world consequences for the future well-being of communities, especially those suffering repression: 'The struggle of man against power', wrote Milan Kundera, 'is the struggle of memory against forgetting'.[8]

[. . .]

The damage caused by conflicts increased with the military inventions of the late nineteenth century and the early twentieth: heavy artillery, the gunboat, the tank and the Zeppelin. The Brussels Declaration of 1874 regarding the law and customs of war was the first international attempt to protect historic monuments from 'wilful damage'. It was never ratified but International Peace Conferences at The Hague in 1899 and 1907 used its concepts to establish the first international treaties to protect cultural property in times of war. The 1907 Hague Convention also agreed on an emblem to be placed on buildings due protection. War from the air and the devastations of both World Wars, however, demonstrated the weakness of the 1907 Convention and the 1954 Hague Convention for the Protection of Cultural Property in the Event of Armed Conflict was designed to tighten up protection. This is the key piece of international legislation under consideration. Its preamble recognizes that:

> cultural property has suffered grave damage during recent armed conflicts, and that, by reason of the developments in the technique of warfare, it is in increasing danger of destruction . . . damage to cultural property belonging to any people whatsoever means damage to the cultural heritage of all mankind, since each people makes its contribution to the culture of the world.[9]

The measures contained in the 1954 Convention are complex but, in short, call on warring parties to avoid damaging cultural property, indeed actively to protect it. This obligation may be disregarded 'only in cases where military necessity imperatively requires such a waiver'. This has served as a generous loophole. In 1977 the Hague Convention's provisions were incorporated into the humanitarian laws of the Geneva Convention and the loophole narrowed somewhat. But still the fatally intertwined experience of genocide and cultural genocide has yet to find its proper place in international law.

A century of protection then, matched by a century of savagery and cultural devastation: the ethnic riots and demolition of mosques in contemporary India; Stalin's destruction of churches; Hitler's destruction of synagogues and the built heritage of the Slavic people; Guernica, Dresden, Cambodia, Bosnia. Wave after thunderous wave of an unparalleled cultural cataclysm. [. . .]

'Who today speaks of the massacre of the Armenians?' Hitler was able to say of the Armenian genocide, accompanied as it had been by the systematic levelling of the Armenians' built heritage.[10] The architectural evidence of a people, and the crimes committed against it, had largely vanished. Protecting the architectural heritage of those targeted for domination or elimination helps ensure that such peoples can never be erased entirely from history despite the determined efforts of their persecutors and destroyers.

Notes

1. See, for example, M. Christine Boyer, *The City of Collective Memory: Its Historic Imagery and Architectural Entertainments* (Cambridge, MA, 1994); and Dolores Hayden, *The Power of Place: Urban Landscape as Public History* (Cambridge, MA, 1995).
2. Hannah Arendt, *The Human Condition: A Study of the Central Dilemma Facing Modern Man* (Chicago, IL, 1958).
3. See, for example, Monica Spiridon, *Spaces of Memory: The City-Text*, European Thematic Network, online publications, www.lingue.unibo.it (undated). See also Rudy J. Koshar, 'Building Pasts: Historic Preservation and Identity in 20th Century Germany', in *Commemorations: The Politics of National Identity*, ed. John Gillis (Princeton, NJ, 1994).
4. Alois Riegl, *Der moderne Denkmalkultus* (Vienna, 1903); part Eng. trans. as 'The Modern Cult of Monuments: Its Character and its Origin', *Oppositions*, 25 (Fall 1982), pp. 21–51.
5. Dario Gamboni, *The Destruction of Art: Iconoclasm and Vandalism since the French Revolution* (London, 1997).
6. Donald L. Horowitz, *The Deadly Ethnic Riot* (Berkeley, CA, 2002), p. 436.
7. Kevin Lynch, *The Image of the City* (Cambridge, MA, 1960).
8. Milan Kundera, *The Book of Laughter and Forgetting* (London, 1988).
9. Jiří Toman, *The Protection of Cultural Property*.
10. Adolf Hitler, meeting at Obersalzburg, 22 August 1939.

Reading

21

Jane Jacobs

The Death and Life of Great American Cities (1961, 1993)

The destruction and transformation of traditional city sectors induced by policies of "slum" clearance and urban renewal, such as those promoted by Commissioner Robert Moses in New York City, were central concerns of a feisty resident of lower Manhattan in the late 1950s, Jane Jacobs, whose passion for maintaining diversity in cities led her to write this seminal work. Jacobs was among the first to propose that sustaining well-established neighborhoods rather than replacing them with new construction can make the difference in creating successful and thriving urban communities. She argued that planners and architects needed to acquire a better understanding of neighborhoods by looking closely at what (and who) was already there. She excoriated planners and urban designers for not paying attention to the city as "laboratory" and for not sufficiently "reweaving projects back into the city." She urged them to listen to those who understand urban neighborhoods best—the residents—and accordingly "plan for vitality."

Foreword to the Modern Library Edition (1993)

When I began work on this book in 1958, I expected merely to describe the civilizing and enjoyable services that good city street life casually provides—and to deplore planning fads and architectural fashions that were expunging these necessities and charms instead of strengthening them. [. . .]

But learning and thinking about city streets and the trickiness of city parks launched me into an unexpected treasure hunt. I quickly found that the valuables in plain sight—streets and parks—were intimately mingled with other clues and keys to other peculiarities of cities. [. . .]

From Jane Jacobs, *The Death and Life of Great American Cities* (New York: Random House, 1961; New York: Modern Library, 1993), xi, xvi–xviii, 5–6, 9–10, 19, 315–16, 511, 531–33.

—~—

[. . .] At some point along the trail I realized I was engaged in studying the ecology of cities. [. . .] [B]y city ecology I mean something different from, yet similar to, natural ecology as students of wilderness address the subject. A natural ecosystem is defined as "composed of physical-chemical-biological processes active within a space-time unit of any magnitude." A city ecosystem is composed of physical-economic-ethical processes active at a given time within a city and its close dependencies. I've made up this definition, by analogy.

The two sorts of ecosystems—one created by nature, the other by human beings—have fundamental principles in common. For instance, both types of ecosystems—assuming they are not barren—require much diversity to sustain themselves. In both cases, the diversity develops organically over time, and the varied components are interdependent in complex ways. The more niches for diversity of life and livelihoods in either kind of ecosystem, the greater its carrying capacity for life. In both types of ecosystems, many small and obscure components—easily overlooked by superficial observation—can be vital to the whole, far out of proportion to their own tininess of scale or aggregate quantities. [. . .] And because of their complex interdependencies of components, both kinds of ecosystems are vulnerable and fragile, easily disrupted or destroyed.

If not fatally disrupted, however, they are tough and resilient. And when their processes are working well, ecosystems appear stable. But in a profound sense, the stability is an illusion. As a Greek philosopher, Heraclitus, observed long ago, everything in the natural world is in flux. When we suppose we see static situations, we actually see processes of beginning and processes of ending occurring simultaneously. Nothing is static. It is the same with cities. Thus, to investigate either natural or city ecosystems demands the same kind of thinking. It does not do to focus on "things" and expect them to explain much in themselves. Processes are always of the essence; things have significances as participants in processes, for better or worse.

[. . .]

[. . .] Cities are in a sense natural ecosystems too—for us. They are not disposable. Whenever and wherever societies have flourished and prospered rather than stagnated and decayed, creative and workable cities have been at the core of the phenomenon; they have pulled their weight and more. It is the same still. Decaying cities, declining economies, and mounting social troubles travel together. The combination is not coincidental.

It is urgent that human beings understand as much as we can about city ecology—starting at any point in city processes.

Introduction

—~—

There is a wistful myth that if only we had enough money to spend [. . .] we could wipe out all our slums in ten years, reverse decay in the great, dull, gray belts that were yesterday's and day-before-yesterday's suburbs, anchor the wandering middle class and its wandering tax money, and perhaps even solve the traffic problem.

But look what we have built with the first several billions: Low-income projects that become worse centers of delinquency, vandalism and general social hopelessness than the slums they were supposed to replace. Middle-income housing projects which are truly marvels of dullness and regimentation, sealed against any buoyancy or vitality of city life. Luxury housing projects that mitigate their inanity, or try to, with a vapid vulgarity. Cultural centers that are unable to support a good bookstore. Civic centers that are avoided by everyone but bums, who have fewer choices of loitering place than others. Commercial centers that are lackluster imitations of standardized suburban chain-store shopping. Promenades that go from no place to nowhere and have no promenaders. Expressways that eviscerate great cities. This is not the rebuilding of cities. This is the sacking of cities.

—∿—

Cities are an immense laboratory of trial and error, failure and success, in city building and city design. This is the laboratory in which city planning should have been learning and forming and testing its theories. Instead the practitioners and teachers of this discipline (if such it can be called) have ignored the study of success and failure in real life, have been incurious about the reasons for unexpected success, and are guided instead by principles derived from the behavior and appearance of towns, suburbs, tuberculosis sanitoria, fairs, and imaginary dream cities—from anything but the cities themselves.

If it appears that the rebuilt portions of cities and the endless new developments spreading beyond the cities are reducing city and countryside alike to a monotonous, unnourishing gruel, this is not strange. It all comes, first-, second-, third- or fourth-hand, out of the same intellectual dish of mush, a mush in which the qualities, necessities, advantages and behavior of great cities have been utterly confused with the qualities, necessities, advantages and behavior of other and more inert types of settlements.

There is nothing economically or socially inevitable about either the decay of old cities or the fresh-minted decadence of the new unurban urbanization. On the contrary, no other aspect of our economy and society has been more purposefully manipulated for a full quarter of a century to achieve precisely what we are getting. Extraordinary governmental financial incentives have been required to achieve this degree of monotony, sterility and vulgarity. Decades of preaching, writing and exhorting by experts have gone into convincing us and our legislators that mush like this must be food for us, as long as it comes bedded with grass.

—∿—

[. . .] The way to get at what goes on in the seemingly mysterious and perverse behavior of cities is, I think, to look closely, and with as little previous expectation as is possible, at the most ordinary scenes and events, and attempt to see what they mean and whether any threads of principle emerge among them. [. . .]

One principle emerges so ubiquitously [. . .] : the need of cities for a most intricate and close-grained diversity of uses that give each other constant mutual support, both economically and socially. The components of this diversity can differ enormously, but they must supplement each other in certain concrete ways.

I think that unsuccessful city areas are areas which lack this kind of intricate mutual support, and that the science of city planning and the art of city design, in real life for real cities, must become the science and art of catalyzing and nourishing these close-grained working relationships. [. . .]

The Self-Destruction of Diversity

—~—

[. . .] The main responsibility of city planning and design should be to develop—insofar as public policy and action can do so—cities that are congenial places for this great range of unofficial plans, ideas and opportunities to flourish, along with the flourishing of the public enterprises. City districts will be economically and socially congenial places for diversity to generate itself and reach its best potential if the districts possess good mixtures of primary uses, frequent streets, a close-grained mingling of different ages in their buildings, and a high concentration of people.

[. . .] [There are] several powerful forces that can influence, for good or for ill, the growth of diversity and vitality in cities, once an area is not crippled by lack of one or more of the four conditions necessary for generating diversity.

These forces, in the form that they work for ill, are: the tendency for outstandingly successful diversity in cities to destroy itself; the tendency for massive single elements in cities (many of which are necessary and otherwise desirable) to cast a deadening influence; the tendency for population instability to counter the growth of diversity; and the tendency for both public and private money either to glut or to starve development and change.

These forces are interrelated, to be sure; all factors in city changes are interrelated with all other factors. Nevertheless, it is possible and useful to look at each of these forces in its own right. The purpose of recognizing and understanding them is to try to combat them or—better yet—convert them into constructive forces. [. . .]

—~—

Salvaging Projects

Reweaving projects back into the city is necessary not only to bring life to dangerous or inert projects themselves. It is also necessary for larger district planning. Cut up physically by projects and their border vacuums, handicapped socially and economically by the isolation of too small neighborhoods, a city district cannot be a district in truth, coherent enough and large enough to count.

The underlying principles for bringing life to a project site itself and to the borders where it must be rejoined with the district are the same as the principles for helping any city area where vitality is low. The planners have to diagnose which conditions for generating diversity are missing here—whether there is a lack of mixed primary uses, whether the blocks are too large, whether there is insufficient mixture in ages and types of buildings, whether the concentration of people is great enough. Then, whatever among those conditions is missing has to be supplied—usually gradually and opportunistically—as best it can be.

Governing and Planning Districts

Planning for vitality must promote continuous networks of local street neighborhoods, whose users and informal proprietors can count to the utmost in keeping the public spaces of the city safe. [. . .]

Planning for vitality must combat the destructive presence of border vacuums, and it must help promote people's identification with city districts that are large enough, and are varied and rich enough in inner and outer contacts to deal with the tough, inescapable, practical problems of big-city life.

Planning for vitality must aim at unslumming the slums, by creating conditions aimed at persuading a high proportion of indigenous residents, whoever they may be, to stay put by choice over time, so there will be a steadily growing diversity among people and a continuity of community both for old residents and for newcomers who assimilate into it.

Planning for vitality must convert the self-destruction of diversity and other cataclysmic uses of money into constructive forces, by hampering the opportunities for destructiveness on the one hand, and on the other hand by stimulating more city territory into possessing a good economic environment for other people's plans.

Planning for vitality must aim at clarifying the visual order of cities, and it must do so by both promoting and illuminating functional order, rather than by obstructing or denying it.

[. . .] [A]ims of this kind cannot be pursued unless those responsible for diagnosis, for devising tactics, for recommending actions and for carrying out actions know what they are doing. They must know it not in some generalized way, but in terms of the precise and unique places in a city with which they are dealing. Much of what they need to know they can learn from no one but the people of the place, because nobody else knows enough about it.

For this kind of planning, it is not enough for administrators in most fields to understand specific *services* and *techniques*. They must understand, and understand thoroughly, specific *places*.

Reading

22

Dinu C. Giurescu

The Razing of Romania's Past (1989)

War and urban renewal are not the only causes of the destruction of the urban heritage. This detailed account by Dinu C. Giurescu, a Romanian historian and politician who spent several years exiled in the United States, examines the loss brought about by nationalistic pride and ideological propaganda. The case in point is the destruction of old Bucharest, initiated in 1984 by Nicolae Ceauşescu, Romania's undisputed leader from 1965 until his execution in 1989. Within the span of five short years, bulldozers flattened more than 250 hectares of historic property, almost 25 percent of old Bucharest. As stated by the Romanian architect and planner Ioana Iosa, this must have been "the largest peacetime urban destruction in recorded history."[1]

THE URBAN ARCHITECTURAL HERITAGE

Planning an overall urban and rural reconstruction.

In September 1985 it was officially stated that by 1990, 90–95 percent of Bucharest's inhabitants would live in new apartment buildings, thus providing a model for other Romanian towns.[1] It was simultaneously announced that the reconstruction of the villages must be completed within the next 15 years.[2] Figures released in March and June 1988 project the disappearance of approximately 900 communes, out of 2,705, and a reduction in the number of villages, from the present level of 13,123, to a maximum of 5,000–6,000. A commune is an administrative unit composed of several separate villages. A village where the town hall and other institutions are located has the rank of commune, whereas the others in the unit remain villages. Time-limit: the year 2000.[3] Thus, approximately 7,000–8,000 rural centers will vanish from Romania's map and the remaining ones will be approximately 90–95 percent demolished and reconstructed. This is the outcome of a process which started in the postwar years.

From Dinu C. Giurescu, *The Razing of Romania's Past* (Washington, DC: US/ICOMOS, 1989), 2–7, 47–49. Reproduced courtesy of World Monuments Fund.

Industrialization and urban expansion.

Romania's industrialization began in 1949–1950; it developed at a rapid pace with people streaming from the countryside into the cities. The urban population rose from 3,486,995 in 1948, 22.0 percent of the total, to 5,667,559 in 1965, 29.8 percent of the total, and to 11,540,494 in 1985, 50.6 percent.[4]

In the late 50's and in the 60's the Romanian communist party and state leadership launched an extensive housing program in order to meet the pressing demands of the new town dwellers. For 15 years, 1955–1970, these apartments extended into the outskirts, built on open fields, in run-down suburban areas and along ring-boulevards and main roads into cities. Proximity to recently built industrial units and better housing opportunities were the main criteria for urban reconstruction in Bucharest and other centers.

In this first phase, up to the early 70's, it is fair to assume that the historic centers were generally not affected. The first major demolition of traditional architecture took place in Suceava,[5] capital city of the state of Moldavia in the 14th–16th centuries; Pitesti;[6] Vaslui;[7] Giurgiu;[8] and Tirgoviste.

Romania's traditional urban architecture.

Sixty-eight towns are documented on Romania's territory between the end of the 10th and the middle of the 15th century. New ones emerged after 1700 and 1800. The one-family house was the basic unit for both the Romanian urban and rural setting. In the central urban zones, along with stores and workshops, the houses were close to one another. In other areas, the dwellings emerged amidst trees, bushes and multicolored flowers expressing the link between the human and the natural environment. This is why travelers from Western Europe viewed Romanian towns as big villages. Churches, monastic complexes, princely and noble residences, all constructed of masonry, formed points and centers of interest in the overall urban image;[9] other buildings were made of inexpensive construction materials.

The states of Wallachia and Moldavia were founded at the beginning and the middle of the 14th century: Wallachia between the Southern Carpathians, the Danube River and the Black Sea; and Moldavia from the Eastern Carpathians to the Danube River, the Dniester River (Nistru) and the Black Sea. The two states were autonomous political bodies within the Ottoman Empire's area of dominance. They were united in 1859–1861 into the modern Romanian state. From the Middle Ages to 1800 the urban population was composed of up to 10 percent of the overall population of the two Romanian states. Unprotected by walls, the towns of Wallachia and Moldavia stretched into the nearby farming land and settlements as their populations increased. The first modern principles of urbanization were implemented in the last decades of the 18th century.

The gradual building up of the modern Romanian society and state[10] brought about extensive town renewal, too. The old dwellings were 80–85 percent replaced by one-family brick houses, in a variety of styles aligned to the European trends and favored by younger generations of owners. Neoclassical, neo-Gothic, eclectic, Art Nouveau, neo-Romanian at the end of the 19th century, and a few old styles prior to 1800–1830 were all included in the urban architecture.

The one-family house and its garden continued to form the basic unit of this large-scale reconstruction and represented a link with the pre-modern town. A second trait of continuity was the street network, which in its chief components remained much the same, though a number of streets disappeared and new ones were opened (for example, the north-south and east-west boulevards in Bucharest).

The apartment buildings, limited to a maximum of 8–10 stories, made their first appearance around 1900 and expanded in the interwar period. In Bucharest the Bratianu Boulevard (now, Nicolae Balcescu and Magheru Boulevards between University and Romana Plazas) was almost entirely remodeled; it represents a well-balanced and harmonic insertion of interwar architecture into the city's fabric. In other areas of the capital or in different towns, these constructions were usually 3–4 floors high with 6–12 apartments. They were in fact a superposition of individual houses with some amenities in common, such as central heating and hot water.

The traditional Romanian urban architecture consists, in short, of churches in the Byzantine tradition, many listed as historic monuments, some with Baroque or neoclassical traits; and houses and other civil buildings, a few built prior to 1800, the others from the 19th century and the interwar period (neoclassical, neo-Gothic, eclectic, neo-Romanian, Bauhaus and Cubist styles). The traditional urban scene also involves the network of streets with old routes and the overall urban fabric which resulted from a centuries-long evolution. The architecture and environment taken as a whole exceeds the values of each of its component parts. This heritage is an intrinsic and essential component of Romanian identity and history and part of the European heritage.

Reconstruction, renovation, restructuring.

As industrialization and urban growth continued, so did the need for more housing. Where and how should one proceed? Architects and urban planners focused on the central areas. The concepts of reconstruction, renovation and restructuring were examined. Answers were given mostly along accepted lines, but with some interpretations, also. The following alternatives were considered:

First, demolition and reconstruction. Is en masse demolition followed by integral reconstruction a solution? How can one control the arbitrariness of decisions that may erase the past? How can gross errors in projections for the future, mainly for traffic, be avoided? Special care should be given to the present architectural fabric, which is a vivid testimony of history, a link between yesterday, today and tomorrow, a genuine component of the national heritage. As has been said often, "A people without history, without a past, is like a boat without a helm plunging windward."

Second, urban renovation applied to whole areas and not to single monuments only.

Third, restructuring with a three-fold approach: preservation of every valuable building; removal of those considered inadequate; new construction, infill, harmonized with the architectural heritage.

Fourth, modernization as required by contemporary standards, the adaptation of towns to increased traffic and the introduction of amenities in old buildings.

Renewed interest in historic town centers.

In the early 70's, some essential questions were raised. Is the high-rise building the only path to progress? Is height a symbol of modernity? What kind of a relationship is there now between humans and the built environment? Encompassed by massive volumes of concrete and bricks, humans could be alienated, crushed and choked by these buildings that were meant to bring about a better quality of life. An out-of-scale architecture never encountered in the country's past could possibly change these humans into automatons of modernity[11]—creatures who only produce, eat and sleep with reflex responses to social commands. In order to avoid such possible trends, a rational set of principles needed to be applied:

- The reappraisal of whole urban areas based on historic, artistic, architectural, cultural, economic and archeological criteria.
- Modernization of present dwellings.
- Evaluation of changes required by traffic and industrial development.
- A higher population density per square kilometer. This refers only to the peripheral and to other town areas with houses made of short-lived materials.
- A multidisciplinary approach and extensive public debate in order to understand the citizens' reactions to the restructuring process.[12]

There was a practical approach for the protection of specific sites. A preliminary study in 25 historic centers was completed by the Institute for Town Planning, Architecture and Standardization, at the request of the Directorate of Historic and Artistic Monuments (Bucharest, 1973).[13] Proposals were set forth to integrate these centers into contemporary active life through restoration, introduction of modern technical installations (water and electricity) where lacking, maintenance of the old street network and of the overall traditional architectural profile, and the establishment of connections between the inherited and the contemporary building stock.

Areas of historic interest were estimated to represent between 4 and 8 percent of the present town surfaces. Money for modernizing the interiors of this heritage was appraised at between 20 and 40 percent of the cost of a new apartment. Speaking of financial aspects, it is noteworthy to recall an official opinion expressed in 1966: the preservation of historic centers is twice or three times less expensive than their total demolition and reconstruction.[14]

"This architectural-historical urban space is our life and our culture: many a time we carry on our professional and cultural activity here."[15] Our present and future civilization "is not based upon a leveling of traditional structures; . . . our cultural activity is channeling its dynamism, its force, toward the awareness of the national traditions . . . and why isn't the architectural heritage able to shape new values," a senior Romanian architect asked in 1973. Some professionals went further to advocate an urban architecture based on the Romanian traditions of the 17th–18th centuries.[16]

Conflicting views on the architectural heritage.

A different perspective was drawn up at the same time. It asserted that old towns with their specific fabric and street network cannot be adjusted to the requirements of contemporary life.[17] The principles to reshape urban areas should be: an increased density, more people per square kilometer; reduction of the surfaces occupied by industries; demolition of run-down parts; new solutions for traffic without a radical change in the road setting; and conservation of cultural and historic properties.

For a time, the old houses should be maintained but the future profile of these centers will be and is already determined by new apartments, erected along main boulevards and around squares.[18]

In 1966, at a symposium held by the union of architects on systematization and reconstruction of the central urban zones, two major categories were established. First, there were towns with important monuments and well-defined dwellings, such as Brasov, Sibiu, Medias, Sighisoara, Bistrita, and Cluj-Napoca (Kolozsvar), all located in Transylvania. These centers were to be maintained, adapted, modernized and connected to the contemporary buildings.

Second, there were the towns with important historic monuments but with no significant architecture (from the second half of the 19th century and post-1900) and with "no clearly designed urban structure," such as Tirgoviste (former capital city of the state of Wallachia), Suceava and Iasi (the capital cities of the state of Moldavia in the 14th–16th centuries), Sebes-Alba and Baia Mare. On this second group a more radical intervention by urban planners is expected (see, for example, Tirgoviste), keeping nevertheless in place historic monuments and possibly some characteristic segments of an old street.[19] The debated alternative was the radical demolition of the existing centers and their reconstruction on a completely different scale and fabric for the following reasons: some architects and urban planners considered the 19th- and 20th-century architecture of no real value; administrators and some specialists viewed modernity and progress as embodied solely in apartment buildings. No town had systematic records of its heritage, and comprehensive studies were missing.

This theoretical alternative became a reality and was put into practice, though not yet pushed to its ultimate consequences, in Suceava, Pitesti, Vaslui, Giurgiu and Tirgoviste centers, in the early 70's, as stated above.

What the statistics reveal.

Other figures were published in 1975.[20] Overall Bucharest area is 9,250 hectares of which there were:

650 hectares of sound constructions prior to 1943; 2,150 hectares of new constructions, 1944–1970; 800 hectares of new constructions, 1971–1975; and 5,650 hectares of the remaining area with old substandard constructions lacking conveniences.

The official viewpoint was therefore that architecture prior to 1943 and in good condition represented 7.02 percent of the town area only, whereas 61 percent was old, substandard, and inconvenient. As for the dwellings, there are 621,000 units with 410,000 (approximately 66 percent) good ones and 211,000 (approximately 34 percent) substandard ones. The meaning of "unit" is not defined in the article. Is it possible to have approximately 61 percent of the surface with substandard constructions and concomitantly 66 percent of the houses to be in good condition?

It was estimated moreover that 54 percent of the dwellings were in good technical condition and 10 percent in an advanced state of decay. Thirty-six percent were supposed to be in intermediate condition though the article does not mention them explicitly.

The conclusions set forth reflect the official perspective. The remodeling process would be directed into the central perimeter of the capital in the 1975–1990 interval. This perimeter is not delineated but a reduction of the built area was announced from 9,250 hectares to 7,800 and even to 6,200 hectares. There would be a rational use of the territory marked by an increase of population density, by better housing conditions and by a change in the street network. Historic monuments, architectural values and older constructions that do not hamper principal urban functions would be maintained and connected to the newly constructed areas.

Present state of urban and rural architectural heritage.

All attempts made in the late 70's and early 80's to stop the destruction of the traditional heritage produced little results.

Up to 1989 at least 29 towns have been razed and 85 to 90 percent reconstructed,[21] namely: Suceava, Botosani, Pascani, Iasi, Roman, Piatra-Neamt, Bacau, Vaslui, Husi, Birlad, Tecuci, Focsani, Galati, Rimnicul-Sarat, Buzau, Mizil, Ploiesti, Pitesti, Slatina, Craiova, Rimnicul Vilcea, Giurgiu, Slobozia, Calarasi, Medgidia, Tulcea, Constanta, Mangalia and Baia Mare (Nagybanya).[22] The traditional architecture and urban fabric have been leveled and replaced by the collective dwelling with multiple apartments and by a different street network. Another urban world has emerged opposite the earlier one with almost no connection to the past, but with isolated historic monuments and a few other buildings kept and sometimes even hidden within the new structures. Rapid demolition is underway in additional 37 towns.

This new concept and trend were emphasized in many articles hailing the achievements throughout the country.[23] Some of the planners promoted the new settlements, excluding any reference to the former town that they leveled.[24] In 1980 the planned new civic center of Bucharest was heralded as a unique epoch-making achievement, the most important project of systematization, construction and architecture ever implemented on Romania's territory.[25] The mass media increased its praise of the improvement of living standards which would result from the new architecture. Now and then photographs of old, poor, decayed houses were released side by side with the tall new constructions. By 1980, too, it was estimated that 3,000 villages with few inhabitants, "a negative demographic evolution" and a "reduced economic basis" should be dismantled in a "lengthy process."[26]

There is no choice left for the citizens living in privately owned houses once demolition has been decided. The former owner must move into a state-owned flat and become a tenant. The new living space is rented according to legal provisions: a studio for one person or a couple without children, irrespective of the size of the expropriated and destroyed house or apartment. The compensation for the lost property, paid after delays, usually represents less than 30 percent of the real value. In the rural areas, a house with its dependencies and a garden is replaced by a rented apartment of one, two or three rooms according to the family size. The amount of compensation paid in rural areas is not yet known. Once the inhabitants have moved and the houses have been bulldozed, the urban area or the village itself, its site and environment, simply vanish from the maps and from memory as if they had never existed.

By 1984 the radical demolition and reconstruction had started in a central residential area of Bucharest bordered by the Dimbovita River (to the north),[27] Avenue George Cosbuc and Calea Rahovei (to the east), Sabinelor Street (to the south) and Izvor Street and 13 Septembrie Avenue (to the west, see map). Everything was leveled to the ground: mansions, villas, one- and two-story houses almost all surrounded by gardens, small constructions of three or four apartments, public buildings, churches, historical monuments (the Mihai Voda Church and a bell tower were moved in 1986 and are the only monuments to have survived the razing), statues and a whole area highly characteristic for Romania's architectural heritage, the Uranus Hill, which for centuries had been one of the city's landmarks.

The economic value of this entire built zone, the large and comfortable housing space it offered since the district proved resistant to the 1977 earthquake—its significance for the country's history and civilization—were not heeded at all.

One year later, in 1985, the destruction advanced to Piata Unirii, alongside the Dimbovita River (to the southeast), Boulevard Marasesti (to the south), Calea Dudesti and part of Mircea Voda Street (to the east) and Calea Calarasi (to the north)—everything was leveled to the ground, including several churches [. . .].

Massive destruction followed in 1986 on the eastern side of the historic central zone (see map), between Dristor, Theodor Sperantia, Locotenent A. Bodea and Rodiei

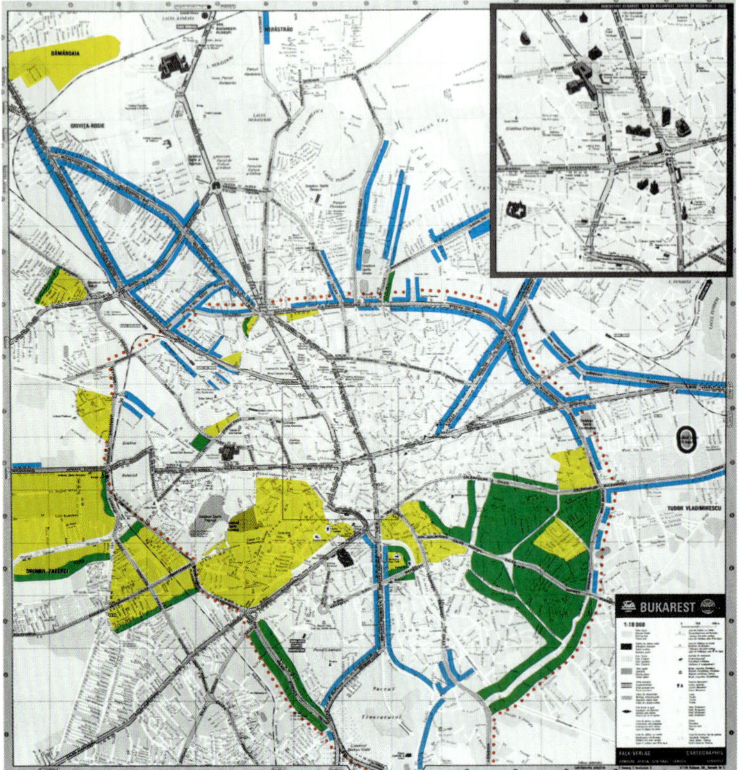

Fig. 1. The northern half of the capital city from the ring boulevards to the demolished central districts (in yellow on the map) is a large area including a whole range of districts highly representative of Romanian traditional architecture. Thousands of valuable structures are still in place in the southern half of Bucharest. *Karthographia u. alle Rechte, Falk-Verlag CmbH, Hamburg*

Streets;[28] also, between Tepes Voda (Vlad the Impaler), Agricultori, Dristor Streets and Mihai Bravu Avenue; from Calea Dudesti (south) alongside Traian Street up to Calea Calarasilor (to the north, see map), advancing eastward to Popa Nan Street, which has not yet been reached. [. . .]

In 1987 other parts within the central zone were torn down. Of approximately 150 buildings in place between Stirbei Voda, Berzei, Virgiliu Streets and Calea Plevnei only four houses and a school building survived the August to October 1987 campaign of demolition. Buzesti Street (up to Pinta Victoriei) and all the buildings close to the Ministry of Foreign Affairs (between Ilie Pintilie Boulevard, and Ana Ipatescu and Clopotarii Vechi Streets) were similarly targeted and pulled down.

Outside the historic zone [. . .] extensive demolition has been carried out on both sides of Calea 13 Septembrie up to Drumul Sarii and Panduri Avenues (southwest Bucharest), whereas the large districts around Drumul Taberei, Emil Bodnaras and Ho Si Min Streets and Armata Poporului Avenue were reconstructed in the 60's and 70's.

The 1986–1987 systematization drive extended also from Grozavesti Avenue over Econom Cezarescu Street toward the new Polytechnic Complex and between Giulesti and Cringasi Avenues. The number of demolished houses is considered a state secret. Individuals and advocacy groups have traced the destruction of churches and other monuments [. . .].

Notes to Introduction

1. Ioana Iosa, *L'Heritage urbain de Ceauşescu: Fardeau ou sant en avant?* (Paris: L'Harmattan, 2006), n.p.

Notes to Reading

1. Speech of the President of the Socialist Republic of Romania, published in *Scinteia*, the official daily of the Romanian Communist Party, Bucharest, September 12, 1985.
2. Ibid.
3. Nicolae Ceaušescu's speech at the National Conference of the Popular Council's presidents, Bucharest, March 3, 1988, *Romania Libera*, XLVI, no. 13, 475, March 4, 1988; Nicolae Ceausescu's speech at the joint session of the Workers' National Council and the Council for Agriculture, *Romania Libera*, XLVI, no. 13, 553, June 3, 1988.
4. *Anuarul Statistic al Republicii Socialiste Romania (Statistical Yearbook of the Socialist Republic of Romania)*, 1987 edition, Directia Centrala de Statistics (Central Direction of Statistics), Bucharest, p. 17, table 15. [. . .]
5. A short reference to these extensive interventions in the town of Suceava in Professor Dr. Arch. Grigore Ionescu, "Sa punem in valoare vechile ansambluri arhitecturale" (Making the most of old architectural developments), A., XIV, 1 (98), 1966, p. 9 (English summary, p. 10).
6. The town of Pitesti was razed and rebuilt in the 1966–1988 interval on the grounds that: "the existing prewar architecture has no special value"; three important buildings needed to be built in the center; and to end the present urban disorder; Cezar Lazarescu, "Studiu pentru sistematizarea zonei centrale a orasului Pitesti" (Study for the planning of the center of Pitesti), A., XIV, 6 (103), 1966, pp. 50–51 and 71 (English summary, p. 2). [. . .]
7. The center of Vaslui was razed and rebuilt in the late 60's and early 70's: a hint in Dr. Ioan Ciobotaru's, "Reconstructie, renovare sau restructurare urbana?" (Reconstruction, renovation or urban restructuring?), A., XXI, 4(143), 1973, p. 60 (English summary, p. 6). [. . .]
8. Giurgiu's center was demolished in the early 70s. One tower survived. [...]
9. Architects Radu Serban and Marilena Serban, "Integrarea imaginii urbane. O incercare de analiza a spatiului urban in partea veche a Bucurestiului" (The integration of the urban image. An attempt to analyse urban space in the historic area of Bucharest), A., XXI, 4 (143), 1973, pp. 92–102 (English summary, pp. 10–11): a study of component elements, their combination and variations which ultimately resulted in a characteristic image of traditional Bucharest architecture, as in most Romanian towns.
10. The gradual evolution of Romanian society toward a market-oriented capitalistic structure which started in the last decades of the 18th century was stepped up in the second half of the 19th century and accelerated in the interwar period (1919–1939). [. . .]
11. Dr. Ioan Ciobotaru, "Reconstructie, renovare sau restrucurare urbana?" (Reconstruction, renovation or urban restructuring?), A., XXI, 4 (143), 1973, pp. 60–62 (English summary, pp. 6–7).
12. Dr. Ioan Ciobotaru, op. cit.; Arch. Alexandro Sandu, "Pentru o intelegere complexa, stiintifica a restructurarii urbane" (For a complex scientific understanding of urban restructuring), A., XXI, 4 (143), 1973, pp. 4–11 (English summary, pp. 2–3): a balanced analysis and rationale of the concept of urban renovation-restructuring; thus, the need for a complex operational, analytical, philosophical and systematic approach. [. . .]

13. Dr. Arch. Virgil Bilciurescu, "Unele probleme in legatura cu valorificarea zonelor istorice" (Some problems in relation to the rehabilitation of historic areas), *A.*, XXI, 4 (143), 1973, pp. 20–23 (English summary, pp. 4–5).
14. Dr. Arch. Virgil Bilciurescu, "Sistematizarea centrelor istorice ale vechilor orase" (Planning of historic centers of our old towns), *A.*, XIV, 6 (103), 1966, pp. 46–49 (see p. 48) (English summary, p. 2). [. . .]
15. Dr. Arch. Virgil Bilciurescu, *A.*, XXI, 4 (143), 1973, p. 23. Cf. Professor Arch. Dr. Grigore Ionescu, "Sa punem in valoare vechile ansambluri arhitecturale" (Making the most of old architectural developments), *A.*, XIV, 1 (98), 1966, pp. 8–9 (English summary, p. 1).
16. Arch. Constantin Joja, "Punerea in valoare a unei vechi arhitecturi urbane romanesti" (How to vitalize old Romanian urban architecture), *A.*, XVI, 4 (113), 1968, pp. 17–21 (different opinions expressed by Arch. Aurel Doicescu, ibid., pp. 22–23, and by Arch. Ion Dumitrescu, ibid., pp. 23–24); Arch. Constantin Joja, "Actualizarea traditiei urbane romanesti," *A.*, XVII, 2 (117), 1969, pp. 32–33.
17. Arch. Cezar Lazarescu, "Probleme actuale ale dezvoltarii oraselor," *A.*, XV, 4 (107), 1967, p. 3, opinion expressed during a plenary session of the Romanian Union of Architects on "Topical problems of town development."
18. Cezar Lazarescu, President of the Union of architects, "Probleme actuale ale urbanizarii in tara noastra" (Present planning problems in our country), *A.*, XXIII, 4 (155), 1975, pp. 9–11 (English summary, pp. 1–2).
19. Dr. Arch. Virgil Bilciurescu, "Sistematizarea si reconstructia zonei centrale a oraselor" (Planning of historic centers of our old towns), *A.*, XIV, 6 (103), 1966, pp. 46–49 (English summary, p. 2).
20. Arch. Constantin Jugurica, "Probleme ale dezvoltarii zonelor centrale ale Municipiului Bucuresti in etapa 1976–1980" (Problems raised by the development of Bucharest central zones during the 1976–1980 stage), *A.*, XXIII, 4 (155), 1975, pp. 34–36 (English summary, p. 3). [. . .]
21. Estimated average, with less (75–80%) in some cases, or more (over 90%). First are enumerated the towns in Eastern Romania (former province of Moldavia), then in the Southern parts (Wallachia and Dobrogea) and in Transylvania (Baia Mare).
22. Large-scale demolition and reconstruction have been carried out in other towns, including: Tirgu Neamt, Adjud, Panciu, Tirgu Ocna and Buhusi in Moldavia; Urziceni, Oltenita, Alexandria, Zimnicea, Rosiorii de Vede, Caracal and Turnu Magurele in Wallachia; and Hirsova, Babadag and Isaccea in Dobrogea. [. . .]
23. Special issues, *A.*, focused on "the Metro in Bucharest," XXVIII, 4 (185), 1980, pp. 10–36; "Romanian planning in other countries," XXVIII, 5 (186), 1980, pp. 9–53, and 6 (187), 1980, pp. 9–31; "Apartment buildings," XXIX, 6 (193), 1981, pp. 10–59; "The reconstruction of the town of Iasi," XXIX, 2–3 (189–190), 1981, pp. 9–81. [. . .]
24. Arch. Nicolae Munteanu, "Centrul Vasluiului" (The center of Vaslui), *A.*, XXIX, 5 (192), 1981, pp. 64–69 (English summary, p. 7). [. . .]
25. Interview with Dr. Arch. Alexandru Budisteanu, chief architect of Bucharest, *A.*, XXVIII, 1–2 (182–183), 1980, pp. 12–17, quotation at p. 15, interview by Architects Andrei Feraru and Mihai Popescu.
26. Arch. Mircea Cardas, "Sistematizarea si reconstructia localitatilor rurale din Romania" (Rural settlement planning and rebuilding in Romania), *A.*, XXVIII, 3 (184), 1980, pp. 10–12 (English summary, p. 3).
27. From the B. P. Hasdeu Street to Piata Unirii.
28. These locations are approximate since the demolitions are advancing at a rapid pace.

Reading

23

Mona Serageldin

Preserving the Historic Urban Fabric in a Context of Fast-Paced Change (2000)

As a professor of urban planning at the Harvard Graduate School of Design, Mona Serageldin has focused her research on land management, strategic planning, urban housing, and community participation, in addition to conducting international work for USAID, the UN Centre for Human Settlement (UNCHS; now UN-Habitat), and the World Bank. This reading is a reflection on the difficulty of preserving the urban heritage in countries experiencing rapid and uncontrolled economic and social transformation. After reviewing the causes and effects of economically and culturally disruptive changes to the traditional city fabric, Serageldin advocates the need to forge new forms of inclusive and active partnerships in historic urban settings involving central authorities, local institutions, civil society, and private entrepreneurs.

This essay addresses the challenge of preserving historic centers in societies experiencing fast-paced change. This situation is commonly encountered in newly independent states, countries undergoing economic restructuring, and nations in difficult political transition.

The cultural heritage in the historic cores of urban settlements is subject to the interplay of two major forces: (1) the dynamics of development and transformation as they affect population movements and real estate markets, and (2) the perceptual and practical links between people and their architectural and cultural heritage.

Rapid economic and institutional transformation subjects the built environment to varying degrees of strain that expose cultural heritage to risk. Concepts of preservation transferred from countries enjoying prolonged stability and growth often prove to be unaffordable and ineffective in preventing the onset of decay in historic cores. National development policies focused on economic issues do not adequately support conserva-

From Mona Serageldin, "Preserving the Historic Urban Fabric in a Context of Fast-Paced Change," in *Values and Heritage Conservation: Research Report,* edited by Erica Avrami, Randall Mason, and Marta de la Torre (Los Angeles: Getty Conservation Institute, 2000), 51–58.

tion objectives and may even clash with them, while the dynamics of real estate markets reinforce disparities in valuation between the old and the new. They create situations in which the value of land in accessible sites is depressed by the condition or present uses of historic buildings standing on the land.

Appreciation of the built environment is partially conditioned by the network of interlinked organizations underlying the social order: family and kin groups; ethnic, religious, and political associations; and even occupation and business interests. Rapid transformation causes strains and dislocations in these structures. Restructuring of production opens new fields and opportunities to acquire status and wealth independently of old systems. Reshaping the institutional and legal frameworks within which new and surviving organizations have to function creates new channels for upward mobility, as well as new symbols of achievement and status. The mechanisms of self- improvement and the experience of personal fulfillment are more or less profoundly altered.

Attitudes toward change span the spectrum from enthusiastic acceptance to outright rejection. The greater the turmoil caused by transformation, the greater the need for anchors to culture as a transformation of identity in the face of globalizing and homogenizing influences. There is a rich body of literature on this important topic. This essay is only intended to stimulate further discussion of the factors underlying the coexistence of a vibrant or revived living culture with a progressively deteriorating historic fabric, in danger of being lost through neglect, collapse, and eventual disappearance.

Changing Context of Development in a Globalized Economy

Since the mid-1970s, cities have had to cope with transformation of unprecedented scale and scope. With little control over the market forces driving this fast-paced change, public authorities are unable to capitalize on the opportunities they open up and unable to mitigate their negative impacts. Developing a capacity to engage citizens is a precondition to addressing these challenges.

Economic transition creates a pervasive sense of insecurity. Globalization brings foreign investment and with it volatility of capital flows. It also brings increased geopolitical interdependence, social mobility, and widening income disparities. People find it hard to accept concepts of national development and increased prosperity that do not translate into gains more or less evenly distributed among social strata. Workers used to relationships of allegiance and solidarity are stunned by offers of employment carrying no stability or hope for advancement.

In developing countries, the effects of transition are compounded by the inability of the domestic economy to create jobs for an increasing number of young entrants into the labor force. Rural migrants drift into the cities, where they join the growing ranks of an urban underclass composed of daily laborers barely earning subsistence wages, hardcore unemployed without hope of finding living-wage jobs, impoverished households, and increasing numbers of homeless and abandoned children.

Between the extremes of affluence and poverty, the backbone of society consists of conservative middle classes struggling to understand the forces that have disrupted their lives. They want to make sense of the present and avoid losing ground. Only the more entrepreneurial welcome change and firmly believe in the promise of a better future made possible by technological innovation. The rest view themselves as the guardians of values and traditions in the face of destabilizing change occurring faster and faster every day.

Emergence of New Spatial Patterns

The dualism that prevailed in the industrial age—between the new affluent sectors and the older, overdensified fabric housing the poor—is fading away as a complex pattern of interlinked districts takes shape. Physical proximity does not overcome social exclusion, while ambiguous transitional zones blur the edges and offer more porous boundaries that allow population movements to restructure the urban area in accordance with the emerging socio-economic order.

Cities are in a perpetual state of crisis management as they struggle to confront multispeed development, exclusion, and violence. Historic districts, bypassed by development, have come to be major recipient areas for the marginalized. The degradation of their urban fabric results in the loss of a rich architectural and urbanistic heritage. Today, as in the past, neglect and misuse are deplored by intellectual elites sensitive to the intrinsic value of cultural heritage. Design professionals attracted by the aesthetic qualities of vernacular architecture and organic settlement patterns tend to associate with this fabric an ideal community life far removed from the harsh realities of life in these settlements—be they Italian hill towns or Balinese villages. They are dismayed at the lack of appreciation of these inherent qualities, as expressed by residents, local representatives, and public officials in charge of managing this vulnerable heritage.

Comparison with Past Episodes of Culturally Disruptive Change

Elite attitudes toward the cultural heritage were colored by the outsider's view of the indigenous. Valuation of worth and benefits was unrelated to the perceptions and experiences of the communities interacting daily with this heritage. In historic centers, this perspective led to a focus on monuments and key buildings as well as on archaeological sites, to the detriment of the context: the historic fabric and the underlying family and community life. Preservation for the tourist and the scholar took precedence over revitalization for the resident.

Value Attached to the Nonmonumental Historic Fabric

Attitudes toward the cultural heritage embody a complex mix of emotional and pragmatic needs. With reference to the architectural and urbanistic heritage, a clear distinction is made between landmarks and nonmonumental buildings that form the historic fabric and provide the setting for monuments. The apparent lack of appreciation of the nonmonumental architectural heritage as a determinant of cultural identity in societies experiencing rapid change is often perplexing to the outsider charmed by its quaint character, distinctive features, and warm sense of place. The factors discussed below account for this attitude.

Loss of use value of the nonmonumental fabric

Traditionally, only the monumental was conceived of as a cultural symbol and built to last as a legacy of political power, religious belief, and flourishing civilization. The nonmonumental environment was utilitarian, built to serve its present users and destined to disappear when it became physically or functionally obsolete. The cultural significance given today to the surviving examples of historic fabrics is not intuitively understood by the communities that inhabit them.

The massive movements of labor that have prevailed since the mid-1970s have created complex rural/urban linkages that spill over national boundaries. The new links have channeled capital and introduced models of modernity that drive an unprecedented transformation of the rural habitat, from Mauritania to Mongolia. Worldwide, there is a convergence toward materials that are convenient to use and toward designs that are economical to build and maintain. Traditional house forms and settlement patterns are demolished and replaced by structures built of durable materials which prominently display the signs of improved social status. Where land is accessible and inexpensive, as in areas bordering on wastelands and deserts or in the vast expanses of steppes and mountains, older, compact settlements are often abandoned and new ones built nearby incorporating the desired features of modernity.

The hilltop villages of Yemen; the oasis settlements of Turfan, Siwa, and Gadàmes; the Ksour range of the Atlas Mountains—to name a few unique and strikingly beautiful historic fabrics that blend perfectly with their natural environment—today stand empty, abandoned by the communities that once inhabited them. People and activities have relocated to adjacent "modern" developments, while national and local authorities struggle to arrest the degradation of the historic sites and promote their touristic value. From the community's perspective, there can be no intrinsic value attached to elements of the built environment that have lost their symbolic meaning and their cultural significance. When they no longer have any use value, they are bound to disappear.

Changes in production methods and their social implications

The mechanization of systems of production undermined the economic base of historic cores as well as their built environment. Handcrafted wares disappeared as household items were replaced by cheaper manufactured goods. At the upper end, handicrafts are part of the arts and luxury markets. Lower-end production, particularly in developing countries, has been reoriented to serve the tourist trade and is today partly mechanized so that products can be offered within the marketable price range defined by middlemen, who reap most of the profit. In developing countries, this process started in the early 1950s and expanded rapidly, as machinery and equipment became more accessible.

[. . .] Progressively displaced by retail, workshops and small production activities gravitate to locations where they can find cheaper and more spacious premises—mostly deteriorating buildings at the edges of residential blocks.

From the viewpoint of preservation of the cultural heritage, the intrusion of workshops in the residential fabric is unwelcome. The erosion of environmental quality undermines the livability of the neighborhood and accelerates the onset of an irreversible cycle of deterioration and abandonment. Invariably the areas around these smaller manufacturing enterprises become pockets of poverty housing, transient labor, and rural migrants whose needs and living patterns are incompatible with the lifestyle and urbanity of families in adjoining quarters; this development then leads to an exodus of longtime residents. The decay of the physical fabric is compounded by the erosion of the community structure.

When asked what they value most in their neighborhoods, old-time residents in historic centers most often refer to "a way of life" and to "social relations"; these remarks highlight the importance of community to an appreciation of the built environment that transcends direct-use benefits. Erosion of the sense of community leads to disintegration of the sense of place and to loss of the significance attached to elements of the physical setting.

Changing roles of civic leaders and community groups

The state (through central or local authorities) gradually assumed fiscal, administrative, and regulatory functions traditionally discharged by local leaders, community associations, and neighborhood groups. This incursion by the state eroded the institutional structure at the community level. This process, which began in Europe in the eighteenth century, occurred in the developing countries mostly in the nineteenth and early twentieth centuries under colonial rule, or as part of national development policies and modernization processes.

The adoption of "modern" planning and design standards for urban layouts and public facilities precluded the use of historic buildings for many functions that they originally housed. Until the late 1960s, preservation practices did not challenge the building codes and bureaucratic norms preventing the more imaginative designers from exploring innovative, adaptive reuse of existing historic buildings. In most developing countries, these strictures are still in place, partly because of fear that restored buildings will be misused and partly because of an inability to conceive and implement an effective awareness-building program for residents in historic districts.

Ambivalence toward the Historic Fabric

[. . .]

In countries in transition, conflicting economic, social, and environmental policies prevail and are sustained by legal and institutional frameworks in a state of flux. Their detrimental effect on the historic fabric endures over prolonged periods and can be devastating.

Residential choice, mobility, and the older housing stock

The former centrally planned economies of Eastern Europe present an interesting example of conservation practices and development policies working at cross-purposes. On one side, ill-advised housing policies allocated the older stock, considered to be of lower quality, to poor families, undermining its desirability and tarnishing the image of historic centers as a place to live and work. [. . .] On the other side, preservation policies extolled the significance of the architectural and urbanistic legacy as a repository of historical memory and a symbol of cultural and ethnic identity. The prohibitive cost of rehabilitating the nonmonumental fabric to the unrealistically high standards mandated by rigid conservation guidelines makes it unaffordable to longtime residents in the absence of significant public assistance. [. . .]

Preservation strategies and practices have yet to be adapted to the politics and decentralized planning, the dynamics of real estate markets, the diversity of institutional actors, and the multitude of individual decisions regarding the refurbishing and use of buildings and spaces. Residents who did not elect to live in the historic centers and do not wish to remain there should be given assistance to relocate.

The rigidity of inherited housing policies and conservation practices is increasingly challenged by a population that views residential choice as an integral component of individual freedom. Many residents perceive that they are denied the opportunity to share in the benefits of growth and affluence and want to move out on that account. An urban fabric that is associated with economic stagnation is bound to lose its attractiveness. Sensitive rehabilitation and revitalization policies could guide the turnover entailed by privatization to reestablish social balance and economic vitality while safeguarding the physical features that give historic environments their special sense of place.

Devalorization of the old urban fabric

The constant exposure to the messages, images, and consumerism of mass culture relayed by the media is powerful enough to affect lifestyles and aspirations everywhere. In developing countries, this exposure has tended to devalorize the historic fabric in the eyes of its inhabitants. Even among those who profess to be traditionalists, varying degrees of ambivalence pervade attitudes, irrespective of political affiliation or level of affluence. Cultural sensitivity can only be inferred from the actual choices and actions of individual households.

Deterred by regulatory controls and the difficulties encountered in penetrating a dense medieval fabric, development since the 1950s has continued to bypass the historic centers. From Lahore to Algiers, the shacks housing the marginalized populations in the older *extramuros* settlements were cleared over time to make way for modern districts and the architectural symbols of a new age. The exodus of local elites, affluent residents, and prosperous businesses to the modern districts deprived historic centers of effective civic leadership and political clout. It also signaled the hopeless obsolescence of the historic fabric and its inability to offer the new generation a desirable living environment able to accommodate their rising aspirations.

The urban middle classes, which constitute the backbone of the population in the historic centers, are the groups most affected by the path and rate of change. The financial hardships they experience during structural adjustment and economic transition are compounded by the restructuring of society and the reallocation of political power that the new order brings. Their ambivalent attitudes toward the cultural heritage reflect a struggle to reconcile the contradictions inherent in acquiring the requisites for participation in the new systems while retaining ties, if not allegiance, to valued aspects of the older order. Caught in a vicious circle of politically legitimized aspirations and frustrated expectations, their disarray is expressed in the search for coherence through ordering principles that simultaneously offer reassurance of cultural continuity, promises of positive change, and hope for self-betterment. Their frustrations are expressed through ethnic, religious, and political extremism, rather than through cultural revival.

Functional obsolescence and unrestrained misuse of the fabric carry a devalorizing message that reinforces the negative image of the old among a youthful population eager to access the conveniences made possible by new technologies—if not to embrace the changes in outlook and lifestyles that new technology could entail. Nor can residents take pride in their civic affiliations when historic quarters remain underserviced and bypassed by development.

Youngsters growing up in the old city quarters find it hard to believe that society at large places a high value on an environment that is allowed to deteriorate through neglect. A schoolboy in Cairo, told of the rich architectural heritage surrounding his house, responded in disbelief. "If these buildings are so important, why are they left in a state of disrepair?" And when he was told that resources were lacking, he remarked, "If there is no money to repair them now, why do people throw garbage around them?" At issue here is the link between obsolescence, neglect, and loss of cultural significance.

[. . .]

Partnerships in the Rehabilitation of Historic Centers

Since the early 1990s, urban development strategies have sought an appropriate balance between public commitment, private investments, and community initiative. [. . .] Worldwide, there is an expanding role for nongovernmental organizations (NGOs) in the rebuilding of community structure and in the sharpening of awareness of the value and appropriate use of the historic fabric. NGOs have the freedom and flexibility to innovate, and they are well positioned to engage citizens through sustained outreach.

The tendency to denigrate or dismiss the potential contribution of public and private local actors is perplexing. Despite the fact that they lack capacity and funding, elected mayors, local councils, and civic groups are the fundamental building blocks of democratic governance and civil society. Their effective interface is the guarantee of sustainability and continuity of initiatives at the community level, including initiatives for conservation of the cultural heritage.

The inability of authorities in developing countries to prevent misuse and deterioration of the cultural heritage is routinely blamed on the inadequacy of the regulatory and institutional framework. Yet the enactment of legislation and the establishment of public and private agencies only rarely result in anticipated improvements. Layers of bureaucracy and overlapping competences multiply without impacting reality on the ground.

The fundamental causes of the ineffectiveness of conservation measures lie in the stress experienced by communities undergoing rapid change. Change, whether desired or imposed, entails geographic mobility, social dislocation, and new economic systems. The imbalance between the quasi-static view of management adopted by conservation agencies and the dynamics of development in societies experiencing rapid transformation becomes untenable. The widening gap between the behavior required by preservation codes and rational individual economic, social, and cultural behavior produces the seeming disregard for the historic fabric deplored by conservation agencies, historic commissions, NGOs, and civic groups whose mandate or mission is preservation of this cultural heritage.

Strategic Management of Change and Development in Historic Settings

The ability to devise effective strategies for historic districts must be grounded in an understanding of their role as a vital component of a living city. How people perceive their heritage at a time when society is undergoing change is critical to this task. When little in the forms and experiences of the past seems relevant to meeting the challenges of survival and upward mobility, the management of change requires an ability to identify opportunities as well as to avoid pitfalls. Public and private institutions involved in historic centers must develop an in-depth understanding of the urban dynamics affecting the fabric they seek to protect. They must view change as a challenge and learn to handle it as an ingredient of strategy, rather than as a force to be contained. Historic cores must be integrated into the economic and social life of the settlement within which they are embedded.

[. . .] Rebuilding communities capable of valuing and protecting their cultural heritage requires balancing diversity and inclusion so that a cohesive mix of socioeconomic groups can be reestablished, and the cycle of impoverishment and environmental degradation can be reversed, as was successfully achieved in the medina of Tunis.

Interestingly, the resurgence of identity as an issue in the developing world does not necessarily entail a renewed attachment to the historic fabric. Respect for the heritage extends only to monuments that symbolize religion and ethnicity, a position often fraught with ambivalence and lacking sensitivity regarding preservation of the integrity of buildings and conservation of their architectural and decorative elements. Garish renovations are a direct consequence of this attitude, as well as a reaffirmation of the link between physical condition and perceived loss of importance and significance.

[. . .]

The progressive loss of significance undergone by the nonmonumental historic fabric has trivialized the architectural and urbanistic heritage, thereby impoverishing society at large. Stripped of meaning, the fabric is reduced to a mass of buildings and spaces to which only use value is attached. When abuse, misuse, encroachment, and neglect gradually erode this value, the objects are discarded. The structures are left to fall into ruin, and the spaces are abandoned. Reversing this pernicious trend involves the dual challenges of inclusion and the building of awareness.

If historic districts are to regain their vitality, they cannot constitute the inexpensive housing stock for the urban underclass and the cheap space for marginal production activities. Rehabilitation with social inclusion, and revitalization accommodating a wide array of informal activities, implies that economic growth and preservation of the cultural heritage should proceed as interlinked facets of development strategy at the community level.

The Challenge of New Patterns of Cultural Interaction

Successful conservation efforts have to recognize and reconcile the different viewpoints of groups who have a right to be heard in the matters affecting the historic urban fabric. In a context of fast-paced change, their voices will express divergent value systems and conflicting interests. Appreciation of cultural heritage by outsiders gives a distorted view of reality. Conversely, exclusive reliance on the perspectives of uninformed local residents dangerously narrows the significance of culture and impoverishes it as well.

Conservation specialists play a catalytic and educational role in assisting responsible authorities to preserve and rehabilitate the heritage they hold in trust for their nation and the world. They are instrumental in saving neglected heritage, whether it be archaeological vestiges to which little importance is attached, buildings considered undesirable symbols of foreign domination or undeserving memorials of oppressive regimes, or cultural expressions somehow perceived as harmful to some locally held value or tradition.

An integrative framework for the rehabilitation of historic centers will seek an approach fostering social cohesiveness, economic sustainability; and political backing. To the extent that they are financially able to renovate and refurbish, unguided by development regulations and unconstrained by formal controls, residents in historic centers will alter the urban fabric and the buildings, sometimes inflicting irreversible damage to the original structures and accelerating the deterioration of the built environment. A sustained outreach effort will be required to build awareness, particularly among the young, of the intrinsic value of the cultural heritage around them, as well as of its economic benefits. Residents must be convinced that the objectives of historic preservation and social inclusion can be reconciled and that rehabilitation and conservation plans will not deny them the opportunities available to citizens living outside the historic core.

In a context of fast-paced change, the challenge for conservation specialists is to devise methods by which cultural heritage can be interpreted, valued, and valorized in light of emerging trends, new perceptions, growing diversity, and divergent attitudes. The importance of their role transcends conservation activities per se. They should contribute to shaping the cultural identity of younger generations caught in the turmoil and crosscurrents of transition, by offering interpretations and strategies that avoid the equally damaging extremes of introspective insulation and confused dilution in a globalized world.

Reading

24

Salvatore Settis

If Venice Dies (2014)

A new plague, comparable in its outcome to what the city experienced during the Black Death of 1630, is annihilating historic Venice: mass tourism. As a result of tourism, the city has lost two-thirds of its residents since 1950. This striking fact is presented at the outset of this reading from Salvatore Settis. With dense and provocative arguments, Settis, a well-known Italian archaeologist and art historian, examines the pernicious outcomes of unrestrained mass tourism on historic cities. He contends that, albeit extreme, Venice can be considered an exemplary case study: it demonstrates that the "flawed insistence on tourism as the ultimate reason why we should preserve our cultural heritage" is a self-defeating strategy that pushes out the residents, deprives the city of its social life and genuine cultural wealth, and turns it into "a theme park of itself," deprived of meaning and historic depth. "If this should ever happen to Venice," Settis warns, "it could happen everywhere else."

According to the current administrative arrangement, the area governed by the municipality of Venice also includes a vast tract of the mainland that comprises the cities of Mestre and Marghera as well as the Marco Polo Airport in Tessera. This is where the majority of Venice's population migrated in the past decades, particularly the younger generations. Concurrent with this internal relocation, the overall population of the entire area fell by over one hundred thousand inhabitants from 1971 to 2011, dropping from 363,062 to 263,996. Yet if one looks at the demographic data from Venice's historical center, as one should, this drop is even more dramatic:

From Salvatore Settis, *Se Venezia muore* (Turin: Giulio Einaudi, 2014). Published in English as *If Venice Dies,* translated by André Naffis-Sahely (New York: New Vessel Press, 2016), 8–10, 68–69, 91–93, 152–53, 165–66, 175–79. Reproduced courtesy of New Vessel Press. English translation by André Naffis-Sahely.

1540 129,971
1624 141,625
1631 98,000 (approx.) (following the plague of 1630)
1760 149,476
1797 137,240 (year the Republic was abolished)
1871 128,787
1951 174,808
1961 137,150
1971 108,426
1981 93,598
1991 76,644
2001 65,695
2012 58,606 (June 30)
2013 57,539 (October 21)
2014 56,684 (June 30)
2015 56,072 (June 30)

As we can see, the only other time Venice experienced a population drop comparable to the present one over the past six centuries was in the aftermath of the plague of 1630, when it took the city's population over a century to return to its previous levels. Although the extant demographic data is less reliable, the plague of 1348 proved to be equally devastating, after which it's estimated that the population dropped from about 120,000 to 58,000: just a little over today's figures. Yet starting in the 1970s, a new kind of plague broke out in Venice. In 1950, the city registered 1,924 births versus 1,932 deaths (more or less the same). In 2000, on the other hand, there were 404 births versus 1,058 deaths. The combined results of an aging population, an exodus to the mainland, the breakup of families, a low birthrate, and other factors paint a portrait of a city on the run from itself. This allows us to understand why the Morelli Pharmacy in Campo San Bartolomeo put up a meter that displays the daily drop in Venice's inhabitants. This dramatic countdown wasn't organized by a public body, but rather by a group of local citizens. One of them, Matteo Secchi, even went so far as to say: "We'll soon celebrate Venice's funeral and carry the coffin in a procession all the way to city hall." Moreover, the Venetians who live in the historic center "don't actually get to elect their own mayor since they are outnumbered three times over by Mestre's inhabitants (who live on the mainland)," according to economist Francesco Giavazzi.

Thus, who are Venice's real inhabitants? What kind of plague is responsible for their annihilation? While the city steadily empties out, the rich and famous continue to flock to it, ready to pay any price to purchase a house—which becomes a status symbol they tend to use for only five days a year. This influx has dramatically distorted the market, raising prices in a manner that drives Venetians out of their own city, making it a capital of second-home owners, who briefly appear with great pomp and flash before vanishing into the ether for months at a time. In the meantime, 8 million tourists pour into Venice's streets and canals each year, for a total of 34 million nights, compared to the city's maximum carrying capacity of 12 million (Giuseppe Tattara, *Contare il crocerismo* / Quantifying Cruising, 2014), meaning that tourists outnumber Venetians 140 to 1. This devastating disproportion has had the impact of a bomb, profoundly altering the population and the economy. A tourist monoculture now dominates a city which banishes its native citizens and shackles the survival of those who remain to their willingness to serve. Venice no longer seems capable of creating anything other than bed-and-breakfasts, hotels and restaurants, real estate agencies, souvenir shops devoted to traditional products (from glass to masks), and staging phony carnivals, thereby applying some melancholy makeup to its features in order to give the city an atmosphere of a perpetual county fair; this briefly allows it to forget the plague which afflicts it and is wiping out its inhabitants while tearing apart its social fabric, cohesion, and civic culture.

—∿—

On the other hand, Venice could maintain its unrivaled forma urbis if it learns how to interpret the paradox of conservation through the prism of its own DNA; if it will learn to employ a poetics of reutilization that doesn't limit itself to mass tourism. If it doesn't stick to the unsuccessful model of an embalmed city, but instead slowly ponders each and every change, ensures that all new structures are both delicate and well thought out, given how even the slightest move might alter its precious fabric. Venice will be able to respect itself only if, in the words of Plutarch, it realizes it can still be "like a living thing . . . a united and continuous whole [which] does not cease to be itself as it changes in growing older, nor does it become one thing after another with the lapse of time." If it will remain "at one with its former self in feeling and identity and must take all blame or credit for what it does or has done in its public character" so that "the community, which is held together by operational links, retains its unity." And let us add a final condition: Venice must know how to creatively construct its own destiny, tailoring each change it makes according to the best possible future for its citizens, and not what the tourists or real estate agencies want.

—∿—

Comparing Venice to Disneyland has now become commonplace; without citing too many examples, simply two will suffice. In 1981, the Italian journal *Urbanistica* published an article which argued, among other things, that "the transformation of Venice into Disneyland could very well signal the transition to a more creative and cheerful way of life." The author in question was a professor of urban planning, had edited *Urbanistica* for seven years, and was subsequently a member of Italy's Higher Council for Cultural Heritage and Landscape. The second example is culled from an advertisement posted on the Internet in February 2014:

> Veniceland, the Disneyland of the Lagoon, is coming to Italy. On the island of Sacca San Biagio, the roller-coaster giant Zamperla will build a theme park dedicated to

> the history and culture of the city, in order to remind visitors of a time when Venice was an international economic powerhouse.

The island this article refers to is situated in the Giudecca Canal, only a step away from the Venice we know and love: yet if one wishes to speak about La Serenissima's history, the city itself isn't enough any more. Instead, one needs a Venice equipped with "educational areas set aside for schools, huge touch-screen displays, performances developed in partnership with the city authorities, a specific area dedicated to the splendid carnival, roller coasters, slides and a large Ferris wheel."

Reproductions of various natural landscapes (the *barene*, or salt marshes) and historical reenactments (the Battle of Lepanto) have been planned, all of which has been granted the seal of approval by the University of Venice, whose rector "offered his university's expertise to the company so that the protection of the city's historical and environmental treasures would be guaranteed. Nobody would think of calling such a place a Luna Park."

Thus, *The Guardian* newspaper was certainly correct when it published a provocative piece in June 2006 entitled "Send for Disney to Save Venice," which argued that if Venice's future lies in cheap, mass-market tourism, then it might as well be entrusted to the Disney Corporation, who would run it better than the city authorities.

No one is safe from such a radical drift. In Pompeii, city authorities are planning a Pompeii Experimental Park, a sort of facsimile of the actual archaeological site, which one can only presume is now deemed too boring. Yet there's nothing new about this idea: back in April 2007, then Minister of Culture Walter Veltroni launched the idea of a Jurassic Pompeii, "made up of gadgets, CDs, recreational areas and virtual games, and created to salvage the deteriorating site of Pompeii, which belongs to our archaeological heritage." All of this would be accomplished in a hurry, of course: according to the minister, it would take only "three years and a special law." Not to mention what Gianni Alemanno cooked up in 2008 when he was mayor of the Italian capital in order to "save Rome from a decline in tourist numbers," namely: "the Disneyland of ancient Rome, featuring virtual reconstructions that will allow visitors to watch shows at the Colosseum, chariot races at the Circus Maximus, explore the catacombs, or take a dip in the Baths of Caracalla."

Even in their most depraved form—for instance, Veniceland—these new coinages and cultural initiatives are seen by some as a democratization of culture, and anyone who dares question them is deemed elitist. [. . .]

—~—

[. . .] Marinetti writes that it would be better to destroy Venice than to see it reduced to a mummified museum-city for the exclusive use of tourists, a process then in its infant stages, and which has now become far more visible. Better a city for the living, Papini adds, than a community of "caretakers of morgues" living off the backs of the dead. Yet whenever we speak of Venice and Florence as museum-cities, occasionally with pride, aren't we essentially agreeing with these taunts and slights? Have we not contemplated turning our most famous and most visited cities into service stations for a hit-and-run sort of tourism? Haven't we degraded the very idea of the city by turning its citizens into servants? The flawed insistence on tourism as the ultimate reason why we should preserve our cultural heritage and landscapes actually overlooks the only point worth considering: that these landscapes and cultural patrimonies don't belong to tourists, they belong to citizens. Indeed, as the Italian Constitution explicitly says, insofar as they are the building blocks of our identity and history, these landscapes and cultural patrimonies are consubstantial to the right of citizenship. They aren't just the heirlooms of our past, but reservoirs of moral energy we'll need to build our future. Citizens—and not tourists—are the real lifeblood of the city, the custodians of its memory, and the architects of its future. A city composed of citizens who are both aware of their own identity as well as their own specific culture, are more hospitable, more interesting, and even more welcoming for the tourists. Cities composed of servants are far less friendly.

Is Venice a "festering carbuncle" of the past, or a prophecy and metaphor of the future? This is up to us: but if its entire life takes place only in the past, a Futurist destruction will become inevitable. The mere passive preservation of the city as a mummified tourist attraction, or a theme park of itself, paradoxically presages and hastens its death. That said, there's certainly no need to tear down its monuments and replace them with smoke-crested factories in order for the city to start living its own life again, and not just scrape a living off its past. The future of the historical city is a vast topic being played out not just in Venice or Italy, but in the rest of the world too, and Venice even as a prophetic vision of Manhattan can be taken as its supreme symbol. With each passing day it becomes increasingly urgent to ask oneself how every city can meld its symbolic capital with its citizens' civic capital and put this to fruitful use. If this should ever happen in Venice, it could happen everywhere else.

[. . .] In Venice's case, no architect in their right mind could argue against the fact that the city is losing all its inhabitants and that it risks turning into a theme park dotted with second and third homes, hemorrhaging not only its people but also its creative energies, social life, and cultural wealth, humbly reducing itself to a movie set for impatient tourists to quickly wander through. Thus, no architect should ever agree to building anything—whether it's a bridge, a terrace, or a window—that might contribute to the death of the historic city by destroying its uniqueness.

No one who truly claims to defend Venice or other historic cities can force them into a state of mummification and keep them eternally the same, or worse, force them to live in a fake paradise of nostalgia. Such a person should instead consider the city and its architectural works as the living embodiment of its citizens, the men and women who live in Venice, or who would like to live there, but are instead forced to flee it. Such a person should treasure the city's physical body as well as its soul, to think of both its material texture as well as the lifeblood of its inhabitants; to consider architecture as an essential component of the right to the city, which also includes the crucial components of the right to work and the social functions of private property. Yet the right to the city must also allow room for the architect's creativity, and his or her ability to put historical spaces back into use or even enhance them with designs which conform to the city's DNA. If only because a Venice without any historic depth would never have inspired something like Manhattan.

—∿—

Venice's gods are far more demanding than those of other cities, because throughout its history its inhabitants were more varied and productive than those elsewhere, and because the city has faced a more difficult challenge from its surrounding environment. This precious, unique, and difficult city—difficult due to its singular relationship to the Lagoon and the mainland, bucking the trend affecting other cities because it is naturally pedestrian-friendly and devoid of cars—is the ultimate symbol of a city built on a human scale. It both challenges us and asks us the following question: Should we preserve this unique way of dealing with space, or should we abandon it by forcing it to adhere to a lone model that will produce identical cities all over the world?

There's nothing more mainstream and politically correct than praising diversity. Diversity of gender, sexual orientation, religion, culture . . . yet although this diversity is highly prized on an individual level, it doesn't apply to cities, which are now under the yoke of a rampant homogenization. The living embodiment of the historic city and its lifestyle, Venice is the litmus test of the process of dissolving the ancient forma urbis, now reduced to a remnant of its former self. Even the fact that the city is losing its inhabitants, a process hastened by the very institutions set up to prevent it, has an undeclared yet obvious aim: to erase its diversity, reducing public spaces to tourist movie sets. Saving the historic city in Venice (and elsewhere) won't happen simply by reviving memories of the city's past or indulging in the pleasures of the present. Even protesting won't be enough: the only effective move will be reenergizing the active practice of citizenship and exercising the right to the city, to then come up with a plan to preserve its uniqueness and put firm rules into place that not only safeguard its framework and environment, but also prioritize the city's use-value over its exchange-value, emphasizing the social function of property, the right of its citizens to gainful employment, and the right of its youngest to both a home and a future.

[. . .]

A new citizenship pact is necessary today, not just in Venice but everywhere else too, both for families native to their city and those who have come from other places. In Venice's case, this new pact will have to begin from a strong sense of commitment to spur politicians and public institutions to adopt a more creative outlook toward the city, to bring the historic city back to life and gear it toward the future, the means to create a new kind of politics to stem the perverse logic causing the exodus of citizens, and to encourage the young to remain via strong incentives such as tax breaks. It would also mean curbing the rampant proliferation of second homes and the transformation of buildings into nothing more than hotels. It would mean encouraging manufacturing and private enterprise as well as generating opportunities for a wider range of creative jobs. It would mean reunifying the historic city, lagoon, and mainland by differentiating their functions, making more agricultural land available and investing in new fisheries, reutilizing old, vacant buildings, incentivizing research, launching new professional training schemes and apprenticeships and investing in universities, chiefly by making it affordable for students to actually live in the city. It would mean developing new models, analyzing situations, evaluating options, and emphasizing initiatives of a higher caliber (like the universities and the Biennale) and not just enslaving the city to "uncontrollable market forces." It would mean enshrining the right to the city and the common good as our first priority.

If we think of Venice as a paradigm of the historic city, its beauty should also be considered a part of this debate. Beauty, after all, isn't a commodity, but is instead part of our spiritual heritage. We cannot acquiesce to a process where:

> subjectivity turns the beautiful into things—the grove into timber, the images into things that have eyes and do not see, ears and do not hear. And if the ideals cannot be reduced to the block and stones of a wholly explicable [*verständig*] reality they are made into fictions. Any connection with the ideals will then appear as a play without substance, or as dependence upon objects and as superstition. (Hegel, *Faith and Knowledge*, 1802)

Thinking about historic cities also means thinking about human communities, the right to work, and the right to the city. Administrators, developers, and architects must renounce any architecture of oppression and show that nonviolent forms of modernity are attainable.

As for Venetians—as well as anyone else who has a special place for that city in their heart—they have serious responsibilities and crucial tasks ahead of them: to prove that the city's beauty and diversity are not just cumbersome legacies of the past, but an extraordinary gift that allows us to embrace the present and an extraordinary endowment for building and securing the future; to prove that Venice doesn't have to transform itself into Chongqing to survive in this century, and that Venice must in fact be its antithesis. That there is room in this world for a wide variety of urban models, culture, and lifestyles; and that the model produced by Venice over the course of centuries entails for itself a right to citizenship, a right to remain alive in this world both now and for generations to come. Because if Venice dies, it won't be the only thing that dies: the very idea of the city—as an open space where diversity and social life can unfold, as the supreme creation of our civilization, as a commitment to and promise of democracy—will also die with it.

Reading

25

Sze Tsung Nicolás Leong

A History of Erasure (2006)

The major urban transformations occurring in China, accompanied by the relentless erasure of the country's historic past, are put into historical perspective by Sze Tsung Nicolás Leong, an American and British artist who has been photographing urban spaces and construction projects in China since 2002. Leong highlights the successive "erasures and rewritings of the past" that have accompanied the centuries-old history of imperial China and discusses the obliteration of the social and material traditions perpetrated by the Communist regime during the Cultural Revolution. He then focuses on the urban destruction that occurred after the introduction in China of a full-fledged market economy controlled by the state. The destruction has been so swift and extensive that it can only be compared to the effects of warfare. The forces behind these irreversible transformations, according to Leong, are a "powerful government ruling with almost limitless authority" and land "transformed into a means for profit."

History is composed as much with the buildings of a city as it is with the words on a page. The writing of history in built form takes shape as a complex sedimentation of time resulting from a slow, dense accumulation of construction. A culture's development can be read through the layers or previous buildings that together form a geological summary of history. The evidence of decades, generations, and centuries becomes part of the city's daily life, making the experience of the present simultaneous with the past.

As slowly as the writing of history accumulates, it can as rapidly be erased. The erasure of built history can happen unintentionally, as with natural disasters, but also occurs intentionally, as with the destructiveness of warfare, the forcefulness of regimes, or the unpredictability of turns in the economy. In all of these cases, history is forced to take sudden changes in course, and the slow sedimentation of buildings—the

From Sze Tsung Nicolás Leong, "A History of Erasure," in *History Images* (Gottingen: Steidl, 2006), 138–40. Reproduced courtesy of the author.

painstaking accumulation of urban form—is interrupted by their sudden eradication. In the environments we live in, history has the potential to be substantially rewritten.

In China, history has been defined by the successive erasures and rewritings of the past. These alterations of history have occurred when the country has shifted from one highly antithetical, contradictory era to another—from dynasty to dynasty, from imperial rule to communism, from communism to the market economy. Each new era attempts to redefine its relationship to tradition, with the hope of shaping an ideal present legitimized and supported by an idealized and carefully formed past.

For the imperial dynasties, the erasure of the past was a way to enforce the continuation of tradition. Emperors would commission their own official histories, rewriting the history of the past then writing their own history, to reinforce the inevitability of their place in the lineage of their predecessors. This practice was not so different with cities, as emperors destroyed conquered cities and replaced them with new ones. This starting anew established the absoluteness of their power by demonstrating their ability to construct entire environments patterned on and legitimized by the urban forms established by history. For the emperors, the shaping of cities provided a means to enforce an absolute order on society and, ultimately, on history itself.

For the communists, the erasure of the past was a way to establish ideological superiority over tradition. History was the antithesis against which to form a new reality, providing the rationale for discrediting past society and destroying its achievements, both social and material. The past was regarded as an enemy to be defeated, humiliated, and obliterated. In the urban realm, this was first realized by Mao Zedong's destruction of Beijing's Ming-era city gates and walls, and his unrealized wish to destroy the capital's Forbidden City. This attitude was the most extreme during the 1966–76 Cultural Revolution, whose goals were encapsulated by the movement, "Smash the Four Olds"—old ideas, old culture, old customs, and old habits. A new society was called forth in the slogan, "Smash the Old World, Build the New World." Yet the Cultural Revolution's enforcers only had raw ideology, not economic or material resources, to drive their revolution. They vandalized and wrecked cultural artifacts, ruined lives, and dismantled social traditions, but their desire to destroy the old world by razing urban environments did not reach the extent that their slogans demanded. Instead of demolishing cities and replacing them with a new world, the communists let their urban fabrics degenerate into slums. The revolutionaries' disdain of their own history was mostly actualized through the deterioration of their cities.

Ironically, China's current economic revolution is completing the physical destruction of history that was called for during the Cultural Revolution. Today, the erasure of the past is carried out simply because much of the traditional past is no longer relevant to the market economy. Scores of traditional neighborhoods, decayed as a result of poverty and imposed ideology, are now defined by the stale as "dangerous" and "dilapidated." Considered impediments to development, these areas hold little economic value except as potential empty land. The new world aspired to by the Cultural Revolution has arrived in the form of developers bearing names such as "New World" (*Xin Shijie*), and commercial developments suffixed by the phrases "New City" (*Xin*

Cheng) or "Century City" (*Shiji Cheng*). When an area is developed, it is almost always cleared of all traces of the past: buildings, streets, residents. The result is an absence of history, within which the components of China's new cities are built out of nothing: luxury apartments, shopping centers, supermarkets, widened roads, tennis courts, office blocks, parking lots.

The motivation for erasing history is ultimately rooted in the drive to shape and manage society. A principal tool of this drive is the design of cities—an activity that involves demolition as much as construction. For the majority of China's history, the destruction of a diverse past enabled the construction of highly planned, rigid urban spaces that facilitated the establishment and administration of social hierarchies. Through urban planning, governing powers could fit society into a fixed order.

The imperial dynasties planned their cities as monolithic, complete entities reflecting the heavenly order with the palace, which symbolized the emperor as the enforcer of the mandate of heaven, placed in the center of the urban plan. Surrounding and radiating from this center, society was structured according to an established hierarchy into strictly defined classes contained within walled and gridded wards. For the communists, erasure was a tool used to suppress any ideology outside the dominant one, and was a method to fit society into a prescribed way of thinking. They believed that society had to be protected from unwanted influences through strict policing. To ensure order, they destroyed buildings and widened streets to facilitate a military movement, as in the case of Chang'an Jie, the main east-west axis on the northern edge of Tiananmen Square. To ensure unpolluted thought, they defaced or tore down the evidence of past societies, and to ensure productivity, they organized and supervised society through its partitioning into work units. In present-day society, erasure is used as a strategy to generate and accommodate new wealth. As traditional neighborhoods yield to private developments, a new but globally familiar urban pattern emerges, based on spatially delineated polarities of income, contoured by the swells of an engulfing economy: former residents of the urban center are pushed to the fringes of the city because they can no longer afford their former neighborhoods; large-scale gated clusters of commercial housing blocks are segregated from the rest of the city; new buildings are left empty or unfinished because of over-construction.

In the photograph *Chunshu, Xuanwu District, Beijing,* a neighborhood dating from the thirteenth-century Yuan Dynasty, but completed during the Qing Dynasty, waits to be destroyed while its condemned and partially destroyed structures still house the area's remaining residents.[1] *Xihuashi Nanli Dongqu, Chongwen District, Beijing* depicts an area that had been entirely cleared of structures and streets, and replaced with commercial housing blocks that surround one remaining rebuilt traditional structure. The same process of urban clearcutting is seen in *Nanshi, Huangpu District, Shanghai. Old Fengdu I, Chongqing Municipality* shows a town on the banks of the Yangtze, with a history dating from at least the second century BCE, completely destroyed as a result of the construction of the Three Gorges Dam, now considered the largest dam in the world. *New Fengdu, Chongqing Municipality* shows the replacement of Fengdu across the river. *Hefang Jie, Shangcheng District, Hangzhou* is a newly renovated traditional-style tourist area nestled in a city once chronicled by Marco Polo as the most beautiful and magnificent in the world, but later destroyed by the Taiping Rebellion of 1861–63. *Xinjiekou, Xuanwu District, Nanjing* portrays the dismantling of China's historical sedimentation by revealing three periods of China's history in varying conditions, layered one on top of another like geological strata: the ruins of houses dating from the imperial period occupy the foreground, partially demolished housing blocks from the socialist period stretch across the middle ground, and new office and residential towers from the latest, capitalist period preside high over the remains of the former two.

Caught in the tenuous period after the end of one history and at the start of another, these landscapes parallel the experience of cities in other locations and other times that have witnessed sudden turns in the writing of their built histories: the extensive reconfiguration of mid-nineteenth century Paris, where wide strips of the city were demolished to create boulevards as symbols of an emperor's command over a city, the wartime reduction to rubble of European cities, where centuries of history disappeared within the span of a few years, the listless spaces resulting from the postwar suburban attenuation of American cities, which were the outcome of efforts to prepare the environment for a new economy. In China, the forces behind the transformation of its cities are similar: a powerful government ruling with almost limitless authority, seeking to realize its vision of an urban order; the sweeping destruction of historic urban areas on a scale and suddenness equal to warfare; and an abrupt change in the economy having substantial repercussions on the environment as land is transformed into a means for profit. It is the confluence of these three forces that makes China's current erasure of the past so swift and extensive.

Notes

1. [Photographs mentioned in this paragraph are not included in the reading.—Ed.]

Part III

Visual Summary: Reactions to the Transformation of Traditional Cities: Three Critical Ruptures

Marco Secchi, *Cruise Ships in Venice*, 2017.

Approximately five hundred cruise ships dock in Venice annually, disgorging roughly 1.4 million tourists, in addition to more than 22 million others who visit the city every year. The number of tourists who arrive in Venice each day exceeds its total population, reduced to 54,000 from 120,000 fifty years ago. While many object to the ships' visual impact, water displacement, and engine pollution (equal to the exhaust from more than 7 million cars), proponents of unrestrained tourism argue that the 1.5 billion euros per year in tourism revenue are essential to the local economy. The case of Venice exemplifies the dilemmas and risks many historic cities face today—that of becoming a museum and a theme park, besieged by tourists, deserted by residents.

Foundation works of La Cité fire station. Paris (IVth arrondissement), 1864–65.
Photograph by Pierre-Ambroise Richebourg (1820–1872).

PLATE III.1

Victor Hugo (reading 17) lamented that "vandalism flourishes and prospers before our eyes," as he witnessed the destruction of Paris's cherished places and monuments. "The hammer that mutilates the face of the country must be stopped," he wrote. However, within twenty short years, Baron Haussmann and Emperor Napoleon III completely transformed the face of medieval Paris. Victor Hugo's warnings in 1837 had become all too real, and irreversible.

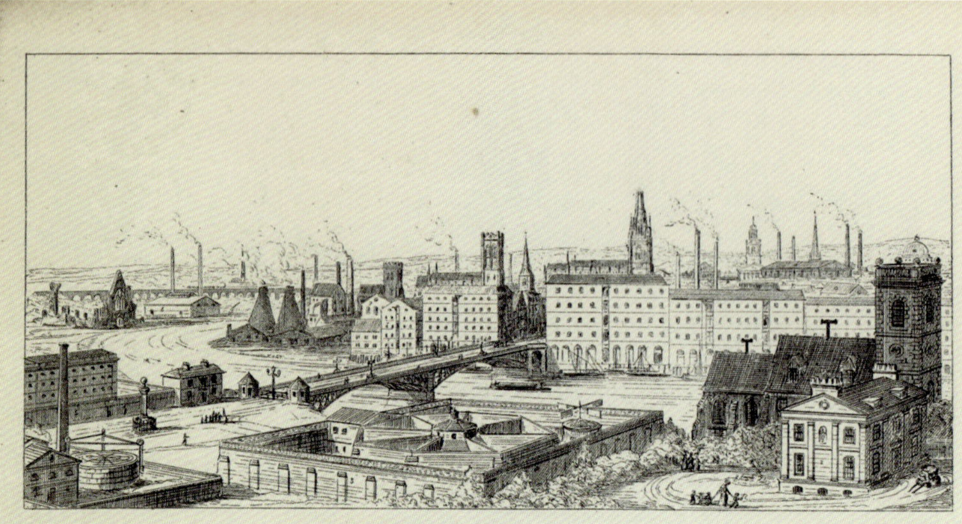

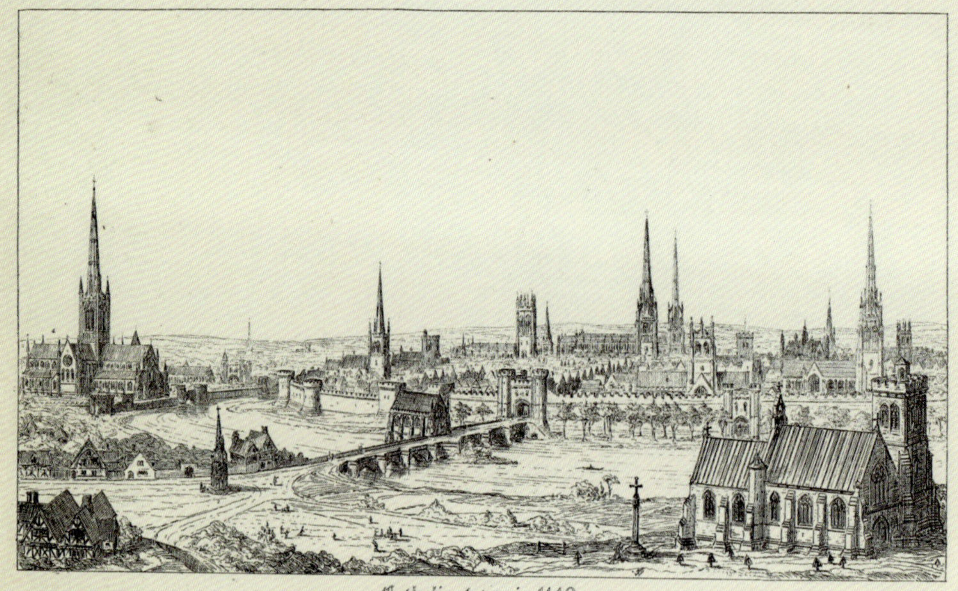

Catholic town in 1440 – This same town in 1840. Drawings by Augustus Pugin, published in 1898.

Watercolor (?), *Ca d'Oro*, by John Ruskin, 1845.

PLATES III.2 AND III.3

Augustus Pugin's two drawings (left), comparing an idyllic English medieval town with its later industrial-age self, where belching smokestacks outnumber bell towers, vividly reveal the despair of some of the most sensitive spirits of the time at how quickly and overwhelmingly the Industrial Revolution was transforming the country's traditional cityscapes.

John Ruskin (reading 18), in his Crystal Palace speech of 1851, was appalled by the "indulgences of magnificence" displayed in the new urban landscape, which founded "all glory upon ruin and [prefaced] all progress with obliteration."

Wonderful City, Building for a Piazza. Painting by Virgilio Marchi, 1919.

PLATE III.4

Writers and artists of the Italian Futurist movement in the early decades of the twentieth century repudiated the past and urged their followers to embrace unconditionally the modern age, often with daring and violent overtones. Filippo Tommaso Marinetti (reading 19) imagined great roads built over the canals of Venice, crisscrossed by trains, streetcars, and automobiles, similar to the new city imagined by Virgilio Marchi in 1919. Marinetti had stern words for lovers of the past: "Throw yourselves down, supine, one upon the other, like sacks of sand to build a bastion at the border, while we prepare a great and strong Venice, with industry, commerce, and military might in the Adriatic, the great Italian sea!"

Part III

VISUAL SUMMARY

Nineteenth-century view of the dome of Dresden's famed Frauenkirche within its city context by Carl August Richter, 1824.

View of Dresden following World War II bombing of the city. Photo by Richard Peter, 1945.

Sketch of central Paris from Le Corbusier's *Plan Voisin*, 1925.

The city of Homs, Syria, in 2014, following cessation of fighting between rebels and government forces.

PLATES III.5, III.6, III.7, AND III.8

Robert Bevan (reading 20) suggests that "cultural cleansing" is a complement to ethnic cleansing, where the destruction of architecture is the means to perpetrate cultural eradication. For Bevan, buildings are "caches of historical memory," which are all too fragile in the face of warfare, as illustrated by these heartbreaking images of Dresden, Germany, and Homs, Syria. Dresden's rich historic heritage—rendered in this unusual early nineteenth-century fish-eye lens view—was obliterated by aerial bombing during World War II. Similarly, the eradication of cultural memory that recently occurred in Homs is a reminder that cultural cleansing remains rampant in the twenty-first century. Le Corbusier's iconic 1925 proposal for the redevelopment of central Paris, known as the Plan Voisin, is a reminder that cultural cleansing can also occur through forms of ideological iconoclasm, often justified as progress for benign social purposes. There were several reasons Le Corbusier's vision of central Paris, complete with high-rise *machines-à-habiter,* was never implemented. If it had been, one would be hard-pressed today to call it "benign."

Part III

VISUAL SUMMARY

Cover of a 1959 brochure advertising the Lower Manhattan Expressway in New York City proposed—but never built—by the urban planner Robert Moses.

The Harbor and Hollywood Freeways under construction in downtown Los Angeles, 1953.

Building boom in Bucharest, Romania, 1989. Photo by Jerome De Perlinghi.

PLATES III.9 AND III.10

Jane Jacobs (reading 21) was moved to write, protest, and act against the wanton destruction of neighborhoods in New York as a result of Robert Moses's (1888–1981) large-scale urban renewal projects built during his tenure as the New York City Parks Commissioner. These images—one a bird's-eye view of Moses's vision for the Lower Manhattan Expressway of 1959 (never built) and the other an aerial photograph of the actual construction in 1953 of the Los Angeles Harbor Freeway—are reminders of what Jacobs found so abhorrent about the major redevelopment schemes implemented in U.S. cities from the 1930s to the 1960s: they ignored "the (pedestrian) street" as "the significant unit" of the neighborhood, which is indispensable for both the economic and the social life of the city. She had harsh words for "planners . . . [who have] a graphic picture of downtown that tells [them] little of significance and much that is misleading." Jacobs's warnings about the myopia of many urban planners are sadly still relevant today, decades after her words were published.

PLATE III.11

This haunting photograph of Bucharest, Romania, taken two weeks after the execution of the Socialist dictator Nicolae Ceauşescu, shows the outcome of Ceauşescu's radical interventions that between 1997 and 1989 led to the demolition of large portions of historic Bucharest and other smaller cities in the country. Ceauşescu obliterated the past by ruthlessly imposing an alien landscape of collectivized, high-rise residential buildings set amid new, oversized boulevards that still convey a sense of staged emptiness and alienation. As lamented by the historian Dinu Giurescu (reading 22), "Another urban world has emerged opposite the earlier one, with almost no connection to the past." This profound disconnect between past and present is symptomatic of the urban ruptures that occurred in Europe and elsewhere during the twentieth century in a misguided and delusional attempt to "modernize" historic settings.

Part III

VISUAL SUMMARY

Building in poor condition in Cairo, Egypt. Photo by Francesco Siravo, circa 2004.

Historic building with tangle of electrical wires, Lahore, Pakistan. Photo by Francesco Siravo, circa 2008.

PLATES III.12 AND III.13

Mona Serageldin (reading 23) suggests that "cities are in a perpetual state of crisis management as they struggle to confront multispeed development, exclusion, and violence." This is particularly true in the centuries-old cities of the developing world where these unprecedented phenomena often result in the relentless and irreversible "degradation of urban fabric." In these images from Cairo (pl. III.12) and Lahore (pl. III.13)—cities distinguished for their monuments and traditional architecture—the combination of lack of maintenance and uncontrolled urban development is vividly manifest in the poor condition of historic structures, often on the verge of collapse, and in the haphazard and disorderly installation of modern infrastructure.

Venice Water Town, Hangzhou, China. Photo by Bianca Bosker, circa 2012.

Proposed design for Palais Lumière, Venice, circa 2013. Photo by Splash News / Alamy Stock Photo.

PLATES III.14 AND III.15

Salvatore Settis (reading 24) laments that Venice has largely followed the model of an "embalmed city," a "Disneyland of the Lagoon," and a city "hemorrhaging not only its people but also its creative energies, social life and cultural wealth." The brand of Venice-as-theme-park has been marketed by developers globally, including in China, where a "Venice Water Town" has been built in Hangzhou (pl. III.14). Venice's city views can also be commercialized, as in the high-rise tower proposed by Pierre Cardin in 2012 in the former industrial area of Porto Marghera (pl. III. 15, Palais Lumière). That plan was shelved in 2015 as a result of public criticism and lack of funding. Today, because of its uniqueness and extraordinary beauty, the traditional fabric of Venice struggles to survive and thrive under the current economic model based on mass tourism and unrestrained commercial development.

Part III

VISUAL SUMMARY

A building sits on its own island in Chongqing Municipality, China, 2007. The home owner refused to sell to a developer, who proceeded with construction around the site.

Bird's-eye view of Beijing in 1958, showing new buildings in the capital. Photo by Li Jilu.

Neon-lit pubs and bars in the French Quarter of downtown New Orleans, 2015.

PLATES III.16 AND III.17

These images of urban destruction in China, 1958 to the present, illustrate the words of the photographer Sze Tsung Nicolás Leong (reading 25): "For the emperors, the shaping of new cities was a means to enforce an absolute order. . . . For the communists, the erasure of the past was a way to establish ideological superiority over tradition . . . [and] today, erasure of the past is carried out simply because much of the traditional past is no longer relevant to the market economy." The so-called Nail House (above left)—the last remaining historic structure amid the burgeoning new construction—is a reminder of often-unsuccessful opposition in the face of heavy political and economic power. Plate III.17 (left) shows the rapidly changing morphology of Beijing during the first decade of the People's Republic, when the city wall had not yet been eradicated on the orders of Mao Zedong.

PLATE III.18

Bourbon Street, in New Orleans, Louisiana, has become a caricature of the "French colonial" presence in the Vieux Carré neighborhood. Especially during Mardi Gras, shown here, hordes of tourists flock to this area, which has been transformed into a virtual theme park. Walt Disney imitated Bourbon Street as one of the components of his original Disneyland. As mass tourism becomes more prevalent in the twenty-first century, historic neighborhoods like Bourbon Street face increasing pressures by investors and myopic city administrators to become attractive but inauthentic lures for tourist dollars.

MONTE
CITORIO
Piaz.Colonna
PIAZZA DI PIETRA
PANTEON
S. Ignazio
FONTANA DI TREVI
Cortile della Panateria
Piazza di
Monte Cav
MINERVA
COLLEGIO ROMANO
PIAZZA DI SCIARRA
S. Marcello
Piaz.della
Pilotta
SS Apostoli
Palazzo
Panfilj
PALAZZO
COLONNA
PALAZ ALTIERI
GESU
Pal. di
Venezia
PIAZZA DI VENEZIA
S. Marco
S. Silvestro
COLON.TRAJANA
SPIRITO SANTO
CAMPIDOGLIO
TOR DE
CONTI
IX

Part IV

Reading the Historic City

A central question of this volume is how one should read the historic city in the context of conserving it. In part IV authors from different cultural contexts grapple with the challenge of linking physical form (i.e., architecture and associated urban space) with social dynamics (i.e., people) related to historic urban neighborhoods and the city writ large. The reading of the city thus entails fully documenting it, understanding its historic and social significance, and ultimately conserving that significance to the maximum possible extent. Many of the readings that follow roughly cluster around two time periods: (1) the mid-1960s to the late 1970s, when several architects, planners, and urban designers (primarily but not exclusively in Western Europe) began to react against modernist assumptions about design without careful concern for historic urban contexts, instead preferring to be creative with what we earlier called the tabula rasa; and (2) the late 1990s to the present, when many astute theorists and practitioners concerned with the global implications of urban change at both the macro- and the microlevel began appropriately to link so-called Western ideas of urban history and the conservation of the urban built environment to a broader range of cultural contexts. We have attempted here to lend proper credence to both "time clusters."

Essentially, many of the authors whose work is presented below find themselves in the conceptual fields of what is sometimes called urban semiotics and urban morphology. As Suzanne Keller wrote in a review of *The City and the Sign,* "Urban semiotics involves the exploration of physical objects and their endowed meanings as mediated through a universe of signs and the symbols they evoke and convey."[1] Advocates of urban semiotics build on the foundational work of Kevin Lynch (*The Image of the City*, 1960), Umberto Eco (*A Theory of Semiotics*, 1976), Roland Barthes (*Mythologies*, 1957; *L'Empire des signes*, 1970; *The Eiffel Tower and Other Mythologies*, 1979), Henri Lefebvre (*The Production of Space*, French ed. 1974, English ed. 1991), and David Harvey (*The Urban Experience*, 1989; *Paris, Capital of Modernity*, 2003), among others. As Anne Vernez Moudon writes in reading 28, "Urban morphology is the study of the

Campo Marzio, central Rome, 1748. Detail. See p. 275.

city as human habitat. Ethnographer Lévi-Strauss . . . described the city as 'the most complex of human interventions, . . . at the confluence of nature and artifact'. Thus, urban morphologists analyze a city's evolution from its formative years to its subsequent transformations, identifying and dissecting its various components. . . . [They] focus on the tangible results of social and economic forces: they study the outcomes of ideas and intentions as they take shape on the ground and mould our cities."

The readings in this part are not intended to encapsulate the still-developing fields of urban semiotics and urban morphology, an impossible task in the space permitted. Instead, we have sought to represent a variety of approaches to the challenges of reading cities that will lead readers of this volume to explore them more deeply. Although most literature associated with urban form stems from European roots—as will be clear from Moudon's reading and several of the other readings selected for this part—much remains to be done regarding the notion of reading historic places outside a Eurocentric conceptual terrain. Hence, as Zeynep Çelik reminds us in reading 26, even though it is critical to reach beyond a Western perspective (recognizing the several connotations of "Western") and "introduce a useful category [i.e., non-Western] that hitherto was generally omitted from the discourse," we should be careful not to create "an attendant train of charged meanings, collapsing most of the world into homogeneity, signifying binary oppositions, and defining by negation." Çelik also reminds us that much of the "new scholarship . . . on non-Western cities . . . is interdisciplinary and brings together methodology and data from various fields." As an astute scholar of Ottoman Empire urbanism, she critiques the notion of the "Islamic city," linking it to the broader, macrolevel discourse related to Orientalism and scrutinizing ways in which a range of authors have read it. As she asserts, "The cities themselves . . . do not stand isolated but are increasingly anchored by the new scholarship to a global framework, triggering questions that challenge the provinciality of former mind-sets." She also links her analysis to the erstwhile, "persistent monopolization of Modernism by 'Western' cultures," citing Marshall Berman's perceptive analysis of "a wide field of intertwined modernities."[2] More recent scholarship has enriched this point even further.[3]

Çelik also pays homage to the architectural historian Sir John Summerson, whose essay "Urban Forms," which appeared in a 1963 edited volume devoted to the historian and the city, is included here. In reading 27, Summerson urges careful inquiry into "the whole physical mass of marble, bricks and mortar, steel and concrete, tarmac and rubble, metal conduits and rails—the total artefact." He asserts that "the tragedy of the modern city is that the processes of creation and recreation have been delegated not to the most responsible but often to the least responsible sections of the community. . . . The growth of cities, the forms into which they grow, the acceptability of those forms by the citizens and . . . the changes in acceptability which these forms undergo . . . are of the very essence of city life and we understand very little about them."

Anne Vernez Moudon's article in the inaugural issue of the journal *Urban Morphology* (1997) explains—more than thirty years after Summerson's lament—that several scholars, architects, and urban designers implicitly embraced Summerson's challenge to "understand the changes in urban forms." She contextualizes the work of three relatively independent "schools of urban morphology"—in England, Italy, and France—that came together following the groundbreaking work of two morphologists, M. R. G. Conzen, a German émigré to the United Kingdom in 1933, and Saverio Muratori (1910–1973), one of whose mentors was Gustavo Giovannoni, whose work is included in part V. As she looks back on these schools, she also attends to her contemporary milieu and discusses how the disparate attempts to read the city coalesced into the International Seminar on Urban Form (ISUF), which persists to the present day and continues to publish *Urban Morphology*. Moudon cogently summarizes the research arising from these schools and from the mentoring roles of Conzen and Muratori that spawned them. Conzen's work—some related to his study of the Northumbrian market town Alnwick and other more synthetic in nature—was written and published in English.[4] Because much of Muratori's work remains untranslated from Italian, it is less well known, although that has been changing recently.[5] In the 1950s, as Muratori elaborated on Giovannoni's example and developed his own theories for an "operative history" (*storia operante*) by studying the urban histories of Venice and Rome, he confronted the complexities of inserting new architecture in multilayered, historic urban fabric. However, despite his own design interventions in Bologna, Rome, and Venice in the 1950s, Muratori never truly resolved the dilemma of how to stitch disparate, new works of architecture into the rich tissue of Italian cities. Thus it remained for Muratori's architectural disciples to build on Muratori's foundation. Chief among them was Gianfranco Caniggia, who developed Muratori's ideas of type, typology, structure, tissue, series, and seriality. Excerpts below from one of Caniggia's 1981 essays reflect this development. Caniggia also elaborated a "processual typology" to help determine how to reuse historic buildings in Italian urban contexts. Moudon explains in her article that "the Italian contribution that was most instrumental in linking the three main schools of urban morphology . . . was the rehabilitation programme of Bologna's historic centre—for which Caniggia was a consultant." However, Bologna's initiative was chiefly coordinated by Pierluigi Cervellati, discussed more fully in part V.

Three French architects in the 1970s, Philippe Panerai, Jean Castex, and Jean-Charles Depaule (reading 29), teaching at the School of Architecture in Versailles, were heavily influenced by what some have called "the Italian Typomorphological School."[6] Ivor Samuels, responsible for the English edition (2003) of Panerai, Castex, and Depaule's influential *Formes urbaines de l'îlot à la barre* (1977), summarized three of the authors' most fundamental contributions to architectural and urban design: "First, [the book] acknowledged the importance of the detailed physical design of our environment in the enabling of populations[,] . . . [using] scaled plans and sections of urban tissues, not diagrams. . . . Secondly, it focuses on the connection between the form of cities and their architecture – especially with respect to ordinary buildings. . . . Thirdly, it brings a genuinely European-wide vision to the topic, . . . [tracking] the remarkable interchange between [Henrik Petrus] Berlage, [Raymond] Unwin, and [Ernest] May and how they were all linked by a common experience."[7] Samuels also explains that prior to this important architectural work by Panerai, Castex, and Depaule, "French town planning was seen . . . as associated to the crude sketches of master plans, general layouts and growth corridors, . . . deviating the treatment of all spatial projects towards an abstract and imprecise dimension."[8] The authors defined "urban tissue [as] the superimposition of several structures acting at different scales . . . [and as] the culminating point of three logical systems: the logic of roads . . . , plot subdivisions . . . and buildings that contain different activities. The old cities, in their own way and each with different modes, ensure the coherence of the tissue." They conclude that we must "come back to this forgotten lesson of the old cities and to the ease of everyday life that they enabled."

Gordon Cullen, a contemporary of Muratori and Caniggia (but working independently in the United Kingdom, as well as in India in 1960), also grappled with how to read and understand the rich dynamics of historic cities. His seminal work, *Townscape* (1961; also *The Concise Townscape*, 1971), parts of which are presented in reading 30, reflect Cullen's concern for "motion (serial vision), position (here and there), and content (this and that)" as he attempts to provide visual coherence and a sense of wonder, surprise, and discovery amid what might at first seem to be a chaotic mix of buildings, streets, and spaces. Cullen asserts that "it is easy to see how the whole city becomes a plastic experience, a journey through pressures and vacuums, a sequence of exposures and enclosures, of constraint and relief." He explains that "a city is more than the sum of its inhabitants. It has the power to generate a surplus of amenity, which is one reason why people like to live in communities rather than in isolation." For Cullen, reading the city calls for feeling its motion, experiencing its surprise, and cohering its vernacular unity.

The Danish urban designer Jan Gehl (reading 31), more of a scholar of history than Cullen, makes similar points about the quality and importance of well-conceived public space. In his book *Life between Buildings: Using Public Space* (1971), Gehl suggests, "With regard to form, seemingly great variations exist between the different city models, especially from an art-historical point of view, yet in reality only two noteworthy radical developments in connection with . . . urban planning ideologies and outdoor activities have occurred: one in relation to the Renaissance and the other in relation to the modern functionalism movement."[9] He explains that "with the exception of a small group of planned late-medieval colonial cities, the [European] cities that grew up in the period from around AD 500 to AD 1500 were not planned in the true sense. . . . [They] evolved through a process that often took hundreds of years, because this slow process permitted continual adjustment and adaptation of the physical environment to the city functions. . . . The result of this process . . . was urban space that even today offers extremely good conditions for life between buildings."[10] In *Cities for People*, Gehl underscores that planners must coordinate their work at three scales; the city writ large, the city as a series of development zones, and the city as experienced at "the small scale, the human landscape."

In another reading focusing on a European cultural context—from the German *Handbuch Städtebauliche Denkmalpflege* (2013; Handbook of Urban Heritage Preservation), edited by Volkmar Eidloth, Gerhard Ongyerth, and Heinrich Walgern (reading 32)—we return to a point suggested near the beginning of this introduction, "systematic preservation of urban heritage emerged in the 1970s": "The interests of historic preservation had to be presented as spatially relevant to residential and cultural landscapes embedded in the contexts of local and national history in order to be recognized and appropriately adhered to by countless new partners: city planners, local politicians, and not least of all, the inhabitants. For the first time, preservationists had to actively participate over the long term in the evolution of planning and its goals." As the editors note in linking initiatives from the 1970s to current urban preservation practice in Germany, "Historical meaning . . . is not only exemplified in art historical contexts, but also comprises technological, economic, or social history, and the history of habitation. It is manifested not only by individual objects, but also in the stratified relationships of monuments, in ensembles of urban and rural monuments, or in cultural landscapes." Furthermore, they write, "factually sound and historically grounded analysis is indispensable: it is capable of providing certainty when demanding preservation while at the same time illuminating where there is room for development." The editors underscore the importance of cartographic analysis to urban heritage preservation, and they emphasize that "indispensable contributions to urban heritage preservation come above all from the history of urban development understood as an architectural history of the city based on archaeology of the city center and building research, and in which it has been rooted since the 1970s."

A key concept from the German context is "monument topography[, which is] . . . classified between a monument inventory and the more in depth scholarly treatment of a survey." Essentially, then, the reading of the city becomes linked to its proper documentation: "The goal of documentation is systematic structuring of information [consisting of] documents like texts, maps/plans, and photographs . . . utilized through description, registration, and cataloging . . . . Comprehensive and irreplaceable as a record of loss in archaeological preservation, [documentation for historic preservation] is deliberately carried out in the planning context and at all stages."

The final two readings in this part—dealing with cities in Japan and Malaysia—reflect ways in which concerns for urban form and space should be linked not only to clearer understandings about urban history but also to the practical implications of utilizing that history as a basis for creating improved, more sustainable urban places. These implications are discussed in greater detail later in this volume, but they also emerge here. In reading 33, Jinnai Hidenobu, reflecting on his native "superb city," Tokyo, laments that "the present-day citizens . . . are discarding the legacy [of the original urban planning of Edo] in the name of functionality and efficiency. We are still obsessed by the illusion of modern city planning. But if there had been no castle-town of Edo on the site of Tokyo and if we had had to build a modern city from a *tabula rasa*, we would have produced a desiccated city devoid of any flavor or expression, one that lacked coherence and failed to carry out even elementary functions." However, he asserts that "by reading the city, we may be able to bring home to ourselves the historical structure of Edo, which we tend to think of as unrelated to present-day Tokyo." Hidenobu suggests that "reconsideration of familiar urban spaces and cityscapes, which places the problems of the city and its environment within the dimensions of ordinary living, should play a major role in promoting the participation of the people of Tokyo in making their own city."

The key linkage between appropriate recognition—or careful reading of the historic urban landscape—and protection or conservation of that landscape is also at the heart of Janet Pillai's (2013) study of cultural mapping. Pillai (reading 34) begins by lamenting that all too often, "government planners and planning institutions in Asia remain prone to ignoring both cultural context and community, resulting in the creation of spaces that are often inappropriate for local cultural use." Instead, she urges more integrative, holistic "cultural planning," which "encourages policymakers to respond to local needs, aspirations and perceptions of place. . . . Rather than viewing culture as an obstruction to development, it utilizes culture as a resource." She then stresses, by summarizing case studies in Malaysia where cultural mapping has been done, that "the complex ecology that sustains human settlements arises from the interlocking relationship between people, place and use [and that] this interconnectedness . . . is created and mediated through the process of cultural adaptation and interaction between man and environment over time."

These nine readings, then, stress the crucial importance of reading the city as an historic organism that—through its buildings, spaces, and places—is a palimpsest that reflects cultural dynamics over time. The understanding of this complex organism, these authors suggest, is fundamental before new layers of change are created by architects, planners, or other decision makers.

Notes

1. Suzanne Keller, "Review of *The City and the Sign: An Introduction to Urban Semiotics*, edited by Mark Gottdiener and Alexander Lagopoulos; New York: Columbia University Press, 1986," *Contemporary Sociology* 17, no. 3 (May 1988): 346.
2. Marshall Berman, *All That Is Solid Melts into Air: The Experience of Modernity* (New York: Penguin, 1988), 346.
3. See, e.g., William S. W. Lim and Jiat-Hwee Chang, eds., *Non West Modernist Past: On Architecture and Modernities* (Singapore: AA Asia and Asian Urban Lab, 2011); and many analyses in *Newsletters* from the International Institute of Asian Studies (particularly research related to its important Urban Knowledge Network Asia), University of Leiden, Netherlands.
4. See M. R. G. Conzen, *Alnwick, Northumberland: A Study in Town Plan Analysis*, Publication no. 27 (London: Institute of British Geographers, 1960; 2nd rev. ed., 1969); J. W. R. Whitehand, ed., *The Urban Landscape: Historical Development and Management: Papers by M. R. G. Conzen*, Institute of British Geographers Special Publication no.13 (London: Academic Press, 1981); Michael P. Conzen, ed.,*Thinking about Urban Form: Papers on Urban Morphology, 1932–1998 / M. R. G. Conzen* (London: Peter Lang, 2004); and J. W. R. Whitehand, "British Urban Morphology: The Conzenian Tradition," *Urban Morphology*, 5, no. 2 (2001): 103–9.
5. See, e.g., Steven Semes, *The Future of the Past: A Conservation Ethic for Architecture, Urbanism and Historic Preservation* (New York: Norton, 2009); Francesco Bandarin and Ron Van Oers, eds., *The Historic Urban Landscape: Managing Heritage in an Urban Century* (Chichester: Wiley-Blackwell, 2012); Giancarlo Cataldi, "Designing in Stages: Theory and Design in the Typological Concept of the Italian School of Saverio Muratori," in *Typological Process and Design Theory*, ed. Attilio Petruccioli (Cambridge, MA: Aga Khan Program for Islamic Architecture at Harvard University and Massachusetts Institute of Technology, 1998), 35–55; Marco Maretto, *Saverio Muratori: Il progetto della città* (Milan: FrancoAngeli, 2012); and Jean Castex, "The City as the Only Model: A Critical Study, a Century after Muratori's Birth," in *Saverio Muratori Architetto,*

a cento anni dalla nascità, ed. Giancarlo Cataldi (Florence: Aion, 2013), 188–95.

6. Michael Darin, "The Study of Urban Form in France," *Urban Morphology* 2, no. 2 (1998): 63–76.
7. As Samuels explains in his introduction, Berlage (1856–1934), an important Dutch architect; Unwin (1863–1940), a highly unfluential British planner and the author of *Town Planning in Practice* (1909); and May (1886–1970), a German planner whose key work ranged from Frankfurt to the Soviet Union and Kenya, at one time worked in the same office.
8. For this final point, Samuels quotes Manuel de Sola-Morales, who wrote the foreword to the Spanish translation of Panerai et al.'s *Urban Forms* in 1977.
9. Jan Gehl, *Life between Buildings: Using Public Space* (Washington, DC: Island Press, 2011), 39.
10. Ibid., 41.

Reading

26

Zeynep Çelik

New Approaches to the "Non-Western" City (1999)

Zeynep Çelik, an architectural and urban historian who was born in Turkey but has taught for many years at the New Jersey Institute of Technology, has focused for much of her career on investigating Istanbul, the Ottoman Empire, and orientalism. One of her seminal works, Empire, Architecture, and the City: French-Ottoman Encounters, 1830–1914 (2008)*, reflects her expertise in the cross-cultural dimensions of historic Mediterranean urbanism. In the reading below, she examines the implications of accepting too simplistically the labels "Western" and "non-Western" in the reading of historic cities.*

The umbrella term "non-Western" has settled comfortably into the current lexicon of architectural and urban history. While introducing a useful category that hitherto was generally omitted from the discourse, it comes with an attendant train of charged meanings, collapsing most of the world into homogeneity, signifying binary oppositions, and defining by negation. It thus perpetuates a hierarchical order with its origins in nineteenth-century European scholarship—a topic that has been scrutinized from different perspectives in various disciplines ever since the publication of Edward Said's *Orientalism* (1978). The post-*Orientalism* discourse has produced its own disputed history with significant implications for architectural and urban history. The resulting intellectual climate created by a broad-based cultural critique (and embodied in the problematic revealed by the now-inevitable term "non-Western") has been instrumental in shaping a number of intriguing contributions to urban history.

[. . .] A noteworthy consequence of the methodological and theoretical convergence with the new writing on "Western" urban history is the gradual reversal of the isolated position of "non-Western" cities as exotic case studies. They are increasingly situated within the context of the broader discourse—a key issue I will come back to.

From Zeynep Çelik, "New Approaches to the 'Non-Western' City," *Journal of the Society of Architectural Historians*, Special Issue "Architectural History 1999/2000," 58, no. 3 (1999): 374–81.

The new scholarship on "non-Western" cities is hence interlocked into venues of urban history in general. Yet, the definition of urban history is not a settled matter and fluctuates significantly depending on the perspective from which it is viewed. [. . .]

[. . .]

In order to bring some restriction to the scope the term "non-Western" implies, I will focus in this essay on the "Islamic City," albeit another highly problematic concept that has been in existence since the 1920s.[1] Measured against the sociocultural norms of the Roman Empire, deemed to represent the ultimate model in the Mediterranean basin, Islamic society was historically understood as static and characterized by the strict separation of the urban dwellers from nomads. Historians saw the "Islamic city" solely as the product of the religion. They attributed to it a fixed physical pattern, defined by the separation of residential and commercial sections, irregular street networks, and a characteristic repertoire of public buildings, namely mosques, souks, and baths. The "Islamic city" formula, thus developed initially by French scholars with implicit reference to North African cities (most prominently Tunis and Fez), and reiterated and consolidated over the next four decades, came under attack from the 1960s on.

[. . .]

Among the revisionist literature, Janet Abu-Lughod's widely acclaimed articles, "The Islamic City—Historic Myth, Islamic Essence, and Contemporary Relevance," published in the *International Journal of Middle Eastern Studies* (May 1987), should be singled out. Abu-Lughod crystallized a range of problems imbued in the concept that have been tackled by scholars sporadically, and synthesized them into a forceful argument. She thus started out by deconstructing the reductive "Islamic city" model of Orientalist scholarship. Abu-Lughod then argued that there were, nevertheless, threads that bound the cities throughout the world of Islam and distinguished among them patterns of everyday life, gendered spaces, and segregation of public and private realms. They were brought about primarily by the Islamic legal and political systems, she maintained, but also by other factors, such as a technology of production and a system of social organization.

The debate on the "Islamic city" continues on the theoretical level, unraveling the fallacies of Orientalist scholarship in abstract terms that lack historic specificity and producing along the way something similar to the genealogy of the "Islamic city" formula. While the reiteration of the critique is useful in dismantling the authority of the formula, the real challenge to its limitations comes from focused studies. [. . .]

—ꟿ—

Today, a more common tendency is to go beyound the academic conventions that valorized research on only the "pure" and "uncontaminated" epochs of Islam. As scholars adopt a more comprehensive view of history, they consider all periods worthy of study. In this light, cities throughout the Ottoman empire are subject to newfound attention. A pioneer work on the Ottoman period is André Raymond's *The Great Arab Cities in the 16th–18th Centuries*.[2] Arguing against the common perception of the Ottoman era as one of decline with regard to urban life, Raymond shows that Arab cities that stretched from Iraq to Algeria underwent a dynamic urban progress. Their populations increased dramatically during these 200 years, trade reached an unprecedented scale due to the creation of an enormous market, and construction activity was rampant. [. . .]

The nineteenth century also features prominently in current literature. Estimated as the ultimate period of degeneration, it had traditionally been shunned by scholars of Islamic civilization. It thus had entered the discourse only sporadically to explain the decline against the background of a powerful Europe and its disabling hegemony that extended from political to technical to cultural fields. According to this viewpoint, modernity belonged only to the "advanced" world and the attempts to take part in the project resulted only in dim mimicry. In contrast, the new scholarship defines this time period as one of dynamism and productive cross-cultural exchange, albeit within the parameters of an unequal power structure.

—∾—

Twentieth-century Modernism also becomes a more entangled phenomenon when the boundaries are redrawn to include "non-Western" cities and when national identity is associated with a modern image. A new wave of scholars are now reading the nationalist penchant for the modern against the background of "Islamic" fabrics. Their nuanced research exposes unforeseen resistances and contestations that transform the spatial and social structure of cities. [. . .]

Finally, focus on colonial urbanism brought an unconventional perspective into the "Islamic city," and French colonial interventions to North African cities emerged as a prolific area. The urban-design policies carefully devised for the occupied territories called for a dual structure that underlined the difference between the colonizer and the colonized, separated them from each other, and aimed to isolate the medinas into controlled zones of subjugation. By the 1930s, the principles were so clear-cut that they could be formulated into a list.[3] As such, French colonial cities gave urban historians interested in the relationship between space and power seemingly crystalline case studies. Nevertheless, each one proved to be highly complicated due to its own specific conditions, and attempts to read their individual complexities revealed much about the dynamics of colonialism and the interchange between cultures, as well as the spatial and social character of the "Islamic" cities. The diversity of issues within the greater colonial agenda comes across in recent books on the cities of Morocco and Algeria (fig. 1).[4]

From the methodological point of view, colonial cities offer an unusual potential: as sites of cultural confrontation and exchange, they call for analyses of the same phenomenon from different perspectives, thereby enabling shifting readings of urban forms and the associated meanings. Furthermore, the increasing awareness of urban-design policies and principles in the colonies enables new readings of the metropoles. Once historians acknowledge the interconnected nature of urban interventions, the piercing of straight arteries in the densely built fabric of Algiers immediately following the French conquest cannot be excluded from the experiments that served as precedents to Haussmann's operations in Paris. Similarly, with a firm understanding of the scale and

Fig. 1. Aerial photograph of Algiers from 1935, showing the juncture of the casbah (*on the right*) and the French quarters (*on the left*), as well as the colonial interventions to the lower part of the casbah, from Zeynep Çelik, *Urban Forms and Colonial Confrontations* (Berkeley, 1997).

content of the modernist experiments in colonial cities (Morocco is the most extensively documented), Marshal Lyautey's famous statement about the colonies as laboratories of Modernism comes under new light, urging historians to rethink the Modern Movement in a broader and more nuanced framework.

There is no distinguishing methodological trait that separates "non-Western" urban history from "Western" urban history. The norms and the format of the discipline have had a universal status for quite some time now, and scholars are not engaged in an "other" way of writing history. In the current intellectual environment that is marked by the fast and easy dissemination of knowledge and by porous boundaries, insisting on alternative methodologies would indeed not be "speaking back" to the dominant discourse (as attempted by *écriture feminine*, for example), but would only reconstruct the exoticism of the "Islamic." The challenge is in the nature of the sources: in a development parallel to "Western" urban history, historians of "non-Western" cities now question the former hierarchies by introducing voices not heard before, such as the modest-income groups and women.

Even a brief overview of the state of the art during the past several decades attests to the new vigor and energy in the literature on the "Islamic city." The questions asked cover multiple terrains; they are heady and intricate. Approaches are diverse and methodologies experimental and often positively eclectic. Source material is innovative. The cities themselves are rich and interesting. Perhaps most important, they do not stand isolated but are increasingly anchored by the new scholarship to a global framework, triggering questions that challenge the provinciality of former mind-sets. The outcome affects all parties. As research on the "non-Western" city produces a substantial repertoire of case studies, the intellectually fragile barriers that created artificial categories start disintegrating. Spiro Kostof's *A History of Architecture* (1984) stands as an early manifestation of this trend. Kostof constructed enduring bridges between "different worlds," showing that the differences stemmed mostly from fixed perceptions. He showed that breaking through the established norms by making associations between Cairo and Florence, between Palladio and Sinan allows for more exciting views.[5]

At the turn of the century, then, historic presences and absences play off against each other, reshaping the field of urban history. Turning to the haunting project of modernity, its origins in cities can now be complicated by drawing in the case of Aleppo in the eighteenth century, for example. The remaking of the European capitals in the nineteenth century can no longer be disassociated from those in the Middle East, urging us to rethink the web of meanings the projects of modernity encompass, as well as the concomitant inequalities. To recognize the global influences disrupts the persistent monopolization of Modernism by "Western" cultures, and, to paraphrase Marshall Berman, "keeping alive . . . the intimate and antagonistic" bonds creates a wide field of intertwined modernities, with a promise for a complex and comprehensive future.[6]

Notes

1. This essay does not claim to be comprehensive, but attempts to outline the arguments that dominated the discourse toward the end of the century. The literature discussed here is a small sample from what I consider to be representative of the state of the art. I would like to alert the readers that I have referred only to literature in English and French-English for obvious reasons and French because of the wealth of literature on the topic in that language and because of its relative accessibility. There is, nevertheless, extensive scholarship in other languages, particularly in German, Turkish, and Arabic.
2. This book comprises four lectures given by Andre Raymond at New York University in the spring of 1983. An expanded version is published in French as *Grandes villes arabes à l'époque ottomane* (Arles, 1985).
3. See: H. Prost, "Rapport général," in J. Royer, ed., *L'Urbanisme aux colonies et dans les pays tropicaux* (La Charité-sur-Loire, 1932), 22–23.
4. On Moroccan cities, see J. Abu-Lughod, *Rabat: Urban Apartheid in Morocco* (Princeton, N.J., 1980); P. Rabinow, *French Modern: Norms and Forms of the Social Environment* (Cambridge, Mass., 1989); and G. Wright, *The Politics of Design in French Colonial Urbanism* (Chicago, 1991) (in addition to Morocco, Wright also looks at cities of Vietnam and Madagascar). On Algerian cities, see D. Prochaska, *Making Algeria French: Colonialism in Bône, 1870–1920* (Cambridge and New York, 1990), and Z. Çelik, *Urban Forms and Colonial Confrontations* (Berkeley, 1997).
5. Kostof pursued the same inclusive approach in his later books, *The City Shaped* (1991) and *The City Assembled* (1992). [. . .]
6. Marshall Berman, *All That Is Solid Melts into Air: The Experience of Modernity* (New York, 1988), 346. I have stretched Berman's "modernities of the past" to modernities in all parts of the world.

Reading

27

Sir John Summerson

Urban Forms (1963)

John Summerson (1904–1992) was an eminent British architectural historian who wrote prolifically about Georgian, Victorian, and modern architecture in the United Kingdom. He served on the Historic Buildings Council (1953–78) and directed and oversaw the protection of Sir John Soane's Museum in London (1945–84). However, his attitude to architectural conservation, according to English Heritage, was "selective, unsentimental and occasionally controversial" (www.english-heritage.org.uk/visit/blue-plaques/summerson-sir-john-1904-1992). Nonetheless, his insightful suggestions on how to read the city by learning lessons from all kinds of urban buildings and infrastructure provide an important conceptual foundation for understanding the dynamics of architectural change in any urban place.

[. . .] The fact is that the history of the fabrics of cities is as yet almost unwritten.

What is the historian's task in dealing with, say, the fabric of one single city? How must he approach it? First, he must learn from the geographers the factors of site and situation and the general morphology of the city as it stands. Next he must take possession of whatever the political, economic, industrial and social historians can give him. After that he must master the whole corpus of topographical material—not only maps, but prints, drawings, photographs and descriptions of lost buildings. Last, he must know the city—know its modern face, its ancient monuments and equally, the scraps and fragments which are neither ancient nor monuments but still significant and instructive flotsam from the past. [. . .]

The bulk of material before the historian of the physical city is, of course, enormous; but if he really is a historian he has got to deal with it all—or, if that sounds too like a catalogue, let us say *be aware* of it all. I stress this because I am disposed to condemn the kind of urban history which concentrates on architecture at the expense of total

Sir John Summerson in *The Historian and the City*, edited by Oscar Handlin and John E. Burchard, published by The MIT Press and Harvard Joint Center for Housing Studies, 1963, www.jchs.harvard.edu, 165–67, 176.

building output; such work may or may not be good architectural history but it is not the history of the city as an artefact. Our historian has to be on terms with the whole physical mass of marble, bricks and mortar, steel and concrete, tarmac and rubble, metal conduits and rails—the total artefact. He has to deal with all this and he has to deal with it within limits. What are these limits?

They are probably best defined in terms of exclusion. Thus our historian must not be primarily concerned either with administration or with social, economic and industrial life of the city. He will have to intrude himself constantly into those fields to discover causes, incentives and controlling factors but they are not for him the main issue. The main issue, all the time, is tangible substance, the stuff of the city, and that implies form. I am not going on from this to say that the historian of the city as an artefact must be an art historian, though it is very nearly true. He must be both less and more than an art historian. If he cannot maintain a lively interest in form or if his interest in form extends only to form which is produced as "art," he cannot possibly write the history of the city as an artefact. It is the study of urban form as the resultant of a complex of social, psychological, and economic forces which is the essence of the kind of history I am postulating. The role of the historian in relation to the city as an artefact lies here.

[. . .]

The outstanding introduction to the study of the city as an organism was, I suppose, Patrick Geddes' *Cities in Evolution*, published in 1915. It did not pretend to be a historical work and was in fact intended to propagate the nascent town-planning movement of its time. But Geddes was the first writer to see the slum not simply as something to be wiped out in the name of hygiene but as a living part of the living city, with an intelligible past and a future which must be rendered intelligible in relation to the whole. In Geddes' eloquent pages the slum became as real, historically speaking, as the great boulevard or the palazzo. Twenty-three years after Geddes, in 1938, came Lewis Mumford's *The Culture of Cities* in which some of Geddes' ideas were taken over and elaborated. Mumford's book is a critical study of cities rather than a history, but for us it is particularly remarkable for the penetrating and imaginative handling of the fabric.

[. . .]

—⁓—

[. . .] Today the sprawl is the city and its history is as important as the history of cathedrals. A city is a community of people who are continually creating and recreating their own environment. The tragedy of the modern city is that the processes of creation and recreation have been delegated not to the most responsible but often to the least responsible sections of the community. But "delegation" is not the right word. It is an oversimplification. The growth of cities, the forms into which they grow, the acceptability of those forms by the citizens and, I would add, the changes in acceptability which these forms undergo—all these matters are of the very essence of city life and we understand very little about them. Nor shall we understand more without strict historical enquiry.

Reading

28

ANNE VERNEZ MOUDON

Urban Morphology as an Emerging Interdisciplinary Field (1997)

Anne Vernez Moudon is Professor of Architecture, Landscape Architecture, and Urban Design and Planning at the University of Washington, Seattle, where she also directs the Urban Form Lab. In this reading from an article that appeared in the inaugural issue of the journal Urban Morphology, *she explains how the disparate roots of this "emerging interdisciplinary field" became interwoven in Europe as a result of efforts to understand urban form by the German scholar M. R. G. Conzen in the United Kingdom; Saverio Muratori, Gianfranco Caniggia, and others in Italy; and Philippe Panerai, Jean Castex, and others in France. She underscores the particular significance of Italian practitioners in this regard.*

Urban morphology is the study of the city as human habitat. Ethnographer Lévi-Strauss (1954, pp. 137–8) described the city as 'the most complex of human inventions, . . . at the confluence of nature and artifact.' Urban morphologists concur: they analyse a city's evolution from its formative years to its subsequent transformations, identifying and dissecting its various components. The city is the accumulation and the integration of many individual and small group actions, themselves governed by cultural traditions and shaped by social and economic forces over time. Urban morphologists focus on the tangible results of social and economic forces: they study the outcomes of ideas and intentions as they take shape on the ground and mould our cities. Buildings, gardens, streets, parks, and monuments, are among the main elements of morphological analysis. These elements, however, are considered as organisms which are constantly used and hence transformed through time. They also exist in a state of tight and dynamic interrelationship: built structures shaping and being shaped by the open spaces around

From ANNE VERNEZ MOUDON, "Urban Morphology as an Emerging Interdisciplinary Field," a series of extracts from *Urban Morphology*, Vol. 1 (1997), pages 3–10.

them, public streets serving and being used by private land owners along them. The dynamic state of the city, and the pervasive relationship between its elements, have led many urban morphologists to prefer the term 'urban morphogenesis' to describe their field of study.

In the summer of 1996, a group of urban morphologists from a variety of disciplines including architecture, geography, history and planning, formalized the International Seminar on Urban Form (ISUF—or *SIFU, Séminaire International de la Forme Urbaine, Seminario Internazzionale de la Forma Urbana*). The group, which included individuals from England, France, Germany, Ireland, Switzerland, Japan, Australia, and the USA, had also met in the previous two summers at the same venue, Lausanne, Switzerland, to explain and compare their work. These meetings acknowledged the expansion of urban morphology beyond its original confines in geography, and its emergence as an interdisciplinary field. They highlighted the need to promote international exchanges and to investigate the scope of the field's theoretical basis.

Three Schools of Urban Morphology

The ISUF meetings confirmed that several generations of scholars had been active in urban morphology, not only in England, but also in Italy and in France, and that many individual researchers from a variety of other countries were contributing to the field. Two individuals figure prominently as seminal instigators of the field: M. R. G. Conzen (b. 1907), a German geographer who migrated to England before the Second World War, first to study and practice urban planning, and then to teach geography; and Saverio Muratori (1910–73), an Italian architect who taught in Venice and then in Rome. Both men were unusual and non-conforming in their respective realms of geography and architecture. Conzen, who is best known for his detailed study of Alnwick (1960), had to weather the post-war quantitative revolution in geography, which largely passed over his inductive and empirical research as lacking in rigour and predictive power. Muratori, on the other hand, who used his self-termed "operational histories" of Venice and Rome (Muratori, 1959, 1963) as the theoretical basis for his architectural design studios, suffered intellectual isolation (and scorn) from his modernist colleagues in architecture.

However, the strengths of Conzen's and Muratori's teachings attracted followers who saw the importance of capturing what the masters had called the city's "genius loci," and its unique mnemonic powers as cultural palimpsest. [. . .]

In Italy, Gianfranco Caniggia (1933–87) took over the mantle of Muratori who had supervised his 1963 study of the city of Como. In his teachings and publications, Caniggia continued the Muratorian tradition, which he called "procedural typology" because of the focus on building types as the elemental root of urban form. Like Muratori, Caniggia put his theory into practice, remaining actively involved in architecture and building throughout his life. His research extended to several cities in Italy and North Africa, conducted with colleagues and students who continue the Muratorian legacy. Today, Giancarlo Cataldi, Gian Luigi Maffei, Maria Grazia Corsini, Paolo Maretto,

Giuseppe Strappa, and others, continue the tradition in Florence, Rome, Genoa, and Siena.

After Conzen and Muratori had seeded the ground for the two early schools of urban morphology, a third school emerged in France in the late 1960s, when architects Philippe Panerai and Jean Castex, together with sociologist Jean-Charles DePaule, founded the School of Architecture in Versailles as part of the dissolution of the Beaux-Arts. Like the Italian School, the French School rose out of a reaction against modernist architecture and its rejection of history. However, it also benefited at the time from the vibrant intellectual discourse on urban life which surpassed architecture and engaged such powerful critics as sociologist Henri Lefebvre and architectural historians Françoise Boudon and André Chastel. While already busy with research on the historical evolution of Parisian neighbourhoods, Panerai and Castex literally stumbled into Muratori's works, then unknown in France, which provided the impetus for further probing the theoretical and methodological dimensions of their work. [. . .]

ISUF: A Genealogy

—∾—

The diffusion of Muratorian ideas followed the general rise in the popularity of Italian architecture throughout the world, particularly with the translation into English of Aldo Rossi's works in the 1980s.[1] Although Rossi chose to remain silent about Muratori's considerable influence on his early professional development, he successfully promoted a return to "traditional" building types, thus kindling a renewed interest in the historic city and promoting its significance in architecture. British, American, and French architects all listened to Rossi's message. They also read another Italian architect. Carlo Aymonino, whose study of Padua and other writings on what he termed "typomorphology" stimulated further interest in the design of the city. Incidentally, but significantly for the structure of ISUF, both Rossi and Aymonino subsequently rejected urban morphology, which they saw as promoting outdated solutions to today's urban problems and impotent in resolving issues of modern architecture.

In retrospect, however, the Italian contribution that was most instrumental in linking the three main schools of urban morphology, and hence in shaping ISUF, was the rehabilitation programme of Bologna's historic centre—for which Caniggia was a consultant. The rapid diffusion of this project, its rich scope and successful implementation, helped to forge contacts between morphologists in several parts of the world.

—∾—

The Theoretical Basis

This coming together of researchers from different language areas and disciplines is founded on common ground. First, there is agreement that the city or town can be "read" and analysed via the medium of its physical form. Further, there is widespread acknowledgment that, at its most elemental level, morphological analysis is based on three principles.

1. Urban form is defined by three fundamental physical elements: buildings and their related open spaces, plots or lots, and streets.
2. Urban form can be understood at different levels of resolution. Commonly, four are recognized, corresponding to the building/lot, the street/block, the city, and the region.
3. Urban form can only be understood historically since the elements of which it is comprised undergo continuous transformation and replacement.

Thus *form*, *resolution*, and *time* constitute the three fundamental components of urban morphological research. These are present in all studies, whether by geographers or architects, and whether they focus on a medieval, baroque, or contemporary city. The smallest cell of the city is recognized as the combination of two elements: the individual parcel of land, together with its building or buildings and open spaces. The characteristics of the cell define the urban form's shape and density, as well as its actual and potential use over time. Studies show that the attributes of the cell and its elements reflect not only a time period of history, but the socio-economic conditions present at the time of land development and building. Over time, these elements are either used differently—for example, by different social classes—transformed physically, eliminated or replaced by new forms. The rate of change in either the function or the form of the cells varies from city to city, but also generally fits into cycles related to the economy and culture. Building and transformation cycles are important processes to explore for city planning and real estate development purposes, yet are rarely studied in contemporary cities.

Studies also focus on what Conzen calls the "plan unit" and what Italians term *tessuto*. Plan units or "tissues" are groups of buildings, open spaces, lots, and streets, which form a cohesive whole either because they were all built at the same time or within the same constraints, or because they underwent a common process of transformation.

Furthermore, while all morphological analysis is carried out for the purposes of theory building, several distinct purposes exist among urban morphological traditions which yield different kinds of theories. The three schools each have had different intentions in their theory building efforts. They are: as follows.

1. The study of urban form for *descriptive* and *explanatory* purposes, with the aim of developing a *theory of city building* (*théorie de l'édification de la ville*). Such studies are concerned with how cities are built and why. This is the primary purpose of geographers, and the Birmingham School in particular. Social scientists in the French School also have this purpose in mind when they carry out morphological studies.

2. The study of urban form for *prescriptive* purposes, with the aim of developing a *theory of city design*. Such studies concentrate on how cities should be built. This is the primary focus of the Italian School which has given this purpose a special direction, namely to develop a theory of building design resting on historical city-building traditions. A few French researchers have had the same intentions in their morphological analyses, seeing the purposes of their work as being to develop a *théorie du projet basée sur les traditions d'édification de la ville*.
3. The study of urban form to assess the *impact of past design theories on city building*. This is in the realm of design criticism, which makes the sophisticated distinction between the *theory of design 'as idea', and the theory of design 'as practised'*. Such studies assess the differences or similarities between stated directives about what should be built (normative theories) and what has actually been built. The French School has championed this use of morphological analysis, tracing successfully the roots of modernism in urban design back to the eighteenth century. However, it remains a difficult mental exercise for many designers and planners. who tend not to spend time assessing the impact of their actions on the long-range life of cities.

Notes

1. For discussions of, and references to, the role of urban morphology in urban design and architecture, see Panerai, Ph., Depaule, J.Ch., Demorgon, M. and Veyrenche, M. (1980) *Eléments d'analyse urbaine* (Éditions Archives d'Architecture Moderne, Brussels); Moudon, A.V. (1992) "A Catholic Approach to Organizing What Urban Designers Should Know," *Journal of Planning Literature* 6, 331–49.

References

Conzen, M. R. G. (1960) *Alnwick, Northumberland: a study in town-plan analysis*. Institute of British Geographers Publication 27 (George Philip, London).

Lévi-Strauss, C. (1955) *Tristes tropiques* (Terre Humaine, Paris).

Muratori, S. (1959) *Studi per una operante storia urbana di Venezia* (Istituto Poligraphico dello Stato, Roma).

Muratori, S., Bollati, R., Bollati, S. and Marinucci, G. (1963) *Studi per una operante storia urbana di Roma* (Consiglio nazionale delle ricerche, Roma).

Reading

29

PHILIPPE PANERAI, JEAN CASTEX, AND
JEAN-CHARLES DEPAULE

Urban Forms: The Death and Life of the Urban Block (1977, 1997)

In the mid-1970s, Philippe Panerai, Jean Castex, and Jean-Charles Depaule, French architects and urbanists born roughly coincident with World War II, collaborated on an analysis of modernist-inspired housing blocks. This investigation resulted in a more far-reaching set of conclusions about the nature and dynamics of îlots, *or urban lots or parcels, and their aggregation in urban blocks. This reading is from the English translation of their seminal* Formes urbaine de l'îlot a la barre *(1977), which Anne Vernez Moudon discusses as it relates to the field of urban morphology (reading 28). Their book became a fundamental text for French architectural students who sought to understand the relationship between individual works of architecture and the urban context.*

CHAPTER 8 BUILDING THE CITY: 1975–95

Because of successive crises, the issue of having to build the city remains at the top of the list of architects' preoccupations and so regularly provides a motive for them to explore new ground in their projects. It is no more the case that developers or public agencies deny a desire to be concerned with the urban environment. But this passage to an urban society does not happen without pain. If, between the difficulties that contemporary cities and their peripheries are faced with, some are without doubt the direct consequences of an economic crisis that mostly goes beyond the domain of architecture and deeply destabilizes society, while others are due to planning errors, from which it is difficult to avoid blaming the profession. Often, these errors have even accentuated and exaggerated the effects of the crisis, creating, locally, some situations that are unsustainable. [. . .]

The Problem of the Urban Tissue

This study has dealt little with the bigger scale of projects. Without denying their importance, it chose to concentrate on an intermediate scale, which is essential for understanding an urban project and which we can call the urban tissue. The concept of tissue, in fact, with the double textile and biological connotations, evokes ideas of interweaving and of connections between parts, together with a capacity for adaptation. It is in contrast to the completed or fixed work and, instead, implies a process of transformations. It can provide a critical response to those problems that we have inherited from recent developments.

The urban tissue, which is the superimposition of several structures acting at different scales, but which appears as a system with linkages in each part of the city, can be defined as the culminating point of three logical systems:

- the logic of roads in their double roles of movement and distribution;
- the logic of plot subdivisions, where land holdings are built up and where private and public initiatives take place; and
- the logic of buildings that contain different activities.

The old cities, in their own way and each with different modes, ensure the coherence of the tissue. The street does not exist without the buildings that define it, and the buildings are built on plots that form the framework of their evolution. Spaces have a status, which determines legal responsibilities as well as possible uses. Systems of reference, orientation are generally legible; activities are mixed and modifications are easy.

[. . .]

The topic of the urban tissue cannot be dissociated from the everyday and ordinary experience of the city, because, even if one prefers Venice to La Grande Motte or Rodez to Cergy-Pontoise, aesthetics are here secondary and it is on the grounds of qualities for the user that we have become interested in the old city and in the analysis of its tissues. Building the city today could mean the wish to find again, perhaps with different forms, the qualities of proximity, mixture and the unexpected, i.e. a public space accessible to all, a variety of mixed activities, a built-up area that keeps adapting and transforming itself in unplanned neighbourhoods.

By dealing with the urban tissue we return to an ability to think once again of the city in other than the functional categories we have inherited. The application of these categories, in spite of any denials has, as an inescapable consequence, produced our cities. Two examples taken from different aspects of our lives can illustrate this subject: our relationship with the car and the programming of activities.

The relationships we have with the car are schizophrenic. Cars are omnipresent and we seem to be incapable of accommodating this presence in new neighbourhoods, or rather we only pretend to take them into account. Paradoxically, this seems easier in old cities, where, once some measures have been taken to moderate speed and control

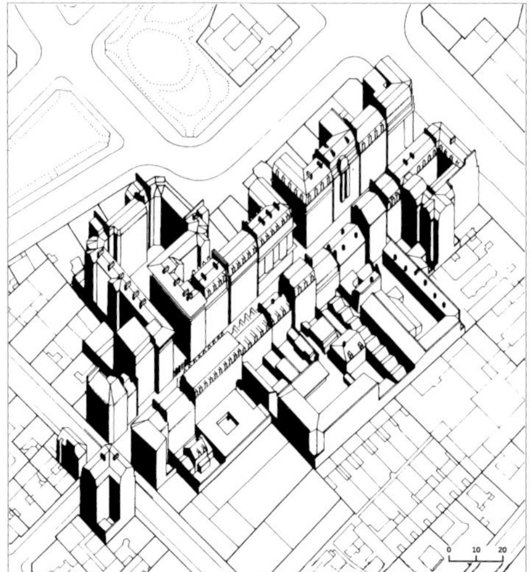

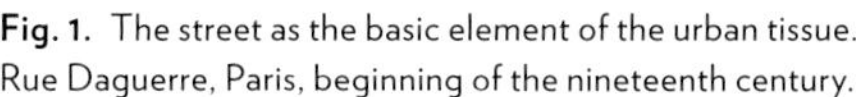

Fig. 1. The street as the basic element of the urban tissue. Rue Daguerre, Paris, beginning of the nineteenth century.

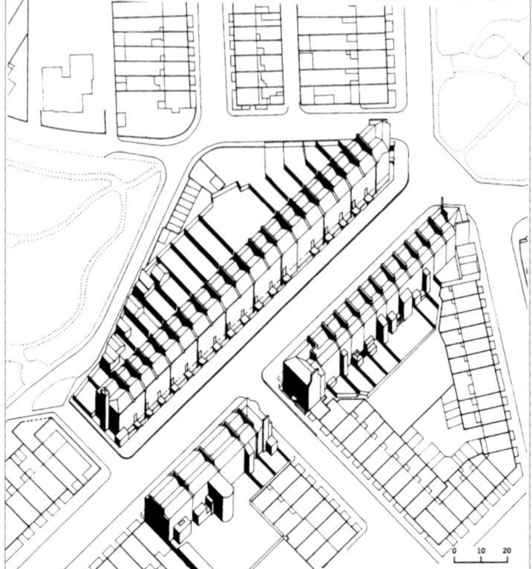

Fig. 2. Row housing as an element producing tissues. Bath, row houses, beginning of the nineteenth century.

parking, the presence of the car does not conflict with normal urban activities. But, in recent urban planning, any attempt to make cars coexist with pedestrians becomes impossible, like combining transit with residential routes, a simple crossing point, delivering goods from a public road and so forth. And, the more density decreases, the more things become complicated. [. . .]

[. . .]

Rather than concern itself excessively with functional changes, which need drastic modifications, the urban project should endeavour to define a set of ground rules with regard to those divisions and simple morphological rules, which constitute a stable basis on which tissues can then be progressively built.

Open Blocks and Closed Blocks

The analysis of the five cases that, from Haussmann to Le Corbusier, mark out the tearing apart of the tissue, which has given rise to different interpretations, the most frequent of which has consisted of linking a desire for urbanity with the taking up again of the so-called traditional block structure. There is here a source of confusion and we therefore need to reiterate some points.

The block (in French, *îlot*, which etymologically means small island) is a part of the urban area "isolated" from the neighbouring parts of the territory by streets. Thus, the block is not an architectural form, but a group of interdependent building plots. It has a proper meaning only when it is in a dialectical relationship with the road network. If we put aside the special cases of facilities or monumental blocks, which consist of only one plot, like just one building, the block of the traditional city is rarely homogeneous and the buildings on its perimeter obey some rules, especially those of that economic logic that has shaped the surrounding streets. Interdependent, but distinctive, the plots provide the construction processes with a fixed legal and real estate framework, which conditions the evolution of buildings and the types of use by the inhabitants. This definition does not influence at all the continuity of the enclosure and the homogeneity of perimeter buildings. Indeed, the old tissues demonstrate a great number of incomplete alignments and heterogeneous fronts, where one can see a large number of buildings of different heights along the streets—and some even recessed—gaps and walls, which shelter courtyards or gardens and allow for planting to be seen. It is often only in the central areas, and as a result of several centuries of progressive densification, that one can find compact built-up blocks and a degree of continuous enclosure.

To think of the block as a whole would be missing the point, and reducing it to a continuous and homogeneous built-up area surrounding an empty centre would be a caricature of reality, where complexity and depth of tissue is ignored to the advantage of a central area of uncertain status or function. [. . .]

[. . .]

Streets and Subdivisions

It is convenient to talk about the block. The block can be read in the plan of the city as the negative of the road layout and the drawing of the roads itself isolates it. But this leads to confusion and the strength of the image of the block risks, as we saw previously,

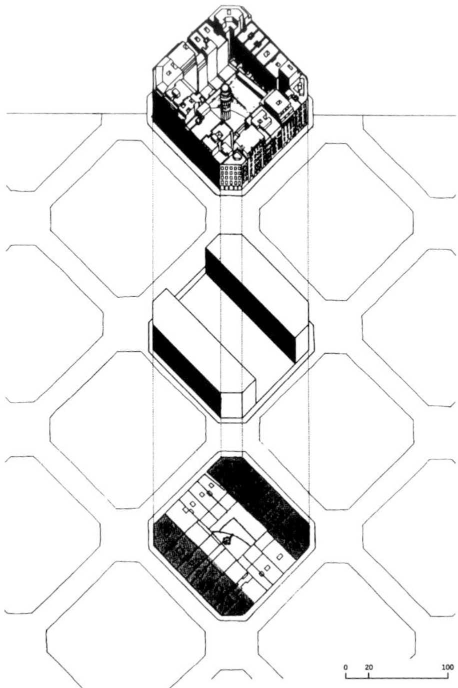

Fig. 3. The block as a large-scale structuring element. Barcelona, the plan by Cerda.

arriving at a reductive reading. In this way a caricatured image appears, where the block becomes a sort of Viennese *Hof* or a Parisian HBM (*habitations à bon marché*) whose interior is reduced to a large more or less controlled courtyard, a distant memory of the courtyard of Florentine Renaissance palaces.

To understand the block, not as an a priori form but as a resulting system, capable of organising parts of the urban territory, implies forgetting for a moment the great regular layouts that, from the chequerboard of Hippodamus to the super blocks of Brasilia, marked the history of spontaneous city planning. It also means abandoning the haunting image of the Roman city, the bastides and Spanish colonial cities, and forgetting Jefferson's chequerboard pattern and Cerda's plan. Or to consider at least that these projects marked the periodic return in history of a global way of thinking, where the logic of the block and that of the road network are fused together in a rationalization of previous experiences. It is only necessary to look at the plans of the very first bastides or the first Spanish attempts at city planning in Latin America, to appreciate the necessary trial and error and vicissitudes, before the codified plans were achieved, which we regard as canonical.

Without negating these interesting proposals or their relevance to the debate on the contemporary city, it is essential to start again from a different viewpoint, in order to rediscover the elementary logic of the urban tissue. Whether it is pre-existing or originates from a new layout, it is the street that distributes, feeds and orders development. The dialectical relationship between street and built plots creates the tissue and it is in the continuation of this relationship—capable of modification, extension and the substitution of buildings—where resides the capacity of the city to adapt to the demographic, economic and cultural changes that mark its evolution. The street layout determines the relationship with site, centre and capacity for extension. The width of plots (their opening on the street) and their depth condition (and are conditioned by) the type of buildings used. To a narrow plot correspond the row house and the small building (the Gothic plot); to larger plots correspond villas and detached houses, houses with courtyards, and apartment buildings. The regrouping of small plots or the subdivision of larger ones, when historical conditions require it, allows for the integration of new types of building. The same block can accommodate different buildings and densities. Courtyards and gardens can coexist with stores and small factories and several functions can be located next to one another.

Modern Urban Architecture

Questioning the city, the urban tissue and plot subdivisions will have some consequences for architectural design. The first of these implies that one will have to locate all programmes and projects in their right place, in the interlocking scales typical of each city, and capture in this way the urban values (often little or badly specified in the briefs), that are connected to the site and the location. Urban planning can no more be reduced to the production of stereotyped solutions, but will have to involve the design of new buildings in an overall concern for the territory and its future transformation. This also means to take on board the inheritance of the Modern Movement, even if it means to have to correct its effects in urban terms.

The second consequence implies a debate on the relative importance of style and to go beyond the contradicting tendencies in professional discussions. Urban architecture is mainly involved in solving problems concerning the city, respecting its logic, whatever its formal aspect. This should lead us to a double rereading. First, of those works of the Modern Movement, which have been able to connect the urban aspect with modernity, and, second, of one exploring older architecture, which has experienced solutions or dispositions that may now respond to our present concerns. [. . .]

Reading

30

GORDON CULLEN

Townscape (1961)

Gordon Cullen emphasized both the visual impact of a city and its environmental qualities. Using words, photographs, and sketches, he convincingly argued that a city was more than the sum of its constituent parts and that the art of environment was necessary to humanize the raw materials of planning and to restore an appropriate relationship between "planner and planee." His approach came at a time, the 1960s and 1970s, when many planners emphasized the technical and statistical aspects of their work, which Cullen considered insufficient and misleading. His examples from historic towns, with their "colour, texture, scale, style, character, personality and uniqueness," came to life in Cullen's compelling sketches. His lessons regarding the need to capture the continuity and intrinsic qualities of historic areas remain valid today.

INTRODUCTION

[. . .]

Now turn to the visual impact which a city has on those who live in it or visit it. [. . .] [B]ring people together and they create a collective surplus of enjoyment; bring buildings together and collectively they can give visual pleasure which none can give separately.

One building standing alone in the countryside is experienced as a work of architecture, but bring half a dozen buildings together and an art other than architecture is made possible. Several things begin to happen in the group which would be impossible for the isolated building. We may walk through and past the buildings, and as a corner is turned an unsuspected building is suddenly revealed. We may be surprised, even astonished (a reaction generated by the composition of the group and not by the individual building). Again, suppose that the buildings have been put together in a

From GORDON CULLEN, *Townscape* (New York: Reinhold, 1961), 9–15, 17, 57.

group so that one can get inside the group, then the space created between the buildings is seen to have a life of its own over and above the buildings which create it and one's reaction is to say 'I am inside IT' or "I am entering IT'. Note also that in this group of half a dozen buildings there may be one which through reason of function does not conform. It may be a bank, a temple or a church amongst houses. Suppose that we are just looking at the temple by itself, it would stand in front of us and all its qualities, size, colour and intricacy, would be evident. But put the temple back amongst the small houses and immediately its size is made more real and more obvious by the comparison between the two scales. Instead of being a big temple it TOWERS. The difference in meaning between bigness and towering is the measure of the relationship.

In fact there is an *art of relationship* just as there is an art of architecture. Its purpose is to take all the elements that go to create the environment: buildings, trees, nature, water, traffic, advertisements and so on, and to weave them together in such a way that drama is released. For a city is a dramatic event in the environment. Look at the research that is put into making a city work: demographers, sociologists, engineers, traffic experts; all co-operating to form the myriad factors into a workable, viable and healthy organization. It is a tremendous human undertaking.

And yet . . . if at the end of it all the city appears dull, uninteresting and soulless, then it is not fulfilling itself. It has failed. The fire has been laid but nobody has put a match to it.

Firstly we have to rid ourselves of the thought that the excitement and drama that we seek can be born automatically out of the scientific research and solutions arrived at by the technical man (or the technical half of the brain). We naturally accept these solutions, but are not entirely bound by them. In fact we cannot be entirely bound by them because the scientific solution is based on the best that can be made of the average: of averages of human behaviour, averages of weather, factors of safety and so on. And these averages do not give an inevitable result for any particular problem. They are, so to speak, wandering facts which may synchronize or, just as likely, may conflict with each other. The upshot is that a town could take one of several patterns and still operate with success, equal success. Here then we discover a pliability in the scientific solution and it is precisely in the *manipulation of this pliability* that the art of relationship is made possible. As will be seen, the aim is not to dictate the shape of the town or environment, but is a modest one: simply to *manipulate within the tolerances.*

This means that we can get no further help from the scientific attitude and that we must therefore turn to other values and other standards.

We turn to the *faculty of sight*, for it is almost entirely through vision that the environment is apprehended. If someone knocks at your door and you open it to let him in, it sometimes happens that a gust of wind comes in too, sweeping round the room, blowing the curtains and making a great fuss. Vision is somewhat the same; we often get more than we bargained for. Glance at the clock to see the time and you see the wallpaper, the clock's carved brown mahogany frame, the fly crawling over the glass and the delicate rapier-like pointers. Cezanne might have made a painting of it. In fact, of course, vision is not only useful but it evokes our memories and experiences, those responsive emotions inside us which have the power to disturb the mind when aroused. It is this unlooked-for surplus that we are dealing with, for clearly if the environment is going to produce an emotional reaction, with or without our volition, it is up to us to try to understand the three ways in which this happens.

I. Concerning OPTICS. Let us suppose that we are walking through a town: here is a straight road off which is a courtyard, at the far side of which another street leads out and bends slightly before reaching a monument. Not very unusual. We take this path and our first view is that of the street. Upon turning into the courtyard the new view is revealed instantaneously at the point of turning, and this view remains with us whilst we walk across the courtyard. Leaving the courtyard we enter the further street. Again a new view is suddenly revealed although we are travelling at a uniform speed. Finally as the road bends the monument swings into view. The significance of all this is that although the pedestrian walks through the town at a uniform speed, the scenery of towns is often revealed in a series of jerks or revelations. This we call SERIAL VISION.

Examine what this means. Our original aim is to manipulate the elements of the town so that an impact on the emotions is achieved. A long straight road has little impact because the initial view is soon digested and becomes monotonous. The human mind reacts to a contrast, to the difference between things, and when two pictures (the street and the courtyard) are in the mind at the same time, a vivid contrast is felt and the town becomes visible in a deeper sense. It comes alive through the drama of juxtaposition. Unless this happens the town will slip past us featureless and inert.

There is a further observation to be made concerning Serial Vision. Although from a scientific or commercial point of view the town may be a unity, from our optical viewpoint we have split it into two elements: the *existing view* and the *emerging view*. In the normal way this is an accidental chain of events and whatever significance may arise out of the linking of views will be fortuitous. Suppose, however, that we take over this linking as a branch of the art of relationship; then we are finding a tool with which human imagination can begin to mould the city into a coherent drama. The process of manipulation has begun to turn the blind facts into a taut emotional situation.

II. Concerning PLACE. This second point is concerned with our reactions to the position of our body in its environment. This is as simple as it appears to be. It means, for instance, that when you go into a room you utter to yourself the unspoken words 'I am outside IT, I am entering IT, I am in the middle of IT'. At this level of consciousness we are dealing with a range of experience stemming from the major impacts of exposure and enclosure (which if taken to their morbid extremes result in the symptoms of agoraphobia and claustrophobia). Place a man on the edge of a 500-ft. cliff and he will have a very lively sense of position, put him at the end of a deep cave and he will react to the fact of enclosure.

Since it is an instinctive and continuous habit of the body to relate itself to the environment, this sense of position cannot be ignored; it becomes a factor in the design of the environment (just as an additional source of light must be reckoned with by a photographer, however annoying it may be). I would go further and say that it should be exploited.

Here is an example. Suppose you are visiting one of the hill towns in the south of France. You climb laboriously up the winding road and eventually find yourself in a tiny village street at the summit. You feel thirsty and go to a nearby restaurant, your drink is served to you on a veranda and as you go out to it you find to your exhilaration or horror that the veranda is cantilevered out over a thousand-foot drop. By this device of the containment (street) and the revelation (cantilever) the fact of height is dramatized and made real.

In a town we do not normally have such a dramatic situation to manipulate but the principle still holds good. There is, for instance, a typical emotional reaction to being below the general ground level and there is another resulting from being above it. There is a reaction to being hemmed in as in a tunnel and another to the wideness of the square. If, therefore, we design our towns from the point of view of the moving person (pedestrian or car-borne) it is easy to see how the whole city becomes a plastic experience, a journey through pressures and vacuums, a sequence of exposures and enclosures, of constraint and relief.

Arising out of this sense of identity or sympathy with the environment, this feeling of a person in street or square that he is in IT or entering IT or leaving IT, we discover that no sooner do we postulate a HERE than automatically we must create a THERE, for you cannot have one without the other. Some of the greatest townscape effects are created by a skilful relationship between the two, and I will name an example in India, where this introduction is being written: the approach from the Central Vista to the Rashtrapathi Bhawan[1] in New Delhi. There is an open-ended courtyard composed of the two Secretariat buildings and, at the end, the Rashtrapathi Bhawan. All this is raised above normal ground level and the approach is by a ramp. At the top of the ramp and in front of the axis building is a tall screen of railings. This is the setting. Travelling through it from the Central Vista we see the two Secretariats in full, but the Rashtrapathi Bhawan is partially hidden by the ramp; only its upper part is visible. This effect of truncation serves to isolate and make remote. The building is withheld. We are Here and it is There. As we climb the ramp the Rashtrapathi Bhawan is gradually revealed, the mystery culminates in fulfilment as it becomes immediate to us, standing on the same floor. But at this point the railing, the wrought iron screen, is inserted; which again creates a form of Here and There by means of the screened vista. A brilliant, if painfully conceived, sequence[2] [. . .].

III. Concerning CONTENT. In this last category we turn to an examination of the fabric of towns: colour, texture, scale, style, character, personality and uniqueness. Accepting the fact that most towns are of old foundation, their fabric will show evidence of differing periods in its architectural styles and also in the various accidents of layout. Many towns do so display this mixture of styles, materials and scales.

Yet there exists at the back of our minds a feeling that could we only start again we would get rid of this hotchpotch and make all new and fine and perfect. We would create an orderly scene with straight roads and with buildings that conformed in height and style. Given a free hand that is what we might do . . . create symmetry, balance, perfection and conformity. After all, that is the popular conception of the purpose of town planning.

But what is this conformity? Let us approach it by a simile. Let us suppose a party in a private house, where are gathered together half a dozen people who are strangers to each other. The early part of the evening is passed in polite conversation on general subjects such as the weather and the current news. Cigarettes are passed and lights offered punctiliously. In fact it is all an exhibition of manners, of how one ought to behave. It is also very boring. This is conformity. However, later on the ice begins to break and out of the straightjacket of orthodox manners and conformity real human beings begin to emerge. It is found that Miss X's sharp but good-natured wit is just the right foil to Major Y's somewhat simple exuberance. And so on. It begins to be fun. Conformity gives way to the agreement to differ within a recognized tolerance of behaviour.

Conformity, from the point of view of the planner, is difficult to avoid but to avoid it deliberately, by creating artificial diversions, is surely worse than the original boredom. Here, for instance, is a programme to rehouse 5,000 people. They are all treated the same, they get the same kind of house. How can one differentiate? Yet if we start from a much wider point of view we will see that tropical housing differs from temperate zone housing, that buildings in a brick country differ from buildings in a stone country, that religion and social manners vary the buildings. And as the field of observation narrows, so our sensitivity to the local gods must grow sharper. There is too much insensitivity in the building of towns, too much reliance on the tank and the armoured car where the telescopic rifle is wanted.

Within a commonly accepted framework—one that produces lucidity and not anarchy—we can manipulate the nuances of scale and style, of texture and colour and of character and individuality, juxtaposing them in order to create collective benefits. In fact the environment thus resolves itself into not conformity but the interplay of This and That.

It is a matter of observation that in a successful contrast of colours not only do we experience the harmony released but, equally, the colours become more truly themselves. In a large landscape by Corot, I forget its name, a landscape of sombre greens, almost a monochrome, there is a small figure in red. It is probably the reddest thing I have ever seen.

Statistics are abstracts: when they are plucked out of the completeness of life and converted into plans and the plans into buildings they will be lifeless. The result will be a three-dimensional diagram in which people are asked to live. In trying to colonize such a wasteland, to translate it from an environment for walking stomachs into a home for human beings, the difficulty lay in finding the point of application, in finding the gateway into the castle. We discovered three gateways, that of motion, that of position and that of content. By the exercise of vision it became apparent that motion was not one simple, measurable progression useful in planning, it was in fact two things, the Existing and the Revealed view. We discovered that the human being is constantly aware of his position in the environment, that he feels the need for a sense of place and that this sense of identity is coupled with an awareness of elsewhere. Conformity

Casebook: Serial Vision

Fig. 1. To walk from one end of the plan to another, at a uniform pace, will provide a sequence of revelations which are suggested in the serial drawings [above], reading from left to right. Each arrow on the plan represents a drawing. The even progress of travel is illuminated by a series of sudden contrasts and so an impact is made on the eye, bringing the plan to life (like nudging a man who is going to sleep in church). My drawings bear no relation to the place itself; I chose it because it seemed an evocative plan. Note that the slightest deviation in alignment and quite small variations in projections or setbacks on plan have a disproportionally powerful effect in the third dimension. Drawings © Gordon Cullen Estate. Reproduced with permission.

killed, whereas the agreement to differ gave life. In this way the void of statistics, of the diagram city, has been split into two parts, whether they be those of Serial Vision, Here and There or This and That. All that remains is to join them together into a new pattern created by warmth and power and vitality of human imagination so that we build the home of man.

That is the theory of the game, the background. In fact the most difficult part lies ahead, the Art of Playing. [. . .]

Casebook: Content

The categories

In this third section of the casebook we are concerned with the intrinsic quality of the various subdivisions of the environment, and start with the great landscape categories of metropolis, town, arcadia, park, industrial, arable and wild nature. These are the traditional categories and there is no certainty that they will continue to exist in the way we know them. On the other hand whatever the future may hold, one thing appears to be certain and that is the principle of categorization; for without distinction between one thing and another all we get is a form of porridge which will maintain life only if one can refrain from vomiting it up. At the present moment of change caused by individual transport and mass communications, the old pattern is breaking down. City centres are dying because they are too densely built for car access, the necessity for people to be in one place in order to do business and trade is lessening due to the various means of communication. Levelling of incomes is breaking up the large country estates, which are being exploited for housing the increased and ever more comfortably placed common man.

This explosion resembles nothing so much as a disturbed ant-hill with brightly enamelled ants moving rapidly in all directions, toot-toot, pip-pip, hooray.

Notes

1. The President's Residence, lately Viceregal Lodge.
2. It was the cause of bitterness between Lutyens and Baker.

Reading

31

JAN GEHL

Cities for People (2010)

The Danish architect Jan Gehl was heavily influenced by the human-scale urbanism advocated in Jane Jacobs's Death and Life of Great American Cities *(1961). Subsequently, he explored urban spaces not only from the perspective of architecture but also by applying his keen insights into sociology, economics, and human psychology. Gehl's incremental interventions in Copenhagen and elsewhere largely focused on pedestrians and cyclists and on the ways they perceive their immediate surroundings, which were vastly different from those of people driving cars. His human scale approach to understanding urban form today and in the past, and to applying its lessons to design, is based on the way in which people use space and experience the city through their senses. Gehl's unconventional and refreshing approach to urban design, set forth in his* Cities for People, *has significantly influenced postmodernist thinking about cities in Europe, North America, and Australia.*

THE BRASILIA SYNDROME

[. . .]

City Scale, Site Planning Scale and Human Scale

Put simply, urban design and city planning can be described as work involving several very different levels of scale.

There is the large scale, which is holistic treatment of the city including quarters, functions and traffic facilities. This is the city as it is seen at a distance or from an aerial perspective.

Then there is the middle scale, the development scale, which describes how the individual segments or quarters of the city should be designed, and how buildings and city space are organized. This is city planning from a low-flying helicopter perspective.

Last but certainly not least is the small scale, the human landscape. This is the city as the people who will use city space experience it at eye level. It is not the large lines of the city or spectacular placement of buildings that are interesting here, but rather the quality of the human landscape as intuited by people walking and staying in the city. This is working with 5 km/h – 3 mph architecture.

Good City Planning Requires Coordinated Work with All Three Scales

In practice, working with the three scales means operating with three very different disciplines, each with its own playing rules and quality criteria. Ideally all three levels of scale should be treated and amalgamated into a convincing whole that provides inviting space for people in the city.

The goal should be total treatment in which the city in its entirety—the skyline, placement of buildings and proportions of city space—are combined on the basis of careful treatment of space sequences, details and furnishing at eye level.

City Planning—from Above and from the Outside

In many cases, this ideal stands in contrast to a planning practice rooted in modernism, which focuses on buildings rather than holism and city space.

Photographs in which the client, mayor and proud architects stand bowed over the model of a new development illustrate the method and the problem. The development is being viewed from an aerial perspective a considerable distance above the model. From that height the elements of the development, the buildings, blocks and roads, can be moved around until the composition is in place and everything looks good—seen from above and from the outside.

Planning cities and developments from above and from the outside typically means that only the two top-level scales—city scale and development scale—are properly addressed.

Many important decisions must be made on the city and site planning scales. On these two scales, a wealth of information as well as specific architectural programs are generally available as support. The most significant financial interests are also concentrated here, and highly specialized planners are available to handle problems on the basis of a large body of experience.

The situation is very different for the human scale, a difficult and rather intangible scale to work with. Both experience and relevant information tend to be scarce, which also means that there are seldom any useful architectural programs available in support. The financial interests tied to the two top-level scales are not as obvious either for the human landscape.

City Life Doesn't Have a Chance with Priorities Ordered Like This: Buildings, Space, Life

There are good rational explanations for why city planning starts from above and from the outside in many situations. Priorities are typically ordered like this: first the large outlines of the city, then the buildings and last the spaces in between. However, experience from decades of city planning shows that this method does not work for the human landscape and the desire to invite people to use city space. On the contrary: in almost all cases it has proved impossible to meet the goal of ensuring good conditions for city life if the majority of planning decisions are made on the top-level scale, and if work with city life is reduced to treating only those areas left over in the larger picture. Unfortunately, the conclusion is that the human dimension is sorely lacking in most new cities and developments.

The Brasilia Syndrome—Using Only the Top-Level Scale

One of the most outstanding examples of modernistic city planning is Brasilia, the capital of Brazil. Planned and developed in 1956 on the basis of Lucio da Costa's winning project in an architectural competition, the city officially became Brazil's capital in 1960 and now has more than three million inhabitants. This new city gives us a good opportunity to assess the consequences of planning focused exclusively on the top-level scale: city and development planning.

Seen from the air, Brasilia is a beautiful composition: designed like an eagle with the government quarters at the head and residential areas in the wings. The composition is still interesting in helicopter perspective, with distinct white government buildings and large housing blocks placed around large squares and green areas. So far, so good.

However, the city is a catastrophe seen at eye level, the scale planners ignored. City spaces are too large and amorphous, streets are too wide, and sidewalks and paths are too long and straight. The large green areas are crisscrossed by trampled footpaths showing how the inhabitants have voted with their feet in protest at the stiff, formal city plan. If you are not on an airplane or in a helicopter or car—and most people who live in Brasilia are not—there is not much to rejoice about.

The Brasilia Syndrome, where the two top-level scales are treated while the small scale is neglected, is unfortunately widespread as a planning principle.

The syndrome is at work in new housing developments in many parts of the world, for example, in China and other fast-growing regions in Asia. In Europe, too, many new urban quarters and developments are plagued by the Brasilia Syndrome, particularly new areas near large cities, such as Oerestad on the outskirts of Copenhagen. [. . .]

Life, Space, Buildings—in That Order

The Necessity of Starting with Life and Waiting with Buildings

If cities and buildings are going to invite people to come and stay, the human scale will require new and consistent treatment. Working with this scale is the most difficult and most sensitive urban planning discipline. If this work is neglected or fails, city life never stands a chance. The widespread practice of planning from above and outside must be replaced with new planning procedures from below and inside, following the principle: first life, then space, then buildings.

Life, Space, Buildings—in That Order, Please

Instead of the reverse order in the planning process that prioritizes buildings, then space and (perhaps) a little life, working with the human dimension requires life and space to be treated before buildings.

In brief, the method involves preparatory work that determines the character and extent of the anticipated life in the development. Then programs are prepared for the city spaces and city structure based on the desired walking and bicycling connections. Once the city space and connections are set, buildings can be positioned to ensure the best possible coexistence between life, spaces and buildings. From this point on, work expands into large developments and large districts, but is always rooted in the requirements for a well-functioning human scale.

Inherent in the order: life, space, buildings are opportunities for formulating requirements for new buildings early in the process to ensure that their functions and design support and enrich city space and city life.

The only successful approach to designing great cities for people must have city life and city space as a point of departure. It is the most important—and the most difficult approach, and it cannot be left until later in the process. If there is to be an order, it must start at eye level and end with a bird's-eye view. Naturally, the best of all worlds is to treat all three scales at the same time, holistically and convincingly.

Traditional City Planning Based on City Life and City Space

The life-space-buildings order is not an innovation: what is new is modernism and modern drawing-board planning using the reverse order. Modernism has only held sway for a period of 60 or 70 years, precisely the period in which the human dimension has been seriously neglected.

Reading

32

Volkmar Eidloth, Gerhard Ongyerth, and Heinrich Walgern

Historic Preservation of Urban Heritage: Its Framework and Fundamental Principles (2013)

This comprehensive handbook presents contemporary German approaches to urban conservation. In addition to discussing the history of urban monument preservation and methods of recording and analysis, the authors, members of a working group on urban heritage conservation, explain the legal framework and planning methodologies underlying urban conservation practice in Germany. They write that "urban heritage preservation perceives the city, town, and cultural landscape as categories of historical space that are more than the sum of their parts."

1. INTRODUCTION

Systematic preservation of urban heritage emerged in the 1970s. The declaration of the Year of European Architectural Heritage in 1975 galvanized great public and political support for the goals of historic preservation. New or amended heritage protection laws in Germany redefined the concept of the historical monument, allowing it to become more comprehensive in its scope than previously understood: it grew to include building ensembles, in particular historic city centers and towns, and large industrial facilities. Efforts to restore historic city centers and towns, and the legal and planning tools simultaneously developed, also demanded new conceptual approaches from historic preservation for the treatment of these "new" monuments. The conservation goals of historic preservation had to be formulated in alignment with urban development or urban design goals (Schulze 2001) and be presented as the protector of the public interest during the process of urban development planning and land consolidation. The interests of historic preservation had to be presented as spatially relevant to residential and cultural landscapes embedded in the contexts of local and national history in order

From Volkmar Eidloth, Gerhard Ongyerth, and Heinrich Walgern, *Handbuch Städtebauliche Denkmalpflege* (Petersberg, Germany: Michael Imhof, 2013), 13–23, 232–35, 297–300. Reproduced courtesy of the authors.

to be recognized and appropriately adhered to by countless new partners: city planners, local politicians, and not least of all, the inhabitants. For the first time, preservationists had to actively participate over the long term in the evolution of planning and its goals. [. . .]

2. Urban Heritage Preservation in the Historic Preservation System

Volkmar Eidloth

Cultural heritage conveys past experiences. A society's treatment of that heritage reflects its relationship to history. Accordingly, historic preservation is society's task and its implementation should be effected by everyone, if possible. The concept of historic preservation describes in concrete terms actual interaction with cultural heritage and comprises all of the corresponding activities and tasks, from research and interpretation to conservation and restoration. Protection of that heritage means exercising existing legal instruments for the exertion of historic preservation as a societal imperative (Martin 2002:7).

Preservation of urban heritage is part of the overall system of historic preservation. The former refers to Manfred Mosel's definition (1993), which encompasses its duality: two aspects that are almost always inextricably bound together in the practice of preservation of urban heritage. On the one hand, a specific, protected object is engaged by the full spectrum of preservation prerogatives, and in particular, the historical tradition in which the object is embedded and how we encounter this tradition, its entwining of a plurality of monuments and the interplay between the monument and its surroundings in the form of cities, rural residential areas, and cultural landscapes. On the other hand, conservation of urban heritage describes a distinct methodological approach: representation and advocacy of the demands of historic preservation during planning processes and at all levels of planning. By contrast, protection of urban cultural heritage would be—notwithstanding the fact that this is the title of a joint federal and state government program for urban renewal within the scope of urban development sponsorship—the introduction of building, planning, and cultural heritage management regulations that realize the ambitions of urban heritage preservation (cf. Martin/Krautzberger 2006:448).

Within the traditional ambit of historic preservation, preservation of urban heritage is located between the acquisition of a monument and practical historic preservation. Its close relationship to inventory results from the need for surveys and their mediating impact. This occurs, however, according to the needs at the time and within the framework of planning objectives and processes. It connects concrete measures to the historic preservation of objects, even when occurring in the future. The "object of treatment" in urban heritage preservation, however, is "not the individual monument, but the oppidan plan itself" (Mosel 1993:10) and its contribution to the preservation of cultural heritage.

Commonalities

The general principles and goals of urban heritage preservation are the same as for historic preservation overall (cf. Eidgenössische Kommission für Denkmalpflege 2007; Vereinigung der Landesdenkmalpfleger 2011). First and foremost is the understanding of a monument as material evidence of history. This historical meaning is not only exemplified in art historical contexts, but also comprises, alongside technological, economic, or social history, the history of habitation. It is manifested not only by individual objects but also in the stratified relationships of monuments, in ensembles of urban and rural monuments, or in cultural landscapes. "The fundamental value of every historic city and every other monument is its historical quality—is the fact that history is visible within it," as clarified by August Gebesseler (1975a:60) in his essay "Old City and Historic Preservation" in the catalog of the traveling exhibition *A Future for Our Past* during the Year of European Architectural Heritage.

In comparison, aesthetic, social, and societal meanings are validated, alongside concepts like milieu and identity, which are not entirely unjustified for urban heritage preservation. Recently, the keywords resource and sustainability have also been added. This purposeful orientation supports without question urban heritage preservation efforts and contributes to preservation (Mörsch 1989b). The value as evidence of history is, however, that which constitutes characterization as a monument, and in the context of a broad, overarching past, provides the basis for urban heritage preservation.

Such a historiographically understood concept of urban heritage preservation presupposes the authenticity of the monument as demonstrated by a substantive historical record. That urban heritage preservation values as generally understood and in pertinent legal texts instead prefer to be associated with the term cityscape or image of place, is a burden indebted to the genesis of the conceptualization of the ensemble, which 19th century terminology and values continue to influence, as demonstrated above all by Tilmann Breuer (1989).

As with images, urban heritage preservation is also concerned with the conservation of an appearance embedded in history. It is, however, dependent on the substantial presence of historical material. This allows the historical image to continually and reliably invoke its historical qualities. The historical imprint of building density and spaces brought forth by age and traces of time on structures, building components, and building materials allows the image of a place to become a valuable, historical document to be protected. If this tangible, visible history of place is increasingly exchanged and ultimately replaced, the historical value is lost, and historic preservation and protection are divested of their own foundation and essentiality (Strobel 1999:12).

Monuments, including urban heritage, always first come into being when their historical significance can be evinced, holding in readiness the object delivered out of the past for the present (Breuer 1982a:13). To acquire and convey knowledge about this significance is the framework of every form of historic preservation; comprehensive understanding of the monument is a prerequisite for every act of conservation. As a consequence, acquisition, analysis, and assessment as well as documentation of its existence, also have to belong to the fundamental principles of urban heritage preservation. [. . .]

Lack of recourse to information and resources is not the reason why urban preservation projects and measures all too often are executed without careful, expert preparation, and without detailed documentation. Rather, a widely disseminated attitude is responsible, which reduces urban heritage preservation to a question of redesigning an urban context, to "new building in old surroundings." Judgment of the formal quality of new buildings is not the primary task of conservation but rather the recognition, description, and preservation of the historical urban quality of city spaces.

Maintaining an intact historical substance during all planning processes and for all interventions is the fundamental priority of urban heritage preservation. Admittedly, this does not mean persistence of the unchangeability of the site. Everything in the urban environment does not possesses the same capability for historical significance, nor is it equally meaningful for the value of a group of monuments. For this reason, factually sound and historically grounded analysis is indispensable: it is capable of providing certainty when demanding preservation while at the same time illuminating where there is room for development, both of which are useful for the necessary and beneficial further evolution of residential areas.

Essential renovations, integrations, and additions also ought to be recognized in urban heritage as contemporary elements, yet should remain appropriate in their function and form. Above all, however, they must flow from the structure of the historic site. Georg Mörsch (1994b:36) describes this necessity: "A response to the surroundings [belongs] to good design, just as a good answer means listening to the questioner." The "dialectic nature of design" with the existing historical surroundings is not measured, however, by the degree of adaptation or harmonization. The creation of "homogenous images of home" cannot be the goal of contemporary urban heritage preservation (Vinken 2008). The particular historical value of the city lies in its historical complexity and not uncommonly is found exactly at the points of fracture and incompatibility in urban settings. Urban heritage preservation is also not at all concerned with the reconstruction of long lost cityscapes, for which the captious term "repair of the city" has recently been newly propagated (cf. Meier 2008).

Distinctive Features

Urban heritage preservation and its working methods have features distinctive from other types of historic preservation (Eidloth 2012). The most significant singularity is its all-encompassing structural approach when defining a monument and carrying out its conservation. Urban heritage preservation perceives the city, town, or cultural landscape as categories of historical space that are more than the sum of their parts, and their historical experiential value is not exhausted in the aesthetic of city, place, or landscape images. [. . .]

Urban structures valued as monuments emerge, however, not only out of the contiguity of buildings and their relationships to one another, but are ultimately manifested [see fig. 1] by the relationship between the built environment and vacant spaces, the placement and shape of streets and town squares, the distribution of water and green spaces, and the patterned parceling of land (cf. Gunzelmann 2008). They reflect earlier social differentiations, economic relationships, and functional connections. Not least of all, the structure and shape of the historical city also express general ideas and motifs as well as the manifestation of political will, which created the urban fabric, weaving it over centuries. Such structures represent an autonomous historical quality that, under the circumstances, does not even require the existence of single monuments.

As a consequence, urban heritage preservation compels more than the preparation of data for planning projects, like the naming and listing of of well-known monuments and ensembles. At the same time, surveying of urban heritage and site descriptions—as opposed to systematic inventories—must always be carried out, in form and content, in reference to the planning goal, the corresponding planning level, and its scale. This can also lead to having to make an informed selection from the entire collection of monuments. The scale in which spatial-structural monument values disclose themselves and in which urban heritage preservation functions is fundamentally smaller than that of the historic preservation of objects. It amounts to about 1:5,000 for planning in dense urban contexts, and from 1:25,000 to 1:50,000 at the regional planning level, and up to 1:100,000 or 1:200,000 in technical contributions to state-wide planning.

Fig. 1. Neustrelitz.

Cartographic illustration is an important tool of urban heritage preservation. Even if maps are admittedly a subjective medium that can be manipulated (Monmonier 1996), they still play an essential role when spatially and temporally complex circumstances are visualized, thereby thwarting the basic problem of urban heritage preservation investigative methods and documentation that tend to dissect the monumental value of the city into individual elements. [. . .]

Necessarily, the spectrum of scientific disciplines and basic principles that sustain historic preservation practice are broadened under urban heritage preservation. Above all, the history of urban development and planning are prominent. Research carried out by Albers (1975) made clear that the history of the discipline of urban development at the outset and over long periods of time is still read as the history of the discipline of urban heritage preservation (cf. also Buch 1985). Indispensable contributions to urban heritage preservation come above all from the history of urban development understood as an architectural history of the city based on archaeology of the city center and building research, and in which it has been rooted since the 1970s (cf. Meckseper 2007).

Historical geography plays a leading role, whose efforts towards spatial-temporal differentiation is particularly close to the questions posed by and tasks of urban heritage preservation (Ongyerth 1996; Eidloth 2001a). Alongside genetic cultural landscape research (cf. Schenk, Fehn, and Denecke 1997), historical-geographical urban research (cf. Denecke 2004) has developed methodical approaches to the acquisition, analysis, and mediation of urban heritage and produced results that have been taken up and made useful by historic preservation. Nevertheless, urban history and historical urban geography are seldom encountered to date in the substantiation of urban heritage assessments as scientific grounds for protection of urban or planning history.

The most distinctive feature of urban heritage preservation compared to other types of historic preservation lies in its pursuit of conservation goals within the framework of public planning. Practical architectural preservation is carried out almost entirely according to the given occasion, and its recommendations react to immediate usage demands, plans for alterations, instances of damage, or the desire to stage history. Urban heritage preservation, on the other hand, anticipates, creating concrete measures for the monument and its preservation, and attempts to influence planning so that favorable conditions are in place for proper preservation of the monument. Urban heritage preservation paves the way for preservation of cultural monuments. Justifiably so, it may be characterized as preventive preservation or, analogous to the system of urban land-use planning, as "preliminary architectural preservation" (Mosel 1998:143). Conversely, the efforts of urban heritage preservation are often at first effected with considerable time delay; its results for the most part cannot be celebrated through striking before and after comparisons. Apparently this makes urban heritage preservation as a field of historic preservation not very attractive.

The participatory act is decisive for the success of urban heritage preservation endeavors. Willibald Sauerländer (1976:13) has already pointed this out: "The historic preservationist must be included as a partner in the very first urban development deliberations. Otherwise, he always takes on the role of the hare who discovers that the tortoise of the planocracy has already won the race." Participation in historic preservation today cannot, however, limit itself to passive participation, but must demand active participation. In view of current planning realities, it is neither sufficient to merely participate as a representative of public interest, nor to be involved only at the level of mandatory urban land-use planning. It is valid to present and formulate historic preservation values and goals in zoning plans and when establishing frameworks for regional and state planning. There is a long list of exemplary models (cf. Walgern 2010), even if involvement of historic preservation at these levels of planning is still not the rule, and standards for content and methodology are still lacking. Informal plans have gained significance, above all because they provide the opportunity to historic preservation to bring "in its own chosen way" its concerns into the planning process before concrete planning goals have been defined (Walgern 2010b:119). The "critical juncture" for dealing with urban heritage "is at the conceptualization phase of development and land-use planning, not first during implementation planning and not at all at the moment of construction" (Mosel 2007:185).

Monument Topography

Claus-Peter Echter, Christophe Schwartzkopf, Gerhard Ongyerth

The published series Monument Topography encompasses and describes monuments within the contexts of place and space, and also occasionally in the cultural landscape. The monuments and ensembles blanketing a tract of land systematically illustrate monument topography through texts, images, and mapping. With the help of this series of surveys, organized by city and county, all monuments in Germany are to be described and documented as uniformly as possible. An instrument for mediation of monuments, monument topography is classified between a monument inventory and the more in-depth scholarly treatment of a survey. Exceptional exemplars of monument topography surveys include the *City Center Atlas* for Baden-Württemberg, the *Eras of Construction Plan* for urban renewal in Bavaria, and the *Dehio Compendium of Artistic Monuments in Germany.*

Monument topography is highly valued in federal and local preservation efforts as a topical method for describing and documenting monuments. Germany's monument topography is unprecedented in Europe in its role as information source for preservation and basis for urban land-use planning. With the help of this series of publications, a catalog of monuments in German states has been systematically published since 1980. At the same time, the series relates fundamental art history and information for current planning and building in cities and counties while promoting awareness of history and monuments to the public.

[. . .]

New requirements have been demanded from monument topography since the 1990s through the incorporation of monumental sites in the historical cultural land-

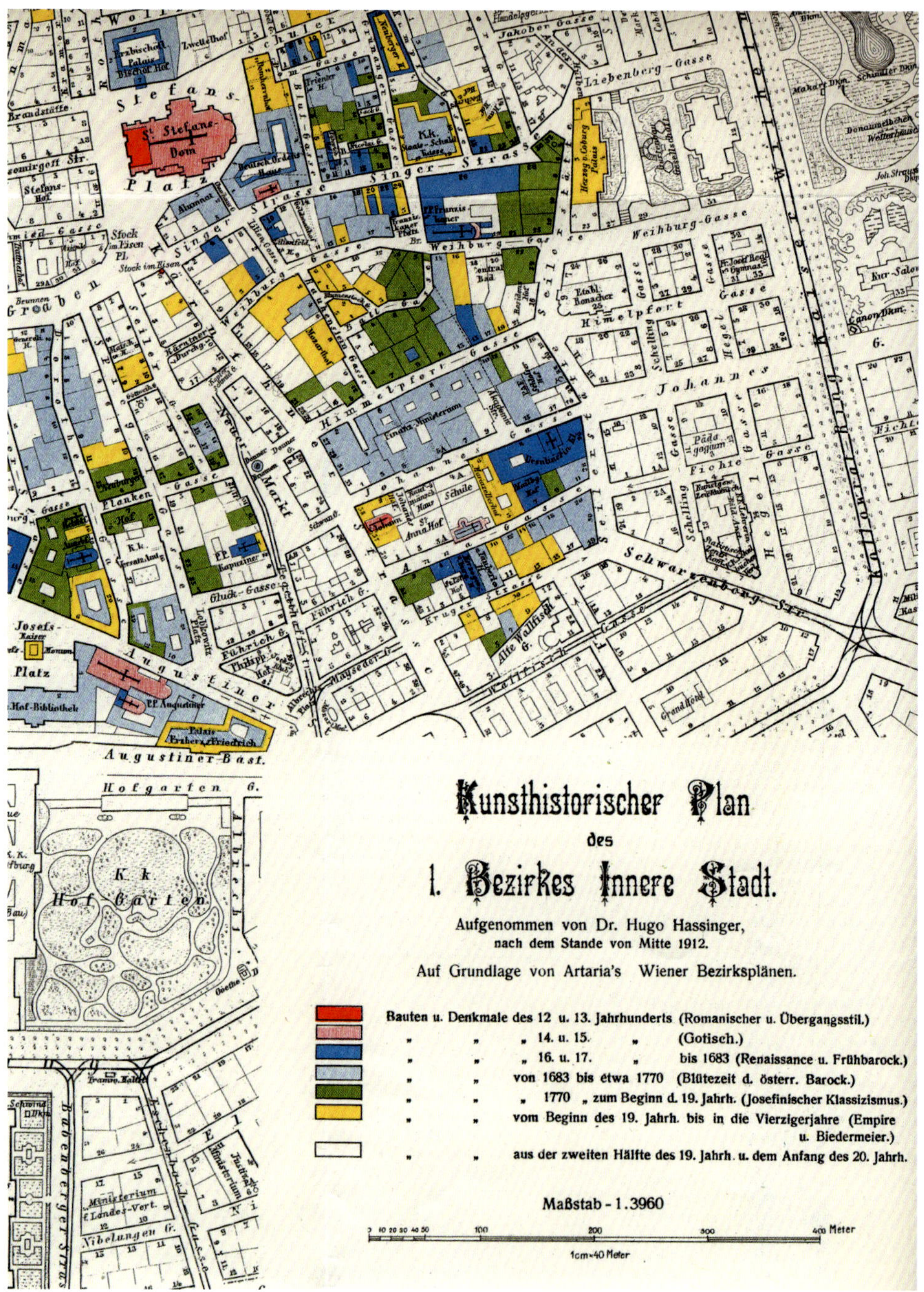

Fig. 2. Art historical map of the imperial city and residence, Vienna, by Hugo Hassinger, 1916 (detail).

scape. In recent topography volumes the preface, which gained considerable meaning in the 1980s, describes exemplarily the historical cultural landscape of each region. The main text of the monument topography comprises analytical characterization of the monuments, which is executed in essays and images of differing forms. In some states, archaeological monuments are also included. [. . .]

The qualities of historical structures, whole facilities, and cities must be captured for the purposes of preventive conservation. In the monument topographies, historians document and communicate necessary values indispensable for all phases of planning. Monument topography is an instrument that communicates historical-urban meaning; it is an information source for everyone connected to building and serves as the fundamental material for preparing urban construction plans, zoning plans, development plans, and preservation statutes. Monument topographies are valuable for understanding the built environment and the prerequisites of developing sustainable concepts for preservation and design planning for cultural heritage. Monument topography guarantees that the requirements of historic preservation are integrated early in public and private planning processes. Monument topography is meaningful as an inventory and aid to planning. –Ech.
References: Echter 2006; Harznetter 2004; Ongyerth 2008; Titze 2011.

Documentation

Documentation makes information about a document or an object, its changes or its state of preservation, useful for the given situation. The goal of documentation is systematic structuring of information that has been acquired and evaluated. Generally, it consists of documents like texts, maps/plans, and photographs containing information that is utilized through description, registration, and cataloging. Documentation for historic preservation is not without a purpose. Comprehensive and irreplaceable as a record of loss in archaeological preservation, it is deliberately carried out in the planning context and at all stages. Proven methods of documentation for historic preservation are building inspections, monument topography, and inventory. Documentation of urban sites contains as a rule systematic explanations based on expert assessments or opinions of the protected object in the form of texts, thematic maps, photographs, and databases.

Documentation is composed mostly of texts, maps, and plans of differing scales, and photographs, or, ideally, an interactive network in a digital document or specialized information system. Urban heritage preservation analog documentation in the form of maps varies: there are topographical overview maps at a scale of 1:50,000 and 1:25,000, place maps at a scale of 1:5,000 and 1:2,500, and historical maps, like the land register maps of the early 19th century and current cadastral maps of the area in question. In addition, there are maps in series or thematic maps for analysis, planning, and documentation as well as a monument map. Series of maps have proven to be useful for communicating the evolution of a place or a cultural landscape by depicting chronological cross sections (e.g., Roman era, Middle Ages, early modern era, first half of the 19th century until the first land surveys, first half of the 20th century before World War I, around 1945–1950, and the present) that are based on historical or current base maps. Special thematic maps, e.g., based on local land registries or property maps, can show the location of historical properties, historical ownership, buildings with special functions, and the historical social topography. The "monument map" is the most important map for documentation. It shows the location, distribution, and spaces surrounding monuments and architectural facilities. Thematic maps often serve planning purposes when documenting urban heritage: alongside the location and distribution of the monument, they reveal historic preservation interests or resources, "structures defining the landscape," "landmark buildings," "constitutive elements," historically significant spatial structures, the edges of areas, and historical green areas. Thematic mapping can be represented like an *Eras of Construction* plan or it can document the assessment of the objects represented as possessing a "special preservation value," "preservation value," or as "expendable." Monument protection acts require verifiability and comparability of the assessment.

Distinctions can be made among thematic maps of historic cultural landscapes: there are acquisition maps based on property maps at a scale of 1:5,000 or for larger districts 1:10,000; site maps based on the current cadastral map portraying all residential, agricultural, industrial, hydraulic, transport, and recreational, as well as religious, federal, military, and "associative cultural landscape" (i.e., views, built environment, intangible historical places) areas at a scale of 1:5,000, or for larger districts analogous to a landscape plan at 1:10,000; and overall views of the historic cultural landscape in the area under examination. This representation can be supplemented with a catalog of features or a database ("inventory of historic cultural landscape"). In every cartographic documentation, a standardized legend explains the content (Vereinigung der Landesdenkmalpfleger 1981). Photography supplements the texts and maps. Analog photographic documentation varies among oblique aerial images, overall views of ensembles or spatial constructions, individual views of buildings, and spatial arrangements. The most modern digital form of documentation of monuments—in principle, however, still mechanical—are databases in specialized information systems for historic preservation, from which texts, themes, types of monuments, and lists of photos can be generated. Databases are information collection and storage systems as well as a tool for evaluation of information and the production of documentation.

—~—

Inventory

Claus-Peter Echter

Inventory is characterized as the listing of components in a group of objects. In historic preservation, this term means comprehensive scholarly acquisition and representation of the aggregate contents of monuments in a given space, or also the components of a monument. Short and long inventories are differentiated according to their level of scholarly exactness, organization, and scope. Inventory is understood as the systematic acquisition and scholarly study of monuments. Its goals are to recognize and interpret art and historic objects through their elucidation and understanding as monuments, to establish the properties of monuments, and to document that which is worth protecting. The results of inventory are official monument lists or monument registries, long inventories, and monument topographies. The term inventory is also used for published surveys.

The term "inventory" came into use at the end of the 19th century. Since its beginnings in the 19th century, historic preservation recognized the scholarly examination of monuments as a necessary foundation for the practice of historic preservation. [. . .]

—~—

With their fundamental and detailed history of building and archival documentation of monuments, in-depth, scholarly long inventories conceived at the end of the 19th century are of great and lasting value. They cannot, however, meet in this form the most recent needs of monument protection and preservation, due to their exhaustive and time-consuming working methods and historical orientation toward the individual object. Integrated historic preservation requires inclusion of archaeological heritage preservation. Since the 1970s, documentation of structures that encompass objects has also become a component of inventories. Topography, urban development, and a city's layout are the subject of discussion. Planning guidelines for urban development and land use for the community under examination are expected to arise from the results of integrated inventories. [. . .]

[. . .]

Survey

Systematic, comprehensive acquisition of monuments as a source of and witness to human history; the description, evaluation, study, and interpretation of the results in word, image, and later also with maps, belong since institutionalization of federal historic preservation to its central, statutory obligations. This scholarly undertaking is characterized as survey. Alongside individual monuments, survey is occupied with ensembles, city neighborhoods, towns, parks, and industrial areas. It should communicate to all those concerned—owners, government authorities, historians, and the public—the ideal and substantive value of the monument.

Completing a survey uses descriptive methods borrowed from the arts and humanities, critically assessing sources and making comparisons. This entails the collection of information, its interpretation, and evaluation. The methodical approach to a survey is fundamentally the same, independent of whether it is the revision of a monument list or a cursory inventory, a single assessment, the creation of a monument topography, or an in-depth inventory. The strategic goals alone may differ, its main focus, and depth. Revision of a monument list primarily fulfills the legal mandate, creating legal certainty, and making possible administrative implementation. The survey documents the extensive results of research, exposing the current state of scholarship concerning the monument. Other instruments of research belong to survey in its broader sense, like historic preservation data entry forms, city center and place atlases, or expert assessment of urban heritage preservation.

References

ALBERS, Gerd (1975): Entwicklungslinien im Städtebau. Ideen, Thesen, Aussagen 1875–1945. – Bauwelt-Fundamente 46. Gütersloh.

BREUER, Tilmann (1982): Erfassen und Dokumentieren. Wissenschaftliche Methoden zur wertenden Darstellung geschichtlicher Überlieferung. – DEUTSCHES NATIONALKOMITEE FÜR DENKMALSCHUTZ (Hrsg.): Erfassen und Dokumentieren im Denkmalschutz. Dokumentation des Colloquiums des Deutschen Nationalkomitees für Denkmalschutz in Zusammenarbeit mit dem Landesdenkmalamt Baden-Württemberg. 4. und 5. März 1982 in der Liederhalle Stuttgart. – Schriftenreihe des Deutschen Nationalkomitees für Denkmalschutz 16. Bonn: 11–16.

BREUER, Tilmann (1989): Ensemble - ein Begriff gegenwärtiger Denkmalkunde und die Hypotheken seines Ursprungs. - MÖRSCH. Georg / STROBEL. Richard (Hrsg.): Die Denkmalpflege als Plage und Frage. Festgabe für August Gebeßler. München: 38–52.

BUCH, Felicitas (1985): Bebaute Bereiche als Geschichtsquellen. Der historische Bestand im Spannungsfeld von Städtebau und Denkmalpflege. - Denkmalpflege in BadenWürttemberg 14: 16–20.

DENECKE, Dietrich (2004): Anwendungsorientierte historisch-geographische Stadtforschung im System Denkmalpflege.- SEGERS-GLOCKE, Christiane (Hrsg.): System Denkmalpflege - Netzwerke für die Zukunft. Bürgerschaftliches Engagement in der Denkmalpflege. Jahrestagung der Vereinigung der Landesdenkmalpfleger in der Bundesrepublik Deutschland vom 22.–25 Juni 2003 in Hannover. – Arbeitshefte zur Denkmalpflege in Niedersachsen 31. Hannover: 360–369.

ECHTER, Claus-Peter (2006): Die Denkmaltopographie als Erfassungsinstrument und kulturgeschichtliches Unternehmen. - Difu-Beiträge zur Stadtforschung 43. Berlin.

EIDGENÖSSISCHE KOMMISSION FÜR DENKMALPFLEGE (2007): Leitsätze zur Denkmalpflege in der Schweiz. Zürich.

EIDLOTH, Volkmar (2001): Angewandte Historische Geograph ie in der Denkmalpflege. - RUPPERT, Godehard (Hrsg): 20 Jahre Historische Geographie in Bamberg (Bamberger Universitätsreden 7). Bamberg: 26–43.

EIDLOTH, Volkmar (2012): Städtebauliche Denkmalpflege - Denkmalpflege der besonderen Art. - SKALECKI, Georg (Hrsg.): Unterwegs in Zwischenräumen. Stadt - Garten - Denkmalpflege. 79. Tag für Denkmalpflege und Jahrestagung der Vereinigung der Landesdenkmalpfleger in der Bundesrepublik Deutschland in Bremen 5.-8. Juni 2011. – Denkmalpflege in Bremen 9. Bremen: 110–120.

GEBESSLER, August (1975): Altstadt und Denkmalpflege. - PETZET. Michael /WOLTERS, Wolfgang (Hrsg.): Eine Zukunft für unsere Vergangenheit. Denkmalschutz und Denkmalpflege in der Bundesrepublik Deutschland. Katalog der Wanderausstellung 1975–76 für das Europäische Denkmalschutzjahr 1975. München: 57–72.

GUNZELMANN, Thomas (2008): Inventarisation und räumliche Strukturen am Beispiel des Inventars Bamberg. - FRANZ, Birgit/ DOLFF-BONEKÄMPER, Gabi (Hrsg.): Sozialer Raum und Denkmalinventar. Vorgehensweisen zwischen Erhalt, Verlust, Wandel und

Fortschreibung (Veröffentlichung des Arbeitskreises Theorie und Lehre der Denkmalpflege 17). Dresden: 36–44.

HARZENETIER, Markus (2004): Denkmaltopographie Bundesrepublik Deutschland: das bayerische Beispiel. – Denkmalpflege Informationen B 127: 84–87.

MARTIN, Dieter (2002): Landesdenkmalgesetze im Vergleich. - PETRA-KELLY-STIFTUNG (Hrsg.): Denkmalschutz: Privatinitiative statt staatlicher Gängelung? Dokumentation einerTagung am 23./24. Januar 2002 inTutzing. – Kommunalpolitische Schriftenreihe 6. Bamberg/ München: 6–12.

MARTIN, Dieter / KRAUTZBERGER, Michael (Hrsg.) (2006): Handbuch Denkmalschutz und Denkmalpflege – einschließlich Archäologie - Recht, fachliche Grundsätze, Verfahren, Finanzierung. 2. erw. Aufl. München.

MECKSEPER, Cord (2007): Stationen undTendenzen stadtbaugeschichtlicher Forschung. - ESCHERICH, Mark / MISCH, Christian/ MÜLLER, Rainer (Hrsg.): Entstehung und Wandel mittelalterlicher Städte in Thüringen. – Erfurter Studien zur Kunst- und Baugeschichte 3. Berlin: 9–20.

MEIER, Hans Rudolf (2008): Stadtreparatur und Denkmalpflege - Die Denkmalpflege 66: 105–117.

MÖRSCH, Georg (1989): Denkmalwerte. - MÖRSCH, Georg/ STROBEL, Richard (Hrsg.): Die Denkmalpflege als Plage und Frage. Festgabe für August Gebeßler. München *I* Berlin: 133–142.

MÖRSCH, Georg (1994): Stadtgestaltung oder Denkmalpflege. Vom falschen Gegensatz und von verpaßten Chancen. - SCHIRMBECK, Egon (Hrsg.): Zukunft der Gegenwart. Internationales Symposium über neues Bauen in historischem Kontext. Universität Stuttgart mitTechnischer Universität Dresden im Auftrag der Wüstenrot Stiftung Deutscher Eigenheimvereine.V, Ludwigsburg. Stuttgart: 23–43.

MONMONIER, Mark (1996): Eins zu einer Million. Die Tricks und Lügen der Kartographen. Basel/ Boston/ Wien.

MOSEL, Manfred (1993): Beitrag der Denkmalpflege zu Erneuerungsplanungen in historischen Siedlungen. - MOSEL, Manfred (Hrsg.): Vereinigung der Landesdenkmalpfleger in der Bundesrepublik Deutschland. Arbeitsgruppe Städtebauliche Denkmalpflege. Serninartagung, Lübeck 30.9. – 2.10.1991, Großer Börsensaal im Rathaus. Vorträge. Hamburg: 10–18 [unveröff. Mskr.].

MOSEL, Manfred (1998): Städtebauliche Denkmalpflege in Bayern. - BÖNING-WEIS, Susanne/ HEMMETER, Karlheinz /LANGENSTEIN, York (Hrsg.): Monumental Festschrift für Michael Petzet zum 65. Geburtstag am 12. April 1998. –Arbeitshefte des Bayerischen Landesamtes für Denkmalpflege 100. München: 141–146.

MOSEL, Manfred (2007): Substanz. Struktur, Bild- konservatorisches Handeln im Ensemble. – REGIERUNGSPRÄSlDIUM STUTTGART. LANDESAMT FÜR DENKMALPFLEGE (Hrsg.): Altstädte unter Denkmalschutz. 50 Jahre Ensembleschutz in Deutschland und den benachbarten Ausland. Internationale Tagung Meersburg, 28.–30. Oktober 2004. - Regierungspräsidium Stuttgart, Landesamt für Denkmalpflege, Arbeitsheft 19. Stuttgart: 177–186.

ONGYERTH, Gerhard (1996): Denkmalpflege und Geographie. Zur Neubewertung geographischer Methoden. – Berichte zur deutschen Landeskunde 70: 115–131.

ONGYERTH, Gerhard (2008): Möglichkeiten und Grenzen der Darstellung von Kulturlandschaft in Denkmaltopographien. - REGIERUNGSPRÄSIDIUM STUTTGART, LANDESAMT FÜR DENKMALPFLEGE (Hrsg.): Das Denkmal als Fragment - das Fragment als Denkmal. Denkmale als Attraktionen. Tagungsband zur Jahrestagung der Vereinigung der Landesdenkmalpfleger in der Bundesrepublik Deutschland und des Verbandes der Landesarchäologen in der Bundesrepublik Deutschland vom 10.–13. Juni 2007 in Esslingen am Neckar. -Arbeitshefte Landesdenkmalamt Baden-Württemberg 21. Stuttgart: 431–441.

SAUERLÄNDER, Willibald (1976): Einführung. –ARBEITSKREIS STÄDTEBAULICHE DENKMALPFLEGE DER FRITZ THYSSEN STIFTUNG (Hrsg.): Die Kunst unsere Städte zu erhalten. Stuttgart: 6–13.

SCHENK, Winfried/ FEHN, Klaus / DENECKE, Dietrich (Hrsg.) (1997): Kulturlandschaftspflege. Beiträge der Geographie zur räumlichen Planung. Stuttgart/ Berlin.

SCHULZE, Jörg (2001): Schein oder Sein. Stadtbildpflege und Ensembleschutz. -VEREINIGUNG DER LANDESDENKMALPFLEGER IN DER BUNDESREPUBLIK DEUTSCHLAND/ LANDESDENKMALAMT BADEN-WÜRTTEMBERG (Hrsg.): Ensembleschutz und städtebauliche Entwicklung. Dokumentation der Seminartagung in Wolfsburg vom 16. bis 18. September 1998. – Berichte zu Forschung und Praxis der Denkmalpflege in Deutschland 9. Stuttgart: 65–73.

STROBEL, Richard (1999): Ortsanalyse und Stadtbildpflege. Grundsätze und Konflikte. - Die Denkmalpflege 57:5–12.

TITZE, Marie (2011): Vom Experiment zur Schwerpunktaufgabe. Die „ Denkmaltopographie Bundesrepublik Deutschland" als Zukunftsproiekt. - Die Denkmalpflege 69: 49–57.

VEREINIGUNG DER LANDESDENKMALPFLEGER IN DER BUNDESREPUBLIK DEUTSCHLAND (1981): Richtlinien der Vereinigung der Landesdenkmalpfleger in der Bundesrepublik Deutschland zur Erstellung einer Denkmaltopographie Bundesrepublik Deutschland. - Deutsche Kunst und Denkmalpflege 39: 69.

VEREINIGUNG DER LANDESDENKMALPFLEGER IN DER BUNDESREPUBLIK DEUTSCHLAND (Hrsg.) (2011): Leitbild Denkmalpflege. Zur Standortbestimmung der Denkmalpflege heute. Bearb. v. Jörg Haspel. Markus Harzenetter. Frank Pieter Hesse und Detlef Karg. Petersberg.

VINKEN, Gerhard (2008): Stadt, Denkmal. Bild. Wider die homogenen Bilder der Heimat. - BRANDT. Sigrid/ MEIER. Hans-Rudolf (Hrsg.): Stadtbild und Denkmalpflege. Konstruktion und Rezeption von Bildern der Stadt: - Stadtentwicklung und Denkmalpflege 11. Berlin: 162–175.

WALGERN, Heinrich (2010): Kulturlandschaftlich-denkmalpflegensche Fachbeiträge zur räumlichen Planung. – BUND HEIMAT UND UMWELT (BHU) (Hrsg.): Kulturlandschaft in der Anwendung. Ergebnisband zum Symposium am 19. März 2009 im Geographischen Institut der Rheinischen Friedrich-Wilhelms-Universität. Bonn: 109–119.

Reading

33

Jinnai Hidenobu

Tokyo: A Spatial Anthropology (1985)

Jinnai Hidenobu is an acclaimed Japanese architectural historian who has walked much of Tokyo searching (with maps and keen senses) for remnants of past urbanism. He identifies three significant periods in the structuring of Tokyo's urban space: the Edo, or Tokugawa, period (1600–1867); the Meiji period (1867–ca. 1920); and the Taishō and Shōwa periods (1920–45), when "Western ideas of city planning were introduced." Yet, Jinnai points out, the adoption of Western cultural elements in the city was gradual, built on the urban form of the past, producing an urban space unique to Japan. What he sees today is a renewed interest in the production of local individuality such as can be found in the groves at local shrines and canal-side landmarks.

Introduction

There is something I always have to explain to foreign visitors in Tokyo.

"Tokyo," I find myself saying, "is an anomaly among the capital cities of the world. You see, it's become difficult here to find a house that's even a century old."

Twice, most of Tokyo was reduced to smoldering ruins, once during the earthquake of 1923, and once again during the Pacific War. Then wholesale demolition and reconstruction followed during the postwar period of rapid growth. The Tokyo cityscape has completely changed. We are now in an unusual position—the only way we can see the Tokyo of the Meiji period (1868–1912), which was built by ravenously adopting Western culture, is in pictures and photographs. Tokyo is a great metropolis that seems to have lost the face of its own past.

—ʌʌʌ—

From Jinnai Hidenobu, *Tokyo: A Spatial Anthropology,* translated by Kimiko Nishimura (Berkeley: University of California Press, 1995), 1–6, 64–65, 214–16. Originally published in Japanese as *Tokyo no kûkan jinruigaku* (Tokyo: Chikuma Shobō, 1985). Reproduced courtesy of the author and Chikuma Shobo.

[. . .] From the standpoint of modern rationalism, with its reverence for clarity, it is truly difficult to form an overall picture of Tokyo's urban space. Increasingly, there are few tasteful old buildings, and the streets and neighborhoods are losing their character. And yet, walking the streets of the city, one is treated to repeated changes in the cityscape. There is unexpected variety in the topography, with the high city's hills and cliffs, winding roads, shrine groves, and large, verdant estates; and the low city's canals and bridges, alleyways and storefront planter pots, and crowded entertainment centers. For the walker in Tokyo, the unexpected is always waiting. Tokyo may not have the old buildings of New York, but each place evokes a distinctive atmosphere nurtured over a long history: this makes Tokyo what it is. Recently, we have also begun to encounter marvelous works of architecture, overflowing with the kind of contemporary sensibility that uses the environmental context to heighten the appeal of the site as a whole. In the rush of our daily lives, however, and accustomed as we are to moving about by subway and automobile, we have few chances to take a leisurely walk around the city. As a result, we are growing insensitive to the appeal of such places.

Under these circumstances, do we simply give up, lamenting that with few buildings left from a century ago, Tokyo has lost the face of its past, its identity? No! To do so would be premature. Instead, we should see that in Tokyo a rich variety of physical locations, along with the urban structure that has filled them since the Edo—or Tokugawa—period (1600–1867), forms the essential framework of today's city. This framework, together with the interweaving of old and new elements that makes up the contents of the city, has produced an urban space that is without parallel in the world. [. . .]

Once, after a number of years of such experiences, I found myself facing an audience of American university students of architecture and landscaping and delivering a series of slide-illustrated lectures (in English, no less) on the emergence of Tokyo. Although I specialize in architectural and urban history, I could not see much value in explaining history as such to a foreign audience. Instead, I decided to incorporate a historical approach into my "reading" of the distinctive features of contemporary Tokyo that had emerged as a result of its development. I entitled my lectures "The Rhetoric of Tokyo's Urban Space," thinking that it might appear novel to my foreign audience, and I made an effort to unlock the secrets of the city's urban space for them. Paying attention to such features of the high and low cities as topography, roads, and land use, I showed that there were continuities from the city of Edo to be found in each, and that the structure of the city worked out during the Edo period serves as the basic stratum of contemporary Tokyo. I then addressed a wide range of issues, including the sense of scale, both in the city and in its architecture; the relations between nature and the city, especially the spatial configuration of the waterside; the use of axes and symmetry within the city; the existence of landmarks; the siting of buildings on lots; and finally, the ways that Japanese and Western elements are combined at various levels, from architectural design to urban space. I was hoping to clarify the logic found in the Japanese style of composing space. This meant that I was interpreting the most quotidian urban space that encompasses us—the sort of interpretation that occurs only when we try to make something comprehensible to a foreign audience. As I talked, it came home to me that once we separate early modern Edo from modern Tokyo, we become totally incapable of grasping the distinctive features of today's Tokyo; Tokyo's characteristic form has to be regarded as the end product of a mixture of elements from both periods.

We need a vantage point that acknowledges the interpretation of the early modern and the modern in the formation of Edo-Tokyo and links the two periods in a single coherent vision. The notion of "Edo-Tokyo Studies" advocated recently by Shinzō[1] counters the tendency to treat the cities as separate entities by proposing that we cut across time and take a three-dimensional view. This is a praiseworthy notion indeed.

This attitude is especially important for our field, because it treats the formation of the city as continuous. Even with the advent of a new era, it is inconceivable that a soundly built city would use a single set of plans to alter its basic form suddenly and completely. It is true that after the Meiji Restoration, Tokyo transformed itself from the many-layered closed system of a castle-town to the open system of a modern city. But it preserved the urban form of the past and modernized in a flexible manner by replacing only the contents of individual lots.

Since the Age of Civilization and Enlightenment in the early Meiji period, Tokyo has taken Western cities as its model. But it would be a mistake to expect that an alien culture could be introduced and accepted as a total system. Western forms of architecture and urban design were incorporated gradually into the context of traditional Japanese cities, first by imitation combined with trial and error, and then by interpretation *à la japonaise*. This process produced an urban space and a cityspace encountered only in Japan. In all likelihood, this mode of adopting alien culture operates in much the same way even today.

In thinking about contemporary Tokyo as part of a single, Edo-Tokyo history, we can identify three important periods in the structuring of urban space.

First, and by far the most important, is the Edo period. The topography provided the most salient reasons for the formation of the city. Overlooking Tokyo Bay and situated at the edge of the Musashino Plain, Edo was favored with ideal conditions for the creation of an urban environment and a cityscape. In addition, this great castle-town used the topography masterfully in developing a system of roads and canals to divide the city into residential areas corresponding to the three major classes of warriors, commoners, and farmers. A residential environment and architectural forms suited to each class emerged: living spaces for the warrior class were created in the high city, with its varied land formations, whereas the commoners made their homes on land reclaimed from the river delta and threaded with canals in the low city.

Broadly speaking, a city can be conceptualized in two ways. It can be seen as an artificial creation, following an urban plan based on the ideas of the rulers or leaders. This process becomes possible only when it is sustained by a definite zeitgeist and urban ideal. Or a city can be seen as the space that its people actually inhabit. The varied activities of the people who live and work there give meaning to urban space and add to it an image of abundance. Literary approaches to the discussion of the city, naturally enough, take this approach.

We can use both conceptions in looking at the formation of the city of Edo. Early Edo developed in accord with administrative intentions as a "planned space" based on a clear ideal of the castle-town. But after the Great Meireki Fire of 1657, and particularly after the middle of the Edo period, the city went beyond the framework of the castle-town, merging with its abundant natural setting as it developed toward the periphery. The high city as a garden city[2] and the low city as a city on water—both became lived-in space that greatly enhanced Edo's appeal.

Tokyo today lives with and through its history. Although Western-style architecture and modes of transport were introduced wholesale to the city in modern times, its basic framework could not be easily destroyed. The city of Edo provided the basic design upon which, layer by layer, the modern and present-day cities of Tokyo were built.

The Meiji period, beginning with the Age of Civilization and Enlightenment, forms the second stage in the city's formation. During this period, a "loose" modernization was carried out by superimposing Western elements onto the legacy of Edo. With the collapse of the Tokugawa government, many daimyō establishments were left vacant. They provided facilities for the variety of urban functions necessary to Tokyo as the capital of a modern state. Although the district divisions and lot configurations—the basic framework of the city—remained virtually unchanged, the city was able to ease its way into the new age by altering the pattern of land use and replacing existing structures with more suitable, Western-style buildings.

As it began to adopt alien, Western cultural elements, Meiji-period Tokyo became a testing ground that was fascinating in its intricate mixture of the new and the old. Curious and original combinations, which are often noted by foreign visitors walking about the city, represent a legacy of Meiji that still thrives today.

In many cases, however, only the individual buildings were made conspicuous by their Western style, while the framework, or context, of the city remained that of Edo. In the end, the people could not conceive of entire districts made up of rows of buildings, or of the city as one great urban space. The problem for them remained how to express the spirit of civilization and enlightenment within the boundaries set by individual buildings and individual lots.

Meiji-period Tokyo succeeded more or less easily to Edo's urban legacy and expressed the spirit of the new age by means of outstanding individual elements. In contrast, during the late Taishō and early Shōwa periods—the 1920s—Western ideas of city planning were introduced and knowledge of its methods of constructing urban space deepened appreciably. At this time the actual framework, or context, of Tokyo as a city was remade along modern lines. We can therefore treat this period as the third stage in the city's formation. Unlike the Meiji period, when the light of civilization and enlightenment shone almost exclusively on buildings belonging to the state and financial combines (*zaibatsu*), modernization in the 1920s made itself felt in the everyday urban spaces surrounding people's actual lives, where designs aimed not only at function and utility but at beauty and comfort as well. The modernist spirit, supported by the ideas of "Taishō democracy," created stylish modern urban spaces throughout Tokyo. Nearly all the urban spaces we enjoy today—the avenues, street corners, plazas, and parks—were built during this period. It was at this time, too, that citizens, experts, and administrators evinced a heightened concern toward Tokyo as a city. It is no exaggeration to say that the prototype of Tokyo as it appears today emerged during this period.

In sum, present-day Tokyo is the result of the layering, one upon the other, of three historically formed strata. Their interaction has given Tokyo an appearance different from that of cities in the West, one unique to itself.

Today, as Tokyo develops into a brilliant, international metropolis, only the dynamic uppermost layer meets the eye. In this book, I wish to apply the anatomist's scalpel to Tokyo from a variety of angles, descending to its deepest level in an effort to describe as fully as possible the distinctive features of its spatial structure. I hope, by uncovering and dissecting the development of Tokyo's urban space and the individuality expressed in its cityscapes, to provide a common ground for discussions of the Tokyo that ought to be. Whether in creating individual urban neighborhoods that make the most of their own special qualities or in designing expensive buildings for individual street-corner sites, I hope that this project will provide an effective guide.

—⁓—

1 THE HIGH CITY: SURFACE AND DEPTHS

Conclusion

Walking and reading the streets of Tokyo with old maps in hand makes it possible for anyone to grasp the fact that ours is a superb city endowed with a cityscape ingeniously created in accord with natural and topographical conditions. Examining the city in this way, we are astonished at the overwhelming number of instances where the urban environment we now enjoy in Tokyo is a legacy of the original urban planning of Edo. And we also come to understand that the city itself faces a crisis because we, the citizens of present-day Tokyo, are discarding this legacy in the name of functionality and efficiency.

We are still obsessed by the illusion of modern city planning. But if there had been no castle-town of Edo on the site of Tokyo and if we had had to build a modern city from a tabula rasa, we would have produced a desiccated city devoid of any flavor or expression, one that lacked coherence and failed to carry out even elementary functions. It was only by inheriting the solid framework of Edo, as well as the Edo people's ingenious sense of land use—of putting things where they belong—that Tokyo, even with its corpulent body, has managed to uphold the quality of its environment and survive to the present. Is it not incumbent on us, before we leap into any further large-scale development using modern technology, to accept this fact with humility?

By reading the city, we may be able to bring home to ourselves the historical structure of Edo, which we tend to think of as unrelated to present-day Tokyo. Even neighborhoods with which we are familiar take on a fresh appearance wherever we look. Although old buildings may no longer be standing, annual growth rings are deeply cut into—and memories are preserved throughout—the city of Tokyo. Gradually we realize that every district is rich in individual expression tied to the historic urban structure and to the local pattern of land use. Are there not genuine possibilities here for the enhancement of Tokyo's identity? It is beyond doubt that the more Tokyo is internationalized, the more we will value this rarest of urban structures in which new and old elements coexist and interact between its surfaces and its depths.

Until now we have tended to be dazzled and unduly influenced by the ceaseless movement of the city. Within the chaos, most people have forgotten who lives where and how; they have lost affection for their own locality. Beautiful cityscapes and wonderful living environments must be fostered slowly and steadily under the gaze of citizens who love and take pride in their land. Now is the time for us to sit down and, using a historical perspective, reacquaint ourselves with the ways our own towns and regions took shape. Until we do, we will not be able to speak concretely of creating a city that truly exists for those who live in it.

I urge you, then, to take up an old map and walk around Tokyo's high city, so rich in historical resources.

4 MODERNISM AND ITS URBAN FORMS

Conclusion: Toward a New Age of the City

[. . .]

[H]ave we not lost our capacity to enjoy city life, as well as our sense of how to create an abundant social environment? A void has persisted ever since the war. The desire to create urban forms has been cut short, and the Tokyo cityscape has been reduced to one of dreary, decontextualized uniformity.

At last, however, history has come full circle. In recent years citizens' demands for a full urban life and beauty in the cityscape have grown stronger. They have fostered a movement that takes greater cognizance of the urban and regional context and designs buildings fully suited to their location. If we are truly to rehabilitate the city, it is necessary—right now, while it is still readily accessible—to pay attention to the urban thinking of the 1920s and to learn as much as we can from this precious historical experience.

And yet, even as we rightly praise the urban forms of modernism, we must consider something else from the standpoint of today: the modernist approach to city-craft was born amid the lofty idealism of the 1920s, which, in its pursuit of social progress and development, was the high point of the modernization process. Its adoption of a new, Western sense of values and planning techniques as models may have been somewhat hasty. To be sure, the small parks and Dōjunkai apartments [. . .] were more than mere imitations of foreign models and in fact displayed a delicate Japanese sensibility in their spatial arrangements. But in general, administrators and experts during this period, in their zeal to elevate the life and culture of the city's people, adopted an attitude (at least at the level of ideals) that rejected the existing history and traditions of the city as premodern relics. As a result, nearly all of the traditional restaurant districts along the Sumida River, as well as the commoner living spaces among the alleyways of the low city, were fated to disappear.

Nevertheless, the dense urban context handed down from Edo remained alive in its essence. People's concern for the city was high, and their concept of chic city life was passed on to modern Tokyo. The result was an attractive urban envirorment composed of a mixture of old and new elements. At some unconscious level, the existing urban context was put to skillful use, and an urban space peculiar to Japanese modernism was elaborated, which included bridgeside plazas and corner lots.

Although administrators and urban experts at the time viewed the city as an organism,[3] their judgment of its historical and cultural values was superficial. Indifference to the city's legacy mounted during the postwar period of economic growth, and technology devoid of intellectual substance dominated. In cities throughout the country, historical neighborhoods and local cultures were razed, while the homogenization of urban space continued relentlessly. Because of a city planning that concentrated on large-scale development, the view of the city as "lived-in space" was suppressed for years.

Today's renascent age of the city is a phase considerably different from the era of modernism. The city's modernization and industrial development exacted a heavy price in the form of a wrecked urban and natural environment, and in the loss of local individuality. From the self-examination that came with this loss have come strong demands for an urban policy that values the quality of citizens' lives. As the slogans—"Culture," "Nature," "History," "Tradition"—adopted by many local governments make clear, groping efforts are under way to create urban localities with their own individual identities.

We are seeing a phenomenon that is the reverse of past experience, an element in the production of local individuality. Attention is now being given to places and urban spaces that somehow slipped through the net of urban planning bent on modernization, to places that have continued without interruption at the everyday level with the tenacity that marks anthropological structures, and to places that lend attractiveness to the cities as they are today. What places are they? They are groves at local shrines, landmarks next to water and vegetation, places that are tied to natural elements such as canals, riversides, and embankments. They are city neighborhoods, living spaces along alleyways, entertainment centers and districts overflowing with excitement—those typically Japanese spaces that give urban life its zip. They are all the places that city planning has virtually ignored.

For cities in Japan, which have assumed a position at the world's economic and technological vanguard, it is becoming increasingly difficult to find foreign models. In fact, we have entered an era when Europeans and Americans, in their search for something that can transcend Western rationalism, are turning an anxious gaze toward Japanese culture, architecture, and sense of urban space.

A way of thinking has emerged that seeks to rediscover the values of the existing urban space and the cityscape, which were formed from people's lives and culture during the long sweep of history from Edo to modern Tokyo. It regards these values as a vital key to the formation of our environment in the years to come. This is an idea that is most welcome indeed, for itself and for its potential contribution to Tokyo as a unique international city. This reconsideration of familiar urban spaces and cityscapes, which places the problems of the city and its environment within the dimensions of everyday living, should play a major role in promoting the participation of the people of Tokyo in making their own city. The problem is how to link this shift in values to the logic and technique of creating urban communities with an individual identity. With patient and sincere effort, and with the people's renewed concern to encourage us, it will surely be possible in the Tokyo of the twenty-first century, which will transcend the age of modernism and be based on a still more pluralistic sense of values.

Notes

1. "Nozomareru Edo-Tōkyō-gaku" (What we should expect from Edo-Tokyo studies; *Bungaku*, April 1983).
2. Kawazoe Noboru, *Tōkyōo no genfūkei* (The original landscape of Tokyo; NHK Books).
3. Ishihara Kenji, *Gendai toshi no keikaku* (Contemporary city planning).

Reading

34

JANET PILLAI

Cultural Mapping: A Guide to Understanding Place, Community and Continuity (2013)

Janet Pillai is a Malaysian sociologist and educator whose interest in urban conservation springs from her interest in how culture, identity, and place intersect. She is also involved with Arts-ED, an organization specializing in heritage education, research, and publications for local communities. Pillai advocates for cultural planning, a perspective on urban planning that takes into account a locality's culturally distinctive assets and its residents' needs and aspirations. Integral to this method is cultural mapping, which complements the physical documentation of heritage assets, thus providing for the benefit of local and nonlocal communities a more comprehensive understanding of what should be conserved.

INTRODUCTION

A community's sense of pride and appreciation of place must necessarily be grounded in the cultural roots and continuity of the locality. Insensitive and decontextualised development in the name of progress robs a place of its cultural integrity and the community its cultural connections. Regretfully, government planners and planning institutions in Asia remain prone to ignoring both cultural context and community, resulting in the creation of spaces that are often inappropriate for local cultural use. [However, there is] a more comprehensive, integrated and cross-disciplinary approach to local and regional development which encompasses the symbiotic relationship between culture, community, and environment—**Cultural Planning.**

Cultural planning is a sensitive and sustainable perspective on urban planning that responds to the culturally distinctive assets and resources of a locality as well as to local needs, aspirations and perceptions of place. It encourages policy makers to

From JANET PILLAI, *Cultural Mapping: A Guide to Understanding Place, Community and Continuity* (Petaling Jaya, Selangor, Malaysia: Strategic Information and Research Development Centre, 2013), 1, 3, 6, 11–12, 18–19, 22–24. Published with permission of Strategic Information and Research Development Centre.

think strategically about applying the culturally distinctive resources of the locality to economic and urban development. It is a place-based approach that utilizes local resources, links local constituencies and interest groups, and fulfils local needs. Its successful application requires a paradigm shift from the supremacy of bureaucratic decision-making to a process of active participation by local players whose culture, cultural energy and cultural creativity have been central to the evolution of the locality and the human settlement within it.

Cultural planning, therefore, has to be based upon thorough knowledge of the cultural character and ecology of the locality. This knowledge and understanding is acquired through **Cultural Mapping** of the site and community.

Cultural mapping is a systematic approach to recording and presenting information that provides an integrated picture of the cultural character, significance, and workings of a place. It employs specific tools and techniques to identify and document the cultural assets and resources of an area, and assess their significance for integrated planning which will retain the cultural integrity of the locality. [. . .]

1 CULTURE-BASED PLANNING

Cultural Planning or culture-based planning is an organic, place-based, and context-specific approach to planning that utilizes local culture as a resource for economic and urban development. This chapter [. . .] underscores the importance of understanding the cultural ecology of a place before developing policies and strategies for urban planning and explains how to draw upon local cultural capital or place-based resources when embarking on rejuvenation, revitalization or development of a site or community.

Cultural Capital

Culture is the product of the reciprocal interaction between people and a particular environment over time. This interaction gives rise to cultural knowledge—factual information, procedures, and skills procured over time in relation to the context. Cultural knowledge includes, among other things, the inhabitants' understanding of the space they occupy; their understanding of actors which influence the underlying dynamics and characteristics of the space; as well as vernacular skills and practices, philosophy, belief and value systems, perceptions, and instincts developed in relation to the place.

Culture comprises tangible and intangible aspects. The tangible aspect of culture (assets) exists as objects and artefacts that can be realized through the senses, while the intangible aspect of culture is that which exists intellectually in the minds of the bearer. While tangible aspects of culture—such as buildings, objects, and products—outlive those who create them, the intangible is fragile and vulnerable by its very nature as its preservation hinges on actors as well as social, environmental, and economic conditions.

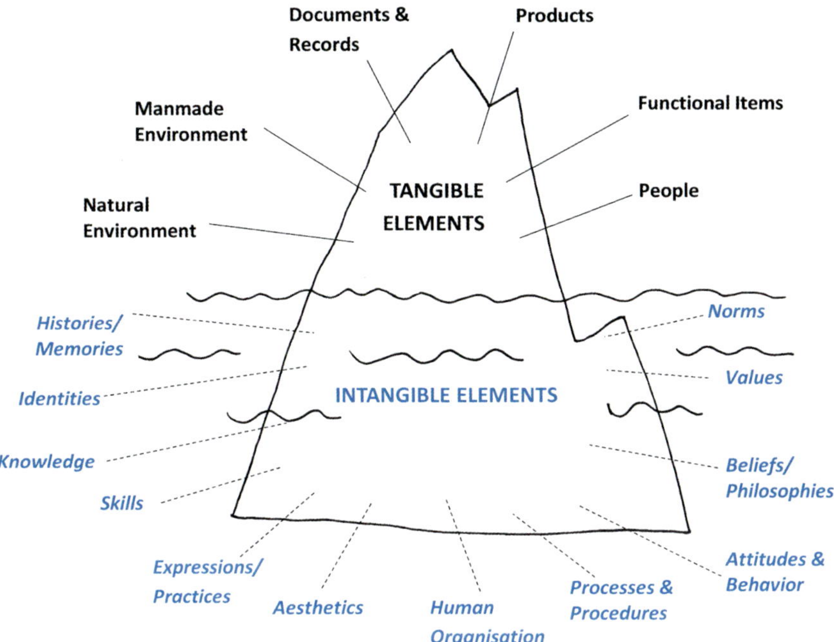

Fig. 1. Tangible and intangible aspects of culture.

Cultural Ecology

[. . .] Cultural planning, as a concept, encourages policymakers to respond to local needs, aspirations, and perceptions of place and to think strategically about the application of the culturally distinctive resources of the locality to economic and urban development. Cultural planning is viewed as a place-based approach which utilizes local resources, links local constituencies and interest groups, and fulfils local needs. Rather than viewing culture as an obstruction to development, it utilizes culture as a resource.

—∾—

City departments, academics, and professionals in the field are being persuaded to move beyond mere physical and economic planning and to incorporate a broader notion of culture as a premise in integrated development. Planning cannot be solely concerned with physical infrastructure and business opportunities which are often unrelated to needs and context. Planning requires a paradigm shift which looks at the context of each settlement with a cultural lens.

Human settlements are sustained by a complex ecology arising from the connectivity between several interrelated dimensions and elements. Intervention in a human settlement would require an integrated planning model that looks at the connectivity of these dimensions and elements in a holistic manner. Planning which takes into consideration the wider anthropological notion of culture requires an integrated and cross-disciplinary approach.

An approach based on the principles of systems thinking is potentially more suitable. Systems thinking requires an understanding of the components of a system, how they are interrelated and how their interdependence contributes to the workings of the complex whole. Optimal functioning of a system requires all component parts to be functioning well in relation to each other, and the whole system functioning in relation to another system. Fallout in one component will impact/affect other components and lead to change or disruption.

The term cultural planning therefore may, to an extent, be used interchangeably with the term **Integrated Planning**. Integrated planning examines all economic, social, and environmental costs and benefits in order to determine the most appropriate option and to plan a suitable course of action. Integrated planning looks at designs and configurations as expressions of the people for whom they are planned. It ensures participation of all stakeholders and affected sectors in joint planning.

2 CULTURAL MAPPING

[. . .] [C]ultural mapping involves identifying and recording the occurrence of cultural elements (tangible/intangible) in a geographical site, and synthesizing and interpreting the data to reveal cultural significance, cultural character or cultural patterns related to the people, place, and environment. The synthesis and analysis of cultural data collected can reveal how cultural ways of thinking and doing impact on the site and affect the social, economic, and environmental manifestations and workings of the site or settlement.

Who Conducts Cultural Mapping?

Cultural mapping may be undertaken on a large scale at the level of town or city planning, where governments or municipalities employ consultancy companies to design and execute the exercise. Such companies may in turn utilize experts to conduct surveys, research, and analysis which are then put forward in a special report. Outputs may be in the form of inventories, cultural statistics, drawn plans of the physical site, analysis, and recommendations. Cultural mapping undertaken in an academic context may be carried out by linguists, archaeologists, anthropologists, ethnographers, sociologists, etc. The mapping may be focused on a specific community or subject matter. Cultural mapping conducted within an academic context provides a deeper understanding of the culture of the selected site and community. Outputs are in the form of papers, articles, books, etc. and may have to be simplified if there is intention to make it accessible to the community.

Both approaches to cultural mapping mentioned above tend to sidestep the potential empowerment that can be generated from the dynamic process of community/stakeholder involvement. If the outcomes of cultural mapping are intended to facilitate uses such as policymaking, planning for conservation or management of cultural assets, or planning for creative industries, then it is critical that members of the community, planners, policymakers, potential investors, local government, etc. be invited to engage in the mapping and planning process.

Community/stakeholders may refer to residents, business groups, associations, local agencies, etc., operating in the cultural site. Engaging different communities and stakeholders as partners in the process of cultural mapping is challenging. Community/stakeholders are more willing to engage in cultural mapping if the process and expected outcomes can be seen to serve their needs or aspirations. Community/stakeholders should be aligned in their desire and commitment to the goals of a larger plan and shared outcomes from cultural mapping. Without expressed desire and support from stakeholders/community, cultural mapping outcomes may remain on a back-burner and become obsolete.

The degree of community or stakeholder involvement can vary depending on the degree of participation required as well as the reasons for wanting community/stakeholders participation. Community/stakeholders, such as a group of residents or a government agency, for example, may act merely as informants or contribute opinions in a mapping project or they may be motivated to conduct the mapping by themselves. The process of stakeholder engagement in mapping should be carefully planned and requires strategic efforts at trust and consensus building.

Increased levels of participation by the community or local agencies in the mapping exercise lead to a proportionate increase in awareness of the state of their assets and resources. This awareness contributes to their ability to make informed decisions. Deep engagement in the process of cultural mapping, planning, and decision-making provides knowledge, appreciation, and inspiration for interested stakeholders to move towards management, maintenance or revitalization of cultural assets.

Cultural mapping may also be initiated and conducted by the community, e.g., for folk art revitalization or conservation of a religious site. The community may be residents; social, religious, cultural and business organizations; administrative bodies; and institutions, which are advantaged by their familiarity, experience, and historical and cultural knowledge of the site.

Selecting What to Map

Mapping should include both tangible and intangible aspects of a culture as each complements the other in terms of form and function. Tangible cultural capital may include buildings, spaces, people, cultural objects or products, while the intangible capital may include organizations, events, activities, perceptions, values, etc. For the purpose of analysis, two major components which impact on cultural creativity, i.e., assets and resources, are mapped and recorded. Where possible, the mapping should include the location and distribution of these tangible and intangible items.

- ***Mapping Assets*** – identifies and records the location and distribution of tangible and intangible cultural items/elements in a site. Tangible assets may include people, buildings, facilities, spaces and landscapes, natural resources, documents, artefacts and products, and movable properties. Intangible items/elements may include business activities, practices, and events. Asset mapping provides a comprehensive database on local tangible and intangible cultural items.
- ***Mapping Resources*** – identifies both material and human resources that may have current application or use in the production and transmission of culture and cultural products. Human resource mapping locates people and their personal professional/political relationships as well as their organizational capacity, cultural knowledge, talents and skills. Resource mapping provides a database of persons, organizations, businesses, institutions, networks or indigenous systems and records that can drive leadership, communication, decision-making or transmission and management of information, knowledge or skills.

[. . .]

Integrated mapping is a holistic approach to mapping which incorporates the economic, social, and environmental dimensions of a human settlement. The three dimensions are treated as interrelated and interdependent components of a complex and unified whole, which includes both tangible and intangible cultural elements. The tangible (which exists as concrete objects) and the intangible (which exists as abstract ideas and beliefs) are interdependent. Together they make up a system. In order to conduct an integrated mapping of this system, it is necessary to map the concepts that underlie it and the system itself.

- ***Mapping Concepts*** – identifies intangible elements of culture such as identity, values, beliefs, and philosophy. Abstract concepts can be discerned from patterns, trends and preferences, behaviour and attitude, or opinions. Concept mapping helps to identify principles, beliefs or values that underlie the expressions and practices of the community. For example, mapping a community's belief and practices in the principles of 'feng shui' may explain the layout pattern, spatial arrangement or physical direction of the built environment, while the character of seasonal festivals, rituals, and foods may be explained by mapping beliefs associated with seasonal agricultural cycles.
- ***Mapping Systems*** – explores the interdependence between the social, economic, and environmental dimensions of an inhabited site. Mapping systems also looks at the connectivity between the tangible and intangible aspects of the culture. The identification of such synergies and interdependent relationships aids our understanding of local ecological systems, local value chains, knowledge trans-

> mission systems, organizational systems, etc. For example, systems mapping can reveal cultural value chains which involve creation, production, distribution, and consumption of a cultural product; explain how topography, climate, and natural resources can affect dwelling structure and architecture or how local plant resources affect culinary and medicinal knowledge, etc. As a complex form of mapping, integrated mapping is best conducted in stages through the collaborative efforts of a multidisciplinary team.

The outcomes of integrated cultural mapping are able to reveal the cultural character of a site, cultural aesthetics of a community, economic value chains or culture cycles. They may reveal intangible cultural concepts such as cultural identity, thus documenting the cultural significance of a site and its assets to the people.

Part IV

Visual Summary: Reading the Historic City

Campo Marzio, central Rome, 1748.

Giambattista Nolli's iconic map of Rome (1748) articulates solids in black, voids in white (known as a figure-ground image) in order to draw distinctions, in plan, between buildings and the spaces around them. He shows the ideal extension of public space into semiprivate enclosed areas and uses symbols (e.g., small circles to indicate columns) and meticulous, plot-by-plot detail to document in plan and in scale all physical structures and the spaces associated with them. After Nolli, urban mapping to read the city would never be the same.

Part IV

VISUAL SUMMARY

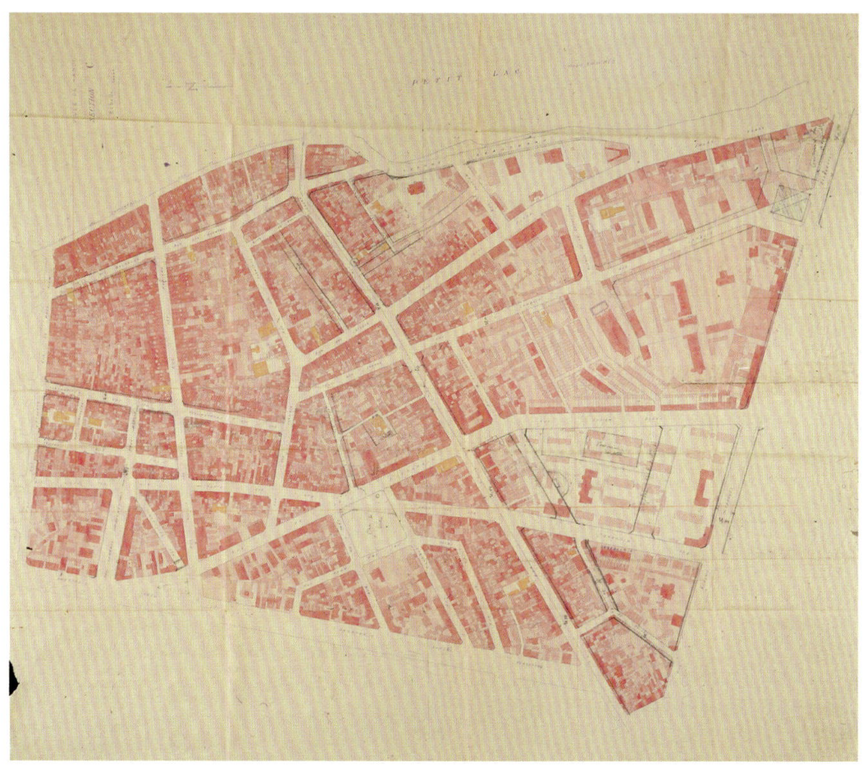

Plan of a neighborhood in Hanoi, Vietnam, by Louis-Georges Pineau, 1942.

General view of Hanoi, Vietnam, 1931.

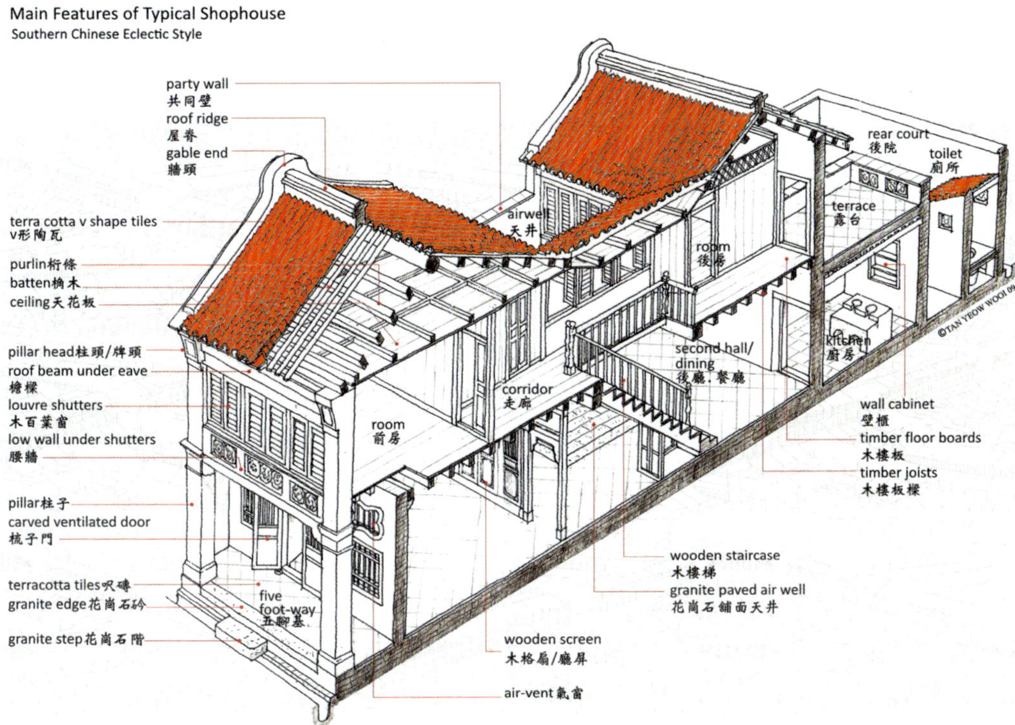

Drawing of a typical southern Chinese shophouse by Tan Yeow Wooi, ca. 2014.

PLATES IV.1, IV.2, AND IV.3

Zeynep Çelik (reading 26) suggests new approaches to achieve a fuller understanding of non-Western cities. These include the French-influenced, colonial cities of North Africa, defined by Çelik as "sites of cultural confrontation and exchange," as well as those of French Indochina, illustrated here by Hanoi's "36 Streets" neighborhood (pl. IV.1). In the 1942 cadastral map of this area, large boulevards intersect an urban fabric of densely clustered shop-houses, approximately 4 meters wide and up to 80 meters deep. An aerial photo from the early 1930s (pl. IV.2) shows roughly the same area, below Hoan Kiem Lake, where there was a preponderance of the shop-house building type, largely occupied by the Vietnamese population. Hanoi's shop-houses reflect confrontation and exchange through the use of Western stylistic elements combined with Asian roof tiles and small courtyard spaces. A similar, although not equivalent confrontation and exchange, occurred in other colonial cities, as shown in the isometric drawing of a typical shophouse in Malaysia (pl. IV.3).

Part IV

VISUAL SUMMARY

A train rumbles through the tight confines of a residential neighborhood on the west side of the Old Quarter of Hanoi.
Photo by Alexander Synaptic.

PLATE IV.4

As suggested by Sir John Summerson (reading 27), the "general morphology" of a city is made not only of its "monuments and modern face" but also of "the scraps and fragments . . . [that are] significant and instructive flotsam from the past." To more fully understand Hanoi's morphology, therefore, it would be crucial to know how and when the city grew while retaining a train link that has become a "street" between residential buildings.

PLATE IV.5

In her explanation of urban morphology, Anne Vernez Moudon (reading 28) emphasizes the dynamic reality of the city, in which buildings, gardens, streets, parks, and monuments are imagined as organisms that inevitably age and change over time. She discusses three schools of urban morphology, in the United Kingdom, Italy, and France. These images center on the Italian school, pioneered by Saverio Muratori (1910–1973), who in the late 1950s and early 1960s published two comprehensive typological analyses of the historic cities of Venice and Rome. Plate IV.5 presents a plan, elevation, and photograph of Venice's Casa Barzizza (Grand Canal at S. Silvestro), dating from the twelfth century. The building's history, up to the twentieth century, is interpreted in the house's incremental evolution over time. Note in particular the building's front elevation, seen in both the drawing and the photograph. Followers of Muratori's method often use plans and elevations to document the evolution of a building type.

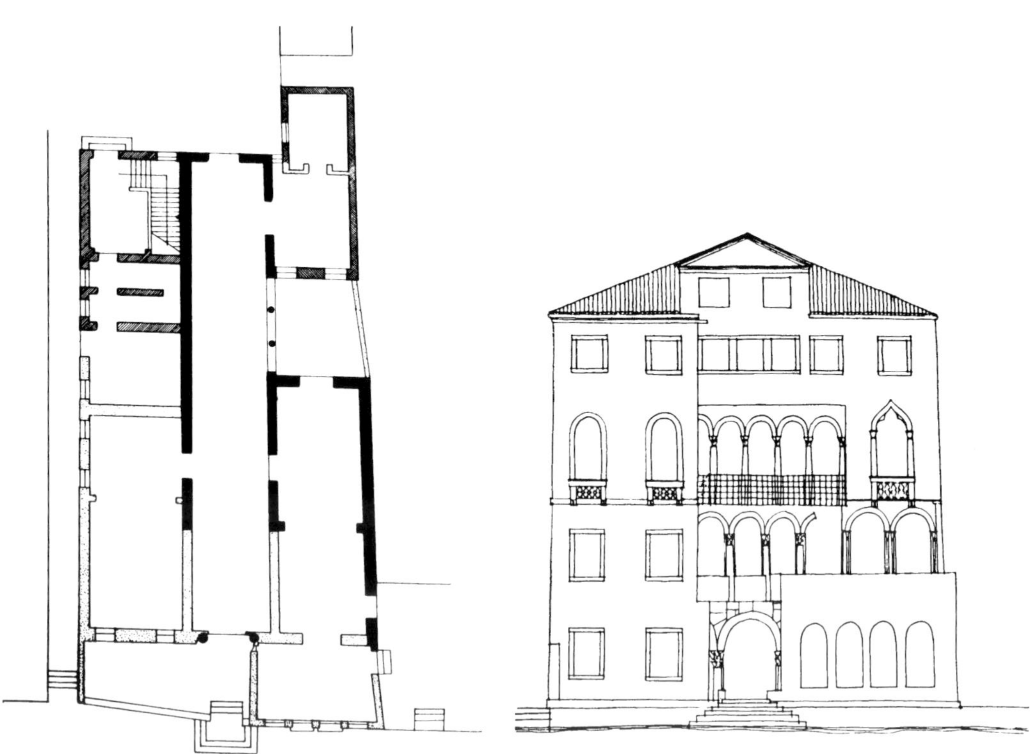

Floor plan of Palazzo Barzizza (top left), erected in the thirteenth century on Venice's Grand Canal (San Silvestro Parish); front elevation (top right) and photograph of the palazzo (seen at far right of photograph) from Saverio Muratori's study of Venice, 1959.

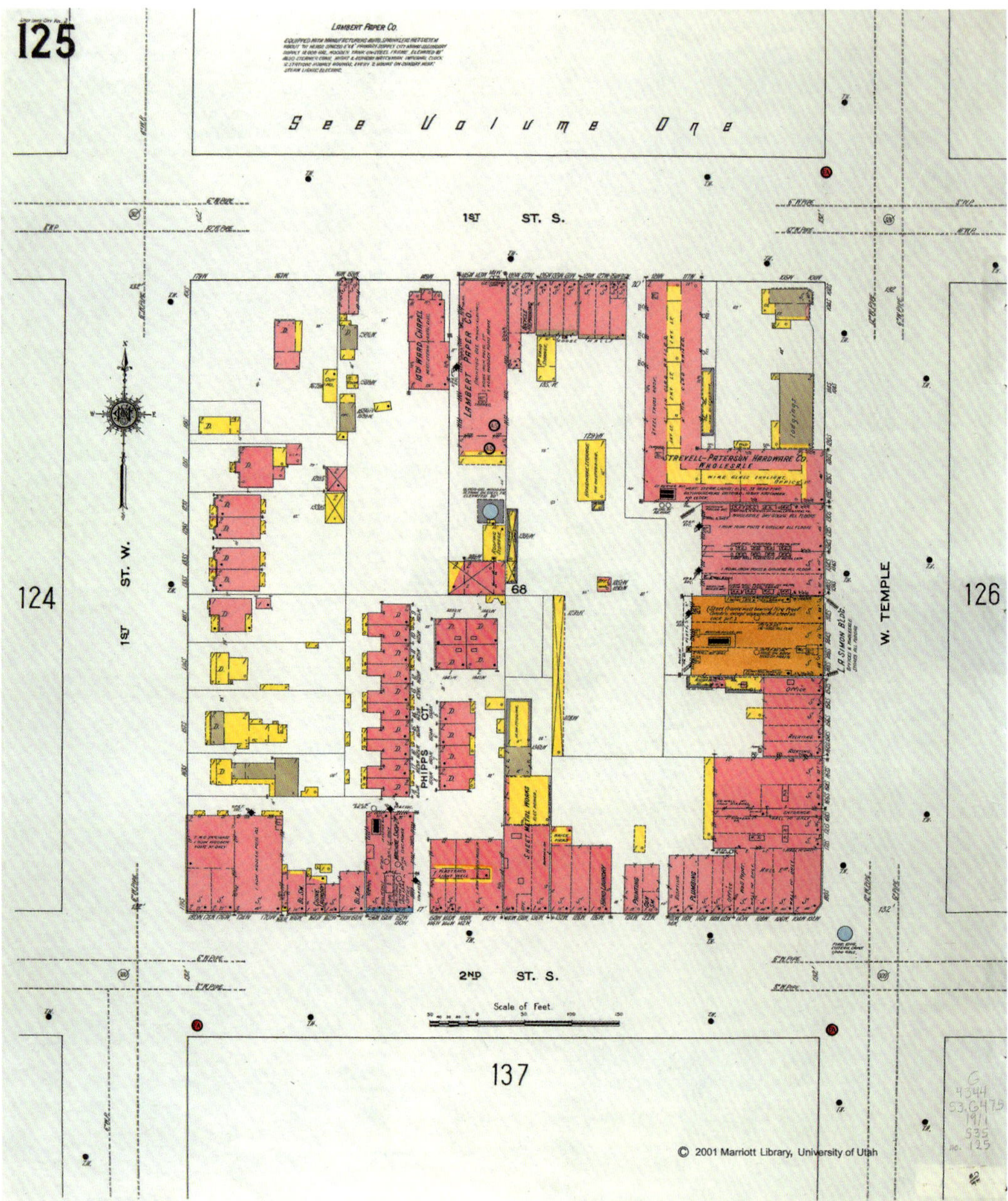

Fire insurance map of Salt Lake City, 1911, by the Sanborn Map Company.

Fire insurance map of Salt Lake City, 1911, by the Sanborn Map Company, with 2018 georeference. Created by Justin Bruce Sorensen, J. Willard Marriott Library, University of Utah.

PLATES IV.6A AND IV.6B

The urban analyses of Philippe Panerai, Jean Castex, and Jean-Charles Depaule (reading 29) exemplify the methods of the French school of urban morphology. This approach is summarized by Moudon, who highlights how "the block" (*l'îlot,* a group of interdependent building plots) is considered by these authors as the key element in understanding and interpreting the urban fabric. These two images relate to urban blocks in Salt Lake City, Utah (USA). On the left is a Sanborn Fire Insurance Map from 1911, where different colors denote building materials for structures that once occupied an urban block. The image above overlays that historic map on a current satellite photograph, which shows the dramatic changes to the block layout where a historical portion of the city once stood, now occupied by a convention center, parking lots, and other structures.

Part IV

VISUAL SUMMARY

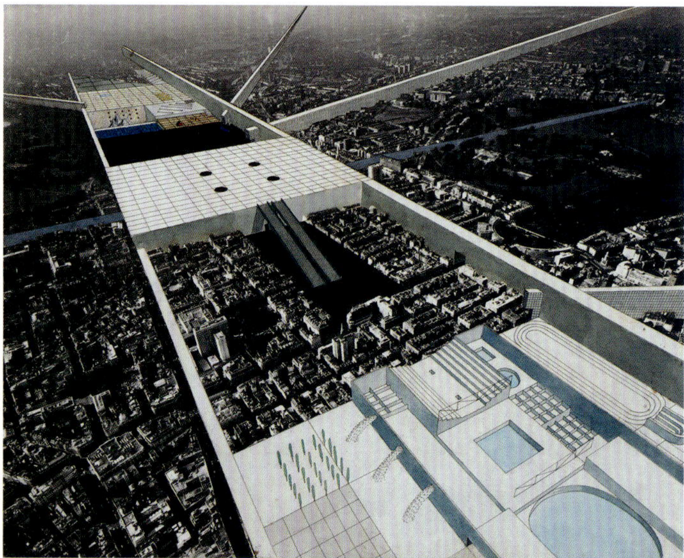

Rem Koolhaas, Elia Zenghelis, Madelon Vreisendorp, and Zoe Zenghelis, *Exodus, or the Voluntary Prisoners of Architecture: The Strip (Aerial Perspective)*, 1972.

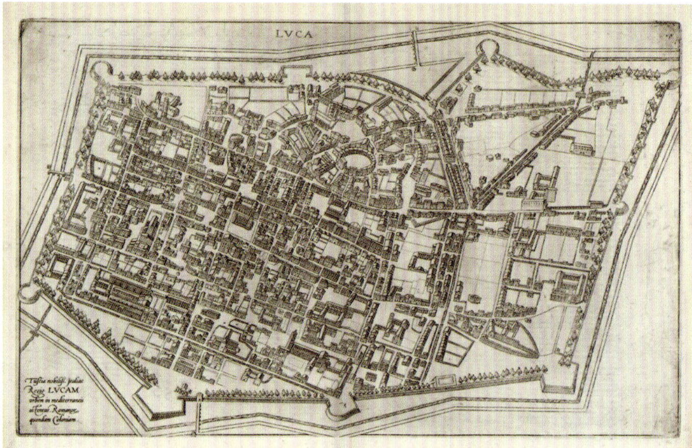

Map of Lucca, Italy, 1588.

PLATES IV.7 AND IV.8

In *Cities for People*, Jan Gehl (reading 31) argues that quality in urban design is achieved through the simultaneous consider-ation of three scales of planning: the aerial view, to gain a holistic vision of the city; the view from a low-flying helicopter, to get a sense of "how buildings and city space are organized"; and the"small scale," to gauge how the city is experienced by people at eye level. Proposals such as that shown here by Koolhaas exemplify formal overreliance on the large scale, often achieved in grand architectural gestures that disregard the complex and often-minute morphology of the existing city (pl. IV.8). Contrary to this approach, the view of Lucca, in Tuscany, exemplifies meticulous attention to the layering of buildings and open spaces found in the historic area (pl. IV.9). This should be the indispensable premise to forms of fine-grained planning mindful of the human dimension.

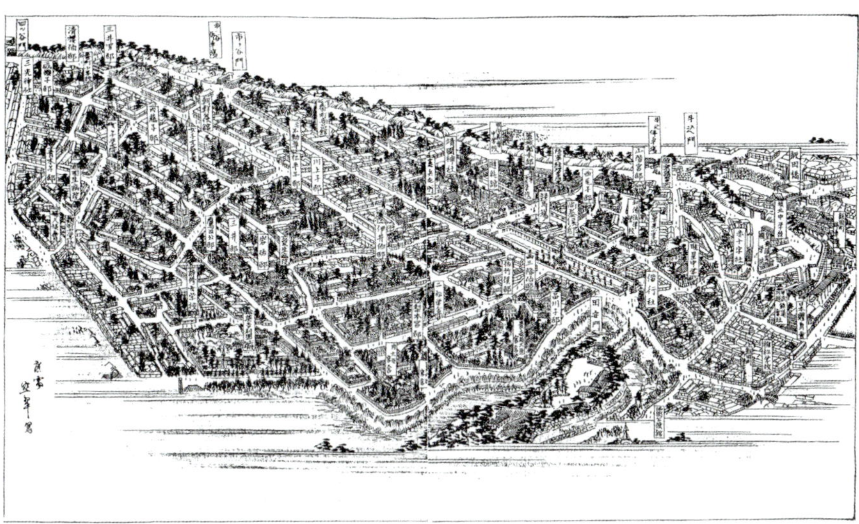

Drawing of Bancho, Tokyo, circa 1897.

Ukiyo-e print of Edo (Tokyo) by Utagawa Kunimori (II), circa mid-nineteenth century.

PLATES IV.9 AND IV.10

Jinnai Hidenobu (reading 33) underscores the spatial and formal links between "modern" Tokyo (post-Meiji Restoration, 1868) and its antecedent, Edo, described as the "many-layered closed system of a castle-town." Although Tokyo became more modern after 1868, it still "preserved the urban form of the past." As with other cities worldwide, a real understanding of either the modern or the contemporary city is predicated on answering a few essential questions: What preceded it? What was destroyed? What is left today?

PHILIPS

Part V

The Search for Contextual Continuities

The first selection in this part, from Françoise Choay (reading 35), explores the birth of the concept of the historic city as a physical and contextual entity distinct from individual monuments. Choay points out that urban space, unlike monuments, was never recognized traditionally as a separate object of conservation. The reasons for this delayed recognition, in Choay's view, lies in the intrinsic complexity of urban structures, which was aggravated, at least until the nineteenth century, by the lack of reliable cartographic references. Moreover, cities were traditionally interpreted as political manifestations symbolized in major monuments rather than spaces that could be appreciated for their physical and aesthetic qualities.

As documented in part III, however, the consideration of historic cities as objects of attention comes to the forefront after the Industrial Revolution, hastened by the awareness of the sudden and irreversible transformation of cherished urban places. John Ruskin is in fact the first to conceptualize the idea of the physical urban heritage as something that has "to be protected unconditionally" in the face of its rapid disappearance. Choay sees in Ruskin's position an acknowledgment of the "memorial" role of the city as a human construct that has the "marvelous power to root its inhabitants in space and in time."[1]

Choay also contextualizes the approaches taken by Camillo Sitte and Gustavo Giovannoni in readings 36 and 38, respectively. As discussed further below, the former saw the preindustrial city and its physical fabric as an ensemble worthy of study and understanding, a position described by Choay as propaedeutic, whereby Sitte strived to rediscover the principles and methods of city building. Giovannoni's position, in Choay's view, represents a "synthesis and surpassing" of that of Ruskin and Sitte. Giovannoni saw the urban heritage handed down from the past simultaneously as a coherent whole, made up of major architecture and its surroundings that were worthy of preservation, and as a living entity that must be reintegrated into present-day life through an intentional process of physical planning. As such, Giovannoni elaborated the first fully devel-

Street in Aibar, Spain, from Bernard Rudofsky, *Architecture Without Architects, 1965*. Detail. See p. 400.

oped doctrine of urban conservation that constitutes his lasting contribution to the field of city planning.

Camillo Sitte's *City Planning According to Artistic Principles* was very influential after its publication in 1889. After analyzing the nature and qualities of the historic urban space, particularly the squares, courts, and streets of European cities, and criticizing the shortcomings of modern city planning, Sitte explored the reconfiguration of public spaces in his hometown, Vienna, outlining expedient solutions based on his observations of traditional city plans. Although it was considered backward-looking and out of touch with contemporary realities by some of the most influential figures of the modern movement,[2] Sitte's work remains important from a methodological standpoint: it represents the beginning of an analytical appreciation of the historic city, considered not as a model to imitate but as the repository of a method that needs to be understood and applied. Only such an understanding, in his opinion, can provide continuity in city building. Sitte advocated the search for a living urban environment in which architecture plays an integral role in determining the form and structure of spaces. He highlighted the complementarity of the practical and the aesthetic found in the historic city while noting the split between function, technology, and aesthetics observed in the contemporary city. This divide persists, and a satisfactory resolution has yet to be found.

Sitte's appreciation of the historic city was mirrored in the work of Patrick Geddes, the Scottish planner and educator (reading 37). Geddes's most influential book, *Evolution in Cities,* published in 1915, expands the consideration of the traditional city by looking at its effect on the well-being of inhabitants. His interpretation is a direct critique of the industrial city. He does not limit himself to the form of the city, as Sitte had, but explores its broader environmental and social aspects, underlining the importance of preserving the environment and maintaining the cultural identity of places. His emphasis is on scientific observation and analysis, considered as an interconnected and ongoing process that gradually helps us evaluate different solutions and eventually identify outcomes that become the very essence of a plan.

In his professional work as an urban planner, Geddes was the first to understand the danger of urban renewal and to foresee the damage that it would inflict on the traditional city. In his plan for the city of Madura (Madurai) in India, for example, he advised against demolishing, reconfiguring, and sanitizing neighborhoods. He advocated instead what he called "conservative surgery," based on a careful reading of the city and attention to detail to improve local housing conditions with minimal interventions and expense and without tearing apart entire communities.

This lesson was lost on his contemporaries, only to resurface several decades later in Jane Jacobs's passionate critique of the slum clearance projects of the 1950s and, more recently, albeit with different connotations, in the writings of Roberta Brandes Gratz with Norman Mintz and Pierluigi Cervellati, readings 42 and 43, respectively. The poor results of urban renewal projects of the mid-twentieth century, with their enormous social and economic costs, are proof of the lasting validity of Geddes's ideas from the 1920s. "There are finer architects than I, and bolder planners too," he wrote, "but none so economical,"[3] and, we might add, with better foresight.

A "conservative" approach to the historic city was advocated also by Gustavo Giovannoni, a well-known Italian architect, engineer, historian, and restorer, in his seminal publication, *Vecchie città ed edilizia nuova*" (New Building in Old Cities), published in 1913 and in an expanded edition in 1931. His background and professional experience was quite different from that of Geddes, a fact that underlines the significance of their shared conclusions based solely on their analytical work and appreciation of the nature of the historic city. Giovannoni's reading demonstrates a full understanding of the speculative mechanisms that were at the root of the many inappropriate transformations he observed in the old fabric of Italian cities. His comments remain valid today.

Giovannoni's theory of *diradamento edilizio,* or selective clearing,[4] is equivalent in many respects to Geddes's "conservative surgery." Giovannoni seeks a compromise between integral preservation and limited forms of intervention. He also called for improving hygienic conditions in traditional housing and the demolition of buildings of no historic or artistic value to make room for new facilities, infrastructure and green areas, as well as to improve views of significant monuments by isolating them from their immediate context.

Today this approach may appear contrary to prevailing notions of urban preservation, but it must be understood in relation to the times, when concerns about unsanitary living conditions in historic city centers were very common. However, Giovannoni's theories and proposals for the Quartiere Rinascimento in Rome and Bergamo's city center are far more modern than those advocated by the modern avant-garde, who ignored the old city and proposed the introduction of new construction in striking contrast to the fine-grained texture of the historic fabric. Contrary to this approach, Giovannoni believed that the new city should live side by side with, not substitute for, the old one. His position was the first to explicitly recognize the need to establish methods and forms of intervention in historic contexts clearly distinct from those applied to the newer parts of the city. He understood that confusing the two spheres of intervention would lead to unnecessary disruption in the highly homogeneous context of old cities and to the imposition of undue constraints on modern developments.

The approach followed by Giovanni Astengo (reading 39) in dealing with historic urban areas, or "centri storici," shared with Giovannoni an understanding of their specific qualities, incompatible with the nature of the contemporary city. His 1955 plan for the old town of Assisi in central Italy remains exemplary in its approach and methodology. Fully illustrated in the pages of *Urbanistica,* the principal Italian journal of urbanism of the time, the plan provided a point of reference for many subsequent interventions in Italian historic urban settings.[5] Astengo recognized the need to "renovate" Assisi,[6] but he opposed introducing new roads and contemporary buildings. Rehabilitation was to be based on recognition of the historic area as a complete, self-contained entity, endowed with its unique and unrepeatable characteristics. In his introductory remarks to the Assisi plan, included here, Astengo stresses the importance of the detailed survey carried out prior to the formulation of the plan, in ways that resemble Geddes's considerations, and underlines the close relationship between the town's traditional layout and buildings and the uses and activities these contained. His plan foresaw a consequent need to ensure a coherent approach across the board—physical, architectural, social, and economic.

Two further innovative aspects must be mentioned in conjunction with the Assisi plan: the holistic approach to the planning of the historic area, which considers it along with its surrounding areas, with controls established to limit conflicting urban expansions; and the establishment of a local public entity charged with preparation of the plan and its subsequent implementation. Astengo was in fact convinced of the pivotal role of the plan and the importance of establishing a permanent planning office, without which the interventions and programs needed to rehabilitate and care for a historic area could be effectively sustained over the long term.

Reliance on a detailed survey is also emphasized in Donald Insall's report and plan for the City of Chester (reading 40), published in 1968.[7] The study was part of four historic town reports commissioned by the British government after passage of the Civic Amenities Act of 1967 and its provisions on the designation of conservation areas.[8] In his introduction to the study and the detailed plans that follow, Insall places Chester in its regional context and assesses foreseeable trends and negative influences that may compromise the town's historic character. The report is exemplary in outlining a methodology for the recognition of townscape and architectural values and defining improvement actions and forms of intervention. It owes a considerable debt to Pevsner's and Cullen's visual planning essays published in the *Architectural Review* from the 1940s on,[9] but it is not limited to a purely visual appreciation of the urban environment. The report deals with issues related to traffic, infrastructure, ownership, and use and condition of buildings. It also contains plans for the functional upgrading of historic structures, particularly underused upper floors, as well as general suggestions for open space improvements in selected areas.

The initial report led to the appointment of a municipal conservation officer—the first such post in the United Kingdom—and to the implementation of a pilot scheme in Chester's Bridgegate Area, including public acquisition of endangered key buildings and the offer of financial aid and advice to owners of historic structures in poor condition. These actions are summarized in the reading below, written forty years after the publication of the Chester report. Of special interest is the summary of degrees of intervention, outlining the different levels of complexity in the rescue of old buildings and neighborhood areas. In the concluding remarks to both the 1968 Chester report and the 2008 publication, Insall underlines the fundamental need for skilled monitoring of historic resources through a continued process of assessment and planning, followed by "energetic performance of constant and consistent daily management."[10]

The notion of the "centro storico" (historic center) is the focus of the "Instructions for the Protection of 'Historic Centers'" (reading 41), an appendix to the Italian restoration charter of 1972.[11] Heavily influenced by Cesare Brandi's theory of restoration, and largely due to Brandi himself, this appendix to the charter contains an extension of the historic area concept to include all human settlements "whose structures, both complete or fragmentary, even if partially transformed over time, have been formed in the past, or, even if developed in more recent times, have special historic value or remarkable urban and architectural qualities."[12] Exceptional quality, however, is not by itself an indispensable requirement for protection and concerted action. The "Instructions" place greater emphasis on the value of settlements as an expression of past urban cultures and structures and recognize in them a significance that is independent and distinct from architecture.

The operational aim of the "Instructions" departs from Brandi's highly theoretical approach to classify the different forms of intervention applicable in historic urban contexts. A clear distinction is made between the urban and architectural levels. These, in turn, are linked to different types of plans envisaged by the Italian planning legislation existing at the time: general plans (*piani regolatori generali*), district plans (*piani particolareggiati*) and detailed sector or neighborhood plans (*piani esecutivi di comparto*).

In line with Astengo's pioneering work in Assisi, Giuseppe Campos Venuti and Pierluigi Cervellati introduced the notion of "integrated conservation" with their plan for the historic center of Bologna (1969). The plan marks an important advance in the planning of historic urban areas. Its main tenet is that conservation of historic ensembles cannot be limited to preservation of their visual and aesthetic character but must also include consideration of the underlying physical, social, and economic structures. Moreover, a plan prepared for a historic area must consider the citywide system that surrounds it in order to ensure coordination of policies and interventions. Further aspects of wide-ranging interest in the Bologna Plan are the importance given to the study of the city's typological and morphological character as a basis for future interventions, the conscious effort to maintain the existing residents in the historic area by establishing a housing rehabilitation program funded by the municipality, and the conversion of monumental and significant historic buildings to house public services (the so-called *contenitori,* in fact, large, empty, religious structures).[13]

The two excerpts from Pierluigi Cervellati included in reading 43 reflect subsequent elaborations on interpretive techniques and urban restoration practices. The first deals with cadastral interpretation as a means to identify the *netto storico,*" literally, the "historic net," in order to distinguish the lots and buildings that have remained unchanged from those that have been modified over time. This operation, coupled with typological analyses, is considered the indispensable methodological premise for establishing uses and forms of intervention that are compatible with the historic fabric. The second excerpt outlines the notion of urban restoration (*restauro urbano*) exemplified by Leonardo Benevolo's proposal for the restoration of Rome's old Borgo neighborhood following the destruction and reconfiguration of the area carried out in the mid-twentieth century.[14] Cervellati and Benevolo oppose the notion that "what is modern today will become historic tomorrow," in favor of a conscious and scientifically founded restitution of parts of the city that have lost their integrity as a result of recent, ill-considered transformations. In a book written more than thirty years after the completion of the Bologna plan, Cervellati proposes to plan the entire city and surrounding countryside by adopting the methodologies of urban and territorial restoration.[15] This approach is based on the recognition that today's environment, both natural and man-made, can hardly be considered a tabula rasa but is the result of a complex system of human adaptations, stratification of uses, and historic developments over time that underwent a significant acceleration after the Industrial Revolution. It is no longer a question of planning for unlimited expansion and transformation but of handling with care and consideration what is already there.[16]

Cervellati's views on city planning, although developed in totally different urban contexts, are remarkably similar to the "urban husbandry" notion introduced by Roberta Brandes Gratz with Norman Mintz (reading 42).[17] Gratz advocates a soft approach to existing urban areas. As outlined in the reading, this notion is opposed to the project-based planning undertakings that "overwhelm and alter what exists." It advocates instead a continuous urban revitalization process of incremental growth and small-scale improvements carried out plot by plot as opportunities arise. This latter process mirrors more closely the long-established cycles of adjustment and organic adaptation in cities than the traumatic, large-scale, high-sounding, and ultimately short-lived developments pursued in recent decades. It recognizes the cumulative value of long-term investment in city centers, and it seeks to channel existing resources and capabilities toward the care and management of what is already there. This process, in her opinion, can be a powerful engine for community revitalization and the growth of local economies. It is also the surest way to preserve and sustain over time the physical and social identity of places. As Gratz explains, "We offer Urban Husbandry as an alternative," a course of action for which the "past offers lessons on which future alternatives can be based."[18]

A review of practices in urban conservation must necessarily consider two aspects that are closely associated with interventions in historic city areas: the introduction of new uses in old buildings and complexes and infill development in historic urban environments. These two topics, and the principles to be followed in either case, are outlined in ways that are clear and sensible in two publications issued by the Heritage Office of New South Wales, Australia (readings 44, 45).

The guidelines on the adaptation of historic buildings and sites stems from the key document guiding conservation in Australia, the Burra Charter, now adopted internationally as a reference for conservation practices. Its main tenets on adaptive use underline compatibility of function, low impact on cultural significance, and minimal changes in the physical fabric of a monument or site. All of these are predicated on an understanding of the significance of a place, without which adaptation becomes a gratuitous formal exercise that detracts from the heritage asset rather than retaining its symbolic value and practical use for the communities concerned. Ultimately, it is a matter of identifying the right mix between preserving the significance of a place, making the functional program compatible and relevant, and introducing only enough changes to enable new uses without compromising the essence and character of a structure and its surrounding context.

Also in the case of infill, the design criteria recommended by the New South Wales Heritage Office make express reference to the Burra Charter, which "requires the retention of an appropriate visual setting and other relationships that contribute to the cultural significance of a place." Accordingly, when justifiable from a general planning standpoint, and provided that no historical remains are destroyed in the process, new infill development should aim at maintaining an area's distinctive identity through the building of contemporary structures that are physically and visually compatible with the surrounding historical context.

The New South Wales guidelines make it clear that contextual design should not be confused with unsubstantiated historical reproductions or outright mimicry. Rather, it is a specific and distinct embodiment of contemporary design made to harmonize with a given context. This can be achieved by establishing analogies in character, scale, form, siting, material and color, and detailing between the old and the new and by maintaining a sense of continuity through the design and positioning of the contemporary structures in the old context.

Continuity is achieved by establishing close analogies with the structure and morphology of the preexisting fabric. These analogies can be established by looking at the constituent components of individual buildings and the urban fabric as a whole. Spacing, the rhythm of bays, modularity, building typology, street patterns, urban morphology, and so on, are some of the aspects that can be considered in analyzing the character of traditional built fabric. These "rules" can be internalized in the design process and help with the definition of a contemporary design that establishes a close relationship with the existing context.

Very often in these cases, discernment and discretion in choosing an appropriate design vocabulary are the best course of action. In particular, it has been noted that the methods and techniques routinely adopted for the harmonious reintegration of lacunae in the case of paintings, archaeological remains, and architecture (hatching, changes in materials, surface treatments, etc.) have not yet been "adjusted" to respond to the need to infill contemporary structures in historic contexts.[19] But the "basic requirements for reintegration and easy identification of the intervention are still valid in this instance."[20] The specific terms of this "creative integration," together with the consideration of the social and economic factors that characterize an urban setting, must be developed on a case-by-case basis "to establish the peculiar rhythm of the old complex and to adjust the scheme of the modern creation to the basic modules and materials that already exist."[21]

The last reading included in part V is a further reflection on the criteria for building in a historic city, as discussed in Rafael Moneo's review of his project for the Previsión Española Insurance Company in Seville (reading 46). The text is of special interest for illustrating the complex set of analytical and design considerations that accompanied Moneo's proposal. These considerations highlight the architect's search for solutions that are based on an explicit analysis of the morphological and textural elements that characterize the old city.

Throughout his remarks, Moneo underlines how the insurance building avoids the deliberate and ultimately gratuitous contrast often found in contemporary infills in favor of a nuanced and sophisticated interpretation of the city's multifaceted stratifications. Revisiting his experience in Seville twenty years later, Moneo notes, "If the historic cities that make up our heritage deserve to be preserved, it is difficult for the architect to disregard an overall vision of the city. Understanding the city, recognizing that any urban intervention involves accepting some hypothesis about what its growth was like and about how one must proceed so as to preserve the character of the existing architecture is something that I still believe to be valid today."

What are the planning lessons to be learned from the planners and cases discussed above? Most examples emphasize the need for thorough appreciation of the historical context and careful review of existing conditions prior to the preparation of a conservation plan. The latter is necessary to formulate a comprehensive vision and coordinate actions and management over the long term. Only the patient, continuous implementation of homogeneous policies and interventions will produce the coherent and consistent results that are so essential for the continuity of historic urban areas. Such continuity cannot be taken for granted but must be cared for and regenerated every day through the minimum possible level of intervention and social disruption.

In addition, the cases presented recognize, either explicitly or implicitly, the mutual relationships and complementarity of the physical, cultural, social, and economic elements embodied in traditional urban contexts and the need to adopt methods and forms of intervention clearly distinct from those applied to the newer parts of the city. While contemporary urban developments are defined by fragmentation and discontinuities, and by the conscious juxtapositions of distinct architectural objects, historic urban areas are increasingly seen as highly integrated systems "based on the recognition of [the] layering and interconnection of [physical and immaterial] values"[22] that make up their individual identities. Awareness of the holistic and integrated nature of old cities is what should inform the search for and implementation of effective actions beyond ideological divisions and instrumental debates aimed at justifying inconsiderate transformations and demolitions. Ultimately, what matters is a better understanding of the nature and qualities of historic areas to ensure continuity of form, compatibility of use, and better management of the irreplaceable urban assets that are increasingly at risk of transformation and disappearance.

Notes

1. See also reading 2, from Joseph Rykwert, *The Idea of a Town*.
2. Siegfried Giedion refers to Sitte as "a kind of troubadour, ineffectively pitting his medieval songs against the din of modern history." *Space, Time and Architecture: The Growth of a New Tradition*, 5th enl. ed. (Cambridge, MA: Harvard University Press, [1941] 2009), 505.
3. Letter to the Dewan of Patiala, 15 September 1922, Geddes Papers MS10516, National Library of Scotland. See Helen Meller, *Social Evolutionist and City Planner* (London: Routledge, 1993), 203; quoted also in Dennis Rodwell, *Conservation and Sustainability in Historic Cities* (Oxford: Wiley-Blackwell, 2007), 32.

4. Literally, "the thinning out of the built fabric."
5. G. Astengo, "Assisi: Salvaguardia e rinascita," *Urbanistica* (1958): 24–25.
6. The term he uses is "rinnovamento."
7. Donald W. Insall and Associates, *Chester, a Study in Conservation* (London: HMSO, 1968).
8. See Rodwell, *Conservation and Sustainability in Historic Cities,* 38–44.
9. See John MacArthur and Mathew Aitchison's essay in Nicholaus Pevsner, *Visual Planning and the Picturesque* (Los Angeles: Getty Publications, 2010).
10. Donald Insall, *Living Buildings. Architectural Conservation: Philosophy, Principles and Practices* (Mulgrave, Victoria, Australia: Images Publishing, 2008), 207.
11. Circolare no. 117, 6 April 1972, issued by the the Ministero della Pubblica Istruzione, subsequently published in Cesare Brandi, *Teoria del restauro* (Torino: Giulio Einaudi, 1977), 151–54.
12. Ibid., 151.
13. Pier Luigi Cervellati and Roberto Scannavini, eds., *Bologna: Politica e metodologia del restauro* (Bologna: Il Mulino, 1973).
14. Leonardo Benevolo, "Lo Sventramento novecentesco e gli indirizzi di un possibile restauro urbano di Borgo," in *San Pietro e la Città di Roma* (Rome: Editori Laterza, 2004), 85–130. On Benevolo's plan, see also Paolo Marconi, *Il recupero della bellezza* (Milan: Skira editore, 2005), 92–99.
15. Pier Luigi Cervellati, *L'arte di curare la città* (Bologna: Società editrice il Mulino, 2000), 105–11.
16. Francesco Scoppola has eloquently advocated the "primacy of archaeology in town planning." See his "Profili di storia del restauro architettonico e della conservation ambientale," *Gazetta Ambiente*, no. 3 (2017): 230–31.
17. Roberta Brandes Gratz, *The Living City* (New York: John Wiley & Sons, 1994), 147–74.
18. Roberta Brandes Gratz with Norman Mintz, *Cities Back from the Edge: New Life for Downtown* (New York: John Wiley & Sons, 1998), 3.
19. Scoppola, "Profili di storia del restauro architettonico e della conservation ambientale," 212.
20. Paul Philippot, "Historic Preservation: Philosophy, Criteria, Guidelines," in *Preservation and Conservation: Principles and Practices,* 374–82.
21. Ibid.
22. Ron Van Oers, "Conclusion: The Way Forward: An Agenda for Reconnecting the City," in *Reconnecting the City: The Historic Urban Landscape Approach and the Future of Urban Heritage* (New York: John Wiley & Sons, 2015), 317.

Reading

35

Françoise Choay

The Invention of the Historic Monument (1992)

Françoise Choay is an influential French architectural and urban historian and theorist who taught at the University of Paris and wrote extensively about the history of urban planning. In her Urbanisme, utopies et réalités: Une anthologie *(1965), she asserted there were two kinds "of spatial projections, of images of the city of the future": the "progressivist" model and the "culturalist" model. Le Corbusier and the Congress of Modern Architecture (CIAM) exemplified the former, while Camillo Sitte, Ebenezer Howard, and Raymond Unwin personified the latter. In her subsequent* Allégorie du patrimoine *(1992), Choay probed further the notion of the urban historic heritage in its evolution from a purely judicial, political, social, and economic construct to the appreciation of the aesthetic and physical dimensions of the city of the past. This reading traces the different approaches to the "physicality" of the historic city and its interpretations as a memorial space (J. Ruskin), as an aesthetic product that still has lessons to offer (C. Sitte), and as a product of history that while respected in its autonomy and constituent elements must be integrated into the more general process of regional and city planning (G. Giovannoni).*

CHAPTER FIVE THE INVENTION OF AN URBAN HERITAGE

Haussmann, whose enemies were as numerous and diverse in his own time as they are today, took exception to the accusation of vandalism levied against him by certain devotees of the old Paris: "But my good gentlemen, who from the depths of your libraries seem to have seen nothing [of the insalubrious state of old Paris and of the metamorphosis that has been brought about], name a single ancient monument worthy of interest, a single building precious for the arts or intriguing by virtue of its memories, that

From Françoise Choay, *The Invention of the Historic Monument,* translated by Lauren M. O'Connell (Cambridge: Cambridge University Press, 2001), 117–25, 128–32, 134–37. Originally published as *L'allégorie du patrimoine* (Paris: Éditions du Seuil, 1992).

has been damaged by my administration or with which it has been involved, if it has not been for the purpose of isolating it and placing it at the greatest possible advantage, in the most beautiful possible perspective."[1] The Baron's protest was made in good faith, and we owe to him, in fact, the conservation of numerous buildings that—like Saint-Germain-d'Auxerrois—were slated for demolition. In this sense, this enlightened bourgeois was indeed the contemporary of Mérimée, whom he used to meet, as a matter of fact, at the Emperor's residence.

Nonetheless, in the name of hygiene, circulation, and even aesthetics, he destroyed entire sections of the ancient fabric of Paris. But in this as well he was a man of his time: in his era most of those in France who defended the monuments of the past with the greatest conviction and energy also agreed on the need for a radical modernization of ancient cities and their fabric. It was in this spirit that Guilhermy published an *Itinéraire archéologique de Paris* in 1855, in which he drew up a detailed inventory of all of the individual monuments that he felt were threatened by the modern age, without concerning himself at all with architectural ensembles or with the urban fabric *per se*. [. . .]

—~—

[. . .] [T]he notion of an urban historic heritage, together with an explicit conservational project, was born in Haussmann's own time, albeit in Great Britain, from the pen of Ruskin. [. . .] Its subsequent evolution and development were difficult, and warrant analysis.

Why this lag of four hundred years between the invention of the historic monument and that of the historic city? Why did the latter have to wait so long before being conceived of as an entirely separate object of conservation, not reducible to the sum of its monuments? Numerous factors contributed to slowing both the objectivization of urban space and its historical conceptualization: on the one hand were its scale, its complexity, and the persistence of a mentality that identified the city with a name, a community, a genealogy, and a kind of personal history—while taking no interest in its physical space; on the other were the absence, until the beginning of the nineteenth century, of reliable[2] cadastral surveys and cartographic documents, and the difficulty of locating archives relevant to the modes of production and transformations of urban space over time.

Up to and including the nineteenth century, learned monographs on cities do not dwell on their physical space except through the mediation of monuments, symbols whose importance varies with the author and the century. The same is true for historical studies; until the second half of the twentieth century their authors were interested in the city from the point of view of its judicial, political and religious institutions and its economic and social structures: space is their great lacuna. Fustel de Coulanges discusses *La Cité antique* (1864) without ever evoking the sites and buildings that are inseparable from the judicial and religious institutions of Greece and Rome. Henri Pirenne was scarcely more loquacious in his *Les Villes du Moyen Age* (1939), his *magnum opus* on the economic origins of the urban phenomenon in the West. The history of architecture, for its part, ignores the city. As Sitte aptly observed in 1889: "Even in modern histories of art, which discuss every insignificant thing, city planning has not been granted the humblest spot."[3] Between the Second World War and the 1980s, one could still count by hand the number of historians and art historians who had worked on urban space.[4]

We are witnessing today, however, a flowering of works on the morphology of preindustrial cities[5] and the agglomerations of the industrial era. This movement has been spurred by developments in the field of urban studies, whose role in the genesis of a genuine history of urban space we should recall.

The conversion of the material city into an object of historical knowledge was provoked by the transformation of urban space wrought by the industrial revolution: a transformation marked by a traumatic upheaval in the traditional environment and the emergence of new circulatory and cadastral scales. Thus it was by way of difference, and in Pugin's lexicon, of contrast, that the ancient city became an object of investigation. Its first scholars, who began to place it into historical perspective, and to study it according to the same criteria as contemporary urban formations, were primarily the creators (architects and engineers) of the new discipline[6] that Cerdá called "urbanism." The same author proposed the first general and structural history of the city.[7]

But to oppose *the cities* of the past to *the city* of the present is not to advocate the conservation of the former. The history of the doctrines of urbanism and their concrete applications does not coincide with the invention of the urban historic heritage and its protection. The two adventures are, however, interdependent. Whether urbanism seeks to destroy ancient urban ensembles or strives to preserve them, it is in the very fact of their becoming obstacles to the free deployment of new modalities of organizing urban space that the ancient formations acquired their conceptual identity. The notion of an urban historic heritage took shape in contradistinction to the dominant process of urbanization. It is the result of a dialectic of history and of historicity which implies three successive figures of (or approaches to) the ancient city. I will qualify these figures respectively as memorial, historical, and historial.

The Memorial Figure

The first figure appears in England, from the pen of Ruskin. Already in the early 1860s, at the very moment when the "*grands travaux*" of Paris were beginning, the poet of the *Stones of Venice* rose up in protest, alerting public opinion to interventions that were altering the structure of ancient cities, that is, their fabric. For him, this texture is the very essence of the city; it makes of the city an intangible patrimonial object, to be protected unconditionally.

This position is rooted in the value and the role that Ruskin assigned to domestic architecture, which he regarded as the constitutive element of the urban fabric. It is the contiguity and the continuity of their modest dwellings—along the banks of their canals and their streets— that render Venice, Florence, Rouen, and Oxford[8] irreducible to the sum of their great religious and civic buildings, their palaces and their colleges, and make of these urban ensembles specific entities.

In such circumstances the ancient city as a whole seems, then, to play the role of historic monument. This is, however, an illusion that Ruskin permits himself to rectify by way of comparison. In the *Seven Lamps*, which is concerned with architecture and not with the city, the historic monument functions, in effect, almost like an authentic intentional monument. On the one hand, it plays a memorial role, here and now and in the present, due to the piety value with which it is invested: but on the other hand, there remains the distance that we have learned, since the Renaissance, to establish with respect to antiquities. But "almost like" does not apply in the case of the ancient city, which is a veritable monument.

Without managing to formulate it explicitly, Ruskin made a discovery that our age is still in the process of discovering. Over the course of the centuries and the civilizations, without those who built or lived in it having intended or been aware of it, the city has played the memorial role of the monument: an object which, paradoxically, was not erected to this end, and which possessed, like all of the world's ancient villages and traditional communities, to a more or less constraining degree, the dual and marvelous power to root its inhabitants in space and in time.[9]

In many regards, in particular in predicting the planet-wide standardization of the great cities, Ruskin reveals a visionary sensibility. However, the cause that he defends, and that William Morris would defend with and after him, is not, properly speaking, that of the conservation of the city and of historic architectural ensembles. Both writers were fighting for the life and the survival of the pre-industrial city of the West.

The Historical Figure: Its Propaedeutic Role

The second figure finds privileged expression in the work of the Viennese architect and historian Camillo Sitte (1843–1903). In it the pre-industrial city emerges as an object belonging to the past, and the historicity of the process of urbanization that is transforming the contemporary city is assumed in all of its fullness and positivity. This vision is thus completely opposed to that of Ruskin, but also to that of Haussmann: the ancient city, rendered obsolete by the industrial society's process of development, is no less recognized and constituted as an original historical figure which calls for reflection.

In 1889, Sitte developed these ideas in a publication that gained instant fame and was later deformed by tendentious readings, *Der Städtebau nach seinen künstlerischen Grundsätzen*, translated into French under the already deceptive title *L'Art de construire les villes.*[10] In the name of the doctrine promulgated by the CIAM congresses, Sigfried Giedion and Le Corbusier had depicted Sitte as the incarnation of the most retrograde attachment to the past,[11] the apostle of the donkey path,[12] the sworn enemy of modern urbanism. And in opposition to that same CIAM doctrine, the *Städtebau* has become, in the last fifteen years, the master work whose authority sanctions all pastiches and diverse variations on the theme of the recaptured city. The two opposite appreciations rest on the same misinterpretation, according to which the *Städtebau* is both dogmatic and passéist, whereas he is actually dedicated to the problems of the present and future city—from which perspective the ancient city possesses the dignity of an historic object in the full sense of the term.

Sitte's book originates in a precise and restricted observation: that of the ugliness of the contemporary city, or, more to the point, its lack of aesthetic quality. This does not in any sense imply a blanket and moral condemnation of contemporary civilization, as with Ruskin. To the contrary, his critique proceeds from a keen awareness of the technical, economic, and social dimensions of the transformation wrought by industrial society and of the spatial transformation that necessarily accompanies it. Technical progress shapes our world: it confers upon built urban space unprecedented extension and scale and grants to it new functions—among which aesthetic pleasure seems no longer to have a place.

> It is above all the enormous size to which our larger cities are growing that has shattered the framework of traditional artistic forms at every point . . . ; the city planner must, like the architect, invent a scale appropriate for the modern city of millions. . . . All these elements must be reckoned with as stated factors that the city planner has to take into account, just as an architect must consider the strength of materials and the laws of statics. . . . Our modern engineers, . . . have literally performed miracles . . . to the benefit of all city dwellers . . . [but] the process of enlarging and laying out cities has become an almost purely technical concern.[13]

For Sitte, the fact of identifying this aesthetic deficiency holds no interest *per se*. Far from amounting to a rueful critique, it becomes the springboard for a process of questioning. Are contemporary metropolises condemned to this ground zero of urban beauty? Can the advent of an urban art in tune with the development of industrial society be conceived and facilitated? Such are the questions that determine the dynamics of the *Städtebau*. They are conditioned by analysis of the organization from which ancient cities derive their beauty—an analysis that makes of Sitte the creator of urban morphology. Using the public squares as a paradigm, and with the help of plans that he himself realized at dozens of ancient sites or city cores, he describes and explains how, from the city (or cities) of classical antiquity to the baroque town, a series of various spatial configurations has never ceased to radiate a kind of beauty that contemporary squares never supply.

The interest of these analyses is not, however, solely historical. There are lessons still to be learned (the term "teaching" reappears constantly in the *Städtebau*) from the ancient city. Contrary to an approach often imputed to Sitte or justified by his authority, he rejects the notion of copying or reproducing these configurations, which respond to societal conditions that no longer exist and have been drained of meaning.[14] The solution of antinomy between present and past, historial and historical, is, however, possible—on the condition that a rational and systematic approach to morphological analysis be applied: "It is absolutely essential to make a positive formulation of the requirements of art because today we can no longer count on an instinctive taste in art; this no longer exists. It is imperative to study the works of the past, and for the artistic tradition that we have lost there must be substituted a theoretical understanding of the reasons for the excellence of ancient layouts."[15] Given the wide diversity of spatial configurations available—granting to each period, whether antique, medieval, or baroque, its own distinctive aesthetic—the investigator will seek out rules and principles that remain constant over time. It is clear that these principles[16] (a keyword in *Städtebau*, accompanied or not by the qualifier "artistic," and used interchangeably with "system")[17] consist in a set of formal characteristics shared by the various examples of ancient public spaces analyzed by Sitte: enclosure, asymmetry, differentiation, and articulation of elements. By virtue of their very intemporality these characteristics are applicable by the urbanism of the waning nineteenth century.

The morphological study of ancient cities, and consequently the formal history of their space, thus constitutes an unparalleled heuristic tool for the urbanist. The rules such study reveals on the organization of solids and voids show him the way to an experimental urban aesthetic. The pedagogical role that this approach assigns to the study of the ancient city, as well as the problems that it raises, call forth a comparison with the propaedeutic, or preparatory and pedagogical, role proposed twenty years or so earlier by Viollet-le-Duc in his *Entretiens sur l'architecture*.[18] In fact, over the course of the second part of his career, the latter was haunted by the search for a "truly contemporary" architecture, as Sitte was by that for an urban art. He draws up a merciless indictment of the historicism and eclecticism of his age and condemns all forms of copying or imitation of the past,[19] while nonetheless rooting his own research firmly in historical investigation. Rational analysis of the great architectural systems of the past (Greek, Roman, Romanesque, Gothic . . .) actually reveals that "these immutable principles that remain true across the centuries . . . [are] applied in different ways by different civilizations"[20] and will help us to elaborate a new system on the basis of the new historical conditions that are our own.

A single certitude emerges from the *Städtebau*, and it concerns the cities of the past: their active role is finished, their plastic beauty remains. The logic of the *Städtebau*'s analyses would seem to point to the notion of conserving the ancient urban ensembles as one conserves museum objects. And yet Sitte did not militate for the preservation of ancient centers. Over the course of his entire book, which was actually inspired by other purposes, only on two occasions does he briefly express a concern for "saving, if there is still time, our old cities from falling prey to continuing demolition."[21]

Others have developed the conservational philosophy implicit in his historical and critical work, and have thus assigned a museal function to the ancient city.

The Historical Figure: Its Museal Role

As a museal figure, the ancient city, threatened with disappearance, is conceived as a rare and fragile object, precious for art and history; like works of art conserved in museums, it should be removed from the orbit of daily life. In becoming historical, it loses its historicity.

This conception of the historical city had been prepared by generations of travelers, scholars or aesthetes. Both the archaeologists, who discovered the dead cities of classical antiquity, and the authors of guides and *ciceroni,* who carved the world of European art into urban slices, contributed to making the museification of the ancient city conceivable.

This unattractive word is not lacking in ambiguity. The city as an entity assimilated to an art object and comparable to a museum piece should not be confused with the museum-city, which contains works of art. The notion of an art city,[22] born at the turning of the century, is vague enough to be understood both ways. Most often, however, it is specified by the quality and the number[23] of art treasures, of historic monuments with their painted and sculpted decor, of museums and collections, that it contains—as though in a great open-air museum. It follows, then, that heterogeneous categories of cities can be considered art cities: capital and provincial, sprawling and minuscule, brimming with life or fast asleep—often without the very configuration of this container being taken into consideration.

The museal city, the center, or the urban quarter brought to our attention by Sitte's analysis impose themselves, to the contrary, as singular totalities, independent of their constituent parts. Their paradigm: the *Grande Place* of Brussels, wrested from the grip of Hausmannization and preserved by its *bourgmestre,* Charles Buls,[24] a fervent admirer of Sitte. As a matter of fact, Buls does not stop at preserving, he restores the historical square and reconstructs its missing parts; the approach takes its place within the catalogue of conservational attitudes as the opposite of Ruskin's pious conservation. The museal conservation of the *Grande Place* bears the imprint of Viollet-le-Duc's historicism, which will likewise inspire numerous small ancient centers and urban fragments in Central Europe.

The metaphor of the museal object remains, however, an approximate one. Ancient cities cannot be preserved under glass, as Viollet-le-Duc jestingly suggested was the unconfessed desire of the inhabitants of Nuremberg. Indeed, how might one actually preserve urban fragments and remove them from everyday circulation, except by depriving them of both their functions and their inhabitants? What is more, how might the visitation or museal touring of such spaces be organized? The contours of the problem begin to emerge; it will not be posed in explicit and legal terms until the Second World War.

However, during the first decades of the twentieth century the museal figure and museal conservation take on a new ethnological dimension, in the context of the colonial experience. When Lyautey, influenced by the example of the English in India, undertakes the urbanization of Morocco, he decides to preserve that country's urban creations—the *medinas*. In contrast to the politics adopted in Algeria, the modernization of Morocco would respect the traditional urban establishments, and cities responding to new Western technical criteria would be created. This course of action stems from a will to preserve—along with their original spatial support—ways of life and a vision of the world that are different from, and judged incompatible with, Western-style urbanism. But aesthetic appreciation also plays a role, albeit secondary, in this will to conservation—perhaps even securing its place in a future art tourism.

It is not thus surprising that the ethnological experience of a different, exotic urban reality should have been transposed, in a reciprocal motion, to the familiar cities of Europe. The history of this conversion remains to be written; it is illustrated by the urbanists Prost, Forestier, and Danger, among others, who were trained by Lyautey. After having left the Maghreb they discovered the ancestral European continent—with the foreigner's eye and in its legitimate strangeness: a territory to be developed at unprecedented scales that Africa had offered the opportunity to test, but also a territory to be protected. The pre-industrial urban framework, and especially the small cities that were still nearly intact, became the fragile and precious vestiges of an original style of life, of a culture in the process of disappearing, to be protected unconditionally and, if necessary, to be placed on reserve, as it were, or museified.

At the time the members of the CIAM rejected the notion of the historical or museal city. Le Corbusier's earlier Plan Voisin (1925)[25] is emblematic of their future positions: it proposes to raze the fabric of the old neighborhoods of Paris and replace it with standardized skycrapers, and preserves only a few disparate monuments: the Cathedral of Notre-Dame, the Arc de Triomphe, the Sacré-Coeur, and the Eiffel Tower—a list that already anticipates the mediatized conception of the signal monument. This *tabula rasa* ideology, which was applied to the treatment of ancient centers during the 1950s, did not officially cease to prevail in France until the creation of the law on protected sectors in 1962, by André Malraux.[26] Indeed, although later modified in its particulars and its thrust, this law was, at its origins, an urgent measure inspired by the museal figure of the city. Meanwhile, the CIAM members, contested in Europe, would nonetheless pursue their iconoclastic project in the developing countries, working toward the deconstruction of some of the most beautiful *medinas* of the Near East, such as those at Damas and Aleppo. Their influence remained strong in the Far East: they are responsible, significantly, for the destruction of a portion of old Singapore.

The Historial Figure

The third figure of the ancient city can be defined as the synthesis and the surpassing of the two prior figures. It constitutes the cornerstone of all present-day interrogation, not only on the future of the ancient urban fabric, but also on the very nature of those human settlements that we continue today to call cities.

This figure first appears—precociously and fully formed—in the theoretical writings and practice of an Italian, G. Giovannoni (1873–1943), who grants to the ancient urban ensembles both a use value and a museal value by integrating them into a general conception of territorial planning and development. The change in scale imposed upon the built environment by improvements in technique ("The city planner must, like the architect, invent a scale appropriate for the modern city of millions")[27] has as its corollary a new mode of conservation with respect to the ancient groupings—for history, for art, and for everyday life. This "urban heritage,"[28] which Giovannoni is no doubt the first to so designate, acquires its meaning and its value not as the autonomous object of a specific discipline, but as an element and constituent of an original doctrine of urbanism. Political and ideological passions[29] have long obscured Giovannoni's significance; it is thus all the more urgent that he be restored to his legitimate place on the historical stage.

The prospective stance and most of the ideas Giovannoni developed in his great book of 1931, *Vecchie città ed edilizia nuova,* were already present in his major article of 1913, published under the same title. He assesses the innovative role of the new modes of transportation and communication and predicts their continued improvement and refinement. Several decades of hindsight allow Giovannoni to conceptualize in terms of "networks" (*rete*) and infrastructures the transformation in urban scales that Viollet-le-Duc and Sitte had made the pivot of their reflection. The term "urbanism" ceases to apply solely to urban and spatially circumscribed spaces, becoming regional in scale. It must now fulfill the calling that characterizes society in the industrial age, the age of "generally diffused communication"—that of moving and communicating in every way possible. The city of the present, and even more that of the future, will be a city in flux.

"A historic city is in itself a monument,"[30] but it is at the same time a living fabric: such is the double postulate that permits a synthesis of the pious and museal figures of urban conservation, and upon which Giovannoni founds a doctrine of conservation and restoration of the urban heritage. It can be summarized in three guiding principles. First, any ancient urban fragment should be integrated into a local, regional, and territorial development plan that symbolizes its relationship with present-day life. In this sense, its use value is legitimated both technically, by its plugging into[31] the great primary networks of development, and humanly, "by maintaining the social character of the population."

Next, the concept of historic monument should not be applied to a single monument independent of the built context in which it is inscribed. The very nature of the city and of traditional urban groupings, their "*ambiente,*"[32] results from this dialectic between "major architecture" and its surroundings. Thus to isolate or "to free" a monument from its context is tantamount, in most cases, to defacing it. The built context of a monument exists in an essential relationship to it.

Finally, once these two conditions have been fulfilled, the ancient urban ensembles call for preservation and restoration procedures similar to those that Boito defined for monuments. Transposed to the dimensions of the urban fragment or nucleus, their essential objectives are to respect its scale and morphology and to preserve the original relationships that linked built parcels and circulation paths. "One must not neglect the tasks of recomposition, reintegration, and isolation."[33] A margin of intervention is thus allowed for, limited by respect for the *ambiente,* this (historical) spirit of the place, materialized in spatial configurations. Reconstitution—provided that it not be deceptive—and, above all, certain acts of destruction, become licit, advisable, even necessary. Giovannoni uses the elegant metaphor of the *diridamento,*[34] which evokes the clearing of a forest or of a too densely planted seedbed, to name the operations of eliminating all parasitic, adventitious, and superfluous constructions:

> The rehabilitation of ancient quarters is achieved more from the interior than from the exterior of blocks, in particular by reestablishing houses and blocks in conditions as close as possible to the original conditions, for dwelling has its own order, its own logic, its own hygiene, and its own dignity.[35]

[. . .]

Nearly alone among twentieth-century theoreticians of urbanism, Giovannoni placed the aesthetic dimension of human settlements at the very core of his concerns. At the scale of technical development networks, which is not our subject, he developed with optimism the premises posed by Viollet-le-Duc. At the neighborhood scale, on the other hand, he was able to link the propaedeutics of forgetting to a critical and conditional conception of the preservation of ancient urban ensembles within the dynamics of development.

This heritage is thus endowed with a dual status—whose antinomy Giovannoni discovered in the work of Viollet-le-Duc and Sitte—and charged with a dual role that neither Sitte nor Viollet-le-Duc wished or was able to assign to it. What is more, this urban heritage, the fragmented and fragmentary basis of a dialectic between history and historicity, finds itself treated according to the complex approaches of Riegl, for whom each patrimonial object constitutes a field of opposed forces between which a state of equilibrium, unique to each situation, must be created. And in managing this conflictual dynamic, Giovannoni recognizes and confers upon the ancient urban fabric the present-day and social value that Ruskin and Morris had granted to it without, however, succeeding in rooting themselves in historicity: the city dweller and his praxis as such assume their place at the very focal point from which emanates the forward-looking stance of the *Vecchie Città ed Edilizia nuova.*

Giovannoni's theory anticipates, with more flexibility and complexity, the various politics of "protected sectors" that have been finalized and applied in Europe since 1960. It bears as well the seeds of their future paradoxes and difficulties.

Notes

1. *Mémoires*, vol. III, Paris, 1893, p. 28.
2. The first European cadastral survey was that made of the Milan region at the end of the eighteenth century. Cartography, which made great strides in the eighteenth century, was used at that time essentially for fortifications and fortified towns. We owe to Haussmann the first operational and global plan of Paris, complete with contour lines.

3. George R. and Christiane Crasemann Collins, *Camillo Sitte: The Birth of Modern City Planning. With a translation of the 1889 Austrian edition of his City Planning according to Artistic Principles*, 2nd edition, New York, Rizzoli, 1986, p. 223.
4. Few are the studies by art historians such as R. Krautheimer's *Rome: Profile of a City, 312–1308*, Princeton University Press, 1980, and his *The Rome of Alexander VII*, Princeton University Press, 1985, as well as the *Système de l'architecture urbaine: Le quartier des Halles à Paris* by F. Boudon, A. Chastel, H. Couzy, and F. Hamon, Paris, Éditions du CNRS, 1977.
5. For the role played by archaeologists in the new historiography of the city, see in particular the publications of the *École française de Rome, Les Cadastres anciens dans les villes et leur traitement par l'informatique*, Rome, 1989, no. 120, and *D'une ville à l'autre: Structures matérielles et organisation de l'espace dans les villes européennes (XII–XVIe siècle)*, Rome, 1989, no. 122.
6. The geographers would follow, such as P. Lavedan, for example, who wrote a history of the planned organization of cities since the Renaissance under the debatable title *Histoire de l'urbanisme*, Paris, Laurens, 1926–52.
7. In his *Teoría general de l'urbanización*, Madrid, 1867, French translation and adaptation by A. Lopez de Aberasturi, Paris, Le Seuil, 1979, which seeks to found urbanism as a science of the city and of its production. Cerdá shows how the evolution of urban forms is linked to that of modes of circulation and transportation.
8. Cf. *supra*, ch. IV, n. 32 and 34. [. . .]
9. On these powers of space, see in particular, for non-urban settlements, Lévi-Strauss, *Anthropologie structurale*, Paris, Pion, 1958, chs. VII and VIII, and P. Bourdieu and A. Sayad, *Le Déracinement*, Paris, Éditions de Minuit, 1964. [. . .]
10. Vienna, Graeser. The first French translation was that of Camille Martin, Geneva, 1902. [. . .]
11. It cannot be denied that the *Städtebau* opens with a nostalgic evocation of the Forum of Pompeii. To my knowledge, this opening motif has never been compared to the first paragraph of "The Lamp of Memory," from which Sitte seems, nonetheless, to have borrowed a poetic and confidential tone that does not reappear in the rest of his book.
12. The expression is that of Le Corbusier, who nonetheless had read and admired Sitte before vilifying him. Cf. P. Turner, *The Readings of Le Corbusier*, French translation, P. Choay, *La Formation de Le Corbusier*, Paris, Macula, 1987.
13. Collins, *op. cit.*, pp. 244–45, 248, 142.
14. "Modern living as well as our modern building techniques no longer permit the faithful imitation of old townscapes." *Ibid.*, p. 249.
15. *Ibid.*, 263.
16. *Ibid.*, pp. 150–51, cf. pp. 2, 11, and 120. [*Translator's note:* These references are to the French translation of the *Städtebau*, as in n. 10, which renders Sitte's terminology more faithfully in this case.]
17. For example, "That Public Squares Should be Enclosed Entities," p. 170. [. . .]
18. Paris, Morel and Co., 1863–1872, 2 vols., reprint Brussels-Liège, Mardaga, 1977.
19. "In ceasing to concern itself above all with the alliance of form with needs and means of construction . . . [architecture] gave itself over to *neo-grec, neo-romanesque, neo-gothic*. . . . It fell prey to fashion," *op. cit.*, vol. 1, Tenth Discourse, p. 451. Viollet-le-Duc himself did not, any more than Sitte, "pretend to offer models to be copied, but only to reveal principles," *ibid.*, vol. 2, Thirteenth Discourse, p. 140.
20. *Entretiens*. "Simple Confessions to the Reader," pp. 6 and 7. For identical formulations, cf. also vol. 1, pp. 99, 324, 432, 447, 456, 458, 476.
21. *Op. cit.*, p. 142. [*Translator's note:* Our translation differs slightly from that of Collins cited here, to capture more closely the spirit of the original German. Cf. the French translation, as in n. 10, p. 4.]
22. Cf. *Città d'arte, Atti dell'incontro di studio "La città d'arte: Significato, ruolo, prospettive in Europa"* (Florence, 1986), Florence, Giunti Barbera, 1988.
23. *Op. cit.*, V. Franchetti Pardo, "Introduzione."

24. Author of *L'Esthétique des villes*, Brussels, Buylant-Christophe, 1893, and of "*La conservation du coeur des anciennes villes*," *Tekne*, nos. 64–66, Brussels, 1912.
25. See M. Smets, *Charles Buls*, Liège, Mardaga, 1995.
26. After the airplane manufacturer, Gabriel Voisin [. . .].
27. As in n. 4.
28. *Vecchie Città ed Edilizia nuova*, Turin, Unione tipografico-editrice, 1931; French translation: *La ville ancienne face à l'urbanism*, trans. J. M. Mandosio, C. Tandille, A. Petita, Introduction by F. Choay, Paris, Seuil, 1998, pp. 113, 129, etc.
29. A portion of Giovannoni's career unfolded under the regime of Mussolini. For this reason he was unfairly implicated in the indictment of fascism after the war, and violently criticized by B. Zevi (*Storia dell'architettura moderna*, Milan, Einaudi, 1995). Furthermore, not having spared certain stars of the modern movement, like Le Corbusier, he was accused of an excessive attachment to the past, at the same time that he was developing the most advanced and technical theories of urbanism. A rehabilitation of Giovannoni's *oeuvre* is currently under way in Italy (cf. G. Zuconi, "*La naissance de l'architecte intégral en ltalie*," French trans. in *Annales de la recherche urbaine*, C. Gaudin, Paris, 1990, as well as F. Ventura's critical reprint of the *Vecchie Città*, Turin, Città Studi Edizioni, 1995).
30. *Op. cit.*
31. *Ibid.*, for example, 66 ff.
32. This term, untranslatable in French, refers to the felicitous effects of the perception of the interconnectedness of the elements of the urban fabric. [. . .]
33. *Ibid.*, "La restauration des monuments en Italie," p. 63.
34. In particular: "Il diradamento edilizio ed I suoi problemi nuovi," *L'Urbanistica*, no. 5–6, 1943, not to mention the numerous passages devoted to the *diradamento* in *Vecchie Città, op. cit.* During the same era, Patrick Geddes speaks of "conservative surgery."
35. *Vecchie Città*, p. 252.

Works Cited

Boudon, F., Chaste, A., Couzy, H. and Hamon, F., *Système de l'architecture urbaine: Le quartier des Halles à Paris*, Paris, Éditions du CNRS, 1977.

Bourdieu, P. and Sayad, A., *Le Déracinement*, Paris, Éditions du Minuit, 1964.

Buls, Ch., *L'Esthétique des villes*, Brussels, Buylant-Christophe, 1893.

Buls, Ch. "La Conservation du coeur des anciennes villes," *Tekne*, nos. 64–66, Brussels, 1912.

Cerdá, I. *Teoría general de l'urbanización*, Madrid, 1867, Fr. trans. and adapt. I. Lopez de Aberasturi, Paris, Le Seuil, 1975.

Città d'arte, Atti dell'incontro di studio "La città d'arte: Significato, ruolo, prospettive in Europa," Firenze, XI, 1986, Florence, Giunti Barbera, 1988.

Conig, H., *Rénovation urbaine et changement social*, Paris, Éditions ouvrières, 1967.

École française de Rome, *Les Cadastres anciens dans les villes et leur traitement pnr l'informatique*, no. 120, Rome, 1989.

École française de Rome, *D'une ville à l'autre: Structures matérielles et organisation de l'espace dans les villes européenes (XIIe–XVIe siècle)*, no. 122, Rome, 1989.

Giovannoni, G., "Vecchi città ed edilizia nuova," *Nuova Antologia*, Milan, 1913, Turin, Unione tipografico-editrice, 1931.

Haussmann, Baron E., *Mémoires*, Paris, Victor-Havard, 1890–93, 3 vols.

Krautheimer, R., *Rome, Profile of a City 312–1308*, Princeton, Princeton University Press, 1980.

Krautheimer, R., *The Rome of Alexander VII, 1655–1667*, Princeton, 1982.

Lavedan, P., *Histoire de l'urbanisme*, Paris, Laurens, 1926–1952.

Lévi-Strauss, C. *Anthropologie structurale*, Paris, Plon, 1958.
Madsen, S. T., *Restoration and Antirestoration*, Oslo, Universitetsforlaget, 1976.
Ruskin, J., "On the Opening of the Crystal Palace," see Madsen, S. T.
Sitte, C., *Der Städtebau nach seinen künstlerischen Grundtsätzen*, Vienna, Greser, 1889. Fr. trans. D. Wieczorek, *L'Art de Bâtir les villes*, Paris, Le Seuil, 1996. Engl. trans. George R. and Christiane Crasemann Collins, *Camillo Sitte: The Birth of Modern City Planning. With a translation of the 1889 Austrian edition of his City Planning according to Artistic Principles*, 2nd edition, New York, Rizzoli, 1986.
Smets, M. *Charles Buls*, Liège, Mardage, 1993.
Turner, P., *The Education of Le Corbusier*, Fr. trans. P. Choay, *La Formation de Le Corbusier*, Paris, Macula, 1987.
Viollet-le-Duc, E. *Entretiens sur l'architecture*, Paris, Morel et Co. 1863–72, 2 vols., Brussels- Liège, Mardaga, 1977.
Webber, M. "The Post City Age," *Daedalus*, New York, Autumn 1968.

Reading

36

Camillo Sitte

City Planning According to Artistic Principles (1889)

Camillo Sitte (1843–1903), an Austrian architect and urban planner, made an important contribution to the reevaluation of the ancient and medieval urban heritage and pioneered the study of the city of the past, which became for the first time a separate field of inquiry. His fame is closely associated with the illustrated book City Planning According to Artistic Principles. *Sitte's arguments go from dismay at the loss of beauty in the new industrial city to a quite new and modern appreciation of the city of the past. According to Sitte, the traditional urban structure is not just the sum of individual monuments; rather it is a coherent ensemble where every element is part of an organic pattern and responds to aesthetic rules that can be observed and analyzed and that continue to offer important lessons to modern-day planners. This reading from his well-known book is typical of Sitte's didactic approach, which compares the planning methods of previous generations, so clearly displayed in the historic city, to the more recent urban developments. Sitte's summing up of the aesthetic impact the modern city has on its users could have been written today: "Everything tends toward the immense, and the constant repetition of identical motifs is enough to dull our senses to such an extent that only the most powerful effects can still make any impression."*

CHAPTER IX: MODERN SYSTEMS

[. . .] We have at our disposal three major methods of city planning, and several sustainability types. The major ones are the *gridiron system,* the *radial system,* and the *triangular system.* The sub-types are mostly hybrids of these three. Artistically speaking, not one of them is of any interest, for in their veins pulses not a single drop of artistic blood. All

From Camillo Sitte, *City Planning According to Artistic Principles,* translated by George R. Collins and Christiane Crasemann Collins (London: Phaidon Press, 1965), 91, 93, 100, 103–4, 106–7, 110–12. Originally published in German as *Der Städte-Bau nach seinen künstlerischen Grundsätzen* (Vienna: Carl Graeser, 1889). Courtesy of Christiane Crasemann Collins and the late George R. Collins.

three are concerned exclusively with the arrangement of *street patterns,* and hence their intention is from the very start a purely technical one. A network of streets always serves only the purposes of communication, never of art, since it can never be comprehended sensorily, can never be grasped as a whole except in a plan of it. [. . .]

—~—

The grid plan is the one most frequently applied. It was carried out already very early with an unrelenting thoroughness at Mannheim, whose plan looks exactly like a checkerboard; there exists not a single exception to the arid rule that all streets intersect perpendicularly and that each one runs straight in both directions until it reaches the countryside beyond the town. [. . .]

—~—

[. . .] [A]s soon as the geometric pattern and the building block became dominant, art was forced into silence. The modernizing of Gotha, Darmstadt, Düsseldorf, the fan-shaped plan of Karlsruhe, etc., are examples of this. The absence of pedestrians on so many modern gigantic streets and plazas (the Ludwigstrasse in Munich, the Rathausplatz in Vienna) in contrast to the crowds in the narrow alleyways of the older parts of towns, demonstrates unequivocally how little the matter of traffic received its due consideration in such city expansions, although supposedly everything was based on just that. Whereas new broad streets are laid out on the periphery of the city where dense traffic is never likely to develop, the old city center remains forever congested.

This should be proof enough that the exponents of an exclusively traffic-oriented point of view, despite occasional success, are not justified in throwing to the winds as useless the assistance of art, the teachings of history, and the great traditions of city building.

—~—

[. . .] The effective enclosure of space, deriving as it does from the historical evolution of an original unbroken street front (such as still exists today in villages), continued to be the basis of all dispositions in the old towns. Modern city planning follows the opposite tendency of dissection into separate blocks—building block, plaza block, garden block—each one being clearly circumscribed by its street frontage. From this develops a powerful force of habit: the desire to see every monument in the center of a vacant space. There is method in this madness. The ideal behind this planning could be defined mathematically as a striving for the maximum of frontage line, and herein would appear to lie the creative impulse behind the modern block system. The value of every building site increases with the length of its street frontage, the maximum value for building lots in the parcelling of land being therefore achieved when the perimeter of each block of buildings is greatest in relation to its area. Thus from a purely geometrical point of view circular blocks of buildings would be the most favorable, and, indeed, in the same configuration as that in which large balls of equal size can be pushed the closest together, namely six around one in the middle. In arranging straight streets of identical width between such blocks, the circular forms would be transformed into regular hexagons, as used in tile patterns or in the honeycomb. One could not believe it humanly possible that an idea of such really oppressive ugliness, of such appalling tediousness, and of such a labyrinthine lack of orientation would actually be carried out. Yet, incredible as it seems, it has become a reality in Chicago.

That then is the essence of the block system! In it art and beauty are no more. [. . .]

CHAPTER X: ARTISTIC LIMITATIONS OF MODERN CITY PLANNING

[. . .]

It is above all the enormous size to which our larger cities are growing that has shattered the framework of traditional artistic forms at every point. The larger the city, the bigger and wider the plazas and streets become, and the higher and bulkier are all structures, until their dimensions, what with their numerous floors and interminable rows of windows, can hardly be organized any more in an artistically effective manner. Everything tends toward the immense, and the constant repetition of identical motifs is enough to dull our senses to such an extent that only the most powerful effects can still make any impression. As this cannot be altered, the city planner must, like the architect, invent a scale appropriate for the modern city of millions. With such an extraordinary concentration of people at one location, real estate values also increase exorbitantly, and it is not possible for an individual person or the local administration to escape the inevitable effects of this increase in value. Everywhere, as if spontaneously, lots are divided up and streets are broken through so that even in the old parts of town more and more side streets result, and something of the obnoxious building-block system surreptitiously takes over. This is a phenomenon which is naturally connected with the current value of real estate and the value of street-frontage lines: hence it cannot be eliminated by decree, least of all by aesthetic considerations. All these elements must be reckoned with as stated factors that the city planner has to take into account just as an architect must consider the strength of materials and the laws of statics—even if they impose the most disagreeable and petty limitations.

The regular parcelling of lots based on purely economic considerations has become such a factor in new plans that its effects can hardly be avoided. In spite of this one should not surrender quite so blindly to the consequences of this universal method, because it is precisely this that has led to mass slaughter of the beauties of city planning. [. . .]

The high price of building lots leads to their utmost utilization, as a result of which a number of effective motifs have been abandoned in recent years. Completely building up each lot always tends to produce the characteristic cubic mass of modern times. Projections, porches, ornamental staircases, arcades, corner turrets, etc., have become for us an unthinkable luxury, even on public buildings; only high up—in the form of balconies and bay windows or on the roof—is the architect allowed to give his imagination free rein, but never below at street level where the 'building-frontage line' alone dominates. This has already become so customary that many splendid motifs, such as the monumental open staircase, no longer please us. And this whole class of architectural elements has retreated from street and plaza into the interior of buildings, yielding to the universal trend of the time—the fear of open spaces. [. . .]

—~—

The innate conflict between the picturesque and the practical cannot be eliminated merely by talking about it; it will always be present as something intrinsic to the very nature of things. This inner struggle between the two opposing demands is not, however, characteristic of town planning alone; it is present in all the arts, even in those apparently the freest, if only as a conflict between their ideal goals and the limiting conditions of the material in which the work of art is supposed to take shape. A work of art that is not subject to these limitations can perhaps be imagined abstractly, but never realized materially. The practical artist is always faced with the necessity of embodying his ideas within the range of technical possibilities. These restraints are narrow or broad according to his technical means or depending on the various ideal aspirations and the practical demands of a given period in time; nobody would deny this who has carefully studied the history of art.

In the field of city planning the limitations on artistry of arrangement have, to be sure, narrowed greatly in our day. Today such a masterpiece of city planning as the Acropolis of Athens is simply unthinkable. That sort of thing is for us, at the moment, an impossibility. Even if the millions were provided that such a project would entail, we would still be unable to create something of the kind, because we lack both the artistic basis for it and any universally valid philosophy of life that has sufficient vigor in the soul of the people to find physical expression in the work. Yet even if the commission be devoid of content and merely decorative—as is the case with art today—it would be frightfully difficult for our realistic man of the nineteenth century. Today's city builder must, before all, acquire the noble virtue of an utmost humility, and, what is remarkable in this case, less for economic considerations than for really basic reasons.

Assuming that in any new development the cityscape [*Stadtbild*] must be made as splendid and pictorial as possible, if only decoratively in order to glorify the locality—such a purpose cannot be accomplished with the ruler or with our geometrically-straight street lines. In order to produce the effects of the old masters, their colors as well must form part of our palette. Sundry curves, twisted streets and irregularities would have to be included artificially in the plan; an affected artlessness, a purposeful unintentionalness. But can the accidents of history over the course of centuries be invented and constructed *ex novo* in the plan? Could one, then, truly and sincerely enjoy such a fabricated ingenuousness, such a studied naturalness? Certainly not. The satisfaction of a spontaneous gaiety is denied to any cultural level in which building does not proceed at apparent random from day to day, but instead constructs its plans intellectually on the drawing board. This whole course of events, moreover, cannot be reversed, and consequently a large portion of the picturesque beauties we have mentioned will probably be irretrievably lost to use in contemporary planning. Modern living as well as modern building techniques no longer permit the faithful imitation of old townscapes, a fact which we cannot overlook without falling prey to barren fantasies. The exemplary creations of the old masters must remain alive with us in some other way than through slavish copying; only if we can determine in what the essentials of these creations consist, and if we can apply these meaningfully to modern conditions, will it be possible to harvest a new and flourishing crop from the apparently sterile soil.

An attempt should be made regardless of obstacles. Even if numerous pictorial beauties must be renounced and extensive consideration be given to the requirements of modern construction, hygiene, and transportation, this should not discourage us to the extent that we simply abandon artistic solutions and settle for purely technical ones, as in the building of a highway or the construction of a machine. The forever edifying impress of artistic perfection cannot be dispensed with in our busy everyday life. One must keep in mind that city planning in particular must allow full and complete participation to art, because it is this type of artistic endeavor, above all, that affects formatively every day and every hour the great mass of the population, whereas the theater and concerts are available only to the wealthier classes. Administrators of public works in cities should turn their attention to this matter. It is therefore desirable to demonstrate how far it might be possible to harmonize the principles of the ancients with our modern requirements [. . .]

Reading

37

Patrick Geddes

Patrick Geddes in India (1947)

Trained as a biologist, Patrick Geddes (1854–1932) believed in the inherent unity of nature and culture, transdisciplinarity and holistic education; and, regarding cities, in "diagnosis before treatment" and "conservative surgery." After applying his ideas to improving slum conditions in Edinburgh, Geddes was invited to India, to advise on reconciling "the need for public improvement and respect for existing social standards." Here, he wrote reports on eighteen Indian cities in which he offered a refreshing view of the role of planners. This reading is composed of portions of the excerpts from Geddes's Official Reports on Indian Cities in 1915–19 published together under the title Patrick Geddes in India. *In Geddes's view, planners should seek to understand the "whole set of existing conditions" and "strive to . . . meet the wants and needs, the ideas and ideals of the place and persons concerned." He saw planning as a means to improve the lives of all people, "from the humblest to the highest." Such an approach is the opposite of prevailing planning methods, in use then as now in many parts of the world, that lack consideration of an area's surroundings, inhabitants, or needs. On a more practical level, Geddes laid out the principles of "conservative surgery," aimed at limiting demolition and "adjusting" the traditional city fabric with minimal and carefully worked out improvements. Geddes's method can be compared to the theory of selective clearing, independently proposed by Gustavo Giovannoni in the same years (see reading 38).*

THE DIAGNOSTIC SURVEY

I. Town Planning in Kapurthala. A Report to H.H. the Maharaja of Kapurthala, 1917 (p. 2).

By what process can a city be remodelled in order to achieve the best results?

From Patrick Geddes, *Patrick Geddes in India,* edited by Jaqueline Tywhitt (London: Lund Humphries, 1947), 24–27, 40–45, 48–53, 75–77.

There are two schools of thought, each containing town planners, architects, and gardeners. The first, and most popular school, which has dominated thought during the last two centuries, holds that the immediate effect is alone worth consideration. Here a street as fine as may be, there a monument as impressive as funds will allow, there again an avenue as extensive or a garden as magnificent as space permits. So far so good, yet the designer possessed only by these ideas exceeds too readily the scale of his surroundings and over-reaches also the requirements of the town. The result has been that, in too many cities, imposing new streets have been laid out without survey of their surrounding quarter and constructed without reference to local needs or potentialities. Similarly, monuments are erected on sites that please the fancy of the designer, instead of at the appropriate climax of the city and the focus of interest. Gardens also have been swept away or created according to the taste or humour, the training or the limitations of the designer.

Happily there is another school of planning, of building and of gardening that investigates and considers the whole set of existing conditions; that studies the whole place as it stands, seeking out how it has grown to be what it is, and recognizing alike its advantages, its difficulties and its defects. This school strives to adapt itself to meet the wants and needs, the ideas and ideals of the place and persons concerned. It seeks to undo as little as possible, while planning to increase the well-being of the people at all levels, from the humblest to the highest. City improvements of this kind are both less expensive to the undertaking and productive of more enjoyment to all concerned.

Although a designer of abstract patterns may appear to be animated solely by aesthetics, his decoration must be related to the use of that which he is ornamenting and must also be expressive of its material. This applies even more strongly to the work of the city designer, the architect, and the gardener. The gardener indeed has the most difficult task of all, for he has to provide a fit setting for the completion of the work of the others. Bacon, long ago in his famous essay on gardens, wrote 'Men build stately before they garden finely, as if gardening were the greater perfection'.

Environment and organism, place and people, are inseparable but, since the essential unit of a city is the home, it will be as well to start by examining its especial requirements. With the dwelling we must consider its occupants, the man, the woman and the child. The child should obviously be strong, healthy, mentally developing, and normally 'good'. The expression of these qualities all together will normally result in child beauty, and full maturity and participation in life will follow. So with the woman, so with the man and so also with the home. This too must be stable and healthy and provide conditions for mental and moral development. It must form as substantial a part of the wealth and glory of the city as may be, with its architecture, artistic character and garden developed accordingly. The same sequence is true for a city, and all others are false.

It may be said that this is common knowledge, but what then is the cause of the frequent aesthetic failure of our results? It is due to the lack of harmony between the advancing phases of western 'science'. Each of the various specialists remains too closely concentrated upon his single specialism, too little awake to those of others.

Each sees clearly and seizes firmly one petal of the six-lobed flower of life and tears it apart from the whole. In the east, on the other hand, it has been the glory of the historic sages and ancient rulers to concentrate their minds and efforts upon life as a whole. As a result, civic beauty in India has existed at all levels, from humble homes and simple shrines to palaces magnificent and temples sublime.

In city planning then, we must constantly keep in view the whole city, old and new alike in all its aspects and at all its levels. The transition in an Indian city, from narrow lanes and earthen dwellings to small streets, great streets and buildings of high importance and architectural beauty, form an inseparably interwoven structure. Once this is understood, the city plan ceases to appear as an involved network of thoroughfares dividing masses of building blocks, but appears instead as a great chessboard on which the manifold game of life is in active progress. As an old student and votary of the game I may be able occasionally to suggest certain advantageous moves; each will, however, result from a survey of the situation as it has arisen and will ignore none of the difficulties, nor shall I avoid them by attempting to make a clean sweep and starting a new game in which I may express my own methods. The problem of city planning, as of chess, is to improve the situation by, as far as may be, turning its very difficulties into opportunities. Results thus obtained are both more economical and more interesting, even aesthetically, than those that are achieved by clearing the board and re-setting all the pieces.

The first school of designers are wont, both in west and east, to start with the greatest things, such as the palace and the chief civic buildings. Only later do they penetrate the old parts of the city and then, too often, only to sweep its past before them.

The method of the diagnostic survey starts quite otherwise. First it seeks to unravel the old city's labyrinth and discern how this has grown up. Though, like all organic growths, this may at first seem confused to our modern eyes, that have for so long been trained to a mechanical order, gradually a higher form of order can be discerned—the order of life in development. This is the method of all evolutionary science and hence the method of the latest and youngest of all social sciences—and yet the most ambitious and most necessary of them all—the science of the city survey.

—~—

CONSERVATIVE SURGERY

I. Report on the Towns in the Madras Presidency, 1915 : Tanjore.

In this town, as usual, it is proposed to drive a new gridiron of forty feet streets through a congested and insanitary area. Again as usual, this dreary and conventional plan is quite unsparing to the old homes and to the neighbourhood life of the area. It leaves fewer housing sites and these mostly narrower than before and the large population thus expelled would, again as usual, be driven into creating worse congestion in other quarters, to the advantage only of the rack-renting interests. This interest often consciously, but sometimes, I am willing to believe, quite unconsciously, is at the bottom of this pretentious but spurious method of 'relieving congestion', which has been practised in European and in Indian cities alike. Nor, so far as my knowledge goes, has the offer of suburban sites met this difficulty ever or anywhere. Even if, as rarely happens, the new site offered is both suitable and acceptable to the people expelled, they are practically excluded by the present cost of building in favour of the more prosperous classes. Hence the result of these would-be improvements is to increase the serious depression of the poor and make this ever more difficult to relieve.

The method of Conservative Surgery, on the other hand, brings out different and encouraging results; first it shows that the new streets prove not to be really required since, by simply enlarging the existing lanes, ample communications already exist; secondly that, with the addition of some vacant lots and the removal of a few of the most dilapidated and insanitary houses, these lanes can be greatly improved and every house

A. Portion of Tanjore Fort. The Municipal Council's proposals for the relief of congestion. Cost about Rs 30,000. Scale 1 cm. equals 100 feet.

B. Portion of Tanjore Fort. A 'diagnostic survey.'

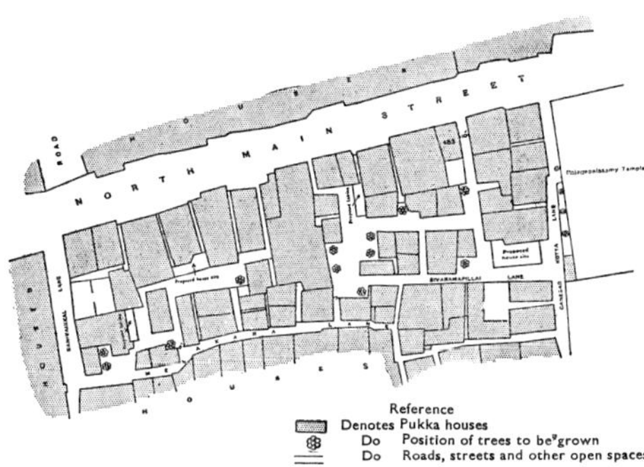

C. Portion of Tanjore Fort. The congested area as it would appear after the application of 'conservative surgery.' Cost about Rs 5,000.

brought within reach of fresh air as well as of material sanitation—a point on which the more pretentious method constantly fails as is evident on every plan. [. . .]

So extreme is the contrast between this simple, economical, yet more thorough method of improvement by conservation, and the customary system of slicing through new sanitary lanes, that I am constantly compelled to wonder how this system, at once so costly and so inefficient, can have become so general both in India and in Europe. True, to the professed utilitarian, the preservation of the old world picturesqueness of these courts and lanes is obviously anathema. It rouses all those deep-seated prejudices and readily excited sentiments towards a coldly fanatical iconoclasm of old-world beauty, which had such disastrous effects during the past century that they are hardly equalled by the savagery of war. Yet, when we realise that not only does this system cost from six to tenfold that of the commonsense methods of Conservative Surgery, but that it is less efficient in the locality and causes an intensification of congestion elsewhere—in fact that the old difficulties persist—surely the awakening of public interest must be at hand.

The conservative method, however, has its difficulties. It requires long and patient study. The work cannot be done in the office with ruler and parallels, for the plan must be sketched out on the spot, after wearying hours of perambulation—commonly amid sights and odours which neither Brahmin nor Briton has generally schooled himself to endure, despite the moral and physical courage of which each is legitimately proud. This type of work also requires maps of a higher degree of detail and accuracy than those hitherto required by law for municipal or governmental use—indeed, in this town, it was found necessary to establish a practical class for engineers and surveyors for this purpose. Even when a detailed and corrected map has been produced (instead of a rude tracing from the revenue atlas, necessarily largely out of date) the task is still difficult. Even after a good deal of experience of the game, one constantly finds oneself in check ; now and then so definitely and persistently as to feel tempted, like the impatient chess-player, to sweep a fist through the pieces which stand in the way. This destructive impatience is, indeed, an old vice of beginners in a position of authority; and their chance of learning the real game is, of course, spoiled by such an abuse of it.

III. Town Planning in Balrampur. A Report to the Honourable the Maharajah Bahadur, 1917.

Some of the principles of conservative surgery can be illustrated in a quarter south of the palace of Balrampur. Here are two plans. The first, a tracing from the Municipal Survey, shows the existing labyrinth which is crowded and dilapidated, dirty and depressed. The second shows a plan that has resulted from an intensive study of the area, house by house as well as lane by lane. It will be seen that the lanes have now become reasonably spacious and orderly, though not formally so, and that open and easy communications exist in every direction.

At first sight it may seem that very extensive demolitions have been proposed entailing costly compensation, but examination on the site will show that this is not so.

Here, as so often, the right starting points have been provided by the existing open spaces, each with its well and temple.

D. Balrampur: The quarter south of the Palace and of Pajawa Tank from the Municipal Plan.

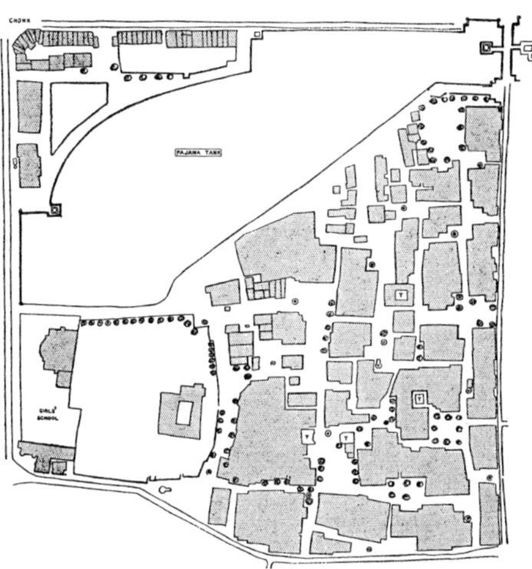

E. Balrampur: The same quarter as improved.

These spaces have been slightly extended by clearing the sites of all fallen buildings and planting trees to protect the enlarged spaces against future encroachment. The open spaces can then be linked by further small clearances, mainly at the expense of ruined and dilapidated buildings.

As this study of the locality proceeds, one is encouraged by the results, alike for sanitation and for beauty. As these depressed and dilapidated old quarters re-open to one another it can be seen that the old village life, with its admirable combination of private simplicity and sacred magnificence, is only awaiting renewal.

Even in the beautiful old cities of the west we have rarely such a wealth either of open spaces or of antique shrines. In fine old European towns, as of Belgium or Italy, the churches are larger and more magnificent, but the great number of these small shrines, with their domes and spires always pleasing and often admirably proportioned and wrought, makes an effect which, though less magnificent, is in a way even more delightful.

IV. Report on the Towns in the Madras Presidency, 1915 : Madura.

North of a wretched cotton slum in a city of Southern India a little Temple, obviously for popular and humble use, has just been built. It is covered with new sculpture and gorgeous with colour. Does this show that 'the citizens do not care for improvements'? Everywhere in the slums we see women toiling and sweeping, each struggling to maintain her poor little home above the distressingly low level of municipal paving and draining in the quarter. The fault does not lie with the people and I have no fear that the people of the cities would not respond to improvements. The immediate problem is for the municipal and central government to understand what improvements really are needed and desired, both domestic and social, spiritual and artistic.

One of the poor quarters of this same town is at present threatened with 'relief of congestion', and we are shown a rough plan in which the usual gridiron of new thoroughfares is hacked through its old-world village life. We are told that this sweeping and costly plan is not the original one, but is regarded as a moderate and even economical substitute for the first one of total demolition, that was happily too expensive to obtain the sanction or support of the Government. It is not suggested that the new thoroughfares to be made through this area are required in any way for city communication; the streets outside the area are amply sufficient for this purpose. This local scheme is only one of 'sanitation'.

We start walking through the district, and find that the very first house doomed to speedy destruction is as substantial, decent, and even pleasing, as one could wish to see. Why then should it be demolished? The explanation is 'straightening the new lane beside it'. This new lane is not intended to be appreciably broader than the present one and the only merit claimed for the destruction is that it will bring the new lane about sixteen degrees nearer to the draughtsman's straight line than at present. In short, the 'sanitary' improvements begin by destroying an excellent home and squandering its value (at least 3000 rupees) for the sole purpose of inclining the present lane from a position slightly oblique to the edge of the drawing board to one strictly parallel to it.

How is such planning to be explained? I take it as a vivid illustration of the 'principle of functional substitution' as it is called by evolutionists. Were this a question of a new conservancy lane or a new latrine I could understand it. These are the sacred shrines of the sanitation engineers who originate these clearances. But draughtsmen care no more for sanitation than do other members of the public. When copying the plans of a sanitarian their prime interest is in its neat straight lines. Thus a crude sanitation plan gives place to a still more elementary aesthetic, and we here do obeisance to the straight lines of the drawing board and the set square.

PLANNING FOR HEALTH

IV. Town Planning in Balrampur. A Report to the Honourable the Maharaja[h] Bahadur, 1917.

Despite the many differences between east and west I continually find the same contrasts as those with which I am familiar at home, between the antique beauty of the simple homes and sacred buildings, which are the best elements of any historic town, and the slum conditions which have in recent times invaded and immersed them. Improvement is not achieved by vainly lamenting the past or by harshly insisting upon the needs of 'progress', but by simply setting to work to clear away the accumulation of miscellaneous rubbish and filth. Thus, with moderate effort and outlay, the conspicuous neglect and dilapidation of a Temple, a well, neighbouring buildings, and a fallen house may all be cleared and the space made over to an attractive open square.

At this stage I am commonly interrupted. I am assured that 'everything has been tried' that 'things constantly relapse into disorder' that 'there is no doing anything with the people' that 'their prejudices are against improvement'. I am even told that 'they prefer dirt'. In fact I am still constantly treated as an inexperienced and Utopian youth instead of a veteran jemadar of sweepers with more than thirty years' experience of the fight against dirt in more cities than I need mention. Yet in every city or town without exception, in east and west alike, I have met the same pessimism and been told much the same story.

What is the explanation? It is always and everywhere the same. There are deep-rooted prejudices: there is obstinate adherence to untidy habits : but—I say it deliberately—the worst of all these prejudices and habits belong to the sanitarians themselves

Fig. 1. 'The dignified isolation of cantonments and Government perambokes is in sharp contrast to the congested confusion of old bazaar towns.' *Old and New Delhi*, 1942.

Fig. 2. 'When an engineer rushes into town planning he too often adopts the simple expedient of drawing straight thoroughfares on the drawing board across the town plan and then sawing them through the town, regardless of cost and consequence.' *Calcutta*, 1942.

and, for the last two generations, have been reducing the effects of their admirable goodwill, their intensive science and their strenuous labours. The overflowing sanitary bucket remains their only shrine and altar ; the hideous iron latrine their only temple ; and their corresponding belief that individuals and cities are only to be sanitated from behind, and from below upwards, is assuredly one of the most depressing of our modern superstitions.

In saying these hard things I am not forgetful of the magnificent services of sanitarians. But, though the provision and care of latrines for an army are fundamental necessities, it is not thus that one effects the recruitment of heroic youth for war, nor thus that its spirit is maintained. This is done by flag and music and by every form of high emotional appeal, as all practical soldiers know and no sanitarian would dare deny. So let the sanitarian no longer refuse to learn this lesson and, open minded as he is on questions of mechanics, chemistry, bacteriology and the rest, let him also give the people's psychology its hearing and trial.

Let the temple flag be hoisted, let the building be repaired and adorned, its flower garden planted or renewed. Let the well be cleansed and cemented. Let the sacred tree have its platform repaired; or if dead and gone, let a new pipal be planted, with the other trees beloved by gods and men—the pleasant Neem, the fruitful Bael, the flowering Kadam—and let them be set in corners of the little squares as space may offer.

From such small material beginnings, begetting delight instead of disgust, a new interest in sanitation would spread. The woman will say 'If this is what they call sanitation, and not merely putting sanitary buckets by our wells and offering us polluting latrines that the Engineer Sahibs will not themselves enter, then there is some good in it after all'. And, as the woman returns from the repaired well, with purer water and uninfected vessel and feet, we can again be of service to her. Let us remove that heap of earth and rubbish from outside her door, which is so plainly beyond her powers, and fill up the nearest mosquito-puddle with it. She may next allow our inspector to criticise gently the heap of broken brickbats within the compound, which her husband has been saving these seven years for something he will never build. Let it be bought if need be—two or three annas may pay for a cartload, for the material is probably by now almost worthless—and let it be used to mend the holes in the lane until the time comes when it can be paved.

Reading

38

Gustavo Giovannoni

New Building in Old Cities (1931)

Gustavo Giovannoni (1873–1943) was an Italian historian, teacher, engineer, architect, and town planner who greatly influenced the Italian debate about architectural history and design and had a major influence on the theory of architectural and urban conservation. His theoretical and practical work saw him engaged in the cities of Rome, Bergamo Alta, Siena, and Bari. His ideas on urban conservation were first formulated in 1913 and subsequently elaborated and expanded in 1931, with the publication of Vecchie città ed edilizia nuova. *This reading documents Giovannoni's position in the debate between "innovators" and "preservationists" and their opposing views about old city areas. Giovannoni advocates for a compromise between these positions to enable the coexistence of new and old parts of the city, each with its own clearly defined and independent characteristics. The reading also shows Giovannoni's uncompromising position on the urban practices and theories of the modern movement, which he considered potentially destructive for "all that exists" and in total conflict with the urban past. Giovannoni saw the challenges represented by the old parts of the city but advised against the prevailing trend of transforming old areas into the center of the new city. Instead he supported the idea of separate and clearly distinct modern centers and, in the old city, "selective clearing"* (diradamento edilizio)*, where "prudent adaptation measures are substituted for destruction, like in an orchard where a good agriculturist proceeds with rational and judicial pruning and grafting of the plants that in turn helps the old plants to regerminate."*

CHAPTER 1. DISCORD AND AGREEMENT

[. . .] The innovators say: cities are not museums or archives, but are made for living in the best way possible, and we cannot compromise development and stop the

From Gustavo Giovannoni, *Vecchie città ed edilizia nuova* (Turin: Unione tipografico-editrice Torinese, 1931), 2–4, 154–58, 166–67, 172–74, 183, 248–49, 252, 254–56, 258, 260–66, 273–74, 276–77, 280.

progress of civilization by shutting new life in between narrow and sad streets only for a poorly understood fetishistic respect for the past. Our needs are completely different from those of our ancestors and we can no longer adapt ourselves to them, just as we are no longer able to wear their clothes, quaint but uncomfortable. Air, light, comfort, cleanliness, this is what we want! The dwellings are comfortable and open; the streets are wide, useful, easy to follow. Should there be important buildings in their path, and works of art, which cannot be moved (of course we are not speaking of exceptional monuments) there is nothing else to do but to demolish them, and at the most, if there is time, preserve their memory through pictorial documentation.

The preservationists respond: life cannot be motivated by a materialistic, utilitarian concept alone, without ideals, without the search for beauty; even less should the life of the individual determine the collective life of the city, which must contain within itself elements of a moral and aesthetic education, with regard for the traditions that embody so much of the nation's glory. Tradition is trampled upon the day that a monument is toppled or defaced: a witness to art and history is removed; or, the physiognomy of an entire neighborhood's environment—slowly engraved by the centuries—which often has a much greater value than that of a single monument, is violently transformed. The reason to exist, the importance and often also the prosperity present in many cities (like Rome, Florence, Venice, Nuremberg, Bruges, Siena, and Verona), is in the light that the past sheds upon them—much more than their current value. Let's not darken it by destroying the ruins of monuments and clouding their character. [. . .]

As often happens when faced with a complex issue (and few human contrivances are more complex than the development of a city), all of the extreme principles, all of the aphorisms it invokes are respectable and correct, but they are theories that approach this serious issue from only one angle. Often indulging in formal terminology, they end up just fighting it out in a vacuum. In practice, instead, particularly now with the recent prevailing building trends and the perfection of numerous "devices" at the service of the city, the question has shifted, and this field is undergoing that which modern culture and modern structures have produced in so many others by unexpectedly changing in the face of what seemed to be insurmountable problems. I do not believe, therefore, that I am an exaggerating optimist when I affirm that one study—completed with a broad perspective, with precise knowledge of the real demands of building and the means at its disposition, and with sincere fondness for art and the memories that a city embodies—is not only almost always capable of finding a compromise between two sets of criteria. [. . .]

[I]t is possible in the historical city—through a series of providential improvements and initiatives, and above all with the methodical study of a kinematic system that replaces the dominant empiricism—to achieve harmonious coexistence between old neighborhoods and new ones, each with its own characteristics, in one large system: a more complex and extremely new organism.

This subject, which new methods and new studies have opened, is vast and magnificent but also contains a gravity and urgency that is frightening. The assertion is not futile, in fact, that the great problems of our cities are banging at the door and perhaps now their fate is being decided: in the past as well as in the future. This means that, in this period of time already well under way, either they will be rendered adaptable to become genuinely great urban centers that accommodate the gradual growth of the population, taking on a scale and nobility worthy of the great traditions, respecting and valuing the exquisite artistic patrimony instilled over the centuries, or the possibility for a broad, organic, fecund development and the salvation of that which is beautiful and dear in our urban heritage will be undermined beyond repair, perpetuating the sad age of disorientation with no guidelines for building, of parasitic speculation on the landscape, of progressive destruction of monuments and their environment.

How many irreparable errors, rendered permanent by the objects constructed, were indeed perpetrated in the last fifty years in the beautiful cities of Italy! The myopia, the incompetence, the rhetoric, the private interests were given free rein to establish a city planning regime built on empiricism and dilettantism: streets without destination and without purpose; regulatory plans conceived only in terms of their geometric function (or, to be more precise, according to a geometry of only two dimensions); eviscerations of old, worthless (or almost worthless) neighborhoods— financially disastrous and ruinous for the character of the ancient city and for the integrity of its monuments—for sanitary reasons because they are the source of new and more grave crowding; embryonic designs for traffic circulation that even before being undertaken are immediately surpassed by the reality of the demands and the transport systems; lacking every elementary concept of zoning in the new neighborhoods, lacking every tendency toward development initiatives that are not immediate, lacking every vision of the city of the future. [. . .] In this way, many of our beautiful cities have lost in part their character and their beauty, without becoming truly modern cities adapted to the new rhythm of life, to the most current and wide-ranging functions of a city. The banality of its appearance matches the insufficiency of the methods of development.

Therefore it is necessary to say "enough" to this path and take the path "less traveled" up until now. [. . .]

—∾—

CHAPTER 5. CHALLENGES ENCOUNTERED IN ANCIENT URBAN CENTERS

All of the problems contemplated a moment ago regarding urban initiatives, whether related to the past or with a far-reaching vision of the future, are related to the truly fundamental challenge of how a new building is grafted onto the ancient city center.

—∾—

Rhetorical phrasing, simplified criteria, and the desire to emulate foreign examples unsuitable for us sometimes coalesce the small and quotidian requirements of an ordinary city administration in strange ways, turning the development plan into a run-of-the-mill work by an anonymous technical office. "We must have wide avenues!"

"We must destroy unsanitary city centers: memorials to the barbaric Middle Ages!" "Away with the indecorous hovels near the palaces!" "In Rome, unite the Pantheon with Augustus's Mausoleum via an avenue as broad as the Tiber!"

We will now cease with these banal and simplistic expressions, even though they are always resurgent and always effective, in an effort to objectively examine the various overarching ideas that are at odds among them.

Encountered most often is the intent to transform the old city—which remains the center of gravity of the new one—into its central nucleus, the business center, the "City."

Le Corbusier recently took up that motif again, claiming that in cities, old or new, it is necessary to:

1. Ease congestion in the center to cope with the demands of traffic circulation;
2. Increase density to create the network required for running businesses;
3. Increase the means of communication;
4. Increase green spaces.

The first and the fourth proposal would seem in fact to fully contradict the second. But Le Corbusier's proposal of a system of many skyscrapers was successful; the buildings were naturally all alike but isolated and detached from one another, enclosed by wide streets and gardens. The solution, as already pointed out, however, is so artificial and absurdly uneconomical that the whole system immediately collapses.

The only criteria, barbaric but logical, that it would require is this: destruction of all that exists for creation of the new order.

But let us return to the average example of the existing city and remember the way in which it was formed. It was born in response to needs that in many respects were completely different from ours but whose pattern is preserved by the continued existence of the plan, even when authentic remains of monuments or minor buildings have become scarce. The city originally had, much more than is believed, its logic and its cleanliness: the small houses did not suffocate the small streets and they breathed through wide and delightful interior gardens. The additions and contamination that took place over the span of centuries, and above all the speculative scheme of rental houses replacing family residences, changed greatly its character, increasing building heights and filling up interior spaces. Nevertheless, the greatest worsening of the conditions of overcrowding and narrowing occurred in recent times with the tendency toward centralization, badly governed, poorly executed, and poorly tempered by still insufficient systems of outward communication.

This clear principle and almost always sad experiment demonstrates that *an old city that has survived is almost always unfit to become the center of the new city.*

Indeed it is enough to compare the current state of an old city with the limitations that it presents with the demands [. . .] of a new one: like a large, complex mechanism whose gears were determined with rigid precision, it demonstrates the conditions of the two organisms to be diverse, antithetical, and incompatible, such that any arrangement is damaging for both, ruining the character of the ancient and impeding adequate development of the new.

—∾—

We instead affirm that in the great majority of cases, *the desire to transform the ancient city center (which other methods could effectively improve) into a vibrant center of mobility and business for the modern city is an immense error, definitive and incurable,* based on sophistry far removed from reality and destined to condemn everything noble and sacred that the city represents, as well as the possibility of a broad, rational, and fervent future development, suffocated without hope in the closed ring of an idea that seems dynamic but instead renders permanent the present discomfort. Ordinarily, this great mistake—disastrous and fundamental—results from the integration of various errors of judgment that distort reality, and the most common are the following:

1. to not take into account the initial development plan, that is, the many possible orientations of the future city, which, albeit considered a new organism, must avoid narrowly radiocentric solutions and gradual deterioration of the interior zones;
2. to not take into account the practical and economic possibilities, the infinite resistance to destruction, and at the very least the equivalently vast difficulties of reconstruction while, at the same time, assuming the theoretically laid out plan to be an organism genuinely viable almost in one go, with its orderly systems, its circuits devoid of interruptions, its neighborhoods expeditiously arranged;
3. to consider new building perfect without seeing the severe ills that invade it and distance it (as we saw in connection with the individual topics) from requirements of sanitation, order, traffic circulation, etc., formulated by scholars, such that it can be said that the orderly and well-made new city is a rare exception;
4. to consider, conversely, old building as only worthy of contempt without realizing that the ills from which it suffers are for the most part connected to inappropriate use and social and planning problems connected to poverty or vice that are not cured with a shovel because they are human diseases to be cured with human wherewithal;
5. to ignore the values that constitute spiritual patrimony—often glorious, often exquisitely beautiful—that live in ancient cities. It may be wise to sacrifice some elements to some carefully scrutinized demands, which, opening the door to further development, save the rest. But to condemn large areas, especially neighborhoods that can be considered a collective work of art, to vanish—tumultuously or gradually—for erroneous experimentation, would be an insane crime that nothing can excuse.

—∾—

[. . .] It is therefore necessary to dive deeper into the study of the issue, whether by analytically examining the various arguments that together form a whole and the discussions that depend on them, or by studying the methods that allow attaining, completely or in part, the goal.

Taking up again the subdivisions that were already put in place for study of the characteristics and conditions of the modern city, the social organism and in particular the demands of sanitation, decency, and the relative well-being of the home, will be initially examined.

Sanitary conditions. — When discussing the building process and demographic crowding that almost always is produced in the central areas of the ancient city, where life continually develops, it was already implicitly demonstrated how much work is still to be done in order to adapt it to modern standards. In reality, secondary cities without excessive decline where life is still carried out in these tranquil central areas are not lacking. They are still composed of the small houses with private gardens that face them flowering onto the streets, and beautiful open courtyards, maintaining together the character of ancient beauty and cleanliness. Much more frequent and deleterious, however, are the cases of progressive cities where conditions are almost intolerable due to the scarcity of air and light, the density of the population, and the poor state of the homes, disturbing the rational arrangement of the area. The necessity for an improvement seems therefore to be evident, but the challenge is how it should be implemented.

—∾—

Indeed, often in these cases, when the problem cannot be resolved as a whole, the builders and the financiers of the eviscerations resolve it *symbolically*. They lay out a wide street in the old habitat and on its margin construct incredibly tall new buildings. They leave the surrounding area as it was but in a condition much worse than before because the new barrier closes them off and suffocates them more than the preexisting hovels did. It would appear that those *linear* systematizations were built not for the townspeople but for the tourists (since they do not miss the lively and picturesque appearance of the ancient city) who, as they walk down the new avenue, which naturally assumes the same type and the same name in all cities, "are easily convinced," according to the ingenuous expressions of Palladio,[1] "that the other streets of the city also correspond with its breadth and beauty."

[. . .]

It is necessary instead to take "the path less traveled" when renewing old neighborhoods, often undeniably necessary, as generally described above: not radical transformations, but minute improvements, diffuse, progressive; not fundamental alterations of the social order that create new contrasts between wealthy and poor areas, but gradual, spontaneous elevations of the class of the population, of the character of the small industries, of commerce, of the cultural centers that are located there. And this improvement, comprising not a line but an entire area, must engage the elements of the street and the house, all elements have to contribute: buildings, better modest than grandiose, that do not disregard the existing type but correspond with it; architecture, with renovation of living spaces and reduction of crowding, starting from the interior rather than the exterior; the provision of sanitary inspectors that establish facilities, activate public services, and gradually negate the habitability of the most unsanitary dwellings, for example, ground floor dwellings, like the "low-rises" of Naples and the *sottani* (cramped living space at ground level or below) in Cagliari; financial provisions to facilitate, by means of building loans and incentives, the initiatives of single proprietors to adapt and restore their own buildings.

[. . .]

Economic factors in the ancient city centers. — Along with the questions now under discussion, and intimately involved with them, are economic factors, presenting from another point of view the dilemma between the tendency toward preservation and that toward destruction and reconstruction.

Arguments for economic order are the battle horse of the demolishers. Transformation of the city's ancient areas, which are often also centrally located, into business areas, shopping centers, and wealthy residences, whether by radical and complete rebuilding, or by organic alteration of single buildings, constitutes a considerable increase in revenue and therefore are of great financial benefit; the architectural and social distribution of the city, taken in its entirety, acquires logic and order. Indeed, construction companies and community authorities turn to this Fata Morgana expecting rivers of gold.

In truth it is undeniable that the potential for profit sometimes has positive roots when applied to the subject of renovation and alteration of building function, but that happens more in isolated cases than in general and systematic applications. Examples of single edifices that have been completely remade are in fact frequent in the great European cities (some as many as three times in forty years in Berlin on Leipzigerstrasse), adapting them to the improved conditions of the location, to the rapidly changing demands of life and therefore, in the final analysis, to the greater potential for revenue. Failure is much easier to come by, however, when the venture encompasses vast areas with the resulting enormous financial transactions and great expense of large systematizations that it requires.

—∿∿—

Mobility in the old city. — The contrast between old and new seems most manifest in the requirements of traffic circulation. As was shown, the entities that facilitate traffic in a modern city correspond directly—by means of width, route, location of roadways, rest stops, and many other elements that comprise the roadways—to the concrete and precise function assigned to them, like mechanical devices in an office, or the pipes, drains, and surge tanks in a hydraulic plant. They must be immediately relevant to the current means of transportation and, if necessary, to those of the future, and exactly for this reason, the structures of the old city are absolutely incapable of being adapted.

The eviscerator's empiricism believes it has found a remedy for this: widening of the streets or existing public squares. As is almost always the case, ratiocination and experience easily demonstrate that this choice is inopportune and insufficient, often resulting in a serious and definitive worsening of the ills that were to be cured.

—∿—

Thus, this erroneous initial undertaking—as is always the case when a system is destroyed and it cannot be replaced with a radically different one, or when one believes one can reconcile two antithetical ends—definitively ruins the ancient without achieving the new; the existing city is mangled and mauled a bit without obtaining traffic conditions adapted to modern mobility or to future conditions required by the growth of building development. The city becomes intolerably enslaved by a center that was not intended to be created. But when the disadvantages of the misguided solution materialize, it is already too late. When the demons of feverish mobility have invaded the streets—here a little old, there a little new—the gradual congestion of movement is inevitable, and the damage is irreparable.

—∿—

Aesthetic problems in old cities. — Ultimately, aesthetic challenges arise in the problematic relationship between old and new, between "life, engraved on the walls, nourished by centuries and generations," and the modern building revolution.

The preceding pages already revealed the conflict between harmony, picturesque and architectural, composed in the ancient building aesthetic, and the modern tendency toward wide, open spaces with no interest in the unique, the abandonment of local character provided by what were until now considered permanent elements, like the climate and construction materials. The solution, the fundamental motif of this study, has already been envisaged: to give each building style its own field, benefiting from the clear division that must be established between traffic arteries and the fabric of residential areas, between old and new zones.

—∿—

It is therefore better, as long as it is possible, to take the path less traveled: limit adaptations in the old city center to a few modest architectural additions respectful of the environment, without introducing material alterations that result in artistic alterations. Instead, initiate new building life and its endeavors—the great speculative deals, the significant architectural expressions of modernity—in the newly built neighborhoods: this is the formula that cleanly separates the camps such that innovators and preservationists must find themselves in agreement.

It is obvious to state how all that has been said on this subject possesses a varying scale of value according to the very different cases that present themselves in reality. They range from extreme environmental conditions (as in Venice) to hybridism between long-standing factories and amorphous houses, or crude ones, resulting from building activities in recent years, that already compromise in part the city's character, the latter taking refuge in a few quiet corners. Furthermore, the demands of modern life, intense or gradual, or late and contrived, play a role.

Proof of the thesis of the aesthetic incompatibility of radical transformations of old neighborhoods remains, however, generally complete. If one does not want Italy to lose its exquisite heritage of urban and architectural monuments that shines in the many gemstones that wreathe its crown, and if one does not want at the same time to constrict and stiffen the possibility for development adapted to our times, it is necessary above all that the illusion is unmasked and tackled. It is the manufacturer of so many calamities, believing to see a valorization of ancient beauty in the encroachment of new building and opening up of wide spaces, the isolation of monuments, the substitution of large new edifices for modest houses: that is, an activity that directly or indirectly ends up almost always in conflict and destruction.

—ʍ—

CHAPTER 10. IMPROVEMENT OF INTERIOR NUCLEI: THE THEORY OF SELECTIVE CLEARING [*DIRADAMENTO*]

The measures of varying types indicated here—whether general initiation of external construction or rational channeling of traffic to exterior routes and to a few potential, well-studied and assessed, cross routes (when it is not possible to avoid it)—remove intense traffic and the causes of excessive congestion from the old residential area. These measures deal with the problems of hygienic, social—and sometimes also aesthetic and economic—renewal, and no longer enmesh them in the complex and hybrid function demanded by a great road network. Rather, they are isolated and viewed directly without exaggeration and without interference.

Such are the problems of improved sanitation: decrease the density of the population, bring air and light into closed-off areas, improve public and residential facilities, combat the filth that settles there, which often the broom does not alone suffice to remove. Such are the problems of social betterment: removal of the poorest living quarters from central areas, the dens of vice, taverns, and hotels of the lowest class; gradual economic and aesthetic valorization; liberation of abrogated artifacts and their restoration, prudently removing formless elements, opening views and returning to the residential area the healthy and fresh beauty of plant life.

All of this is carried out "with patience and love": not wanting to do too much or alter in essence the typology, the order of the neighborhood; diffusing as opposed to constructing linear systematizations; liberating without adding on; bettering without radically transforming; all by means of small, local measures without grand gestures.

The solution that can achieve the goal, that reconciles the three factors of systematization—local mobility, local artistic appearance, and desire for sanitation—is in most cases the systematization of the practice of *diradamento*[2] [selective clearing of the built fabric].

It is characterized by an irregular broadening rather than the uniform regularity of new streets, and demolition here and there of a house or a group of houses that is replaced by a small public square with a garden inside it: a small lung in the old neighborhood. Streets grow smaller only to widen again in a moment, bringing a variety of movement, including contrasting effects of the original type of building that persist in this way in all its artistic and environmental character. Only by making way for some rays of the sun, some new views, do the old houses, too closely bound together, open and breathe again.

In other words, the method is embodied in demolition of small separate sections, leaving open areas behind and rebuilding little or nothing at all, and in this way reducing to a minimum the introduction of new elements that are almost always out of tune with the old. It is embodied by the choice of the area to be improved among the most suitable without preconceived geometry of straight streets and constant compartmentalization, demolishing the buildings of no interest, opening the city blocks most dense and filthy. It is embodied by careful consideration of the new vistas that are created, in which major monuments or characteristic groupings of small houses are framed.

In this way, sanitary and artistic advantages progress together and the basis for future development does not exceed or threaten current development. It is permissible to distribute the advantages of redevelopment to an entire vast region without settling them on one street or public square. The picturesque character remains, and is also perhaps emphasized, that resides in variegated groupings, in the contrast of shadows and light. General conditions are improved without radically altering the economic order, without, that is, wanting to transform the neighborhood into something which it never could be. It allows, finally, for gradual implementation that continues year after year with funds regularly allocated to the community budget.

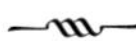

In this way, a holistic study of the city should be at once broad—encompassing the neighborhoods that are being expanded and the main traffic arteries—as well as simple and restricted, carried out step by step with great care for systematization of interior areas. Above all, it is necessary to establish—with precise understanding of the various kinds of elements: streets and houses, art and historical events—the immutable cornerstones: edifices with historical and artistic character that must be preserved, works and groupings whose environment must be respected. The possibility of selective clearing must be considered from the point of view of maximum yield of light and air that a partial demolition can bring to the nearby houses, of the effect on the local panorama, which will result in the composition of new views, and for the traffic network. Consequently, sometimes small incisions uniting two streets via a small public square, removing surplus bodies that produce bottlenecks, or that simply round off a corner, can, as mentioned elsewhere, be sufficient to restore balance to the flow of traffic congested in places. [. . .]

And the new constructions should exhibit maximum respect for the environment, coinciding with the requirement of maximum simplicity in the architectural lines. When possible, they continue the motifs of the remaining parts of the same building, but the new elements should have nothing pseudo-medieval, nothing "à la mode," nothing arti-

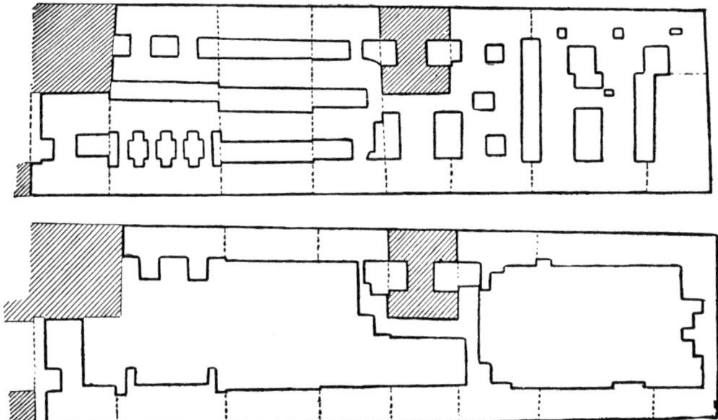

Fig. 1. Interior systematization of a group of buildings in Via Emanuele Filiberto in Rome, attained through the demolition of internal structures and reassembly of small courtyards constituting large, organized garden spaces. Schematic planimetry before and after systematization.

ficially decorated with plaster: only possibly door and window casings in stone. If it is not known how to create a new kind of art adapted to the surroundings, recourse can be taken in simple forms, closer to us, from the Renaissance. Folklorism unfolds not in architectural camouflage but in elements, like balconies, loggias, railings, planters, etc.

Restoration of individual buildings is the last issue that must be addressed. It can constitute two types, just like the duality found in the criterion informing proposals for architectural, sanitary, and artistic systematization.

First, just as the swaths opened by thinning bring air and light into the urban fabric, one must investigate how to bring air and light into living spaces through a series of internal adaptations: opening of the courtyards, creating space between buildings, partial lowering of joined floors, improvement of staircases, building new lavatories, structural renovation that fights humidity and saltpeter, absolute exclusion of ground floor living spaces—the so-called *bassi*—or only when they have been raised by at least 60 cm from street level and completely satisfy the required sanitary conditions.

In fact, it is necessary to reiterate these concepts: renewal of old neighborhoods is achieved more from the inside of the building blocks than from the outside, and this is often attained by restoring the houses and building blocks to conditions that are close to the original because, as it has been said, the old dwelling had its order, its logic, its cleanliness, and its dignity. If the streets were narrow, the houses were almost always as low as possible, such that the proportion was often better than in the streets of the modern neighborhoods, and the dwellings could breathe inside through the courtyards and gardens.[3] [. . .]

—∾—

This kind of restoration, undertaken with pure artistic intentions, and the other kind, having as a goal the salubrity of the dwelling, can be carried out in the same building without irreducible conflicts arising between the two because the original layout of the houses was ordinarily much more sound and rational than that which it has now become after centuries of poor adaptations. Restoration to the original type is already a big step on the path of organic renewal, and at times also on the path of practical usefulness corresponding to the changed terms of use.

Projects that aim to partially or completely liberate monuments now hidden or altered also enter into this subject directly. Just as the notion is vulgar, dangerous, and often disastrous—above all strongly challenged—of isolating monuments in large spaces, which, intending to promote them changes their environment and mutates the primitive conditions of appreciation through transformations that end up clumsy falsifications, is instead the prudent project that, without exaggeration, seeks to return to those monuments a view equal or similar to the original surroundings. By removing amorphous superstructures or constructions that conceal lines that were made to appear on the exterior, by opening wide spaces responsive to the building style that avoid at the same time the reconstruction of new intrusive, speculative buildings, one can achieve results that are happily artistic, interconnecting, or not, with the measure of selective clearing of the built environment. [. . .]

These concepts and proposals for the reuse of renewed old neighborhoods assure us that the ideas now laid bare are not the unobtainable dream of idealists with their heads in the clouds, but concrete and practical possibilities, because the financial payoff—an essential and dynamic element—supports their attainment. [. . .] Prudent adaptation measures are substituted for destruction, like on a plantation where a good agriculturist proceeds with rational and judicial pruning and grafting of the plants that in turn helps the old plants to regerminate.

The current prejudice is that it is more practical and economical to construct a new house than fix up an old one. But this often could not be further from the truth. When one deserts the empiricism and lackadaisical nature of a few professionals who do not want to strain themselves too much when seeking out meticulous solutions, and who do not care to keep up with the technical and industrial advancements of the day, a conscientious and rational study can be completed. Now is the time to establish a kind of "restoration specialist" (who the skeptics would gladly compare to the technicians in a *maison de beauté*) whose normal activity would be the complex project of aesthetic, sanitary, and practical improvement of "ruined" houses, adapting them to the functions of modern life in a way that is not radically and absurdly transformative, but such that it complies with the building type and finds ample economic benefit in the correspondence between the changed use and central location.

[. . .]

The local authorities can and should complete the construction part of the systematization: the gradual execution of selective clearing, improvement of all public services, preparation of special building regulations that govern new works, avoiding, as it has been mentioned, that they benefit only a few in the end. And furthermore, their most essential task is to provide all public services, particularly water supply and sewage systems, as well as regular cleaning and maintenance of the streets. These things, which seem to be elementary, are instead often neglected in the old neighborhoods,[4] left in a dirty and abandoned state. They can facilitate financial incentives for owners who improve and restore their buildings, and the means of facilitation can be varied: an exemption for restored buildings from the building tax for an extended time period, exemptions from levies for construction materials necessary for the restoration, cash awards to be allocated each year to those owners who complete the best restorations. [. . .]

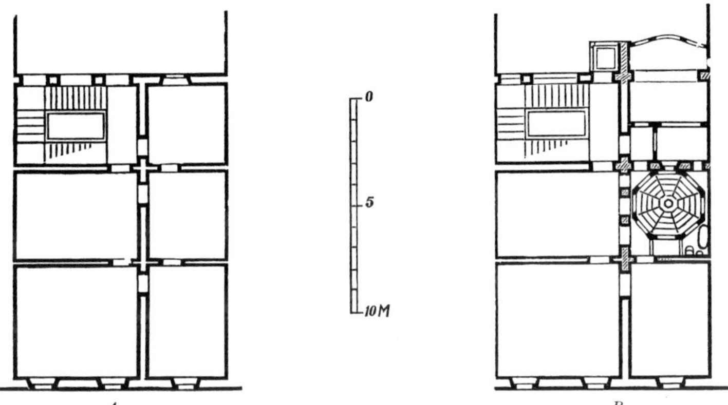

Fig. 2. A, B. Floor plan of the first floor of a small house in Rome before and after its transformation.

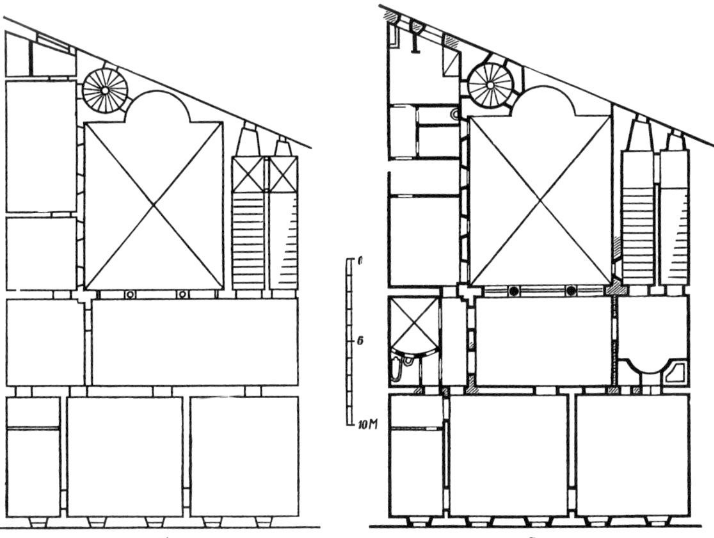

Fig. 3. A, B. Floor plan of the first floor of a sixteenth-century house in Rome (Via Giulia) before and after its transformation.

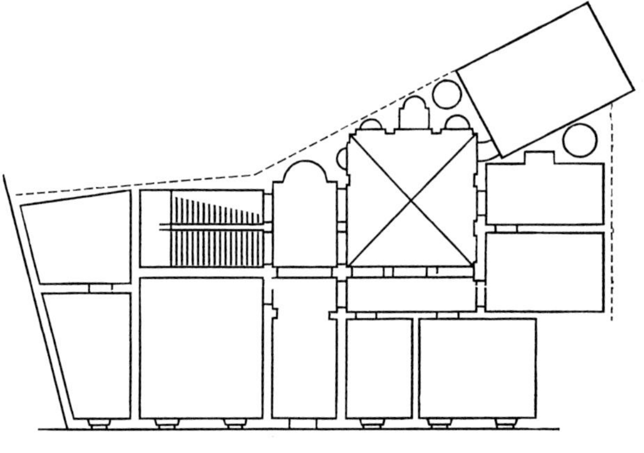

Fig. 4. Floor plan of the ground floor of a building according to the designs of Antonio Sangallo.

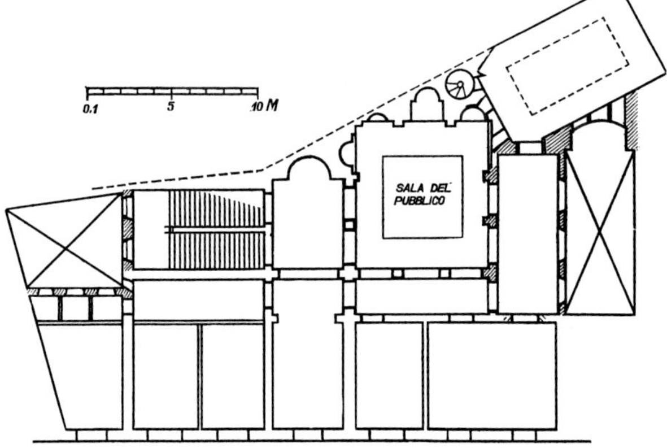

Fig. 5. Floor plan of the same building in part adapted for the needs of a small bank.

[. . .]

It is necessary, moreover, in this instance, to be wary of the private building industry, the direct auxiliary and natural executor of the task of new construction. The impulse of self-interest to delay the process is too great; too numerous are the temptations to do more than is necessary, turning restoration initiatives to one's own advantage, selecting only those that appear financially beneficial and that entail primarily building, without any standard other than profit for radical reconstructions, particularly those buildings that lack any artistic value. The latter, while they seem to allow full freedom for new activities, instead require no less care and no fewer safeguards due to the proximity of more admirable structures and their environmental association. The well-controlled efforts of a private speculator can be used for a single project but inevitably becomes very dangerous if it presides (with the concessions that the public authorities so abuse) over the systematization of an entire area.

The only solution, in this typical and essential example, is the creation of a dedicated, autonomous agency, free from any financial gain, and only concerned with judicious administration in the public interest, to whom is conferred all of the powers that all of the competencies depend on: powers derived from special legislative and regulatory provisions for expropriation for the public good and the possibility to buy or sell the buildings; historical and artistic competencies allowing partial delegation of the supervision of monuments to the public authorities, administrative competencies for communication with financial entities and with public housing and sanitation institutes on behalf of or by intervention of the local authority.

This agency has a dual role: to spur on and help private owners and to work directly in their stead.

Likewise for the private owners: establishment of building and architectural consortia under the supervision of the special agency, the latter aiding the processing of paperwork, equipping projects at no cost, procuring directly or indirectly building loans at good rates, allocating subsidies to be granted to projects that are not cost-effective, necessarily establishing this with grants corresponding to some extent to general interest in the individual restoration.

—∾—

The measures vary greatly in type, and the project, so imagined, is complex and manifold, to be conducted with prudence, through a gradual evolution, and with an integrated vision that does not lose sight of any of the different proposed goals. But the result will certainly be positive if it is pursued with the continuity of a practical program enlivened by the continuity of tradition and an idea, a noble and dignified goal: to emancipate so many distinctive parts of our ancient cities, saving them from the international vulgarity that renders everything the same. One smiles at the thought of the newest agglomerations spreading out over the sweet countryside in areas cheerfully green and sunlit, while inside the cities that have lived through so much, science and modern art unite to reawaken, not to violate, "the soul of the centuries."

After the theory, examples, or works performed, or proposals and typical and significant projects.

—∾—

All of this is, and more must clearly become again, heritage for all. But it takes on its greatest value for the scholars and artists who can read, not only in the great monuments, but also perhaps in the small structures that respond directly to the practical needs and spiritual requirements of civil life, the entire shaping and evolution of architecture in a period in which it was—and still is through its surviving manifestations—a teacher to the world.

—∾—

The research was initiated, as should be standard in such cases, by the evaluation of a certain kind of historic-artistic cadastre in order to determine all of the building units that, according to their value and interest, are to be maintained unchanged in their form and environment. An overview map resulted in which many groups of buildings with black cross-hatching specify areas of "no trespassing."

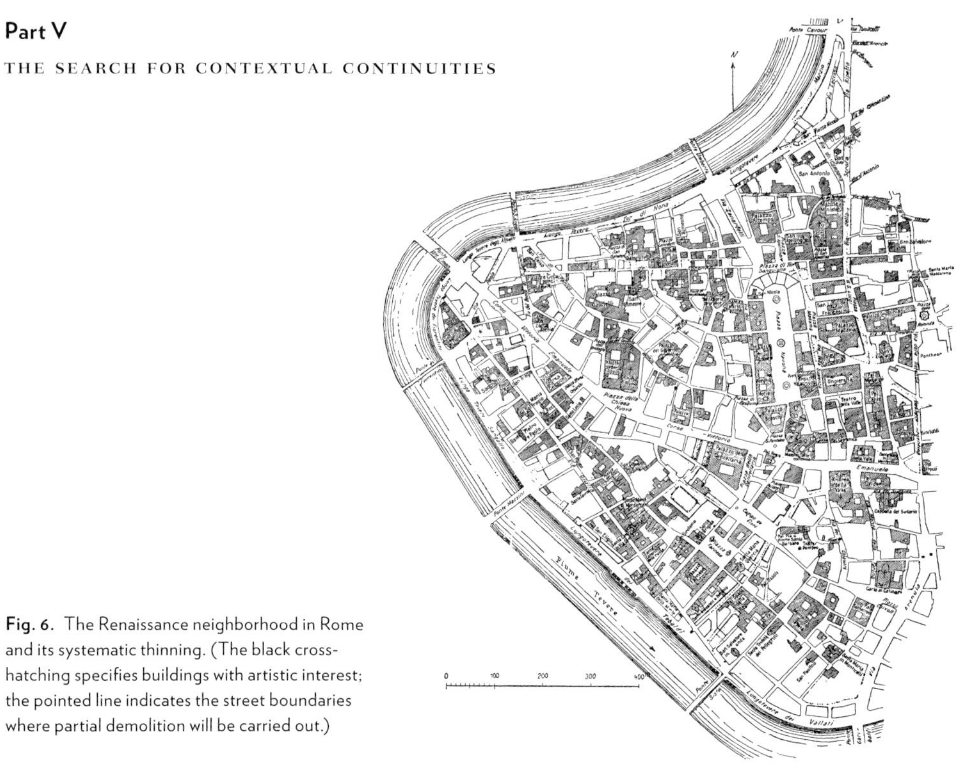

Fig. 6. The Renaissance neighborhood in Rome and its systematic thinning. (The black cross-hatching specifies buildings with artistic interest; the pointed line indicates the street boundaries where partial demolition will be carried out.)

In this way, the study proceeds from corner to corner and from house to house without preconceptions, with patience and detailed experimental research, resolving at every step a historical question, an artistic problem, and practical economic difficulties. The theory fragments and is then rekindled among a thousand concrete circumstances of reality. But it is then necessary that a program of gradual implementation is prepared and is properly carried out with an analog sentiment of careful vigilance, with corresponding responsiveness to the means and ends, if one does not wish that the proposal remain a "wishful desire for ancient beauty." [. . .]

Notes

1. A. Palladio, *The Third Book of Architecture*, chapter 2.
2. This text follows the first treatment of this discourse by G. Giovannoni, *The Theory of Thinning the Urban Environment, etc.* (Nuova Antologia, July 1, 1913), and an essay on the same topic about the work of the Commission for Systematization of the Built Environment in Renaissance Neighborhoods in Rome (published by the Commune of Rome in 1920). The essay by L. Piccinato follows these studies closely, without citing its sources: *Systematization of Cities with Historical Character* (Proceedings of the International Congress on Housing and Town Planning, held in Rome in 1929).
3. This fact is easily proved by the many iconographic maps and elevation drawings of old cities that are still preserved and that would be of great interest to systematically collect.
4. A typical example is the old town in Bari. All that was required was the intervention of a positive outlook because in one year the small streets and porticoed sidewalks changed completely from their filthy state. If now a proper sewage system were put in place and the *bassi* dwellings were vacated, even before any architectural improvements were completed, the old town would become one of the nicest in the city.

Reading

39

Giovanni Astengo

Assisi: Preservation and Rebirth (1958)

Giovanni Astengo, an Italian planner and university professor, was at the forefront of planning research and practice for more than fifty years. Astengo's professional engagements include the preparation of the regional plan for the Piedmont region, followed, among many others, by plans for the cities of Ancona, Assisi, Bergamo, Genova, Gubbio, Pavia, Pisa, Pistoia, and Turin. Of special relevance is the plan for Assisi, a medium-size historic center in central Italy, on which he worked through various vicissitudes in 1955 and 1956. Although unsuccessful in its implementation, the plan remains a model of methodological rigor and one of the first urban plans, in Italy as well as internationally, to be explicitly formulated around a comprehensive conservation program. The excerpt and plans presented here illustrate in a cogent sequence the methodological steps Astengo followed: "knowing, understanding, evaluating, and intervening." The report proceeds from an assessment of the city's historic structure to the meticulous survey of the city's outstanding architectural and urban values to the formulation of the plan for the walled city, which includes guidelines for restoration and detailed plans for the principal public open areas and individual residential blocks.

Assisi is justifiably considered one of the cities richest in historical significance due to its art, landscape, and environmental surroundings. When it was included in the first list of one hundred communities that required preservation plans, it proved to be one of the most sought-after locations for the urban planner. The outcome of this fascinating theme is a study imbued in its entirety with the exceptional nature of its subject. When its execution became my task in 1955, at the behest of the local governing authority, it seemed only proper to me that it should be thoroughly documented.
[. . .]

From Giovanni Astengo, "Assisi: Salvaguardia e rinascita," *Urbanistica* 28, no. 24–25 (September 1958): 10–12, 38, 41, 52–54, 62, 94, 108–9, 117. Reproduced courtesy of INU - INU Editions, Rome.

It was apparent from the beginning that the general urban development plan by definition would be expected to lay down basic guidelines for transformation of the entire territory and general terms for the preservation of the landscape and would have to be supplemented with detailed plans for precise codification of conservation and transformation of individual constitutive elements in the existing urban environment and characterization of expansion beyond the city walls. Study of the particulars would have to proceed apace with the general study, and indeed in some aspects precede it in such a way that the general plan and the detailed plan should be delivered together to the city administration so that they could be deliberated and implemented together.

In this way, the demands of conservation and renewal, which clearly constitute the plan's two fundamental yet dramatically contrasting objectives existing in a continual indissoluble correlation, would necessarily have to substantiate the entire plan for Assisi in all of its most vital aspects, and could be present from the outset in the two distinct yet integrated planning instruments.

It may be interesting to know that the study was conducted almost entirely on site through direct and continuously verified investigation. [. . .]

[. . .]

The architectural value of the urban environment was evaluated to define the conservation conditions and propose key interventions for urban renewal. Above all, experience gained directly with the building commission during the initial phase made it possible to evaluate the cultural perspective of local planners and get to know in depth the psychological environment of businesspeople and proprietors, such that norms and conditions could be fitted to the effective lack of preparation and self-restraint of the construction companies.

This report provides a brief history of the events surrounding establishment and adoption of the plan. [. . .]

With ardent supporters and opponents, presentation of the plan and its adoption aroused mixed feelings among the local inhabitants, a fact that may also be of interest.[1]

[. . .] In the end, these doubts can only ultimately result in demonstrating the necessity of the plan. Not only as a measure of needed oversight but also, and fundamentally, as the only possible instrument of rebirth.

[. . .]

But for this to happen, the renewal must above all emanate from within, from the self-awareness of the most responsible citizens.

Giovanni Astengo

GENERAL URBAN DEVELOPMENT PLAN FOR ASSISI

1. The Urban Structure

The city today, still existing within the mostly intact circular fourteenth-century walls, is the result of a continuous sequence of events—construction and destruction—that, uninterrupted from the ancient Umbrian settlement until today, had as its home and "theater" the narrow and precipitous western slope of Mount Asio, the last offshoot of the Subasio mountain range in the direction of the Tescio valley.

The superimposition of generations of events has not, however, changed significantly the basic layout—the structure—of the city. We need only remember that the forum in Asisium, the Roman municipality, occupying with its walls an area certainly smaller than that of the fourteenth-century city, was also located in the Piazza del Comune: the urban center of gravity remained, therefore, unchanged over two millennia. The route of a few access roads to the forum also remain in large part unchanged.

[. . .]

[. . .]

City walls, in part pre-Roman, terraces, retaining walls, paved roads, the Sanguinone acqueduct, cisterns and drainage systems, made up the basic structure of the Roman city, upon which, high above ground, the city's buildings must have been preeminent among such elevated habitations: the plastered villas decorated with frescoes; the public administration and religious buildings with their red stonework and decoration in blond travertine carved out of the foot of the mountain below Valecchi, an exalted symbol of which is the Temple of Minerva, standing in the Piazza del Comune not as a ruin but as an architectural organism, merged with its environment, alive and contemporary.

The temple of Minerva is, however, an exception, and with the city gates and thick walls, it is all that survives of the elevated Roman city, emptied and disintegrated in the decadence resulting from the "escape from the city," devastated and destroyed in the cry of the barbarian invasions.

[. . .]

Churches, towers, houses, and castles emerged in large part on top of or close to the Roman buildings using salvaged materials, which in great abundance could have been obtained from the ruined buildings or by demolition of the remaining intact buildings, as is demonstrated by the use of Roman columns for crypts and altars and the use of large travertine blocks for construction of the oldest towers.

During this intense work between the fifth and ninth centuries, the foundation of the medieval city was laid, materializing through the reuse of the principal Roman structures at its base.

The Piazza del Foro remained the central square of the medieval city, the principal roads remained, as well as the aqueducts and drainage system, but the complex that was coming into being was a completely new organization of living, of its forms and architectural structures. [. . .]

[. . .]

A century will have to pass before momentum starts to build with the first stirrings of communal liberty (1054) and the constructive and innovative fervor that will form, in a short time, new cities.

[. . .] The decree of Frederick I (1160) establishes the confines of Assisi within his territory. [. . .] During these few years straddling the twelfth and thirteenth centuries, the city arises as a free municipality, destroys feudal castles, strips aristocratic towers, and moves the war to Perugia where it is defeated at Collestrada in 1202; in 1203 peace is declared between the *boni homines* and *homines populi,* which, in 1210, is called the Peace of Assisi.

2. The Recent Ruin of Assisi

The genuine medieval and baroque atmosphere would not last long in its entirety.

Railways (1865–70) broke through Assisi's isolation, bringing the first tourists and with them the construction of the first modern hotels.

The series of new buildings begins in 1870 with the Subasio, inserting its massive bulk between the S. Francesco Gate and the portico of the pilgrims in the piazza behind the basilica, marking the first violent blow to the ancient urban landscape. Another indirect consequence of the railroad connection was the attempt to introduce modifications to the street plan in order to make different sites accessible by carriage. [. . .]

[. . .]

The Subasio Hotel and evisceration signal without a doubt the beginning of a disruption in which problems are resolved too simplistically and without respect for the preexisting environment. [. . .]

And results begin to appear, in twos, with the new century. From 1900, the new Giotto Hotel—an unappealing and howling mass of banality set down in the urban landscape—which, notwithstanding all of the different paint colors tested to date to render it less ostentatious, will never succeed in fitting in with its surroundings. A little later, in 1911, arrives another anonymous yet domineering parallelepiped, the Windsor-Savoia, which completes, with the Subasio and Giotto, the group around the San Francisco gate.

[. . .]

But the worst is yet to come. After World War I it arrived, and was called a rhetorical composition *in stile,* invented restoration, demolition of authentic architecture, an arbitrary addition, and absolute contempt for the natural and urban landscape.

In 1923–25 the placement of the Convitto Nazionale, a large residential high school for rural students, in Piazza Nova, designed by the architect Armanni—an enormous mass of stone, arches, and mullioned windows—is a giant parody of the modest, graceful, and authentic medieval houses demolished to make room for this monstrous barrack.

—⁂—

The result of these enormous masses and false arches from that period are now present in the organism of the city, like just as many foreign bodies. The unified and genuine atmosphere has been broken, the greater eyesores have given birth to the lesser ones, such that everyone feels authorized to open windows and shop windows, add a story to their house, build terraces or bathrooms.

—⁂—

3. Survey of the Architectural and Urban Values of the City inside the Walls

The chaotic situation generated in the recent past by overlapping interventions contradictory to the surroundings or detrimental to authentic architectural values created the need for a preliminary critical evaluation of the individual buildings. The survey served as the departure point for every decision about future development and intervention, and was characteristic of our generation's soul-searching when faced with the past.

Critical evaluation of a significant mass of buildings, their examination from all sides (comprising over 1,200 cadastral lots), necessarily had to be conducted by clustering buildings according to analogous characteristics and by a classification system.

The adopted classification system consisted essentially in discriminating between *negative, neutral,* or *positive* buildings or features of buildings from the point of view of architectural and urban planning criticism. They are considered *negative* when the building or feature is determined to be in glaring contrast to the environment understood in its widest possible meaning: the natural or built environment. The "eyesores" belong to this category: buildings of recent construction, the fruit of inept design in which one perceives a lack or confusion of compositional ideas. Whether a recent addition, superimposed, or juxtaposed with ancient structures, it is conceived with total disregard for the architectural values in its vicinity, and is almost always followed by the employment of vile materials (perforated masonry or plaster) or with clumsily laid stonework.

[. . .]

Those buildings or parts of ancient or recent buildings are considered *neutral* that, although having modest or almost no architectural value, seem at least to fit into the environment or in any case are not in glaring contrast to it, whether because of the modesty of their dimensions and the elements employed or because of the correct and honest use of construction materials.

[. . .] The buildings, which are assessed as neutral in architectural criticism, nevertheless bear the important environmental burden of forming the connective tissue, the foundation on which the authentic *positive* values stand out. These last clearly constitute the richness of the urban architectural landscape in the built environment and are classified based on a hierarchy of values that take into account diverse factors. To the lowest level we can allocate those structures, or more often parts of structures, that are made of authentic medieval elements that have been defaced by transformations, subsequent modifications, or clumsy restoration, or have remained unchanged but in a state of advanced disrepair. [. . .]

Another category of structures includes medieval buildings deemed to have some architectural interest for compositional reasons and the craftsmanship of elements that are in a decent state of conservation, or in any case can easily be consolidated, or elements that are incorporated into subsequent transformations or in acceptable restorations, or buildings of other periods of notable architectural value.

The second, in conclusion, comprises Roman, medieval, or buildings of other periods of the highest possible architectural value and which, due to the organic nature and originality of the composition and the craftsmanship evident in their single parts, can be considered architectural "monuments" of great value.

[. . .]

In conclusion, the spatial boundaries of the areas most relevant to the planning of urban conservation and renewal are indicated in a summary form, characterizing in a precise and indispensable way the external spaces of greatest environmental importance.

Detailed Plan No. 1 for the City Within the Walls

The urban arrangement of the city within the walls could not be configured solely according to the rules of the general plan. The architectural and urban elements that make it up, and which are revealed through features subject to minute and frequent variations in a range of spaces – even very tiny ones – are numerous. Numerous are also the economic and social needs of the population that resides there, the monuments and natural and built environments under consideration, and the points from which every part of the city is seen, such that differentiated, minute, and detailed specifications and provisions that can only be set out in the detailed plan are required. Even the same planimetry at a scale of 1:1,000 derived from the cadastral map from which the detailed plan was drafted, is – in many respects – insufficient, whether due to the smallness of the representation, or because the altimetrical details[2] are missing, such that one must resort to magnifications and topographic surveys at a scale of 1:200.

The surveys, conducted with sufficient accuracy, have allowed for the establishment of provisions for every existing building pertaining to hygienic and structural renovation of the interiors, restoration the exterior, and removal of the worst eyesores (additions, superstructures, imitation stylistic elements) that today disfigure particular sections of the environment and whose eradication would allow for enhancement of the authentic, ancient character of the environment.[3] [. . .]

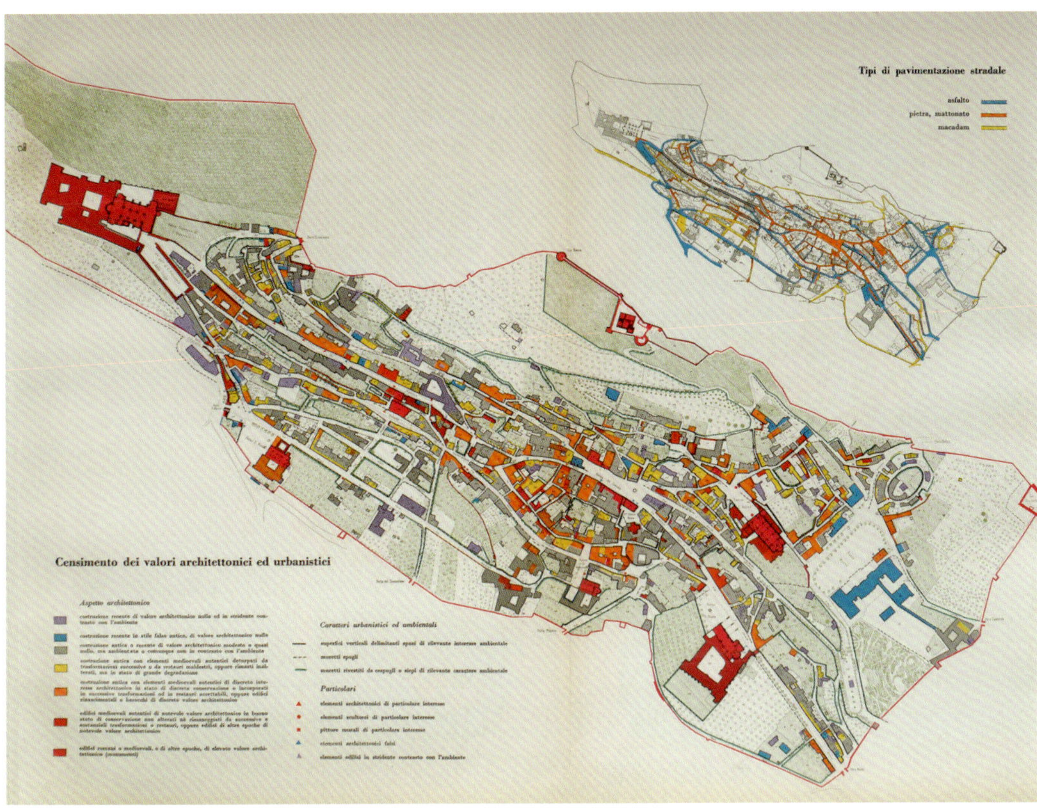

Fig. 1. Master Plan of Assisi by Architect Giovanni Astengo

Legend

Survey of Architectural and Urban Values (Censimento dei valori architettonici e urbanistici)

Architectural Assessment (Aspetto architettonico)

- recent construction of no architectural value, in stark contrast to the historic surroundings
- recent construction imitating an ancient style of no architectural value
- old or recent construction of little or modest architectural value, but adapted to or at least not contrasting with the historic surroundings
- old structure with authentic medieval elements disfigured by successive transformations or by inappropriate restoration, or having remained unchanged, but in a state of great degradation
- old constructions with authentic medieval elements of fair architectural value in an acceptable state of conservation; or incorporated into successive transformations or acceptable restorations; or Renaissance or Baroque buildings of fair architectural value
- authentic medieval buildings of considerable architectural value in a good state of conservation, either unchanged or unaltered in spite of substantial transformations or restorations; or buildings from other time periods of considerable architectural value
- Roman or medieval buildings, or buildings from other time periods, of great architectural value (monuments)

Urban and Environmental Character (Caratteri urbanistici ed ambientali)

- vertical surfaces (walls) delimiting spaces of significant environmental interest
- bare walls
- walls covered with vegetation of significant environmental character

Features (Particolari)

- architectural elements of particular interest
- sculptural elements of particular interest
- wall paintings of particular interest
- imitation architectural elements
- building elements in stark contrast with the historic surroundings

Types of Street Pavement (Tipi di pavimentazione stradale)

- asphalt
- stone, brick
- macadam

Renovation and Restoration

In particular, mention must be made of the planning and implementation of renovation and restoration procedures prescribed by the plan for existing buildings. [. . .]

The greatest risks posed to these buildings are those that can be read on the selfsame walls of the city. The greatest danger is clearly complete demolition, carried out under cover of night and under the pretext of a feigned threat of a perilous instability, followed by reconstruction *in stile*[4] out of new, vigorously and roughly hewn stone, applied alternately in white and pink. Even if today the danger of this second intervention is greatly diminished, one must keep a watchful eye out for the first, because it is always possible, to a greater or lesser degree.[5]

The character of authentic buildings in various states of decay are no less threatened, even if a restoration plan has been drawn up that takes into account local customs, as well as the following two factors. The first is instrumental in nature: local planners do not tend to promote detailed plans,[6] which grants contractors leeway when interpreting imprecise project designs. The second, which in reality is the principal factor, is cultural in nature: the architectural value of the buildings which many planners – for the most part graduates of technical colleges – are asked to work on, is to a great extent not understood and not perceived, or distorted by vague historical and critical notions.

It should not be surprising, therefore, that from this cultural unpreparedness, horrendous solutions have arisen, however self-assured, that range from minor to major in their destructiveness: arches sliced open to let in more light, the breaking of new openings into venerable walls, imitation arches, attaching new balconies, hanging latrines, and so forth, to the most grave transformations academic in flavor,[7] like, for example, additional storeys with earthenware tile reminiscent of the fifteenth-century, or the nonchalant insertion of bizarre stylistic elements onto ancient architecture.

—ɯ—

Having, therefore, to configure architectural restoration and building renovation projects in many zones of the ancient city, it is necessary to specify a few fundamental principles that are essentially of service to the planners, executors, members of the local building commission, and the functionaries responsible for supervising implementation. In short, they are summarized in the following rule:

To restore means to statically stabilize authentic elements without introducing additions or using imitations or falsifications.[8]

From this definition it follows that it is valid to open closed arches only if they are complete and composed entirely of authentic ashlar; if they are incomplete, then only if it is possible to recover authentic ashlar from the demolition of stone walls or internal walls that is suitable for filling the gaps.[9] Conversely, it is not valid to complete authentic arches – even if lacking a few elements – with masonry or jambs of fresh stone or worse, to open arches made entirely of fresh stone from Assisi. The very varied design of the ashlar, the hammering and coloring of the stone of the authentic elements, are absolute facts, inimitable. So varied and refined was the production during the two golden centuries of Assisi's civil architecture.

—~—

Likewise, "recovery" – or the task of elimination of the transformations that thirteenth-century architecture underwent in the following centuries, or the transplanting of later styles – is absolutely not valid.

—~—

Almost all of these later transformations of thirteenth-century architecture belong by now to history, to the culture of the city, and as a rule – except in the cases in which it is critically demonstrable that it is a disfigurement and therefore dispensable – should be accepted, respected, and established as absolute fact. How absurd it would be to think of being able to return the city as a whole to its thirteenth-century state, dismantling everything that was not datable with certainty to that period. Thus, in the details, it is absurd, antihistorical, and anticultural to think of destroying the various manifestations of the subsequent culture superimposed on the background.

—~—

Finally, from this position of critique it follows that if, when renovating, there were exterior transformations to be made due to unavoidable functional needs arising from the redistribution of interior spaces, the single principle that can legitimately be of guidance in that case is to execute the transformations with the most suitable stylistic elements of our time, rejecting any inducement to mimicry or deception.

—~—

And it must be said at once that another serious danger facing restoration work is that it takes place precisely through the juxtaposition of individual restoration projects that encompass great detail, are planned by different planners, are carried out independently of one another close together in time and yet distinct, and that relate to the various properties that subdivide a parcel of land or a dense city block.

[. . .]

To avoid the grave danger of fragmentation that stems from the current lack of a reliable architectural language and from widespread cultural unpreparedness, it is considered essential to introduce an intermediate procedure between the requirements of the detailed plan and every individual renovation and restoration task.

The Renovation Sector

The coordination of planning for individual interior renovation and restoration interventions can be accomplished by using the institution of the *sector*[10] – required by urban planning law for the formation of *building units, including unbuilt areas and structures*

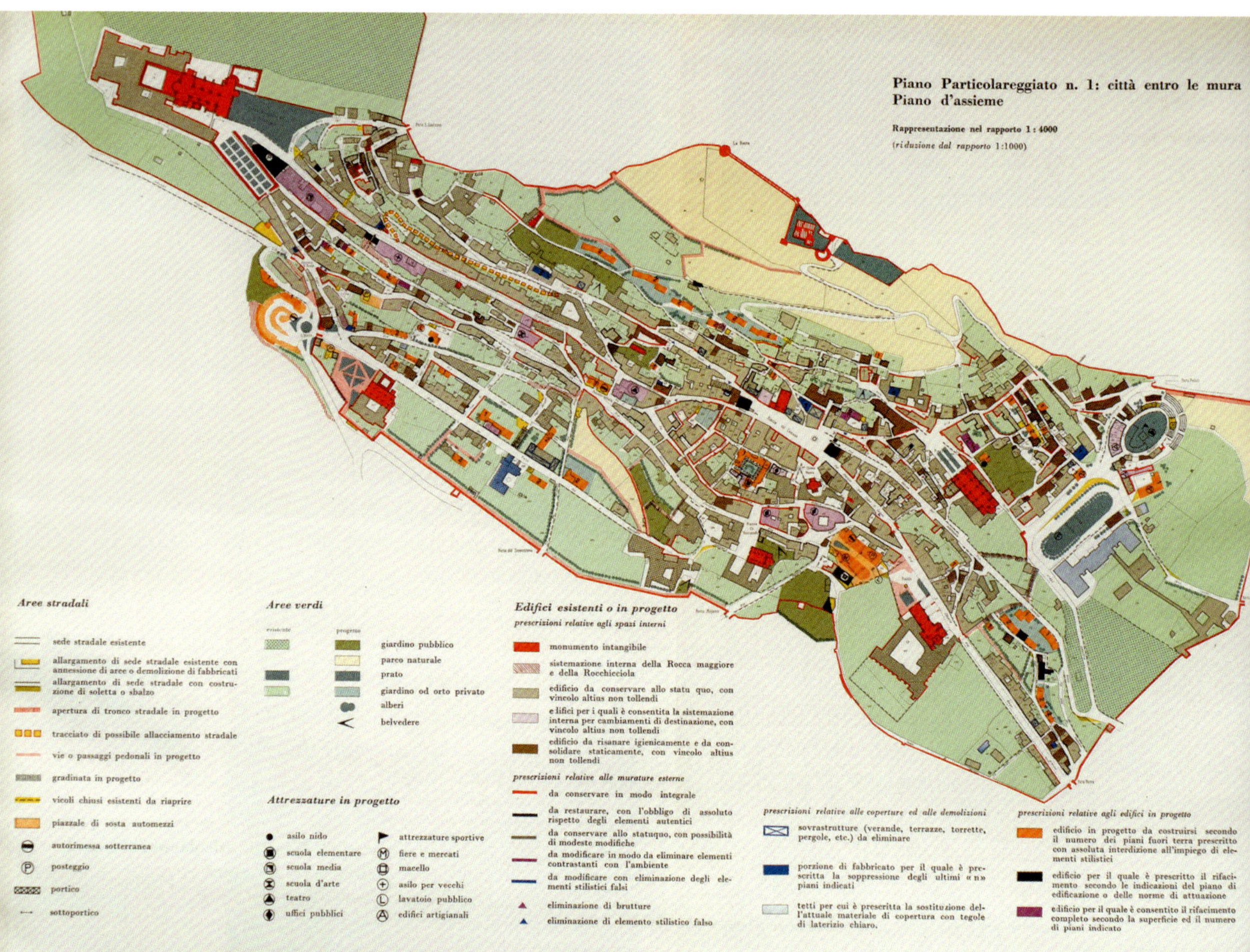

Fig. 2. Assisi: Detailed Area Plan for Zone No.1: Proposals for the city within the walls.

Legend

Roadways
(Aree stradali)

- existing roads
- enlargement of the existing roads, including annexation of areas or demolition of buildings
- enlargement of roadbed with construction of reinforced slab or cantilever
- construction of approved road section
- possible routes for future connecting roads
- planned pedestrian streets or passages
- planned flight of steps
- blocked alleyways in need of repair
- vehicle parking area
- underground garage
- car parking
- portico (covered walkway)
- covered passage

Green Areas
(Aree verdi)

existing

- public garden
- lawn
- private garden / orchard

planned

- public garden
- park
- lawn
- private garden/orchard
- trees
- panoramic viewpoint

Planned Facilities
(Attrezzature in progetto)

- nursery
- elementary school
- middle school
- vocational art school
- theater
- public offices
- sport facilities
- markets and fairground
- slaughterhouse
- retirement home
- public lavatory
- artisans' workshops

Existing or planned buildings
(Edifici esistenti o in progetto)

Prescriptions regarding interior spaces

- protected cultural heritage
- interior remodeling of the Rocca Maggiore and Rocchicciola
- building to be preserved in its entirety including height (*servitus altius non tollendi*)
- building whose interior layout may be adapted to a change in function; no alteration in height allowed (*servitus altius non tollendi*)
- building earmarked for hygienic and structural upgrading; no alteration in height allowed (*servitus altius non tollendi*)

Prescriptions regarding exterior wall treatments

- to be preserved in its entirety
- to be restored with the requirement of absolute respect for the authentic elements
- to be conserved as is, with the possibility of modest alterations
- to be modified in order to eliminate elements contrasting with the historic fabric
- to be modified in order to remove false historical elements
- removal of eyesores
- removal of imitation historical elements

Prescriptions regarding roofs and demolitions

- superstructures (verandas, terraces, small towers, pergolas, etc.) to be removed
- buildings with added ("n") stories to be demolished
- roofs made of inappropriate materials to be replaced with traditional light-colored terracotta tiles

Prescriptions for approved new buildings

- new building to be constructed up to the prescribed height; no imitation architectural details are permitted
- building to be developed in accordance with the approved municipal plans and building regulations
- building envelope to conform with the prescribed surface areas and number of floors

to be transformed according to special ordinances – which can receive, for our purposes, the specific characterization of the **renovation and restoration sector**.

A preliminary assembly study that comprises the transition from the urban development plan to the architectural building project will be prepared for each sector made up of a few blocks of buildings forming homogeneous nuclei.

The plan for the sector,[11] once approved by the council and the superintendency for monuments, should typically be of service to the individual building and architectural

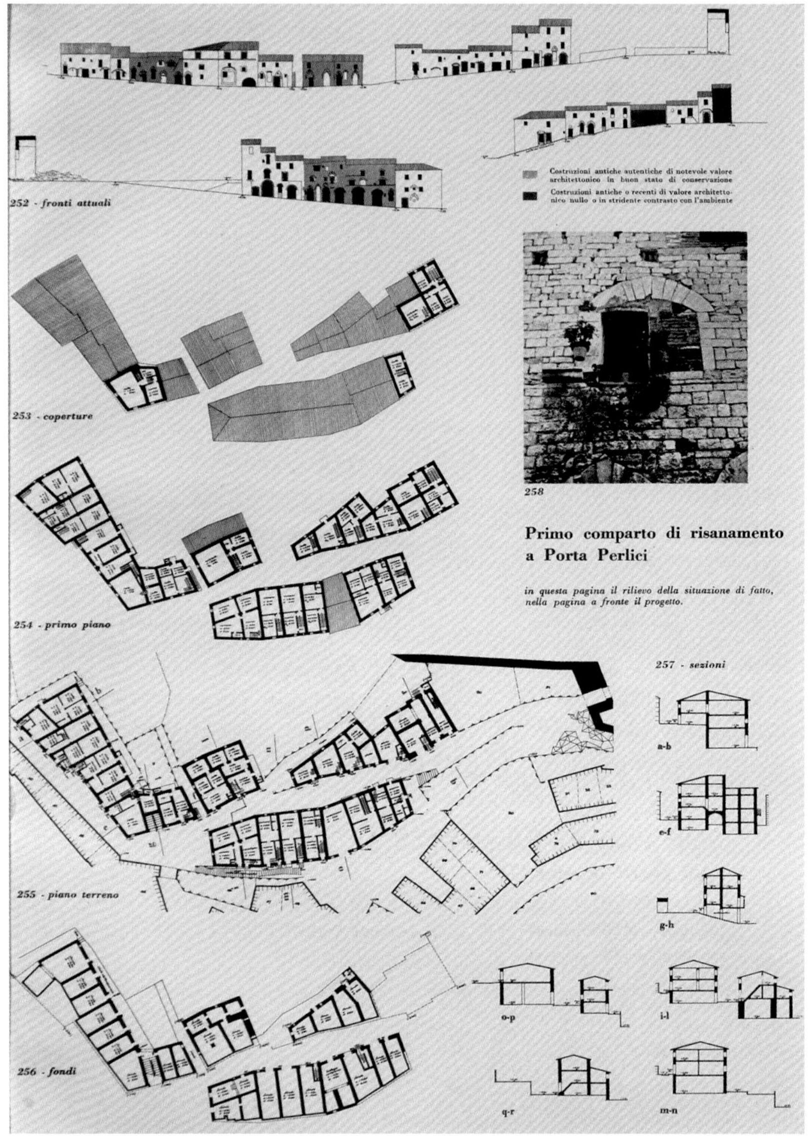

Fig. 3. Assisi: Detailed Area Plan for Zone No.1: the City within the walls – the Porta Perlici area.

Existing Conditions

252 – Existing elevations
253 – Roof plan
254 – First floor plan
255 – Ground floor plan
256 – Basement plan
257 – Sections

Legend (upper right)

- Old constructions of considerable architectural value in good state of conservation
- Old or recent constructions of little architectural value or in stark contrast to the historic surroundings

In the Porta Perlici neighborhood a group of four blocks was selected as a pilot rehabilitation area. Porta Perlici is located near the city gate and is an area of great architectural interest, with a number of exquisite medieval buildings that are in need of urgent stabilization and restoration. These blocks present also some of the most unsanitary conditions in Assisi. The four blocks are currently subdivided into 20 cadastral parcels inhabited by 32 families, for a total of 118 residents; 7 apartments are without toilets and 7 present unsanitary latrines; almost all lack connections to a direct water supply.

designs that will develop and interpret in detail and as broadly as possible the guidelines contained in it.

Notes

1. Twenty-nine local technicians, engineers, architects, and geometers joined together to protest the conditions of the plan, signing a common objection, while the board of directors of the Accademia Properziana del Subasio, comprised of medical doctors, professors, teachers, and scholars from the O.F.M. officially expressed their endorsement.
2. It would have been very appropriate to accompany the 1:1,000 scale planimetry of the city within the walls with an elevation map. Unfortunately, this mapping could not be carried out due to the high cost associated with it. We therefore had to content ourselves with limited altimetric surveys of the areas subject to intervention and continuous on-site inspections.
3. First and foremost, the greatest eyesore in Assisi is the Spagnoli building, which is supposed to be set up as a school for hotel administration. This crude construction is volumetrically incorrect and the only possible solution would be demolition of the top three floors of the structure facing the valley, and complete demolition of the structure facing the mountain.
4. As it is said to have happened more than once, for example, in via Borgo Aretino and in Piazza San Pietro.
5. Especially when there will be numerous renovation and restoration building sites during implementation of the plan and in the application of the special law for Assisi.
6. Meanwhile, during restoration it is necessary to plan the whole at a scale of 1:50, and the details at a scale of 1:10 with developments at 1:1. These scales are entirely unknown. Due to inveterate habits, projects have always been executed at a scale of 1:100 without elevation, and often without the fundamental projections. To remedy the situation, I had to propose a series of rules for presentation of building projects; rules that on March 3, 1956 were deliberated in the City Council and made enforceable with the approval of the G.P.A. (Giunta Provinciale Amministrativa /Provincial Administration Committee). The rules instituted the "rough estimate opinion" with the urban planning and construction assessment and determined that it was obligatory to present key documents at a scale of 1:50 when requesting a building permit. I am well aware that these rules have rarely been respected, and that the majority of projects continue to be presented in the simplified way of the past, even when they constitute restoration. It can be argued that the architectural value of a project can also be independent of the scale in which it is drafted, but those who are familiar with serious planning are well aware that only at certain scales is it possible to accurately define the structural elements of a building.
7. The surviving nineteenth-century teachings of the Academy of Fine Arts – based on copying plaster casts, on *in stile* design and archaic aesthetic prejudices – molded in turn the many "architectural design professors" that were working, not only in Assisi, before the School of Architecture was founded.
8. For the rule corresponding to the first point in the Athens Charter (1931), see Carlo Perogalli, *Monumenti e metodi di valorizzazione* (Monuments and Methods of Valorization), Milan: Tamburini, 1954.
9. Since the thirteenth century, ashlars from arches belonging to houses or towers demolished by fire or pillage have been reused, such that one was often led to doubt the contemporaneity of the coexisting elements. This procedure is, within certain limits, valid even today: if it is directed, for example, at the completion of well-defined openings without any ashlar. For this purpose it would be necessary to establish a municipal warehouse with authentic ashlars retrieved from demolition sites and which usually end up in public landfills or are employed as elements in masonry for wall building.

10. Article 23 of the urban planning law of August 17, 1942, n. 1150.
11. That due to the delicacy of the subject matter must be signed by a qualified designer, expert in urban planning and restoration. Since there are no official post-graduate specializations outside the qualification for university teaching of the individual subjects, it is proposed that the assignment of these projects be entrusted to free professors in one of the following subjects: architectural composition, urban planning, restoration.

Reading

40

Donald Insall

Living Buildings: Architectural Conservation: Philosophy, Principles and Practice (2008)

*Donald Insall, a British architect and planner, can be considered the doyen of British conservation practice, with an impressive range of projects that include the conservation of individual monuments and buildings, urban interventions, infill programs, and the development of an exemplary conservation plan for old Chester commissioned in 1966 and adopted by the city in 1969. This reading includes Insall's account of the development and significant features of the Chester plan. Prepared in 1968, it was explicitly aimed at providing a comprehensive assessment of the city of Chester and making very detailed recommendations for a general conservation program, as well as specific interventions in individual sections of the city. The report accompanying the plan (*Chester: A Study in Conservation *[London: HMSO, 1968]) remains a methodological model for a comprehensive analysis and proposal extended to an entire conservation area, including a general assessment of the Greater Chester area, a critique of new buildings and prevailing development patterns both in the center and in its proximity, and a program for the reconditioning of historic buildings, in particular, residential properties. The reading concludes with a summary of types and degrees of intervention, from those applicable to individual buildings to more complex rehabilitation, renewal, and new building projects in historic settings.*

10. Conservation in a Changing Historic Area

In 1966 the Government decided to commission four pioneer pilot studies of historic towns. One of these, which we were invited to undertake, was for the historic city of Chester. We were set a very open brief, which was to "study and report on the implications of a conservation policy," designed 'to preserve, promote and enhance the

From Donald Insall, *Living Buildings. Architectural Conservation: Philosophy, Principles and Practice* (Mulgrave, Vic.: Images Publishing Group, 2008), 195–209. Reproduced courtesy of Donald Insall Associates.

architectural and historical quality of the area', and 'to maintain its life and economic buoyancy'.

We spent six busy months on this survey, and another six in producing our report. [. . .] We examined first the regional setting, its pressures and implications. In the time dimension, we explored the historical continuity within which the city had grown and is alive today. We set out to analyse the specific character of the place, and to identify its key features and elements. [. . .] We recognised the strong dynamic pressures and forces acting upon the city, including social change, movement patterns and shifting economic demand.

Next, we gave more detailed study to specific smaller areas, selected for their neighborhood identity. The method we developed in each area was to appraise first the townscape, then the architectural quality of its buildings and spaces, and finally their individual ownership, use and condition. [. . .]

We drew up our recommendations in the form of a phased and costed conservation programme. This proposed firstly the designation of a conservation area, evaluating and mapping its historic buildings in detail and advancing a firm but imaginative policy of control. Recognising that change and redevelopment in any city are continuous, we suggested undertaking pilot schemes in deteriorating areas and we identified some possible agencies who could help in achieving them. These included the city itself (as owner, or in consortium with developers), private owners and also semi-public bodies such as local housing associations/societies. In some instances encouragement might also be sought from national resources. In this way, identifying the major ways and means, we set up a tabulated programme for the reconditioning of historic buildings, phased respectively over one year, five years and 15 years, and preceded in specific cases by urgent first-aid action.

Following our brief in broader terms, and in wide consultation with many national organisations, including every major planning authority, we carried out an analysis of current legal powers and set out recommendations for nation-wide action. [. . .] We further advanced specific proposals for improved and more positive procedures in local planning, in allocating grant aid, and in securing better encouragement and efficiency in day-to-day conservation practices nation-wide. [. . .]

Meanwhile, the report was carefully considered by Chester's city council. After what seemed a nerve-racking silence (ideas do need time to take root), the council came to a fundamental and important decision — it would indeed adopt and support a declared policy of conservation in Chester. Further, and as the first city in the country to do so, it decided in December 1969 to back this policy by making a definitive financial allocation in each year from the general rate fund, to help in setting up and pursuing a conservation programme. [. . .] In their various ways these decisions, and Chester's energy in following them, have been basic to the remarkable success of the ensuing conservation programme. The appointment of a Conservation Officer has become widely accepted and adopted in local government planning offices, leading to the establishment, in fact, of a new profession.

Fig. 1. Chester's characteristic black and white buildings.

Fig. 2. The Bridgegate conservation action area.

—~—

The main message that emerges from the Bridgegate [conservation action area] experience has been the positive power of commitment, allied with a refusal to give up, and coordinating every possible resource into concerted action. City initiative, aided by central government support, has led in turn to company and private investment, sometimes backed by housing association, county and other funds, to the extent that an entirely new financial buoyancy has been created. In the city centre nearby, the same has been true for once-neglected areas like King Street, now busy and prospering again.

Renewal and replacement constantly take place in the patchwork of any city, and architects are not always adept at integrating new buildings with old ones. Individual replacements are in many cases easier to design appropriately, rather than entire cleared streets or building groups, so the City has suffered less than some others, and has a strong policy of design guidance and some interesting new architecture.

What has been the result of all this concerted activity, both for Chester and for the conservation movement at large? There is no doubt that the city itself has prospered in extraordinary measure. Despite changing national fortunes and the competition of other towns, trade and tourism here are at a high level and Chester's physical appearance and presence have benefited immensely. To judge from old photographs, the general condition of its buildings has perhaps never been better. Change has continued, but under firm guidance. Despite changing shopping habits, the Rows still present a lively variety. Pedestrian priority has been greatly improved, stage-by-stage, until the central streets of the Rows area echo once more to the sound of human conversation and human feet. [. . .]

[. . .] The keynote of the conservation exercise has been the success of its positive and remarkable teamwork.

Conservation and enhancement at this end of the graded scale are closely linked. They can and must accommodate continuing change, but this can only be achieved by first recognising and underlining existing merits, and then by an energetic performance of constant and consistent daily management.

Urban conservation is a dynamic and a continuing exercise, and cannot be achieved overnight. Decades later the conservation programme is still alive and active in Chester, meeting ever-new changes and challenges. It has sufficient vital momentum to carry it forward long beyond present lifetimes.

Degree of Intervention: A Review

To summarise the lesson of these examples and to recapitulate:

It has been illuminating to remind ourselves how many differing degrees of intervention are available, remembering that in practice the whole range of these varied degrees may occur alongside one another.

1. **Regular daily care** must always take pride of place. To prevent decay is more sensible than to delay and then attempt to remedy it.
2. **Programmed maintenance** becomes possible for a group of buildings in single care, and again brings high dividends.
3. **Major but conservative repairs** may still be made without significant architectural alteration, for example, when structural emergencies and functional changes overtake prudent advance planning.
4. **Repairs incorporating changes** may have to be combined, when even essential repairs and adaptations accumulate, delayed by the disturbance they bring, or by raising funds.
5. **More radical interventions and alteration** are sometimes essential to secure a building's continuing life.
6. **Restoration** to a building's original or previous form calls for yet more replacement and renewal. Actual physical identity of its fabric may then yield place to accurate replication.
7. **A rehabilitation programme** involves higher degrees of intervention and change. Its aim is to retain character and features, but within extensive adaptation to new purposes.
8. **Renewal incorporating existing buildings or elements**, whose continuity is for one reason or another adjudged as being of value, brings yet more change.
9. **Completely new buildings** gain hugely by considering their context, crediting and complementing existing neighbours, and even if themselves totally new.
10. **Urban change, involving property in multi-ownership**, brings strong challenges and yet a vibrant opportunity for proactive and dynamic management.

Reading

41

Charter of Restoration 1972

Appendix D. Instructions for the Protection of "Historic Centers"

Cesare Brandi (1906–1988) was a major Italian theorist of conservation who published several seminal works, including the well-known Teoria del Restauro *(1963 and 1977), and strongly influenced conservation practice in Italy and beyond. He was the principal editor of the* Carta del Restauro 1972*, a set of instructions issued to the regional superintendents responsible for the protection of the national heritage. Appendix D of the 1972 Charter, dealing with the preservation of historic and urban areas, is reproduced here in its entirety. After a premise that recognizes the intrinsic value of major and minor urban ensembles, independent of the presence of special landmarks or monuments, and the importance of coordinating their conservation with the totality of the city and territorial contexts, the document identifies conservative rehabilitation* (risanamento conservativo) *as the universal, recommended form of intervention. A distinction is then made between interventions at the urban scale and interventions on individual buildings, together with the types of actions and limitations applicable to each type. This succinct document provides a coherent overview of the objectives and methodology applicable to the conservation of urban ensembles and offers a guide for the formulation of general plans and building interventions in historic city contexts.*

When identifying historic city centers, not only the traditionally recognized old urban "centers" are taken into consideration. More generally it includes all human settlements whose structures, unitary or fragmentary, even if partially transformed over time, that were built up in the past or, among later ones, those possibly having a particular historical value as a testament or a pronounced urban or architectonic quality.

Historic character is attributed to the meaning that the aforementioned settlements present, whose testaments of past civilizations and evidence of urban culture possess significance and value, not only as architecture, but also as an urban structure

From Carta del Restauro 1972, in Cesare Brandi, *Teoria del Restauro,* 2nd ed. (Torino: Giulio Einaudi editore, 1977), 151–54.

of and in itself—independent of their intrinsic artistic or formal merit or the particular appearance of their surroundings, which can further enrich or exalt that value.

The goal of restoration interventions in historic urban centers is to guarantee—by ordinary and extraordinary means and tools—persistence over time of the qualities that characterize these aggregate structures. Restoration, therefore, is not limited to operations intended only to conserve the formal character of single buildings or individual environments, but extends to material conservation of the characteristics of the entire network that is the urban organism and all elements that take part in the definition of said characteristics.

The ability to adequately preserve the urban organism in question, its continuity over time and the modern and civil life enacted in it, requires above all reorganization of historic centers in their broadest urban and regional contexts, as well as their relationships and connections with future developments: this also aims to coordinate city planning actions in such a way as to achieve protection and recovery of the historic center, starting with the outer city, and by means of planning adapted to regional interventions. In this way, it is possible to configure (carried out by means of planning tools) a new urban organism through such interventions, where functions that are not congenial to its recovery in terms of conservative rehabilitation [*risanamento conservativo*] are removed from the historic center.

Implementation is also considered in relation to the need for preservation of the most general, regional context of the surroundings, above all when this has assumed qualities of particular significance closely connected to the historic structures as they come to us (for example, the hilltops wreathing Florence, the Venetian lagoon, the Roman land divisions of the Po Valley, the *trulli,* or stone huts with conical roofs, in Apulia, etc.).

As for the individual elements through which preservation of the whole organism is realized, built elements as well as other elements constituting external (streets, squares, etc.) and internal (courtyards, gardens, open areas, etc.) spaces are to be taken into consideration, along with other significant structures (walls, doors, stones, etc.) and natural elements that accompany the whole, characterizing it more or less through accentuating aspects (natural contours, flowing water, geomorphological singularities, etc.).

Built elements within the whole are conserved not only in their formal aspects, which define architectonic expression, or that of the surroundings, but also in their typological character inasmuch as it is an expression of functions that characterized over time the use of those elements.

Every restoration intervention is preceded by a careful and critical historical reading, whose goal is apprehension of all qualities: urban, architectonic, environmental, typological, structural, etc. The results of this analysis are not directed so much at establishing operative differentiations—because then one would have to work with homogeneous criteria for the entire area defined as a historic center—but rather at identification of the many varying degrees of intervention, at the city planning level and the building level, distinguishing the necessary "conservative rehabilitation" [*risanamento conservativo*].

For this reason, it is necessary to specify that conservative rehabilitation must be understood, above all, as maintenance of the network of roads and buildings in general (maintenance of the layout, conservation of the maze of streets, the perimeter of the city blocks, etc.), including maintenance of the general character of the surroundings. The latter requires integral conservation of the most significant monumental and environmental features, and adaptation of other elements or single built organisms to the demands of modern life, taking into consideration substitutions, in whole or in part, of the elements themselves as the only exception, and then only proportional to and compatible with conservation of the general character of the structures in the historic center.

The principal city planning interventions are:

a) *Urban renewal.* This entails verification of the relationships that unite the historic center with regional or urban structures, and eventually to rectify them where they are lacking. Of particular importance is analysis of the regional and functional role that the historic center develops over time and into the present. In this way, special attention is placed on analysis and renewal of existing relationships between the historic center and urban development and contemporaneous construction, above all, from a functional point of view, with particular respect for compatibility with commercial uses. To avoid the chaotic and demeaning effects of all purposes, functional and technological in nature, in the historic center, urban renewal as an intervention should be concerned with the general liberation of the center from utility.
b) *Reorganization of traffic routes.* This refers to analysis and revision of street connections and traffic patterns that run through a structure with the primary goal of reducing pathological aspects and returning functions compatible with structures of the past to the historic center.

   Worth consideration is the possibility of inclusion of facilities and public services closely connected to the demands of life in the city center.
c) *Inspection of urban infrastructure.* This concerns streets, squares, and all existing open spaces (courtyards, internal spaces, gardens, etc.) with the aim of a homogeneous connection between the buildings and external spaces.

The principal types of building interventions are:

1) *Static and hygienic rehabilitation of buildings,* geared to maintenance of their structure and balanced use. Such an intervention is effected according to the techniques, methods, and instructions of the practice of architectonic restoration. In this type of intervention, it is of particular importance to respect typological, structural, and functional qualities of the organism, avoiding those transformations that alter its character.
2) *Functional renovation* of internal systems, permitted only in those places where they are indispensable to everyday maintenance of the building. With this type of

intervention, respect for the typological and structural qualities of buildings is of fundamental importance, prohibiting any interventions that change their character, like, for example, emptying of buildings or introducing functions that excessively deform the typological-structural balance of the organism.

Basic operative tools of the types of intervention listed above are essentially:

- general city plans that restructure the relationship between the region and the historic center and between the city and the historic center as a whole;
- detailed plans pertaining to renewal of the most significant elements of the historic urban center;
- executive plans organized in sections that cover one city block or a group of elements organically assembled together.

Reading

42

ROBERTA BRANDES GRATZ WITH NORMAN MINTZ

Cities Back from the Edge: New Life for Downtown (1998)

Roberta Brandes Gratz is a journalist and urban critic who has written and lectured extensively on city development issues and was greatly influenced by the work and ideas of Jane Jacobs. In Cities Back from the Edge: New Life for Downtown, *Gratz and Norman Mintz elaborate the notion of urban husbandry, first introduced by Gratz in* The Living City *(1989). Their arguments begin from Jane Jacobs' passionate struggle against car-induced demolitions, "slum clearances," and urban renewal projects that took place in American cities from the 1930s to the 1970s. In opposition to this approach, whose fundamentals are still pursued through "Project Planning" initiatives designed to "overwhelm and alter what exists" through large-scale projects, the authors advocate a different course of action. They convincingly argue that assets that are already in place, instead of being replaced, can "be reinvigorated and built onto in order to stimulate a place-based rejuvenation that adds to the long-evolving, existing strengths." This approach can be summed up in a single sentence: "Many small initiatives, over time, do add up to big change without massive development overwhelming and replacing a functional place."*

CHAPTER 3. PROJECT PLANNING OR URBAN HUSBANDRY: THE CHOICE

Two approaches invariably conflict in each story of downtown change. The first and most prevalent is the project approach to rebirth, what I call *Project Planning*. The fundamentals are always recognizable.

This approach assumes that a void exists that can be filled with a project. The planning process is designed to achieve the project, market it, sell it, and involve the public in selecting a predetermined solution—in other words, the project. The Project Planning process should not be confused with a problem-solving process. A problem-solving

From ROBERTA BRANDES GRATZ with NORMAN MINTZ, *Cities Back from the Edge: New Life for Downtown* (New York: John Wiley & Sons, 1998), 59–63, 65–68, 71, 78, 82–83. Reproduced courtesy of Wiley and Roberta Brandes Gratz.

process may or may not involve a project. Project-based Planning does. The problem, if there was one, remains unsolved.

Under Project-based Planning, a project must be big to be meaningful. Big projects require big, experienced developers, big contractors, big government agencies, big public financial support, and lots of investment banking and legal fees. Under this Project-based Planning, the new is added at a large enough scale to overwhelm and alter what exists. What exists may be wiped out entirely, as with urban renewal. Something radically replaces it. Few clues are left as to what has been lost and what alternative strategy has been missed.

—~—

Inevitably, designers working over a drawing board fall prey to an illusion: They begin to think of the world or of the future as if it were a piece of blank paper. The completed project, projected into the future, becomes the singular focus. The setting of the work, the existing conditions in the field, are often reduced to information at the margins of the paper. Everything else that might be happening at the same time is closed off from view as the engineer draws his or her finger along the project timeline.

We are all now captives of Project Planning, without recognizing the way it narrows our understanding of the world. Accountability is reduced to complete implementation of a pre-existing plan. No matter how hard we try to do "master planning," taking account of more and more variables and contingencies, using more and more complex software planning programs, we harden ourselves against an awareness of what places are really like—where people live, work, own property and businesses—and how they persist, change, and evolve around the tyranny of our plans. Project Planning is a scientific approach to change, based on data,[1] calculations, and projections.

The key word is science, a science based on calculations, projections, and formulas. Planning has become science-like, a practice based on theory, statistical data, demographics, and projections. A project gets planned, measured, calculated, projected. It gets implemented in well-planned stages. And then it is done, finished, completed, occupied, or used. Perfect for ribbon-cutting. Cities, downtowns, and active places, however, defy scientific assessments. They cannot be reduced to scientific formulas. Urbanism is an art, not a science. Urbanism, not urbanology.

When city problems are approached scientifically, the complexity that is the essence of urbanism is unrecognized, ignored, or lost. [. . .]

[. . .]

Project Planners dominate the citadels of power. Planning professionals, developers, Wall Street investors, and the like consider Project Planning the only approach worth talking about, the only one requiring complicated financial packages. Only Project Planning, of course, is dependent on *them*. Project Planners dismiss anything else as irrelevant, anything that places more confidence in the judgment of citizen users. Downtowns are pockmarked with their accomplishments. Only Project Planners, their followers, and the public persuaded by their rhetoric define these downtowns as reborn. *Rebuilt, yes; reborn, hardly.*

Opponents of Project Planning recognize and celebrate [. . .] complexity. [. . .] We call them *Urban Husbanders*. Urban Husbanders is a term I introduced and summarized in *The Living City*.[2] Urban Husbanders assume that assets are already in place to be reinvigorated and built onto in order to stimulate a place-based rejuvenation that *adds* to the long-evolving, existing strengths, instead of *replacing* them. Planning is meant to be about problem solving, relying heavily on the expertise of citizen users, the accumulated experience and wisdom of the community. Building on resources to diminish or overcome problems is the chosen route, instead of projects that obliterate those worthy resources. Urban Husbanders advocate introducing change incrementally and monitoring it carefully, providing a great opportunity to learn from each step. Urban Husbanders are the initiators of most of the downtown successes in this book.

Proponents of Urban Husbandry strengthen what exists before adding anything new. They involve many entrepreneurs of various sizes, not just one big developer. Urban Husbanders rely only on modest doses of government support, if any. Urban Husbanders are the most frequent opponents of Project Planners. They work to add a layer of organic urban growth, rather than replace what has taken decades to grow. This layer may look and feel in many ways radically different from what was there before but, fundamentally, the connection between before and after is not broken.

[. . .]

Urbanology versus Urbanism

Project Planners don't need to worry much about the people or businesses in place or the existing garden when they devise a downtown redevelopment policy. People and businesses get relocated or "plowed under." Plants are transplanted, perhaps to a garden with a different, less compatible soil. Sometimes they are torn out from their roots and discarded. The garden is replaced.

—~—

An Urban Husbander would have found creative ways to enhance what little urban fabric is left in that downtown into a lively, diverse place that reflects the city of Indianapolis instead of the developer of the mall. Boston's Newberry Street, Pasadena's Colorado Boulevard, or New York's Columbus Avenue. Denver's Lower Downtown, New York's SoHo, or San Francisco's South of Market. These are streets and districts that distinguish a place. They nurture urbanism and foster its spread. An enclosed mall does the reverse. Indianapolis and the multitude of other over-projected, becalmed cities need this kind of nurturing desperately, if they actually have any authentic urban fabric left to nurture. [. . .]

—~—

Urban Husbandry considers existing life first, respects it, views it as an asset, not a problem, and determines with local users what remedies could improve things. It examines problems from the site, not from a color-coded map, looks at where people live and work, where physical and non-physical impacts will be felt. Urban Husbandry starts with a strategy or a vision that possibly, eventually, but not at first, may include projects of modest scale, projects that repair and add but don't overwhelm. The strategy is adjusted as conditions change.

Process, Not Projects

Again, the garden analogy is applicable. This is the way a community, a downtown, a neighborhood, a city grows. New things get planted, grow, run out of space, move to new space, and the cycle repeats itself. Things grow at their own pace. This is what is exciting about cities, why they change, grow, evolve. Nothing is frozen in a city. Continuous change is a sign of health in a complex and vibrant downtown. People can move around, according to life requirements. A single person can start in a small apartment, move to a larger one, or even a house, after marriage. With children, larger space may be needed. Alternatives are readily available. Similarly, a business might start small in one district, expand to another with growth, and yet another with more growth, and, perhaps, leave town with maturity and expansion. In a healthy city, businesses move and leave town, but new emerging businesses take their place. Variety of opportunity—the variety within the garden—nurtures the new. This variety gives the city, the community, the neighborhood its strength.

—~—

Urban Husbanders, in many places, fought for the future of downtown, the local economy, and community values in the face of surrounding mall proliferation. Burlington, Iowa; Holland, Michigan; Franklin, Tennessee; Sheboygan Falls, Wisconsin; and hundreds of other communities of all sizes have successfully followed this route by following the rebirth strategy developed by the National Main Street Center (of the National Trust for Historic Presevation) that starts from the premise that the historic buildings, existing infrastructure, and functioning local businesses are an undervalued resource on which new growth can occur. A rebirth momentum often emerges from the Main Street approach to withstand the competition of surrounding or nearby malls. The rebirth naturally reflects the personality of its place, its local garden.

[. . .]

When city problems are approached mechanistically, the complexity that is the essence of urbanism is misunderstood, ignored, or lost. Most significantly, the ability of a city to renew itself without big, publicly financed interventions is lost. The public cost factor is always rationalized. *But it takes more money to damage a downtown with overwhelming Project Plans than to strengthen it and let diverse activities flourish.*

—~—

Project Planners don't know how to respond to natural urban change. When challenged, they throw up their hands and say, "The market will take care of it." A fundamental inconsistency marks this view. For almost 30 years, for example, Manhattan's

SoHo underwent gradual, evolutionary change. No public incentive or public investment was involved. SoHo had, by the mid-1990s, reached a level of success unsurpassed by any other old manufacturing neighborhood in the country [. . .] . By the mid-1990s, however, the art center character appeared threatened. Art galleries were moving out and big retail chains, looking for opportunities in interesting urban locations, were anxious to come in. Planning and elected officials advocated increasing the size limitation of retail businesses from the current 10,000 square feet. The zoning restrictions, planners argued, had not preserved the artistic quality of the district. The market prevails anyway, they said.

Facts contradict this view. Restrictions, in fact, had, up to that point, done a good job limiting *excessive* change. The idea of "no change" was never an option, and can't be achieved anyway. But removing those restraints would surely accelerate unavoidable erosion of the arts-based community and local economic uses. Attributing future change to the "market, anyway" removes responsibility from the city for the zoning changes that would accelerate continued loss of artistic character and guarantee that loss. Inconsistently, in another part of town, the Wall Street area, planners argued on behalf of developer incentives and zoning adjustments to *spur renewal*. Zoning rules could be relied on to encourage developers and spur the market downtown, but not to discourage development and modify the market in SoHo. Zoning can—and does—work both ways. Restraints work to prevent overly large flowers, or killer weeds, from pushing out smaller flowers in a garden. Incentives work to fertilize. The issue with incentives is what is being fertilized, and to what end.

[. . .]

[. . .] *Project Planners expedite real estate development. They do not foster rebirth. Project Planners argue the two are the same. They are not.* The Project Planning story seems to repeat itself, differing in scale and form, but not too much in substance.

—ᴧᴧᴧ—

Waiting for Disney

—ᴧᴧᴧ—

Natural agglomerations do not survive getting spiffed up, moved around, or added to with big projects. Projects replace. They don't add. Once a garden is uprooted, it is hard to replant after the replacement falls short. Project Planning undermines the organic process, instead of nourishing it. Natural districts are misinterpreted today and translated into "themes" and "clusters" that never add up to more than "themes" and "clusters." Contrivances can't endure. Districts cannot be created or imposed. They can only evolve. The legendary 42nd Street evolved. Nobody planned it. No consultant picked its uses and screened its entrepreneurs. It grew in small and large pieces and, for a long time, adapted easily to constantly changing times.

—ᴧᴧᴧ—

The Lessons

[. . .] If the right lessons are learned, it may demonstrate the folly of developing "centers," the products of decades of planning and development thinking that turned its back on streets and brought life inside and killed it outside. Instead of centers of activity, the direction must go back to streets of life that evolve into districts and connect with the larger place.

—∿—

Pieces, remnants, a few treasured landmarks, local businesses, persevering residents, and special uses remain in every downtown, the varied plants of the traditional urban garden. If not further eroded or totally rebuilt, the surviving plants can be cultivated into a garden again. Some downtowns have more surviving plants than others. They are the fortunate ones, best positioned to be the star performers of the 21st century. In each downtown, these enduring precincts, sustained functions, resilient businesses, committed downtowners, determined place defenders, community activists, neighborhood developers, landmark preservationists, and human-scale advocates will be the building blocks of a brighter future, the special offerings that will lend degrees of character and credential to what follows.

Grand plans and inflated visions will continue in new configurations. The need for public resistance will not cease. But advocates for more modest and appropriate visions, people who understand and use cities, are increasing in number and influence. Only if they succeed will downtowns survive. These are instinctivists, citizen users, Urban Husbanders—the enlightened opposition to excessive Project Plans, the people who are the best experts about cities and towns.

Notes

1. Macro data do not reflect micro differences. Plans based on macro data do not consider the micro impacts. All macro decisions have micro impacts. A national or state decision based on macro data affects localities where conditions may be antithetical. Similarly, a citywide decision translates into neighborhood impacts. [. . .]
2. Chapter 6. Urban Husbandry: The Economy of Wisdom, was contrasted with Planned Shrinkage (an early form of Project Planning): The Economy of Waste.

Reading

43

Pier Luigi Cervellati

Historical Systems (2009)

Pier Luigi Cervellati is best known internationally for his participation in the preparation of the 1969 plan for the historic city of Bologna, a seminal plan that introduced the social dimension and the notion of integrated conservation for heritage areas. More recently, Cervellati has advocated an approach very similar to that of Gratz. According to Cervellati, the priority today is no longer to build anew but to repair and curate what is already there by learning patiently the art of restoring and maintaining the city. In the reading below, Cervellati starts with the definition of historic center *to propose an extension of the concept to cover the built and natural environments, planning for which, in his view, should be carried out using similar methodological criteria. He then discusses the interpretation of past cadastral plans to define the "historical net," or ensemble of city elements that remain unchanged after comparing the historic sequence of cadastres. These elements should be the object of ad hoc conservation measures, in association with a thorough typological analysis of individual structures, illustrated here with an example from Venice. The reading concludes with a discussion of urban restoration, exemplified by the plan for the area of Borgo in Rome. (L. Benevolo,* San Pietro e la città di Roma, *2004). The plan proposes the recovery or reinstatement of something that is no longer there or has been severely altered. For Cervellati, restoration of a historic area is a process that shuns arbitrary and "creative" interventions and focuses instead on the maintenance of what is already there and on the gradual and patient recovery of what has been lost.*

From City to Historic Center / From Urban Center to Historic City

Preface

It was a mistake to define the "historic center" as the city of the past: the city, often enclosed by walls, where its dwellers live together according to the same laws (as

From Pier Luigi Cervellati, "I sistemi storici," in *Il nuovo manuale di urbanistica,* vol. 1, edited by Leonardo Benevolo (Rome: Gruppo Mancosu Editore, 2009), E60–E93, passim. Authorization granted by Carlo Mancosu publisher.

expressed by Nicolò Tommaseo in the second half of the nineteenth century). The city, after the so-called industrial revolution and great social upheaval, expanded beyond those walls. And while expanding, it almost always tore them down.

It became an "urban aggregate" whose center had to coexist with the ancient city. A modern periphery without a core. An urban "center" erected and established over the span of centuries taking on functions incompatible with its structure. Whereas the periphery is always more diffuse, marginal, and extrinsic precisely because it was built separate from the center in which it is unrecognizable. A center that it makes use of but does not inhabit.

The historic city, the preindustrial city, had its own core, and usually it coincided with the main public square, together with many other places of reference. The churches, (other) squares, and streets with their hierarchies, the abbeys and seats of power, formed the city through their entirety, where the relationship between inhabitants and the physical landscape was very close. Beyond the walls was the countryside and little else.

Extending into the countryside, the urban aggregate, the modern periphery, continued to use and misuse all of the structures of the historic city. Efforts at modernization included the insertion of new buildings, widened streets, and the installation of new functions. The inhabitants were pushed out, and the city of the past, rich in works of art, a monument in and of itself due to its specificity and identity, ended up being turned into an urban center of gravity in order to be adapted and become modern. Treating the ancient city as equivalent to a "center" contributed to the deformation of the very meaning of the city. The "center" insofar as it is a historic one, is not equivalent to the city. The periphery has never been described as such.

There was as a result a transition from city to historic center. We are now concerned with designing/planning a redevelopment: from urban center to historic city.

The Perimeter of the Historic City

An aerial photograph of an Italian city often reveals the perimeter of the ancient city center.

Pistoia can be considered equivalent to other historical Italian cities where the city wall is still for the most part intact. In this specific case, in addition to the Medicean walls of the fifteenth and sixteenth centuries, signs of the Roman and medieval city structures are still legible. The presence of the walls simplifies recognition of the ancient city. Aerial photographs of the urban aggregate demonstrate—like the rings in the trunk of a tree—the stages of the successive expansions. [. . .] The geodetic cadastre (generally drawn up from the mid-nineteenth century) reflects the final phase of the ancient city: the relationship that the city still has with the surrounding countryside as well as the internal balance between built areas and open spaces, cultivated fields and gardens.

The comparison of two maps from the Italian Military Geographic Institute from the end of the nineteenth and twentieth centuries demonstrates Pistoia's transition to a historic center. At the beginning of the last century, city and countryside constituted two distinct entities through the presence of the quadrangular walls whose vertices are connected to the main thoroughfares of the city. The feeling of entrance and exit to and from the city is strongly represented by the city gates.

At the beginning of the third millennium, the perimeter of the medieval walls is still legible ([see] fig. 1) and is considered the boundary of the ancient city, while the area between the two perimeters is assessed as modern, even where the walls are still present. [. . .] One must always deepen the analysis, observing and comparing historical cartography with the current. [. . .] Through this comparison, a plan for restoration of the historic city gains validity. It is necessary to undertake identification of the perimeter. In summary, the area (territory) and the period (time frame) when the formation of the ancient city can be considered complete must be identified. The moment and scale at which the city becomes a historic center.

—⁂—

Interpreting the Cadastral Surveys

The first geodetic cadastre completed for the city dates to 1837. The churches are in blue and in red are all other buildings, regardless of their function. The urban plan is almost identical to the cartography of the preceding centuries. Albeit belated, this cadastre—in its design and compilation of associated "sommarioni" (lists recording the owner of a plot of land, its size, and the activities—residential, commercial, administrative, etc.—that are carried out there)—does not differ from the Napoleonic, pontifical, or Leopoldine cadastres, drawn up at the outset of the 19th century. The descriptive precision of the planimetry of the buildings and the streets as well as the warpage of the fields (cultivated areas or gardens on the margins of the Medicean walls) and of the internal canals, allows for a perfect reading of the urban plan of the ancient city. After another hundred years have passed, the urban plan is still analogous to the preceding one. But the band of green tangential to the walls filled with gardens and properties belonging to the abbeys (and later to plant nurseries) is diminished by new buildings. The city has expanded beyond the walls that have remained almost intact. [. . .]

Comparison of the Historic Cadastral Surveys and the Current Regional Topographic Map

When comparing the two cadastres one can picture the metamorphosis that has occurred. In red are the new buildings and in yellow those destroyed. It is the same between the cadastre and the regional topographic map. During the fifty years that separate the two maps, the number and size of new buildings is greater than that identified in the one hundred years separating the first and second cadastral surveys.

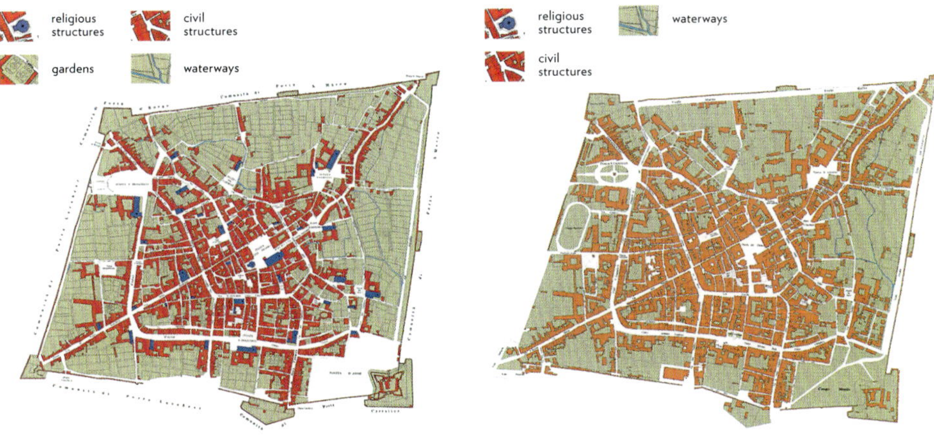

Fig. 1. Urban cadastre of Pistoia from 1837.

Fig. 2. Urban cadastre of Pistoia from 1953.

Fig. 3. Comparison of the 1953 and 1837 cadastres.

Fig. 4. Comparison of the regional topographic map and the 1953 cadastre.

The Historical Net

By superimposing these two comparisons, that which has been defined as the "historical net" is obtained. Historical net means the accumulation of buildings, streets, public squares, cultivated fields and gardens, canals, and everything else that remains (like plots of land) unaltered. In the specific case of Pistoia, the "invariable" elements from the first cadastral survey in 1837 to the regional topographic map of 2000 are documented. The historical net is therefore the areas that were not cadastrally modified; invariably, they have remained intact. The cadastral plots that remain unaltered are now to be subdivided according to the typology to which they belong.

buildings in 1873
buildings in 1953
buildings after 1953
waterways
waterways from 1873, now disappeared

Fig. 5. Plan for the historical city of Pistoia, historical net.

For Pistoia [. . .] the cadastral survey of 1837 was taken as the reference point for the period of completion of the historic city.

Atlas of Building Typologies and Open Spaces

Three cadastral maps and updated aerial photography evidence four periods that correspond to the salient moments in the urban history of Venice over the past two centuries. The Napoleonic cadastre (dated 1802–10) represents the actual state of the city in the lagoon during the final years of the Repubblica Serenissima.

The Combatti map (dated to 1850) and the following "Austrian" cadastre document the interventions realized over fifty-two years of Austrian government. The cadastre drafted in the 1930s (and 1940s)—called the first (or new) plan, those preceding being derived from the Italian-Austrian plan—constitutes an irreplaceable document useful for identifying the changes that occurred during the Kingdom of Italy. Ultimately, the aerial photography (at a scale of 1/2000) of 1982, suitably updated, illustrates the last fifty years of republican government.

Comparing the maps, the temporal evolution of urban change is illustrated. The historical net (as was seen in the case of Pistoia) is also obtained.

The historical net coincides with the "invariable elements" or more simply the persistence of the historical city. The cadastral comparison was verified through relevant on-site inspections. The cartography that resulted formed the basis for identifying the atlas of building typologies and open spaces (cultivated fields, gardens, public squares, and *campielli*). [. . .] Most important, the buildings belonging to two specialized "typologies" are defined: the structures associated with religious matters—churches, synagogues, convents, devotional schools, chapels, etc.—and civil structures, like the Doge's Palace, the old and new *procuratie* in St. Mark's Square, theaters and administrative offices of the city-state, such as the mint, jails, warehouses, *squeri* (workshops for storing and repairing gondolas), mills, etc. Specialized typologies, civil and religious, insofar as they are architecturally related to residential typologies, take on specific importance in the urban context.

The residential typologies, on the other hand, consist of three identifiable models. This "concentration" of residential building types is undoubtedly reductive. On the basis of unsurpassed research by Caniggia, only the fundamental types have been identified, leaving aside the various articulations and evolutions that Venetian houses underwent over the centuries.

The *fondaco* (storehouse and family residence) is a dominant residential typology. According to Caniggia, this typology represents the evolution of the Roman *domus* created by subsequent obstruction of the original building lot.

—ꟿ—

The multifamily house constitutes an important presence for understanding the position and residential "quality" of Venice during the long reign of the Repubblica Serenissima, whether the two-family version with a separate stairway or, in particular, when the presence of the "Leonardian" stairway allows independence from the single house. The Leonardian stairway occurs in the two- and three-room structures, as well as in "block" structures and terraced houses.

[. . .]

Serial houses and/or row houses occur in serial groups of individual two-room structures, but they are also identified in connection with courtyards or gardens. Nine variants have been identified (see P. Maretto, *The Venetian House*).

—ꟿ—

Fig. 6. Details of the map of building typologies drafted for the "historical net" obtained by means of cadastral comparisons and the topographic map.

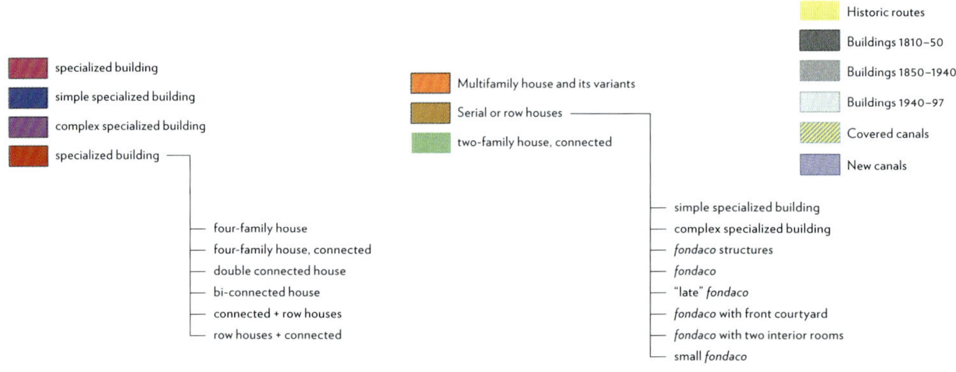

The creation of the atlas of building typologies provides a technical basis indispensable for formulating the categories of interventions and the possible intended uses. In practice, an operational category corresponds to each typology.

Ordinary and extraordinary maintenance. (Maintenance, provided that it is adjusted to the constructive and distributive typology of the edifice.)

"Restoration" (particularly for the specialized categories and in the case of Venice for the entirety of residential typologies). Up to philological and typological recovery. Also "restructuring" of the built environment can be inferred from typological analysis. Like the multicolor plan often drafted beyond the plausible methodological criteria.

For buildings that do not belong to a typology, one can refer to case studies of urban restoration.

—∾—

Articulation of Open Spaces (Courtyards and Venetian Gardens)

Typological interpretation of the configuration of the Venetian garden distinguishes characteristics derived over the centuries from precise rules and through repetition (although with stylistic variants) from elements that establish their specificity. Inside a space typically narrow and elongated, organization of the garden occurs behind the edifice. The layout is generally articulated by pathways that distribute the vegetal and decorative elements aligned on the principal perspective axis. Passage from enclosed areas (the entrance hall of the palazzo) to those partially open (portico) culminates in the courtyard. From the courtyard to the real and true garden. The vegetal area is located right next to the courtyard (M. Cunico 1989) but is separated from it by means of a gap or an access gate that separates the two domains. This separation, or *caesura*, between the two principal areas is emphasized: the paved courtyard filled with statues and vases and the cultivated area with flowerbeds and tall trees. An axial path, with a pergola and espalier, traverses the entire length between the multicolored parterres of the "flower garden" reaching the door to the canal, which is made distinct in various ways: by a loggia, a small house, or another architectural element.

The path from the entrance hall to the portico, from the courtyard to the garden, constitutes the compositional backbone from which the lateral flower beds extend. These are shaped by the principal path, which is usually covered with a pergola, and by orthogonal paths that intersect it and terminate at the enclosing wall often with architectural elements. In the 1900s, the romantic English garden transforms the order that had remained essentially unchanged since the 15th century. In addition to the wide variety of tree species, the gardens themselves in many instances no longer represented the typology of the *palazzo fondaco*.

[. . .]

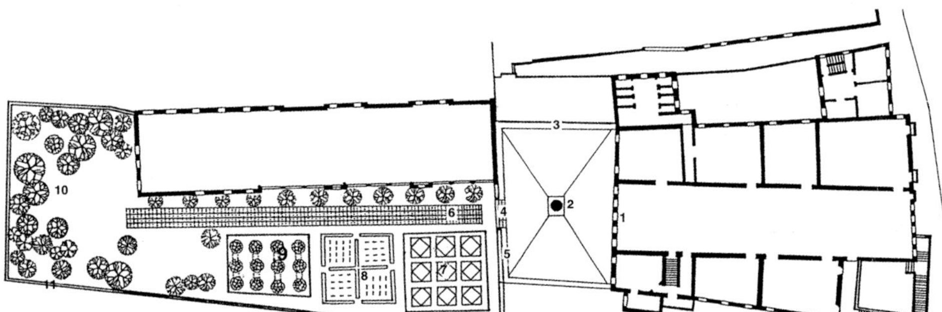

Fig. 7. The fifteenth-century garden.
Palazzo Ariani all'Angelo Raffaele: 1. portico; 2. courtyard; 4/5. access-caesura; 6. pergola; 7. flowerbeds; 8. vegetable garden; 9. fruit orchard

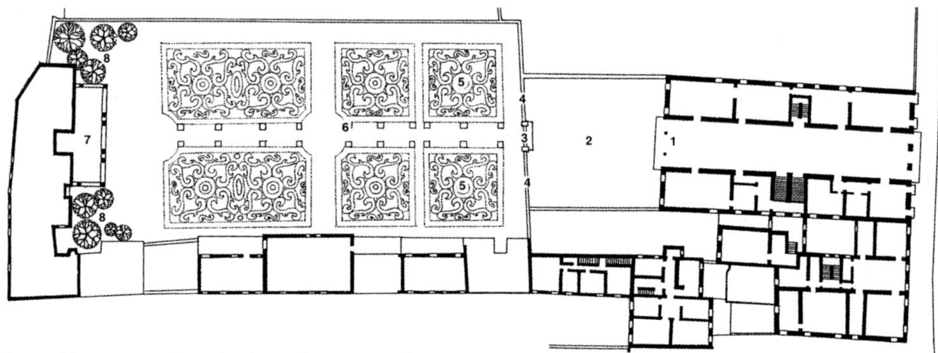

Fig. 8. The seventeenth- and eighteenth-century garden.
Palazzo Soranzo Cappello in Rio Marin: 1. portico; 2. courtyard; 3/4. access-caesura; 5. parterre with flowers; 6. statues; 7. loggia

Urban Restoration

Having defined the perimeter of the historic city and formulated the atlas of typologies, the project of urban restoration can be pursued. The objective of urban restoration is no longer the isolated edifice but the systematization of the areas where interventions have altered the original framework. The case studies under consideration all have the same methodological model.

1) Historical reconstruction of the design sequence of the area—whether street, public square, or group of buildings—that should be restored. Documentation of the reconstruction must be detailed and exhaustive, making use of official archival materials, cadastres, and historical maps, elevation views and pictorial representations, architectural drawings and planning documents (if they exist), historical photographs, as well as literary descriptions, and newspaper and magazine articles contemporary with the period of the alterations.

2) Presentation of the current condition, equally as detailed, possibly with reference to the plan of replacement, evisceration, and/or alteration. The aim is to identify not only the logic and objectives of the original project, its purpose, justifications, the volumetric separations, and the perspectives that had been established, but also to define that which still remains of the original framework after the alterations were carried out. Not to mention to objectively measure the extent of reversibility of the replacement.
3) Alteration of the architectural fabric is always justified as an act of modernization of the area, the street, the public square, or the group of structures that are the object of transformation. The objective of urban restoration is instead that of constructing an effective modernization, realistically and historically aware of recovering—returning—the altered area to the remainder of the historical city that is still intact. It is a process that connects history, criticism, and planning. It is not about recovering the origins—perhaps archeological—of the place, but rather to recover the framework established before the historical city was transformed into a "historic center." Before the transformations/systematizations considered "modern."

The evisceration of the Borghi neighborhoods around St. Peter's Basilica, carried out around the middle of the twentieth century, is an emblematic case. The urban restoration plan in this case does not strive to achieve a scenographic reconstruction of Bernini's design but rather to recover a Baroque urban masterpiece. Opposers of the

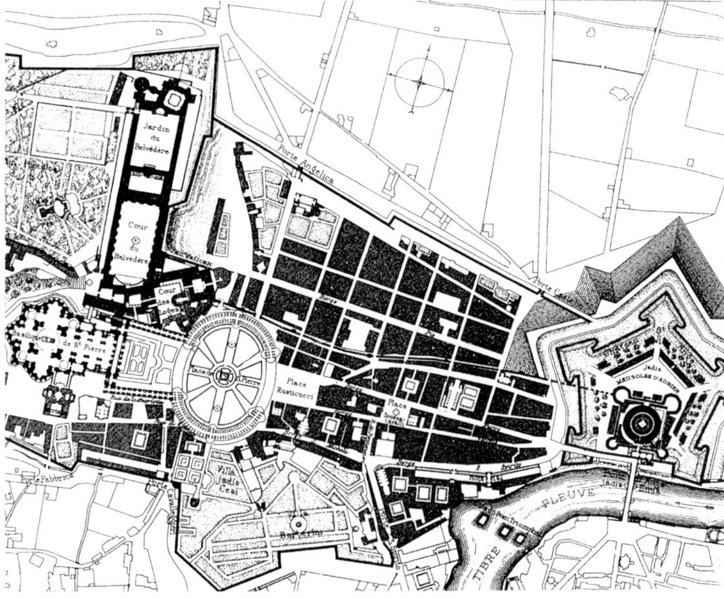

Fig. 9. Restoration of Borgo San Pietro in Rome. The Borgo neighborhood depicted in the map by G. B. Nolli from 1748.

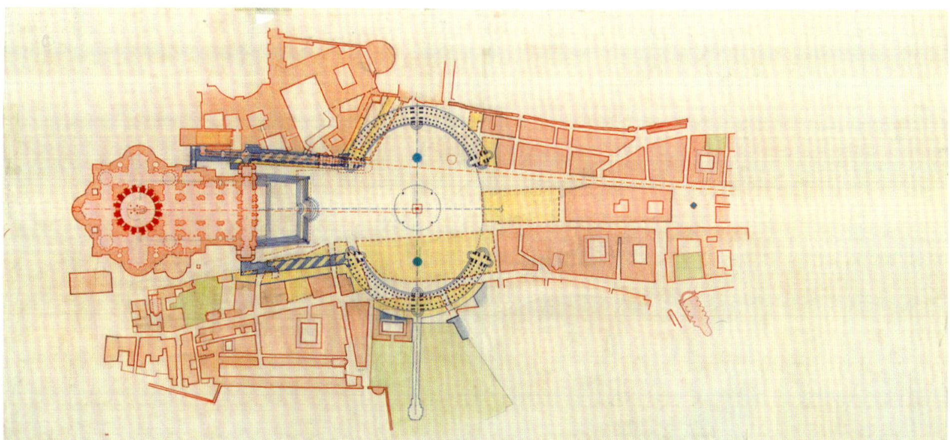

Fig. 10. Bernini's intervention in St. Peter's Square in a drawing by L. Benevolo. In purple are the preserved buildings, in blue the new ones, and in yellow those that have been demolished. Courtesy Studio Architetti Benevolo.

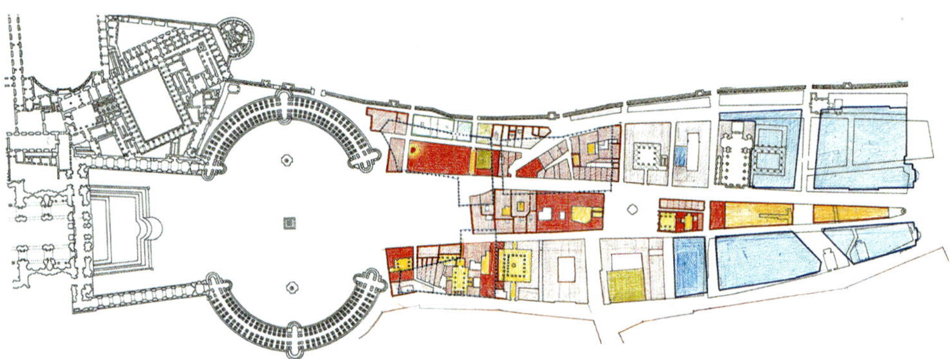

Fig. 11. Urban restoration of the area of via della Conciliazione in a drawing by L. Benevolo. In red are the philological reconstructions, in purple the typological reconstructions, in blue volumetric reconstructions (see L. Benevolo, *San Pietro and the City of Rome,* Laterza, Bari-Roma, 2004). Courtesy Studio Architetti Benevolo.

urban restoration make reference to a constant "historicizing" of the city. *That which today is modern tomorrow will be historical*: a senseless assertion if one considers the metamorphosis of the so-called modern city that replaced the urban center with the city of the past, which must be considered in its entirety and be brought back, precisely through interventions of urban restoration, to its original configuration.

[The] examples refer to the twentieth-century evisceration of the Borgo neighborhood for the opening of via della Conciliazione in Rome [. . .] [and the] recovery of the Jewish ghetto in Senigallia.

Research for Rome's urban restoration plan was completed by L. Benevolo over the span of a quarter century and below only its most significant proposals are included. [. . .] The recovery of the Jewish Ghetto in Senigallia is from 2003 (Cervellati, Floris).

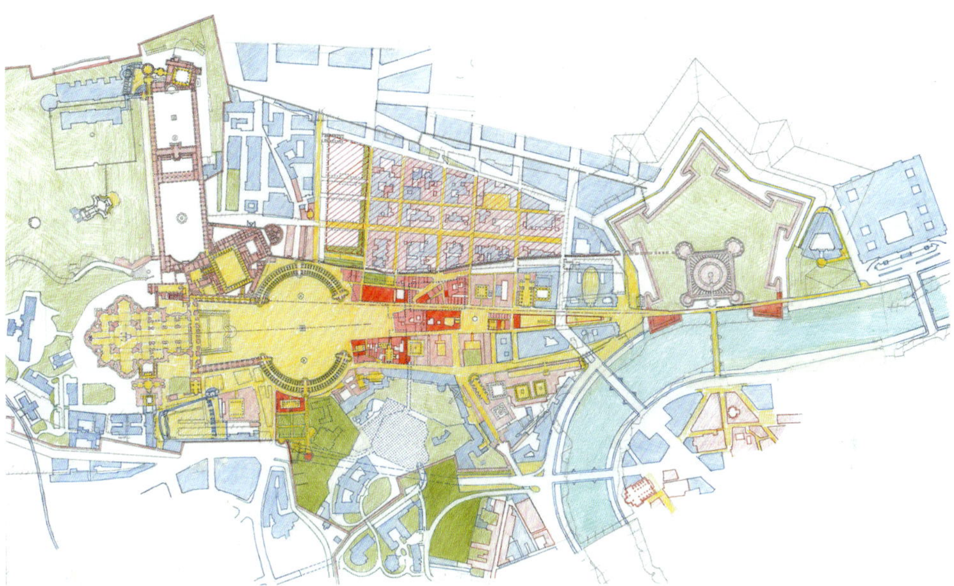

Fig. 12. Urban restoration of all the Borgo neighborhood. To be compared with its condition before 1870, when the area was enclosed by a wall in the form of a loop, for the most part surrounded by open spaces. Courtesy Studio Architetti Benevolo.

Recovery of the Jewish Ghetto in Senigallia

Demolished at the end of the nineteenth century, the edifices that composed the ghetto formed a public square that altered the weave of the walled city's street network. Rich iconographic documentation of the size and shape of the buildings from the seventeenth and eighteenth centuries, not to mention the group of cadastral maps of which the first is the pontifical map from 1821 to the so-called Mastai Ferretti map of 1840, evidence the compactness of the built environment. One must add to the pictorial documentation the no less meaningful photographic documentation. In its current state, the new public square (G. Simoncelli) discredits the size of the Piazza del Ducca opposite the fortress and renders the urban structure incomprehensible. The proposed plan of recovery recomposes the historical framework of structures and voids, reinstating also in this case the urban structure accumulated over centuries. The act of restoration is facilitated by the iconographic documentation and the very simple typology of construction. At street level are found small shops and stands, and the upper floors contain multifamily dwellings. The plane trees that decorate the square today never existed inside the walled city. Especially in this part of the thirteenth-century fortress. The use of this tree to beautify eviscerations or incongruous insertions represents a precise historical period.

Fig. 13. Pontifical cadastre (1821).

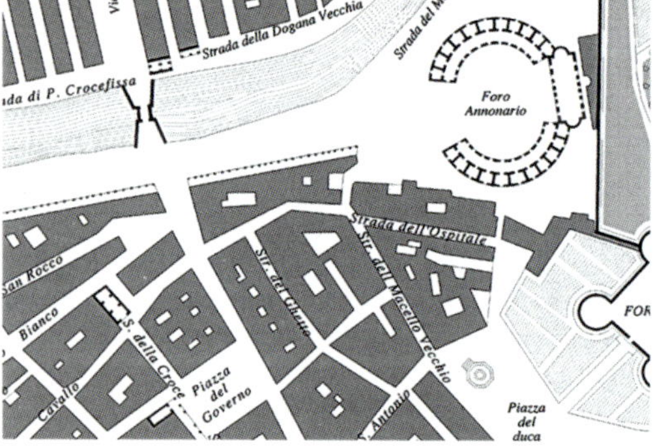

Fig. 14. Map of Senigallia, said to be from Pope Pius IX (1841).

Fig. 15. 1931 cadastre.

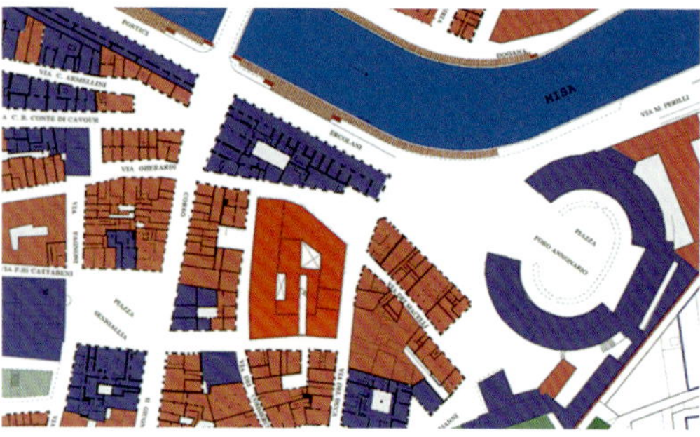

Fig. 16. Project to recover the ghetto.

Reading

44

NSW (Australia) Heritage Office

Design in Context: Guidelines for Infill Development in the Historic Environment (2005)

In 2005, when this work was published, the Heritage Office was the New South Wales State Government's authority on heritage matters and was responsible for administering the Heritage Act (Act 136 of 1977, as amended). Design in Context *sets out practical guidelines on infill development for architects, property owners, developers, and others so that "architects can contribute to the future in a creative and inspiring way." Further, the "guidelines do not seek to exclude the extraordinary but to improve the ordinary. They encourage quality while demanding respect for the existing context." NSW Heritage intends to publish a revised volume, in late 2018 or 2019, that will combine some of the context of this reading and reading 45.*

Introduction

[. . .]

An important aspect of any good design is to understand the context of a place and respond to it. Heritage items are a response to their cultural, social, historical, political, economic and physical environments. Similarly, new development affecting an established and valued setting such as a conservation area should understand and respond to that place in a positive way that is of its own time.

The relationships between a building and its setting contribute to that place's special character. That setting can be a cultural, natural, urban, suburban or rural landscape. Depending on its design and position, a new building can have a beneficial or detrimental effect on its setting or an adjacent valued building. Infill buildings should aim to provide continuity in the built form rather than seeking to create an iconic or individualistic building.

From NSW (Australia) Heritage Office, *Design in Context: Guidelines for Infill Development in the Historic Environment* (Sydney: Heritage Office, 2005), 2–3, 6, 8, 10–16. Reproduced courtesy of Heritage Division, NSW Office of Environment and Heritage for the Heritage Council of NSW.

In shaping our built environment we have a responsibility to past, present and future generations. Infill work or design in a historic context links the past to the present and projects into the future. This is an exciting challenge and an opportunity for professional design teams to demonstrate their skills and artistry. Our greatest buildings are those that respond positively to their cultural and physical environment.

Despite improvement in the quality of new buildings in valued historic contexts, there is still misunderstanding about what is appropriate development in sensitive places. In response to the community perception that too much valued urban, suburban and rural fabric is being lost, planning policy has been developed to identify areas and places of special character and quality. Legislation at national, state and local government levels attempts to encourage new development that positively contributes to the historic context and does not devalue it.

We now recognise that it is not necessary to prevent development in these areas in order to conserve them. Nor should new development directly copy the architecture of the existing buildings. At the same time, new development that makes no reference to the established and valued setting is unlikely to be approved. Both approaches can erode and detract from the historic context: the first through superficial echoing of architectural features, the second through disregard for the historic context.

New design should respond to its historic context through an understanding and informed analysis of its character and quality. This will include elements such as its grain, existing patterns of development, important views, scale, materials and building methods. As a consequence, the resulting design should create new relationships between the building, its neighbours and its setting.

The replacement of intrusive or non-contributory items within conservation areas provides an opportunity to interpret that area's special character and qualities and enhance it. The various elements that contribute to an area's heritage significance can be the catalyst for a successful contemporary design.

Infill development can accommodate a rich variety of interpretations and expressions. Each place will require different solutions. These guidelines advocate that the use of the design criteria can result in a multitude of architectural outcomes. Some designers may adopt a more traditional or vernacular approach, others may wish to explore a highly contemporary solution. Both are equally valid. It is the quality of the response that is the key.

Design Criteria

Designing in context does not mean imitation or following inflexible design rules. A wide range of solutions may emerge for any design problem after careful analysis of surrounding buildings and sympathetic interpretation of their design elements.

To achieve a successful infill design new development must be appropriate under the following design criteria:

01. character;
02. scale;
03. form;
04. siting;
05. materials and colour; and
06. detailing.

01. Character

All built environments have their own special character, but not all are valued as representing our history and culture. Changes to the built environment over time break the links between the past and the present and this frequently results in an environment without harmony or unity.

In contrast, places that are valued for their historic character convey a sense of continuity with the past. They may be places that developed over a relatively short time, so that the majority of the buildings are of a similar architectural style. [. . .] They may be places that have responded to, or reinforced, locally distinct patterns of development over time. [. . .] They may be places that respond in a unique way to a distinctive landscape. [. . .]

[. . .]

Infill design requires careful analysis and evaluation of the historic context to identify the important elements of the overall heritage character. The character of a place is shaped by many contributing factors such as:

- the underlying natural landforms;
- distinctive landscape elements;
- the date and style of the buildings;
- the scale and form of the buildings;
- street and subdivision patterns;
- setbacks of the buildings;
- materials, building techniques and details;
- views, vistas and skylines.

The character of an individual building or group of buildings is also shaped by the solid to void relationships, the play of light and shadow on the façades, and the proportions of openings.

Each of the other five criteria described in these guidelines contributes to the overall character but can be identified separately.

[. . .]

02. *Scale*

The scale of a building is its size in relation to surrounding buildings or landscape. Infill design should recognise the predominant scale (height, bulk, density, grain) of the setting and then respond sympathetically. The impact of an inappropriately scaled building cannot be compensated for by building form, design or detailing.

The grain, or pattern of arrangement and size of buildings in a precinct or conservation area, can be an important part of its character. The subdivision patterns and layouts of the streets provide the predominant scale and rhythm of building frontages. Any re-subdivision of lots within conservation areas should reinforce the townscape pattern. Where a subdivision pattern contributes to the significance of a conservation area, consolidation of lots within it will have a negative impact on the place.

Infill buildings that are of necessity larger than the surroundings can have their scale reduced by breaking long walls into bays, or by arranging openings in the walls so that their size and shape reflect the structure and openings of their neighbours. Where the scale of the roof is much larger than that of adjacent buildings, it may be broken up into smaller elements to reduce the bulk. Setbacks to upper levels can help to provide a transition between adjacent buildings of different scales.

03. *Form*

The form of a building is its overall shape and volume and the arrangement of its parts. Infill design should be sympathetic with the predominant form of its neighbours. Where a building form is highly repetitive within an area, variations to this form appear discordant. For example, the form of a new house in the context of a conservation area of typical federation bungalows should not interrupt the cohesiveness of the streetscape.

The roofline may play an important part in determining neighbourhood character. Infill buildings should respond to, or reinforce, existing ridge or parapet lines, roof slopes and other features such as party walls and chimneys.

The treatment of the façade in terms of the proportion, material and number of openings affects how a new building relates to its neighbours. The form need not copy that of the neighbours but should relate to it positively.

04. *Siting*

New buildings in a valued historic context should add sympathetically to the local streetscape and the grain of the area. The qualities of the streetscape can be reinforced by conforming to existing front and side setbacks and the general location of new buildings on site and the complementary treatment of street edges. Fences should be related to those of adjacent properties.

Most older buildings are oriented to their street frontage. New buildings should not be oriented across sites in a manner that is contrary to the established pattern. Where the façades create a more or less continuous line, this pattern of setbacks should be repeated when new buildings are added. Similarly, garages and carports should not be permitted to break a consistent building line. The dominance of garages and outbuildings to the streetscape can be ameliorated by soft landscaping.

Where there is an established pattern of side setbacks that contribute to the character of the streetscape this should also be reinforced by new buildings. Building with minimum setbacks to the boundaries on both sides, where this is not the pattern, can increase the bulk of the building and have an obtrusive and unacceptable impact.

Where side access is available, garages and carports should be located behind the building line to minimise their impact on the streetscape. Where there is no side access, an unroofed hard-stand area at the front of the dwelling may be appropriate if it does not impact negatively on the streetscape.

In rural settings, waterfront properties or in areas of twentieth-century housing buildings may have been deliberately not orientated to the street frontage. In an area where the position of buildings on sites contributes to the area's significant character, new buildings should respond to their sites in a similar way.

This principle also applies to the rear of infill buildings. New buildings should conform to the predominant building alignment where it contributes to significance.

New buildings should allow for the retention of significant views and vistas to and from the building, a townscape or a landscape. Natural features of significance should be retained, such as natural foreshore features and mature trees. In the latter case, new buildings should be sited beyond the drip line.

Sites where significant archaeological remains are to be retained in situ may require innovative approaches to the new placement of buildings or structural systems. [. . .]

05. *Materials and Colour*

Within a locality of consistent character there are usually predominant building materials, textures and ranges of colour, particularly in detail and decoration. Good infill buildings should recognise characteristic materials, textures and colours used locally and in adjacent buildings. These should be re-interpreted and incorporated as part of the new building.

Materials and colours of surrounding buildings need not be simply copied but used as a point of reference. Modern materials can be used if their proportions and details are harmonious within the surrounding historic context. Colour, texture and tonal contrast can be unifying elements.

The quality of new materials should be commensurate with those of the existing buildings.

06. *Detailing*

Common details within an area establish neighbourly resemblance and contribute to its special character. Verandahs, chimneys and shutters, for example, are often distinctive features of nineteenth-century housing. The lack of details in many contemporary buildings can accentuate their difference within their historic context and disrupt the harmony of the area.

Details that contribute to the character of a conservation area or heritage item should be identified. They can inform or inspire the design of the new building. Modern details can reinterpret traditional details and create new relationships between new and old. Contemporary detailing of materials and junctions can provide levels of visual interest that contribute positively to the character of a place.

Landscape details such as fences, garden walls and planting treatments can play an important role in defining local character. New fences and walls should relate to adjacent properties. Where such features remain and contribute to the streetscape's heritage significance they should be retained.

Some areas have consistent planting schemes or plant types that contribute to their character. New planting schemes should recognise and reinforce their height, form and character.

New requirements for ecologically sustainable design such as solar panels and water tanks should be sensitively located and designed in a manner that does not intrude on the cohesiveness of the area.

Assessing New Development in a Historic Context

Assessors take a number of aspects into account when appraising development applications. When assessing heritage impact the assessor will check that the development meets the design criteria outlined in these guidelines. Design quality will be an important element. Given that most heritage buildings and conservation areas have been listed for their historic and/or architectural (aesthetic) significance, it is almost impossible to ignore design quality in the assessment process. Heritage assessment is often accused of being subjective, and to some extent there will be a subjective element to the process. It is possible, however, to define objectives for assessing development within an established and valued historic context. The design criteria put forward in these guidelines attempt to do this.

This checklist [pp. 385–87] assists designers, applicants and assessors to determine whether the proposal is appropriate. It encompasses both the qualitative aspects of the design of the building and the quality of its contribution to its historic context.

Assessing New Development in a Historic Context: Checklist for Applicants and Assessors

PART A **Documents to Be Included**	**Applicant's Confirmation**	**Assessor's Comments**
Date of submission		
Statement of heritage impact statement (SOHI) Include a statement of significance for any heritage item, precinct or conservation area affected by the new development Respond to the design criteria described in **Design in Context** in graphic and written point form (see Part B of this checklist)		
Site plan Showing setting including adjacent properties, buildings, trees and structures such as fences 1:200 scale min.		
Landscape plan 1:100 scale		
Floor plans 1:100 scale		
Section and details 1:100 scale minimum		
Elevations 1:100 scale minimum		
Fencing details 1:50 scale minimum		
External materials and colours Provide schedule and, where required, a sample board		
Working model 1:200 scale minimum		

PART B **Checklist for Inclusion in Heritage Impact Statement: Response to Design Criteria**	**Applicant's Confirmation**	**Assessor's Comments**
01. Character Use annotated diagrams, photographs and/or sketches to describe the factors which contribute to the character of the historic context, including: • topography of site and its surroundings; • distinctive landscape elements and quality; • street and subdivision patterns; • date and style of built form; • figure/ground and figure/landscape qualities; • views, vistas and skylines; • local culture and traditions; • uses; • consistency or repetition of above factors.		
02. Scale Annotate drawings, photographs of model or photomontages to describe the relationship between the proposed new development and the context, in terms of the following design criteria: • scale of buildings; • building and wall heights; • massing; • density — pattern of arrangement of buildings and size of buildings; • proportions; • rhythm of buildings and landscape; • floor-to-floor heights and relationship to ground or street plane; • modulation of walls, openings and roof planes in response to the scale of neighbouring buildings; • transition between different heights (for example, through the use of setbacks).		
03. Form Annotate drawings, photographs of model or photomontages to describe the relationship between the proposed new development and the context, in terms of the following design criteria: • predominant form of neighbours; • roof form and skyline—ridge and parapet lines, roof slopes, punctuation by party walls, chimneys and lanterns or skylights; • proportion and number of openings; • solid to void ratios; • relationship between internal and external spaces.		

continued on next page

PART B Checklist (cont.)	Applicant's Confirmation	Assessor's Comments
04. Siting Annotate drawings, photographs of model or photomontages to describe the relationship between the proposed new development and the context, in terms of the following design criteria: • predominant setbacks — front, side and rear; • boundary walls and fences; • orientation and address of buildings; • location and dimensions of driveways and garages and design strategies to reduce their visual and physical impact on the streetscape; • retention of views and vistas to and from the new development, across townscape or landscape; • retention of natural features of significance; • retention of significant archaeological remains; • quality of spaces created between existing and new.		
05. Materials and colours Annotate drawings, photographs of model or photomontages to describe the relationship between the proposed new development and the context, in terms of the following design criteria: • response to predominant materials, textures and colour palette—harmonious, complementary, contrasting; • commensurate quality of new materials; • qualities of light and shadow; • hierarchy of material use (for example, solid masonry base and lightweight upper levels); • relationship between skeleton or structure and skin.		
06. Detailing Annotate drawings, photographs of model or photomontages to describe the relationship between the proposed new development and the context, in terms of the following design criteria: • response to distinctive details of neighbouring existing buildings—reinterpretation in contemporary materials, contrast; • relationship of new fences, garden walls, planting and landscape elements to important existing details; • unobtrusive design of new service elements, such as solar panels and water tanks.		

Reading

45

NSW (Australia) Heritage Office

New Uses for Heritage Places: Guidelines for the Adaptation of Historic Buildings and Sites (2008)

The NSW Heritage Office (now the NSW Heritage Council within the Government's Department of Planning) published New Uses for Heritage Places *as a set of guidelines for adaptive reuse of heritage places, similar in intent to* Design in Context (2005)*, which this publication sought to complement. As Frank Sartor, New South Wales minister for planning, explained in the foreword, "Heritage buildings need to be used, [but] once a building's function becomes redundant, adapting it to a new use provides for its future." These guidelines, illustrated with examples from salient case studies, provided practical advice for architects and other stakeholders about how to achieve high-quality results that were both architecturally creative and sensitive to the cultural significance of the heritage place.*

Introduction

The best way to conserve a heritage building, structure or site is to use it. Adaptation or adaptive reuse offers new uses for old places. The new use needs to be compatible with the building, retain its historic character and conserve significant fabric, but it can still introduce new services, as well as modifications and additions.

Each generation contributes to the constantly evolving historic environment in its own way. Architects, building designers and developers are crucial to the outcome of such change. They have a responsibility to future generations to ensure that their contributions enrich, rather than diminish, the environment. They need to understand the significance of a place and respond to it. Heritage items are a response to their cultural, social, historical, political, economic and physical environments. Adaptation

From NSW (Australia) Heritage Office, *New Uses for Heritage Places: Guidelines for the Adaptation of Historic Buildings and Sites* (Sydney: Heritage Office, 2008), 4, 10–14, 17–18. Reproduced courtesy of Heritage Division, NSW Office of Environment and Heritage for the Heritage Council of NSW.

projects link the past to the present and project into the future. This provides both a challenge and an opportunity for professional design teams to demonstrate their skills and creativity.

Adaptation usually requires some element of new work, but this work should be informed by an understanding and analysis of a heritage building's significance, its character and quality. It should result in a design which creates a relationship between the existing and the new work, its neighbours and its setting.

As with infill development, adaptation can accommodate a rich variety of interpretation and expression. Some designers may adopt a more traditional or vernacular approach; others may wish to explore a highly contemporary solution. Both are valid. It is the quality of the response that is the key and the relationship between the old and the new—a respect for the old and the inspiration it provides for the new work.

Heritage-Led Urban Regeneration

[. . .]

The key to heritage-led regeneration is understanding the heritage significance of the place, and how the different features of the site contribute to its significance. [. . .]

Specialist knowledge can contribute to the success of heritage-led regeneration projects at every stage: during the initial planning and assessment, master or concept planning stages; and the construction and completion phases of the project. The potential to conserve, provide long-term sustainable uses, and interpret the heritage values of the place can be integrated into the project, thereby increasing the potential for long-term benefits.

Engaging appropriate professional advice from the outset, and consulting the local council [. . .] early will help develop a common understanding about what is considered appropriate. Engaging with the local community early in the project will avoid resistance to the project at a later stage and can provide fruitful local support and partnerships, as well as contribute vital information to the interpretation of the place.

Principles for the Adaptation of Historic Buildings and Sites to New Uses

[. . .]

Adaptation does not mean imitation or following inflexible rules. A wide range of solutions to a design problem may emerge after careful analysis and sympathetic interpretation.

The owner of the item and the statutory authorities may need to adopt a flexible approach to planning to retain the significance of the heritage item. [. . .]

Large projects that involve major development of a heritage place need to demonstrate that the change of use, and associated work, provides long-term sustainability for the heritage place. It should not be a one-off project that makes the place vulnerable to uncertainty and ongoing change. Legally-binding management mechanisms that secure the future maintenance and care of the place (such as a heritage agreement) may be required as part of the project.

To achieve a successful adaptation, new work must be appropriate and accord with the following seven principles:

1. *Understand the Significance of the Place*

Understanding what is important about a place is the first stage of any project. The analysis of the heritage values and the fabric should result in a clear statement of heritage significance, and identify significant fabric.

2. *Find a Use Which Is Appropriate to the Heritage Significance of the Place*

Retain the existing use when it is integral to the heritage significance:

- Retain or re-establish the relationship between the heritage place and its use.
- Continue practices or associations that contribute to the cultural significance of the place.
- Continue public access to heritage places that have historically been accessible to the public.

A new use should be compatible with heritage significance and involve minimal changes to significant fabric, layout and setting.

- Reuse the heritage place and significant elements of the place in the new use in preference to constructing major new additions. Where aspects of the new use would have an unacceptable heritage impact, consider accommodating them in sympathetic modest additions.
- Continue significant associations and meanings in any new use.

Inappropriate uses are those where:

- Extensive changes are required to accommodate the new use, resulting in a loss of heritage significance. In this case, either the functional requirements need to be reduced, or an alternative use must be found.
- Changes of use require major structural upgrading that negatively impacts on heritage significance. Changes of use should be compatible with the structural capabilities of the item.
- Changes of use negatively affect the technical performance and durability of the fabric.
- Changes of use require major new services that impact negatively on the heritage significance of the site.

3. Determine a Level of Change Which Is Appropriate to the Significance of the Place

Minimise impact on significant fabric.

Minimise impact on significant interiors, interior planning (circulation patterns and use of rooms) and decorative schemes and finishes.

- Locate new services and service areas so they do not impact on significant spaces or fabric.

[. . .]

4. Provide for the Change to be Reversed and for the Place's Future Conservation

- Adaptation and development should not prevent the future conservation of a heritage item.
- New additions and adjacent or related new construction should be undertaken in such a way that, if they are removed in the future, the essential form and integrity of the historic place is unimpaired.
- Non-reversible changes to a heritage place will only be considered when there is no alternative way of retaining the place as a viable asset.
- Existing fabric, use, associations and meanings should be recorded and archived before changes are made. [. . .]

5. Conserve the Relationship between the Setting and Preserve Significant Views to and from the Heritage Place

- Where the relationship between the heritage item and its setting contributes to its significance, this relationship should be preserved. Views that have been identified as contributing to the significance of the place should also be retained.

6. Provide for the Long-Term Management and Viability of the Heritage Place

- Secure ongoing funds to maintain the heritage place in the future as part of the project. The benefits from the project will then offset the change of use.
- Link conservation works and proposed new works together by conditions of approval, a heritage agreement, or other appropriate mechanism, so that the conservation works are integral to the project.
- Prevent fragmentation of the management of the heritage place in large-scale adaptations. Where there is a fragmentation of ownership through lease or sale, a legally binding overarching management framework should be put in place (such as a heritage agreement). This will ensure that the heritage values of the place are appropriately managed.

7. Reveal and Interpret the Heritage Significance of the Place as an Integral and Meaningful Part of the Adaptation Project

Interpretation communicates the history and previous uses of a building to its occupants and visitors and helps to explain how and why the adaptive reuse changes have been made. Retaining historic signs, the layout of internal spaces and the physical evidence of past uses contributes to greater understanding of the significance of the place. [. . .]

Interpretation is a key element of the adaptive reuse process, as it helps people to understand how the new life of the building has added a new chapter to its story, providing a sense of continuity from the past to the present. It adds to the uniqueness of the property, providing appealing selling points in the competitive real estate market. [. . .]

Assessing Adaptation Projects

This section provides information about how statutory bodies assess development applications for adaptation projects, involving a heritage listed item.

Assessors consider a number of issues when appraising development applications. The assessor will check that the development meets the principles for adaptation outlined in these guidelines. Given that most heritage buildings and conservation areas have been listed for their historic and/or aesthetic qualities/aspects (including architectural), design quality is an important part of the assessment process. For this reason, there will be a subjective element to the process. It is important, therefore, to define objectives for assessing development of a heritage item, as these guidelines attempt to do.

Consulting early with statutory approval authorities improves understanding and outcomes. [. . .]

Documentation

Sufficient information needs to be provided with any application for an adaptation project. The checklist that follows will help designers, applicants and assessors decide whether or not the proposal is appropriate. It also lists the documentation required. It encompasses both the qualitative aspects of the design of the new elements of the building, and the quality of their relationship with its significant fabric.

Where a change of use is being considered for a heritage item, a conservation management plan or conservation management strategy should be prepared. This should identify a compatible use and any constraints on a new use. [. . .]

PART A Documents to Be Included	Applicant's Confirmation	Assessor's Comments
Date of submission		
Conservation Management Plan (CMP) or Conservation Management Strategy (CMS) A CMS may be sufficient where no major intervention is proposed or as an interim planning document while a CMP is prepared.		
Statement of Heritage Impact (SOHI) Include a statement of significance for any heritage item, precinct or conservation area affected by the new development Address the *Adaptation Principles* described in the *Guidelines* in graphic and written point form (see Part B of this checklist).		
Drawings Show clearly existing fabric, extent of demolition and/or alterations and additions, including the information below:		
Site plan showing setting, view lines and cones, including adjacent properties (buildings, trees and structures such as fences) 1:200 scale min.		
Landscape plan 1:100 scale		
Floor plans 1:100 scale		
Sections and details 1:100 scale minimum		
Elevations 1:100 scale minimum		
External materials and colours Provide schedule and, where required, a sample board		
Working model 1:200 scale minimum		

PART B **Checklist for inclusion in Heritage Impact Statement: response to adaptation principles**	**Applicant's Confirmation**	**Assessor's Comments**
1. Does the project demonstrate that the significance of the place has been understood? • Is there a CMP or CMS that provides policies for change? • Is the proposal consistent with the CMP/CMS policies?		
2. Is the use appropriate to the identified significance? • Where use is significant, is it retained? • Is the new use compatible with significance—explain how? • Are practices or associations that contribute to the site's significance continued? • Is public access retained where this has been available? • Does the project involve minimal change to significant fabric?		
3. Is the level of change appropriate to the significance of the place? • Is significant fabric appropriately conserved or adapted? • Are any new elements sited appropriately? • Are significant interiors conserved? • Are significant associations and meanings conserved? • Do the proposed works affect the structural or technical performance of the buildings? • If the works have a major impact on the significance of the place, describe the alternative solutions examined.		
4. Does the project allow for the place to be returned at a later time to its former uses or for significant fabric to be conserved? • Are additions sited so that if they are removed at a later date, the essential form would be restored? • Are non-reversible changes proposed to significant fabric—if so, is there no other feasible alternative? • Is adequate recording proposed?		
5. Does the proposal conserve the setting and preserve significant views?		
6. Does the proposal provide for the long-term management and viability of the heritage place? • Are conservation works to the place part of the project? How are they secured as part of the project? • Does the project involve fragmenting the site through subdivision? If so, what mechanisms are proposed that secure overarching management to conserve related aspects of the site?		
7. How does the proposal reveal and interpret the significance of the place in an integrated and meaningful way?		

Reading

46

Rafael Moneo

Remarks on 21 Works (2010)

Rafael Moneo (1937–) is a Spanish architect who was awarded the Pritzker Prize in Architecture (1996) and the Royal Institute of British Architects' Gold Medal (2003). A longtime studio teacher of architecture as well as a design architect, Moneo first achieved international notoriety in 1986 because of his National Museum of Roman Art in Mérida, Spain, whose structural arches were inspired by ancient Roman design. Moneo's designs often relate creatively to their historic context, as was the case in Sevilla, where he designed the Previsión Española Insurance Company building (1982–1987), on which Moneo reflects in this reading, as well as the extension of the City Hall in Murcia (1991–1998), illustrated in the Visual Summary at the end of this part. Besides his architectural work, Moneo's sensitive writings are noteworthy for providing creative insights about designing new architecture in historic contexts.

Previsión Española Insurance Company
Conditions for building in a historic city: a discussion of the notion of character, Seville, Spain, 1982–1987

One of the most pressing concerns for architects who, like me, graduated in the early 1960s was the question of how to build in historic cities, how to proceed in places where the *preesistenze ambientali* abounded. And I deliberately use the Italian term, since it was unquestionably in Italy where the problem emerged with greatest clarity. The issue became a priority in that country because of the wealth of Italy's heritage and the emphasis that leading architectural theorists were placing on history at the time. As they saw it, the modern movement had not succeeded in finding appropriate solutions for interventions in historic cities. In many instances, indiscriminate construc-

From *Rafael Moneo: Remarks on 21 Works,* edited by Laura Martínez de Guereñu (London: Thames & Hudson, 2010), 137, 139–41, 143, 145, 147, 149–50.

tion based on the principles of modern architecture had produced catastrophic results, destroying cohesive urban atmospheres and well-defined architectural spaces.

—∿—

The echoes of this discussion were still alive in the early 1980s, when I designed the Previsión Española Insurance Company Headquarters in Seville. With these thoughts in mind, I conceived it as a work of architecture capable of fitting into the historic city, moving beyond strictly stylistic criteria and exploring the underlying formal matrixes that could be perceived in the urban environment. I believed that understanding the formal principles that inspire the architecture of a city such as Seville was the key to building within it. The vision of the city seen as a whole prevailed over a vision confined to one single context, since only considering a specific area always implies the risk of becoming trapped by its constraints, subjected to the mimesis of its stylistic features. This was the spirit that drove the project.

[. . .]

Like many great metropolises, Seville enjoys the richness that comes from the accumulation of layers over time, although its appearance today has little to do with what it was in the past. The city has an extensive historic quarter that has preserved much of the layout from the time of Muslim rule, but this district now includes a large number of interventions that were made either to improve the streets or to incorporate new urban areas. [. . .]

The site where the Previsión Española headquarters was to be built was on the edge of the old city, in a neighborhood surrounding the former mint, the Casa de la Moneda, an area bounded by streets that follow the alignments of the old city walls (figure 1). It was split in two, since the city plan foresaw a connection between the Constitución Avenue from the Pasco de Colón by means of a street designed in the nineteenth century, a solution that implied doing away with the remains of the Casa de la Moneda. Vestiges of the medieval city walls remained on the site, as the buildings that had been constructed on it had not concealed their layout. The plan of the site also allowed for preserving the remains of the ramparts that led to the Torre de la Plata, as well as the neatly arranged orthogonal space that surrounded this tower (figure 2).

The first decision in the project was to merge the two sites proposed in the city plan into one, a decision that led to introducing two passages, one on the far northeast end of the site, along Almirante Lobo Street, and another along what had historically been the passage that connected the Torre del Oro, a military watchtower, with the city walls. In fact, the significance of the project lies in the way in which the new building succeeded in consolidating the alignments of the old city walls and in stressing the importance that these ramparts had in giving form to the city. The new building closed and completed the existing block in a way that accepted its alignments, revealed what had been the layout of the city walls, and gave access from the passages to the stretch of rampart that is now hidden by the buildings that mask the Torre de la Plata (figure 3). In this way, Previsión Española has become the building that once again defines the perimeter of the old city, as the ramparts had done before and the road circumnavigat-

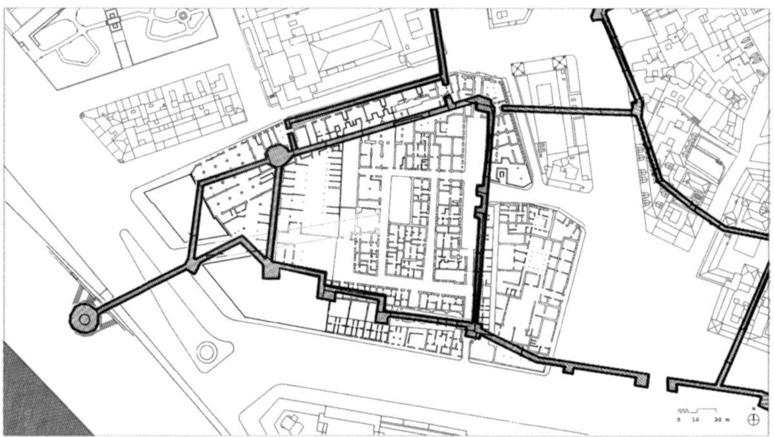

Fig. 1. Plan of Seville in the sixteenth century with the superimposed outline of Previsión Española.

Fig. 2. Plan of initial site conditions with the proposed connection to the city.

Fig. 3. Site plan with ground floor plan of Previsión Española, Torre del Oro, and Torre de la Plata.

ing the old city manages to do today. Therefore, Previsión Española should be viewed as a work of architecture that respects its context yet, above all, helps consolidate the city's structure, defining the perimeter of what once had been the old city.

[. . .]

The horizontal condition is at the origin of the building's organization and configuration. As can be seen in some palaces of Seville, Previsión Española makes a tripartite horizontal structure—plinth, piano nobile, and upper floor—the identifying feature of its architecture. As in many other cases, the main entrance becomes a key element in the facade. It is a facade that unfolds, that can be virtually extended, yet it was endowed with a unique, unexpected character by the way in which its two flanks come together, strengthening and emphasizing the corner where the main entrance is placed. This corner is conceived as a gentle break where the walls, the facades, are entrusted with what this architecture wants to be: a building faithful to the underlying formal matrixes that are the basis of the city's architectural character. This corner also anticipates—and, in a sense, resolves—the character of the building's interior spaces, as a void is created behind it that acts as the keystone articulating the two flanks produced by the alignments. The corner serves as the starting point of a series of facades whose texture was treated with the utmost care.

[. . .]

This meticulous combination of different materials on the facade was crucial for making the new construction fit into the city's architectural heritage without exaggeration, without overstating its presence. Instead of pursuing a mimetic approach, we strove to go along with what we considered to be the city's most unique feature: the special attention given to the small scale through the elements used in its architecture. This is why the textures and patterns in the surfaces are so important in Previsión Española. The patterns are defined by many different components, which does not prevent their integration into the building and ultimately into the city as a whole. The stratification of the facade enables it to include a range of very diverse materials while highlighting the distinct character of each of the floors according to their respective uses: reception and customer service on the ground floor, management on the piano nobile, and offices and administration on the upper floors.

Craftsmanship is very much alive in the architecture of this structure, and I made the choice to incorporate it with full understanding of the difficulties involved in going against current trends. I was well aware of the decline of the crafts tradition in the last quarter of the twentieth century; it was actually considered an anachronism by some. My choice was a deliberate gesture. Working traditional craftsmanship into the project was precisely the way in which I believed that the building could merge into the architecture of the historic city without causing a controversy, avoiding disturbing contrasts. Therefore, Previsión Española should be viewed taking into account the value of all its different elements, designed as if they were formally self-sufficient. It should be perceived as a composite building, the result of taking on highly diverse elements one by one, independently, each endowed with its own intrinsic value.

[. . .]

Accepting the diversity of elements and materials is a way of approaching Previsión Española that is contrary to the uniform or monolithic nature so prevalent in the architecture of today. This attitude leads immediately to considering the meaning that the term "realism" can have in architecture when it is associated with the practice of rational construction. Clearly a monolithic approach contributes to conceiving a built object in a way that strengthens its abstract nature, and therefore, in those projects where the urge to emphasize the underlying abstract principles prevails, architects tend to focus on using one single material. According to the opposite view, the built object has the ability to absorb and integrate different materials and elements, and given how rarely this approach is pursued, the result can be quite bold. I chose this path for Previsión Española because diverse materials and elements have characterized Seville's architecture since the seventeenth century. The idea was to explore the less obvious and somewhat forgotten formal structures and matrixes, confronting at the same time the stylistic simplification of the historic legacy of the surrounding architecture that we were trying to honor. The careful use of textures and craftsmanship created affinity with other less obvious architectures. This was the attitude at the origin of an architecture that strove to fit into an environment where historic architecture prevails.

Other architectural principles were equally important, such as respecting the existing alignments, as one can clearly see in the floor plans. In fact, the floor plans were laid out following the alignments; in other words, paying homage to the city itself. Thus the project's conception relies on the interpretation of the city's growth process. [. . .]

This attempt to build the city with a work of architecture that finds its place within the whole may be the product of a certain idealism. However, if the historic cities that make up our heritage deserve to be preserved, it is difficult for the architect to disregard an overall vision of the city. Understanding the city, recognizing that any urban intervention involves accepting some hypothesis about what its growth was like and about how one must proceed so as to preserve the character of the existing architecture is something that I still believe to be valid today. The Previsión Española project has proven its ability to integrate itself with a city like Seville. The building has been kept intact, just as it was constructed and the craft techniques have given the expected results. However, under a new owner, a change of the name on the facade using a different typography—substituting Helvetia for Previsión Española—has not been resolved with the precision and attention that I would have liked. The case of Previsión Española reveals that the inevitable and continuous changes of ownership that are common today cannot be easily absorbed by works of architecture in which the importance of signage is quite apparent.

Part V

Visual Summary: The Search for Contextual Continuities

A street in Aibar, Navarra, Spain, from Bernard Rudofsky, *Architecture Without Architects*, 1965.

Bernard Rudofsky's seminal exhibition, *Architecture without Architects*, at New York's Museum of Modern Art in 1964 was a testament to the beauty and variety of global vernacular architecture. A wealth of images exemplified the ingenuity and inventiveness of anonymous builders. The exhibition (and Rudofsky's book, published soon thereafter) provided some of the last glimpses of traditional historic places that, more than half a century later, have either disappeared or been dwarfed by radical urban transformations induced by a mistaken notion of progress.

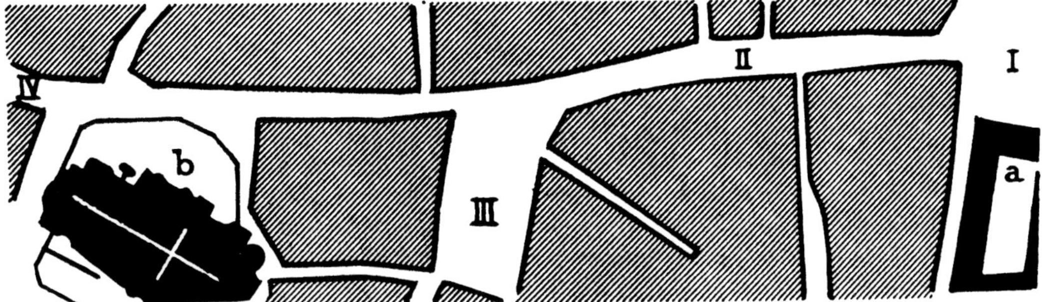

Plan of Bruges, Belgium, circa 1918. I. Grand'Place – II. Rue des Pierres – III. Place Stevin – IV. Rue du Sablon – a. Market halls – b. Cathedral of Saint-Sauveur.

Brügge, Rue des Pierres, circa 1902. Drawing by F. Puetzer. First published in Camillo Sitte, *L'Art de batir les villes: Notes et réflexions d'un architecte*, 1902, 1918.

PLATES V.1 AND V.2

When Camillo Sitte embarked on his study of principles that might assist his late nineteenth-century contemporaries to design aesthetically pleasing cities, he traveled through Europe to observe how public spaces, streets, plazas, churches, and fountains traditionally had been integrated to form a coherent whole. Using a sketchbook, he often employed two architectural conventions in depicting and interpreting the form and details of streetscapes and other urban spaces: figure-ground plans, variants of Giambattista Nolli's drawings of Rome in the 1740s (see part IV, opening image); and perspective views. These two drawings of Bruges, Belgium, demonstrate the way in which Sitte used black-and-white sketches to convey his ideas about urban space and city planning according to artistic principles.

The village of Roccatamburo in Poggiodomo, Valnerina, Umbria Region, Italy, 1974. Photo by Italo Insolera.

Pizzoferrato, Abruzzo Region, Italy, 1958. Photo by Italo Insolera.

PLATES V.3 AND V.4

These photographs of vernacular Italian settlements celebrate some of the ordinary and often-overlooked components of the traditional city fabric. They also illustrate the Charter of Restoration 1972's "Instructions on the Preservation of Historic Urban Areas," which states that "restoration . . . extends to material conservation of the characteristics of the entire . . . urban organism" (reading 41). That entirety includes, as shown here, stone paving, external masonry stairs, tiled roofs, and bending alleyways that open into small, accidental piazzas created incrementally over time.

PLATE V.5

Roberta Brandes Gratz and Norman Mintz (reading 42) distinguish between project planning and urban husbandry, arguing in favor of the latter. They assert that urban husbandry "considers existing life first, respects it, views it as an asset, not a problem, and determines with local users what remedies could improve things." In two of their simple, Sitte-esque drawings (right), they depict how an ordinary parking lot might be redesigned as a place that residents can use for other functions. It is a "project of modest scale that repairs and adds but doesn't overwhelm."

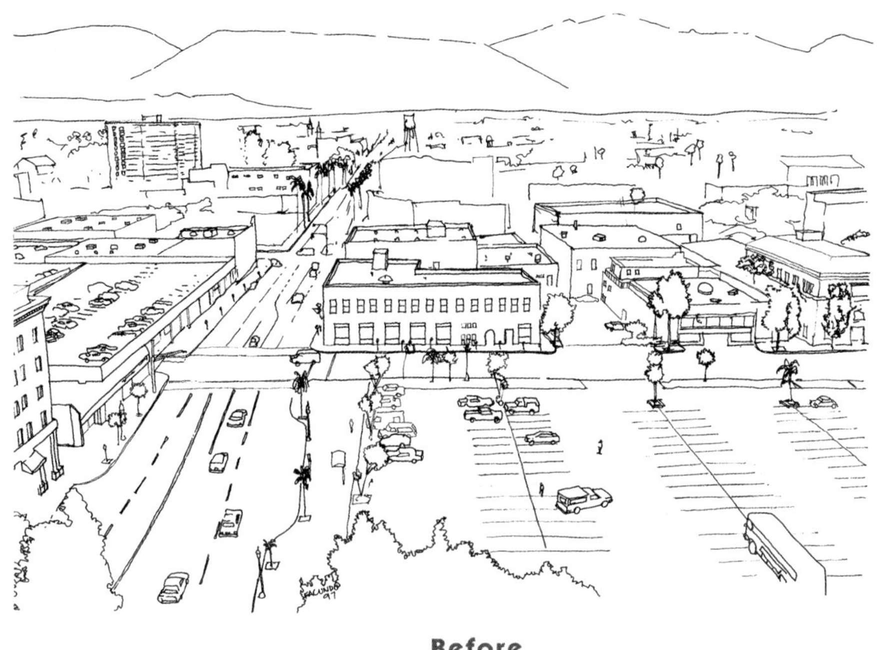

Before

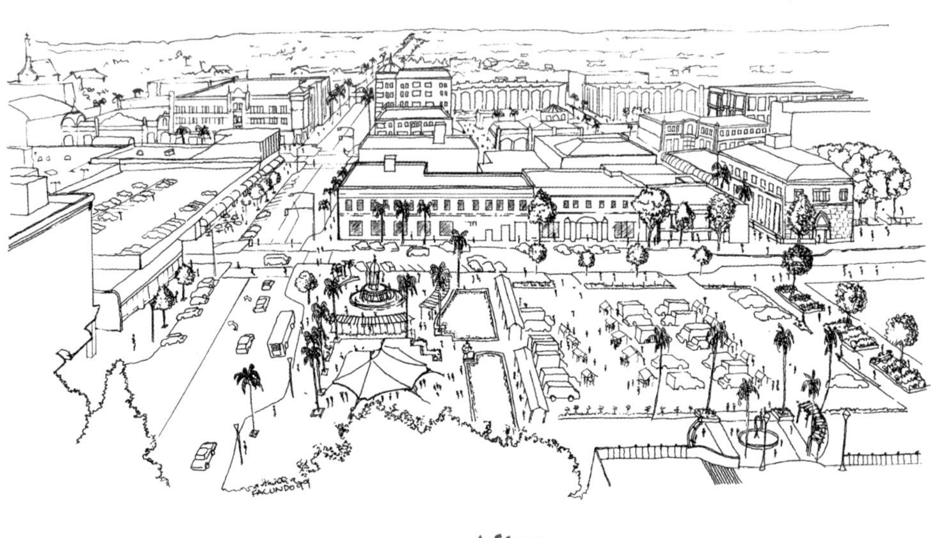

After

Returning a center to San Bernadino: from parking lot to place.

Transforming a parking lot into a vibrant civic space in San Bernardino, California.

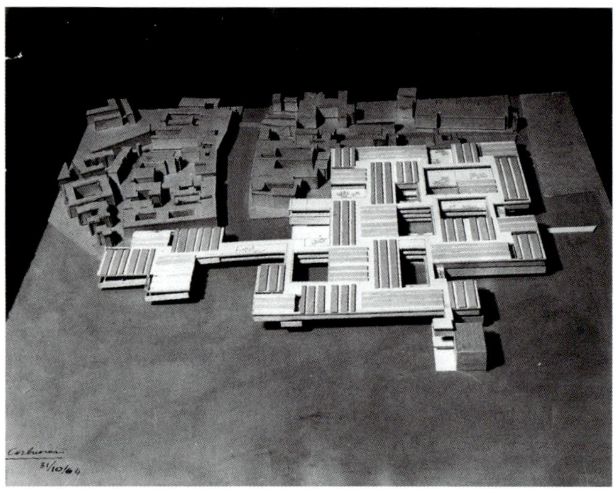

Design model for a hospital in Venice (1964), Le Corbusier, architect.

Sharp Center for Design, Toronto, Canada (1921, 1956–62, 2004). Photo by Richard Johnson.

PLATES V.6 AND V.7 (ABOVE)

The infill guidelines drafted by heritage planners in New South Wales are predicated on the assumption that "our greatest buildings are those that respond positively to their cultural and physical environment." If true, then how to respond when introducing a new building to an existing context? "New design," according to the NSW Heritage Office (reading 44), "should respond to the historic context through an understanding and informed analysis of its character and quality. This includes its grain, recurring patterns, important views, scale, materials and building methods." These two examples reflect opposite approaches: one stems from an informed analysis; the other thumbs its nose at the existing physical context. Le Corbusier's 1964 design for a hospital in Venice (never realized) reflects a mature approach to designing in a historic context, very different from the radical urban transformation he had proposed earlier in the Plan Voisin (1922–25) (see p. 200). Instead of the bold, iconic landmark one might have expected, Le Corbusier proposed a low-rise structure on pilotis that integrates seamlessly into Venice's unique city fabric. Conversely, the Toronto intervention negates the existing environment in favor of brazen architectural hubris. It would not meet the standards of quality advocated by New South Wales planners.

PLATES V.8, V.9, AND V.10 (RIGHT)

The NSW guidelines suggest that "adaptation . . . should result in a design which creates a relationship between the existing and the new work, its neighbors and its setting" (reading 45). The Stony Island Arts Bank—inspired by the vision, actions, wisdom, and community engagement of Theaster Gates—meets this test by transforming a Beaux-Arts bank structure on Chicago's South Side into an arts and African American heritage center in an impoverished neighborhood. Inspired by Samuel Mockbee's Rural Studio (Alabama) and Rick Lowe's Project Row House (Texas), Gates created the Rebuild Foundation, aimed at rebuilding the cultural foundation of underinvested neighborhoods. The initiative resulted in a series of adaptive reuse projects under the name "Dorchester Projects" that empathize with the nature and character of their settings. A contrasting example—in the form of facadism—is seen in the Altolusso (High Luxury) Apartments: a late nineteenth-century building was demolished, with the exception of a facade that served as the veneer for high-rise towers. Although widely discredited in the conservation field, this approach was quite popular in the 1980s. But even today, the so-called facadomies continue to be carried out, thus creating new and improbable contextual relationships fraught with cosmetic kitsch and totally alienated from their settings.

Stony Island Arts Bank, Chicago. Photo by Tom Harris.

The library of the Stony Island Arts Bank, Chicago. Photo by A.J. LaTrace.

Altolusso Apartments, Cardiff, Wales (1890s facade of college retained, 2005 facadism).

Part V

VISUAL SUMMARY

City Hall Extension, Murcia, Spain, 1991–98. Photo by Michael Moran.

Ait Ben Haddou, Morocco. Photo © Getty Conservation Institute, 2011.

PLATES V.11 AND V.12

In determining how to build in historic cities, Rafael Moneo (reading 46) avoids "strictly stylistic criteria" and explores instead "the underlying formal matrixes . . . perceived in the urban environment." A case in point is the design for an addition to Murcia's historic city hall, where Moneo first sought to understand "the square's volumetrics" and then conceived his addition as a counterpoint with a strongly independent identity. Moneo wanted the facade to face the cathedral head-on. The settlement of Ait Ben Haddou, Morocco, on the other hand, reflects a less contrast-driven approach to new design within historic environments; there the living tradition of building with earthen materials has continued to inspire new builders to add the new to the old in a seamless connection with the past.

SWEETY HOME

Part VI

The Search for Significant Values

In the waning years of the twentieth century, a seismic shift occurred in the conservation field globally as practitioners began employing (and scholars began studying) "values-based" approaches both to understand "significance" and to meet the increasingly complex array of challenges associated with heritage conservation.[1] The adoption of the Burra Charter by Australia ICOMOS in 1979—a result of a review centering on how the Venice Charter (1966) related to Australian practice—marked a milestone in ongoing debates about what constitutes heritage, why a place is significant, and how values (or meanings, perceptions, qualities, etc.) that people attach to places relate to their significance.[2] As the conceptual and practical dimensions of what constitutes "heritage" have expanded in the past forty years, some abstract concepts related to the widening scope of heritage (and the evolution of "World Heritage") have increasingly been questioned: authenticity, integrity, tangible/intangible heritage, community, outstanding universal value, and cultural landscapes, to name some of the most problematic. As one of the authors in this part, Gustavo Araoz, expressed this trend, "In the 1990s the adoption of new heritage categories . . . provoked an intense global discussion on the meaning of authenticity, . . . which opened the way to the attribution of cultural values to both material fabric and immaterial characteristics in a site, [and has] led . . . to extensive explorations into the domain of safeguarding the intangible aspects of built heritage."[3] In 1994, the Nara Document on Authenticity was another catalyst for "intense global discussion," as was the adoption by UNESCO in 2003 of the Convention for the Safeguarding of the Intangible Cultural Heritage. The implications of these discussions have already been far-reaching in terms of practice and pedagogy: "critical heritage studies," "critical conservation," and charges of elitism by what has been called an authorized heritage discourse suggest ongoing tensions and questions about what constitutes heritage, who lays claim to it, and thus who should be involved in its conservation.[4] As two analysts have recently observed, "To operate effectively in the thoroughly politicized global society of the last 50 years, . . . conservation profession-

Sule Pagoda, central Yangon, Myanmar, 2013. Detail. See p. 463.

als have been challenged to broaden their perspective, engage new partners, reframe inherited theories, and engage with political, economic, and cultural dynamics of the society-writ-large as part of the problem of conservation."[5]

As dynamic, socially charged places, cities figure prominently in what we call here the search for significant values. Our initial focus is on three readings that frame the broader-based historical, theoretical, and (at times) World Heritage contexts in which this search has arisen and persisted. After thus setting the stage, the six other readings cohere around one of four key concepts that stem from the "search for values" and pervade effective, contemporary urban conservation practices. These concepts are intangible heritage, authenticity, social value (including community participation), and the safeguarding of traditional building practices. Our intention, therefore, is to highlight insightful ways in which often abstract concepts (not always clearly translated into other cultures and languages) can be better understood by referring to actual practices, in this case largely from Asia and Africa but with global implications.

The first of the three introductory readings is from Jean-Louis Luxen (reading 47), a former secretary general of ICOMOS (1993–2002), who delivered a commentary on the intangible dimension of monuments and sites at ICOMOS's 14th General Assembly (2003). His remarks help to probe one of the provocative concepts—intangible heritage—that continues to be debated in the context of its supposed opposite, tangible heritage. (Recall here that, in Part IV, Janet Pillai points out how intertwined the two concepts are in the context of cultural mapping.) Luxen calls the distinction between tangible and intangible heritage "artificial," and as one way out of the confusion, he proposes two "complementary approaches: one, seeking to reveal the intangible dimension of a physical construction; [and another] seeking to incarnate an intangible form of heritage in a material object." The two readings that follow, from Gustavo Araoz (secretary general of ICOMOS, 2009–17) (reading 48) and from John Pendlebury, Michael Short, and Aidan While (reading 49) (U.K. professors), were written approximately five years after Luxen's commentary. Araoz asserts that because of "the ongoing debate on intangibility . . . heritage conservation in and of historic cities [has] faced new challenges [that] spring from two unrelated trends, . . . a conceptual shift in the perception of the nature of heritage places; and . . . the accelerating demographic pressure to increase urban density." He also reflects on the important shift that resulted from applying the "cultural landscapes" concept to cities, exemplified by the Vienna Memorandum on World Heritage and Contemporary Architecture of 2005, in which the term "historic urban landscapes" superseded "historic towns." Pendlebury, Short, and While also discuss urban World Heritage sites—while also referring to many more cities not branded by "World Heritage"—as they emphasize that it is "problematic" to "translate core concepts such as 'authenticity' to the urban spatial scale." They explain how changing approaches to urban conservation challenges can be recognized in analyzing memoranda, declarations, or charters drafted by international "experts." (See the appendix for key international conventions, recommendations, and charters.) Finally, Pendlebury, Short, and While raise crucial questions about the thorny concept of authenticity, especially when linked to another complex term linked to World Heritage listing, "outstanding universal value" (OUV).[6]

Reading 50, from Bernard M. Feilden and Jukka Jokilehto's 1998 ICCROM publication, not only scrutinizes the notion of authenticity applied to the tangible heritage (which they see in terms of materials, workmanship, design, and setting) but also provides a useful template that poses questions about the evidence attesting to the authenticity of a resource (or city), the aim of a proposed treatment, and how implementation might occur. They caution, however, that "while aspects are presented separately, care should be taken to guarantee a balanced judgement in treatments in order to maintain the authenticity as well as the historic character and significance of the heritage resource." Authenticity is also a main concern of Michael Turner and Tal Tomer (reading 51), specifically, as it refers to community values and interpretations, even as they emphasize how "loosely defined" the term "community" remains. In particular, they advocate an inclusive notion of urban heritage, not belonging exclusively to those who have "created" it, but also to the communities that over time have settled in the same city and have given a different interpretation and a new dimension to historic places. The importance of accepting the "other" is not seen as a way to dilute or make irrelevant the authenticity and integrity of a place, but, on the contrary, as a way to give it additional and unexpected dimensions. The values of a place, as they explain, are often negotiated over time by different "neighbors." This is a healthy process that, rather than leading to an aggressive affirmation of identities, can highlight a wider spectrum of values and memories in a conservation setting. Ultimately, a sustained participatory debate is necessary to harmonize "particularistic ideas in a universal context" through mutual understanding and respect.

A compelling cluster of four readings follows. These works by less well known authors were selected not only because they exemplify provocative searches for "significant values" and try to relate abstract concepts of heritage to practical realities but also because their terrain for scrutiny falls outside a Eurocentric norm: Accra (Ghana), Djenne (Mali), and Shanghai and southern Guangdong (China). In Senam Okudzeto's analysis of Accra's drastic transformations (reading 52), we confront a proliferation of dubious and largely artificial new values imposed (as slogans) by the ruling elite. The result—overwrought kitsch—is indicative of many public "beautification" projects throughout Africa. Put starkly, these kinds of projects often grease the wheels of corruption and give a false sense of national unity and strength, often mimicking superficial, "Western-style" developments, all at the expense of established residents who see their familiar places obliterated and radically transformed. Okudzeto also takes issue with the slippery term "heritage": "since it is a mutable concept, [it is] vulnerable to abuse in the context of nationalist polemics." She eschews trite labels and instead emphasizes a point that is often obscure to casual observers of Accra—that "social, traditional and historic uses of space are encoded in buildings. Although built in brick, an essentially Danish vernacular, the social division of space in the homes is distinctly African, whereby each home has a 'male' and 'female' quarter and the remains of earlier ancestors remain interred within the compound of the home." She proposes that conservation should help create "a radical public history," whereby not only physical structures would be rehabilitated and protected, but "the communities that have grown along with the structures [would be] supported and maintained."

The disconnect between "communities" and "buildings" is also at the heart of the anthropological analysis in reading 53 by Non Arkaraprasertkul and Matthew Williams of Shanghai's traditional *lilong* (neighborhood lanes) housing, which until the early 1990s represented a majority of this megacity's residential building stock. However, in the past twenty years most of this urban fabric has been eradicated, with local residents "giving up their space for the privileged classes as a pragmatic way to sustain their life," albeit often with great challenges, in high-rise flats far from their cherished neighborhoods. As they correctly note, "Historic laneways live through the interactions of their residents, the people who embody the stories of their district and their city." Inadvertently echoing Okudzeto's points about Accra, Arkaraprasertkul and Williams assert that the community's "presence and history cannot be replaced by newly polished facades and kitsch advertising campaigns which ironically romanticize a past rendered all but sterile by forcing out its most essential ingredient—the people who embody the history of the laneway houses themselves." They then urge "community preservation" as opposed to "historic preservation" and suggest "methods of group preservation." In their conclusion they stress that "destroying heritage destroys memory, community and a sense of place."

If memory is destroyed, can it ever be reinvigorated? This is one of the cardinal questions of Carmen C. M. Tsui's analysis of the city of Huizhou (Guangdong), China (reading 54). She explores the methods psychologists use when they work with patients suffering from amnesia, and she attempts to derive methods for providing "memory cues" in the dramatically transformed environments of this little-known historic settlement. First, however, she searches for the significant values of the place, finding in her interviews with residents genuine reverence for places in the city reminiscent of Song dynasty landscape paintings and other distinctive scenes that were historically linked to the city and its geomantically derived setting. As Tsui explains, "The Chinese . . . extracted and highlighted the distinctiveness of the landscape, place and scenes by using text. From the tangible memory cues (landscape and place) we can devise those intangible ones (scenes and text), which are deeply processed and encoded in the people's collective memory of Guangdong cities." She suggests that the "intangible memory cues help us to recreate the physical environment that once stored the collective memory of the people."

Linking ephemeral memory to mutable place is also central to Trevor H. J. Marchand's analysis, focusing on Djenne in Mali and San'a' in Yemen, of how and why traditional building practices are protected and transmitted (reading 55). He excoriates a "museological view of culture as property," asserting that "cultures are effectively reduced to, and constrained by, a positivist discourse that reconfigures cultural resources as classifiable and quantifiable objects." Instead, he emphasizes process over product: "process is constituted by skilled performance and expert knowledge, both of which give rise to the production and reproduction of material entities." Marchand is primarily interested in knowledge, which he views as the "primary interest for the field of conservation." He recognizes the immense importance of objects, of course, but seeks "to compel recognition of the factor that bestows those objects with importance in the first place: human thought, and the knowledge it yields." In a plea that echoes several readings in this part, Marchand passionately argues that "we must look to the people —the producers and users who, through their engagement in production and use, effectively generate knowledge about artifacts, architecture, and landscapes."

The overlapping conservation concerns about safeguarding the city as physical object while not destroying the city as memory reservoir pose striking challenges in whatever cultural context we seek to understand and protect. The readings in Part VI do not provide easily digestible recipes for how, precisely, to navigate through the shoals of corrupt politics, superficial place-making, rising or falling urban densities, and myriad other factors that mitigate against easy solutions for the conservation of historic urban landscapes. (Questions, and some answers, regarding economics, sustainability, governance and management in historic cities are broached in parts VII and VIII.) Here the focus is on the implications for urban conservation of the remarkable widening of what constitutes "heritage" in the early twenty-first century. Intangible, authentic, significant, values-based, museological, memorable: despite the confusion these English words engender—often sparking multiple connotations and frequent confusion, especially when translated into other languages—they provide thoughtful practitioners with helpful conceptual guides about what to heed in the quest for effective, community-focused, and socially valuable conservation. The broad conceptual scope represented by the nine authors in this part mirrors the equally broad spectrum of issues that practitioners must confront in the search for significant urban values.

Notes

1. The Getty Conservation Institute has been instrumental in probing the depths of these challenges where "values-based" approaches are concerned. See Erica Avrami and Randall Mason, eds., *Values and Heritage Conservation: Research Report* (2000); Marta de la Torre, ed., *Assessing the Values of Cultural Heritage: Research Report* (2002); Marta de la Torre, ed., *Heritage Values in Site Management: Four Case Studies* (2005); and *Symposium on Values in Heritage Management: Emerging Approaches and Research Directions* (forthcoming).
2. For a brief history of the Burra Charter, which was last revised in 2013, see Meredith Walker, "The Development of the Australia ICOMOS Burra Charter," *APT Bulletin* 45, no. 2–3 (2014): 9–18.
3. Gustavo Araoz, "World-Heritage Historic Urban Landscapes," *APT Bulletin* 39, no. 2–3 (2008): 33.
4. See, e.g., Laurajane Smith, *The Uses of Heritage* (London: Routledge, 2006).
5. Erica Avrami and Randall Mason, "Mapping the Issues of Values," unpublished paper delivered at the GCI-sponsored Symposium on Values in Heritage Management, February 2017, 2.
6. Since the publication of Pendlebury, Short, and While's article, and especially after ICOMOS adopted "historic urban landscapes" as an operative concept in 2011, there have been many attempts to translate this three-word concept (sometimes referred to as HUL) into the "more robust mechanism" that the authors hoped for. Ron Van Oers, formerly of the World Heritage Centre and one of the most ardent proponents of the HUL approach, was a crucial human catalyst in this regard, working with cities such as Hangzhou (China), Rawalpindi (Pakistan), and Ballarat (Australia) before his tragic death in 2015.

Reading
47

Jean-Louis Luxen

The Intangible Dimension of Monuments and Sites with Reference to the UNESCO World Heritage List (2001)

Jean-Louis Luxen, an eminent conservation practitioner, lawyer, and university educator from Belgium, served as secretary general of ICOMOS from 1993 to 2002 and has written extensively about the relationship between heritage conservation and economic development, as well as the synergies between tangible and intangible heritage. In the reading below, he focuses on the dynamic tension between tangibility and intangibility with reference to sites inscribed on the World Heritage List.

Context

Over the past thirty years, the concept of cultural heritage has been continually broadened. The *Venice Charter* made reference to "monuments and sites" and dealt with architectural heritage. The question rapidly expanded to cover groups of buildings, vernacular architecture, industrial or 20th-century built heritage. Over and above the study of historic gardens, the concept of cultural landscape highlighted the interpenetration of culture and nature. Today an anthropological approach to heritage leads us to consider it as a social ensemble of many different, complex and interdependent manifestations, reflecting the culture of a human community. Conservation represents an insistence on harmony over time between a social group and its environment, whether natural or man-made, while the protection of this lifestyle is perceived as a major aspect of sustainable human development.

Recently the question of authenticity has attracted our particular attention. The diversity of heritage categories, the building materials used and the methods of construction or adaptation have led to the establishment of variable standards of authentic conservation. At the same time, it was also necessary to take into account differing

From Jean-Louis Luxen, "The Intangible Dimension of Monuments and Sites with Reference to the UNESCO World Heritage List," in *Authenticity and Integrity in an African Context: Expert Meeting, Great Zimbabwe, Zimbabwe, 26–29 May 2000*, edited by Galia Saouma-Forero (Paris: UNESCO, 2001), 25–29. Reproduced courtesy of UNESCO.

interpretations, in the light of different cultural traditions, of the very concept of authenticity itself. The *Nara Document* introduces a form of compensation for a certain relativism of concepts by the universal requirement for explicit reference to the values that a cultural property represents in the eyes of the human community concerned.

These changes have led conservation professionals to go beyond the question of: how to conserve? to more fundamental questions: why conserve? conserve for whom? what is the meaning of conservation? The quest for the message of cultural properties requires us to identify the ethical values, social customs, beliefs or myths of which physical heritage is the sign, the expression, in time and space. Values of authenticity or identity are advanced in order to reveal the significance of architectural or urban constructions and transformation of the natural landscape through human intervention. In the end, the concept or social representation of the cultural property is more important than the object itself: the intangible dimension prevails.

The result is a more comprehensive approach designed to give a better appreciation of the uniqueness of cultural properties, the presiding genius of a cultural group and its roots, against a background of rapid social change and openness to external influences. This approach is based on a lucid awareness and dynamic mobilisation of a community. However, it also carries with it the risk of excessive and even chauvinistic or conflictual affirmation of identity, if it loses sight of universal values and the richness of dialogue between cultures and openness to others.

The distinction between physical heritage and intangible heritage is now seen as artificial. Physical heritage only attains its true significance when it sheds light on its underlying values. Conversely, intangible heritage must be made incarnate in tangible manifestations, in visible signs, if it is to be conserved. This dialectic may prove particularly fruitful in providing greater representation for those cultures of the world which place more importance on the oral tradition than on the written, on folk arts and traditions rather than sophisticated artistic expression. The geo-cultural regions that stand to benefit in particular are Africa and Oceania, whose physical heritage consists of more humble works in perishable materials, a heritage that the monumentalist approach has for too long neglected. Yet the specific contribution made by these cultures represents a significant enrichment of the global heritage catalogue.

A precise definition of cultural properties is nonetheless indispensable as an operational basis for an appropriate conservation policy in all its various dimensions: identification and cataloguing, legal protection, conservation and restoration, management and promotion, public awareness and professional training. Some form of materiality is essential for a significant relationship between intangible heritage and the natural landscape altered, or buildings constructed, by man. [. . .]

Precautions

In any exploration of this intangible dimension of heritage, it is important to remain in touch with our fields of specialisation. We must take care to consider the intangible dimensions in the context of their relationship to physical heritage, i.e. to the monuments and sites that are our field of study and action. It is only on this condition that our contribution to the general debate will be most fruitful. Let us not become distracted by analysis of the various aspects of intangible heritage such as customs and traditions, music, language, poetry and other forms of human expression, fields which lie outside the professional competencies of most of our members.

Techniques and Know-How

The conservation of heritage construction also constitutes a conservatory of specialised construction techniques or traditional technologies, whose ingenuity merits recognition and protection. Such recognition is, indeed, often indispensable in ensuring the survival of many edifices or modifications of the landscape inherited from the past, and whose adaptation to local climatic and economic needs is the product of centuries-old tradition.
[. . .]

Intangible References

Two complementary approaches are recommended: one, seeking to reveal the intangible dimension of a physical construction; the second, seeking to incarnate an intangible form of heritage in a material object.

It is interesting as part of this twofold approach to distinguish from the World Heritage List those physical cultural properties that have acquired an intangible reference from those that have not, however justified it might seem, and those that might be eligible for such a reference. This, based on very distinct references:

Spiritual reference

—~—

Reference to the origins of man

—~—

Political reference

—~—

Social reference

—~—

Explorations and migrations

—~—

Artistic reference

—~—

Gathering-places

—~—

Sacred natural sites

—~—

Limits of the Exercise

At the close of this analysis, it is apparent that progress must be made towards the identification of intangible elements to be associated with physical heritage, in order to bring out the fullest expression of its spiritual, cultural and artistic values. No doubt imagination and creativity will also be required in inventing new procedures, according to the example of the Japanese who have developed an original policy for the protection of "living national treasures," masters possessing the gift of knowledge and major cultural and artistic traditions.

Reading

48

Gustavo F. Araoz

World-Heritage Historic Urban Landscapes: Defining and Protecting Authenticity (2008)

Gustavo Araoz has been extensively involved with heritage conservation, both in the United States and worldwide, as a private practitioner, a university professor, and an institutional leader. He served as executive director of US/ICOMOS from 1995 to 2009, after which he was elected president of ICOMOS. In this reading, he reflects on the historical context in the conservation field of intangible heritage and authenticity, particularly as they have related to urban conservation efforts since the late twentieth century.

[. . .]

In looking at the last 50 years of the heritage-conservation movement, one can detect that during each decade the international preservation community concentrated on unraveling one or two major challenges that, while not to the exclusion of other concerns, marked the period indelibly. Thus, the 1960s could be said to be the decade of building theoretical consensus; the 1970s was the decade of heritage inventories; the 1980s was the decade of site management; and in the 1990s the adoption of new heritage categories, such as cultural landscapes, sacred sites, and vernacular settlements, provoked an intense global discussion on the meaning of authenticity, which became the leitmotif for that decade. The conclusions reached in the 1990s about authenticity, which opened the way to the attribution of cultural values to both material fabric and immaterial characteristics in a site, have led during the current decade to extensive explorations into the domain of safeguarding the intangible aspects of the built heritage.

As part of the ongoing debate on intangibility, and particularly its implications on dynamic-heritage categories such as cultural landscapes, the theory and practice of heritage conservation in and of historic cities have faced new challenges that in essence may be said to spring from two unrelated trends. The first is a conceptual shift in the

From Gustavo F. Araoz, "World-Heritage Historic Urban Landscapes: Defining and Protecting Authenticity," *APT Bulletin: Journal of Preservation Technology* 39, no. 2–3 (2008): 33–36. Reprinted courtesy of the Association for Preservation Technology International.

perception of the nature of heritage places; and the second trend is related to the accelerating demographic pressure to increase urban density. Further propelled by the triumphal emergence of the market economy as the preferred development model and by the transfer of traditional public authority to the private sector as aftershocks of the collapse of socialist models, historic cities are being treated as laboratories where mega-experiments on urban density are being tested.

—∿∿—

The concern of the various professional disciplines of the global heritage community of ICOMOS in dealing with the complex issues of conservation in the face of growth has varied in intensity and level of alarm, but there is basic agreement that the authenticity and integrity of the world's urban heritage is under serious threat.[1] To some that threat includes the paradigmatic shift from "historic town" to "historic urban landscape" proposed by the Vienna Memorandum, which, inter alia, would expand the values inherent in historic urban districts to include its dynamic historic patterns of evolution and change, thereby shifting the objective of conservation from preserving the authenticity of material form to protecting the historical processes and patterns of urbanization.

The appreciation of the dynamic nature of heritage resources in continuing use, and the fact that the process of change can indeed add to their value, or even be one, did not originate in the Vienna Memorandum; it merely focused the spotlight on the challenges posed by it. The traditional materials-based approach and practices of the heritage-conservation field had been challenged earlier by the acceptance and codification into theory of vernacular settlements and cultural landscapes as heritage categories that are dependent not on conservation but on the perpetual renewal of their form according to historically established patterns. Managing the authenticity of such places is an ongoing process that has undergone several stages and will continue to do so into the foreseeable future.

—∿∿—

When contemporary approaches to heritage conservation began to take shape in the early nineteenth century, it was axiomatic that the intangible aesthetic and historic values that were attributed to a place (or to anifacts, in the case of moveable property) lay on the extant material elements. In spite of the broad range of divergent views of the time, exemplified in their most extreme opposition by the work and writings of Viollet-le-Duc and Ruskin, all approaches converged on the materiality of heritage. When Cesare Brandi, recognized throughout Europe as the most influential conservation theorist of the twentieth century, finally reconciled all philosophical oppositions at the middle of the twentieth century, his entire theory of critical conservation continued to rest on the tacit assumption that all values attributed to a place ultimately rested on its material evidence.[2]

—∿∿—

Just when the world seemed to have achieved a perfect theoretical balance that would sustain the appropriate evaluation and protection of the authenticity of heritage place, the application of the World Heritage Convention opened a whole new set of controversial conceptual issues about the nature of heritage and its authenticity.
[. . .]

During the convention's early years, when the universally known, iconic sites were being inscribed, authenticity as being material based went unchallenged, since the individual monuments being nominated were the object of static conservation and the cities inscribed were being controlled by principles derived from the theories of Giovannoni.

The 1980s, however, were a particularly fertile time in the evolution of the field of heritage. New categories of heritage sites, such as cultural landscapes and places of memory, emerged whose conservation defied then-prevailing theories and practices and, more serious yet, seemed to undermine the accepted meaning of authenticity. Issues such as the replacement of ephemeral construction materials, first raised by Japan, defied the principle that authenticity resides exclusively in the original construction materials. It was proposed instead that authenticity rested as much on the intangible ancient traditions of reconstruction and replacement of deteriorating parts as it did on the physical elements. While a perfectly logical concept, this was a major theoretical tectonic movement that almost inadvertently shifted the resting place of values from the material evidence to the intangible (and even unconservable) intellectual construct of ancestral communal memory.

Other new types of heritage categories with intangible carriers of significance for which the test for authenticity proved ambiguous were emerging in the context of the World Heritage Convention.

Notes

1. According to the most recent edition of the World Heritage Operational Guidelines, authenticy in terms of the material evidence refers to the originality of the extant historic fabric as a carrier of values. Integrity refers to the amount of extant authentic historic fabric and its ability to convey the full significance of the place.
2. Cesare Brandi, *Teoria del Restauro* (Torino: G. Einaudi, 1963).

Reading

49

John Pendlebury, Michael Short, and Aidan While

Urban World Heritage Sites and the Problem of Authenticity (2009)

John Pendlebury (Newcastle University) was a town planner involved in urban conservation in the United Kingdom before he began teaching in 1996. Michael Short teaches planning, architecture, and urban design at the Bartlett School for Planning (University College London), and Aidan While teaches urban studies and planning at the University of Sheffield. Their perceptive reflection on the thorny challenges of retaining authenticity in the context of urban World Heritage Sites complements the preceding essay by Araoz. The authors also offer comments on "scientific" principles established by key international documents related to urban conservation in the 1970s and 1980s (e.g., the Amsterdam Declaration, 1975, and the Washington Charter, 1987). They make the important point that the translation of "core concepts such as 'authenticity' to the urban spatial scale remains problematic."

Authenticity, Integrity and Cultural Value at the Urban Scale

[. . .]

As town planning activity extended across the historic city in the post-war period, intensified during the 1960s and re-ordered to a much more conservation-based approach following the rejection of architectural modernism, conservation objectives increasingly had to be articulated at very different scales—at the level of a city, town, village or smaller area within these (see e.g. Larkham, 2003; Pendlebury, 2003). In addition to responses within individual countries, such as the legislation enabling the designation of conservation areas in the UK (the Civic Amenities Act 1967), international bodies began to focus their concern and efforts on conservation at an urban scale. Two important international declarations were made in the mid-1970s; one by the Council of

Reprinted from *Cities*, vol. 26, John Pendlebury, Michael Short, and Aidan While, "Urban World Heritage Sites and the Problem of Authenticity," pp. 351–52, 357, © 2009, with permission from Elsevier.

Europe, *The Amsterdam Declaration* (Council of Europe, 1975); the other by UNESCO from its meeting in Nairobi (UNESCO, 1976). Subsequently ICOMOS adopted the *Washington Charter* for historic towns and urban areas in 1987 (ICOMOS, 1987). All three statements echoed established 'scientific' principles, emphasising the importance of research and of sustaining authenticity. All emphasised the importance of the integration between conservation and town planning at the urban scale, the significance of public opinion and support, and the need for works of conservation to be socially progressive. This fusion of conservation and planning processes is what the Council of Europe terms 'integrated conservation'. However, it is a set of principles which are principally concerned with process.

Thus, from a conservation perspective, how to translate core concepts such as 'authenticity' to the urban spatial scale remain problematic. In seeking to conserve an ever changing city, authenticity cannot just rest on the integrity of individual buildings and monuments. This was acknowledged during the discussions on the Nara Document (*The Nara Document on Authenticity,* ICOMOS, 1994), which recognised the need for urban areas to evolve and experience socio-cultural change (Assi, 2000). Conservation becomes not so much the protection of architectural fabric but a key element in the processes of urban management.

In 2005, the *Vienna Memorandum* ("World Heritage and Contemporary Architecture—Managing the Historic Urban Landscape," UNESCO, 2005) was addressed at the integration of contemporary architecture into historic context. It focused on the following principles:

- Concept of historic urban landscape.
- Importance of understanding place.
- Avoid pseudo-historical design.
- New development should minimise direct impacts on historic elements.
- Contemporary architecture should be complementary to the values of the historic urban landscape.
- Cultural or Visual Impact Assessment.

This was not a radical statement. It introduced a new, but rather undefined concept (historic urban landscape), extended traditional conservation tropes (e.g. on issues of architectural style and assertion) and reiterated familiar processes (e.g. the importance of research and appraisal).

[. . .]

Strategic work within UNESCO is on-going, mobilised around the concept of 'historic urban landscapes'. Underpinned by a perception of the need to get away from thinking of cities as monuments and a need to see cities as first and foremost places where people live, this concept incorporates elements such as, for example, cityscape, urban morphology, functionality, authenticity and integrity, *genius loci* and intangible values (Rodwell, 2008; Rodwell and van Oers, 2007). The 2008 ICOMOS *Quebec Declaration on the Preservation of the Spirit of Place* (ICOMOS, 2008) sought to connect ideas of intangible heritage with non-tangible concepts of material place, such as *genius loci*, under the concept of spirit of place.

Thus the development pressures experienced by urban World Heritage Sites have increasingly become an issue preoccupying the international regulatory bodies. Beneath the concern with individual proposals are critical issues over the nature of conservation objectives at the urban scale. The objective for UNESCO is to sustain authenticity and integrity based on the defined OUV of a site. However, this is occurring within a context of constant urban evolution. Furthermore, although some elements of the urban landscape are more important than others, it is precisely the combination of different elements from different time-scales—the totality in all its messiness—that is the object of conservation. In other words, management of the urban WHS becomes partly about conserving individual structures and artefacts, but also involves judgements about the spirit of place as a living entity from the past, in the present, and for the future. There is understood to be a fundamental need to embrace change, even if the extent and form of this change remains difficult to define.

—ꟿ—

Conclusions

—ꟿ—

[There] is a weakly defined sense of what the authenticity of OUV means at an urban scale which, in turn, exists in competition with different locally held visions of the city. The concept of a WHS as a 'historic urban landscape' is interesting but remains sketchy at best. This is an urgent problem for UNESCO/ICOMOS. It is evident that the problems of urban WHS management we have described are not unique to the United Kingdom but common throughout the developed world. This has placed stress upon the international bodies both in terms of the resources required for active monitoring and intervention in site-management (through missions) and politically in terms of the need to demonstrate the seriousness of the regime through, for example, removing Dresden from the list. Furthermore, even if it is possible for 'historic urban landscapes' to develop into a more robust mechanism it will inevitably be part of a universalising approach to heritage which denies space to, or at least exists in competition with, locally produced notions of heritage, authenticity and sense of place.

References

Assi, E (2000) Searching for the Concept of Authenticity: Implementation Guidelines. *Journal of Architectural Conservation* 6(3), 60–69.

Council of Europe (1975) *European Charter of the Architectural Heritage*. Council of Europe, Amsterdam.

ICOMOS (1987) *Charter on the Conservation of Historic Towns and Urban Areas: "The Washingtan Charter."* ICOMOS, Paris.

ICOMOS (1994) *The Nara Document on Authenticity*. ICOMOS, Paris.

ICOMOS (2008) *Quebec Declaration on the Preservation of the Spirit of Place*. ICOMOS, Paris. p. 4.

Larkham, PJ (2003) The Place of Urban Conservation in the UK Reconstruction Plans of 1942–1952. *Planning Perspectives* 18(3), 295–324.

Pendlebury, J (2003) Planning the Historic City: 1940s Reconstruction Plans in Britain. *Town Planning Review* 74(4), 371–393.

Rodwell, D (2008) Urban Regeneration and the Management of Change: Liverpool and the Historic Urban Landscape. *Journal of Architectural Conservation* 14(2), 83–106.

Rodwell, D and van-Oers, R (2007) *Management and Preservation of Historic Centers of Cities Inscribed on the World Heritage List (summary report)*. Paris, World Heritage Centre. http://whc.unesco.org/uploads/activities/documents/activity-47.7.pdf.

UNESCO (1976) *Recommendation Concerning the Safeguarding and Contemporary Role of Historic Areas*. UNESCO, Nairobi.

UNESCO (2005) *Vienna Memorandum on "World Heritage and Contemporary Architecture—Managing the Historic Urban Landscape."* World Heritage Centre, Paris. p. 6. http://whc.unesco.org/en/activities/48.

Reading

50

Bernard M. Feilden and Jukka Jokilehto

Management Guidelines for World Cultural Heritage Sites (1998)

Bernard M. Feilden's and Jukka Jokilehto's collaborations—at ICCROM in particular—afforded them the opportunity to impart a multitude of lessons related to conservation practice and theory to the conservation field. Feilden's major book, The Conservation of Historic Buildings *(1982), and Jokilehto's equally influential monograph,* The History of Architectural Conservation *(1999), are benchmarks in the field. In this brief reading about authenticity in three key aspects (materials, workmanship, and design) from an unfortunately out-of-print text published by ICCROM, Feilden and Jokilehto underscore both the complexity and the importance of authenticity as they relate to World Heritage Sites.*

8.2 How Does Treatment Relate to Authenticity?

[. . .]

[. . .] The following summary briefly characterizes those aspects of the cultural resource that relate to its different forms of authenticity and appropriate conservation actions. It is emphasized, however, that while the aspects are here presented separately, care should be taken to guarantee a balanced judgement in treatments in order to maintain the authenticity as well as the historic character and significance of the heritage resource.

Authenticity in materials:

Evidence: Original building material, historical stratigraphy, evidence and marks made by impact of significant phases in history, and the process of ageing (patina of age).

From Bernard M. Feilden and Jukka Jokilehto, *Management Guidelines for World Cultural Heritage Sites,* 2nd ed. (Rome: ICCROM, 1998), 66–68.

Aim of treatment: To respect historic material, to distinguish new material from historic so as not to fake or to mislead the observer; in historic areas or towns, material should be understood as referring to the physical structures, the fabric of which the area consists.

Implementation: Maintenance and conservation of material substance related to periods of construction. In historic areas or towns this would mean maintaining the historic fabric, and avoiding replacement of even the oldest structures so far as these form the historical continuity of the area.

Authenticity in workmanship:

Evidence: Substance and signs of original building technology and techniques of treatment in historic structures and materials.

Aim of treatment: To respect evidence of original workmanship in building materials and structural systems.

Implementation: Conservation and maintenance of original material and structures, with creation of harmony between repairs and eventual new parts by using traditional workmanship.

Authenticity in design:

Evidence: Elements or aspects in which the artistic, architectural, engineering or functional design of the heritage resource and its setting are manifest (the original meaning and message, the artistic and functional idea, the commemorative aspect). In historic sites, areas or landscapes, design should be referred to the larger context as relevant to each case.

Aim of treatment: To respect the design conception as expressed and documented in the historic forms of the original structure, architecture, urban or rural complex.

Implementation: Conservation, maintenance, repair, consolidation, restoration or anastylosis of historic structures, and harmonization of any eventual new constructions with the design conceptions expressed in historic forms.

Authenticity in setting:

Evidence: The site or setting of the resource related to the periods of construction; historic park or garden; historic or cultural landscape; townscape value; and group value.

Aim of treatment: To keep the heritage resource *in situ* in its original site, and to maintain the relationship of the site to its surroundings.
Implementation: Planning control, urban or territorial conservation planning, and integrated conservation.

While the questions of authenticity and appropriate treatments mentioned here are mainly conceived in relation to historic structures, it is necessary to give serious consideration to traditional settlements especially in rural areas, such as villages and cultural landscapes characterized by traditional forms of life and functions, including gradual change and construction activities. In such cases, the continuation of traditional crafts and skills may be an essential part of the relevant management policy in order to guarantee coherence within a traditional economic system, life style and habitat. Attention should be paid to ensuring genuine quality in such crafts, and avoiding substitution with industrial products or methods. Furthermore, experience has shown that traditional types of materials should generally be recommended, especially when new paint, mortar, etc., need to be applied, in order to guarantee physical and aesthetic coherence with the existing structure.

Reading

51

MICHAEL TURNER AND TAL TOMER

Community Participation and the Tangible and Intangible Values of Urban Heritage (2013)

Michael Turner, a UNESCO professor at Israel's Bezalel's Academy of Art and Design in Jerusalem, also served for several years as the chair of Israel's UNESCO World Heritage Committee. Tal Tomer is an architect who received his training at Bezalel's Academy from 2008 to 2013. In this perceptive commentary, Turner and Tomer begin by emphasizing the turbulent nature of urban change in the recent past and then address two key questions about community: "Who are the urban communities in this dramatically changing scene? How are their voices heard in order to generate an enriching symphony rather than a cacophony of sounds?" In so doing, they underscore the importance of community participation in the context of urban conservation.

Introduction

While cultural and urban continuity is being debated, the revolutions affecting the city have multiplied exponentially, creating a dissonance between people and place. These revolutions have included the industrial revolution of the eighteenth century, the social and economic revolutions of the nineteenth century, the environmental revolutions of the twentieth century, and the technological revolutions of the past decade.

At each point in time, these revolutions have impacted the city with figures that are sometimes mind-boggling. The various projections from the current statistics indicate that some 50 percent of the world's population are living in cities and escalate to a figure of over 75 percent that will be living in cities by 2050 (Seetharam 2010), a doubling of urban neophytes in the developing world. Whether it is a decade before or after 2050 is irrelevant; it is more than poignant to view the changes in Shanghai during the twenty years 1990–2010—a view that speaks for itself.

From MICHAEL TURNER and TAL TOMER, "Community Participation and the Tangible and Intangible Values of Urban Heritage," *Heritage & Society* 6, no. 2 (2013): 187–93, 195–98. Reprinted by permission of the publisher Taylor & Francis Ltd, http://www.tandfonline.com.

These transformations have created a changing context, losing tradition and continuity, with old and new pressures on the urban landscape changing the setting. This has, in terms that have been identified in the UNESCO Recommendation on the Historic Urban Landscape,[1] changed the mindset of conservation from the objects of the monuments to the subjects of the living cities.

Who are the urban communities in this dramatically changing scene? How are their voices heard in order to generate an enriching symphony rather than a cacophony of sounds? The urban complexities challenge the single client-user in the managing of the site, as the multiplicity of stakeholders, including the custodians, has now to develop tools for managing not only the site but the people living and working in our cities. But, it is the first subparagraph of Article 5 in the World Heritage Convention that outlines the obligations of States Parties to the Convention. The article determines that States Parties adopt a general policy that aims to give the cultural and natural heritage a function in the life of the community and to integrate the protection of that heritage into comprehensive planning programs (UNESCO 1972).

However, community is loosely defined in the World Heritage Convention and the Operational Guidelines. Many terms are used interchangeably and include "International community," "Stakeholders," "Site managers, local and regional governments," "present and future generations of all humanity," and "local communities, non-governmental organizations (NGOs) and other interested parties and partners, general public, civil society, local people."[2]

Further references are made in the Nara Document,[3] where it is indicated that all cultures and societies are rooted in the particular forms and means of tangible and intangible expression that constitute their heritage and that these should be respected; and that the management of cultural heritage belongs, in the first place, to the cultural community that has generated it, and subsequently to that which cares for it.[4]

Levels of participation

Dealing with the heritage of past, present, and future questions the responsibilities and representations of the two communities identified in the Nara Document—those who created the heritage and those who should be currently caring for it. This simplistic formula is acceptable for a monument or a site, but the urban complexities need clearer guidelines. The creation of such guidelines would need to include the changing social patterns that adapted, hijacked, or ransomed the original fabric, while the structure of urban responsibilities lies in a web of stakeholder connections between central and local government on one side and the residents, neighbors, and visitors, pilgrims, or tourists on the other. An urban Nara Document is urgently needed that might build on the new UNESCO Recommendation for Historic Landscapes.

These situations can be seen and possibly redefined as compromise or co-existence. Is a compromise a watering down of our values? Not if the layering and evolution of the city is the essence of the value. The dimensions of culture, place, people and time provide us with a matrix to cross-reference these urban reactions.

—᠁—

We are fooling ourselves with a single idyllic image of the European City. In this context, how many people live in the city where they were born? In confronting changing societies, there is a need to transcend time and place. If the newcomers might embrace place, then the old-timers will need to provide space, in recognition of the changing heritage of today. Are we willing to accept syncretism or symbiosis, coexistence or compromise? Will a North African living now by Notre Dame claim this as his or her heritage, and will the displaced French living in their manor accept this? Similar situations can be seen with the Albanian community in the historic center of Naples and the Turkish communities in Berlin. All this puts a new perspective on the meaning of "local communities."

Increasing public awareness of this fundamental dimension of heritage is an absolute necessity in order to arrive at concrete measures for safeguarding the vestiges of the past. This means developing a greater understanding of the values represented by the cultural properties themselves with their urban attributes, as well as respecting the role such monuments and sites play in contemporary society.

Parallel to this, the conceptual debate on the paradox of universalism and particularism can be understood within the definitions of Outstanding Universal Value of the World Heritage Convention on one side and the renegotiating of values in the Burra Charter on the other.

Values, beliefs (standards), which have significance for a cultural group or an individual, often include, but are not limited to spiritual, political, religious and moral beliefs. Places may have a range of values for different individuals or groups, and values are continually renegotiated (ICOMOS 1999).

[. . .]

We need to reflect not only on the changing social structures but also the evolving interpretations of the values and political opinions of the populace. The values that have been identified within the past, present, and future are dependent on interpretations and the cultural connections through time of place and people.

It is not enough to agree on the values, which strangely enough might be quite unproblematic, but to debate the interpretations of these values is many times the *casus belli*. [. . .]

It is not just the inanimate physical object of still life, of the monument, but also the integration of the spirit of place, the context and setting as the physiognomy through the palimpsest of intangible traditions and tangible urban fabric. For the intangible, it is the Convention on the Protection and Promotion of the Diversity of Cultural Expressions (UNESCO 2005) that has extended our understanding of criterion (5) of the Operational Guidelines and provided a more structured format for understanding the components of cultural continuity and diversity. These might include typologies, chronologies, topologies, anthropologies, philologies, and themes.

The diversity of cultures and heritage in our world is an irreplaceable source of spiritual and intellectual richness for all humankind. The protection and enhancement of cultural and heritage diversity in our world should be actively promoted as an essential aspect of human development,[5] which can be achieved through participatory processes. This is not restricted to any one culture; the community participation for the Japanese town in the concept of Machinami,[6] the pillow of poetry in Uta-makura, and the climate and culture in Fudo are all evidence of these values.

Cultural heritage diversity exists in time and space and demands respect for other cultures and all aspects of their belief systems. In cases where cultural values appear to be in conflict, respect for cultural diversity demands acknowledgment of the legitimacy of the cultural values of all parties.[7] After the Nara Document opened new vistas on cultural diversities, it was the Burra Charter (ICOMOS 1999) that generated the next debate, focusing on the assumptions that:

1. The healthy management of cultural difference is the responsibility of society as a whole;
2. In a pluralist society, value differences exist and contain the potential for conflict; and
3. Ethical practice is necessary for the just and effective management of places of diverse cultural significance.

—∿—

Authenticity and integrity

—∿—

The UNESCO Recommendation on Historic Urban Landscape is the approach that should now be harnessed to develop a new language for community participation and urban heritage. [. . .]

The value of the layering of space (Tuan 1979) of the urban fabric has been discussed viewing Hopi space and time through the subjective and objective realms and the northern city of Peking as an *axis mundi*. Within this layering the city is rebuilt by, over, instead of. It is absorbed, occupied, and even hijacked. It is the difference between the concepts of the seven cities of Delhi with New Delhi, each built by the other, and the layering of the archaeological mound as the famous Tel Megiddo, with each city stacked above the water source.

How can these situations be evaluated through participatory processes? The Environmental Impact Assessment (EIA) has gone a long way in developing a body of knowledge in these fields with participation and responsibilities, while the addition of the Heritage Impact Assessment (HIA) (ICOMOS 2011) can bring together an integrative approach by defining the problems and stakeholders and developing a process that includes:

Screening → Scoping → Alternatives → Assessing → Reviewing → Decision → Monitoring[8]

Lingua franca

The Himeji Recommendations provides a clear light, not in just reviewing the definitions of authenticity but also in emphasizing the importance of the continuing debate on the need for the involvement of communities.

The Himeji Recommendations of 2012 states that:

> The attribution of values to heritage is a social rather than a scientific or technical process involving multiple individuals and groups. Further discussion is needed on the relationship between values and authenticity, and specifically on the way in which the integration of local and global values can inform the authenticity and significance of heritage; also, on how to understand the range of communities that are relevant to the identification and management of heritage, and how best to involve them in this process (Japanese Agency for Cultural Affairs and Himeji City 2012).

This reaffirms the need for greater emphasis to be placed on developing processes, tools, and frameworks that can enable community participation in the negotiation of integrated heritage management strategies and the development of an Esperanto-promoting dialogue.

The Rosetta Stone at Memphis in 196 BCE on behalf of King Ptolemy V at the British Museum is surely the epitome of how we might develop a local language and meaning and share particularistic ideas in a universal context. It also embodies the needed transparency that all local vernaculars were respected.

"The proverbial wisdom of the populace in the streets, on the roads, and in the markets, instructs the ear of him who studies man more fully than a thousand rules ostentatiously arranged."[9]

Notes

1. Approved by the UNESCO General Conference in November 2011.
2. These terms appear in the Operational Guidelines of the World Heritage Convention as follows: International community (para 6, 15, 49, 269) Stakeholders (para 3, 12, 40, 64, 111, 117, 119, 123, Annex 5, 6, 9) Site managers, local and regional governments (para 3, 12, 64, 123, 168, Annex 6) present and future generations of all humanity (para 7, 15, 49, 109, 170n, Annex 5, 7) local communities, non-governmental organizations (NGOs) and other interested parties and partners, general public, civil society, local people (para 12, 38, 40, 64, 90, 123, Annex 3,6)
3. Appearing as Annex 4—Authenticity in Relation to the World Heritage Convention.
4. Nara Document on [Diversity] Authenticity, 1994.
5. Para 5, The Nara Document on [Diversity] Authenticity, 1994.

6. The "Machinami Charter"—A Charter for the Conservation of Historic Towns and Settlements in Japan (adopted by Japanese ICOMOS Committee in 2000) gives the following definitions: "Machinami, usually translated as 'Historic Town,' is a Japanese word that includes a nuance of the historic core, in both its tangible and intangible factors, its physical and spiritual aspects, that would be created by a 'bond of spirits.' It also contains the tone of making a line, hand-in-hand, that applies both to buildings and to people. Shuuraku, the Japanese word for 'settlement,' is often translated as village. In this Charter it also contains an idea of a community's surrounding natural and cultural environment."
7. Para 6, The Nara Document on [Diversity] Authenticity, 1994.
8. Flowchart of key steps in the environmental impact assessment procedure (from UNEP/CBD/SBSTTA/7/13 and Ramsar Wise Use Handbook 11).
9. *Source: Proverbs, or the Manual of Wisdom, on the title page, printed for Tabart & Co., London (1804).*

References

ICOMOS 1999 *The Burra Charter—The Australia ICOMOS Charter for Places of Cultural Significance.* Electronic document, http://australia.icomos.org/wp-content/uploads/BURRA_CHARTER.pdf, accessed April 12, 2013.

ICOMOS 2011 *Guidance on Heritage Impact Assessments for Cultural World Heritage Properties.* Electronic document, http://www.icomos.org/world_heritage/HIA_20110201.pdf, accessed April 12, 2013.

Japanese Agency for Cultural Affairs and Himeji City 2012 *2012 Himeji Recommendations from the Meeting of Experts on Heritage and Societies—Toward the 20th Anniversary of the Nara Document and Beyond.* Electronic document, http://nara2014.wordpress.com/himeji-recommendation, accessed April 20, 2013.

Seetharam, Kallidaikurichi 2010 *Developing Living Cities: From Analysis to Action.* World Scientific, Singapore.

Tuan, Yi-Fu 1979 "Space and Place: Humanistic Perspective." In *Philosophy in Geography,* edited by Stephen Gale and Gunnar Olsson, pp. 387–427. Springer, Dordrecht.

UNESCO 1972 *Convention Concerning the Protection of the World Cultural and Natural Heritage Adopted by the General Conference at Its Seventeenth Session.* Electronic document, http://whc.unesco.org/en/convention text, accessed April 12, 2013.

UNESCO 2005 *Convention on the Protection and Promotion of the Diversity of Cultural Expressions.* Electronic document, http://unesdoc.unesco.org/images/0014/001429/142919e.pdf, accessed April 12, 2013.

Reading

52

Senam Okudzeto

Remembering African Cities: Rethinking Urban Conservation as Radical Public History (2017)

Senam Okudzeto, originally from Accra, Ghana, is an award-winning artist based in London and Basel. She frequently returns to Accra, where she remains engaged with various community groups, journalists, educators, and government agencies. There she has been active in promoting artistic creativity as well as working to protect the rich architectural heritage of Ghana as the country evolves in unpredictable ways. In this reading, commissioned for this volume, Okudzeto reflects on recent experiences in Accra related to urban conservation, heritage interpretation, and community participation.

What values are currently ascribed to historic structures and communities in African cities and how can people be more fully engaged with the heritage of an often underappreciated urban past? Given the little-discussed history of African urban spaces, what characterizes the public understanding of architectural or urban conservation in the West African context? A popular prejudice views authentic sub-Saharan Africa as rural and the urban as an invention of twentieth-century colonial Europeans.[1] Urban Africa is sometimes assumed to be a young, new place of defiant modernity, where fashion and music thrive as a deliberate but recent affront to urban squalor (e.g., *African Catwalk* or *Gentlemen of Bacongo*).[2] However, as cities expand, ancient urban communities are often the first places to become overcrowded and underdeveloped, putting these areas at greater risk. A dystopian picture of an overcrowded African urban future prevails: even larger cities with even greater social inequality and proliferating informal economies.[3] What challenges do these changes pose for historic communities, given that heritage conservation initiatives within African nations are invariably justified by their ability to promise social and fiscal returns, even when designed and funded within the constraints of contemporary social development models and institutions? Throughout the continent, Africans are eager for new and normalized narratives that challenge

Senam Okudzeto, "Remembering African Cities: Rethinking Urban Conservation as Radical Public History" (2017). Previously unpublished, written for this volume.

the perception of their everyday lives as forever stuck in the shadow of war, crisis, and the "development curse." Beyond scholarly research, what tools are available to inspire ordinary people to gain new understandings of their own potential to transform civil society, particularly in contrast to the idea of being "developed" (by the West)?

What follows is an attempt to answer these questions, drawing on my experience as an artist, academic, and organizer of a two-day conference, in Accra, Ghana, in March 2010. Our goal was to create a national campaign to promote awareness about Ghana's urban and architectural heritage and outline its various forms. At the time of the conference, the challenges of living in Accra were being visibly compounded by unprecedented growth. The city's expansion was largely unregulated, too rapid for the government, which remained heavily underfunded after recently emerging from severe recession from the 1960s to the 1980s.[4] A. R. Harrunah Attah, editor of the *Daily Mail*, described a national capital "defined largely by haphazard planning" and "disgruntled city dwellers who have lost faith in their cities systems and structures."[5] In addition to the anticipated rural poor migrating to the city in search of opportunity, there was an immense Ghanaian populace of returnees from a diaspora, those who had left to escape the recession and were now returning to build self-designed dream homes.[6] As a result, massive urban sprawl occurred, characterized by strange houses that often mimicked the prefabricated homes of suburban American gated communities. Our project was particularly concerned with the future of several public monuments, key modernist structures dating from the period of national independence in the early 1960s and the communities who inhabited the remarkable private buildings and family homes of the fifteenth- and sixteenth-century historic districts of Danish Osu and Jamestown, Accra, substantial parts of which had been designated as slums in need of "upgrading."[7]

In 2007 the mania for haphazard building spread to the Ghana government, initially due to the yearlong fiftieth anniversary celebration of national independence. The nation became center stage throughout the continent for its role as the first sub-Saharan nation to gain independence from European colonialism. The country itself became a monument, the capital city its crown. An extensive Accra beautification project was launched by the government, whereby public circles and monuments would be enhanced and decorated for the yearlong festivities. This was the first national engagement with the capital city's urban heritage since the dawn of independence, but what should have been a massive restoration project instead became a travesty of misused public funds and visual atrocities. Ancient trees lining major thoroughfares were abruptly felled, replaced by plants the city had neither the resources nor the staff to maintain, a particular affront to the urban working class that traveled on foot rather than in air-conditioned cars and relied on their shade in this equatorial city.[8] Because the budget of US$20 million was considered low, the majority of work regarding rehabilitation of monuments was turned over to private enterprise. Essentially, the government sold free advertising space in return for civic maintenance. In some cases companies commissioned garish new statues rendered in molded metallic plastic, modeled to resemble copper, accompanied by strategically placed placards reading, for example, "GUINNESS IS GOOD FOR YOU."

The race to reclad and, in the most horrific circumstances, demolish and reconstruct showed no respect for original design principles, thereby flattening the historical landscape and eliminating vernacular accents in design. Waves of anguish swept through the design community as the capital's grandeur was erased seemingly overnight and replaced with the gaudy strip lighting of an overnight boomtown. It became clear that the preservation of urban heritage was merely an unintended consequence of the nation's previous years of poverty rather than because of any conscious strategic planning by government authorities. Many journalists had already criticized the Accra Beautification Project, but their analysis focused primarily on its financial aspects. We aimed to equip journalists with better tools to archive, record, and present the city's historical strata in the national media and, in so doing, ascribe informed values to its structures in the public eye.

Largely theoretical discussions during the conference's first day were tested during a daylong tour of historic Accra, in particular, its ancient districts of Danish Osu and British and Dutch Jamestown and their growth in relation to the transatlantic slave trade.[9] One of the aims of the project was to argue for the recognition of important structures that remained unofficial heritage. Apart from the journalists who took part in the tour, we were able to introduce the regional director of the UNESCO office to several critical sixteenth- and seventeenth-century structures that heretofore had not been officially recognized as heritage.[10]

The historic communities we visited are densely crowded, and the majority of houses have no indoor plumbing. Few have sanitation facilities outside of public bathhouses, meaning a huge part of historic Accra is designated as a slum. The area also contains a large number of important structures that combine European and African vernacular styles as well as social traditions.[11] A key observation often lost to outsiders is the way in which social, traditional, and historic uses of space are encoded in buildings.[12] Although built in brick, an essentially Danish vernacular, the social division of space in the homes is distinctly African: each home has a male and a female quarter and the remains of earlier ancestors are interred within the compound of the home. Intramural sepulture, the practice of burying ancestors within the confines of the family compound, was outlawed in Accra by the British in the early twentieth century.

The chaotic appearance of the city center was also a marker of the slave trade, as the community deliberately designed their homes to become an unfathomable maze to outsiders in order to frustrate slave traders.

The tour concluded with mid-twentieth-century International Style modernist projects strategically located on sites of former British colonial power.[13] These buildings could be read historically as defining the nation's goals to reclaim its colonized territories and assert its importance on the world stage.[14] All were commissioned at the point of national independence, although not all were sponsored by the Ghana government.

Despite my interest in urban conservation efforts, I am somewhat critical of the term "heritage," since it is a mutable concept, vulnerable to abuse in the context of nationalist polemics.[15] However, the nationalist discourses of West Africa are comparatively recent and rarely take into account the essential role of urban spaces in anticolonialistt movements and consequent nation-building projects. In the case of the conference, participants identified Ghanaian urban heritage very closely with social uses of space and ongoing cultural traditions. They wanted to identify and retain the memories associated with those traditions. Historic structures, including recent ones, are the physical vessels in which social traditions can survive. These are places where new traditions have evolved in dialogue with the old. Tragically, though, many important structures (and the traditions they are linked with) are in danger of being destroyed, as the "constitutive nature of power and complexity in the city" is played out.[16] Those who hold economic power in the city too often hope that the rehabilitation of quarters that have fallen into disrepair will bring about the removal of the urban poor through gentrification.[17] Approaching urban conservation with the idea of creating a radical public history aims to not only restore structures but also maintain and support the communities that have grown through them. In the context of the urban heritage of Ghana, there is an urgent need for new practical methods to address the challenges of being contemporary African citizens, so that people feel they have political agency, that they are valued, connected to each other, and capable of authoring the future of their civic and national histories without creating new forms of jingoism, kitsch, or nationalist fervor.[18]

Notes

1. For a cursory understanding of historic African urbanism, see Jérôme Chenal, *The West African City: Urban Space and Models of Urban Planning* (London: Routledge, 2014); T. Falola and S. J. Salm, *African Urban Spaces in Historical Perspective,* Rochester Studies in African History and the Diaspora, no. 21, 2005.
2. Per Anders Petterson, *African Catwalk* (Heidelberg: Kehrer Verlag, 2016); Daniele Tamagni, *Gentlemen of Bacongo* (London: Trolley, 2009).
3. See Mike Davis, *Planet of Slums* (London: Verso, 2006); AbdouMaliq Simone and Abouhani Abdelghani, eds., *Urban Africa: Changing Contours of Survival in the City* (London: Zed Books, 2005).
4. While Accra grew almost exponentially, government expenditure was almost inversely proportional. See www1.worldbank.org/publicsector/pe/Ghana%20HIPC_AA__final.pdf.
5. A. R. Harruna Atta and Obed Boafo, "Accra's Hidden Treasures in Public Spaces," *The Mail* (Ghana), April 9, 2010.
6. Millions of Ghanaians emigrated during the recession of the 1970s and 1980s. In 2011 it was estimated that 7.5 million people, of a population of 26 million, were living abroad. See Jamilla Hamidu, "Are Ghanaian Dispora a Middle Class? Liking Class to Political Participation and Stability in Ghana," *Africa Development* 40, no. 1 (2015): 139–57.
7. Accra's historic center has been a fishing and trading community since the fifteenth century. Its urban identity originated from the communities of (Danish) Osu and (British) Jamestown, which expanded through commerce with local European trading posts, later upgraded to forts. UN-Habitat has identified Jamestown as a key focus for its Slum Upgrading Facility established in 2004. See UN-Habitat report, "Ghana Slums Lined Up for Investment," Accra, January 4, 2004. http://mirror.unhabitat.org/content.asp?cid=2438&catid=542&typeid=6.
8. Many Neem trees from before the period of independence were felled unnecessarily. Taking decades to grow, they provided working-class locals with folk remedies for malaria as well as much-needed shade. See Naa Lamiley Bentil, "Tree Cutting at Cantonments: Parks and

Gardens Explain," *Daily Graphic* online, February 13, 2007, www.modernghana.com/news/123884/1/tree-cutting-at-cantonments-parks-and-gardens-expl.html.

9. On Accra's historic communities, see Nii-Adziri H. Wellington, *Stones Tell Stories at Osu: Memories of a Host Community at the Danish Trans-Atlantic Slave Trade* (Accra: Sub Saharan Publishers, Legon, 2011); John Parker, *Making the Town: Ga State and Society in Early Colonial Accra* (Portsmouth, NH: Heinemann, 2000).
10. We visited the ruins of Franklin House in Jamestown, situated on Tabon Lane, named for Jamestown's remarkable Afro-Brazilian community, which evolved from a group of Afro-Brazilian slaves deported to West Africa from Bahia in the late 1880s following a bloody slave revolt.
11. For example, the late eighteenth-century and early nineteenth-century Afro-Danish homes, Ni Okantse We and the Richter Fort in Osu.
12. This is particularly true of public spaces and monuments associated with the modernist Black Star Square Stadium and Independence Arch in Accra, which are completely transformed during concerts, public holidays, and traditional festivals.
13. Janet Berry Hess, "Imagining Architecture: The Structure of Nationalism in Accra, Ghana," *Africa Today*. 47, no. 2 (Spring 2000): 35–58.
14. These sites also reflected Ghana's changing political alliances; see Lukasz Stanek, "Architects from Socialist Countries in Ghana (1957–67): Modern Architecture and Mondialisation," *JSAH* 74, no. 4 (December 2015); Mark Crinson, *Modern Architecture at the End of Empire* (London: Ashgate, 2003).
15. See Pippo Ciorra, "(Un)political," in *This Thing Called Theory*, ed. Teresa Stoppani and Giorgio Ponzo (London: Routledge, Taylor and Francis, 2016); Pippo Ciorra, "Patrimony," in *Recycled Theory, Illustrated Dictionary* (Macerata: Quodlibet, 2016), 218–26; Thordis Arrenhius, *The Fragile Monument: On Conservation and Modernity* (London: Artifice Books, 2012). Arrhenius argues that "conservation is a modern phenomenon, generated out of the events that radically transformed society around 1800," linking it to a need to establish stability and political legitimacy following the French Revolution.
16. Edgar Pieterse, *City Futures: Confronting the Crisis of Urban Development* (London: Zed Books, 2008).
17. Ghanaian politicians, especially those in Accra, pay particular attention to their constituents. The citizens of historic districts have a contradictory cultural status, representing both the urban poor and a cultural aristocracy.
18. For example, the groundbreaking *African Cities Reader*, ed. Ntone Edjabe and Edgar Pieterse published by the African Center for Cities and *Chimurenga* magazine, South Africa, www.africancitiesreader.org.za.

Reading

53

Non Arkaraprasertkul and Matthew Williams

The Death and Life of Shanghai's Alleyway Houses: Re-thinking Community and Historic Preservation (2015)

Non Arkaraprasertkul, originally from Thailand, is an architect, urban designer, historian, and anthropologist who teaches at the Jagiellonian University in Krakow, Poland. His transdisciplinary research interests lie at the crossroads between design and the social sciences. Matthew Williams received his PhD from the Australian National University and specializes in the cultural implications of the rising use of the automobile in Thailand and China. This perceptive commentary about Shanghai's lilong *(alley) houses and the challenges associated with their conservation is largely based on fieldwork conducted by Arkaraprasertkul for his PhD dissertation (Harvard University). In this reading, they draw an important distinction between historic preservation and community preservation, which has implications reaching well beyond Shanghai.*

This article was originally written to honor the life and work of Tess Johnston, a true historian of Shanghai's architectural development and a friend of the authors whose contributions to the knowledge of the subject spans over four decades.

Housing and Heritage

One of the most urgent contemporary problems in cities occurs when the need to preserve monuments of the past clashes with the need to house large numbers of people.[1] As Shanghai focuses on developing its service economy to bolster its global city status, it must build housing for the new workers, from low-income migrant workers, to blue-collar and white-collar skilled workers and foreign workers. Shanghai today is the largest city by population in the world, and has been growing at an exceptionally fast rate of about 10% annually since the late 1980s.[2] At the same time city officials are growing increasingly aware of the brand value in preserving the city's heritage buildings. In cities that have achieved a global status, such as New York, London, Paris, Tokyo (and perhaps also

From Non Arkaraprasertkul and Matthew Williams, "The Death and Life of Shanghai's Alleyway Houses: Re-thinking Community and Historic Preservation," *Revista de Cultura/Review of Culture* 50 (2015): 139–44, 146–50. Reproduced courtesy of the authors.

Fig. 1. Alleys of a *shikumen* (the most popular style of the *lilong* houses) compound in Siwen Lane, one of Shanghai's largest lane neighbourhoods housing at its height, 700 families. Located in the prime downtown area of Jing'An district, the compound has since been slowly demolished to make way for a museum and new residential corporate buildings.

Hong Kong), there is a dynamic co-existence between economic modernity and state-of-the-art conservation of the remnants of the past. An obvious question arises: what is the use of historic buildings in the era of economic modernity? Responses to this dilemma have varied across the globe. Some have attempted experimental schemes for engaging local populations in historic conservation and site management. Others have simply pushed for mass evictions, often accompanied by police or gang brutality, 'legitimised' in the name of a weakly defined 'common good', but practically oriented toward enriching real estate developers and local politicians.[3]

In arguably the most important doctrine of urbanism in the last century, *The Death and Life of Great American Cities*,[4] the late urbanist Jane Jacobs (1916–2006) attacks modern architecture, namely high-rise buildings and large-scale urban planning, for ignoring existing social conditions, advocating instead for the status quo of small-scaled and dense urban neighbourhoods that better provide the residents with a sense of community, security and sustainable form of economy built on social capital. [. . .]

[. . .] However, by advocating a strict adherence to the status quo, in her hope of maintaining the sense of community, Jacobs precluded the natural demographic cycles and evolving needs of a community. Demographically speaking, residents move in and out; family numbers naturally increase or decrease with each birth or death; and people move around as their needs and lifestyles change. All of these are individual factors that, over time, collectively alter the structure of the neighbourhood's population. In a similar way, buildings, edifices, and structures are built to last for a certain period of time, depending on the materials, construction technology, maintenance, and so on. Often, removing old, rundown, energy-inefficient and spatially inefficient buildings is more financially feasible, and more physically beneficial to the residents than keeping them, or trying to refurbish them to look as if nothing has changed. By advocating sentimentalism for a traditional lifestyle, Jacobs overlooked the fact that to resist change entirely is inimical to the natural and desirable development of a city. [. . .]

[. . .] [L]ike Greenwich Village, the traditional Shanghainese alleyway houses of today are very different from what they were like a century ago, not only in terms of their contemporary usage, but also the population residing within them. This is despite the fact that there has been no shortage of literature, newspapers, magazines, exhibitions, and reminiscing about the romantic past of these alleyway houses. [. . .]
[. . .]

Preservation and Its Discontents

During the Communist period before reform and opening up (1949–1978), to accommodate the large-scale redistribution of residents and housing, interior rooms were divided and sub-divided as families grew over the decades, to the point that the square footage per person had diminished to barely legal limits. With scarce housing resources, intensive use of existing buildings exacerbated the deterioration of the buildings. They included informal structures such as cooking stations or sheds that were added to the building by residents pressed for more working space, without any concern (nor technical knowledge) of the building's structural integrity, let alone concern for stylistic and aesthetic uniformity. The combined changes also undermine fire safety. Additionally, there are multiple problems as a result of the lack of regular maintenance: rainwater leaks through the roof and wall; careless wiring and punctured walls to make way for electrical and telephone cables, and deteriorating wooden floors and structures, to name a few. They all contributed to shortening building lifespans at a hyperbolic speed. Many of these buildings are no longer structurally safe, nor sufficiently hygienic to serve as adequate accommodation for most residents.

Thankfully, the urban development process in Shanghai has slowed down during the first decade of the 21st century, owing to the combined efforts of local Shanghainese architectural perservationists who have made their voice heard by the municipal government.[5] These preservationists have demanded that a selected number of edifices and neighborhoods should be kept intact to prevent Shanghai from turning into another generic city with no historical signficance, let alone unique urban characteristics. [. . .] [T]he preservation program is only concerned with the maintenance of the façade, with only nominal concern for the condition of the interior. [. . .]

[. . .] Having weighed the pros and cons, the residents see giving up their space for the privileged classes as a pragmatic way to sustain their life. This affects the whole sense of urbanity, as the city becomes more and more internationalised without any true sense of belonging to hold on to. If the central core of Shanghai, where sophisticated heritage edifices stand, is occupied only by expatriates and wealthy Chinese, what is the point then of being there? Many criticise the "Disney Land" approach to preservation simply because it only preserves, in some extreme cases recreating the architectural façade, but not the social structure. [. . .]

[. . .] Historic laneways live through the interactions of their residents, the people who embody the stories of their district and their city. Their presence and history cannot be replaced by newly polished façades and kitsch advertising campaigns which ironically romanticise a past rendered all but sterile by forcing out its most essential ingredient—the people who embody the history of the laneway houses themselves.

Practical Strategies: Affordibility, Diversity, and Livelihood

[. . .] [W]e propose a practical strategy by which both heritage and livelihood can coexist. [. . .] Shanghai has many heritage buildings that could be put into better use. The prevailing trend to date has been to turn them into luxury retail shops to make up for the loss of profit should the building be torn down and replaced instead by high-rise buildings. In Shanghai, the high-end retail district known as Xintiandi (lit. "The New Heaven and Earth") is the epitome of this trend. Once a traditional *lilong* neighborhood in the former French Concession, the architect of the project envisioned the crisscrossing alleyways in the same fashion of the mountainous alleyways of Siena, when he was planning the revamping process. Eventually, through what the architect himself calls 'adaptive reuse', the result is a hyper-luxury low-rise retail compound that is both nostalgic to the local residents and unique to visitors in a city where a modern vision of high-rise buildings has dominated its urban redevelopment for decades.[6]

This approach, while refreshing and in some ways protective of the city's history, is problematic on many levels. First, the project only serves select groups of people, namely customers for high-end shops who can afford to buy brand name products, furthering the segregation between the upper middle class and the rest. [. . .] Second, by way of what economists would call the 'network effect', the popularity of an urban renewal project such as Xintiandi gives the impression to both the developers and the visitors alike that this is the 'only way' to revitalise traditional alleyway house neighbourhoods. In recent years, retail compounds such as Xintiandi have mushroomed all over Shanghai, as well as other parts of China, hoping to replicate the success of the heritage industry—or 'tradition-for-sale tourism', another epithet by which it is known. As recent studies show, the popularity of Xintiandi is partly due to its newness and uniqueness, but once replicas of it are widespread, the excitement seems to dissipate. [. . .]

As the use of heritage structures for high-end shopping is in decline, there is growing interest in local industry focussed on the experience of quotidian Shanghainese life.

Fig. 2. *Shikumen* alley gossip: Residents gossip in the *shikumen* lanes of Siwen Lane compound, a key artery of community interaction and public household activity.

Fig. 3. *Shikumen* demolition: A *shikumen* house left standing amidst a mostly demolished *lilong* compound in a prime area near Xintandi.

For instance, the recent success stories of a handful of creative zones and neighbourhoods originate from the ways in which low-budget artists and creative entrepreneurs themelves make use of traditional alleyway houses.[7] The attraction of these zones and neighbourhoods, as we have observed, is rooted in the experience of actual everyday life, and the anti-corporatism sentiment associated with them. In a specific *lilong* neighbourhood in central Shanghai where we have been conducting research,[8] most customers of small businesses there said that they prefer this neighbourhood to a reconstructed compound such as Xintiandi because it is not only more affordable, but also, in a broader sense, 'more real'. This neighbourhood has been undergoing a gradual diversification process thanks to its popularity. [. . .]

Group Preservation, and Diversification from Within

[. . .] [T]he Shanghai government regards historic preservation of select sites, including the traditional alleyway, as essential to the branding of a city with global ambitions. Yet, there is little consideration of how the existing residents of said 'historical monuments' fit into the overall architectural preservation of the sites. Hence, we are seeing more of an interest in architectural preservation, rather than a preservation of culture and a way of life. [. . .] [T]he Shanghai government handpicks select "worthy" structures to preserve, which makes the "unworthy" structures available for immediate bulldozing. Hence, you get many 'preserved historic sites' left in the middle of surrounding high-rise buildings, and the remaining residents, who are mostly older, find such encroachment to be daunting. They used to shopping at cheap street markets but, due to the new urban development, find themselves surrounded by high-rises where fruits and vegetables in their modem supermarkets cost ten times more. The same applies to the social life the residents used to share with neighbours from nearby communities. Once the network of cross-community neighbours is gone, remaining residents are unable to maintain the sense of neighbourhood. After a time this may affect their sense of personhood, encouraging them to eventually move.

[. . .] [T]here has been little to no effort on the government's part to maintain the sense of community. The government's primary focus has been on revamping the facade of the edifices. [. . .]

[. . .]

[T]here is a possibility for the preservation of both architecture and community culture together—the middle way. [. . .]

Conclusion

[. . .] [I]f we create a livable environment for the residents, they will want to stick around to tell stories of their past to the younger generation and the newcomers to the city. Isn't that what preservation is all about? [. . .]

Finding the middle way between community and historic preservation means that cities must strike a balance between preserving their heritage and being open to change. Destroying heritage destroys memory, community, and a sense of place. Refusing to change can render the city a glamorous but stultifying museum. In finding the ideal balance, we must operate from the paradigm that places residents first. [. . .] We advocate the methods of 'group preservation' and 'diversification from within', which would require efforts from both the local authorities and residents working together. To find the correct balance between preservation and change, both the local authorities and residents need to have a mutual understanding of both the bigger picture, and the ethnographic details of everyday life. Ultimately, what is a city but a collection of diverse individuals drawn together? As Montgomery poignantly reminds us: "Most of all, [a city] should enable us to build and strengthen the bonds between friends, families and strangers that give life meaning, bonds that represent the city's greatest achievement." In cities which strike this balance, there is a heightened sense of vitality as residents' participate in, what Jacobs herself would call, an intricate 'street ballet'—a pattern of observable comprehensive human activity, that nourishes our sense of belonging and common purpose.

Notes

1. See Michael Herzfeld, 'Heritage and the Right to the City: When Securing the Past Creats Insecurity in the Present', *Heritage & Society* 8, no. 1 (2015).
2. World Population Review, 'Shanghai Population 2015' (2014).
3. See Michael Herzfeld, 'Spatial Cleansing: Monumental Vacuity and the Idea of the West', *Journal of Material Culture* 11, no. 1/2 (2006); Hyun Bang Shin, 'The Right to the City and Critical Reflections on China's Property Rights Activism', *Antipode* (2013); Qin Shao, *Shanghai Gone: Domicide and Defiance in a Chinese Megacity*, State and Society in East Asia (2013).
4. Jacobs, *Death and Life*.
5. Yang, 'Shikumen Pledged'.
6. Greg Yager and Scott Kilbourn, 'Lessons from Shanghai Xintiandi: China's Retail Success Story', *Urban Land Asia* (2004); Fulong Wu and Shenjing He, 'Property-Led Redevelopment in Post-Reform China: A Case Study of Xintiandi Redevelopment Project in Shanghai', *Journal of Urban Affairs* 27, no. 1 (2005); see Xuefei Ren, 'Forward to the Past: Historical Preservation in Globalizing Shanghai', *City & Community* 7, no. 1 (2008).
7. See Xuefei Ren and Meng Sun, 'Artistic Urbanization: Creative Industries and Creative Control in Beijing', *International Journal of Urban and Regional Research* 36, no. 3 (2012); Esther Hiu Kwan Yung, Edwin Hon Wan Chan, and Ying Xu, 'Sustainable Development and the Rehabilitation of a Historic Urban District—Social Sustainability in the Case of Tianzifang in Shanghai', *Sustainable Development* 22, no. 2 (2014).
8. See Non Arkaraprasertkul, 'Shanghai Urban Future: Urbanization, Heritage Industry, and the Political Economy of Urban Space', in *The 2014 Annual Meeting of the American Anthropological Association*, ed. Sean Mallin, Nicholas Lawrence Caverly, and Erik I. Harms (Washington D.C., 2014): 'Traditionalism'.

Bibliography

Arkaraprasertkul, Non. 'Shanghai Urban Future: Urbanization, Heritage Industry, and the Political Economy of Urban Space'. In *The 2014 Annual Meeting of the American Anthropological Association*, ed. Sean Mallin, Nicholas Lawrence Caverly and Erik I. Harms (Washington D.C., 2014): 'Traditionalism'.

Herzfeld, Michael. 'Heritage and the Right to the City: When Securing the Past Creates Insecurity in the Present'. *Heritage & Society* 8, no. 1 (2015): 3–23.

———. 'Spatial Cleansing: Monumental Vacuity and the Idea of the West'. *Journal of Material Culture* 11, no. 1/2 (2006), pp. 127–149.

Jacobs, Jane. *The Death and Life of Great American Cities*. New York: Vintage Books, 1961.

Ren, Xuefei. 'Forward to the Past: Historical Preservation in Globalizing Shanghai'. *City & Community* 7, no. 1 (2008), pp. 23–43.

——— and Meng Sun. 'Artistic Urbanization: Creative Industries and Creative Control in Beijing'. *International Journal of Urban and Regional Research* 36, no. 3 (2012), pp. 504–521.

World Population Review. 'Shanghai Population 2015' (2014).

Wu, Fulong, and Shenjing He. 'Property-Led Redevelopment in Post-Reform China: A Case Study of Xintiandi Redevelopment Project in Shanghai'. *Journal of Urban Affairs* 27, no. 1 (2005).

Yager, Greg, and Scott Kilbourn. 'Lessons from Shanghai Xintiandi: China's Retail Success Story'. *Urban Land Asia*, 2004, pp. 34–37.

Yang, Jian. "Shikumen Pledge Extra Protection after Readers Offer City Suggestions." *Shanghai Daily*, August 25, 2014, 2013, A4.

Yung, Esther Hiu Kwan, Edwin Hon Wan Chan, and Ying Xu. 'Sustainable Development and the Rehabilitation of a Historic Urban Distric—Social Sustainability in the Case of Tianzifang in Shanghai'. *Sustainable Development* 22, no. 2 (2014), pp. 95–112.

Reading

54

Carmen C. M. Tsui

Revitalizing Effective Memory Cues in a Chinese City: Urban Conservation Principles for Huizhou (Guangdong) (2002)

Carmen C. M. Tsui, an architectural historian from Hong Kong who received her PhD from the University of California, Berkeley, currently teaches at the City University of Hong Kong. This reading is taken from field research she conducted in Huizhou, a city east of Guangzhou, China, with a rich historic past. Tsui attempts to find innovative methods to conserve historic places in this rapidly expanding city, such that "memory cues" might spark reengagement with the past, in ways similar to how medical doctors try to resurrect memories in amnesia patients.

Effective Memory Cues: The Keys to Retrieve Collective Memory

[. . .] Ever since the declaration of the Nara Document of Authenticity in 1994 during the 16th meeting of the World Heritage Committee, ideas about "authentic" conservation and the significance of "intangible heritage" have awakened many conservationists. [. . .] However, how to translate these two notions into an effective conservation strategy is still an outstanding question that challenges many conservationists.

[. . .] In Imperial China people had neither the concept nor the practice of conservation. [. . .]

The Chinese respect for the past is not manifested in conservation efforts on historic structures. Chinese philosophers suggest that all tangible materials will disappear one day and cannot be preserved; only intangible values can remain eternal.[1] Instead, their fondness of the past is manifested in a high respect for the ancients, and in their inevitable duties to transmit traditions. The Chinese shoulder a natural-born duty to transmit what they have inherited from the ancients. "Transmission" is in fact the pivotal central mechanism in Chinese culture.

Adapted for this volume from Carmen C. M. Tsui, "Revitalizing Effective Memory Cues in a Chinese City: Urban Conservation Principles for Huizhou (Guangdong)" (MA thesis, 2002), various pages. Reproduced courtesy of the Chinese University of Hong Kong.

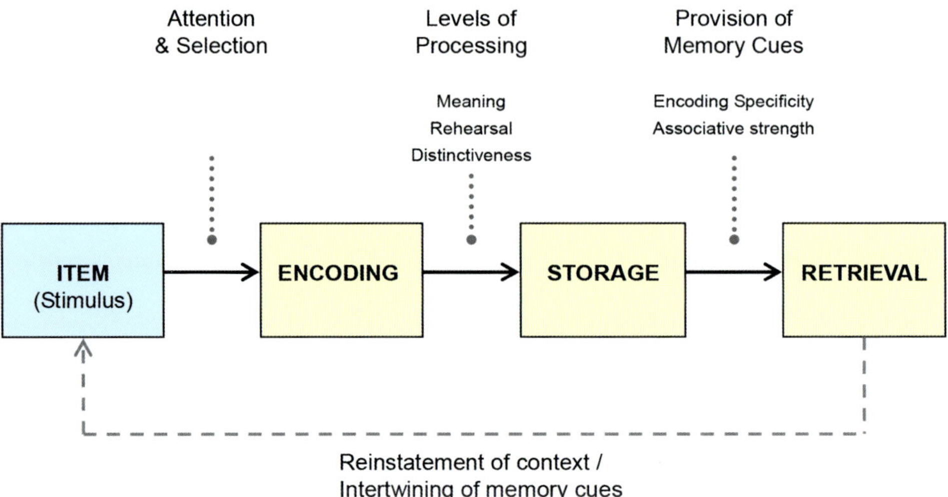

Fig. 1. Summary diagram on the memory process.

To allow "transmission," memory is an essential element to the Chinese. It is memory that links present-day Chinese to their pasts. Only when they retrieve their memories of their pasts, are they able to inherit traditions. And in return, the present-day Chinese will also be remembered by their later-born, and this allows tradition to be transmitted from generation to generation. This creates a sustainable chain of memory that spans time and links generations. The Chinese revive their pasts from memory and apply them to the modern. This prevents Chinese culture from freezing in nostalgia, but instead propels it in a sustainable manner. While transmission is the central mechanism in Chinese culture, the sustaining of memory is the joint of this transmission. Therefore, what has to be conserved are the elements that lead to the sustaining of memory—a memory shared by a common culture, one that simply can be called "collective memory."

Collective memory is the memory of the past shared by a common culture.[2] [. . .] Collective memory is not necessarily personal experience; in other words, it is reconstructed by the society. Through reading history, listening to others' experience, participating in rituals, and so on, a person is stimulated to reconstruct the memory of the past. In this case, the past is stored and interpreted by the society.

Several psychologists have argued that the memory process involves three stages: encoding, storage, and retrieval. Encoding refers to initial learning or acquisition of information; storage refers to maintaining information over time; while retrieval refers to accessing stored information.

—᠁—

Memory cannot be sustained if people fail to retrieve the stored information of the past into current consciousness. As Frederic C. Bartlett already demonstrated in the early 1930s, retrieval is a reconstruction process whereby aspects of the content of previously presented materials will be woven into a coherent whole, with the aid of preexisting knowledge.[3] Our memory is not an accurate, literal representation of the past, but it is instead reconstructed in accordance with our present desires and needs.

To allow the reconstruction of memory to happen, Tulving discovered that the provision of a memory cue is essential. A memory cue is a fragment or a representational form of the original item that can be used to evoke memory. [. . .] Information can be recalled only when memory cues are provided along with the information at the time of learning. The likelihood of memory recall depends on the extent to which the memory cue was reinstated or matched the original encoding.

—᠁—

Are there any cues better than others in recalling our memory? Ever since Tulving raised the importance of memory cues in retrieval, psychologists have continued to investigate the effectiveness of the memory cues. [. . .]

To apply this to urban study, the effective memory cues in the city are those fragments or representational forms that are specifically encoded in the city's distinctiveness, are highly associated to it and/or frequently occur within the city's history. [. . .]

[M]emory cues have immense importance in sustaining the collective memory to Chinese cities. Therefore, it should be conserved or revitalized to allow the transmission of Chinese culture and traditions. To achieve this, the ultimate task is to ensure its continuous provision in the city.

—᠁—

Extracting Tangible Memory Cues to Intangible Memory Cues

[. . .]

[T]he landscape setting and places in cities are not the two major distinctive elements only of Guangdong, but also the tangible cues that could be effective in retrieving the collective memory to the province.

—᠁—

[I]n Guangdong, it has been the province's characteristic landscape setting that has provided its cities with high defensibility and easy accessibility.

—᠁—

The landscape provides a reference for the distribution and location of the Guangdong cities. The cities are so located to fit into the natural landscape, and the Cantonese utilize the characteristic landscape setting to benefit the cities' defensive power and accessibility, thereby also enhancing its economic situation.

—w—

Although landscape provides the reference that guided the physical form of Guangdong cities, it is difficult for one to be aware of the characteristic landscape setting when one is put inside the vast city. What a person can experience, instead, is individual place and its urban artifacts; what a person can sense is the spirit of the place.
[. . .]

A place is not merely a physical environment, but is instead a coherent whole constituted by an overlaying of elements. In Australia's Burra Charter a place is defined as a "site, area, buildings or other work, group of buildings or other works together with associated contents and surrounds."[4] Revisiting a place allows us to recall what has happened. But why are some places more memorable than others? This is because every place has its own spirit, and it is the maintenance of this spirit of a place that helps us to recall our past—what had "taken place" in the place.

—w—

Two elements are crucial to this landscape-place relationship: distinctive scenes and text. [. . .]

The Cantonese highly value their natural environment.[5] Because of such appreciation, they like to identify the distinctive scenes generated by the beautiful landscape.
[. . .]

The tradition of listing the city's distinctive scenes did not originate in Guangdong. Instead, it started in the Song Dynasty at Xiaoxiang 瀟湘 (present Hunnan 湖南 Province).[6] A famous artist Song Di 宋迪 captured the most outstanding scenes in the city in his landscape paintings. People later named those scenes as the Xiaoxiang Ba Jing 瀟湘八景 (Eight Scenes in Xiaoxing) and this formed the first list of distinctive scenes in China. Later, with an appreciation to Song Di's paintings, the calligrapher Mi Fu 米芾 inscribed a poem for each of them. Because of his fame, Mi Fu accidentally made the list famous to the whole country. From then on people everywhere in China copied him by listing the distinctive scenes in their own city.

—w—

The Chinese visualized the picturesque landscape and ingenious place through their distinctive scenes. And they extracted and highlighted the distinctiveness of the landscape, place and scenes by using text. From the tangible memory cues (landscape and place) we can devise those intangible ones (scenes and text), which are deeply processed and encoded in the people's collective memory of Guangdong cities.

—w—

[. . .] When we traced back to the first list of distinctive scenes in China, the Xiaoxiang Ba Jing, we found that the scenes are made famous after they are depicted by the text composed by Mi Fu and the painting by Song Di. This shows that people are aware of the scenes only after they are extracted into readable forms: the text and the paintings. The distinctive scenes help encode the landscape and the place, while the text and paintings help encode the distinctive scene.

—⁓—

Text occupies immense importance in Chinese culture. Unlike in Western culture, where people build magnificent structures such as triumphal arches and pyramids as memorials, the Chinese instead inscribe texts on tablets to memorialize special events. In Imperial China, text is also the official medium to document the city.[7] Despite its diversified meanings, text, if it applies to the city, serves as an intangible memory cue that indicates a specific place and highlights its character.

[. . .]

The most basic yet significant function of the text is to indicate a targeted item. Among all kind of texts, the "name 名" is the simplest and direct form that can achieve this task. "Naming" the item with text is crucial to our communication because it provides us a common ground for discussions. It is also an effective cue in retrieving our memories: we start to recall a person, a place or an object when someone mentions its name. Then, we are able to recall the details associated with that name—the story about the person, our experience in that place or the appearance of that object. The high associative strength of the name has made it the most powerful retrieval cue.

When the Chinese name a place, they are not merely creating a symbol that indicates a specific site or location. Rather, the place's name usually has embedded meanings. Some of the names reflect the place's geographical settings and natural environment, such as the ancient name of Guangdong—Lingnan 嶺南—which describes the region's southern location to the mountain range. Or the name reflects the people's wishes about a place. [. . .]

Once a name is used to indicate a place, unless under special circumstances it usually persists through time. [. . .] It becomes a ritual for people to associate a specific name with a specific place, and such high associative strength and encoding specificity of the name has led to effective memory retrieval.

[. . .]

Though not as common as the text, the landscape painting is another effective medium to depict the distinctive scenes in imperial Guangdong. In many Guangdong cities, people illustrated distinctive scenes in paintings. [. . .] The paintings provide people with vivid visualizations of the scenes, and serve as valuable records for later generations like us to remember the past. [. . .]

The text and the paintings are not merely depictions of distinctive scenes. In fact, they serve two additional roles: first, they are a readable form of distinctive scenes; and second, they are a communicable form for people to learn and discuss the scenes. However, as times change, new forms of visualization and communication are emerging

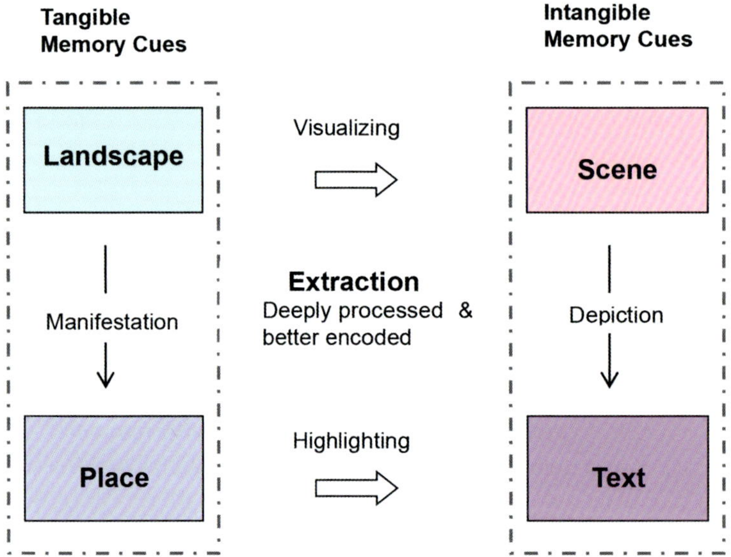

Fig. 2. The extraction from tangible memory cues to intangible ones.

today. The relative positioning of scenes is now presented in a touristic map. Photographs have replaced landscape paintings to provide better visualization of distinctive scenes, for better encoding will lead to better retrieval of memory. In many Guangdong cities, such as Huizhou and Chaozhou, the local government even posts the list of distinctive scenes on the Internet as propaganda about the city's tourism.

—ɱ—

Just as the scenes visualized the landscape and the place, the text highlighted the distinctiveness of the landscape and place.

—ɱ—

From the tangible memory cues (landscape and place) we are able to devise those intangible ones (scene and text). The intangible memory cues are deeply processed and better encoded as they involve the extraction and understanding of meanings behind the tangible forms (fig. 2).

[. . .] These four effective memory cues, either tangible or intangible, are all important in retrieving the collective memory of Guangdong cities.

Incarnating Intangible Memory Cues into Tangible Ones: The Formation of New Places

Intangible memory cues are those better remembered by people because of its encoding specificity and associative strength. However, two reasons urge us to incarnate them into physical forms. Firstly, the intangible memory cues must be made incarnate as tangible manifestations if they are to be conserved. Secondly, since the intangible memory cues reflect greatly the people's collective memory of their city, they therefore hint to us those distinctive elements and desirable qualities in the city that people enjoyed. Therefore, the intangible memory cues help us to recreate the physical environment that once was stored in the collective memory of the people. They serve as important guidance for our future design.

The tangible memory cues can be incarnated in two ways. The most straightforward way is to recreate the physical material that they described. [. . .]

To incarnate the texts and the dinctive scenes, the landscape and the places that are associated with them should be revitalized. [. . .] Those that have already disappeared should be reconstructed if possible. Another way of incarnation requires the translation and transformation of the conceptual meanings embedded in the intangible ones.

[. . .]

Huizhou's side-name Yuedong Zhongzhen, for example, captures the city's significant position in eastern Guangdong. Having understood that the side-name is gained because of Huizhou's strategic geographical locations, then how can it affect the city's future development? To take Huizhou as the contemporary Yuedong Zhongzhen therefore requires the translation of the side-name's embedded meanings into design guidelines that suit contemporary taste. Strategy should be developed to help Huizhou maintain its position as the contemporary Yuedong Zhongzhen.

Conclusions

The tangible and intangible memory cues in Guangdong cities are indispensable to each other. Therefore, to sustain the collective memory, we should ensure the continuous provisions of these effective memory cues in the city and maintain their interrelationships. In other words, the essence for revitalizing the effective memory cues is to recreate and reinforce the relationships between them.

1. Extracting tangible memory cues into intangible ones. The tangible heritage only attains its true significance when it sheds light on underlying values.[8] Therefore, to allow better encoding and deeper processing, we should extract the tangible memory cues into the intangible ones which involve the understanding of meanings and values. The listing of the distinctive scenes, the naming of places, the highlighting of city characters and the generation of sayings are good examples of extraction.
2. Incarnating intangible memory cues into tangible ones. The intangible heritage must be made incarnate into tangible manifestations, if it is to be conserved.[9] Since the intangible memory cues are deeply processed and better encoded, they provide good reference that reflects what has been stored in people's collective memory of their city. If they can be incarnated in tangible form, then the

immaterial distinctive characters of the city can be manifested in the physical environment.

3. Enhancing the intertwining of multiple memory cues. In most cases, the effective memory cues, either tangible or intangible, do not exist in the city in a discrete manner. They are intertwined with each other in the city and form multiple cues that have stronger retrieval power. We should therefore enhance the intertwining of the effective memory cues, and identify those intertwined ones for conservation.

Notes

1. For example, the "Three Immortals" suggested by the Chinese are virtues, merits, and words 立德`立功 `立言.
2. The term "collective memory" (*memoire collective*) first appeared in Halbwachs' landmark work *Les cadres sociaux de la memoire* (The Social Framework of Memory, 1925). Following this he wroter other works related to the topic, including "La memoire collective chez les musiciens," *Revue Philosophique* 127 (1939), 136–165; *La topographie legendaire des Evangiles en Terre Sainte* (The Legendary Topography of the Gospels in the Holy Land, 1941); and *La memoire collective* (1950).
3. Sir Frederic Charles Bartlett (1886–1969) was Britain's most outstanding psychologist between the World Wars. He has profoundly affected the ideas of memory research in the field of experimental psychology. His landmark work *Remembering: A Study in Experimental and Social Psychology* published in 1932 has changed the perspective of memory psychologists everywhere. He claimed that remembering is an act of reconstruction, not an act of reproduction. Frederic. C. Bartlett, *Remembering: A Study in Experimental and Social Psychology* (New York: Macmillan, 1932).
4. See Article 1.1 in the Australia ICOMOS charter for the conservation of places of cultural significance (the Burra Charter).
5. In the gazetteer of any Guangdong city, it has a whole Chapter *Shan Chuan* 山川 documented in text all the mountains and water bodies in the city. The one of Huizhou even devotes two sections in the chapter to the prefecture's two major landscape features: Mt. Luofu 羅浮山 and the West Lake 西湖.
6. In the introduction to *Yancheng Ba Jing* 羊城八景, the author Li Zhen describes that "the eight scenes starts from Xiaoxiang and spreads to the whole world 八景起於瀟湘而綿延於天下."
7. Textual records on the city are mainly concentrated in three areas: its history, geography, and customs. The gazetteer—the provincial gazetteer *Tongzhi* 通志, the prefectural gazetteer *Fuzhi* 府志 and the county gazetteer *Xianzhi* 縣志—is the most informative and detailed record onto one particular city. Other textual materials, such as the historic record *Tongshi* 通史, geographical record *Di Li Zhi* 地理志, also help people in understanding the city. There are also some significant historic texts related to Guangdong, such as *Ling Baio Lu Yi* 嶺表錄異, *Yue Da Ji* 粵大記, *Guangdong Xin Yu* 廣東新語, *Yangcheng Gu Chao* 羊城古鈔, etc.
8. Jean-Louis Luxen, "The Intangible Dimension of Monuments and Site with Reference to the UNESCO World Heritage List," www.international.icomos.org/luxen_eng.htm.
9. Ibid.

Reading

55

Trevor H. J. Marchand

Process over Product: Case Studies of Traditional Building Practices in Djenné, Mali, and San'a', Yemen (2003)

Trevor H. J. Marchand is professor emeritus at the School of Oriental and African Studies (SOAS), University of London. After training as an architect, he researched traditional masonry in Nigeria and then embarked on social anthropological research in Yemen related to his PhD. Long engaged in understanding the complex relationships between the human brain and craft work, Marchand has studied masons in Djenné, Mali, and woodworkers in the United Kingdom. In the work presented here, he stresses the importance of understanding the conservation of heritage—specifically, traditional knowledge—from a process-oriented, grassroots perspective, using examples from Mali and Yemen.

The internalization of ownership and responsibility by indigenous peoples is regarded as a vital component in conservation efforts, effectively guaranteeing the transmission of the object's "cultural essence" for the foreseeable future. This requires local populations to share, or adopt, Western definitions of "cultural property" as consisting of those material artifacts that are inseparable from identity. It also espouses notions of authenticity and beliefs about the irreplaceable nature of the "original." [. . .] In discussing the impact of the "museological view of culture"—described "as sensory experienced object rather than as meaning"—Rowlands (2005) notes the pervasive influence of international legislation on late-twentieth-century notions of cultural property, fueled by the perceived threat of globalization to the survival of local cultures. Identity politics thrive in this climate. Claims to rights over cultural property instigate and perpetuate struggles to define and maintain bounded ethnic, linguistic, and nationalist enclaves. Rowlands is part of the wave of late-twentieth- and early-twenty-first-century anthropologists who embrace the discipline's return to a serious consideration of essen-

---

From Trevor H. J. Marchand, "Process over Product: Case Studies of Traditional Building Practices in Djenné, Mali, and San'a', Yemen," in *Managing Change: Sustainable Approaches to the Conservation of the Built Environment,* ed. Jeanne Marie Teutonico and Frank Matero (Los Angeles: Getty Conservation Institute, 2003), 137–41, 145–46, 148–50, 155–59.

tialist theories of material culture that no longer "oppose objects to persons or relations to things."[1] He believes that this perspective is "the key to understanding how a bridge can be made between the studies of the construction of persons and the value that is placed on the protection of culture and tradition."

This theory of culture, as embodied in the materiality of things, is highly complementary to the aims of the conservationist invested in the preservation of the "object." The object (whether artifact, architecture, or landscape) is bequeathed the status of "cultural resource," and resources are deemed to possess both a physicality and a value that may be claimed, owned, and cared for in the interests of the collective identity. It is not always clear, however, who this collective is and therefore who has the right to manage these resources. Despite claims that international guidelines (set forth by such bodies as UNESCO) serve to safeguard the local in the face of globalization, declarations of "world heritage" render the distinction between the two realms ambiguous. Struggles over the possession and conservation of these cultural resources are played out between the often disenfranchised populations of postcolonial locales and teams of Western-trained specialists (archaeologists, art historians, architects, engineers, scientists, conservators, museum curators, and government officials). This issue, however, is not my principal focus here. My aim is to draw attention to some of the serious consequences that result from underscoring the tangible, physical properties of cultural capital to the near exclusion of all else.

When the scope of cultural property is reduced to the physical, it can be thoroughly dissected and discerned. "Things," by virtue of their physicality, may be subjected to a positivist framework that classifies, quantifies, and qualifies, ultimately generating a specific, and scientific, form of knowledge (Feyerabend 1975). Those who control this knowledge command a privileged position from where decisions may be made and plans executed that directly affect the present and future state of the artifact, architecture, or landscape in question. Indeed, control over things is dangerously vulnerable to being wrested away from the original producers, owners, and inhabitants, and one must critically question which collective entity of people is ultimately the true and rightful possessor of the cultural resource: the locals, scientists, or global tourists. If the museological view of "culture as property" is prevalent, and culture is actually conceived as something that one can have more or less of, then, by extension, the declaration, conservation, and monitoring of World Heritage Sites must certainly (at least to some considerable degree) dispossess local populations of exclusive ownership and redistribute custody of that cultural resource within an international arena of competing interests. In short, it would seem that the practice of prioritizing the material by (largely) Western-trained specialists is vested with (potentially neoimperialist) ambitions to monopolize what has been constructed as a tangible resource. Cultures are effectively reduced to, and constrained by, a positivist discourse that reconfigures cultural resources as classifiable and quantifiable objects.

[. . .] [M]y main objective is to counter this claim and illustrate that "process," not simply product, should be of (perhaps greater) concern to conservationists and be rightly regarded as a precious resource in its own right. Process is constituted by skilled performance and expert knowledge, both of which give rise to the production and reproduction of material entities. These qualities are possessed by people, not things, and they combine through normally complex regimes of socialization and training to generate competent agents with distinct roles and recognized status in a given society. For the most part, socially designated experts possessing skills and knowledge (i.e., artisans, builders, sorcerers, philosophers, etc.) are responsible for the transmission of their expertise to select members of younger generations. Thus, logically, the conservation of systems that produce and proliferate this knowledge, such as apprenticeship, and the maintenance of socioeconomic parameters necessary for production, equates to the most promising scenario for sustaining desirable cultural resources.

Practices and processes may not be tangible in the sense of being material artifacts that can be scientifically scrutinized and reduced to analytic descriptions of their chemical composition and physical properties, but they are nevertheless "sensibly experienced" and "passed along." As cultural resources, traditional processes are "regenerated" each time production and reproduction (of, for instance, the material object, the rite or ritual, the sacred word or incantation) takes place. Furthermore, traditional practices and processes—constituted by specialized trade and technical knowledge; engagement in skilled performance; the knowledge of one's identity, status, and social responsibility as an "expert" and moral agent; and the public manifestation of an expert discourse—are "historical" in the sense that they are rooted in a specific social, cultural, political, and economic history. Regeneration and historical constitution in no way imply a static reproduction of either the process or the product but instead indicate that both are anchored in a dynamic, living tradition that continues to harbor value for them, thereby sanctioning their survival. What has perhaps kept traditional practices and the processes of production peripheral to conservationist concerns is precisely their nontangible and dynamic qualities that render them elusive to effective control and manipulation.

[. . .]

An Anthropological Approach to the Built Environment

[. . .] My interest is in knowledge, and it is "knowledge" that I am advocating as the primary interest for the field of conservation. This is not to discredit the immense importance of objects but rather to compel recognition of the factor that bestows those objects with importance in the first place: human thought, and the knowledge it yields. Without the knowledge that produces, uses, or even discards an object, the object, on its own, falls prey to new, decontextualized designations of meaning. Meaning, like the knowledge that each of us possesses about the world, is a product of thought: it is derived from what we think about people, things, and other ideas, and it is amenable to change. Objects do not have meaning unto themselves because an object cannot think about what it is—an object cannot think about anything. Objects cannot "contain" meaning or memory because these belong to the realm of thought, and thought, as a property, belongs to humans (or other living species). If all this seems obvious and a little heavy-handed, then it should. I am merely reinforcing my position that in no conceivable way can objects be regarded as inherently containing values, essence, meaning, memory, or culture.

[. . .] We must look to the people—the producers and users who, through their engagement in production and use, effectively generate knowledge about artifacts, architecture, and landscapes. The cultural memory is embodied "in" these practices, not in the object. As I asserted at the outset, a conservation of this knowledge, as it becomes manifest in the processes of production (and of use), is perhaps the most viable way of guaranteeing the renewal of salient resources. Anthropology provides an effective means of engaging with these more elusive cultural assets and would undoubtedly play a highly complementary role in relation to other conservation efforts.

More specifically, in dealing with the built environment, anthropology provides a framework for critically assessing the social, cultural, and historical significance of concepts such as space, place, and architecture. By considering the historical evolution of Western theories of space, from Aristotle through medieval Christianity and the Renaissance and via Descartes and later Enlightenment figures such as Newton, it becomes evident how space emerged conceptually as a reified, quantifiable entity in our society (Casey 1996; Lefebvre 1991). Its cultural construction becomes all the more evident in cross-cultural studies of spatial cognition (see, e.g., Gumperz and Levinson 1996; Marchand 2001; Senft 1997). Inspired by Heidegger's essay "Building, Dwelling, Thinking" (1977) and Merleau-Ponty's *Phenomenology of Perception* (1962), there has been mounting advocation by scholars during the past decade for recognizing the primacy of place over space (Casey 1996; Gregotti 1996:69; Hirsch and O'Hanlon 1995). As a result, space might be better understood as a conceptual extension of our emplacement-in-the-world as sentient beings: first and foremost, we are always "in place." Our emplacement is by virtue of our perpetual immersion in, embodied experience of, and engagement with our surroundings. Taking a theory of place seriously incites a closer examination of the processes that make place both a physical and a meaningful entity. An anthropology of space, place, and architecture investigates this "making" as comprising the competing discourses between builders, suppliers, architects, planners, governing bodies, conservationists (in the case of heritage sites), and inhabitants (whereby the notion of discourse encompasses engagement in all forms of practice).

My concern here is architecture, and more particularly building processes, at two UNESCO World Heritage Sites, Djenné, Mali, and San'a', Yemen. In both of these Islamic and urban settings, traditional builders—defined here as those employing indigenous materials and construction methods and deriving their expert knowledge through apprenticeship as opposed to a technical or formalized education process (Marchand 2001:73)—are still largely responsible for much (if not the majority)[2] of the construction in their cities, and they continue to transmit their expertise to younger generations of craftsmen in the trade.

Traditional Builders: Toward a Sustainable Conservation of Process

The Case of San'a'

—~—

[T]he perpetuation of the apprenticeship system, and by consequence the master-apprentice relation, is vital to the conservation of trade knowledge and the regeneration of San'a''s architectural heritage. Therefore, it is the apprenticeship process—defined as the transmission of technical skills, social and moral responsibility, and professional status—that I am regarding as the legitimate object of conservation. Various planning specialists and architects concerned with the preservation of the built environment in San'a' have proposed the establishment of trade schools. The rationale for such government-run (or conservation organization–affiliated) institutions is the training of a younger generation of craftsmen to reproduce those building skills deemed at risk of disappearing (see Lewcock 1986:115; Marchand 2001:181–82 and notes 112, 113 [pp. 265–66]); Studio Quaroni in Piepenberg 1987:104). I hope that I have demonstrated, even in this summarized description of apprenticeship, that trade schools that aim to objectify and codify knowledge for efficient technical reproduction could not feasibly replace the complexity of knowledge inculcated in the young builder under the yoke of his master. The slow transmission of knowledge via the master-apprentice relation has the capacity to distill a fine balance between reason and imagination. This balance, in turn, fosters the possibility for a creative regeneration (of both the architectural heritage and the expert knowledge), configured within a discourse of continuity and tradition.

The Case of Djenné

At the start of 2001, I commenced new fieldwork with a team of traditional builders in Djenné in order to make a comparative study of building processes and apprenticeship. This was the first of several phases of projected research with Djenné masons. [. . .]

Djenné is an ancient trade city located in the Inland Niger Delta of Mali and connected to the nearby Bani River (a major tributary of the Niger River) by a network of waterways. Historically, it served as a major junction for the trade in gold, ivory, kola, and slaves heading north from the southern forests and savannah and for the salt, copper, and Mediterranean goods coming across the Sahara via Timbuktu. [. . .]

—~—

The production of Djenné's built environment and the dissemination of the style throughout the region must be attributed to the city's organization of masons, the *barey ton*. The term *ton* is a Mande designation for either age set associations (Durán 1995:113; Imperato 1977:40) or professional organizations, such as that for hunters (*donson ton*) (McNaughton 1982:54), or builders. Fairhead and Leach (1999) note interestingly that the term is synonymous with the word for termite mound (*ton*); termites are revered throughout West Africa for their disciplined coordination. [. . .]
[. . .]

In an attempt to protect Djenné's heritage, UNESCO declared the city and its surrounding archaeological sites a World Monument in 1988, and the Malian authorities set up a Mission Culturelle with the aim of safeguarding the monument and educating the local population about heritage and conservation. Following from this, and based on an extensive body of Dutch research in the region (most important, the meticulous study of Djenné's architecture and urban environment by Maas and Mommersteeg [1992] and Bedaux's vast archaeological expertise), the Dutch Embassy in Bamako requested the Rijksmuseum voor Volkenkunde, Leiden, to draft a plan for the restoration of the city. [. . .]

[. . .] Of main concern to my argument here promoting process over product is the project's astute regard for the role of the traditional masons and the transmission of technical knowledge as integral to the restoration program. [. . .] One criticism I reserve for the conservation efforts, however, is the continued reliance on a constructed notion of "authenticity" invested in the building-as-object over and above building-as-process. Despite a recognition by the project directors that the classification as a UNESCO World Heritage Site, in combination with protective Malian laws regarding classified monuments, immobilizes the "living city . . . in its own armour of architectural tradition," a rather "inflexible and rigid set of rules" is perpetuated for those houses chosen for restoration by their scientific committee (Bedaux et al. 2000:204). The project "proposes not to classify all of Jenné's buildings, but only those that are significant for its architectural image," in the hope that these will "serve as a source of inspiration for future developments" (p. 204). It is felt that "as much as possible of the original parts of any monument" should be retained, and the documentation produced for these houses should be used to ascertain a "reasonable control of future alterations" (p. 204). Original floor plans should be "reconstructed when possible" based on existing documentation and the coherent oral accounts of changes offered by house owners (p. 205). Also, despite the fact that traditional restoration methods entailed demolition and reconstruction (due to the inherent instability of the old-style cylindrical mud bricks), original walls should be retained whenever it is structurally feasible since there are "only a few really old walls left in the city" (p. 205; Bedaux, Diaby, and Maas pers. com. 2001).

Households that agree to participate in the project are expected to make no further structural or planning modifications to their homes. In theory, they are legally bound to the agreement and may be tried under Malian law for noncompliance. In my view, the house takes on the status of protected monument above and beyond its function as a home and is effectively rendered impotent in the face of changing family needs and transforming social values. It is therefore difficult to imagine how the already selected and restored houses will inspire other households to partake in a restoration agenda that is largely premised on an idealized authenticity arbitrarily rooted in Dubois's photographs and other turn-of-the-century colonial documentation (Bedaux et al. 2000:205). [. . .]

Conclusion

[. . .] In my critique of a museological view of the built-environment-as-object, I have championed a conservation of process over product. Process, in the sense that I have considered it here, has been most notably defined by the knowledge possessed and transmitted by the traditional builder. I have not, however, advocated a fetishization of expert knowledge that would seek to "harness the exotic and cabalistic power of otherness . . . and veil it . . . in a shroud of mysticism" (Law 1999:101). Knowledge surely cannot, and should not, be preserved as a static objectified thing, alienated from its producer. Rather, it is knowledge recognized as a dynamic process responsible for regenerating social agents, architecture, and meaning that must be conserved.

[. . .] The contemporary traditional builder, through his apprenticeship, is inculcated with the technical and social knowledge necessary for innovatively responding to change while simultaneously reproducing a discourse of locality, continuity, and tradition. In short, it is this expertise that sustains a sense of place. If through legislation and cultural politics (Western-inspired) conservation efforts incapacitate contemporary traditional builders and inhabitants in responding to changing needs and social values, their architectural heritage will inevitably lose its utility and meaning for the living local population, and thus also its authenticity as a valued cultural commodity.

Notes

1. Appadurai's book, *The Social Life of Things* (1986), played a major role in coercing an anthropological reconsideration of essentialist theories of material culture. Other important contributors to this wave of thinking include Gell (1998), Strathern (1988, 1990), Weiner (1992), and Godelier (1999). Gell advocates an appreciation of iconic objects as indexes of agency that, in particular, can occupy positions in the networks of human social agency. See Rowlands (2005) for a more comprehensive overview of twentieth-century anthropological positions with regard to essentialism.
2. In Djenné, the traditional masons maintain (essentially complete) control over all building in the town. The building of government projects, such as the recently constructed hospital, may, however, be shared among teams of builders from other cities such as Bamako (the nation's capital) and Mopti (the regional capital) who are specialized in modern (read: Western) construction methods. In San'a', on the other hand, the traditional building trade has been heavily encroached on by architects, engineers, and Western-style contractors who employ (often unskilled) wage laborers. Depite the renegotiation of the power share, Yemen's traditional builders have nevertheless managed to preserve their upper hand in the competitive discourse (Marchand 2000a, 2001).

References

Appadurai, A. 1986. *The Social Life of Things*. Cambridge: Cambridge University Press.

Bedaux, R., B. Diaby, P. Maas, and S Sidibe. 2000. "The Restoration of Jenne, Mali: African Aesthetics and Western Paradigms." In *Terra* 2000, 201–7. London: James & James Scientific Publishers.

Casey, E. 1996. "How to Get from Space to Place in a Fairly Short Stretch of Time: Phenomenological Prolegomena." In *Senses of Place*, ed. S. Feld and K. Basso, 13–52. Santa Fe, New Mex.: School of American Research Press.

Duran, L. 1995. "Birds of Wasulu: Freedom of Expression and Expression of Freedom in the Popular Music of Southern Mali." *British Journal of Ethnomusicology* 4:101–34.
Fairhead, J., and M. Leach. 1999. "Termites, Society and Ecology: Perspectives from West Africa." In *Cultural and Spiritual Values of Biodiversity*, ed. D. Posey. 235–42. London: UNBP and I.T. Books.
Feyerabend, P. 1975. *Against Method: Outline of an Anarchistic Theory of Knowledge*. London: Verso.
Gell, A. 1998. *Art and Agency: An Anthropological Theory*. Cambridge: Cambridge University Press.
Godelier, M. 1999. *The Enigma of the Gift*. Cambridge: Polity.
Gregotti, V. 1996. *Inside Architecture*. London: MIT Press.
Gumperz, S., and S. Levinson, eds. 1996. *Rethinking Linguistic Relativity*. Cambridge: Cambridge University Press.
Heidegger, M. 1977. "Building, Dwelling, Thinking." In *Basic Writings*, 319–39. San Francisco: Harper San Francisco.
Hirsch, E., and M. O'Hanlon, eds. 1995. *The Anthropology of Landscape: Perspectives on Place and Space*. Oxford: Clarendon Press.
Imperato, P. J. 1977. *African Folk Medicine: Practices and Beliefs of the Bambara and Other Peoples*. Baltimore, Md.: York Press.
Law, J. 1999. "The Storyteller." In *Liberated Voices: Contemporary Art from South Africa*, ed. P. Herreman, 92–109. London and New York: Museum for African Art.
Lefebvre, H. 1991. *The Production of Space*. Trans. D. Nicholson Smith. Oxford: Blackwell.
Lewcock, R. 1986. *The Old Walled City of Sana*. Paris: UNESCO.
Maas, P., and G. Mommersteeg. 1992. *Djenné: Chef d'oeuvre architecturale*. Eindhoven: Université de Technologie.
Marchand, T. 2000a. "The Lore of the Master Builder: Working with Local Materials and Local Knowledge in San'a', Yemen." In *Traditional Knowledge: Learning from Experience*. IASTE Working Paper, vol. 137:1–17. University of California, Berkeley.
———. 2001. *Minaret Building and Apprenticeship in Yemen*. London: Curzon.
McNaughton, P. R. 1982. "The Shirts that Mande Hunters Wear." *African Arts*, no. 3 (May): 54–58.
Merleau-Ponty, M. 1962. *Phenomenology of Perception*. London: Routledge.
Piepenberg. P. 1987. "Sana'a' al-Qadeema: The Challenge of Modernisation." In *The Middle East City*, ed. Abdulaziz Y. Saqqaf, 93–113. New York: Paragon House.
Rowlands, M. 2005. "Value and the Cultural Transmissions of Things." In *Commodities and the Value of Things*, ed. P. Geschiere. Durham: Duke University Press.
Senft, G. 1997. *Referring to Space: Studies in Austronesian and Papuan Languages*. Oxford: Clarendon Press.
Strathern, M. 1988. *The Gender of the Gift*. Berkeley: University of California Press.
———. 1990. "Artefacts of History." In *Culture and History in the Pacific*, ed. J. Siikala, 25–44. Helsinki: Finnish Anthropological Society.
Weiner, A. 1992. *Inalienable Possessions*. Berkeley: University of California Press.

Part VI

Visual Summary: The Search for Significant Values

Sule Pagoda, central Yangon, Myanmar, 2013. Photo by Jeff Cody.

Sule Pagoda, central Yangon, Myanmar. This sacred place was used as "mile 0" by nineteenth-century British colonizers when laying out a rectilinear, European-derived grid.

Part VI

VISUAL SUMMARY

West Kowloon Opera, Hong Kong.

Hong Kong Opera. Photo by Jeff Cody, circa 2003.

PLATES VI.1 AND VI.2

Traditional *yueju* (Cantonese opera) in Hong Kong is a remarkable example of intangible cultural heritage embodied in physical form. Traditional Chinese opera remains extremely popular today and is often performed in temporary structures, such as the ones in Hong Kong shown here, erected periodically during the year. Jean-Louis Luxen (reading 47) argues that "intangible heritage must be made incarnate in tangible manifestations, in visible signs, if it is to be conserved."

Part VI

VISUAL SUMMARY

Kintaikyo Bridge, Iwakuni, Yamaguchi Prefecture, Japan. Photo by Jeff Cody, 2006.

PLATE VI.3

The Kintaikyo Bridge in Iwakuni, one of three celebrated bridges in Japan, was first built in 1673. It has been replicated—with new materials—three times, most recently in 2004. Similarly, temple structures in Japan and other Asian countries are periodically built anew with materials and forms identical to the originals, raising important issues regarding the meaning of authenticity. Gustavo F. Araoz (reading 48) contends that the 1990s were a pivotal decade in which these issues were reconsidered, primarily because of the Nara Document on Authenticity (1994) and its implications concerning whether only original materials should be considered authentic.

Part VI

VISUAL SUMMARY

Yangon, Myanmar, street scene. Photo by Jeff Cody, 2013.

PLATE VI.4

This view of central Yangon, Myanmar, exemplifies the thorny challenge of disorderly and unsympathetic urban development in proximity to significant historic sites. John Pendlebury, Michael Short, and Aidan While (reading 49) underscore a key point about the difficulty of conserving authenticity in "a context of constant urban evolution." While suggesting that "it is precisely the combination of different elements from different time-scales—the totality in all its messiness—that is the object of conservation," they also underline the importance of a value judgment about "the spirit of place as a living entity from the past, in the present, and for the future." Ultimately, evaluating a place and determining an acceptable balance between preserving heritage values and accepting change constitutes the greatest challenge of urban conservation.

Aerial photo of Mexicaltitán de Uribe, Mexico. Photo by Georg Gerster.

PLATE VI.5

The island-village of Mexicaltitán de Uribe (Nayarit), Mexico, which some historians believe is the place Aztec culture originated, is a compelling example of a relatively pristine urban landscape in need of management in the face of mounting pressures from tourism and modern development. In their discussion of authenticity of setting, Bernard M. Feilden and Jukka Jokilehto (reading 50) suggest that "the continuation of traditional crafts and skills may be an essential part of the relevant management policy in order to guarantee coherence within a traditional economic system, life style and habitat."

View of traditional Japanese houses in Higashi Chaya old geisha district, Kanazawa, Japan. Photo by Ben Bryant, 2017.

PLATE VI.6

Kanazawa, Japan, is a city where active community engagement has lived up to the ideals of the Machinami Charter (2000), adopted by the Japanese ICOMOS Committee to conserve Japan's historic towns (see Appendix). The Japanese word *machinami* refers to a historic town in both its physical and spiritual senses. A similar holistic approach is advocated by Michael Turner and Tal Tomer (reading 51), who consider that the true physiognomy of a place can be fully understood only "through the palimpsest of intangible traditions and tangible urban fabric." They advocate the active participation of the resident community as a means to identify and protect the genuine values of a place.

Sekondi Beachfront, Sekondi-Takoradi, Ghana. Photo by Christine Badgley.

PLATE VI.7

This incongruous fish sculpture marking a roundabout in Sekondi, Ghana, illustrates Senam Okudzeto's observation (reading 52) that so-called beautification projects in African cities often become "travesties of misused public funds and visual atrocities." She calls for "urban conservation with a mind towards creating a radical public history," in which the residents are directly involved in the decision-making process.

Part VI

VISUAL SUMMARY

View of Shanghai. Photo by Jeff Cody, circa 1998.

PLATE VI.8

In their essay about the prospects for conserving Shanghai's *lilong* housing, the traditional back-alley structures and communities removed from the traffic and commercial frenzy of the downtown area, Non Arkaraprasertkul and Matthew Williams (reading 53) state that "there is a possibility for the preservation of both architecture and community culture together—the middle way." But they introduce a caveat: this is possible only if there is a genuine will to preserve not just the buildings but also the distinct way of life of these communities. It is an effort that requires the active engagement of both local authorities and residents. Plate VI.8, above, depicts the eradication of a *lilong* neighborhood in the 1990s, when rampant demolition of such neighborhoods was a by-product of overheated development.

A man riding his bike on the Dongxin Bridge in the direction of Hejiang Pavilion and Qiaodong subdistrict in Huizhou, China. Photo by Chintung Lee, 2017.

PLATE VI.9

Huizhou, located on the coast of southern China's Guangdong Province, is one of the country's distinct landscapes, deeply embedded in the memory of the people. Carmen C. M. Tsui (reading 54) explains how "the Chinese visualized . . . landscape and . . . place through their distinctive scenes and extracted and highlighted the distinctiveness of the landscape, place, and scenes by using text."

FACTORY

Part VII

The Sustainability of Urban Conservation

The sustainability of urban conservation is a much-debated issue that has often placed in opposition those who apply strict economic (or fiscal) criteria in evaluating the viability of preserving heritage assets against those who consider cultural assets of such paramount importance that they should be independent of purely fiscal considerations. The first reading, from David Throsby's essay on the economics of cultural heritage (reading 56), confronts these differing standpoints and looks at the concepts of cultural value and sustainability as being essential to reconciling the two positions. In Throsby's view, clarifying these concepts is fundamental if we want to "link an economic approach to heritage with the essential cultural purposes that the conservation profession strives to achieve." In particular, with regard to heritage assets, *non-use* values[1] are as important as their direct financial value and contribute considerably to the aggregate value of a heritage item through its different and not necessarily mutually exclusive levels of significance (aesthetic, spiritual, social, historical, and symbolic).

The sustainability of heritage assets, on the other hand, hinges on establishing the conditions for the long-term preservation of cultural capital through the generation of tangible and intangible benefits, intergenerational equity, socially equitable distribution of returns, maintenance of diversity, avoidance of irreversible change, and recognition of the role that individual heritage assets play in the larger context of a city, region, or country. Of special relevance in Throsby's paper is the search for a methodology to measure the dual economic and cultural value of heritage assets, evaluate their prospects for sustainability, and discuss how these various components can contribute to shaping decisions concerning heritage.

In the selection that follows, Christian Ost expands on Throsby's definitions and methodology to develop an economic assessment of heritage that can be applied more specifically to the urban context (reading 57). Such an extension cannot omit consideration of the spatial system that defines public spaces and binds together the built fabric, as well as the intangible heritage, which constitutes a fundamental component

Winsor McCay, *Technocracy*, 1933. Detail. See p. 532.

in any living city. The latter includes traditions, rituals, festivities, sports events, know-how, crafts, and customs that apply to a specific cultural and contextual setting.[2]

As Ost explains, the extension of the cultural heritage concept to an entire urban context covers a much wider, multifaceted range of components than in the case of individual heritage assets. However, by expanding the scope to conserve more than an individual heritage asset, one needs to include aspects of immaterial and/or social significance that may be difficult to assess and quantify in strict economic terms. Nevertheless, the importance of these intangible elements for the well-being and sustainability of whole communities is now fully acknowledged and demands that social and environmental indicators be considered on a par with economic ones. This is important because the consideration and activation of the assets that form the cultural capital of a city has a direct impact on residents' quality of life and visitor satisfaction. These, in turn, provide "larger economic outcomes for the city as a whole."

Because non-use values are difficult to measure, particularly when dealing with cultural and public goods in a large heritage context, there is a need to identify valuation methods based on hypothetical market conditions, user preferences, willingness to pay, and the assessment of customer satisfaction indicators.[3]

Ost identifies in the recognition of cultural significance and activation of assets a two-step management process necessary to generate economic benefits in a city context. In his view, responsibility for identifying suitable cultural policies should rest with the city representatives and administration, while the activation of assets is an economic decision that can be furthered either through private investment or through a combination of private and public resources. Based on these premises, Ost puts forward the idea of a portfolio approach to managing cultural and economic assets in a heritage city. As in the case of risk management of portfolio investments, the mixing and balancing of different urban assets is meant to identify the best possible returns achievable in the long term. In this perspective, an integrated approach to the development of cultural and economic resources should consider the city holistically and move from a strategic understanding of the correlation between its different components to the identification of a suitable diversification of assets. The resulting portfolio may be defined as "a collection of built, moveable, intangible, and spatial assets, with historic and cultural significance, which are active such as to generate inclusive and sustainable economic assets."

Activating heritage projects, in the case of both individual buildings and large urban initiatives, is predicated on a clear understanding of the financial tools that are available and most effective in the conservation and appropriate development of heritage assets. In reading 58, Donovan Rypkema offers a clear and concise illustration of the rationale for the use of financial tools, what they are, why they are needed, and how they can be employed to best advantage in urban conservation. Financial tools that have proved especially effective include grants, micro loans, property tax reductions and credits, transferable development rights, and public-private partnerships. Each is discussed on its merit and its potential to promote heritage investment. The conclusion acknowledges that the Historic Urban Landscape recommendations, adopted at the UNESCO General Conference of 2011, if furthered through the various national legislations, can provide the comprehensive urban development framework and stable investment climate conducive to the use of financial tools that encourage "growth and new development in parts of the city while maintaining the quality and character of heritage areas."[4]

The consideration of cultural and economic values, even if identified by criteria aimed at inclusiveness and sustainability, leaves open the question, whose values are they? Are they a fair and balanced representation of community interests, or are they imposed from the top by politicians, administrators, interest groups, and conservation experts? In this respect, it must be recognized that interventions that appear to be perfectly legitimate and well justified on economic grounds have often resulted in gentrification and the creation of tourist enclaves that transform historic areas in ways that are contrary to the interests of the residents and the community at large.

Accordingly, the readings that follow discuss how to ensure that the identification of values is the result of a genuine process of urban appraisal grounded in the living community and outline ways in which the worst effects of gentrification and tourism can be avoided or curbed to minimize physical change and achieve acceptable results for the populations concerned. They thus point to the complementary aspects that must be taken into account when evaluating the sustainability of urban conservation, aspects that go beyond purely cultural and economic criteria to consider the wider social context and the direct engagement of local communities.

In reading 59, Julian Smith offers a number of stimulating arguments in favor of an in-depth understanding of the multiple realities of a city, including its human activities and behavioral patterns. Smith advocates a complete shift in the way of seeing and understanding the city. It should move away from an appraisal limited to its physical form and aesthetic attributes to include an appreciation of the "cultural experience as basic to sense of place and sense of identity." After discussing the nature and significance of cultural mapping, an exercise that combines memory and imagination, Smith looks at the importance of developing an ecological view of the city, intended as an ensemble of locally based practices and activities that determine a specific cultural behavior in any given urban setting.

Moving on to consider how these interpretations and findings can help develop a sustainable community-based design strategy in existing city areas, Smith advocates that communities take the lead in "defining the present and then choosing interventions that strengthen its positives and weaken its negatives" rather than envisioning a preconceived and often fanciful notion of their future.[5] This more realistic "ecological" or "organic" approach, as defined by Smith, is totally opposed to the now-fashionable concept of management of change, a notion that in fact assumes that "change is a given."[6] To the contrary, what seems more important is to learn how to manage continuity, intended as "finding the healthy equilibrium that thrives on diversity but achieves a larger whole that has a certain stability and sustainability." In this perspective, change may be relatively contained, mostly focused on adjusting existing conditions to reassert a healthy equilibrium between the different components of the urban landscape. Smith's concluding remarks advocate, contrary to the modernist and utopian viewpoint that has prevailed so far, a return to "some of the fundamental values that have inspired previous generations."

The issue of reconciling conservation, tourism, and sustainable development, in particular, the question of the sustainability of heritage tourism, is discussed by Noha Nasser in reading 60. Moving from the realization that mass tourism has proven harmful to culture, the environment, and built resources, Nasser reviews the concept of sustainable tourism as an alternative, capable, at least in principle, of retaining cultural values while benefiting local economies. Heritage tourism, a form of tourism based on small-scale, locally owned activities and on the premise of nonconsumptive, renewable use of resources has the potential to further both conservation and local development requirements. In order to fulfill this potential, however, it must be integrated with forms of long-term, responsible planning, accept change within a framework of continuity—thus avoiding the risk of irreversible transformations—maintain local control over the revenues generated from tourism, and be firmly grounded in local participation. The conclusion is that heritage tourism can and should play a compatible and complementary role in the conservation effort through careful management of cultural resources, quality of development, and close integration with the sociocultural needs and expectations of the local community.

The final selection in part VII, from Stephanie Brown (reading 61), tackles the issue of gentrification in the context of urban revitalization projects, both as a source of conflict and as a process of community transformation that must be understood and managed to avoid the worst effects of physical and social displacement of lower-income residents and local businesses. Contrary to most literature on the subject, which focuses exclusively on the negative aspects of gentrification, Brown's article provides a helpful framework for understanding the problem and a realistic proposal for managing the process in ways that help achieve a healthier and more inclusive model of social coexistence in existing urban areas. It should be noted in this respect that traditional cities, with the notable exception of ghettos, such as those of Venice or Rome, were in most cases functionally and socially mixed, a factor that explains the vibrant and varied character of historic urban areas. Recent transformations resulting in extreme forms of gentrification or overly restored tourist enclaves have in fact obliterated urban diversity by displacing long-established residents and businesses and imposing the "disturbing sameness"[7] conveyed by many historic cities today.

Notes

1. "Non-use values" refers to economic outputs not observable by market data.
2. A classic example is the Palio, the horse race that takes place in the center of Siena, which is a centuries-old tradition deeply associated with local rituals and rivalries between different town neighborhoods, the so-called *contrade*.
3. On the economic valuation of urban sites, see Anna Alberini, Patrizia Riganti, and Alberto Longo, "Can People Value the Aesthetic and Use Services of Urban Sites? Evidence from a Survey of Belfast Residents," Fondazione Eni Enrico Mattei, September 2002 (NOTA DI LAVORO 70.2002).

4. See also D. Ripkema, "Devising Financial Tools for Urban Conservation," in *Reconnecting the City: The Historic Urban Landscape Approach and the Future of Urban Heritage* (New York: John Wiley & Sons, 2015), 283–90. On economic analysis and financial tools, see F. Bandarin and R. van Oers, *The Historic Urban Landscape: Managing Heritage in an Urban Century* (New York: John Wiley & Sons, 2014), 171–74.
5. On the subject of community values in the management of heritage assets, see Harriet Deacon and Rieks Smeets, "Authenticity, Value and Community Involvement in Heritage Management under the World Heritage and Intangible Heritage Conventions," *Heritage & Society* 6, no. 2 (2013): 129–43.
6. The point that "conservation is the management of continuity" as opposed to the "management of change" was also expressed by Jukka Jokilehto at the 2014 Annual School of the U.K. Institute of Historic Building Conservation (IHBC), held in Edinburgh (quoted by D. Rodwell in in his keynote presentation at the International Cultural Heritage Forum, Vilnius, December 4–6, 2014).
7. Michele Lamprakos, "The Idea of the Historic City," *Change Over Time* 4, no. 1 (Spring 2014): 8–38.

Reading

56

David Throsby

Cultural Capital and Sustainability Concepts in the Economics of Cultural Heritage (2002)

David Throsby, a cultural economist, is Distinguished Professor of Economics at Macquarie University in Sydney. Two of his books, Economics and Culture *(2001) and* The Economics of Cultural Policy *(2010), are classics in the field of cultural economics. Throsby was one of the first professionals to propose and examine the notion of cultural capital in the context of heritage economics. In this reading, in addition to an exposition of the meaning of cultural capital and sustainability in terms of their application to the economics of cultural heritage, Throsby considers ways to make them operational for real-world phenomena.*

Introduction

Traditionally, the work of conservationists in the field of tangible cultural heritage[1] has covered a range of tasks, including identification, classification, certification, interpretation, protection, maintenance, and restoration. The decisions that they make concerning, for example, what counts as heritage or which items should be accorded privileged status (e.g., as listed buildings) have been based on their professional and technical expertise. Economists have recently begun to ask questions about the economic ramifications of such decisions. [. . .]

At the same time, when economists themselves become involved in heritage matters, they have been accused by conservationists of adopting a narrow economizing attitude to heritage decisions, turning attention away from the essential cultural values of heritage toward a more market-driven approach. [. . .]

[. . .] We could characterize conservationists as interpreting heritage items as stores of cultural value—that is, as things that have been inherited from the past which are valuable in themselves and which yield value to those who enjoy them in one way or

From David Throsby, "Cultural Capital and Sustainability Concepts in the Economics of Cultural Heritage," in *Assessing the Values of Cultural Heritage,* edited by Marta de la Torre (Los Angeles: Getty Conservation Institute, 2002), 101–4, 107, 109–11, 113–17.

another, both now and in the future.[2] Economists in turn can readily comprehend that artifacts, artworks, buildings, sites, and so on have the characteristics of capital assets and that the depreciation, maintenance, restoration, and so of such assets can be analyzed as economic processes.[3] Given that heritage as capital has some characteristics (such as the production of cultural value) that are different from those of other sorts of capital, it seems that a notion of "cultural capital" to describe heritage might be able to integrate its principal economic and cultural characteristics.

Moreover, both conservationists and economists are concerned with the long-term nature of decisions relating to significant capital items, invoking the notion of "sustainability."[4] This concept has specific connotations in an environmental context that relate especially to the preservation of natural assets for future generations; so, for example, the harvesting of fish stock is "sustainable" if the catch is controlled so that the total population of fish is maintained into the future. In more general usage, a sustainable solution to a problem is one that is not a quick fix but is likely to provide a more permanent or lasting remedy. The antithesis of sustainability—namely, "unsustainability"—is also widely recognized. For example, a country's rapid rate of economic growth in the short term might be described as unsustainable if it is not based on fundamental strength and is not likely therefore to be maintained over a longer period. It is thus not difficult to see that since the very same principles of long-term decision making, concern for future generations, and so on are important for the disciplines of both conservation and economics in their respective analyses of cultural heritage, the idea of sustainability could well provide a link between the economist's and the conservationist's approach to the problem.

The task of this paper, then, is to sharpen the analytical articulation of these two concepts—cultural capital and sustainability—in their application to the economics of cultural heritage, and to consider ways of making them operational so that they can be applied to real-world phenomena. The latter requirement means confronting problems of empirical measurement—i.e., how can we assess the economic and cultural value of heritage and of the services that heritage produces, and how can those values be incorporated into an empirical analysis of decisions relating to cultural heritage, such that sustainability principles are effectively served?
[. . .]

Cultural Capital

Definitional Issues

The concept of capital in economics is almost as old as the discipline itself. In formal terms, capital can be defined as a stock of goods that gives rise to further goods and services over time. The principal form of capital identified in economics is *physical capital*, meaning plant, machinery, buildings, equipment, and so on, all of which provide a flow of services yielding other commodities that may be consumed or may themselves be capital items leading to still further commodities. [. . .]

In economics the concept of capital invokes the notion of investment, which is the process of adding to the capital stock. At the beginning of any time period, individuals, firms, or the economy as a whole are assumed to possess an endowment of capital goods, which may depreciate or deteriorate through wear and tear and which may be replaced or augmented by new investment during the time period under consideration.

Economists also identify two further forms of capital: human and natural capital. [. . .]

In conisdering the phenomenon of capital in economics, we must be clear about the distinction between stocks and flows.[5] The *stock* of capital, as its name suggests, refers to the quantity of capital in existence at a given time, measurable as the number or value of capital items in a given situation. This capital stock gives rise over time to a *flow* of services that, as noted above, may enter final consumption immediately or be combined with other inputs to yield further goods and services. Take the historic town center of Dublin, for example, a precinct that has been redeveloped as a cultural and commercial center that preserves the architectural features of the original buildings. The collection of buildings and the relationships among them make up the capital stock, and the flow of services they provide can be seen in the continuing benefits enjoyed by those who visit the precinct or use it during their everyday lives. In any analysis of capital in economics, it is essential to identify whether the capital concept being used refers to a stock or a flow variable.

It should not be difficult to accept that tangible cultural heritage of the sort described above can be considered a form of capital. Heritage items such as a painting by Rembrandt or a historic building can be seen as assets: both required investment of physical and human resources in their original manufacture and construction; both will deteriorate over time unless resources are devoted to their maintenance and upkeep; and both give rise to a flow of services over time that may enter the final consumption of individuals directly (e.g., when people view the painting in a museum or visit the historic building) or that may contribute to the production of further goods and services (e.g., when the painting inspires the creation of new artworks or when the historic building is used as a commercial office space). In other words, heritage items can be interpreted as capital assets with the standard characteristics of ordinary physical capital in economics.

Is it sufficient simply to classify tangible heritage as physical capital, or is there something else about heritage items that distinguishes them from other items of physical capital? Recently, suggestions have been made that heritage items are members of a class of capital that is indeed distinct from other forms of capital; this class has been called *cultural capital*.[6] The distinction lies in the type of value that is embodied in these assets and is yielded by the goods and services they produce. [. . .]

[W]e can provide a formal definition of cultural capital as an asset that embodies a store of cultural value, separable from whatever economic value it might possess; the asset gives rise to a flow of goods and services over time which may also have cultural value (i.e., which are themselves cultural goods and services). The stock of tangible cultural capital thus defined comprises cultural heritage as specified above. Intangible cultural capital exists in ideas, traditions, beliefs, and customs shared by a group of people, and it also includes intellectual capital, which exists as language, literature, music, and so on. In this paper, as noted above, we restrict attention to tangible cultural capital.

Questions of Value

Bearing in mind that the value of an item of cultural capital may relate to its asset value as a stock of capital or to the value of the flow of services to which it gives rise, let us turn attention to the types of economic value attributable to heritage assets. We can distinguish between use and nonuse values. *Use value* refers to the direct valuation of the asset's services by those who consume those services—the entry fees paid by visitors to historic sites, for example. *Nonuse value* refers to the value placed upon a range of nonrival and nonexcludable public-good characteristics[7] typically possessed by cultural heritage. In brief, these nonuse values may relate to the asset's existence value (people value the existence of the heritage item even though they themselves may not consume its services directly); its *option* value (people wish to preserve the option that they or others might consume the asset's services at some future time); and its bequest value (people may wish to bequeath the asset to future generations). These nonuse values are not observable in market transactions, since no market exists on which the rights to them can be exchanged, although their magnitude can nevertheless be evaluated, for example, by asking people how much they are willing to pay to ensure that these benefits will continue to be available to them. Because these values arise outside of market processes, they can be referred to as examples of *nonmarket* values.

Taken together, the use and nonuse values defined above make up what we refer to as the *economic value* of a heritage asset or of the goods and services to which it gives rise, i.e., the value of these items as assessed by an economic analysis. It is important to note that economic value in this sense differs from *financial* value ("the bottom line") since the latter does not include nonmarket effects. Nevertheless, both are expressed in the same terms, i.e., in monetary units.

The different types of economic values identified above can be illustrated with reference to Venice. A range of direct economic impacts can be attributed to this historic city, including the contribution of its cultural capital stock to the net value of the output of goods and services produced by the city's economy. A significant proportion of these direct use values is generated by tourism, which provides the tangible revenue base upon which the local economy is sustained. In addition, Venice gives rise to all three of the nonmarket benefits noted above: people all over the world care deeply about the continued existence of Venice, even if they have never been there; many would be willing to pay something simply to preserve the option of visiting it as some time; and the city is surely regarded as part of Italy's and the world's cultural patrimony, which must be passed on intact to future generations. All of these use and nonuse values can be identified for Venice as a whole and, at a more specific level, for individual components of Venice, such as particular buildings or (collections of) artworks contained within its boundaries.

—~—

Sustainability

Definitional Issues

The concept of sustainability is most often invoked in the context of the environment, where the term *sustainable* is generally linked with the word *development*. *Sustainable development* marries the ideas of sustainable *economic* development, meaning development that will not slow down or wither away but will be, in some sense, self-perpetuating, and *ecological* sustainability, meaning the preservation and enhancement of a range of environmental values through the maintenance of ecosystems in the natural world. Furthermore, the term *sustainable development* embraces an interpretation of "economic development" that supersedes former notions of economic growth measured only in terms of increases in per capita GDP; sustainability in this context embraces the wider concept of "human development," focused on the individual as both the instrument and the object of development and measured by a variety of indicators of quality of life and standards of living that go well beyond measuring simply material progress.

[. . .]

It is apparent from the accepted definition of sustainable development that a key element of this concept is equity in the treatment of different generations over time. The term *intergenerational equity*, or *intertemporal distributive justice*, is used to refer to fairness in the distribution of welfare, utility, or resources between generations. Although the principles of intergenerational equity can be applied to relations between any series of generations at any time, practical interest in it has focused, not surprisingly, on the concern among those of us alive today for the well-being of future generations. Intergenerational equity can be considered in relation to cultural capital because the stock of cultural capital is what we have inherited from our forebears and what we will hand on to future generations. Intertemporal equity issues arise in regard to access to that capital; in fact, it may be suggested that equity of access to cultural capital should be regarded as just as important as equity in the intergenerational distribution of benefits from any other sort of capital.

—~—

The Application of Sustainability Principles to Cultural Capital

While intergenerational equity is a key element of sustainability, the long-running debate about ecologically sustainable development has indicated that other criteria need to be taken into account in making the concept relevant and operational. Therefore, let us now broaden the scope of sustainability to incorporate other aspects of this concept and consider their application to cultural heritage. [. . .]

The suggested criteria are as follows:

Generation of Tangible and Intangible Benefits

As we have noted, cultural capital generates a time stream of benefits that provide the rationale for the investment project under consideration. A generalized cost-benefit approach may be taken in order to estimate the overall impact of the project. In this assessment, sustainability would require the analysis of net benefits to take account of *both* use *and* nonuse values, and of both economic and cultural value generated by the project.
[. . .]

Intergenerational Equity

This principle requires that the interests of future generations be acknowledged. [. . .]

Intragenerational Equity

Heritage decisions have significant effects on the welfare of the present generation. Consideration should be given to the distributional impacts of the costs of the investment project under study, in case a regressive incidence can be identified. [. . .]

Maintenance of Diversity

Just as biodiversity is seen as significant in the natural world, so also is cultural diversity important in maintaining cultural systems. The diversity of ideas, beliefs, traditions, and values yields a flow of cultural services that is quite distinct from the services provided by the individual components. Indeed, diversity could be seen as one of the most important attributes of cultural capital in the large, because it has the capacity to yield new capital formation. For example, to the extent that creative works are inspired by the existing stock of cultural resources, a greater diversity of resources will lead to the creation of more varied and more culturally valuable artistic works in the future. [. . .]

Precautionary Principle

As a general proposition, the precautionary principle states that decisions that may lead to irreversible change should be approached with extreme caution and from a strongly risk-averse position, because of the imponderability of the consequences of such decisions. [. . .]

Recognition of Interdependence

Finally, an overarching principle of sustainability is the proposition that no part of any system exists independently of other parts and that the interconnectedness between specific items of cultural capital and the benefits they bestow should be examined in any project appraisal. In other words, the role of heritage items as components of what might be termed the cultural infrastructure of a city, a region, or a country should,

according to this principle, be explicitly recognized and its importance be identified as a distinct element of the analysis.
[. . .]

Application

The Task Ahead

The concept of cultural capital as a means of representing heritage and the principles of sustainability that we have enumerated above provide a solid theoretical foundation that links the economist's and the conservationist's approaches to heritage decisions. The next step is to give these theoretical ideas some practical reality. How can they be made operational in a way that continues to recognize the importance of both an economic and a cultural interpretation of heritage in the real world of conservation?

In order to focus the analysis, let us suppose that the task ahead of us—that is, the decision to be made—concerns a project. For example, a project might involve:
[. . .]

- The redevelopment (and possible reuse) of a historic or cultural site, precinct, location, urban space, and so on

[. . .] The questions to be asked can be framed as follows:

- What are the economic and cultural returns to that investment?
- Does the project meet the sustainability criteria?
- Do the economic and cultural returns justify proceeding with the project, in comparison with alternative ways of using the same economic and cultural inputs?

To address these questions, we need to develop measures of the economic and cultural value of the project. [. . .]

Methodologies for Cultural Assessment

It has been a theme of this paper that, in parallel with any assessment of the economic value of cultural heritage, an assessment of the cultural value of the project must be carried out, and that the cultural evaluation should be accorded, in some sense, an equal weighting with the economic analysis. We suggested earlier that, in principle, a "cultural cost-benefit analysis" might be imagined, where time streams of cultural benefits might be compared with the cultural resources devoted as inputs to the project.

To move from the theoretically plausible to the operationally feasible in this respect is a sizable jump, because, as we have already noted, no simple or universal metric for representing cultural value is available in the same way as money can be used as a means of aggregating economic worth.

Notes

1. For the purposes of this paper, cultural heritage is defined as movable artifacts, artworks, and other items such as are contained in museums and other collections, and immovable heritage such as archaeological sites, buildings, or groups of buildings, locations, precincts, etc., of historical or cultural importance (Throsby 1997b). For further discussion of the definition of heritage, see contributions to Hutter and Rizzo (1997) and to Schuster, de Moncheaux, and Riley (1997); see also Prott (1998) and Klamer and Zuidhof (1999). For the cultural criteria used in World Heritage classification, see *Operational Guidelines for the Implementation of the World Heritage Convention* as promulgated by UNESCO.
2. See, for example, President's Committee on the Arts and the Humanities (1997).
3. See Throsby (1999); Barker (1999).
4. Some examples of cases where sustainability is seen as important from a heritage conservationist perspective are English Heritage (1997) and Rosvall (1999).
5. This distinction was originally created by Irving Fisher, who referred to the flow as "income" deriving from the capital stock; see Fisher (1927), 51ff.
6. The use of the term *cultural capital* in economics differs from the concept now widely used in sociology following Bourdieu (1986), where cultural capital refers to an individual's competence in high-status culture. Bourdieu's usage relates to characteristics of human beings and, as such, is very close to the economic concept of human capital (Becker 1964). For further discussion of the use of the term both within and beyond economics, see Throsby (1997a, 1999).
7. A *public good* is defined in economics as a good characterized by nonrivalness (one person's consumption does not diminish another's) and nonexcludability (once the good is provided for one person, it is available to all, and no one can be excluded from consuming it). National defense is often cited as a paradigmatic case of a pure public good.

References

Barker, G. 1999. *Cultural Capital and Policy*. New Zealand Film Commission.

Becker, G. S. 1964. *Human Capital*. New York: Columbia University Press.

Bourdieu, P. 1986. Forms of capital. In *Handbook of Theory and Research for the Sociology of Education*, ed. J. G. Richardson, 241–60. New York: Greenwood.

English Heritage. 1997. *Sustaining the Historic Environment: New Perspectives on the Future*. London: English Heritage.

Fisher, I. 1927. *The Nature of Capital and Income*. New York: Macmillan.

Getty Conservation Institute (GCI). 1999. *Economics and Heritage Conservation: A Meeting Organized by the Getty Conservation Institute, December 1998*, ed. R. Mason. Los Angeles: Getty Conservation Institute.

Hutter, M., and I. Rizzo, eds. 1997. *Economic Perspectives on Cultural Heritage*. London: Macmillan.

Klamer, A., and P.-W. Zuidhof. 1999. The values of cultural heritage: Merging economic and cultural appraisals. In GCI 1999, 23–61.

President's Committee on the Arts and the Humanities (John Brademas, chair). 1997. *Creative America*. Washington, D.C.: National Endowment for the Arts.

Prott, L. V. 1998. International standards for cultural heritage. In *World Culture Report: Culture, Creativity, and Markets*, 222–36. Paris: UNESCO.

Rosvall, J. 1999. The heritage restoration facing a new challenge: Sustained development. Paper presented at the International Congress on European Historical Heritage as Employment Generating Source, Caceres, Spain, April 28–30.

Schuster, J. M., J. de Monchaux, and C. Riley, eds. 1997. *Preserving the Built Heritage: Tools for Implementation.* Hanover, N.H.: University Press of New England.

Throsby, D. 1997a. Sustainability and culture: Some theoretical issues. *International Journal of Cultural Policy* 4: 7–20.

———. 1997b. Seven questions in the economics of cultural heritage. In Hutter and Rizzo 1997, 13–30.

———. 1999. Cultural capital. *Journal of Cultural Economics* 23: 3–12.

Reading

57

Christian Ost

A Macroeconomic and Strategic Perspective on Historic Conservation (2013)

Christian Ost teaches at the ICHEC Brussels Management School (where he was dean in 2000–2008) and the Raymond Lemaire International Center for Conservation at the Catholic University of Leuven. Ost is a highly regarded heritage economist who has taught at ICCROM and has contributed actively to ICOMOS. Here he proposes a new paradigm for embracing economics and heritage conservation as complementary human endeavors. He ends his piece by asserting, "The aim is to 'make the economy your friend' and to put emphasis on the competitive market, the heritage as a cultural asset, conservation as an investment process, the differentiator of heritage places to attract new investment and creative industries and ultimately the improvement of livability."

1. Macroeconomics and Conservation

The tools developed by economics as a science address a vast array of human activities, given that these are characterized as the satisfaction of needs covered by the use of resources. Economics is therefore about managing scarcity and non-renewable resources. Cultural heritage is a limited resource because it cannot be replaced or substituted. Yet the need to enjoy its beauty or to use it for human activities is growing fast. According to such a definition, heritage conservation is also clearly an economic choice.

In economics, the word "Capital" refers to wealth capable of generating more wealth over a period of time. Among different types of capital, there is physical capital, financial capital, human capital, social capital, and cultural capital. It should not be difficult to accept that tangible cultural heritage can be considered a form of capital. Investment is the process that maintains and develops any form of capital in the economy. Hence conservation is an investment process of allocating resources over time.

From Christian Ost, "A Macroeconomic and Strategic Perspective on Historic Conservation," in *Reflections on Preventive Conservation, Maintenance and Monitoring by the PRECOMOS UNESCO Chair,* edited by Koenraad Van Balen and Aziliz Vandesande (Leuven: Acco, 2013), 101–5. Reproduced courtesy of Acco.

The investment decision entails redirecting resources from being consumed today, so they may satisfy needs in the future. Conservation is therefore an economic process of allocating resources today in order to maintain and/or obtain higher economic values tomorrow. Given the definition of heritage as a cultural capital, and the definition of conservation as an investment process, economists are able to apply conventional asset management techniques and investment theory when evaluating conservation projects.

Macroeconomic investment is a key variable for long-term growth and development. Through technological innovations and market opportunities, investment provides a new framework for economic growth. Conservation achieves similar objectives in re-using heritage buildings for modern activities, in developing sustainable tourism, and in promoting and diffusing state-of-the-art techniques of restoration.

Acting as macroeconomic policymakers, city authorities need to collect information relevant to the planning and managing of heritage conservation. The primary responsibility of city authorities is to coordinate the successive steps of the information process: collecting and producing data, recording and processing data, updating data and finally communicating and sharing data with stakeholders. The objective of heritage economics is two-fold: assessing the contribution of the heritage to the growth and welfare of the city, and providing information to the decision-making process when heritage conservation is at stake.

2. A Long-Wave Perspective on Conservation

Today there is no doubt that the preserved heritage can represent a very high economic value compared to closed mines or useless factories, especially when these latter assets become themselves a modern economic opportunity as part of the industrial heritage. Key factors in modern industries no longer rely on geographical conditions. Business can be successful anywhere on the planet to the extent that we provide high-tech state-of-the-art communication conditions. It is amazing how cultural heritage can be successful today in attracting companies and people, almost liberating an area from the constraints of the economic and geographical factors of the industrial era. Speaking of economic resources, cultural heritage becomes the finest in terms of quality of life in providing shelter to information or communication businesses, financial and entrepreneur services, leisure activities and many other modern activities.

[. . .] [L]inking cultural heritage, local resources, sustainable tourism and growth calls for adequate policies and management on behalf of private and public actors. Cultural heritage policies must not remain only in the hand of cultural authorities. Mass tourism and its intricate implications call for a vast array of reflections for a wide range of disciplines. Globalization is not an economic feature, it is a cultural (in a broader meaning) revolution and goes beyond everything that we have known in the history of preservation. Policies are no longer effective in dealing with such feature, it is the prerequisite of the success of these future challenges.

—∞—

3. Economic and Strategic Analysis of the Heritage in Historic Cities

Today everybody agrees that the cultural built heritage as well as the natural heritage becomes an effective and powerful resource in the allocation process that tends to satisfy people's growing needs; not only in terms of its symbolic, historic or educational value, but also in terms of its use value. From housing in developing countries to more prestigious activities, there is no limitation to the functions that can be provided by heritage in the future.

Economists currently have the ability to perform strong evaluation of impact, costs and benefits from conservation or preservation decisions. However, methodological requirements sometimes make appraisal of the results of these evaluations difficult for non-economists. Even economists cannot isolate or define with scientific precision impacts generated by the symbolic value of the heritage nor conclusively measure the intangibles. As urban-planning implications from a cost-benefit or from a multi-criteria analysis need to be visualized, we have to rely on innovative tools to show decision-makers how, where and when the appearance, growth or decline of economic impacts occurs.

A theoretical and empirical guide for town planning in historic cities using economics of conservation methodology is intended to help the decision-making process of town planners, architects and local authorities. Important decisions include conservation, tourism management, transportation and accommodations in historic cities, access to the sites, guided tours, budgetary and fiscal implications, job opportunities and local development.

The methodological process includes:

- Assessment of values in the city produced as a result of the current or future state of heritage, or as a result of conservation activities. Values are expressed in economic terms in the context of sustainable development;
- Selection, description and evaluation of the most relevant indicators. It also considers the use of dashboards of indicators or composite indexes, in order to help monitor the city heritage. An important issue is to feed strategic analysis with economic indicators. Strategic tools are in turn a prerequisite to decision-making tools;
- Conversion of data or indicators into maps, aiming at a spatial distribution of values, and at economic landscapes. Heritage indicators and maps also provide useful information for assessing the magnitude of impacts expected from projects or alternative options for projects.

Indicators are consistently used these days as an integrated approach to measuring and monitoring cities. They are considered a perfect tool to test a city's performance. Indicators are used to communicate information and to make predictions for future performances. The use of indicators cannot be a substitute for the use of databases. It is however a very effective and pragmatic approach when direct documentation is costly and time intensive.

Heritage performance as a contributor to economic values can be measured by indicators. Non-use values are directly related to the cultural value of the heritage. The urban values that justify designation as world heritage city can be expected to generate high non-use values. Hence, the existence, option or bequest values should be high. In fact, experience in the field confirms a correlation between cultural values, non-use values and collective values. Hence, non-use values will be high and will have a great potential to create marketable use values.

Non-use value indicators are identifiable for outstanding buildings or monuments, as well as the historic city taken as a whole. Non-market valuation techniques are used to build these indicators, and can be classified into two categories: Firstly, revealed-preference methods that draw and analyze data from existing market or past behaviour for heritage-related goods and services and secondly, stated-preference methods that rely on the creation of hypothetical markets in which survey respondents are asked to make hypothetical choices.

The measure of the economic value for heritage-related expenditures is a long tally of many individual data. Induced spending measurement also requires complex techniques. Alternative indicators related to these categories of expenditure help identify the magnitude of these use values. These indicators also reveal how heritage economics are integrated in local city economies. Suggested indicators include indicators related to the expenditures (lodging, food, retail shops, transportation) made by tourists or residents who participate in heritage-related events in the city (carnivals, festivals); property value of non-heritage buildings (the premium of property value for non-heritage buildings as a result of their proximity to the heritage); and induced spending from conservation works or heritage-related investments. Heritage-related expenditures by tourists or by residents are commonly estimated by sampling categories of expenditures measured at different locations in the city.

4. SWOT Analysis Applied to Heritage

Although the content of a guide for conservation of the cultural heritage heavily relies on scientific research, the presentation can be "user-friendly" with simple guidelines mixed in with practical information to help decision-makers in their day-to-day urban management activities.

This includes classification criteria to describe each historic city in terms of its strengths, weaknesses, opportunities and threats (SWOT analysis applied to the heritage factor). As a practical guide intended to improve conservation in historic cities, the outcome of the project will be available to everyone seeking information and methodology in this complex field. It becomes essential to accurately assess opportunities and threats, implied by the protection of the historic city. As an example, a strategic analysis could indicate that tourism revenues are not the expected panacea for the economy, but neither a meagre source of growth. Applying a SWOT analysis (Strengths, Weaknesses, Opportunities, Threats) to historic cities that are candidates to be nominated could help city authorities and caretakers with the process of candidacy.

In historic cities, the macroeconomic decision-making is often distributed between local government and upper-level public governance and impacts fiscal and budget management, and heritage management and conservation. Ultimately, the city administration is the authority politically committed to improve the quality of life in the city and the welfare of its inhabitants. It is responsible for enhancing its heritage by improving economic values within the context of sustainable development. From a macroeconomic perspective, the city administration can increase economic values by increasing the aggregate demand for the heritage.

The responsibility of city authorities is to coordinate the successive steps of the information process: collecting and producing data, recording and processing data, updating data, communicating and sharing data with stakeholders. Cultural and economic decisions may not be compatible when resources are allocated inadequately. Sustainability cannot be achieved either when a lack of resources cannot provide both social and economic results. In other words, developing countries may see conservation policies as restrictive measures preventing their historic cities from developing new economic opportunities. Resources allocated in conservation are competing with other needed resources; on the contrary, industrialized countries consider heritage resources as additional growth opportunities.

As an example, protected areas in historic cities may, depending on the circumstances, appear as an additional incentive for growth (see the historic districts in European capitals), or as a constraint and competitor to the needs for city development. Protected areas and conservation rules have to be considered flexible and adjustable tools. To ensure sustainable development, the protection of historic cities in developing countries should not follow the same requirements applied to rich countries.

5. Towards a New Paradigm for the Economics of Urban Conservation

Economics of conservation should focus on historic cities rather than on major monuments whose protection is better guaranteed, and whose financing is generally provided through public resources, international funds, and cultural tourism. If mass tourism threatens monuments, economics is able to provide useful and relatively easy tools to manage this market issue. This should however not be a priority for economics of conservation.

Emphasis should instead be put on the protection of the historical urban fabric in medium-size towns, metropolises and megacities faced with a changing context of urbanization, concerns for sustainability and market-dominant forces. The new paradigm, based on the historic urban landscape, implies an intrinsic coupling of conservation and economics. Conservation economics is no more merely providing a toolkit to achieve cultural goals, but aims to decide with conservation specialists and urban planners which resources are to be allocated and how.

The fundamentals of conservation economics are partnership agreements, with a clear delimitation of public-private involvement in the decision. The public sector provides the legal framework, the fiscal incentives mechanisms, and the long-term guarantee that decisions will be implemented. It also provides the democratic platform for the decisions. The private sector includes the homeowners, the retail sector, the financial and business sector, and the developers. They must be part of the decisions too. They provide the economic resources and the management skills.

Conservation economics puts emphasis on the use and the development of heritage in line with the needs of the city. The aim is to "*make the economy your friend*" and to put emphasis on the competitive market, the heritage as a cultural asset, conservation as an investment process, the differentiator of heritage places to attract new investment and creative industries and ultimately the improvement of livability.

Reading

58

Donovan Rypkema

Devising Financial Tools for Urban Conservation (2015)

Donovan Rypkema is president of PlaceEconomics, a Washington, DC–based consulting firm specializing in the economic revitalization of city centers and the development of historic properties. Rypkema has vast experience worldwide with the realities of economics in the context of heritage conservation. As the definition of heritage has become more inclusive, governments do not have the requisite funds to restore and conserve the heritage within their jurisdictions. Therefore, Rypkema states, in order for the heritage to survive, these funds will have to come from the private sector, owners, and, to some extent, institutions, and this will require financial tools. He discusses the financial tools required, what they should do, the characteristics of the most effective of such tools, and examples and how they work.

Introduction

In the not-too-distant past "heritage conservation" referred primarily to individual, majestic landmarks. [. . .]

But as the heritage conservation movement has grown and the definition of heritage broadened, added to the list of historic structures worthy of preservation have been more modest buildings, vernacular architecture, and often entire neighborhoods. In the latter case the individual components of the neighborhood might not make a 'landmarks' list, but as an ensemble they add to the distinctiveness of the place and tell an important story about a city, its history and its evolution. [. . .]

These 'lesser landmarks' differ, however, from their major monument cousins in more than just size and grandeur. These buildings are often in private ownership and the access, at least to the interiors, is frequently limited to the individual owner and specifically invited guests or clients.

From Donovan Rypkema, "Devising Financial Tools for Urban Conservation," in *Reconnecting the City: The Historic Urban Landscape Approach and the Future of Urban Heritage,* edited by Francesco Bandarin and Ron van Oers (Oxford: Wiley Blackwell, 2015), 283–90. Reproduced courtesy of Wiley.

This broadening of the definition of heritage has also forced the recognition of an important fiscal reality: not even the most prosperous governments in the world have available (or the political will to provide) the financial resources necessary to restore and maintain all of the heritage buildings worthy of conservation. If the public coffers are not going to provide all of the funds necessary so that heritage buildings survive for future generations, where will that money come from? It will have to come from the private sector, from owners, and, to a lesser degree, from institutions. The corollary is that financial tools will be necessary to attract capital from those non-public sources. Consequently, this chapter will try to answer four questions:

1. Why are financial tools required?
2. What do financial tools do?
3. What are the characteristics of the most effective financial tools?
4. What are some examples of financial tools and how do they work?

[. . .]

Why Are Financial Tools Required?

To understand the need for financial tools, it is first necessary to understand the concepts of *cost* and *value* and further to recognise the multiple values that heritage buildings possess (see fig. 1).

In real estate economics, *value* refers to the monetary amount that a property is likely to command if sold in the marketplace, or the capitalised stream of income that the property generates in net rents. [. . .] *Cost* is the sum of the euros (or dollars or pounds or yen) that need to be spent to prepare a property to be sold, rented or occupied. *Cost* includes the price of acquisition, plus construction costs, fees, professional services, and other expenditures necessary to bring a property to the market.

To expect capital to invest on an on-going basis in a property when there is an economic gap is to ask them to act irrationally and against their own best financial interest. Ultimately capital will simply look for alternative investments where the amount of *cost* of the investment is at least equal to the *value* of the investment. Around the world when heritage buildings are left to deteriorate and sometimes abandoned, it is a clear statement that the current owners have reached the conclusion that the *value* restored and well maintained is less than the *cost* of restoring it.

But heritage conservation is driven by the fact that historic buildings have 'values' above and beyond their economic value—symbolic value, social value, environmental value, educational value, cultural value, aesthetic value, and others. However, the building owner is not the primary beneficiary owner of these values—the larger community is. Sometimes the 'community' means others in the same city; sometimes the benefitting community is the world's population. [. . .]

Box 12.1

In market and quasi-market economies, when *value* exceeds *cost*, capital will usually act without intervention (that is incentives or other stimulus). But when *cost* exceeds *value*, capital (at least private capital) will either not act or act only with some incentive to do so. When *cost* exceeds *value*, the difference is referred to as the *gap*.

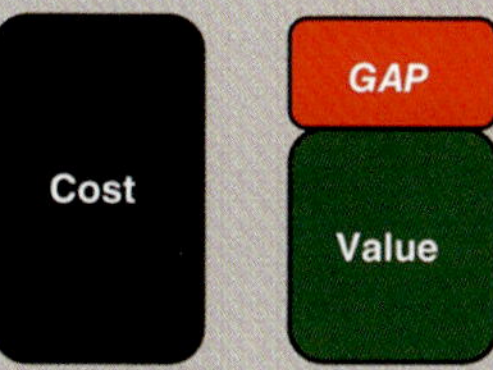

A primary purpose of financial tools, especially of the incentive variety, is to close the *gap* between *cost* and *value*.

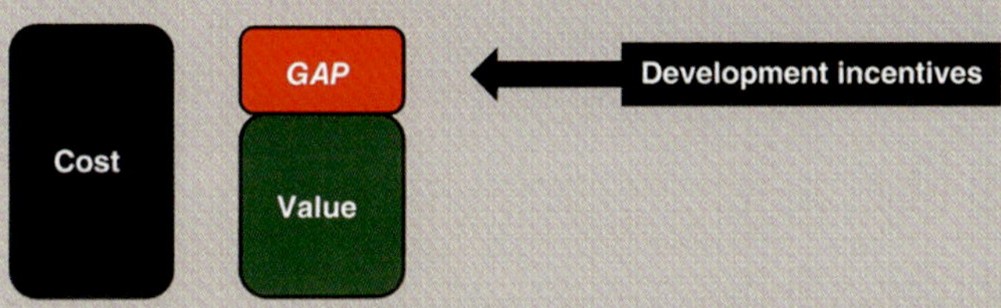

The point is this – there are values of heritage in addition to the economic value that accrues to the building owner. These multiple values might be represented as shown here:

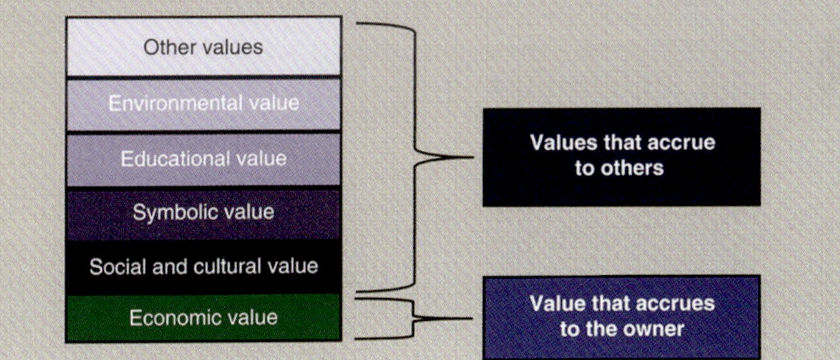

Fig. 1. In market and quasi-market economies, when *value* exceeds *cost*, capital will usually act without intervention (that is incentives or other stimulus). But when cost exceeds *value*, capital (at least private capital) will either not act or act only with some incentive to do so. When *cost* exceeds *value*, the difference is referred to as the *gap*. A primary purpose of financial tools, especially of the incentive variety, is to close the *gap* between *cost* and *value*. The point is this—there are values of heritage in addition to the economic value that accrues to the building owner. These multiple values might be represented as shown here.

Considered in this fashion, the logic of creating financial tools for heritage becomes clearer:

1. For multiple reasons the *cost* of restoring and maintaining a heritage building may exceed the *economic value* of doing so.

2. However, there are additional *values* to the heritage of which the owner is only a negligible recipient.
3. [F]inancial tools may be necessary to close the *gap* between cost and value in recognition that there will be *values* received by the larger community.

Of course, for some properties in some markets there is no gap for the heritage building: the owner is receiving sufficient benefit from ownership that the cost of rehabilitation and maintenance is fully retrieved through net income, sales price, and/or the value of occupancy. Is there ever a need for financial tools in that instance? Yes, in at least four circumstances:

- When a higher quality of restoration and greater sustainability of the heritage building can be obtained as part of the requirements for using the financial tool than would otherwise likely be the case.
- When the property is one where interior public access is important but would not be typically available. [. . .]
- When the zoning district within which the heritage building exists would allow a much larger building. It is not uncommon, particularly in city centres, for 20, or 30, or 40 storey buildings to be permitted. In those cases there is often great pressure to demolish a two or three storey heritage building. The use of a financial tool such as the Transferable Development Rights might be appropriate even though the current heritage building does not have a demonstrable financial *gap*.
- When development of a particular building is seen as a catalyst for additional nearby development.

What Do Financial Tools Do?

Worldwide there are literally hundreds of financial tools developed to encourage investment in heritage. But there are actually only a finite number of impacts tools might have:

- **Reduce costs**: In some countries the Value Added Tax (VAT, elsewhere called sales tax) is waived for materials purchased for a heritage building restoration. This reduces the total cost of the project.
- **Reduce cash required**: A grant awarded for heritage building restoration would be an example of reducing the cash required. [. . .]
- **Increase income**: For commercial properties, the economic value is directly related to the amount of net income the property produces. An incentive that subsidises the rents for small business willing to locate in a heritage building could well increase income and thereby increase value. Increasing value or reducing cost will both have the effect of reducing the *gap*.

- **Reduce expenses**: Some countries levy lower property tax rates on heritage buildings. Since property taxes are an operating cost for a property, reducing that expense will have the effect of increasing net income and thereby increasing property value.
- **Improve financing**: In most of the world the feasibility of real estate investment (including in heritage buildings) is contingent upon the availability of borrowed money and the amount, interest rate, and loan term (payback period) of those funds. Low interest loans, favourable subordinate financing and loan guarantees are all examples of financial tools that may direct capital to heritage buildings.
- **Reduce risk**: In the investment world there is a relationship between risk and reward—the greater the risk, the higher return that investors will demand. [. . .] Some financial tools can be used to reduce risk on the investment in heritage buildings. A long-term lease by a credit worthy government agency for space in the heritage building could significantly reduce the risk. This reduced risk would mean the project would be looked on more favourably by both equity (ownership investment) and debt (borrowed funds) meaning that raising investment capital and securing a loan would both be easier.
- **Increase occupancy levels**: Having space ready and available for tenants (or buyers) but having inadequate demand in the marketplace is one of the fundamental risks in the ownership of real estate, including heritage buildings. [. . .]
- **Clear title**: In many parts of the developing world there is not yet an adequate system of records and chain of title processes so that individual ownership of a particular parcel of land can be indisputably demonstrated. A process of 'clearing title' should be considered a financial tool, in that without clear title it may be difficult to secure either debt or equity to invest in the heritage of building. [. . .]
- **Improve investment environment**: Over the last two decades, the Inter-American Development Bank (IDB) has funded numerous heritage-based city centre revitalisation efforts in Latin America. Often one of the early uses of IDB funds is to improve both the infrastructure and the publically owned heritage buildigns in the city centre. [. . .]

What Are the Characteristics of the Most Effective Financial Tools?

There has now been enough experimentation and subsequent implementation of heritage financial tools that general characteristics can be identified as to when those tools are most effective:

- **Directed to a particular need**: Instead of thinking of financial tools as simply a set of programmes to encourage investment in heritage, tools should be developed that are directed to a particular need. [. . .]
- **Directly related to the gap**: When a financial tool takes the form of an incentive, its primary purpose is to close the gap between cost and value as discussed

earlier. The incentive, then, should be directly related to the gap both in the amount of the incentive and the target of the incentive. [. . .]

- **Paired with appropriate regulations**: The user of a heritage financial tool is most commonly the owner of the building. But the resources to provide that tool (whether changes in public policies, incentives, specific programmes, etc.) most often come from the public sector. Therefore the public as well is entitled to a "return" on their investment in the heritage building. That return might not be in financial payment, but rather in compliance with regulations or restrictions geared toward protecting the heritage building into the future. [. . .]
- **Clearly communicated and actively marketed**: It is insufficient for a government simply to enact or authorise a given financial tool and then sit and wait for prospective users to take advantage of it. There needs to be an aggressive and effective programme to communicate and market the use of the tool. [. . .]
- **Simple in implementation**: This is one example of a principle where there may by necessity, be a distinction between a financial tool that is an *incentive* and one that is a transactional or ownership vehicle. An incentive like a property tax abatement, a low interest loan, or design assistance should be easy for a potential user to understand and relatively easy to utilise. For a transactions tool like a Public-Private Partnership, however, there will be often be a degree of complexity that may preclude meeting the "simple to implement" principle.
- **Within an overall public policy objective**: Financial tools should not be ad hoc or designed for a particular project. Rather the tools should be seen as part of an implementation strategy for an overall public policy objective.
  For example, a city council might establish as a policy objective, *'We want a heritage-based city centre revitalisation programme'* or *'We want to encourage the development of affordable housing in historic buildings'* and then specific financial tools are created, authorised, and funded to meet these public policy objectives.
- **Depoliticised**: Both the goals of heritage in general and the credibility of a specific financial tool in particular will be diminished if there is a sense that the use of the tool is limited to those with influence with government workers or elected officials. [. . .]

[. . .]

What Are Some Examples of Financial Tools and How Do They Work?

There are hundreds of financial tools that have been developed in recent years to encourage investment in heritage buildings. [. . .] Six are discussed below which represent a range of tools that some countries have found effective in promoting heritage investment:

1. **Grants**: An award, usually in cash, to a project generally for a specific purpose and subject to certain requirements. [. . .]
2. **Micro loans**: The difference between a grant and a loan is that the loan typically has to be repaid. Micro loans are usually made when the borrower might not qualify for a loan from a bank or other traditional lending institution because of no credit history, no equity capital available and/or because the size of the proposed project is simply too small to be of interest to a bank. [. . .]
3. **Property tax reductions**: In many parts of the world taxes are levied on real estate as one source of funding for the operation of government, usually local government. Generally (although not always) these are *ad valorem* taxes that are the amount of tax increase based on the value of the property being taxed. This sometimes has the unintended consequence of discouraging investment in heritage buildings. [. . .]
4. **Tax credits**: This is a direct offset of taxes that would otherwise be payable. Tax credits usually are used in relation to income taxes, but could also be used for property taxes, VAT, or other forms of taxation. [. . .]
5. **Transferable development rights (TDRs)**: This is a regulatory tool that allows governments to authorise the transfer of allowable density from one building or site to another. [. . .] In most TDR legistlation there will be identified a 'sending zone', often a heritage precinct, from which these *development rights* can be sold and a 'receiving zone', the area where the additional density will be transferred.
6. **Public-private partnerships (PPPs)**: These are increasingly used around the world, particularly for major infrastructure projects like airports, highways, water systems, and power generation plants. But there is also a great opportunity for Heritage PPPs. [. . .]

[. . .] This does not mean that a PPP is always the answer or that using a PPP is either fast or easy. A government using this tool needs to have expertise in the use and operations of a PPP, however PPPs are currently an underutilised financial tool for heritage and more governments should consider their appropriateness.

Conclusion

Over the last three decades, both the successes and the failures of heritage conservation have taught us that a broader, more comprehensive approach must be taken. The Historic Urban Landscape approach is an important and positive shift in how cities need to think about and manage their heritage resources.

[. . .] As the Historic Urban Landscape approach is adopted at national levels and implemented into local strategies, there are at least four likely outcomes:

1. It is not risk but uncertainty that is the deterrent to much real estate investment. As heritage conservation is integrated into a larger urban development context,

the level of uncertainty as to permits, regulations, and the ability to proceed is reduced and investor confidence is increased.

2. This reduced uncertainty will have an even greater impact among those who currently own or are planning reinvestment in heritage buildings. The long term investment horizon that is often necessary for heritage buildings is enhanced with the confidence that the context, the view sheds, the streetscapes and other locational variables will not be rapidly changed in a manner that significantly and adversely affects the individual heritage building.
3. When uncertainty is reduced for equity investors there is a corresponding reduction in uncertainty for lenders. Banks and other financial institutions can be expected to respond positively about funding availability and the rates and terms those loans will command.
4. The speculative premium that is often generated in situations of rapid change and uncertainty can be expected to diminish. It is this speculative premium—which attaches to land, not buildings—that is often the motivation for the demolition of heritage properties. While real estate speculators may not be happy with that consequence, long term owners, investors and proponents of stable economic growth will all be beneficiaries.

[. . .]

To expect either the public sector to fund all of the heritage conservation that is required, or to expect private owners to restore and adequately maintain heritage buildings without useful financial tools is unrealistic. Central to the implementation of the Historic Urban Landscape approach will be the availability and effectiveness of the financial tools available. The bad news is that there are insufficient and inadequate tools currently available in many historic cities. The good news is that we have learned what works, how they work, and how they can be effective.

Reading

59

JULIAN SMITH

Civic Engagement Tools for Urban Conservation (2015)

Julian Smith (Order of Canada) is an architect and passionate conservation educator who, in 2006, founded the Willowbank Centre (also known as the Willowbank School of Restoration Arts) in Ontario, Canada. Smith's dynamic career has involved conserving culturally significant places across Canada, the United States, France, Italy, India, Sri Lanka, and Japan. At Willowbank he instituted a unique curriculum that integrates crafts-based skills with planning, design, and cultural landscape practices. In this reading, he scrutinizes the meaning of sustainability, cultural mapping, urban diversity, and community engagement.

Introduction

The 2011 UNESCO *Recommendation on the Historic Urban Landscape* [. . .] creates the basis for a synergy between three major perspectives that to date have operated somewhat independently—the contemporary design and development perspective, the environmental perspective, and the heritage conservation perspective.

Where the heritage conservation community can make its strongest contribution is in the area of reading and interpreting the existing urban landscape. This is fundamental to developing interventions that strengthen existing values and re-calibrate traditional and current patterns. The legibility must be related not only to the visual morphology of the city, but to the cultural practices that have created that morphology and that continue to animate it.

[. . .]

[. . .] There is a growing realisation that ecology in its broadest sense—the creation of self-sustaining communities that live within a balance of natural and cultural

From JULIAN SMITH, "Civic Engagement Tools for Urban Conservation," in *Reconnecting the City: The Historic Urban Landscape Approach and the Future of Urban Heritage*, edited by Francesco Bandarin and Ron van Oers (Oxford: Wiley Blackwell, 2015), 221–31, 234–35. Reproduced courtesy of Wiley.

resources—is closely tied to traditional knowledge and the long experience in many communities of living with limited resources. Ecological initiatives gain increasing priority as we realise that unsustainable patterns endanger our very survival.

—w—

The following are some of the tools available to researchers in what is essentially a cultural landscape approach to the urban situation.

Ways of Seeing

The emphasis in understanding historic urban districts has tended to be on the documentation of physical form. [. . .]

[O]ne must move beyond the outward morphology of the city to understand how it is experienced from within. A physical form is experienced through the rituals of inhabitation, and it is these rituals that create a cumulative experience of the urban landscape that is essential to both its understanding and its sustainability. These rituals include not only the daily and seasonal lives of its inhabitants and visitors, but the rituals of shaping and reshaping the physical form itself, over time (fig. 1). [. . .]

Fig. 1. Skyline, Cairo.

[T]he thrust of cultural tourism has already shifted from observation to experience, with increasing emphasis on understanding place through participation. This can sometimes be a problem for host cultures. [. . .]

The documentation of experience rather than observation cannot be so easily captured through more and more exact recording and documentation. Although laser technologies and other advances have seemed to open new ground for collecting and sorting massive amounts of data, this data is still about the observable form of the monument or the city. One can exhaust oneself with measurement and still not approach the recording of experience.

The documentation of experience relies on a broader set of media, and a different set of organising frameworks. In terms of media, it benefits from video and film, which add the dimension of time and the experience of movement, and allow narrative and artefact to coalesce. It also benefits from the insights of poets and novelists who translate the urban experience into frames that capture an emotional as well as intellectual response. It benefits from storytelling and narrative in the oral tradition, and an appreciation for the insights of what is sometimes referred to as 'traditional knowledge' can be understood more simply as the knowledge born of experience. And it can benefit from recording sacred or secular rituals that interpret the urban landscape through stylised and heightened powers of movement. One of the wonderful discoveries of such documentation is the importance of other senses beyond the visual—sound, smell, touch, taste. [. . .]

Cultural Mapping

If the experiential quality of the historic urban landscape is as important as the visual reading of that landscape, there remains the question of what form the documentation of the city can take, in order to be useful to conservators and interveners.

[. . .] Geographic information system (GIS)-based mapping is useful for coordinating visual data and capturing the visual morphology of the city, but it has its limitations when recording the urban experience.

The answer is to supplement these maps and photographs and drawings with images that may seem to distort the city but in fact often come closer to its truths. [. . .]

In India, the representation of urban landscape in the *mandala* can be directly correlated to the ritual mapping of the city through a seasonal round of religious festivals, particularly in South India. The elaborations of the *mandala,* not only in their formal expressions but in the informal *kolams* of everyday life, can reveal an experience of the urban landscape that is truer to the experience of the city than any Cartesian map (fig. 2). The field of cognitive mapping has been developed by environmental psychologists and others to elucidate the urban experience, and it plays a key role in expanding the recording of the city beyond observation.

It is also important, in experiential mapping, to break down assumptions about public and private space, and about exterior and interior space. [. . .]

[. . .] One of the impressive aspects of cognitive maps is that they exist at the intersection of these two centrals concepts—memory and imagination. Neither one can be found in the simple physical documentation of the urban landscape. It is not possible, no matter how detailed the observation, to record how people remember the place, nor how they imagine it yesterday, today or tomorrow. In neuroscience terms, memory and imagination are strikingly similar brain functions, and these cognitive maps, by calling

Fig. 2. Kolam exploration by a young girl in South India.

both into play, create the framework for a dynamic understanding of the city over time. [. . .]

One final aspect of cultural mapping is not related to normal forms of documentations at all, but to knowledge that is instinctive rather than self-conscious. This is the understanding of the historic urban landscape by form-givers working within a particular place and a particular tradition. These people—simultaneously designers and builders—are part of the cultural and natural environment they inhabit. They are masons, carpenters, adobe-builders, glassworkers, and metal smiths, who carry design traditions and instincts within their hands. They both repair the old and build the new, and their particular blend of memory and imagination is fundamental to the ecology of place. The results of their work can be photographed and measured, but the design-build skills themselves take a lifetime to understand. So part of the cultural mapping is simply recognising their presence, recording their names and their skills and their ways of working, and giving them a place of honour within the urban landscape.

The Concepts of Equilibrium and Resilience

The Historic Urban Landscape approach considers cultural diversity and creativity as key assets for human, social and economic development, and provides tools to manage physical and social transformations and to ensure that contemporary inter-

ventions are harmoniously integrated with heritage in a historic setting and take into account regional contexts.[1]

Both the definition and this reference to the essential role of diversity and creativity shift the paradigm for understanding the city from static to dynamic, from utopian to organic. And this is as much a necessity to rescue heritage conservation from an increasingly irrelevant sidebar position of isolated monuments, as it is a necessity to rescue contemporary city planning from its own static and utopian goals.

—~—

The key in understanding the city is to map this diversity of practices and skills, and to have the humility to understand that marginalised communities often carry valuable insights not readily visible in the dominant forms and facades.

Sustainable Diversity

It is fine to say that more creative mapping of the city is possible, using a variety of voices, but there are still questions about how such information can be condensed and articulated in ways that become useful for design and development.

One of the answers is to move beyond the twentieth century reliance on legal boundaries and definitions to a more fluid definition of boundary conditions and a shift to mediation from legal confrontation as ways to develop true community-based design and development. First Nations communities in a number of countries have pioneered both this concept of more fluid boundaries, and the related interest in mediation and dispute resolution. It is essential that these new tools become more integrated into the planning framework.

The most important step is to displace the utopian imperatives of twentieth century modernism with the more flexible organic ideas of urban growth and transformation. The utopian city relies on zoning as its primary tool for decision-making, and zoning is a tool that favours monoculture. It can only comprehend one memory and one imagination. It is necessary to summarise the findings of historic urban landscape research in ways that do not rely on this end product.

[. . .]

If the multiple realities of the city are not recognised and documented, it will always be the dominant reality that shapes the on-going evolution. Tourism, for example, is often a contemporary intrusion into a historic context. If one simply assumes that the host community and the tourist community are engaging with the same reality, then there will be one design solution for both that will inevitably displace historic patterns with new patterns—even though the phsyical form appears to remain relatively constant. In this situation, the international weight of the tourism industry will often override the local interests, and eventually the host community will feel alienated. If, on the other hand, it is understood that the cultural landscape of the tourist community and the cultural landscape of the host community are very different, then it becomes possible to modify the phyiscal form to satisfy both sets of rituals. This requires that very careful mapping of experience, a mapping that recognises both cultural landscapes individually, as well as a shared cultural landscape of overlap and intersection. And tourists can be treated as simply one more complicating layer within the political, economic and cultural layers that already share the city's form.

The fact that the multiple boundaries of memory and imagination will spread beyond the notion of "historic centre" to encompass the broader urban landscape is the *quid pro quo* of the Historic Urban Landscape Recommendation. Yes, there will be a more dynamic interpretation of the historic centre, and the possibility of a contemporary layer within the existing layered setting. But at the same time, those layers and those patterns will influence the evolution of the city around them. It is essential that the reading of the historic urban landscape be a tool not only to understand the past and the present, but as a necessary narrative for framing the future.

There has already been a shift in accepting the environmental imperative as a new and necessary part of contemporary urban planning. The cultural imperative is following—it is showing early signs of success in cities such as Hanoi, which are choosing to use the historic urban landscape as a framework within which to understand a distinctive and rich future.

[. . .]

Influences of Civic Engagement: Towards Community-Based Design and Development

[. . .]

In addition to the shift from a modernist and utopian viewpoint, to a more layered and organic understanding of the city, there is an equally significant transformation at work. That is the re-evaluation of the role of the 'expert'. Just as the shift from a static to a dynamic view of the historic urban landscape is seen by some as a threat, so too is the displacement of the role of the expert to an increased role for civic engagement. Experience is impossible for the expert to document, other than through the knowledge of those who inhabit the city. And in order to understand diversity and layering, it is necessary to experience the city through the knowledge of multiple cultures and subcultures.

This requires significant humility on the part of experts, who are more accustomed to having full control of both the documentation and the analysis. The architect and the architectural historian can do their work by gathering photographs and undertaking recording activities of various kinds. The cultural historian can use historical sources and secondary materials to craft a reasonable narrative. But the ecological complexity of the city is not reachable through these media alone.

This means that the process of producing cognitive maps and recording traditional knowledge and understanding embedded rituals requires a different level of community engagement.

Successful engagement of this kind will almost always lead to expectations by the community—expectations that its involvement will extend beyond documenting the place to identifying values to framing future design and development. [. . .]

Community-based design and development is the traditional way that communities have created a sustainble environment for themselves. It is a paradoxical but important fact that a community that relies on sustainability 'experts' is not a sustainable community. Sustainability has to be grounded within the community, and this begins by understanding the past interactions between nature, culture, memory and imagination.

The goal of sustainable community-based design and development is not to advance towards a certain vision. This utopian approach requires defining the future, and then moving towards it. The organic approach, or what one might call a true ecological approach, requires defining the present then choosing interventions that strengthen its positives and weaken its negatives. The future simply emerges as a sum total of these interventions. The point of reference is the present, not the future.

—~—

Civic engagement within an ecological framework is a necessary part of sustainability. It is the community that understands its experience, that maps this experience onto the urban environment, and that can identify where the relationships are fragile and need to be strengthened or changed. It is the community that can identify the true landmarks, not always the most highly visible points in the landscape. And it is the community that can respond most creatively to threats.

[. . .]

In terms of sustaining and evolving the physical morphology of the historic urban landscape, there is a required role in community-based design and development for the master-builder tradition, the skilled craftsman-designer who for millennia has been the primary creator of the urban landscape. The rise of professional architects and planners in the modernist framework of the twentieth century has not only led to an unfortunate separation between design and build, but also to a tendency to standardise rather than differentiate. Community-based design-build is an essential component of sustaining and reviving the traditions of vernacular architecture and urbanism. [. . .]

Conclusion

The 2011 Historic Urban Landscape Recommendation is a starting point for a new set of principles that applies equally to conserving the past as to planning for the future. The heritage conservation field has a long and proud tradition of working with local communities and understanding the significance of civic engagement. As the field became more professionalised in the late twentieth century, however, it began to adopt some of the patterns of its fellow disciplines in the contemporary design and development communities. It tended to privilege the role of the expert and focus on the object—the building or artefact—as the basis for organising its systems of documentation and regulation. This made it compatible with what architects and planners were doing but did not help develop a more ecological approach.

In the twenty first century, there is an impatience to change these systems and create a more ecological and sustainable perspective. For some, this is a brave new world, but for those in the heritage conservation field it is also a return to some of the fundamental values that have inspired previous generations to value the historic urban landscape. It is not a remnant of a past that is quickly disappearing; it is increasingly a model for a future that is reconnecting with past practices. It is a more dynamic view, but also a more sustainable view.

The greatest strength of the heritage conservation field is that it can still read the past, and because of this it can understand the present. These skills have never been more important. They require the engagement of the communities involved, and from this shared understanding comes the basis for consensus on how to move forward.

Notes

1. UNESCO (2011) *Recommendation on the Historic Urban Landscape*: para. 12.

Reading

60

Noha Nasser

Planning for Urban Heritage Places: Reconciling Conservation, Tourism, and Sustainable Development (2003)

Noha Nasser, architect, urban designer, and educator, is the founding director of MELA Social Enterprise (London, U.K.), which serves as a vehicle for bridging cultures through the creative use and design of public spaces. Formerly, she taught at the University of Birmingham's Urban Morphology Research Group. Her doctoral dissertation examined the historical and cultural processes attributed to Islam-dominant dynasties in the development of the walled city of Cairo. These processes were reconsidered in light of the degradation of historic Cairo due to the lack of conservation planning and unchecked heritage tourism to provide a framework for urban regeneration. Here Nasser provides a critical analysis of the ecological, economic, and social equity implications of conservation and heritage. She presents the idea of sustainability as an overarching framework for managing tourism in heritage places based on the balance between sociocultural needs, economic gain, and the protection of the heritage resource.

Globalising forces inherent in the shift from production to consumption are influencing changes in the built environment and in their local cultures. This is most acute in places of heritage value where the local culture with its built heritage is being transformed into a product for tourist consumption. The global scale of tourism and its accrued uniformity are increasingly evident, particularly the proliferation of standardised hotel architecture, restaurant chains, and street furniture. Similarly, local cultures are losing their local identities as global "cultural industries" dominate (Oncu and Weyland 1997). With the emergence of a greater number of destinations competing for unique tourist experiences, traditional historic places are undergoing a redefinition and reinterpretation of their cultural heritage in order to be competitive and attractive. By doing this, however, heritage places are responding to the commercial forces of consumer demand, and in many cases conservation and cultural values are being compromised. This article

From Noha Nasser, "Planning for Urban Heritage Places: Reconciling Conservation, Tourism, and Sustainable Development," *Journal of Planning Literature* 17, no. 4 (May 2003): 467–79.

provides a critical analysis of ecological, economic, and social equity implications of conservation and heritage. It presents the idea of sustainability as an overarching framework for managing tourism in heritage places based on the balance between sociocultural needs, economic gain, and the protection of the heritage resource.
[. . .]

This article highlights the various concepts associated with heritage places that should be considered in any sustainable planning for these areas. The first concept discusses building preservation and conservation in which the primary concern is protecting the built and cultural heritage. The second concept revolves around the exploitative nature of heritage tourism in which commercial gain has created an imbalance in conservation and cultural values. The third and final concept is that of sustainable tourism that argues for an alternative tourism that will contribute to both conservation and development objectives, as well as safeguard social equity and cultural values.

—𝔴—

Since the 1960s, shifts in the approach toward conservation widened the object of attention to ensembles and areas, as opposed to the previous approach, focusing on buildings or their remnants as monuments. The presence of an overall architectural quality or historical association would define an area, often denoting a significant historical and social relationship to the rest of the town. The major changes and different pressures on historic towns in the last half of the twentieth century, reflected by a wealthier society and a transportation revolution, was increasingly in need of both architectural and socioeconomic protection.

Therefore, urban conservation has three interrelated objectives; physical, spatial, and social (Orbasli 2000). Physically, it is linked to building preservation and the type of new development to ensure that a town's past, its present, and its future combine to create a recognisable unit, so that its growth can be seen and felt to be continuous (Worskett 1969). This involves seeking to improve old environments and bring them into modern use by adapting the townscape, but as Larkham (1996) suggests, this is hard to achieve without wasting some of the investment of previous societies. Spatially, it is viewing the townscape as a holistic entity, with its relationships between spaces and their use, as well as circulation and traffic. The third objective, and most neglected, is social, which concerns the users, local community, and the urban population. Orbasli (2000) argues that although the social dimension is the most difficult to define, it is the most important, as continuity in conservation can be achieved only through the continuation of urban life.

The literature on urban conservation reflects the gap in integrating the social dimension. [. . .]

—𝔴—

Until very recently, social attitudes depicted in the case of conservation were those of the ruling class, the élite intellectual force. These élite claimed to represent public opinion, but were small in proportion to the general population, and tended to focus their attention on major monuments and areas of high land values. However, rising academic pressure has forced local amenity groups to consider vernacular heritage as worthy of conservation as the heritage of the social elite (Ashworth 1990).

Changes in preferred styles have had significant consequences for the urban cores being conserved. Extensive developments are often given façades that attempt to give the appearance of comprising more than one building of traditional plot widths. Larkham (1990) describes, in the case of Britain, the approach of "façadism": rebuilding in forms suitable for modern functions behind a restored and retained façade. Such techniques retain the visual appearance of historic areas, although they may obliterate much of the historical and architectural significance of individual buildings and lead to the loss of the townscape "grain" through plot amalgamation (Larkham 1990). Nevertheless, Hubbard (1993) has examined the reactions of residents toward this approach and has found that they do not perceive this as a problem but consider external appearance as more important than authenticity or originality. This rekindles the "authenticity" debate: the need to identify a building's architecture as an accurate revelation of the past as a fixed truth. In a key contribution to the literature, Ashworth and Tunbridge's *The Tourist-Historic City* (1990) argues that authenticity as it is defined needs to be replaced by a more flexible concept. Their argument revolves around the idea that the existing stock of old buildings are a result of survival over time, dependent on such factors as building type, materials, districts and towns, natural catastrophes, and socioeconomic pressures. Hence, a range of fundamental biases exist that distort authenticity of conservation as an accurate revelation of the past, before it has begun. In their words,

> If authenticity is the accurate reflection of the past through its architecture, then skilful reconstruction may be more authentic than scattered remnant relics. Most old urban structures are the result of much adaptive reuse. Restoration therefore faces the problem of choosing which past from many should be restored. (Ashworth and Turnbridge 1990, 24)

The Shift to the Heritage Approach

Heritage is the most modern phase of conservation. It is the concept that provides "the link between the preservation of the past for its intrinsic value, and as a resource for the modern community as a commercial activity" (Ashworth and Tunbridge 1990, 24). In some cases, this approach has been referred to as "exploitation" where "there is an apparent shift to a market orientation that focuses upon the relics of history as a product, selected according to criteria of consumer demand and managed through the intervention in the market" (Ashworth and Larkham 1994, 16). On the other hand, preservation and conservation have no such direct implication and focus on the artefact or area itself. This distinction has consequences in the approaches to historic city management.

Ashworth (1992) argues that heritage is the product of a "commodification" process in which selection is central: heritage conservation is creation and not preservation of what already exists. The nature of the final product (as heritage) is not determined by the resources endowment, nor can it reflect any supposedly accurate factual record of the past. Schouten (1995) adds that heritage is a product and, as a product, it is subject to difference in validation and interpretation as the historical process itself. Heritage changes over time in the way it is presented and also in the ways in which the public reacts to its presentation. Hence, there is a tendency to change the past to suit changing requirements; relics can be adapted, added to, copied, and interpreted, all of which idealise the past.

—∿—

The Tourism-Heritage Relationship

Although increasing wealth and leisure time have led to increased tourism, which has been the impetus for heritage planning, the relationship between planning, heritage, and tourism is one of paradox (Urry 1990). As with any economic activity, tourism makes use of resources and produces an environmental impact that amounts to exploitation if the quantity and quality of those resources are degraded. Newby (1994) identifies a complex relationship between heritage and tourism in which culture evolves from being a shared entity, to being exploited, and in extreme cases created. When culture is shared, tourism and heritage coexist so that tourism revenues can be used to sustain and conserve environments of heritage value. However, when culture is exploited or created, there is an explicit domination of commercial values over conservation values as tourism becomes central to the local economy. In this instance, the cultural heritage becomes a consumer product susceptible to a selection process restricted by the choice, fashion, and taste of international organisations involved in the marketing of the heritage product, and the consumers.

—∿—

[. . .] [T]he preeminence of economic forces generated by tourism means that frequently commercial activities, often with a leisure or tourist dimension, conflict with form (Newby 1994). This conflict between whether conservation is concerned with a building as a structure or as a shape raises questions on authenticity. Significant structural changes to historic buildings often indicate that more value is placed on the exterior to generate revenues from the progressive commercialisation of tourist activities, rather than valuing the building as an integral whole.

[. . .]

More recently, urban theorists have drawn attention to the ways in which tourism conflicts with the living culture. Where culture is made to serve tourism and is simultaneously transformed into a market-oriented commodity, a revalued or sanitised history results (Larkham 1995). According to Herbert (1995), locals are in danger of

becoming part of the "spectacle" of tourism, gazed upon by outsiders who know little or nothing about their culture or society. Some of the social and cultural problems that arise stem from the different cultural norms and assumptions perceived by both the tourists and locals on such issues as child labour, the role of women, religion, alcohol, and so on that may be shocking or offensive to either side. The greatest conflict between host and visitor occurs in the different cultural uses of urban space. Private space, such as those associated with residential areas, as well as religious space are the most sensitive to tourist intervention (Orbasli 2000). Thus, the development of heritage places and the increase of tourist numbers may bring with them an invasion of privacy. Tourism, which has been heralded as a means of cross-cultural understanding, can also be the cause of cultural confrontation, augmented by the lack of cultural awareness on the visitor's behalf. In addition, this cultural confrontation can be unintentionally exacerbated by displays of wealth and consumerism that may be disruptive to locals. Tourism also induces changes in local lifestyles and cultures. Imported ideas on heritage induced by cliché images that become symbolic of certain cultures, such as dragons or belly dancers, promote the vulgarisation of culture (Dahlan 1990). [. . .]
[. . .]

Can Heritage Tourism Be Sustainable?

The realisation that mass tourism in many cases is destructive of culture, the environment, and the built resources has contributed to the development of alternative forms of tourism. Viewed as a form of alternative tourism, the concept of sustainable tourism has been motivated by the growth in environmental awareness among many people and the recognition among conservationists that tourism is one method of capturing conservation values for conservation purposes. However, the term *sustainability* has become a catchphrase, which, partly because of its imprecision, has attracted widespread interest from proponents and opponents. The ambiguity lies in the potential conflict in terms: *sustainable* implies a state that can be maintained, is ongoing, perhaps even unchanging, whereas *tourism* implies the dynamic process of change to suit consumer demands. On the other hand, the ambiguity also potentially permits flexibility and fine-tuning to meet the needs of different places and cultures.

From its inception, the concept of *sustainability* has revolved around managing current and future development by reconciling the three e's: environment, economy, and an equitable society. One of the first definitions was given in 1987 by the Brundtland Report (the World Commission on Environment and Development) as "development which meets the needs of the future without compromising the ability of future generations to meet their own needs" (p. 8). This underpins the basic precept of intergenerational equity that calls for natural resource conservation and environmental protection for the good of future generations (Jepson 2001). But equity is not just about the distribution of resources, services, and opportunities. It also includes issues of quality of life and community participation in decision making as advocated by Beatley and Manning (1997). Jacobs (1991) defines *sustainability* as the capacity of the environment to accept demands without irreversible or otherwise unacceptable change. In this view, the ecological concept is one of defining the *carrying capacity* of an environment to sustain a certain population, and beyond that level, the species will collapse (Beatley and Manning 1997). Sisman (1994) suggests a concept of sustainability entailing a long-term objective when he argues that sustainability must include a working partnership that blends good environmental practice and profitable business for mutual long-term advantages. Therefore, sustainability acknowledges a "critical natural capital" that must be maintained for future generations. This does not, however, rule out change. As English Nature (1992) suggests, there are other conservation elements of lesser value that are "compensatable." That is, they themselves could be damaged or lost, but they could be replaced by other elements of equivalent worth to ensure "constant environmental assets." From an ecological perspective, the system is capable of reproducing itself on the long term through renewal and recycling, as well as creative innovation (Campbell 1996).

Sustainable tourism is rooted in sustainable development, in the sense that if tourism is to contribute to sustainable development, it must be economically viable, environmentally sensitive, and culturally appropriate. Two schools of thought have developed views on sustainable tourism. The first argument reflects the functional approach of analysing tourism and its impact on the tourist destination as a cultural resource, whereas the second is referred to as the political economy approach, which takes the view that in order to minimise the worst examples of exploitation, host countries and populations need to seek public ownership of the tourist industry and direct marketing of the product (Lea 1988). Wall (1997) supports the first approach and is skeptical when he argues that

> few see tourism as a pollution-free industry which is environmentally benign, although any would accept that it is in the long-term interests of the tourist industry to assure the longevity of the resources on which it depends. But this is easier said than done, for tourism exhibits many of the attributes of common property resources, with most money being spent on transportation, accommodation, and food and beverages, and relatively little being directed to the maintenance of the natural and cultural heritage resources on which tourism ultimately depends. (P. 46)

Nevertheless, proponents of sustainble tourism believe that if development is founded on small-scale, locally owned activities, tourism can fulfil a nonconsumptive use of resources, which appears to have the potential to serve both conservation and local development roles as well (Furze, De Lacy, Birckhead 1996). In this case, the benefits are threefold. First, there will be less need for financial investment in infrastructure and superstructure facilities compared to conventional mass tourism. Second, locally owned and operated businesses will not have to conform to the corporate Western identity of multinational tourism concerns and therefore can have a much higher input of local products, materials, and labour. Third, the profits made should accrue locally instead of flowing back to the state of foreign organisations (Cater 1994).

—w—

Finally, the most vital factor to ensure sustainability of tourism development is to increase local involvement. There has been a growing consensus among scholars of the importance of local involvement to ensure sustainability. [. . .]

There are sound reasons for local involvement other than the moral obligation to incorporate people in shaping their own destiny. In terms of the conservation of the cultural resource base, the local population's time perspective is longer than that of outside entrepreneurs concerned with early profits. The longer view is also likely to ensure that traditions and lifestyles are respected. There are also sound reasons in terms of creating local employment and reviving the local economy. The nature of involvement should take many forms, not just the provision of schools, hospitals, and social services financed from tourism but also through the replacement of alternative economic livelihoods, if the traditional is being removed from the community (Cater 1994). Such an involvement extends beyond economic survival, environmental conservation, and sociocultural integrity, but it allows the community to appreciate its own resources (Furze, de Lacy, and Birckhead 1996).

Both approaches to conceptualising tourism's place in development are, in theory, not in complete opposition to each other. They are both useful in highlighting the diversity of the subject. The functional approach emphasises the considerable economic importance of the industry to all participants and on ways to improve its efficiency and minimise its adverse effects through good management and appropriate policy measures. The political-economy approach sees the need for the tourism industry to take more financial responsibility for the long-term maintenance of the heritage resources on which it depends, by allowing governments and local communities to hold higher stakes in tourism and in the management of their historic resources.

Conclusions

On the whole, there is consensus that sustainability and planning are both compatible and complementary (Campbell 1996; Jepson 2001), although there remains a continued lack of a balanced, holistic approach to guiding development and moving toward sustainability (Berk and Conroy 2000). The focus is primarily on creating more liveable built environments rather than integrating a more holistic view of community development. The absence of a social and cultural perspective is also evident in the conservation and heritage planning literature, in which the physical product forms the principal focus. This has raised philosophical problems of selectivity, authenticity, interpretation, and re-creation of the cultural heritage that have defined and redefined the meaning and significance of the cultural resource. More practical problems stem from the dichotomous relationship between preservation for posterity and change and development necessary for keeping heritage places alive and attractive.

[. . .]

[T]o plan for an agenda for heritage places as an integrated part of a holistic view of community development two interrelated approaches should be realised. The first approach is to reunite urban form, that is, the buildings and urban spaces, with the activities and uses that take place within them. The second approach is to integrate land use planning with social ideals (Campbell 1996; Jepson 2001). In heritage places, this means managing and resolving the dominance of tourist activities over local needs and aspirations, reflected in the transformation of land uses and buildings, the disruptive use of public and private space, changing ownership patterns, and the externalising of the local economy.

Within this framework, the management of change is crucial to the long-term survival of heritage places. Change associated with historic buildings should involve adaptive reuse and reconstruction in order to combat both structural and functional obsolescence in accordance with changing social needs. This process of renewal and recycling has two objectives. First, it protects a critical capital of cultural assets for future generations, and second, it preserves the genius loci and sense of place that gives historic areas their individuality. The process of renewal also redefines the concept of authenticity from one that is focused only on the past to one that views the present as part of the continuum. Skilful reconstruction rather than restoration, therefore, contributes to the added value of the building and forms part of its evolution (and survival). Compatible uses also raise the building's economic viability, promoting the efficiency of local economic activities and its social benefits. The degree of change to the historic fabric is defined by the selection and legal designation of conservation-worthy buildings. However, this article has also highlighted that too much legislated protection can restrict essential growth and modernisation, pushing development to peripheral areas. To a large extent, this can be controlled by integrating conservation areas within comprehensive development plans to promote a strategy for transportation, environment, energy, land use and design, and public facilities that applies not only to local areas but to the city scale (Berke and Conroy 2000).

[. . .]

In terms of the sustainability of heritage places, managing tourism can have substantial inherent potential to underpin sustainable development and conservation. First, tourism can yield economic development at the local, regional, and national levels, creating jobs and bringing in much-needed foreign income. However, mechanisms for ensuring equitable access to social and economic resources and their distribution among all social groups of the local community require careful management. One area of sustainability that has received markedly less attention is that of financial resource mechanisms. Revenues generated from tourism should feed back into the local community through mechanisms of cross-subsidisation such as revolving trusts to refurbish and reclaim buildings or enforced entrance fees to tourist attractions. These revenues could operate to improve local incomes, saving and enhancing whole areas of towns. Second, tourism also has the potential to create more demand for conserving buildings including less valued monuments and overlooked traditional environments (Orbasli 2000). Third, tourism can create uses for redundant buildings, which if carefully managed, can contribute to preservation. Fourth, tourism can also increase an appreciation for the historic environment, contributing to greater local and cross-cultural understanding.

References

Ashworth, Gregory J. 1992. Heritage and tourism: An argument, two problems and three solutions. In *Spatial implications of tourism*, C.A.M. Fleischer van Roojen, ed. Groningen, the Netherlands: Geo Pers.

———. 1990. Can places be sold for tourism? In *Marketing tourism places*, G. J. Ashworth and B. Goodall, eds. London: Routledge.

Ashworth, Gregory J. and Peter J. Larkham. 1994. A heritage for Europe: The need, the task, the contribution. In *Building a new heritage: Tourism, culture and identity*, G. J. Ashworth and P. J. Larkham, eds. London: Routledge.

Ashworth, Gregory J., and J. E. Tunbridge. 1990. *The tourist-historic city*. London: Belhaven.

Beatley, Timothy, and Kristy Manning. 1997. *The ecology of place: Planning for environment, economy and community*. Washington, DC: Island Press.

Berke, Philip R., and Maria M. Conroy. 2000. Are we planning for sustainable development? An evaluation of 30 comprehensive plans. *Journal of the American Planning Association*, 66, 1: 21–33.

Campbell, Scott. 1996. Green cities, growing cities, just cities? Urban planning and the contradictions of sustainable development. *Journal of the American Planning Association* 62, 3: 296–312.

Cater, Erlet. 1994. Ecotourism in the third world—Problems and prospects for sustainability. In *Ecotourism: A sustainable option?* E. Cater and G. Lowman, eds. Chichester, UK: Wiley.

Dahlan, H. 1990. In what way can culture serve tourism? *Borneo Review* 1: 129–48.

English Nature. 1992. Strategic planning and sustainable development. Consultation paper. David Tyldesley Associates on behalf of English Nature, Peterborough, UK.

Furze, Brian, Terry de Lacy, and Jim Birckhead. 1996. *Culture, conservation, and biodiversity*. Chichester, UK: Wiley.

Herbert, David T. 1995. Heritage places, leisure and tourism. In *Heritage, tourism and society*, D. T. Herbert, ed. London: Mansell.

Hubbard, Phil. 1993. The value of conservation: A critical review of behavioural research. *Town Planning Review* 64, 4: 359–73.

Jacobs, Michael. 1991. *The green economy: Environment, sustainable development, and the politics of the future*. Concord, MA: Pluto.

Jepson, Edward J. 2001. Sustainability and planning: Diverse concepts and close associations. *Journal of Planning Literature* 15, 4: 499–510.

Larkham, Peter J. 1996. *Conservation and the city*. London: Routledge.

———. 1995. Heritage as planned and conserved. In *Heritage, tourism and society*, D. T. Herbert, ed. London: Mansell.

———. 1990. Conservation and the management of historical townscapes. In *The built form of Western cities*, T. R. Slater, ed. Leicester, UK: Leicester University Press.

Lea, John. 1988. *Tourism and development in the third world*. New York: Routledge.

Newby, Peter T. 1994. Tourism—Support or threat to heritage. In *Building a new heritage: Tourism, culture, and identity*, G. J. Ashworth and P. J. Larkham, eds. London: Routledge.

Oncu, Ayse, and Petra Weyland. 1997. Struggles over *Lebenstraum* social identities in globalising cities. In *Space, culture and power: New identities in globalising cities*, A. Oncu and P. Weyland, eds. London: Zed Books.

Orbasli, Aylin. 2000. *Tourists in historic towns: Urban conservation and heritage management*. London and New York: E & FN Spon.

Schouten, Frans J. 1995. Heritage as historical reality. In *Heritage, tourism and society*, D. T. Herbert, ed. London: Mansell.

Sisman, Richard. 1994. Tourism: Environmental relevance in ecotourism. In *Ecotourism–A sustainable option?* E. Cater and G. Lowman, eds. Chichester, UK: Wiley.

Urry, John. 1990. *The tourist gaze: Leisure and travel in contemporary societies*. London: Sage.

Wall, Geoffrey. 1997. Sustainable tourism—Unsustainable development. In *Tourism, development and growth*, S. Wahab and J. J. Pigram, eds. London: Routledge.

World Commission on Environment and Development. 1987. Our common future: The report of the World Commission on Environment and Development. Oxford, UK: Oxford University Press.

Worskett, Roy. 1969. *The character of towns—An approach to conservation*. London: Architectural Press.

Reading

61

Stephanie Brown

Beyond Gentrification: Strategies for Guiding the Conversation and Redirecting the Outcomes of Community Transition (2014)

Stephanie Brown received a master's degree in urban planning from Harvard's Graduate School of Design in 2012. In this paper, based on her thesis, Brown provides "a framework for understanding the costs and benefits [associated with gentrification] and the processes that produce them." Mitigating the social displacement that often accompanies higher property values in historic areas experiencing new investments is a worldwide challenge. Here Brown explores three "process models" associated with gentrification, using two studies, in Jamaica Plain in Boston and Columbia Heights in Washington DC. She pays particular attention to an "inclusionary" model, whereby existing residents and other stakeholders are brought into the development process early, so that "the negative consequences of neighborhood transition" can, ideally, be mitigated against.

Overview of the Problem

Gentrification has become the sticking point for many urban revitalization efforts—the specter which hangs over the efforts of community organizations, the rallying point for apprehensive community members, and the dubious label for new residents. Gentrification, or the perception thereof, has been a source of conflict, confusion, and seemingly competing value systems for transitioning communities. It pits community members against each other and generates dissension amongst leadership. Yet for a word which means so much, too often it is a process poorly defined and poorly understood.

In order to manage this type of community transition well, community organizations and leaders must be able to identify and understand the forces at work and develop a new level of engagement with the broader transition process. A complex and contradictory set of costs and benefits for the community are subsumed under the term

From Stephanie Brown, "Beyond Gentrification: Strategies for Guiding the Conversation and Redirecting the Outcomes of Community Transition," Paper submitted to Harvard University, Joint Center for Housing Studies and Neighbor Works America, July 2014, 1–2, 4, 6–12, 14, 16, 19, 28–41, 43.

"gentrification." This paper sets out to provide a framework for understanding those costs and benefits and the processes that produce them. Building on this framework, the paper then provides recommendations for how community leaders in the public and private sectors can begin to maximize the benefits and minimize the costs. In particular, it seeks to:

- **Understand challenges** to partnerships in mixed-income, multi-cultural communities.
- **Identify strategies** to build community and forge alliances between disparate populations in distressed neighborhoods experiencing an influx of higher-income residents.
- **Develop replicable guidelines** for neighborhoods approaching or undergoing such a period of transition.

Methodology

This research took a case study approach, relying primarily on in-depth interviews with various stakeholders in two communities, supplemented by less extensive interviews in communities around the country to provide broader perspective. This research was supported by a literature review and additional academic interviews. The two primary case studies took place in transitioning urban neighborhoods: Jamaica Plain in Boston, MA and Columbia Heights in Washington, DC.

The Jamaica Plain and Columbia Heights neighborhoods are similarly situated. Both are long-standing neighborhoods annexed by their central cities just over a century ago. Both were initially wealthier neighborhoods on the edge of the city; due to this position between the early suburbs and a central city that underwent economic decline in the mid-twentieth century, both have historically contained an economically and racially diverse population. Both currently have a relatively high percentage of affordable housing and active community groups. In recent decades, public transportation lines have been extended through both communities, catalyzing further development. Most importantly, both have recently experienced dramatic social and demographic changes leading to a community-wide conversation about gentrification.

Theoretical Framework

[I]t is vital to acknowledge that gentrification is not a value-neutral term, and the frame in which it is generally discussed reflects the concerns with the phenomenon. Those who have a more positive view of neighborhood transition persistently refer to this transformation as revitalization, reinvestment, development, or any other carefully selected phrase which avoids the dreaded "g-word."

In its recommendations, this paper attempts to move beyond that connotation-heavy debate over "gentrification" versus "revitalization" and acknowledge that community transformation, neither entirely bad nor wholly welcome, brings with it positive and negative developments. Because the word gentrification can so instantly polarize a discussion, its use limits the ability of a community to reshape itself in a thoughtful and unified manner. [. . .]

Nonetheless, the depth of academic examination of gentrification and its social prevalence warrants a more thorough discussion of the term's varying definitions, its use, and its implications. The concept of gentrification has a long history in popular and academic discourse. The word itself dates back to Ruth Glass, a British sociologist who coined the term in 1964 in a discussion of urban transformation in the London neighborhood of North Kensington. The phrase rose to prominence in the academic community in the late 1970s and 1980s, yet despite its long usage, definitions of the term remain imprecise and varied. In its most simplistic definition, gentrification involves significant numbers of the "gentry," a broadly-defined wealthier class, moving into a poorer community and converting it for their own use. The process is also overwhelmingly associated with an increase of property values and the threat of displacement for poorer residents.

—~—

In the context of this paper, the following type of transitioning or transforming community will be examined:

> *communities experiencing a physical, economic, and cultural process wherein the population of a neighborhood shifts towards wealthier and more educated residents, potentially leading to the physical and/or social displacement of lower-income residents and businesses*

The paper's findings have implications for multiple types of community transformation, but the analysis will consistently focus on communities where the shift is towards increasing wealth, neighborhoods many would consider to be gentrifying.

—~—

Root Causes

Transforming neighborhoods are likely to share several characteristics—they often have older homes with higher quality architecture, they are proximate to the central city, and often have access to public transportation. From these commonalities and the trends identified above, two primary theories have risen as to the cause of such change. In 1987, Neil Smith developed the supply-side theory of the "rent gap." This theory argues that in certain communities, the exchange value of the structures and/or the actual rent received begins to fall far below the potential value of that piece of land. Once the potential of the ground rent increases sufficiently above the value of the sale price of the structure on it, a "rent gap" emerges so that it becomes a profitable investment for someone to come in and purchase or flip the property. This trend can be particularly potent in those neighborhoods with unique or high-quality architecture which are well-situated in regards to the downtown core. This potential attracts investors, but also may make a neighborhood appealing for someone who desires a certain type or size of home and would be unable to afford it in a wealthier district.

Another theory, popularized by Richard Florida, looks instead to the demand side of the equation and argues that the type of creative, entrepreneurial professionals who are emerging today want to live closer to urban centers and are more open and attracted to "edgy" environments which have a diverse, funky vibe (Florida 2002). Additionally, these individuals are often at the early stages of their career and so may initially need lower-rent housing options, yet are on track to quickly increase their income and disposable cash. [. . .]

Finally, neighborhood transformation is increasingly triggered by large-scale investment projects. In many cases, as will be seen in Columbia Heights, this takes the form of a city-driven revitalization effort which has a transformative impact for the community. These efforts can also be public-private partnerships, or, somewhat more rarely, purely private developments. Oftentimes these investments are coordinated with work in adjacent neighborhoods or new public transit or infrastructure investment. In these instances, the threat of displacement comes not only from increasing property values, but through the potential use of eminent domain to group properties into large enough parcels for significant development projects. [. . .]

Controversies

Three aspects of this transformation in particular can be alarming, the first being the potential displacement of long-term or original residents. [. . .]

The second category of debate concerns the relative merits of economic and racial diversity. [. . .]

Finally, a third question concerns the real benefits of increased urban development. These benefits come in many forms, including safer streets, better access to resources, better transportation, greater convenience, cleaner parks and streets, and potentially better schools. For the city coffers, another undeniable benefit is the increased property taxes collected as assessed value rises. These benefits are juxtaposed, however, with the challenges of affordability in these communities. Affordability challenges come primarily in the form of increased rents, but can also be seen in the prices of local goods and services. [. . .]

Process Models

[. . .] I have identified two models to explain the primary types of community transition occurring today, which I call "organic" and "accelerated." The **organic model** more closely mirrors the traditional understanding of gentrification rooted in sociological studies from the 1980s. The **accelerated model** blends traditional gentrification with new build gentrification and looks at how the process shifts when there is a significant infusion of public or private funds for development purposes (Lees, Slater, and Wyly 2008). Finally, I also offer a third model, the **inclusionary model**, as an ideal prototype. This model seeks to avoid the traditional endpoint of community transition in a homogeneously upper middle class urban neighborhood and instead redirect the culmination towards a diverse community which preserves affordable housing and retains neighborhood amenities. The aims and processes of this model will be further fleshed out in the final recommendations.

Organic Model

The organic process of transition, as its name implies, is slow and subtle, and its tipping points can be very difficult to discern. The four steps of the organic model—start-up, buy-in, take-off, and fill-in—frame the general process but often overlap in communities. This model originates with Wanda Coston's delineation of the stages in her Columbus, Ohio case study, *Stages of Gentrification and Neighborhood Revitalization* (1984), but also relies on the work of Phillip Clay (1979) and contains aspects of later work on the "third wave of gentrification" by scholars such as Neil Smith (1987). Generally speaking, the organic model is more dependent on the typical set of preconditions (high quality architecture, proximity to the urban core, and access to public transportation) than its accelerated counterpart. Buildings are often in deteriorating condition but have the potential for rehabilitation, either as single family homes or as an industrial-residential conversion.

—⁓—

Accelerated Model

The accelerated model of transition occurs when a significant infusion of new development dramatically and rapidly alters the landscape of the neighborhood. Development may take the form of a large-scale mixed used development, a new transit line, or perhaps even the demolition of a significant area to make way for new development. This model shares a number of features with the organic model, but differs in the main driver of change. The speed of transformation certainly changes, but so too do key stakeholders: local government and/or large developers emerge as the key players in the process. Indications of this change are more apparent in city planning documents, municipal conversations, and quiet real estate accumulation than on the streets of the neighborhood. The results of the accelerated and organic models, however, are remarkably similar.

Summary Table—Community Transition Process Models

	Organic	Inclusive	Accelerated
I	Small scale rehabs with sweat labor Low-income, risk oblivious newcomers	Initial market or investment signs appear Adjacent neighborhoods shift *Track neighborhood change*	Small scale investments may be occurring, but are not necessary to trigger the investment in the next state
II	Subtle promotion and internal discussion Entrepeneurs and speculators reduce vacancies	**Best Moment for Intervention** Beginning of community "visioning"	Rumors of pending development Land assembled and held Formal planning effort and/or design charrettes
III	Major media interest develops Established developers and investors proliferate Tensions increase and affordable housing resisted	New development occurs with active community participation Affordable housing policies enacted Community activities build upon renewed local identity	Large-scale public/private investment occurs Highly visible and concentrated redevelopment Neighborhood seen as safe investment option
IV	Rents and property taxes spike Public legal controls on properties sought Risk-oblivious and major chains move in freely	Community stabilizes with economic and racial mix Cohesive identity promotes diversity Increased neighborhood amenities	Prices rise rapidly as physical landscape changes Neighborhood may polarize

Inclusionary Model

The inclusionary model aims at capturing the benefits of increased investment in the neighborhood—safer streets, better schools, more shopping options, fewer vacancies—while mitigating the potential for harm done through physical and psychological displacement of the existing population. It acknowledges that many of these long-term residents want these benefits, in many cases have actively worked to bring them about, but do not want them at all costs. In order to incorporate the positive and mitigate the negative consequences of neighborhood transition, the inclusionary model overlays both the organic and accelerated models with a focused "moment of intervention" during stage two, when the pending change becomes more evident. From that point it seeks to redirect outcomes, using a series of tactics identified later in this paper, and move towards a new framework for healthier transitions.

—~—

Steps for Pursuing the Inclusionary Model

[. . .]

The following five recommendations are offered as guidelines for action in communities which are experiencing community transformation or for those which believe that this type of transition may lie in their future. Derived from both communities, as well as from other successful neighborhoods around the country, they provide a menu of options for promoting the inclusionary model of transformation.

The applicability of these recommendations will vary by both timing and actor. For example, for communities lacking a robust nonprofit network, it will be particularly important for city officials to diligently monitor the pace and nature of community change, and it may be more appropriate to pursue policy-based and top-down solutions. Many of these recommendations are targeted to nonprofits such as community development corporations rather than to direct service organizations, but case studies have repeatedly revealed that nonprofits and organizations of all types need to actively intervene in community transformation in order to ensure a balanced development path. Timing also matters when implementing these recommendations: policies designed to increase the availability of affordable housing may have a detrimental impact on a community's economic development prospects if pursued too early. More details on timing and actors are discussed in the context of the following recommendations.

1.) Anticipate and proactively respond to change.

Though residents and observers often experience neighborhood change as a sudden event, it never actually takes place overnight. While every neighborhood possesses unique characteristics, many aspects of this transition are identifiable and generalizable. [. . .]

—~—

- *Conduct physical surveys of neighborhood properties.*
  Some changes will not appear readily in data analysis. It is therefore important to recognize physical upgrades in the neighborhood and conduct brief surveys of the neighborhood on an annual basis. This allows community leaders to remain systematically informed of whether new homeowners are upgrading their properties considerably, vacancies are declining, and unused properties are being purchased. [. . .]

- *Stay informed of city plans, including city and neighborhood master plans, transportation proposals and funding requests, and requests for proposals (RFPs) related to development opportunities.*
  Most of this information is readily available online and oftentimes conscientiously distributed to the neighborhood. However, sometimes that distribution comes at too late a point in the process to effect significant change. Particularly in communities where the city has not built trust with their community planning efforts, many interviewees spoke of the importance of proactively seeking out information from city officials. [. . .]

- *Use ACS and other data to monitor demographic changes.*
  The American Communities Survey provides new data on neighborhood demographics more frequently than the traditional census. Local governments may distribute this information, but it can also be obtained directly on the Census website. [. . .]

- *Monitor trends in adjacent communities.*
  New research has shown that the communities most likely to experience housing price shocks are those directly adjacent to communities where prices have recently risen (Guerrieri, Hartley, and Hurst 2010). This spillover effect is common enough to be one of the strongest indicators of change. [. . .]

2.) Develop a shared narrative around which the community can coalesce.

Internal community narratives offer the basis for stability and self-policing. Local mores and norms help guide and protect a community, but a shared identity also offers an invitation to newcomers. As in Richard Florida's theory of the "creative class," many new residents may be coming to a community looking for a unique experience (Florida 2002). Those residents tend to welcome and embrace the history and character of a community. Because of this, residents who might otherwise only serve to drive up rent prices can also be mobilized to preserve and protect the neighborhood's traditional character or identity. [. . .]

[. . .] The following tools are useful in developing the shared narrative:

- *Community visioning or planning meetings.*
  Community planning meetings may be initiated by local government or a socially-minded developer, but [. . .] community groups can conduct their own planning meetings as well. [. . .]

- *Neighborhood gatherings: block parties, festivals, community events.*
  It is always helpful to remind a neighborhood that it is, in fact, a community, and celebratory events are an excellent way of doing so. [. . .]

- *History trails, markers, and tours.*
  While history trails and similar efforts are generally the purview of specialized groups rather than of community development organizations, they can play a vital role in crafting a shared community narrative. [. . .]

3.) Forge active partnerships.

Strong collaboration between community organizations was one of the greatest strengths of Jamaica Plain. These organizations did not always share the same priorities and sometimes disagreed with one another, but more often than not they were able to work together productively. In Columbia Heights, long-established community groups such as the Development Corporation of Columbia Heights (DCCH) and Latin American Youth Center (LAYC) have operated at more of a distance from the newly emerging civic associations and social action groups. The absence of closer partnerships may have inadvertently reinforced stereotypes of both long-term and new residents. Building partnerships across social issues and organizations can strengthen the shared vision described above and enable more concerted action. [. . .]

- *Keep the focus local and specific.*
  Partnerships are difficult to build and to manage, but the more targeted in scope they are, the more successful they will be. For all the differences we see across communities, there are certain universal desires—basic safety, opportunities for kids, and convenient access to needed amenities—which will pull together disparate parties. [. . .]

- *Be open to temporary and non-traditional partnerships.*
  While strong, lasting partnerships certainly have a place in community development, the firm ideological alignment they require is somewhat rare; openness to looser partnerships creates more frequent opportunities to benefit from them. [. . .]

- *Ensure blended representation on committees and board of directors.*
  A board of directors requires a combination of technical and issue-based expertise, fundraising prowess, and community representation; a deficit in any of these three areas will weaken the organization. [. . .]

- *Invest actively in business alliances.*
  Community transformation is not simply a question of housing, though many of the preservation recommendations focus on affordable housing. Businesses have a stake in this transition as well. [. . .]

- *Recruit locally for donors and volunteers.*
  Oftentimes, the wellsprings for both donors and volunteers lie outside the community. In both Jamaica Plain and Columbia Heights, universities located beyond the neighborhood boundaries provided excellent recruitment grounds. This is natural, efficient, and effective outreach. [. . .]

4.) Develop conflict mediation mechanisms.

Community transformation is rarely bloodless. Racial and socioeconomic tensions go to the heart of embedded narratives far broader and deeper than the story of any one community. When local change rubs against this nerve, tensions can flare quickly. These conflicts are deep and important, and should not be ignored. At the same time, they can obfuscate the particular nuances of the local issues at hand.

Community conflict, however, is not limited to issues of deep moral or social significance. Small squabbles, old grudges, and personal conflict can spill over to an entire community and disrupt a multitude of neighborhood projects. None of this is news to community leaders and organizers, but it remains difficult to push through the noise of conflict, meaningfully address the core issues, and move forward with the task at hand. [. . .] The best strategies seek to build trust early and resolve tensions before they become full-blown conflicts, but also include mechanisms to deal with conflicts when they erupt:

- *Open avenues of communication through facilitated, friendly discussions.*
  Conflict mediation begins with positive, cooperative conversations that happen well in advance of specific troubles, so that residents and leaders have relationships in place to fall back upon in moments of strife. [. . .]

- *Train leaders and foster political participation.*
  Training local leaders is a crucial aspect of community development for several reasons. Strong conflict mediation and cross-cultural communication components make such training particularly beneficial. [. . .]

- *Designate a point person or create a formal plan in mixed-income developments.*
  For organizations concerned with affordable housing, the development of mixed-income communities provides a different type of space for conflict mediation. [. . .]

- *Understand the role of social media.*
  Social media also contributes to the speed at which conflicts can spread. The added buffer provided by impersonal mediums such as email lists and message boards can also increase the vitriol of such conversations. [. . .]

5.) Advocate for legal tools to preserve affordability.

Using different tactics, both Columbia Heights and Jamaica Plain were able to preserve a considerable supply of affordable housing in the face of price increases. [. . .]

Several policy tools [. . .] are available to communities to preserve affordability. [. . .]

- *Tax abatement.*
  Tax abatement policies are undertaken at the local level and can be written in a variety of ways. In each case, however, the goal is to reduce the property tax burden experienced when housing values rise. This financial burden can become too much for homeowners or can spur landlords to increase rent prices. While most tax abatement policies are written solely for owners, there are ways to carefully shape such legislation for landlords as well. Tax abatement policies are most frequently offered for elderly residents who live on fixed incomes, but have also been developed for low-income residents and for those who invest in remodeling. [. . .]

- *Tenant opportunity to purchase.*
  Legislation in both Boston and Washington give building tenants the first right of refusal to purchase their building collectively before it is sold to a private developer. The opportunity to purchase can be crucial when owners of low-rent apartment buildings look to sell their buildings for conversion to more expensive condo properties. [. . .]

- *Inclusionary zoning.*
  Affordable housing legislation can be instituted on the state and local level, and local governments can create a similar impact through housing trust funds and other developer exactions. [. . .]

- *Homeownership counseling and assistance.*
  The best time for low and moderate income individuals to purchase property is right at the beginning of a neighborhood transition. As home values rise, low-income families will likely be unable to purchase and may also find it more difficult to rent. [. . .]

- *Awareness campaigns.*
  Finally, community organizations can increase support for affordable housing policies through awareness campaigns. Because many of the above policies require direct political action and public support, their effective implementation requires broad-based coalition building. Awareness campaigns should therefore build on the community's shared narrative (discussed above) in order to mobilize people to action. [. . .]

Conclusion

I began this paper arguing against the use of "gentrification" as a rhetorical tool to warn long-term residents of the changes brought on by their newer, wealthier neighbors. Such a strategy—no matter how effective politically in the short term—serves to categorize community members and create walls between neighbors. Yet in arguing against the use of this divisive term, I do not want to downplay the challenges faced by lower-income residents during community transitions. I want to be very clear—the pangs of community transition are real and deep. Residents may be financially unable to stay in their own homes or feel so disconnected from new trends that they are left adrift and are uninterested in staying. Our efforts to promote equitable, prosperous, sustainable communities are rooted in the hope that all residents will have a stake in their neighborhoods, and full access to their amenities. To exclude those long-term residents who have borne the worst of times in inner-city neighborhoods from new opportunities and resources in these communities would be the height of injustice.

And, yet, neighborhoods change. This is an inevitable facet of the urban experience, and the neighborhoods now wrapped up in the gentrification debate have seen several distinct permutations of community life in prior generations, across both ethnic and economic divisions. This is the lifeblood of cities, the mechanism for their growth, and their hope for the future. A community preservation strategy which aims to freeze demographics in place is neither realistic nor desirable. Moreover, long-term residents in disadvantaged communities are often the very people fighting the hardest for change—improved public safety, better local schools, more transit options, increased retail availability. New attention and new residents, particularly ones with more disposable income, bring the resources needed to accomplish just such goals.

We need a third way. This paper has sought to identify tested strategies which mitigate transition costs to long-term residents while still capturing the fiscal and political benefits for the broader community. These strategies are a menu of options rather than a fixed path, and should be used in the combination most sensible for each distinct neighborhood. Despite their diversity, the strategies on this menu share the goal of forging a new, blended community in the midst of transition. Achieving that goal requires conflict, compromise, and conciliation. It is neither an easy nor a swift path, and there will always be individuals, both long-term residents and newcomers, who dismiss or resist their neighbors. The vast majority of residents, however, simply want a secure and sustaining home. That's a fight no one has to lose for everyone to win.

Works Consulted

Clay, Phillip L. 1979. *Neighborhood Renewal: Middle-class Resettlement and Incumbent Upgrading in American Neighborhoods*. Lexington, MA: Lexington Books.

Coston, Wanda Brendette. 1984. *The Stages of Gentrification and Neighborhood Revitalization: A Case Study of the Dennison Place and Victorian Village Neighborhoods, the Near North Side Community, Columbus, Ohio*. Columbus: Ohio State University Press.

Florida, Richard. 2002. *The Rise of the Creative Class*. New York: Basic Books.

Guerrieri, Veronica, Daniel Hartley, and Erik Hurst. 2010. "Endogenous Gentrification and Housing Price Dynamics." University of Chicago and NBER, May 6 (http://popcenter.uchicago.edu/pdf/housing_stanford_final_erik.pdf).

Lees, Loretta, Tom Slater, and Elvin K. Wyly. 2008. *Gentrification*. New York: Routledge/Taylor & Francis Group.

Smith, Neil. 1987. "Gentrification and the Rent Gap." *Annals of the Association of American Geographers*, 77, no. 3: 462–65.

Part VII

Visual Summary: The Sustainability of Urban Conservation

Winsor McCay, *Technocracy*, 1933.

In the twenty-first century—roughly eighty-five years since the graphic artist Winsor McCay created this ghoulish image of a machine monster running rampant over rooftops—the daunting challenges related to the conservation of significant historic places in urban contexts worldwide remain. Globalizing multinational firms, mounting tourism, intensifying urbanization, climate change, and rising economic inequalities exemplify some of these challenges, which prompted the delegates to the UN's Habitat III conference held in Quito, Ecuador, in October 2016 to propose the "New Urban Agenda," whereby it was hoped that "national urban policies, urban legislation and regulations, urban planning and design, local economy and municipal finance, and local implementation" would lead to "a better and more sustainable future."

Hong Kong from North Point to Causeway Bay. From Yu Yuan-chia, *A Panorama of Hong Kong on Scrolls* (Hong Kong: Joint Publishing Company, 1995).

PLATE VII.1

This forest of high-rise buildings in Hong Kong (Kowloon in the foreground) attests to the power of economic capital to transform in just a few years the face of what was already one of the world's densest cities. The resulting impact on city landmarks within the traditional fabric has often been irreversible, such as in the case of the Wong Tai Sin Temple (seen in painting above, at lower left), which today is dwarfed by Hong Kong's city towers. Both David Throsby (reading 56) and Christian Ost (reading 57) make the case for the cultural capital embodied in and by heritage buildings. This makes them valuable in themselves as well as in relation to their context and their immaterial value, a fact that is generally ignored or overlooked in evaluating the economic impact of urban projects in old city settings.

Part VII

VISUAL SUMMARY

The Manifesto Building, Lisbon (Mouraria District). Before intervention. Photo by Camilla Watson.

The Manifesto Building, Lisbon (Mouraria District). After intervention. Photo by Rui Pinheiro.

PLATES VII.2A AND VII.2B

A grant from Lisbon's city council was the catalyst for rehabilitating this previously vacant structure into a vibrant community center, with extensive input from local residents. This is an example of what Donovan Rypkema (reading 58) calls a lesser landmark for which a "financial tool"—in this case, a grant—was employed to revitalize the social, environmental, and cultural value of an under-utilized historic asset with the support and for the use of the larger community.

Street scene in Madurai (Tamil Nadu), India. Drawing by Manohar Devadoss, 2007.

PLATE VII.3

The busy pedestrian quality of this traditional street scene in Madurai illustrates the role local residents can play in the challenging process of urban conservation. Julian Smith (reading 59) underlines this point by urging us to "move beyond the outward morphology of the city to understand how it is experienced from within." He calls for a more "layered and organic understanding of the city"—in part, derived from engaging with local inhabitants who know their city well—so that more "community-based design and development" can occur.

Part VII

VISUAL SUMMARY

The Gods Cried Again from the Hut in Me, pencil on paper drawing by Nancy Wolf, 1983.

PLATE VII.4

In this drawing, Nancy Wolf highlights the vivid contrast between indigenous heritage and traditions and the most apparent and sought-after symbols of modernity, represented here by a cluster of Western-inspired high-rises. These two worlds often collide because of a misguided notion of modernity and faulty interpretations of tourists' expectations. As Noha Nasser (reading 60) explains, "The greatest conflict between host and visitor occurs in the different cultural uses of urban space." Nasser stresses that "the most vital factor to ensure sustainability of tourism development is to increase local involvement." Without greater cross-cultural understanding and sensitivity, the authenticity of long-lasting traditions risks being obliterated by the latest wave of fashionable newness.

The Mars Bar in the East Village of New York City is now a bank. Photos by James and Karla Murray.

PLATES VII.5A AND VII.5B

The word *gentrification* was coined by a British sociologist in 1964 to characterize urban transformation and social displacement of local residents by wealthier new owners. Residents in cities worldwide struggle with this kind of stark transformation, and Stephanie Brown (reading 61) probes their roots and effects. She proposes an ideal "inclusionary model" (without suggesting a one-size-fits-all approach) so that local residents and others can be proactive about proposed changes and thereby "develop a shared narrative around which the community can coalesce."

Part VIII

Managing Historic Cities

The six readings in this final part suggest that because cities are dynamic creations, their management in the face of inevitable change is likewise characterized by constant political, economic, and social adjustments and transformations. In light of the impact of macro-scale events, the authors included in part VIII attempt to determine how to "manage" both predictable and unpredictable transformations arising from within and without historic cities at various levels and in different cultural contexts. With the exception of one reading from 2002, the readings presented here date from the past decade, reflecting contemporary commentaries not only on management but also on the concomitant issues of integrated and/or value-driven approaches to urban conservation. They also explore community participation in the complex web of urban systems and power structures that often marginalize the genuine involvement of all "stakeholders"—to use a common but sometimes problematic term—in making decisions about urban continuity and change. We have sought to offer a selection of readings that are comprehensive in scope and sufficiently pragmatic to address issues of general concern rather than still another example of "experts talking to experts," a criticism raised in previous publications on the management of urban conservation.[1]

Before highlighting key points and practical suggestions in the readings, however, it is important to confront the thorny issue of what "management" means and implies. As a 2013 UNESCO publication suggests, "The term 'management' has been used widely in the heritage sector: as issues become more complex, there is a need to be more precise."[2] And yet the word, with its many connotations, seems to elude precise definition. In one sense, management concerns processes—the judicious use of means to accomplish an end—deriving from the Italian word *maneggiare,* "to handle, manage, touch, treat," which in turn derives from the Latin *manus,* "hand." The term "cultural resource management" came into use in the conservation field in the early 1970s and

Inadequately maintained historic buildings in Chikan (Guangdong), China. Detail. See p. 578.

increasingly was used in the United Kingdom and the United States through the 1980s to denote "research, planning and stewardship."[3] Thus for at least the past forty years in the conservation profession, "management" has implied an integrative, holistic, and generally positive approach to harmonizing disparate and uncoordinated policies, programs, and initiatives. In another sense, and more recently, as questions emerge about heritage conservation and its links to "neoliberalist" agendas for "economic and social transformation under the free market," the term "new public management" has arisen, connoting what one scholar calls "part of the market-based welfare policies that exacerbate social divisions in society."[4] As the anthropologist Lynn Meskell has observed, "Heritage places and practices also require managing, governing, translating, and capitalizing, such that new political economies have developed around heritage that entail a new generation of interdisciplinary scholarship."[5] For many scholars of this new generation, management is intended as a pejorative term, associated with neoliberal market forces. Hence the concept of management may take different and sometime opposite connotations, even if we confine this discussion to the English literature on the subject; the term's meaning becomes even more elusive if one uses it in other linguistic and cultural contexts.

One urban conservation professional who always sought clarity in his international, practical work and teaching was Herbert Stovel (reading 62), whose discussion of urban management in the reading below provides clarity about what constitutes a well-managed historic city amid the divergent interpretations of management suggested above. Stovel identifies twelve indicators of a well-managed city; for example, it authentically reflects its heritage values, ensures community participation in decision making, and draws on its heritage values as the key reference in the evaluation of development options.

How should a well-managed historic city become a reality? One way, urban conservation specialists have argued since the 1970s, is through an integrated approach, as pointed out by Jukka Jokilehto, a colleague of Herb Stovel in ICCROM's Integrated Territorial and Urban Conservation (ITUC) training program. Jokilehto explains, "*The European Charter of the Architectural Heritage,* adopted by the Committee of Ministers of the Council of Europe in September 1975, recognized that 'the groups of lesser buildings in our old towns and characteristic villages in their natural or manmade settings' were part of European architectural heritage. The charter [. . .] recommended 'integrated conservation'[, which] [. . .] should depend on legal, administrative, financial and technical support, and could only succeed with the co-operation of all citizens. The *Amsterdam Declaration* of the *European Architectural Heritage Year,* October 1975, gave further weight to the concept of 'integrated conservation' of urban and rural areas."[6] (For this declaration and other charters, see also the Appendix.)

Matthias Ripp and Dennis Rodwell, in their insightful analysis of the governance of urban heritage (reading 63), also recognize the importance of the Council of Europe's Charter of 1975 and explore why and how more integrative management approaches to urban conservation should be instituted. They assert that "the challenges facing cities in the twenty-first century do not stop at the borders of a specialism within one sector;

they impact across several parts of an inter-related system. The key to greater efficiency, more innovation and advancing the steps towards making cities more resilient, is to organize both the administration and the communication network in an integrated way."[7] Further, they point out that the participation of a broad spectrum of stakeholders is fundamental to this process.

Eduardo Rojas, in his discussion of urban governance as it relates to urban conservation planning (reading 64), likewise emphasizes the urgent need to genuinely encourage "local communities, organizations of the civil society, and private citizens [who are already] participating in the designation and protection of urban heritage areas as promoters and supporters." Rojas, speaking primarily from a Latin American context—Rodwell and Ripp mainly (but not exclusively) discuss a range of European examples—points out, however, that this "poses governance problems: difficulties harmonizing the often conflicting goals and expectations of the variety of stakeholders, and the slow involvement of private investors and individuals in the process." He proposes specific strategies to mitigate these challenges. One of those strategies, as suggested by Arkaraprasertkul and Williams (reading 53, part VI), is to "place the residents first" in the process.

An even more dramatic reevaluation of an existing urban conservation paradigm has occurred in the past decade, as reflected in the adoption in 2011—by UNESCO, ICOMOS, and many conservation practitioners worldwide—of the historic urban landscape (HUL) approach to urban conservation. Ron van Oers, who until his untimely death in 2015 was at the forefront of efforts to articulate and operationalize the HUL notion, characterized it as "a way forward [to] reconnect the city." Van Oers (reading 65) spoke and wrote passionately about and worked assiduously to implement "integration [of the] different disciplines for the analysis and planning of the urban conservation process, in order not to separate it from the planning and development of the contemporary city." He points out that, beginning in 1992 with the adoption of Agenda 21, the United Nations articulated the need "to position local communities center-stage in the decision-making process, a gradual shift in development thinking . . . away from a focus on *managing* cities to one of *governing* them [original emphasis]. . . . There is an urgent need to involve a broader constituency comprised of other groups than the usual suspects." In this regard, van Oers and many others employing the HUL approach are in agreement with the interpretation of "management" outlined by several of the authors in this selection.

However, the selections from Rojas and Ripp and Rodwell also demonstrate the pressing concern that urban conservation professionals have to ensure that the voice of all stakeholders is not only heard but also integrated in a more positive mode of urban governance. As noted in the 2013 UNESCO publication cited above, "Information from the field shows that, in practice, heritage management systems are often failing to involve local counterparts. Even when community involvement does take place, the level of participation in decision-making and the capacity of local stakeholders actually to engage and make contributions are often limited. However, there are many factors that can hinder a participatory approach and render ineffective attempts at local community involvement in heritage properties: the management system itself, a power imbalance between stakeholders or political and socio-economic factors in the wider environment (poverty and civil unrest, or even deep-seated cultural values), are some examples. Furthermore, a participatory approach that fails to engage all interest groups, particularly those who are often marginalized – women, youth and indigenous peoples are common examples – can actually do more damage than good. It can lead to flawed projects because heritage specialists may have failed to be properly informed about important aspects, or because of misunderstandings that then delay or block projects" (18). Van Oers spells out the assumptions, objectives, strategies, and implications of the HUL notion, which derives inspiration partially from an extension of the "cultural landscapes" approach to the urban conservation field. The HUL notion remains a highly significant but as yet not fully operationalized methodology extensively tested in the field. As this volume goes to press, several cities on different continents—following the leadership provided by Ron van Oers and his colleague and former World Heritage Centre director, Francesco Bandarin—are seeking to root this approach in specific urban contexts and monitor its hopefully positive implications.

In reading 66, an excerpt from a 2013 interview, Jukka Jokilehto shares some of his reflections about the HUL notion, as well as the management of change and continuity and the insertion of modern architecture in historic urban areas. He emphasizes the balance that needs to be struck between often-unheard voices from the community and "professionals who assist in clarifying the meanings and creating a basis for the legal and administrative tools needed for the control and management of such resources." Jokilehto underlines that "management must necessarily take into account the general social-economic and cultural aspects of the territory, and guide development without undermining the continuity of traditional qualities in the protected areas." Finally, with respect to accommodating new architectural development in historic cities, Jokilehto asserts, "It is not necessary to produce something that is completely out of place in relation to the traditional urban morphology. . . . It is a question of common sense." Unfortunately, however, what seems like "common sense" to several scholars is highly contested by the many who are involved in the profit-related amalgam of global urban development.

The book's final reading (67), from Shannon Mattern, urges caution about managing a city through "smart," digital, algorithm-based, or computer-driven approaches. She poses a crucial question, "what are the non-textual, un-recordable forms of cultural memory" that a computer might ignore? It is crucial, she says, to "think about urban epistemologies that embrace memory and history." The reduction of a city's history to algorithms, data points, or other derivatives of 'technology" (in the early twenty-first-century connotation of that word) is antithetical to the richly textured, human-based notions of memory, history, culture, and urban form that we have underscored throughout this book. The readings in this final part of the book ultimately underline the need to reconcile diverging interests, manage change and its impact, and meld the old with the new so that the benefits of what we have inherited from the urban past can not only survive into the future, but provide renewed inspirations for those who follow us.

Notes

1. Bob Kindred, Book review of *Managing Historic Cities* by UNESCO World Heritage Centre, *World Heritage Papers* 27, UNESCO, 2010, *Journal of Architectural Conservation* (July 2012): 100–101.
2. Gamini Wijesuriya, Jane Thompson, and Christopher Young (lead authors), *Managing Cultural World Heritage: World Heritage Resource Manual* (Paris: UNESCO, 2013), 15.
3. See the National Park Service's Cultural Resource Management Guideline (NPS-28; www.nps.gov/history/history/online_books/nps28/28contents.htm), which indicates that "cultural resource management involves *research*, to identify, evaluate, document, register, and establish other basic information about cultural resources; *planning*, to ensure that this information is well integrated into management processes for making decisions and setting priorities; and *stewardship*, under which planning decisions are carried out and resources are preserved, protected, and interpreted to the public.'
4. John Michael Roberts, "Neoliberalism and New Public Management," in his *New Media and Public Activism: Neoliberalism, the State and Radical Protest in the Public Sphere* (Policy Press, 2014). Also see Sophie Bessant, Zoe Robinson, and R. Mark Ormerod, "Neoliberalism, New Public Management and the Sustainable Development Agenda of Higher Education: History, Contradictions And Synergies," *Environmental Education Research* 21, no. 3 (2015): 417–32.
5. Lynn Meskell, ed., *Global Heritage: A Reader* (Hoboken, NJ: Wiley-Blackwell, 2015), 2.
6. Jukka Jokilehto, "ICCROM Integrated Territorial and Urban Conservation, ITUC, Programme – Phase I (1994–1998), Summary Report," unpublished, January 1999.
7. Dennis Rodwell and Matthias Ripp, "The Governance of Urban Heritage," *Historic Environment: Policy & Practice* 7, no. 1 (2016): 84.

Reading
62

Herbert Stovel

Approaches to Managing Urban Transformation for Historic Cities (2002)

Herbert Stovel was a titan in the conservation field. A Canadian who possessed unbridled curiosity and knowledge about global cultural heritage, Stovel worked tirelessly at ICCROM and ICOMOS, as well as being engaged in conservation training. His involvement with the Nara Document on Authenticity *(1994) and his publications regarding conservation increased his impact on the field. In this relatively obscure, sharply focused essay, he concisely articulates how best to manage the challenging practices of urban conservation in the context of inevitable transformations.*

Purpose

This paper is intended to look at the ways in which we define and examine management performance for historic cities. [. . .] It attempts to identify relevant indicators of management performance by reviewing considerations important in a number of complementary perspectives available for appreciating and understanding transformation in historic cities.

—~—

Overview of Results of Recent Conservation Efforts for Historic Cities

An overview of efforts to safeguard historic cities over the last thirty-five years does not provide great confidence in the overall effectiveness of the many measures introduced for protecting urban heritage. This period—the era of modern conservation we might say—which began with the creation of ICOMOS, ICCROM, and the UNESCO instruments focussed on cultural heritage (the UNESCO International Campaigns of the 1960s, and the 1972 World Heritage Convention) has seen a range of very serious

From Herbert Stovel, "Approaches to Managing Urban Transformation for Historic Cities," *Revista de Cultura,* 3rd ser., 4 (2002): 35, 37–44.

efforts to strengthen capacity for urban conservation. Several hundred international and regional meetings have resulted in resolutions, declarations, recommendations, charters and meeting reports which have identified principles intended to guide decision-making towards greater respect for the heritage values of historic cities. These meetings and the efforts of those responsible for management of historic cities have also resulted in the development of many innovative approaches to heritage management in historic cities: historic building inventory and classification systems, master plans and conservation plans intended to guide use and development in heritage sensitive directions, systems of grants and incentives tied to careful treatment of historic buildings.

While these measures have undoubtedly strengthened efforts to retain historic buildings and street patterns in many particular contexts, at the same time, we can recognize that they have proved inadequate in other contexts. In the end, we can realize that it is not the charters or the conservation tools *per se*, that ensure conservation, it is political will. [. . .] If we stand back to assess the overall effectiveness of our collective efforts, it is difficult not to recognize that in many regions, we continue to be at risk of slowly losing the battle for retention of the heritage values of our historic cities. [. . .]

The Situation in Asia

This seems particularly true in Asia. There are many examples of Asian historic cities overwhelmed by the forces of contemporary change and development, and this often in spite of considerable efforts to promote conservation. [. . .]

—~—

The Nara Seminar on the "Development and the Integrity of Historic Cities" of March, 1999 [. . .] identified a number of major issues which have an "adverse effect on the conservation and maintenance of the historic fabric" in conserving *"the special historic character of historic cities in Asia:*

- *degradation in the quality of life of the inhabitants resulting from excessive pressures due to rapid urbanisation*
- *depopulation of small and secondary cities weakening their social and economic viability*
- *changes in the way of life which have led to new requirements in housing and services*
- *focus on the conservation of single monuments*
- *over-emphasis on the catering for the demands of tourism*
- *neglect of the inter-relationships between the historic areas, the wider urban context and the rural hinterland."*

Alternative Frameworks for Reviewing Management Effectiveness

If then, an historic retrospective directed at the evolution of contemporary conservation practice does not seem to yield proven practices effective in urban management, then we will have to look elsewhere to find alternative means of understanding—and therefore guiding—urban transformation towards greater respect for heritage values.

Several alternative perspectives may be useful in carrying out this search:

- Many of the historic cities we persevere to save with our modern instruments and methods arrived as objects of preservation interest after several centuries — even millennia—of evolution during which those conservation instruments were absent. What can we understand of the forces guiding changes during those past centuries that we can build into present practice?
- Many contemporary historic cities are immensely satisfying for visitors in their ability to continually change and mutate without impairing their heritage values. What appear to be the key factors being respected in guiding change over time in such successes, at least as seen from the viewpoint of external visitors?
- Cities change as the result of hundreds and thousands of decisions made inside and outside of formal and informal decision-making frameworks. In essence, conservation success appears to have more to do with the ability of historic cities to manage these processes of "dynamic" change, than the effectiveness of the "static" protective instruments (lists, inventories, prohibitions, supports and incentives) normally employed within the conservation community. It is worth asking to what extent we can identify and describe the nature of the dynamic development processes which best contribute toward realisation of conservation objectives.
- Many contemporary historic cities, concerned about developing sensible and ethical approaches to city development, which offer quality of life to their citizens and optimize use of available resources, now commit themselves to management visions which can support retention of historic resources. Examples would be cities which may choose to adopt policies promoting "sustainability," "ecological soundness," "liveability," or "risk sensitivity," etc.

1. ***A well managed historic city will maintain and strengthen its craft traditions.***
   Assessment should look at the degree to which traditional craftsmanship and related support systems have been sustained and made available to strengthen maintenance of the existing and a base for contemporary expression.
2. ***A well managed historic city will ensure contemporary planning efforts which reflect traditional patterns and layouts.***

Assessment should look at the degree to which contemporary planning and design is based on efforts to understand and to meaningfully re-employ existing urban forms, building vestiges and patterns.

—᠁—

3. ***The attributes of a well managed historic city will authentically reflect its significant heritage values.***
AUTHENTICITY: Assessment here looks at the degree to which the attributes (design, material, setting, workmanship, function, traditions) of the historic city may be seen to reflect the significant heritage values of the historic city.
4. ***A well managed historic city will maintain and strengthen the integrity of its components, its systems and the relationship between them.***
INTEGRITY: Assessment here looks at the degree to which wholeness and intactness of the historic city and its operating systems may be seen to be present.
5. ***A well managed historic city will maintain and strengthen its sources of continuity.***
CONTINUITY: Assessment here will look at the degree to which continuity of form, layout, living traditions and patterns of use are present in the historic city.

—᠁—

6. ***A well managed historic city will ensure community participation in decision-making.***
Assessment involves looking at the edges of involvement of the community in defining heritage values and in determining forms of appropriate care.
7. ***A well managed historic city will support self-help strategies for its improvement.***
Assessment involves looking at the degree to which planning promotes use of self-help policies and strategies in achieving conservation goals.
8. ***A well managed historic city will ensure its defined heritage values serve as the key reference in evaluating development options.***
Assessment involves looking at the degree to which the values of the historic city serve as a core criterion in evaluating development options.

—᠁—

9. ***A well managed historic city will have mechanisms in place to strengthen decision-making at local levels.***
Assessment involves looking at the degree to which decision-making has been moved to the local level (and therefore the degree to which local heritage interest has been strengthened and local ownership assured).
10. ***A well managed historic city will promote heritage conservation as an instrument of social inclusion.***

Assessment involves looking at the degree to which conservation policy and programmes promote social and cultural respect, mutual respect and sustained co-existence.

11. ***A well managed historic city will optimize retention of programme and project profits within the local community.***
Assessment involves looking at the degree to which development profits are retained within individuals and institutions within the local community.
12. ***A well managed historic city will ensure high levels of risk preparedness in its institutions and municipal agencies.***
Assessment involves looking at the degree to which management regimes incorporate policies, strategies and programmes for improving risk preparedness.

Conclusion

The above dozen subject focuses are merely illustrative of possible subject areas for review for historic cities in assessing management effectiveness qualitatively, and indeed there could be many more. As well, the precise choice of subjects to be assessed will depend on the particular qualities of the historic city and the political, economic and social circumstances in which it is proposed to realize heritage objectives. Each community needs to debate its choice of the areas in which indicators are to be established, in the context of their particular circumstances, in building up effective management systems which will preserve their particular heritage values.

In the end, it is difficult to escape the conclusion that the modern instruments invented by the public sector to protect urban heritage values have not proved fully adequate in the face of the economic, social and political forces confronting historic cities today.

Bibliography

1. *Operational Guidelines for the Implementation of the World Heritage Convention,* March 1999, WHC.99/2.UNESCO.
2. *Report of The Nara Seminar on the "Development and the Integrity of Historic Cities".* 5–7 March, 1999. Information document prepared for the World Heritage Bureau, Paris, July 5–10, 1999. WHC-99/CONF.204/INF.5, UNESCO.
3. *Report of the Suzhou (China) Conference - "International Conference for the Mayors of Historic Cities in China and the European Union".* April 1998. Information document prepared for the World Heritage Committee, Kyoto, 30 November–5 December, 1998. WHC-98/CONF.203/INF.12, UNESCO.
4. Giles Macdonough, *"Fresh look at an historic face",* Financial Times, "City Break Berlin", Aug. 3, 2002.
5. *The Nara Document on Authenticity,* Nov. 1994. Adopted by ICOMOS (1999). Consulted in US/ICOMOS Scientific Journal, Volume 1, Number 1, 1999. "ICOMOS Charters and other international doctrinal documents".
6. *The Declaration of Amsterdam,* 1975. Congress on the European Architectural Heritage 21–25 October, 1975. Consulted in US/ I CO MOS Scientific Journal, Volume 1, Number 1, 1999. "ICOMOS Charters and other international doctrinal documents".

Reading

63

Matthias Ripp and Dennis Rodwell

The Governance of Urban Heritage (2016)

Matthias Ripp, whose background is in historical geography, is a senior heritage manager for the World Heritage city of Regensburg, Germany. Dennis Rodwell, author of Conservation and Sustainability in Historic Cities *(Blackwell, 2007), is an independent scholar and international consultant with extensive experience in urban conservation, regeneration, and planning, particularly but not exclusively in Europe. In this reading, Ripp and Rodwell argue that "governance at the municipal level is the key to integrated urban planning policy and practice." They also maintain that for truly integrated practice, planners and geographers need to work not only with each other but also with professionals from other disciplines. This article is complemented by an equally compelling article, "The Geography of Urban Heritage" (2015), also published in* The Historic Environment.

Introduction

In the context of Europe, the long-term survival of the spectrum of urban heritage is predicted, its contribution to wider societal agendas is increasingly acknowledged, and the four complementary values of community, heritage, resource and usefulness, harnessed to common purpose, provide indicators for a potent combination in the wider heritage interest.

Notwithstanding, urban heritage is arguably under greater threat today than hitherto, in major part, the result of a failure to comprehend its multiple connections and relationships. These include: a mind-set that is still working to early post–Second World War models that only predicated the survival of highly selected designated heritage; a lack of association with the positive aspects of migration and demographic change; an absence of assimilation with today's global agendas of sustainable develop-

From Matthias Ripp and Dennis Rodwell, "The Governance of Urban Heritage," *The Historic Environment: Policy & Practice* 7, no. 1 (2016): 81–82, 84, 86–87, 89, 93, 97–98, 100, 103–8. Reprinted by permission of the publisher Taylor & Francis Ltd, http://www.tandfonline.com.

ment and climate change; and a failure to embrace the correspondence between conservation and new construction as two complementary forms of development.

In order to realise its full potential, urban heritage requires to move beyond its traditional, ring-fenced comfort zone and position itself centrally within urban planning policy: professionally, politically and in the public mind. Reciprocally, geography, the core discipline of urban planning, has yet to fully embrace heritage as a significant component of the urban environment and condition. The mainstreaming of urban heritage requires a two-way comprehension of common purpose allied to a recognition that the complexity of urban heritage calls for systems rather than linear approach to challenges and opportunities.

—~—

Integrated Urban Development and Governance

The challenges facing cities in the twenty-first century do not stop at the borders of a specialism within one sector; rather, they impact across several parts of an interrelated system. The key to greater efficiency, more innovation and advancing the steps towards making cities more resilient, is to organise both the administration and the communication network in an integrated way.[1]

—~—

Within city administrations, a series of preconditions can be implemented to make more effective and integrated use of 'conventional planning tools'.[2] The starting point is experienced personnel with a broad range of background skills. With cross-cutting topics becoming more important, there is not only the need for more thematic experts but also for generalists who have a better understanding of how different subjects, factors, professions and interests are interconnected. [. . .]

To create such an atmosphere is not easy and requires a strong commitment at all hierarchical levels. The benefit is the flow of creative and innovative ideas, and the exploration and establishing of unconventional solutions. Tools that can be useful in this context include integrated planning methodologies, stakeholder collaboration management, and specific moderation techniques focused on identifying and harnessing common objectives rather than consolidating opposing starting points.[3] The appropriate mind-set of the involved persons will help to ensure successful implementation.[4] Participation is a key word in this process, and a broad spectrum of stakeholders needs to be involved.[5] Adopting a bottom-up approach in contrast to classic top–down planning procedures can transmit the case for heritage across the whole urban population in ways that heritage-focused professionals find difficult: often for the simplest of reasons, including adherence to terminology with which they, but not their audiences, are most familiar.

—~—

[. . .] Management plans can be a powerful tool, but they are only as strong as the management system within which they operate and is responsible for the implementation, continuous evaluation, and updating of the plan.[6]

Lists of tools are easily published without fully understanding the critical importance of the personnel on the ground who will implement them. Much attention has been given to tools, especially Management Plans. [. . .] What it lacked, however, was guidance on how to start the process with a good scoping, how to design the process of participation, definition of the vital role of heritage managers and how implementation and monitoring can be guaranteed.[7] If heritage is understood as a key component of a complex system, the human factor deserves far more attention.
[. . .]

Integrated Heritage Management: Regensburg and the HerO Project

The City of Regensburg prepared a first version of its World Heritage management plan for the nomination to UNESCO in 2004.[8] After inscription as a World Heritage Site in 2006, and the establishment of a special unit in charge of World Heritage issues in 2007, the city council decided as early as 2008 to review its management plan using an integrated and participatory approach.

The whole process was integrated into the European Commission URBACT II Project, Heritage as Opportunity (HerO), launched in 2009.[9] The objective of the HerO Project was to develop a methodology for designing integrated management plans including local stakeholders and citizens. Nine differently sized European cities worked together to test and adapt this methodology.[10] Its guiding principle, inspired by the 2005 UNESCO Vienna Memorandum,[11] was that historic urban landscapes need to be considered as living organisms which can only survive if all their functions are addressed equally.[12] Emphasis was placed on managing conflicting usage interests and capitalising on the potential of cultural heritage assets for economic, social and cultural activities.[13]

[. . .] The project group defined eight fields of action: tangible cultural heritage, culture and tourism, economic development, housing, mobility, urban planning and development, environment and leisure, and awareness-raising and research.[14]

Because of strong interest in this process, the working group started with 10 members but expanded to 35. For this reason, a special moderator was chosen among the members for each of the eight fields of action. The role of these moderators was to collate the comments for each field, to assist with the editing work at the end of the process, to moderate between conflicting interests within the over-arching working group and to moderate the fields of action within an event for wider citizens' participation. [. . .]
[. . .]

Lessons from the HerO Project

The main lessons learnt from HerO were:

- Through the integrated approach, a broad basis of common objectives to safeguard and sustainably develop urban heritage sites was defined, and the identification and motivation for urban heritage was extended.
- Structuring specific actions that are ready for implementation and discussed with a broad variety of stakeholders makes the result of the process very tangible.
- Through the early integration of the responsible authorities for European, national and regional programmes, the chances of obtaining funding for the defined actions are enhanced.
- The relationship between local governments and the managing authorities in charge of European, national and regional funding was improved.

The HerO project proved a major step towards an improved urban governance focused on urban heritage. The methodology helped to bring all stakeholders together to discuss potential and existing conflicts openly, understand the complex needs of different sections of the population and interest groups and form a common vision and understanding of the nine cities' heritage. The logical next step is to build on this experience and enhance the individual cities' management plans, including the many urban layers that were lacking—such as overarching cultural mapping—to coordinate more closely with the broader issues of urban geography and to adapt organisational structures for better urban resilience.

The experiences of projects such as HerO demonstrate the need for cities to reorganise how they deal with the major cross-cutting challenges. The only effective way to find resilient solutions is through integrated planning approaches, to define sustainable objectives, and establish new ways of organising administrations with a stronger focus on integrating the diverse cross-cutting topics. The success of the HerO methodology shows that the potential benefits can be substantial.[15]

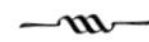

[. . .] The term *historic urban landscape* does not communicate well, the methodologies anticipated in the approach are largely traditional to the heritage sector, and the quintessential need for integration with urban planning and the broad discipline of geography is not expressed. Indeed, by failing to innovate decisively, to break out of the 'conservation container' and advance a new agenda for the twenty-first century, the UNESCO initiative communicates as a lost opportunity for advancing the cause of integrated urban heritage management. For as long as the heritage community continues to regard its remit as highly selective, the urban geographer will assume that urban heritage's relevance is limited: to archaeological (in the broad sense) and aesthetic interest, and as a marketing tool for high-end regeneration and tourism.

The promotion of a comprehensive understanding of urban heritage values, coupled with cross-sectoral governance issues at the operational, municipal level, are essential starting points. Proactive engagement with civil society is crucial.

This article has presented a selection of initiatives from the heritage perspective, mostly top-end, and identified a number of areas where clarity is lacking.

These include:

- Coordinating the management of sites that have been designated as physical 'properties' in tandem with their essential role as evolving human spaces in contemporary society; including the need for comprehensive cultural mapping.
- The role and qualifications of coordinators, greatly expanded beyond the traditional role of 'conservators'. [. . .]

The process of 'top–down—bottom–up' moderation of heritage values in a community involves:

- Asking different sectors and age groups in any given community what is important about their place to them—children, youths, parents, the retired—and listen.
- Not pre-judging the outcome by using 'loaded' words like heritage and values.
- Anticipating that most of the responses will focus on friends, family, community and the familiar. These are the keys to establishing common ground.
- Comprehending that *heritage* and *culture*, in the widest sense (but not defined as such) are an integral part of the everyday social exchanges within a community and valued instinctively as such.
- Not representing top–down and essentially selective understandings until after citizens have represented the values that are vital to them.
- Building from the bottom up in order to establish the common ground.
- Showing respect for the values articulated by the community as an indispensable foundation for soliciting their respect for yours.

Two target groups, amongst the least considered at present, are especially important: First, school children, a sector of the population that has multi-generational extended family relationships and influence, is open-minded, highly creative *and* encapsulates the future.

[. . .]

Second, a sector of the population that is often regarded as one of the most challenging to access: youths with poor educational qualifications in post-industrial urban communities where unemployment levels are high and often three or four generational.

Conclusion

[. . .] For sound governance, integrated approaches within over-arching urban and regional planning are more relevant and successful than approaches that focus on selected 'heritage assets'—be they individual buildings, groupings or districts—that do not necessarily have the same meaning for today's communities as they do for academics.

Whereas certain cities possess a heritage value that has a higher grade of importance in the eyes of heritage professionals, all historic cities—as established multi-generational inhabited places—have a broad set of values in the eyes of their citizens; this range of values is not currently integrated into urban planning policy and practice, to the result that neither urban heritage nor urban planning are in a position to realise their potential in the face of twenty-first century global agendas.

For this, urban governance needs to progress from compartmentalised, reductionist, linear approaches to sectoral management, to a systems approach embracing interdisciplinary, societal coordination and facilitation.

Notes

1. Ripp, "Krisen: Chancen für die Altstadt?" (*Crisis: an Opportunity for Historical Cities?*).
2. The O'Donnell and Turner list includes: planning for conservation of natural and cultural resources, tree protection ordinance and long-term lease of heritage properties.
3. Rodwell, "Reconciling Conservation and Development."
4. Ripp, *HerO—Heritage as Opportunity*.
5. This can be done through a variety of methods, including future labs (a methodology to integrate ideas and needs of citizens in urban planning), round tables in a certain district, direct and informal feedback. Choosing the right format and the right persons to moderate and answer questions from the citizens is crucial for success. See: Ripp, "Der Regensburger Welterbe-Managementplan."
6. There is also an unfortunate tendency, in compliance with UNESCO Operational Guidelines, to regard the preparation of a Management Plan as an end in itself—to satisfy a 'tick a box' mentality. There needs to be a far more rigorous monitoring of Management Plans after a World Heritage Site has been inscribed. The saga of the Liverpool—Maritime Mercantile City is a case in point: see Gaillard and Rodwell, "A Failure of Process?"
7. Ringbeck, *Management Plans for World Heritage*.
8. Stadt Regensburg, *Old Town of Regensburg*.
9. URBACT: promoting sustainable urban development.
10. The nine cities were: the capital cities Valletta (Malta) and Vilnius (Lithuania); the port cities Liverpool (United Kingdom) and Naples (Italy); and the provincial cities of Lublin (Poland), Poitiers (France), Regensburg (Germany) and Sighișoara (Romania).
11. UNESCO, *Vienna Memorandum*.
12. Ripp and Bühler, "'HerO' Fast Track Network."
13. Bühler and Ripp, "Das Urbact II thematische Netzwerk HerO."
14. Stadt Regensburg, *Management Plan*, 50.
15. Smith et al., *Road to Success*.

References

Bühler, B., and M. Ripp. "Das Urbact II thematische Netzwerk HerO—Heritage as Opportunity [The Urbact II Network HerO—Heritage as Opportunity]." *ISG-Magazin* 4 (2009): 4–6.

Gaillard, B., and D. Rodwell. "A Failure of Process? Comprehending the Issues Fostering Heritage Conflict in Dresden Elbe Valley and Liverpool—Maritime Mercantile City World Heritage Sites." *The Historic Environment: Policy and Practice* 6 (2015): 16–40. doi:10.1179/1756750515Z.00000000066.

O'Donnell, P. M., and M. Turner. *The Historic Urban Landscape Recommendation: A New UNESCO Tool for a Sustainable Future*. Cape Town: IFLA, 2012. http://www.heritagelandscapes.com/SiteImages/IFLA-Cape%20Town-HUL%20ODonnell-Turner%2028July2012(1).pdf.

Ringbeck, B. *Management Plans for World Heritage Sites—A Practical Guide*. Bonn: German Commission for UNESCO, 2008.

Ripp, M. "Der Regensburger Welterbe-Managementplan. Gestaltung einer Welterbe-Strategiegemeinsam mit den Bürgern [The Management Plan for Regensburg. Developing a Joint World Heritage Strategy Together with the Citizens]." In *Arbeitskreis Regensburger Herbstsymposion: "Zum Teufel mit den Baudenkmälern"—200 Jahre Denkmalschutz in Regensburg* [Regensburg Autumn Symposium Working Group: "To Hell with Listed Buildings"—200 years of Preservation in Regensburg], edited by E. Trapp, P. Morsbach, A. Hubel, J. Buck, W. Schöller, E. König, L.-M. Dallmeier, M. Ripp, and I. Scheurmann, 83–86. Regensburg: Dr. Morsbach Verlag, 2011.

———, ed. *HerO—Heritage as Opportunity. The Road to Success: Integrated Management of Historic Towns*. Regensburg: Stadt Regensburg, 2011.

———. "Krisen: Chancen für die Altstadt? Zur Rolle des gebauten Kulturerbes als urbaner Resilienzfaktor [Crisis: an Opportunity for Historical Cities? Built Cultural Heritage as a Factor of Urban Resilience]." In *Forum Stadt. Vierteljahreszeitschrift für Stadtgeschichte, Stadtsoziologie, Denkmalpflege und Stadtentwicklung* [City Forum: Quarterly Journal for Urban History, Urban Sociology, Preservation and Urban Development], edited by R. Kaltenbrunner and M. Ripp, no. 2 (2013): 149–161.

Ripp, M., and B. Bühler. "The 'HerO' Fast Track Network: Cultural Heritage as Opportunity." In *Regions for Economic Change—Networking for Results*, edited by European Commission, Directorate-General for Regional Policy, 16–17. Brussels: European Commission, 2009.

Rodwell, D. "Reconciling Conservation and Development." *Context* 122 (2011): 31.

Smith, B., N. Scheffler, and M. Ripp, eds. *The Road to Success—A New Approach to the Management of Historic Towns. Policy Recommendations* (Urbact II Project HerO—Heritage as Opportunity). Regensburg: Stadt Regensburg, 2011.

Stadt Regensburg. *Old Town of Regensburg with Stadtamhof: Nomination for Inscription on the UNESCO World Heritage List; Management Plan*. Unpublished, 2004.

———. *Management Plan UNESCO World Heritage Site "Old Town of Regensburg with Stadtamhof."* Regensburg: Stadt Regensburg, 2012.

UNESCO. *Vienna Memorandum*. Vienna: UNESCO, 2005. http://whc.unesco.org/uploads/activities/documents/activity-47-2.pdf.

URBACT: A European Exchange and Learning Programme Promoting Sustainable Urban Development, 2009. http://urbact.eu/; also, within URBACT, the HerO Project: http://urbact.eu/hero.

Reading

64

Eduardo Rojas

The Conservation of Urban Heritage: A Sustainable Development Opportunity for Cities (2017)

Eduardo Rojas, a Chilean architect who also trained as a planner in Edinburgh, received an MBA from Johns Hopkins University and was awarded a Doctor of Urbanism at the Universidade Lusófona in Lisbon, Portugal. Currently he is an independent consultant on urban development and heritage conservation and teaches at the University of Pennsylvania. Previously, he was a principal specialist in urban development and housing at the Inter American Development Bank (IDB), where he worked throughout Latin America on implementing urban rehabilitation projects and managing municipal loans and technical cooperation projects. In this paper, commissioned for this book, Rojas situates urban conservation practice in the context of sustainable development, as also outlined in UNESCO's Habitat III conference (2016).

Sustainable development needs sustainable cities; not only because the majority of the population lives in cities but also because urban areas produce the majority of the goods and services that ensure good living conditions for the population (McKinsey 2011).[1] Thus, it is not surprising that the Sustainable Development Goals (SDGs) recently approved by the United Nations commit member states to "make cities inclusive, safe, resilient and sustainable" (United Nations, 2015), objectives reiterated in the recommendations that emerged from HABITAT III (UN HABITAT 2016). The current state of knowledge indicates that attaining this goal requires enhancing access to the human development opportunities offered by cities to all citizens (inclusive cities), guaranteeing that all city dwellers can live free of threats of violence (safe cities) and natural disasters (resilient cities), and ensuring that satisfying current needs does not endanger the right of future generations to satisfy their own (sustainable cities) (Rojas 2016c). In addition to investing in economic and social development and new urban infrastructures and facilities it is necessary to safeguard and make good use of the

Eduardo Rojas, "The Conservation of Urban Heritage: A Sustainable Development Opportunity for Cities," unpublished paper written for this volume (2017).

cities' inheritance: the intangible and tangible assets that are the "common wealth" of every city (O'Donnell 2016) and the "brace" linking the economic, social and environmental dimensions of development (Turner 2016).

Recounting the social and economic consequences of losing urban heritage underscores the importance of its conservation. The loss of immaterial heritage can disrupt community life. The breaking of individual values, such as righteousness, industry, or the higher incidence of crime due to the loss of social capital in the community, reduces the city's capacity to provide good living conditions for its population. A city with a fractured community composed of an archipelago of individuals pulling in their own direction does not function and is not capable of creating, producing, and distributing the goods and services that it needs to sustain its development. The depletion of the material urban heritage also has significant negative impacts on the social and economic development of cities. The loss of monuments deprives communities of the valued symbols of a shared history; the loss of residential, office or commercial properties in urban heritage areas deny a community the enjoyment of their aesthetic or historic values and to their owners their use values forcing the society to build space anew with the consequent consumption of resources (Rojas 2016c).

The complex role of heritage in cities is recognized by UNESCO's Recommendation on the Historic Urban Landscape (HUL) (UNESCO, 2011) that acknowledges the dynamic nature of cities and the complexity of their urban heritage that is embodied in the historic layering of elements of the urban fabric, values, cultures, traditions and experiences. The meaning of cultural heritage has expanded from single monuments identified as objects of art to whole cultural landscapes. This approach has significant implications for the governance of the urban development process that must care for the city's inheritance.

The Governance Challenge

Bell's definition of governance as "the use of institutions and structures of authority to allocate resources and coordinate or control activities in society, or in any other relevant environment, including the economy" (2002:1) calls attention to two issues that are particularly complex in managing the conservation of the urban heritage. The first is the "legitimacy" of the structures of authority that regulate interventions regarding the urban heritage assets. To be acceptable to affected communities, the adoption of conservation regulations requires the involvement of different local stakeholders who are not only the main users and owners of the urban heritage but also are the most likely to pay many of the costs related to its conservation. The second issue relates to the capacity of the institutions in charge of conducting the conservation effort to deal with local demands for change and development, and to manage any conflicts they create as a result of the conservation of the urban heritage. Experience shows that the closer these institutions are to the local communities the more able they are to respond to local needs, but also the more vulnerable they become to short-term pressures by land owners and developers. Attaining the right balance between responding to local needs and safeguarding the local, national, or universal values of the urban heritage lies at the core of the governance challenge.

Many communities today are increasingly aware of the wide range of sociocultural and economic values of the urban heritage. However, the canonical processes of identifying and valuing the urban heritage—central government led and elite based—only rarely incorporate the views and preferences of the communities even though they are directly affected by these decisions. Nominations of urban heritage areas to the national or international heritage lists usually represent the views and interests of the cultural elite or government officials. The full involvement of the community in identifying the heritage to be protected and how much change they are ready to accept in the future is central to their commitment to conservation and their willingness to bear the associated costs. Not surprisingly, community engagement is the first of the 4 tool groups considered in the HUL in addition to: knowledge and planning, regulatory systems, and finance (UNESCO 2011). The "values approach to urban heritage assessment" (Throsby 2012) provides a solid conceptual foundation to address these issues.

The Multiple Dimensions of Urban Heritage

Individuals and communities value relations, events, or objects for the benefits that they provide. Focusing on these benefits, Throsby (2012) describes the heritage as a capital capable of producing a stream of benefits either sociocultural or economic, using the term "heritage asset" to refer to the inheritance of cities or communities. The intangible heritage as a societal asset brings many benefits. For instance, communal celebrations (festive, religious, or commemorative) provide individuals with opportunities to interact with other members of the community, building relationships that enhance the social capital of the group. The places where these events take place—squares, community centers or temples—are valued as the physical platforms for accessing the benefits of this intangible heritage, acquiring what Throsby (2012) calls social, spiritual, or symbolic sociocultural values. Even the corner store in a neighborhood may acquire sociocultural meanings beyond its economic use-value as a source of supplies when it is the frequent gathering place for residents in a neighborhood and a source of informal services to them, a process well described by Jacobs (1961) in her analysis of New York's Greenwich Village.

The material heritage of cities also has economic use values providing built space to accommodate residential, commercial and productive activities. The economic flows (rents) generated by the use values of the urban heritage benefit owners and the services provided by the buildings' benefit users. Public buildings have similar economic use values for the community. The adaptive rehabilitation of these assets to satisfy current needs is not only proving to be a viable conservation strategy but also is an approach that raises complex issues of governance, particularly with respect to the management of the ensuing trade-offs between conservation and adaptation. The allocation of public resources to finance conservation expenditures also poses complex governance issues. Urban heritage areas contain pieces of the urban heritage valued by the rest of the city or the nation. They are usually the concern of the cultural elite that seeks to prevent the loss of historic, aesthetic, scientific or spiritual values that they embody. In most countries the government joins in to prevent their disappearance (what is called their existence value) so their sociocultural values are either transferred to future generations (bequest value) or at least that they will be available for future generations to enjoy even if today's generation do not know what to do with them (option value) (Throsby 2012). Who should pay for the conservation and stewardship of this heritage is only one of the many challenging questions.

Governance for the Sustainable Conservation of the Urban Heritage

Simply finding a place for urban heritage in the development agenda is not sufficient. There is also the need to ensure that the material and intangible assets provided by urban heritage are well managed—that is, that they are put to work for their developmental purposes. The good management of these assets should ensure that the heritage of cities contributes to enhance the quality of life of the population. Material heritage provides physical space to support new and expanded economic activities, good quality housing and urban amenities; the intangible heritage enhances the capacity of community members to work and cooperate in the production and distribution of cultural and material goods and services. The characteristics of the material urban heritage pose significant challenges to the achievement of this goal. Although some buildings are privately owned and access to some of the benefits generated by the urban heritage are transacted in markets and have a price, the most important attributes of this cultural heritage—those that generate the bulk of the sociocultural values—are available to all members of the urban society and to a great extent are held in common. Similarly, the conservation and enhancement of the immaterial heritage requires interventions in education, law enforcement, and community building that fall in the public realm. The management of the commons has always been problematic for societies. Urban heritage is no exception, requiring a complex set of regulations and market-based interventions.

The conservation of the characteristics that make urban heritage culturally valuable requires that special regulations be imposed on its use, limitations that are always regarded by private owners as barriers to development. Commonly, the rules and regulations are justified only in relation to the conservation of a limited set of sociocultural values (historic, aesthetic, symbolic, spiritual) and the conservation of the urban heritage sites is attempted almost invariably by calling for the investment of public resources. This approach leads to a situation in which the urban heritage is regarded as a planning and fiscal liability for development and it is opposed or—in the better circumstances—regarded with indifference by the champions of economic development.

In most developing countries, local governments lack the human, institutional, and financial resources necessary to preserve their community's monuments. They are rarely capable of assisting private owners to preserve the attributes of their properties that confer them their heritage value, and they are seldom able to either regulate the use of or maintain the public spaces used daily in the heritage areas of their cities. The result is a laxity in imposing regulations and an absence of direct action, which ultimately leads to either the deterioration or the abandonment of the material heritage.

When neither the market nor the government alone can properly manage a commons such as urban heritage, it is necessary to find alternative solutions. A development-focused approach to conservation needs to expand the range of stakeholders involved in the decisions (thus enhancing legitimacy), as well as reaching out more proactively to local stakeholders who might invest and benefit from the conservation effort (thus increasing the volume of resources involved in the conservation effort) (Rojas 2016b). In addition to the traditional stakeholders—the cultural elite and the central government—it is necessary to attract private sector actors by allowing and encouraging the adaptive rehabilitation of heritage properties for contemporary uses. This approach turns the heritage into an asset for the city's social and economic development (a material capital capable of producing a sustained flow of sociocultural and economic benefits). However, to accomplish this goal the governance of urban heritage conservation—that is the structures of authority, institutions, and financial arrangements—require major adjustments.

The institutions and most of the structures of authority needed are directly linked to the management of the community's local affairs. This is in direct contrast to current practice where urban heritage conservation is mostly in the hands of national or regional agencies while local actors are confined to purely passive roles, although they bear the largest burden in the process (development limitations and expenditure of public resources) and should have a large voice in these decisions. It follows that urban heritage conservation needs to be fully integrated with the governance of the urban development process of each city—a responsibility of the local government—with national and regional cultural entities playing a subsidiary role by taking care of the monuments of national and regional importance, and providing the legal and operational support and supervision for local decisions (Rojas 2016c). In terms of the conceptual framework proposed by Throsby (2012) the reforms advocated above involves putting into play—in addition to the central government resources to conserve the existence, option, or bequest values—the economic direct use values of the urban heritage capable of bringing in resources from a wide variety of stakeholders that are not usually active in the traditional approach: consumers, households, landowners, developers, entrepreneurs, and merchants. They will do so if the heritage area is an attractive place for living and conducting business. Attaining this condition is in part a government task, as it requires effective infrastructure and public spaces, good accessibility and citizen safety, and a flexible and efficient urban management structure for regulating the adaptive rehabilitation and the operation of the new business in urban heritage areas and mitigating the worst effects of gentrification. This implies the need to engage the contributions of different stakeholders and establishing institutions capable of coordinating the activities of different government entities and a range of public and private actors, including private sector stakeholders. Strong forms of public-public coordination exist in cases either where public urban development corporations are devoted to the task or when the different public actors agree to contracts that implement the conservation plans. Mixed-capital corporations entering in partnerships with property owners and investors have managed to coordinate public and private interventions in urban heritage areas. A well-defined and broadly accepted conservation plan is a powerful mechanism to promote private-private coordination.

Lessons from Latin American Experiences

A study of the governance structures used in the heritage conservation programs of Oaxaca (Mexico), Quito (Ecuador), Salvador (Brazil), and Valparaíso (Chile) found cause for optimism despite the shortcomings and challenges identified in each (Rojas 2014). Among the various and fragmented efforts where public and private actors did not connect, the study revealed the gains made by the conservation effort of the historic center of Oaxaca, whose progress was the result of the early participation of concerned citizens. They organized and financed foundations to promote and invest in the conservation of the historic center and motivated the different levels of government to contribute to this effort. The Municipality of Quito also sought the involvement of a wide variety of social actors in the conservation of its historic center and tried to organize their efforts by establishing a strong coordination mechanism under the form of a mixed-capital corporation to work in conjunction with both private owners and investors. These are but two examples of the types of fruitful cooperation that took place among various stakeholders that endeavored to protect the urban heritage and leverage it into a significant contributor to the wealth of the city. In each of these two examples municipal governments created institutions, regulations, and procedures that established a fruitful cooperation process among a wide variety of stakeholders and also channeled their contributions to the sustainable conservation and development of their heritage. As a result the cities were able to incorporate additional assets into their social and economic development process, resulting in many positive impacts.

The Rojas (2014) study found that in their early stages the conservation efforts in Salvador and Valparaíso corresponded quite closely to the traditional pattern of a process driven mostly by the historic and aesthetic sociocultural values of the heritage with a reduced set of stakeholders involved. Fundamentally, it was the regional government (Salvador) and the national government (Valparaíso) that made most crucial decisions and supplied the financing. This resulted in a conservation process highly dependent on the resources and endeavors of higher tiers of government, with the local communities perceiving the conservation of the heritage as an alien objective that had little connection to their needs and objectives.

Urban Policy Implications

The successful governance of the urban heritage conservation process based on the adaptive rehabilitation of urban heritage sites requires weighing and effectively reaching agreements on the trade-offs among conservation, adaptation, and development.

The simplest legal structures for conservation based on regulations lead to weak and unsustainable conservation. At the other end of the spectrum are the legal and administrative arrangements that allow the government to lead the conservation process involving a wide variety of stakeholders bringing their financial and management capabilities into the effort. The evidence collected by Rojas (2014) suggests that the latter approach is more sustainable. The effectiveness of the financial resources in achieving the expected results depends heavily on the efficient operation of the institutional mechanisms that allow all actors to contribute according to their best interest and relative advantages, and to do so according to their individual capacity to bear the risks and capture the socio-cultural or economic returns of the conservation process. These are local challenges that must be solved locally. Thus they must be incorporated fully in the city's development plans with the regional and national governments playing a subsidiary role assisting city governments in achieving their conservation objectives while providing resources to conserve urban heritage sites of regional or national importance.

Notes

1. The topics discussed in this document were presented at a talk delivered by the author as James Marston Fitch Historic Preservationist in Residence to the American Academy in Rome on September 30, 2015. The ideas presented have been discussed in other publications by the authors that are referred to in the text.

References

Bell, S., ed. 2002. *Economic Governance and Institutional Dynamics.* Melbourne: Oxford University Press.

Jacobs, J. 1961. *The Death and Life of Great American Cities.* New York: Vintage Books.

McKinsey Global Institute. 2011. "Urban World: Mapping the Economic Power of Cities." www.mckinsey.com/insights/urbanization/urban_world.

O'Donnell, P. 2016. "Enabling Access to Public Spaces to Advance Economic, Environmental and Social Benefits." In *UNESCO Culture: Urban Future. Global Report/or Sustainable Urban Development*, 185–91. Paris: UNESCO.

Rojas, E. 2014. "Governance Matters for the Conservation of the Urban Heritage: The Case of Four World Heritage Sites in Latin America." Thesis, Universidade Lusófona de Humanidades e Tecnologias. http://recil.grupolusofona.pt/handle/10437/6112?show=full.

———. 2016a. "Governance." In *Tabula Rasa: Forms of Urban Preservation,* ed. B. Roberts, 38–44. Zurich: Lars Müller.

———. 2016b. "The Sustainable Conservation of Urban Heritage: A Concern of All Social Actors." In *Urban Heritage, Development and Sustainability: International Frameworks, National and Local Governance,* ed. S. Labadi and W. Logan, 236–55. Oxford: Routledge.

———. 2016c. "Urban Heritage for Sustainable Development." In *UNESCO Culture: Urban Future. Global Report for Sustainable Urban Development,* 193–99. Paris: UNESCO.

Throsby, D. 2012. "Heritage Economics: A Conceptual Approach" In *The Economics of Uniqueness: Investing in Historic Cores and Cultural Heritage Assets for Sustainable Development,* ed. G. Licciardi and R. Amirtahmasebi, 45–73. Washington, DC: World Bank.

Turner, M. 2016. “Heritage Cities: Culture-based Solutions to Environmental Concerns.” In *UNESCO Culture: Urban Future. Global Report for Sustainable Urban Development*, 177–83. Paris: UNESCO.

United Nations. 2015. “Sustainable Development Goals.” New York. www.un.org/sustainabledevelopment/sustainable-development-goals/.

UNESCO. 2011. *Recommendation on the Historic Urban Landscape*. Paris: UNESCO. http://whc.unesco.org/en/activities/638.

UN HABITAT 2016. Habitat III Conference, Ecuador, Quito, 17–20 October 2016. www.habitat3.org/node/532167.

Reading

65

Ron van Oers

The Way Forward: An Agenda for Reconnecting the City (2015)

Ron van Oers was a highly influential Dutch urban conservation specialist, whose untimely death in 2015 shocked many in the conservation field. Trained as a planner at TU-Delft, he worked under the supervision of Fritz van Voorden to complete his PhD (2000), after which he worked most notably and in varying capacities at UNESCO's World Heritage Centre in Paris, until 2012, when he became vice director of the World Heritage Institute for Training and Research – Asia Pacific (WHITRAP) in Shanghai. In addition to his passionate lecturing about heritage conservation and his broad international perspective, van Oers contributed significantly to the field of urban conservation by collaborating with Francesco Bandarin in articulating the rationales for and operationalizing of the Historic Urban Landscape (HUL) approach, which is the central focus of this reading, from one of two books on which Bandarin and van Oers collaborated.

Managing the City as a Living Heritage

The Historic Urban Landscape is an updated heritage management approach based on the recognition and identification of a layering and interconnection of values—natural and cultural, tangible and intangible, international as well as local—that are present in any city. It is based also on the need to integrate the different disciplines for the analysis and planning of the urban conservation process, in order not to separate it from the planning and development of the contemporary city. In other words, the Historic Urban Landscape approach seeks to reconnect heritage precincts with the modern city; the city with its wider setting and hinterland; urban conservation with the process of city planning and regional development; new architecture with the historic context; and the different cultural traditions, including migrant and traditionally resident, with

From Ron van Oers, "The Way Forward: An Agenda for Reconnecting the City," in *Reconnecting the City: The Historic Urban Approach and the Future of Urban Heritage*, edited by Francesco Bandarin and Ron van Oers (Oxford: Wiley Blackwell, 2015), 317–23, 325–28, 330–32. Reproduced courtesy of Wiley.

each other and with the socio-economic trends that are evolving in the contemporary city. All this is part of the day-to-day running of the city in order to respond timely and adequately to the dynamics of the twenty-first century urban condition, which is always in a state of flux and seemingly accelerating. With many competing demands for attention and investment of efforts and resources it can be hard to focus and determine priorities.

The Historic Urban Landscape approach focuses on the identity and values embedded in any city. In socio-cultural terms these are a key determinant of quality of life, while in economic terms they can be a strong component of competitiveness in the global marketplace.[1] Both quality of life and competitiveness are required to attract young talent and entrepreneurial citizens, as well as inward investment and businesses. In a process of mutual dependency, these actors will create a virtuous cycle characterised by a self-strengthening process that cares for the environment, ensures creativity and innovation, drives development, and further reinforces the identity of the city.

—⁓—

Identity and Sense of Place

[. . .]

The complex layering of natural, cultural, built, intangible and local heritage, superimposed on and interacting with each other, and connecting the physical with the socio-economic and cultural environment, is what can be labelled as the historic urban landscape of a city—it is the critical underpinning of its sense of place, or *genius loci*. A thorough identification, inventory and assessment of natural, cultural and community resources of the city, therefore, through a process of cultural mapping, stakeholder consultations and participatory planning, among others, should provide the basis for a better understanding of the city's character and identity, and its broader sense of place. This should inform management of the city, including policymaking and enforcement towards the conservation of key resources (among which its urban heritage), as well as towards the planning and design of new extensions and infill. [. . .]

—⁓—

Local Heritage and Corporate Image

[. . .]

[U]rban heritage has come to be bound more to place than to people. The hypermobility of goods, ideas and people that characterises globalisation in the twenty first century puts a premium on fixed assets to place, and urban heritage is paramount among these. [. . .]

—⁓—

The City as Repository of Urban Experiences

Next to heritage becoming place rather than population bound, hyper-mobility introduces another challenge, that is of a new architecture in the historic context. Our fast and consumerist society, where the average shelf-life of products has diminished significantly in tune with the innovations in Information and Communication Technologies (ICTs), has stopped building cities. [. . .]

—~—

If architectural education and training does not include instruction and reflection on the sociocultural context or historical achievements of previous generations of builders, including of vernacular dwellings,[2] how then can we expect any sensitivity, even from the most gifted among the architects, towards the values and potential of urban heritage? It came all the more as a surprise (or, did it?), that the 2012 Pritzker Prize, the highest international recognition in architecture, was awarded to Wang Shu, the first Chinese architect ever to receive this. He is critical of China's rush to urbanisation and wholesale importation of Western-style architecture, which distorts age-old physical and social structures, as he reveals in the interview in this book (conducted just before he received his prestigious award). Wang Shu is recognised foremost for his modest, 'anti-starchitecture' approach, which includes renovation of existing buildings and reuse of building materials.[3] All this signals the need for a renewed encouragement and confidence in the reconnection and integration of different disciplines and professional practices that converge in the historic city.

Integrating Disciplines and Professional Practices

The conservation and rehabilitation of the historic city needs to go beyond the expert opinion of the conservation specialists only. There is an urgent need to involve a broader constituency comprised of other groups than the usual suspects, such as residents, youth, entrepreneurs, urban planners and managers, artists and the media, among others, in order to forge collaborative alliances, reduce conflicts and optimise creative use of the historic city. Moreover, this should be extended toward providing direction for the planning and design of the city's contemporary parts.

—~—

[. . .] [The] field of urban heritage management [is] seriously compartmentalised, much to the detriment of the historic city and its potential to contribute to the development of the contemporary city. With a view to de-compartmentalise and reconnect the city's human, social and cultural capital, some of the more successful cities of today, including Turin, Portland, Bilbao, Seattle and Barcelona, to name a few, have created a one-stop-shop for the management of their urban environment.

Since the adoption of Agenda 21 in 1992, when the United Nations framed sustainable development and put forward the need to position local communities centre-stage in the decision-making process, a gradual shift in development thinking has occurred away from a focus on *managing* cities to one on *governing* cities. The latter places greater importance on the quality and sensitivity of local government and signals a shift towards 'participative culture'.[4]

—∾—

Future Challenges of Urban Conservation

—∾—

Fifty years of conservation experiences have created a vast inventory of practices and policies. In spite of the uniformity of the doctrinal principles descending from the professional Charters and UNESCO Regulations, these practices vary from place to place, and have evolved along the years, reflecting a shift of perceptions of heritage values and an evolution of the needs, linked to the demands of social and economic actors. However, the different practices developed in Europe and in other regions are not fully documented. There is still a lack of national and international research in the field of urban conservation.

—∾—

The Critical Path: Historic Urban Landscape Action Plan

[. . .]

In order to facilitate the implementation of the new UNESCO *Recommendation on the Historic Urban Landscape* by local governments and city councils, and to seek a reconnection between disciplines and professional practices to create synergies, a six-step Historic Urban Landscape Action Plan was elaborated. The action plan was included in the General Conference Resolution on the Historic Urban Landscape and suggests the following set of actions:[5]

While stressing the need to take account of the singularity of the context of each historic city and urban settlement, which will result in a different approach to its management, nevertheless six critical steps can be identified for Member States to consider when implementing the Historic Urban Landscape approach. They would include the following:

1. *Undertake comprehensive surveys and mapping of the city's natural, cultural and human resources (such as water catchment areas, green spaces, monuments and sites, view sheds, local communities with their living cultural traditions).*
2. *Reach consensus using participatory planning and stakeholder consultations on what values to protect and to transmit to future generations and to determine the attributes that carry these values.*
3. *Assess vulnerability of these attributes to socio-economic stresses, as well as impacts of climate change.*

4. *With these in hand, and only then, develop a city development strategy (CDS) or a city conservation strategy (CCS) to integrate urban heritage values and their vulnerability status into a wider framework of city development, the overlay of which will indicate (a) strictly no-go areas; (b) sensitive areas that require careful attention to planning, design and implementation; and, (c) opportunities for development (among which high-rise constructions).*
5. *Prioritise policies and actions for conservation and development.*
6. *Establish the appropriate partnerships and local management frameworks for each of the identified projects for conservation and development in the CDS/CCS, as well as to develop mechanisms for the coordination of the various activities between different actors, both public and private.*

[. . .]

Historic Urban Landscape: A Stepped Approach

The Historic Urban Landscape Action Plan acknowledges the need to map and assess the local economic context, and subsequently to elaborate a CDS, which is *'critical to both good city management and economic performance'*, as promoted by the Cities Alliance.[6] The benefits of engaging in a CDS process go far beyond the drafting of a document alone, and include the participation of a wide range of public, private and civil society leaders, who normally do not have many occasions to meet and work together, and the cross-sectoral communication that ensues in order to align the city's social, economic and environmental interests.[7] The Historic Urban Landscape Action Plan, therefore, aims to align itself with this process.

—∾—

[. . .] The main challenge is to integrate this action plan into the city's (or nation's) planning framework. This may involve significant consultations, with adaptations, this time at higher government levels. As this framework may be favouring certain dominant cultural groups in society and their preconceptions, such an integration will likely constitute a major overhaul of the framework itself, its relevant legislation and all related components, such as the structure and conduct of Public-Private Partnerships (PPPs), etc. While challenging indeed, it will also constitute an important occasion to progressively move forward to the next stage in making the planning framework a true instrument of twenty first century forward-looking, proactive, inclusive and participative decision-making.

Interdisciplinary Context and Operational Coordination

—∾—

The Historic Urban Landscape approach aims at re-establishing the connection between management of the historic environment, contemporary urban development and the geological context, in order to ensure a higher degree of sustainability and risk control, as well as harmony and continuity in urban forms, building structures and materials. [. . .]

The *Recommendation on the Historic Urban Landscape* aims to give relevance, among other things, to the 'time dimension' in the management of historic cities, and recognises in the archaeological methods a principal source of knowledge and management practice. A landscape approach aims to integrate this dimension in the urban planning, conservation and development process. [. . .]

—∾—

The Historic Urban Landscape approach aims at giving a proper place to intangible heritage values in the process of interpretation, planning and conservation of historic cities. This is to ensure that a full understanding of the role that intangible heritage values can play is associated to planning methodologies and decisions related to the management of the urban environment. [. . .]

In addition to giving a proper place to intangible heritage values, the Historic Urban Landscape approach also stresses the need to pay greater attention to the role that local communities play, both in the process of conservation and in maintaining the sense of place, the importance of their values and knowledge, as well as their creative capacity. [. . .]

—∾—

[I]f there is one overriding message [. . .], it would be that the Historic Urban Landscape has different meanings in different places that are shaped by different environmental, economic, social and cultural conditions—these should be recognised and respected in order to fulfil its potential to reconnect the historic city to its urban context and to the dynamics of the urban century.

Notes

1. PricewaterhouseCoopers (2005) *Cities of Opportunity*. New York City: 52.
2. See for this argument also: Van Oers, R. (2006) Preventing the Goose with the Golden Eggs from Catching Bird Flu—UNESCO's Efforts *in Safeguarding the Historic Urban Landscape. Cities between Integration and Disintegration: Opportunities and Challenges*, ISoCaRP Review 02, Sitges: 21.
3. See also: "The Local Architect/Wang Shu," at http://www.archdaily.com/212424/the-localarchitect-wang-shu/, February 2012; and "Modern Architect with a Traditional Vision," International Herald Tribune, August 2012: 18.
4. Cumberlidge, C. and Musgrave, L. (2007) *Design and Landscape for People—New Approaches to Renewal*, London: Thames & Hudson: 16.
5. UNESCO (2011) General Conference Resolution [2011] 36 GC/41 Historic Urban Landscape, Paris: 1.
6. The Cities Alliance (2007) *Understanding Your Local Economy—A Resource Guide for Cities*, Washington DC: The World Bank.
7. *Aden: Commercial Capital of Yemen—Local Economic Development Strategy*, AdenGovernorate Local Council and The Cities Alliance, n.d.

Reading

66

Jukka Jokilehto

Interview by Branka Šekarić (2013)

Jukka Jokilehto was trained as an architect and town planner in his native Helsinki, but his work was transformed beginning in 1971 when he attended ICCROM's architectural conservation course, followed by training at the Institute of Advanced Architectural Studies at the University of York (U.K.), where he began to collaborate with Bernard Feilden (see reading 50, part VI). In 1973 Jokilehto returned to ICCROM to direct the Integrated Training in Urban Conservation (ITUC) course, which he continued for more than a quarter century. Jokilehto has made enormous contributions to the field of conservation through his written work (e.g., A History of Architectural Conservation, *1999; rev. ed. 2017), his work at ICCROM and with other international conservation organizations, and in other domains of practice. In this brief interview, Jokilehto articulates the importance of "maintaining continuity" in urban contexts, a fundamental lesson in terms of heritage management.*

Conservation and development in historic urban areas? The identification of the limits of change and what should be preserved—whose responsibility in this decision-making process?

First of all, we should focus on the **management of continuity** and understand what are the essential issues that collectively form references for the recognized significance of heritage. It is only then that the limits of change can be discussed. Indeed, the conservation of heritage resources can be referred to the decision-making process. However, the process must necessarily involve multiple stakeholders. Each of them will have a specific responsibility. Even though it is often said that the community is responsible for its heritage, there is need for the professionals who assist in clarifying the meanings and creating a basis for legal and administrative tools needed for the control and management of such resources. This is particularly important when dealing

Published in B. Šekarić, ed., "Interview with Jukka Jokilehto," *Модерна Конзервација (Modern Conservation)* 1 (2013): 225–36. Belgrade: National Committee ICOMOS Serbia.

with historic urban areas. It is well known that the world's population is in constant rise. In March 2012, it exceeded 7 billion (= seven thousand million), out of which 2.7 billion are in Asia.

In 2008, the world's urban population surpassed rural population, having more than 50% of the total. In the future, urban population will continue to rise more than the rural population, creating an increasing number of metropolises. The increase can take place by expanding the urban area to the surrounding rural territory, thus transforming it into semi-urban or sub-urban territory. Therefore, the traditional character of rural cultural landscape tends to be lost. The other possibility is that the increase will take place inside the existing urban areas, resulting in high-rise constructions, one of the headaches of conservation-minded people. How to react to these challenges? It is difficult to say. In any case, certainly there is need to look at the territory as a whole, and make balanced judgements about future developments. Such developments do not only depend on public authority either. Indeed, the current tendency is that the decisions are taken by the private sector, and the current legal and administrative frameworks are not always—or rarely—capable of responding.

The concept of ***historic urban landscape*** *as a new approach to the preservation of the historic urban heritage? Do you see this concept as* ***an essential step forward*** *in the matter of urban conservation?*

Yes, I do think that the instruments proposed by the 2011 UNESCO Recommendation on Historic Urban Landscape (HUL) are a step in the right direction. In fact, this recommendation is not so much another tool for urban conservation, but rather an encouragement of developing suitable planning and management tools for the control of the non-protected territory. For example, in the World Heritage context, where a constant monitoring is being implied for inscribed properties, it has become clear that more often than not the problems faced by such areas come from the outside. In principle, the buffer zone should already provide an instrument to control what happens in the surroundings of World Heritage properties. In practice, however, it does not seem to be enough. In fact, the World Heritage justification of a property, such as a part of an historic urban area, normally highlights the excellences of that area. It does not touch on commonalities. Indeed, we could say that the World Heritage is not "democratic." At the same time, it is still part of a larger territory and as such subject to pressures of everyday life and business. The economics are an essential part of this though too often forgotten. The question is about "levels" of management. It is not enough to focus on the often rather restricted area recognized for its OUV. Rather, management must necessarily take into account the general social-economic and cultural aspects of the territory, and guide development without undermining the continuity of traditional qualities in the protected areas.

Relation between old and new, what do you think about the ***intervention of modern architecture*** *in the* ***historical context****, and what is your attitude towards the increasingly actual phenomenon—international "stars" of contemporary architecture and their works within the historical urban areas?*
I am not against modern architecture in historical context. However, one should take into account the physical and social-cultural context, as well as the visual integrity of the place. There are many ways of designing modern architecture of good quality. It is not necessary to produce something that is completely out of place in relation to the traditional urban morphology, as was the case of the Graz Kulturhaus. If such a building was needed, it would have been advisable to choose a location where it did not destroy the qualities for which the historic centre of Graz had been recognized as World Heritage, i.e., its "harmonious blend of the architectural styles and artistic movements that have succeeded each other from the Middle Ages until the 18th century. . . ." It is a question of common sense.

Earlier, at least in Finland, architects were normally trained to understand and take into account the character of the context where a new building was designed. Indeed, there was and I believe still is, in Finland, a commission that verifies the suitability of each new project. It is a shame for the architects if they have forgotten this. It is also a shame for the Municipal Council if they have forgotten this. The problem is that we tend to have been contaminated by the "Dubai symptom." We should remember that the city of Dubai has practically no historic fabric left. Consequently, it has been possible to build adventurous high-rise buildings, including the latest 828m tall tower. Curiously, Dubai has also decided to build a brand new "historic town centre"! At the same time, in the neighbouring Sultanate of Oman, the Sultan has ordered a maximum height for new constructions, also to be built in a style sympathetic to the overall image.

Reading

67

Shannon Mattern

A City Is Not a Computer (2017)

Shannon Mattern is an associate professor of media studies at the New School in New York, where she teaches and conducts research on archives, libraries, and "spatial epistemologies." She is the author of Deep Mapping the Media City *(2015) and other works related to urban media. In this reading, she confronts the so-called smart city of the early twenty-first century, stating clearly: the city is not a computer. Instead, as has been argued throughout this book, the city is a place for, by, and with human beings whose identities, memories, and histories give their lives greater meaning, even if the cities they inhabit are not "smart."*

"How should we measure the effectiveness of a city (what are its KPIs)?" That's Key Performance Indicators, for those not steeped in business intelligence jargon. There was hardly any mention of the urban designers, planners, and scholars who have been asking the big questions for centuries: How do cities function, and how can they function better?

—~—

Dreams of Informatic Urbanism

[. . .] The idea of the "new city" certainly isn't new, and the model now emerging in the United States has precedents in Asian and Middle Eastern countries, where Cisco, Siemens, and IBM have partnered with real-estate developers and governments to build "smart cities" *tabula rasa*.

We don't know how these urban experiments will fare. Since they are in a constant state of development, always "versioning" toward an optimized model ever on the horizon, they are not easily evaluated or critiqued.[1] If you believe the marketing

From Shannon Mattern, "A City Is Not a Computer" (February 2017). First published by *Places Journal*. https://placesjournal.org.

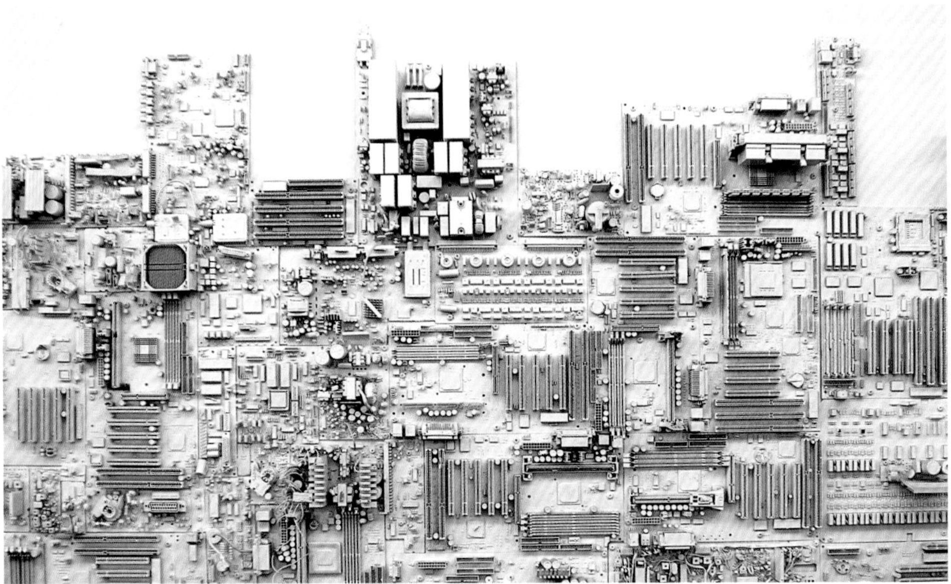

Fig. 1. A wall in Bairro Alto, Lisbon, covered with circuit boards painted white. Daniel Gonçalves. https://www.flickr.com/photos/domiriel/6692364895/.

hype, though, we're on the cusp of an urban future in which embedded sensors, ubiquitous cameras and beacons, networked smartphones, and the operating systems that link them all together, will produce unprecedented efficiency, connectivity, and social harmony. We're transforming the idealized topology of the open web and Internet of Things into urban form.

Programmer and tech writer Paul McFedries explains this thinking:

> The city is a computer, the streetscape is the interface, you are the cursor, and your smartphone is the input device. This is the user-based, bottom-up version of the city-as-computer idea, but there's also a top-down version, which is systems-based. It looks at urban systems such as transit, garbage, and water and wonders whether the city could be more efficient and better organized if these systems were "smart."[2]

[. . .] Modernist designers and futurists saw morphological parallels between urban forms and circuit boards. Just as new modes of telecommunication have always reshaped physical terrains and political economies, new computational methods have informed urban planning, modeling, and administration.[3]

Modernity is good at renewing metaphors, from the city as machine, to the city as organism or ecology, to the city as cyborgian merger of the technological and the organic.[4] Our current paradigm, the *city as computer*, appeals because it frames the messiness of urban life as programmable and subject to rational order. [. . .]

—~—

[. . .] *The city is not a computer.* This seems an obvious truth, but it is being challenged now (again) by technologists (and political actors) who speak as if they could reduce urban planning to algorithms.[5]
[. . .]

Informational Ecologies of the City

—~—

[. . .] We need to ask: What place-based "information" doesn't fit on a shelf or in a database? What are the non-textual, un-recordable forms of cultural memory? These questions are especially relevant for marginalized populations, indigenous cultures, and developing nations. Performance studies scholar Diana Taylor urges us to acknowledge ephemeral, performative forms of knowledge, such as dance, ritual, cooking, sports, and speech.[6] These forms cannot be reduced to "information," nor can they be "processed," stored, or transmitted via fiber-optic cable. Yet they are vital urban intelligences that live within bodies, minds, and communities.

Finally, consider data of the environmental, ambient, "immanent" kind. Malcolm McCullough has shown that our cities are full of fixed architectures, persistent terrains, and reliable environmental patterns that anchor all the unstructured data and image streams that float on top.[7] What can we learn from the "nonsemantic information" inherent in shadows, wind, rust, in the signs of wear on a well-trodden staircase, the creaks of a battered bridge—all the indexical messages of our material environments? I'd argue that the intellectual value of this ambient, immanent information exceeds its function as stable ground for the city's digital flux. Environmental data are just as much figure as they are ground. They remind us of necessary truths: that urban intelligence comes in multiple forms, that it is produced within environmental as well as cultural contexts, that it is reshaped over the *longue durée* by elemental exposure and urban development, that it can be lost or forgotten. These data remind us to think on a climatic scale, a geologic scale, as opposed to the scale of financial markets, transit patterns, and news cycles.

The Case Against Information Processing

—~—

The *city as computer* model [. . .] conditions urban design, planning, policy, and administration—even residents' everyday experience—in ways that hinder the development of healthy, just, and resilient cities. [. . .] We have seen that urban ecologies "process" data by means that are not strictly algorithmic, and that not all urban intelligences can be called "information." One can't "process" the local cultural effects of long-term weather patterns or derive insights from the generational evolution of a neighborhood without a degree of sensitivity that exceeds mere computation. Urban intelligence of this kind involves site-based experience, participant observation, sensory engagement. We need new models for thinking about cities that *do not compute*, and we need new terminology. In contemporary urban discourses, where "data" rhetoric is often frothy and fetishistic, we seem to have lost critical perspective on how urban data become meaningful spatial information or translate into place-based knowledge.

We need to expand our *repertoire* (to borrow a term from Diana Taylor) of urban intelligences, to draw upon the wisdom of information scientists and theorists, archivists, librarians, intellectual historians, cognitive scientists, philosophers, and others who think about the management of information and the production of knowledge.[8] They can help us better understand the breadth of intelligences that are integrated within our cities, which would be greatly impoverished if they were to be rebuilt, or built anew, with computational logic as their prevailing epistemology.

We could also be better attuned to the lifecycles of urban information resources—to their creation, curation, provision, preservation, and destruction—and to the assemblages of urban sites and subjects that make up our cities' intellectual ecologies. "If we think of the city as a long-term construct, with more complex behaviors and processes of formation, feedback, and processing," architect Tom Verebes proposes, then we can imagine it as an organization, or even an organism, that can learn.[9] [. . .]

Instead of more gratuitous parametric modeling, we need to think about urban epistemologies that embrace memory and history; that recognize spatial intelligence as sensory and experiential; that consider other species' ways of knowing; that appreciate the wisdom of local crowds and communities; that acknowledge the information embedded in the city's facades, flora, statuary, and stairways; that aim to integrate forms of distributed cognition paralleling our brains' own distributed cognitive processes.

We must also recognize the shortcomings in models that presume the objectivity of urban data and conveniently delegate critical, often ethical decisions to the machine. We, humans, *make* urban information by various means: through sensory experience, through long-term exposure to a place, and, yes, by systematically filtering data. It's essential to make space in our cities for those diverse methods of knowledge production. And we have to grapple with the political and ethical implications of our methods and models, embedded in all acts of planning and design. *City-making* is always, simultaneously, an enactment of *city-knowing*—which cannot be reduced to computation.

Notes

1. Orit Halpern and Robert Mitchell, "The Smartness Mandate: Notes Toward a Critique," *Grey Room* (forthcoming).
2. Paul McFedries, "The City as System [Technically Speaking]," *IEEE Spectrum* 51:4 (April 2014): 36, https://doi.org/10.1109/MSPEC.2014.6776302.
3. Stephen Graham and Simon Marvin, *Telecommunications and the City: Electronic Spaces, Urban Places* (New York: Routledge, 1996); Jennifer Light, *From Warfare to Welfare: Defense Intellectuals and Urban Problems in Cold War America* (Baltimore: Johns Hopkins University Press, 2004); Mark Vallianatos, "Uncovering the Early History of 'Big Data' and 'Smart City' in Los Angeles," *Boom California* (June 2015).
4. Some argue that the city-as-machine has a much deeper history, as evidenced by use of grid

layouts, linear patterns, and regular geometric forms since ancient times, and by the use of standardized patterns for colonial urban development. See, for instance, Kevin Lynch, *Good City Form* (Cambridge: MIT Press, 1981): 81–88. See also Matthew Gandy, "Cyborg Urbanization: Complexity and Monstrosity in the Contemporary City," *International Journal of Urban and Regional Research* 29: (March 2005): 26–49, https://doi.org/10.1111/j.1468-2427.2005.00568.x; Peter Nientied, "Metaphor and Urban Studies: A Crossover, Theory and a Case Study of SS Rotterdam," *City, Territory and Architecture* 3:21 (2016), https://doi.org.10.1186/s40410-016-0051-z; William Solesbury, "How Metaphors Help Us Understand Cities," *Geography* 99:3 (Autumn 2014): 139–42; Tom Verebes, "The Interactive Urban Model: Histories and Legacies Related to Prototyping the Twenty-First Century City," *Frontiers in Digital Humanities* 3 (February 2016), https://doi.org/10.3389/fdigh.2016.00001.

5. For more on the algorithm as a timely conceptual model, see Massimo Mazzotti, "Algorithmic Life," *Los Angeles Review of Books*, January 22, 2017.
6. Diana Taylor, *The Archive and the Repertoire: Performing Cultural Memory in the Americas* (Durham, NC: Duke University Press, 2003).
7. Malcolm McCullough, *Ambient Commons: Attention in the Age of Embodied Information* (Cambridge: MIT Press, 2013): 36, 42.
8. Marcus Foth, Nancy Odendaal, and Gregory N. Hearn, "The View from Everywhere: Towards an Epistemology for Urbanites," in *Proceedings of the 4th International Conference on Intellectual Capital, Knowledge Management and Organizational Learning*, Cape Town, South Africa, 2007.
9. Tom Verebes, "The Interactive Urban Model: Histories and Legacies Related to Prototyping the Twenty-First Century City," *Frontiers in Digital Humanities* 3, February 2016, https://doi.org/10.3389/fdigh.2016.00001.

Part VIII

Visual Summary: Managing Historic Cities

Inadequately maintained historic buildings in Chikan (Guangdong), China.

In Chikan (Guangdong Province), China, clusters of historic buildings in the urban core were neither well-maintained nor carefully managed. As a result, degradation and demolition became more likely.

Part VIII

VISUAL SUMMARY

Lost City, pencil on paper drawing by Nancy Wolf, 1988.

PLATE VIII.1

This imaginary depiction of the ruins of a "lost city" engulfed by the Cartesian grid and high-rise towers of a modern metropolis evokes the point expressed by Herbert Stovel (reading 62) when he lamented, "It is difficult to escape the conclusion that the modern instruments invented by the public sector to protect urban heritage values have not proved fully adequate in the face of the economic, social and political forces confronting historic cities today."

Valparaíso, Chile. Elevated view of the historic quarter Cerro Concepción, declared a UNESCO World Heritage Site in 2003. Photo by Karol Kozlowski.

PLATE VIII.2

Valparaíso, the Chilean port town that flourished in the nineteenth century as a result of maritime trade, is today partially inscribed on the World Heritage List. This has contributed to significant stakeholder involvement to harmonize local expectations with general conservation principles. In Eduardo Rojas's (reading 64) view, "Attaining the right balance between responding to local needs and safeguarding the local, national, or universal values of the urban heritage lies at the core of the governance challenge."

Rawalpindi, Pakistan. View of the old city from Sujan Singh haveli. Photo by Saif Tahir.

PLATE VIII.3

Rawalpindi, Pakistan, famous for its traditional mansions (*havelis*), is contending with issues of rapid urban development. Ron van Oers (reading 65) worked here before his sudden death in 2015. As an ardent proponent of the Historic Urban Landscape approach, a new way to conceptualize the conservation of the urban heritage, he sought to bridge the divide between the traditional and the contemporary city. This approach, he writes, "seeks to reconnect heritage precincts with the modern city; the city with its wider setting and hinterland; urban conservation with the process of city planning and regional development; new architecture with the historic context; and the different cultural traditions, including migrant and traditional resident, with each other and with the socio-economic trends that are evolving in the contemporary city."

Kunsthaus, also known as the Friendly Alien. Blob architecture by Peter Cook and Colin Fournier, Museum of Contemporary Art, Graz, Austria.

PLATE VIII.4

The Graz Kunsthaus, designed by Peter Cook and Colin Fournier (1999–2003), is intentionally meant to contrast rather than harmonize with its context. Jukka Jokilehto remarks, contrary to this approach: "It is not necessary to produce something that is completely out of place in relation to the traditional urban morphology." In this case, a more appropriate location outside of Graz's historic area could have been found. Jokilehto (reading 66) points out that it is a matter of common sense. He advocates "managing continuity" in historic urban areas rather than subscribing to the prevailing and often abused concept of conservation as "management of change."

Metropolis II, 2010, by Chris Burden.

PLATE VIII.5

Shannon Mattern (reading 67) observes that "modernist designers and futurists saw morphological parallels between urban forms and circuit boards. . . . Our current paradigm, the *city as computer*, appeals because it frames the messiness of urban life as programmable and subject to rational order." Chris Burden's mechanical assemblage in *Metropolis II* is a reminder of how the present urban form is sometimes an inspiration for artistic creativity. Yet, Mattern cautions, "urban planning cannot be reduced to algorithms." Instead, she argues, "we need to think about urban epistemologies that embrace memory and history."

Appendix

Francesco Siravo

Key International Conventions, Recommendations, and Charters Related to Urban Conservation

Conservation Principles and Practices Shared in an International Context

The cultural heritage conventions and charters promoted by regional and international entities trace the evolution of conservation principles and disciplines formulated and diffused internationally. These documents not only reflect advanced theories and practices in a national context, but they also serve as drafts at an international level that guide conservation legislation and policies implemented in individual countries.

Several international documents on restoration and conservation followed the 1931 Athens Charter for the Restoration of Historic Monuments and subsequently after the establishment in 1964 of the Venice Charter for the Conservation and Restoration of Monuments and Sites. (See, below, further commentaries related to these two fundamental charters.) These documents have enabled the dissemination of fundamental principles and the designation of guidelines and practical procedures for interventions. They have also promoted dialogue between diverse populations and cultures, sometimes within the borders of a single country. Nevertheless, an understandable difficulty exists in orienting oneself among these documents, and in many instances they are so general, repetitive, and at times contradictory that they are ignored at the national level. Furthermore, the disparity of opinions and regional approaches risks the creation of fractures and tensions that undermine the foundations of a search for universal principles and practices. They make clear the distance that separates theories and general principles from substantive results. The documents and their contents demonstrate an excess of abstraction and an inability to confront problems and difficulties that one often encounters in the field. In reality, many of the observed shortcomings and contradictions do not concern the documents in question but are the result of the rapid expansion of the disciplines involved and the same international difficulties of implementing effective protection of cultural property. It suffices to remember the pressure generated by mass tourism and by enormous economic and social transformations, the tremendous differences that separate developed countries from the rest of the world, the conflicts existing between national identities and diverse groups, and the same crisis situation besieging international institutions. It is nevertheless necessary to recognize that—faced with such a panorama—the totality of international documents on conservation constitutes a generally coherent and potentially effective theoretical and practical frame of reference, above all, if opportunely selected and used with care. In this way, international conventions and charters remain essential instruments for promoting dialogue and understanding between diverse cultures and regions around the world. What follows, therefore, is a summary of the most important of these international documents related to urban conservation practice. This is not a comprehensive list of all such documents; moreover, the creation of new documents will undoubtedly occur. The final section enumerates the principal regional or national documents focusing on urban conservation as of late 2017. For a more extensive list of international documents related to cultural heritage conservation, see www.getty.edu/conservation/publications_resources/research_resources/charters.html.

Definitions: Conventions, Recommendations, and International Charters

To achieve clarity, it is first necessary to specify the range, significance, and principal contributions of the many types of documents one finds in the urban conservation field. A first distinction concerns the terminology and legal force of these documents. Thus, it is necessary to distinguish between "conventions," "recommendations," and international "charters." Conventions are prepared by international institutions, such as UNESCO and the Council of Europe, and then submitted for signature by individual governments; after ratification, they are made binding for all the signatory states. Recommendations, although not binding, are nevertheless the result of broad consultations among member states and have a strong prescriptive value. "Charters" do not have the force of law, but they do hold authority as well as ethical and moral value, because they contain principles, codes of conduct, and guidelines established by consensus among area specialists. Naturally, the more authoritative and diversified the participating experts, the greater is the disciplinary import and the international diffusion of the charter in question. It is furthermore critical that renowned international organizations—and not national governments—be perceived as institutions free of political motives and partisanship in the drafting of the charter. For this reason, those promoted by UNESCO and ICOMOS over decades on behalf of cultural heritage are among the most respected international charters that have had the widest dissemination. However, in the early twenty-first century, as these organizations have been increasingly affected by global politics, they have sometimes been assailed by critics who question the motives and methods of their actions.

Athens and Venice Charters, Related to Architectural Restoration

International charters and pronouncements initially focused on issues tied to restoration of monuments in keeping with developments in conservation disciplines and as a response to transformations brought about by industrial development and war during the twentieth century.

The Athens Charters (1931 and 1933)

These are the first documents of international scope concerned with issues of conservation. The first of the two, the *Athens Charter for the Restoration of Historic Monuments*, was initiated by the International Museums Office (an agency within the League of Nations) and is most closely concerned with the restoration of monuments:

a) monuments should be subjected to maintenance more than restoration;
b) all historic periods and styles present in the monument are to be respected;
c) it is essential to respect the character of monuments and to avoid incongruous use;
d) ruins are to be scrupulously respected (and the practice of conjectural restorations is to be consequently abandoned), even if it is acceptable to carry out anastylosis if the intervention remains clearly identifiable; and
e) if the conservation of uncovered archaeological ruins cannot be guaranteed, they should be carefully documented and reburied. For the first time, this document, international in scope, recognizes that restoration is to be entrusted to specialists and that they must collaborate (e.g., with archaeologists, architects, chemists, experts in the natural sciences, etc.) and that every act of restoration or conservation must be preceded by a full and well-documented study of the monument.

In 1933, again in Athens, the International Congress of Modern Architecture (CIAM) was held, which presented a second charter concerned with urban planning issues (the Town Planning Charter). In it, the objectives are stated: to safeguard monuments and their immediate context during urban development and restructuring, to modify or deviate the route of highways and busy traffic arteries that may be planned in the proximity of monuments, and to integrate contemporary architecture into historical areas rather than build in a historical style. Through the 1950s, the Athens Charters constituted the principal international reference documents for conservation for countries embedded in the Western tradition.

The Venice Charter for the Conservation and Restoration of Monuments and Sites, 1964

This resolution was published following the Second International Congress of Architects and Specialists of Historic Buildings, when ICOMOS was also instituted. The document cited the 1931 Athens Charter whose principles it aims to clarify and whose scope of applicability it aims to expand. In that regard, the Venice Charter does not constitute a substantive modification of basic principles but rather their reconsideration in the light of experience gained since the promulgation of the Athens Charters more than thirty years earlier. The first definition concerns the monument, expanding it from a single architectural structure of an exceptional nature to every urban or rural place that constitutes evidence of a civilization, a significant development, or a historical event. The definition "monument" is therefore applied "not only to great works of art but also to the most modest works from the past that, with the passage of time, have acquired cultural relevance."

The charter also established a distinction between "conservation" and "restoration." "Conservation" should be generalized and comprise all operations necessary to secure on a permanent basis the maintenance of the monument, including its immediate context, preserving the scale and relationships of the whole. Possible changes to a monument's functional use, preferably for the public, are permitted but only if they do not entail modifications of the planimetric layout or decorative components. Not permitted—except for exceptional cases and only if it is the only means to guarantee their conservation—is the removal of statues, paintings, and other decorative elements, which should always be considered part of the monument. "Restoration," a highly specialized undertaking, might be necessary in the aftermath of exceptional events or radical transformations, but it must be preceded and followed by an archaeological and historical study. Therefore, restoration is based on respect for original documentation and materials and has the objective of preserving and rendering legible the historical and aesthetic significance of the monument. "Restoration stops where conjecture begins." Accordingly, every addition that is considered indispensable but that is not justified as a historical and documented reintegration is to be made clearly distinct from the original architectural composition.

The document reiterates, moreover, that contributions from all historical periods must be respected, declaring explicitly that "unity of style is not the objective of restoration." When a building presents stratifications attributable to diverse historical periods, the elimination of later transformations in favor of a preceding manifestation of the monument can be justified only in exceptional instances: only if the parts to be eliminated possess very little value and their removal reveals a greater historical, archaeological, and aesthetic value, uncovering as a result a state of substantial wholeness. Every substitution of missing parts must be harmoniously integrated with the whole yet be clearly distinguishable from the original, to avoid falsification of historical and artistic evidence. Possible additions are not permitted, with the exception of cases in which they do not impede meaningful appreciation of the building and its relationship with the context.

Burra Charter, 1979, and Nara Document, 1994

After more than fifty years, the Venice Charter remains the principal reference document in the international arena regarding issues in architectural restoration. Although many have called for its revision, the current attitude is that the fundamental principles of the Venice Charter remain valid but that it is necessary to integrate the document with appropriate specifications and definitions pertinent to questions that have emerged in recent years.

The Burra Charter, 1979 (Australian ICOMOS Charter for the Conservation of Places of Cultural Significance)

Resulting from the work done by the Australian committee of ICOMOS to adapt the principles of the Venice Charter to the specific conditions of the continent, it immediately acquired international relevance, to the extent that it was revised and supplemented in 1981, 1988, 1999, and 2013, along with the addition of guidelines. Above all, it emphasizes that a monument comprises the much larger idea of "place," also in relation to the nature of Australian cultural heritage that comprises numerous aboriginal sites. In this sense, it is applicable to the most diverse conditions and situations and is therefore widely generalizable at an international level, encompassing "place" to mean "site, area, land, landscape, building or other work, group of buildings or other works, and may include components, contents, spaces and views." Even the term "conservation" is understood in its widest sense, defined as the totality of processes aimed at ensuring the care of a site to preserve its "cultural significance," that is, the totality of values associated with it (historical, artistic, social, spiritual, etc.). Depending on the circumstances, conservation can comprise only maintenance or more complex interventions, and is often a combination of both, including restoration, reconstruction, and transformation of use.

The charter distinguishes principles, processes, and practices of conservation. The principles derive from the ultimate goal of the work of conservation, which is to preserve and/or reestablish the "cultural significance" of the place and to implement the necessary conditions to guarantee its security, maintenance, and future existence. The act of conservation is therefore understood not as a finite event but as a process carried out over time that must also comprise long-term management of the site or artifact that is the object of conservation. A list of principles follows, which mirror substantially those of the Venice Charter but are more explicit and direct in form. Among them, the act of conservation based on absolute respect for the existing fabric is emphasized, with the minimum possible intervention so as to preserve the place's original character as much as possible.

Under the title "Conservation Processes," the charter groups and defines for the first time the diverse forms that intervention applied to a place can take, distinguishing between preservation, restoration, reconstruction, and adaptation. It is to be noted that (a) preservation is appropriate where the existing fabric or its condition constitutes evidence of cultural significance, or where insufficient evidence is available to allow other conservation processes to be carried out; (b) restoration is appropriate only if there is sufficient evidence of an earlier state of the fabric and if the return to that state leads to rediscovery of the original cultural significance; (c) reconstruction is appropriate only where a place is incomplete due to damage or alteration and its completion is necessary to guarantee survival or total recovery of its cultural significance; and (d) adaptation is acceptable in cases in which conservation of the site is otherwise impossible and it is does not detract from or substantially alter the cultural significance. Finally, the practices and methods of conservation listed by the charter reiterate the substance of preceding international pronouncements with regard to the participation of experts, the drawing up of preliminary studies, the collection of adequate documentation, etc.

The Nara Document on Authenticity, 1994

This is the result of a conference held in Nara, Japan, organized by the Japanese government in cooperation with UNESCO, ICCROM, and ICOMOS. The conference recalled the international spirit of the Venice Charter and the need to enlarge boundaries in response to new demands and concerns in the area of conservation, with particular attention to globalization and a parallel search for cultural identity on the part of emerging countries and minority groups.

Although the document does not deal with specific questions within the related disciplines (for which one refers to the Venice Charter), it nevertheless places in the foreground three fundamental issues. First, the diversity of cultures and cultural heritage, whether physical or intangible, must be protected and promoted as an essential and crucial aspect of every human society. The safeguarding of such heritage is not only the direct obligation of the society that produced it and cares for it but also and above all a common responsibility of humanity in keeping with the international conventions and charters in this area and with respect for cultural values and convictions of each community and social group. Second, decisive and central to the process of conservation is the idea of "authenticity," which plays a fundamental part in the recognition of the value of the property and which must be based on credible and truthful sources. The assessment of values attributable to cultural artifacts and the credibility of the sources differs from society to society and even within a single society. As a result, absolute criteria for assessment do not exist, but, on the contrary, the respect due each society requires that the value of each artifact must be assessed in conjunction with the cultural context to which it belongs, Third, it is of the utmost urgency that each society recognize the particular nature of its own cultural heritage and, at the same time, the credibility and truthfulness of the information that validates its authenticity. According to the artifact under consideration, the assessment of authenticity can concern formal, spiritual, and environmental values or aspects tied to materials, uses, and local traditions that, individually or in combination, determine the specific dimensions and artistic, historical, social, and scientific significance of the cultural heritage in question.

Major International Documents Related to Urban Conservation

These documents first came into being as statements of principle drafted at the regional level (The Quito Norms for Latin America and the Convention for the Protection of the Architectural Heritage of Europe) in response to the concerns and inclinations of groups of nations. They were later systematized in the charters of international breadth initiated by ICOMOS and other international entities. Their contents also aid in the gradual refinement of the idea of the urban area from a general category to recognition of the specificity of smaller centers and towns with a rural character. Finally, the contribution of international pronouncements promoting and monitoring cultural tourism should be noted, with their consideration of norms and recommendations for managing areas with a historical and artistic character.

The Quito Norms, 1967
(Meeting on the Preservation and Utilization of Monuments and Sites of Artistic and Historical Value)

This document assembles the summaries of deliberations by the Organization of American States in a meeting organized in Quito. It was the first to raise, in an international context and in Latin America in particular, the issue of protection expanded to large archaeological sites and the totality of ancient cities. The document denounced the derelict state of the region's cultural heritage and the destruction caused by uncontrolled industrial development. Particularly severe was the assessment of the destruction inflicted on ancient cities in the "name of poorly understood and poorly managed concepts of urban development." "It is no exaggeration to state that the potential wealth destroyed by these irresponsible acts of urban vandalism in many cities of the hemisphere [South America] far exceeds the benefits to the national economy (of every country) derived from the installations and infrastructural improvements claimed as justification for such acts." This document is also one of the first international pronouncements to declare explicitly that monuments are destined to satisfy a social function and to bring economic benefit to the respective national states, even if the excessive focus attributed by the Norms to their use for commercial purposes and tourism was gradually abandoned in later international documents. Finally, it should be noted that the recommendation contained in the Norms to expand the concept of *monument* to buildings and cultural expressions of the nineteenth and twentieth centuries —today considered obvious—was a relatively new concept at the end of the 1960s.

Resolution of the Symposium on the Introduction of Contemporary Architecture into Ancient Groups of Buildings, 1972

The objective of the symposium, organized by ICOMOS in Budapest at the time of its general assembly, was the admissibility of contemporary architecture projects in historic contexts. Cautious presenters recognized the importance of granting architecture of the past an active role in contemporary life while allowing for the possibility of introducing new architecture into ancient contexts, yet always such that this occurs within the framework of town planning that protects and accepts the rightful permanence and integrity of the existing historic fabric. The introduction of such architecture should therefore avoid falsification or imitation of architecture of the past and orient itself instead to harmonious integration with the existing fabric by means of compatible forms and treatment of the facades, scale, and volumetrics. The introduction of new uses for historical buildings is legitimate and admissible on the condition that it does not pose adverse effects, either external or internal, on their structural and aesthetic integrity.

Declaration of Amsterdam and the European Charter on Architectural Heritage, 1975

These two documents result from the European Architectural Year (1975), and both are principally concerned with built historic heritage, understood in the widest sense of these terms, including not only monuments but also smaller buildings found in historical cities and villages. These are the expression of the history and culture of past societies and an indispensable resource for understanding the present. The relevance that they have for contemporary society resides in their being simultaneously indispensable to the collective memory of nations; bearers of irreplaceable spiritual, culture, social, and economic values; and privileged places of integration of social groups and differentiated urban functions.

A solution can only emerge from implementation of an integrated idea of conservation through the use of suitable restoration techniques and the selection of uses compatible with historic buildings. The charter emphasizes the need to rehabilitate residential built heritage in a spirit of social justice, thus trying to avoid the expulsion of poorer inhabitants from historic urban areas. The methods for implementing a policy of integrated conservation are (a) legal (by applying and strengthening laws in this area), (b) administrative (with the creation of dedicated technical offices), (c) financial (with direct aid and fiscal incentives), and (d) technical (with the enhancement of skills and training in restoration). However, above all, integrated conservation requires the involvement of residents in the decisions that directly concern their living environment. Finally, every generation has the responsibility to impart a shared European heritage to future generations. The two texts, more than technical documents, constitute a manifesto of goals for the policies to be adopted in the European sphere for conservation and recovery of historic urban areas.

Resolution of the International Symposium on the Conservation of Smaller Historic Towns, 1975

This is the first international document to address the urban fabric of small towns. The resolution describes the characteristics and problems in such areas, from depopulation to lack of economic activity, phenomena particularly severe in developing countries. A list follows of the strategies to be implemented to combat such tendencies, comprising planning instruments coordinated at various levels, fair economic policies that align preservation with development, and projects for raising awareness among residents that foster appreciation and redevelopment of historic and landscape heritage. The resolution emphasizes that conservation of towns cannot rely solely on public and private initiatives at the local level, which are considered too limited with respect to the extent of the problems, but must also involve legislative instruments and assistance on the part of regional and national authorities.

Charter of Cultural Tourism, 1976

This is the result of a meeting between various cultural and tourism entities organized by ICOMOS in Brussels with the goal of endorsing a shared statement concerning the cultural implications of tourism. The document begins by stating that tourism is an irreversible phenomenon whose influence on historic heritage in cities and throughout the land will only increase over time. It therefore urges individual states to assume responsibility for the containment of the negative effects of the phenomenon, integrating management of cultural heritage within a planning framework at the local and national levels with cooperation among them so that international conventions on the conservation of cultural and natural heritage can be adopted. Of particular importance is the statement that therespect owed to cultural heritage and its need for protection must take absolute precedence over any other social, political, or economic considerations.

Recommendations Concerning the Safeguarding and Contemporary Role of Historic Areas, 1976

Adopted at the general meeting of UNESCO in Nairobi, these Recommendations constitute a highly significant international document regarding interventions in historic areas. Perhaps due to its length and detailed contents, it has not been widely disseminated and was subsequently replaced by other, more concise resolutions. It remains, nevertheless, the principal point of reference for all international deliberations that have followed it. The preamble of the document is an explicit and direct denunciation of the dangers that threaten architectural historic heritage. It is a reminder of the responsibility of individuals and member states to prevent the loss of groups of artifacts that, confronted with ever more massive processes of standardization and cultural leveling, remain the primary evidence of the diversity, richness, and identity of human societies. The definition of that which constitutes such heritage is detailed and all-encompassing. Under the heading "Areas of Historical and Architectural Importance" are urban and rural settlements, archaeological and paleontological finds, and anything else recognizable as aesthetically, historically, socially, and/or culturally valuable.

Among the general principles of intervention, the explicit designation of the implementation of an integrated plan stands out, which encompasses, in addition to buildings, the organization of space and environmental aspects. The strategic profile indicates the need to go beyond simple, passive protection of built heritage and actively combat, with preventive planning documents and with the application of scientific methods of restoration, potential undesirable transformations and foreseeable environmental damage. National, regional, and local planning policies must take into account such guidelines with appropriate legal, technical, economic, and social measures, stimulating as much as possible active participation on the part of individuals and private enterprises. A detailed exposition of the measures and methods to be adopted for safeguarding follows, among them (a) the specification to connect planning norms and laws for housing to policies of rehabilitation and safeguarding of historic heritage at the national level (IV.9); (b) a description of the content and nature of the requirements to include in conservation planning documents (IV.10, 11); and (c) the request to identify the authorities responsible for conservation programs at the various planning stages, to involve interdisciplinary groups in the preparation of the plans, and to provide public technical offices with the necessary technical and financial resources (IV.17).

From a more strictly technical and operational standpoint: (d) the recommendation to define, on the part of the public authorities, a complete inventory of the protected areas and the associated intervention priorities (IV.18); (e) the nature and sequence of surveys and operational plans to be completed before drafting the plan (IV.19–21); (f) the recommendation to expand safeguarding measures to all historical periods, and to subject any proposal for demolition to prior, careful scrutiny (IV.23, 24); (g) the implementation of inspections and limitations on technological installations, street furniture, paved areas, motorized vehicles, and parking spaces (IV.30–32). Finally, regarding social and financial issues: (l) the request to maintain and support traditional activities and promote cultural and social events using cultural heritage in urban and rural settings (IV.33, 34); (m) the promotion of participation at all levels of the community and the formation of voluntary advocacy organizations for heritage (IV.35, 36); (n) the allocation of public monies to be directed toward rehabilitation and conservation efforts, as well as forms of subsidization, subsidized loans, and fiscal incentives supporting cooperatives and private citizens (IV.37–42); (o) the creation of nonprofit agencies, financial institutions, and associations tasked with stimulating recovery efforts by means of loans, utilization of public funds, private donations, direct interventions, and so on (IV.43–45); and (p) the institution of aid aimed at supporting residential usage and the traditional economic activities of low-income groups to avoid expulsion of residents and transformation of the existing social composition within historic areas (IV.46). The document concludes with a series of recommendations for launching research, education, and awareness-building activities (V.47–53) and for the development of a network of collaborators and international assistance for rehabilitation of architectural historical heritage.

The Tlaxcala Declaration on the Revitalization of Small Settlements, 1982

This document resulted from an initiative promoted by the Mexican committee of ICOMOS with the participation of various Latin American countries and is the second international document that confronts the issue of small historic settlements. Although reflecting a series of regional preoccupations and priorities, the declaration emphasizes a few aspects of international relevance taken up again in later years, in particular, the importance of interventions respecting the cultural traditions of the original indigenous community, the reinforcement of local building traditions, and discouragement of the indiscriminate introduction of consumer models and unsustainable, inappropriate housing. Finally, the declaration emphasizes the importance of protecting vernacular forms, industries, and building systems, guaranteeing their perseverance and survival through the organization of training programs and the introduction of opportune technical manufacturing improvements. These last aspects are reiterated and broadened in 1999 with publication of the ICOMOS Charter on the Built Vernacular Heritage (161).

The Appleton Charter for the Protection and Enhancement of the Built Environment, 1983

Published by the Canadian committee of ICOMOS, this charter explicitly connects the Venice and Burra Charters, expanding the criteria and groups of buildings to entire sites and historic contexts. This charter is significant because it synthesized preceding enunciations of principles, with the clarification of scales and levels of intervention, and the definition of rehabilitation, with a specification of types of intervention, subdivided into continuous actions (maintenance) and occasional actions (stabilization, removal and/or integration of parts). Specifications of the principles and practices of good intervention follow. The latter clarify the role of fundamental documentation (required before each intervention), material and techniques of restoration (preferably traditional), respect for patina (but forbidding its falsification), the reversibility of interventions (leaving open possibilities for future corrective actions), and absolute respect for the integrity of the heritage (not only aesthetic but also structural and technological).

The ICOMOS Charter for the Conservation of Historic Towns and Urban Areas, the Washington Charter, 1987

This charter was adopted following the ICOMOS General Assembly in Washington, DC. Its objective is to provide general specifications for interventions in historic urban areas. The charter is presented as complementary to the Venice Charter for issues tied to interventions in historic urban contexts and explicitly references the 1976 UNESCO recommendations. From its premise, the document recognizes that interventions on historic urban fabric can make use of planning methods and different forms of protection, also in relation to the diverse developments that each settlement experienced during its postindustrial phases of growth. As a result, shared principles and objectives exist for all interventions. In particular, it emphasizes the need to integrate conservation activities into a coherent framework of development and planning policies at the regional urban level. The properties to be protected comprise physical and material aspects, including streets and blocks of buildings, relationships between buildings and green spaces, formal and decorative elements associated with single edifices, historic viewsheds, and relationships with the surrounding context. Creating awareness among residents and their direct participation are considered integral to programming activities and implementation of the conservation plan. The charter ends with a list of appropriate methods and instruments for ensuring protection and suitable utilization of the historic areas in the broadest context of contemporary cities.

The Vienna Memorandum on World Heritage and Contemporary Architecture: Managing the Historic Urban Landscape, 2005

This is the result of a meeting of six hundred experts and professionals organized in Vienna by the Center for World Heritage under the auspices of UNESCO. The meeting stemmed from the need to establish appraisal criteria for the examination (and reexamination) of historic cities nominated for or already included in the World Heritage List in response to concerns regarding the insertion of modern architecture in historic urban contexts.

Central among the themes contained in the memorandum is the urgent need to grant significant attention to structural and environmental aspects of the historic urban context (morphology, typology, materials, uses, etc.). In this regard, the concept "historic urban landscape" was introduced to designate values of cohesion, continuity, and properties that bond residents to their environment, which must be analyzed and reconstructed before implementing eventual urban planning and development transformations. Particularly criticized over the course of the meeting was the addition of tall buildings in historic contexts in northern Europe that threaten the latter's spatial integrity and alter contextual and visual relationships. Particularly stressed was the need for a profound understanding of the history, culture, and architecture of historic cities instead of an undiscriminating acceptance of independently conceived architectural models. Future evaluation of the transformation of historic areas should therefore be framed in a general management plan, which contains analysis, framework laws, construction regulations, and implementation mechanisms provided by the Operation Guidelines for the Implementation of the World Heritage Convention. Eventual insertions of contemporary architecture must furthermore be preceded by an assessment of their impact on the historic urban context.

Convention for the Safeguarding of Intangible Cultural Heritage, 2003

The initial recommendations of 1989 (Recommendation on the Safeguarding of Traditional Culture and Folklore became the object of an international convention promoted by UNESCO with the goal of defining the measures that member states must implement to safeguard intangible cultural heritage (ICH). It adds cosmological conceptions and spiritual practices of indigenous groups to the first definition of that which constitutes this heritage, together with their associated material elements and rituals. This expansion reflects the priorities of many communities in various parts of the world whose beliefs and practices, long marginalized, are today being rediscovered and appreciated. The convention confirms the action strategies already specified in the preceding recommendations for protection of intangible heritage.

Recommendation on the Historic Urban Landscape, 2011

Adopted November 10, 2011, by UNESCO's General Conference, this Recommendation was the first document focusing on the urban historic environment since the Recommendations Concerning the Safeguarding and Contemporary Role of Historic Areas adopted in Nairobi in 1976. The document expands on many of the subjects and themes first identified and debated during the preparation of the Vienna Memorandum of 2005, including the very concept "historic urban landscape." At the same time, while recognizing the relevance of all previous pronouncements on the subject, the Recommendation explicitly refers to the urgent need to address new challenges and threats to the urban heritage stemming from rapid and uncontrolled urbanization, mass tourism, market exploitation of historic resources, and climate change. These challenges can only be addressed in ways that "better integrate and frame urban heritage conservation strategies within the larger goals of overall sustainable development."

As defined by UNESCO (paragraphs 8 and 9), "The historic urban landscape is the urban area understood as the result of a historic layering of cultural and natural values and attributes, extending beyond the notion of 'historic centre' or 'ensemble' to include the broader urban context and its geographical setting. This wider context includes . . . topography, geomorphology, hydrology and natural features, its built environment[,] . . . its infrastructure above and below ground, its open spaces and gardens, its land use patterns and spatial organization, perceptions and visual relationships[,] . . . [including] social and cultural practices and values, economic processes and the intangible dimensions of heritage as related to diversity and identity." Although both the Nairobi Recommendations and the preceding Amsterdam Declaration on Integrated Conservation had strongly advocated the need for a holistic, integrated approach to urban conservation practice, in reality this approach proved to be illusory, partially because of the disconnect between the various public and private actors engaged in the management and transformation of heritage areas. The HUL approach (as it is often referred to) sought to catalyze a process of *actual* integration of efforts and actions by all concerned, including heritage conservation organizations, public institutions, and private entities, including private owners and property developers. Such coordination is undoubtedly necessary, but to date it has remained a fairly elusive goal that the HUL approach proposes to address more explicitly and directly than any previous international pronouncement on the subject. From a holistic standpoint, the HUL process assumed that conservation was more than safeguarding physical assets; instead, taking inspiration from a multitude of efforts to protect the intangible heritage (embodied in the 2003 Convention), the landscape approach focused on the entire social and cultural environment, where local community values—and local solutions—would be validated under the umbrella of "sustainability," as ratified in 2016 at the UNESCO's Habitat III conference in Quito, Ecuador.

Since HUL's promulgation, an important challenge has been to "operationalize" the Recommendation's ambitious goals to ensure that both local and national governments take specific actions to achieve a more effective integration of policies in historic urban areas for the benefit of all stakeholders. One kind of answer has been to look at positive precedents—such as Ballarat (Australia), Hangzhou (China), or Rawalpindi (Pakistan)—where local governments have been attempting to implement the HUL approach. A second answer stems from specific recommendations by UNESCO that seek to distill the HUL process into a number of practical steps:

1. Undertake a full assessment of resources;
2. Use participatory planning to determine conservation aims and actions;
3. Assess the vulnerability of urban heritage to socioeconomic pressures and climate change;
4. Integrate urban heritage values into a wider framework of urban development;
5. Prioritize policies and actions for conservation and development;
6. Establish public-private partnerships and local management frameworks; and
7. Develop mechanisms for coordination among varied stakeholders.[1]

Roughly coincident with the HUL Recommendation was the Valletta Principles for the Safeguarding and Management of Historic Cities, Towns and Urban Areas, adopted by the 17th ICOMOS General Assembly in Paris, two weeks after UNESCO ratified HUL.

Other Regional and National Documents Related to Urban Conservation

A number of other charters and pronouncements have been created to tailor urban conservation policies to specific needs and requirements at the regional or country level. These have enriched the general debate on urban conservation and have often introduced new perspectives on themes and notions that too often have been based exclusively on Western values. Below is a list of the principal ones.

- The Itaipava Principles, Brazil (1987)
- Fez Charter (1993), Organization of World Heritage Cities (OWHC)
- The Charter of European Sustainable Cities and Towns Towards Sustainability, also known as the Aalborg Charter, Denmark (1994)
- Bergen Protocol (1995), OWHC
- Charter on the Built Vernacular Heritage (1999), CIAV (International Committee for Vernacular Architecture)
- Charter for the Conservation of Historic Towns and Settlements of Japan (also known as the Machinami Charter), Japan ICOMOS (2000)
- China Principles for the Conservation of Heritage Sites (2015), China ICOMOS
- Hoi An Declaration on Urban Heritage Conservation and Development in Asia (2017)

Notes

1. These seven action measures are outlined in UNESCO's *New Life for Historic Cities;* see http://whc.unesco.hul.

About the Editors

Jeff Cody is an architectural historian with a background in historic preservation planning. His professional degrees are from Amherst College (BA) and Cornell University (MA and PhD). Beginning in the mid-1980s at Cornell, Cody began more intense research on twentieth-century architectural and urban history in China, which initially led to his teaching in Cornell's Graduate Program in Historic Preservation Planning (1989–95) and then to his teaching architectural history and elective courses in architectural and urban conservation at the Chinese University of Hong Kong (1995–2004). While teaching and researching historical issues related to Chinese urbanism and conservation, he was an occasional consultant on historic impact assessments and, from 2001 to 2004, a member of Hong Kong's Antiquities Advisory Board. Cody became a senior project specialist at the Getty Conservation Institute in 2004, when he began coordinating a series of conservation training activities, mainly for Southeast Asian conservation professionals engaged in built heritage but also for mayors of World Heritage cities and archaeologists in Tunisia and Southeast Asia. As a fellow at the American Academy in Rome in 2016, he researched urban conservation efforts in Italy after World War II. At the GCI, Cody directs "Old Cities, New Challenges," an urban conservation training course in Penang, Malaysia, for heritage professionals from ASEAN countries. He is the author of *Building in China: Henry Murphy's "Adaptive Architecture"* (2001) and *Exporting American Architecture, 1870–2000* (2003) and coeditor of *Chinese Architecture and the Beaux-Arts* (2011) and *Brush & Shutter: Early Photography in China* (2011).

Francesco Siravo is an Italian architect specializing in historic preservation and town planning. He received his professional degrees from the University of Rome, La Sapienza, and specialized in historic preservation at the College of Europe, Bruges, and Columbia University, New York. Since 1991, he has worked for the Historic Cities Programme of the Aga Khan Trust for Culture, a foundation promoting urban conservation in the Muslim world, and has been responsible for major planning and building projects in cities that include Zanzibar, Cairo, Samarkand, Lahore, and Mostar. Before joining the Historic Cities Programme, he consulted for local municipalities as well as governmental and international organizations, including UNESCO, ICCROM, the World Bank, and the GCI. Previous work includes participation in the preparation of conservation plans for the historical areas of Rome, Lucca, Urbino, and Anagni in Italy and for the old town of Lamu in Kenya. He has been visiting lecturer at the University of Rome (2005–8), the University of Pennsylvania (1996–97), and ICCROM (1987–92) and written books, articles, and papers on various architectural conservation and town planning subjects, including *Zanzibar: A Plan for the Historic Stone Town* (1996) and *Planning Lamu: Conservation of an East African Seaport* (1986).

Illustration Credits

Plate I.0; p. 53: Private Collection. Photo © The Fine Art Society, London, UK / Bridgeman Images. **Plate I.1a:** Su concessione dell'Archivio Cederna - Capo di Bove, Parco Archeologico dell'Appia Antica, MiBACT, /1206.2/1206.2_000_000_005. **Plate I.1b:** Su concessione dell'Archivio Cederna - Capo di Bove, Parco Archeologico dell'Appia Antica, MiBACT, /1206.2/1206.2_000_000_006. **Plate I.2:** Su concessione dell'Archivio Cederna - Capo di Bove, Parco Archeologico dell'Appia Antica, MiBACT, F.44/F.44_013. **Plates I.3, VII.3:** Manohar Devadoss, *Multiple Facets of My Madurai* (Chennai: EastWest Books (Madras) Pvt. Ltd., 2007), p. 63, p. 113. **Plate I.4:** ÖNB / Wien, Cod. 2554. **Plate I.5; reading 12 figs. 1–3:** © Vibhuti Sachdev and Giles Tillotson. **Plate I.7; p. 126:** Photo Charles J. Sharp, Wikimedia, CC-BY-SA 3.0. **Plates I.8, V.10:** Wikimedia Commons. **Plate I.10:** Framepool RS. **Plate I.12:** Jörg Müller, Hier fällt ein Haus, dort steht ein Kran und ewig droht der Baggerzahn oder Die Veränderung der Stadt. © Fischer Kinder-und Jugendbuch GmbH, Frankfurt am Main 2018. Originally published by Sauerländer Verlag in 1976. **Plate II.0:** Photo Scala / Art Resource, NY. **Plate II.1:** Palazzo Pubblico, Siena, Italy De Agostini Picture Library / Bridgeman Images. **Plate II.2:** Paul Mellon Collection, in Honor of the 50th Anniversary of the National Gallery of Art Courtesy National Gallery of Art, Washington. **Plate II.3:** Prints & Photographs Division, Library of Congress, LC-DIG-pga-03399. **Plate II.4:** Courtesy of Bonnie Campbell Lilienfeld. **Plate II.6:** Newberry Library, Chicago Ayer 655.51.C8. **Plate II.7:** Klaus Herdeg papers, 1963–1992, Avery Architectural & Fine Arts Library, Columbia University. **Plates II.8, VI.5:** Georg Gerster / Science Source. **Plate II.9:** © George Steinmetz. **Plate II.10; reading 13 fig. 1:** Courtesy Professor Yinong Xu. **Plate II.12:** Getty Research Institute, Los Angeles (2003.R.22). **Plate II.13:** www.lacma.org. Gift of Carl Holmes (M.71.100.152). **Plate II.14:** Courtesy of the University of Texas Libraries, The University of Texas at Austin. **Plate II.15:** Gisele Taxil. **Plate II.16:** © Gordon Clarke, Institute of Nomadic Architecture. **Plate II.17:** Drawing by Francesco Siravo. **Plate II.18:** Johnny Miller / Unequal Scenes. **Plate II.19:** Nigel Pavitt, *Kenya: A Country in the Making 1880–1940*. **Plate III.0; p. 198:** Cris Foto / Shutterstock. **Plate III.1:** Pierre-Ambroise Richebourg / THE IMAGE WORKS, INC. **Plate III.2:** Getty Research Institute, Los Angeles (NA440.P85). **Plate III.3:** Ruskin Foundation (Ruskin Library, Lancaster University). **Plate III.4:** © CNAC / MNAM / Dist. RMN-Grand Palais / Art Resource, NY. **Plate III.5:** Getty Research Institute, Los Angeles (2012.PR.17). **Plate III.6:** Richard Peter / Deutsche Fotothek / picture-alliance / dpa / AP Images. **Plates III.7, V.6:** © F.L.C. / ADAGP, Paris / Artists Rights Society (ARS), New York 2019. **Plate III.8:** REUTERS / Ghassan Najjar. **Plate III.9:** Courtesy of MTA Bridges and Tunnels Special Archive. **Plate III.10:** UCLA Department of Geography, Benjamin and Gladys Thomas Air Photo Archives, Fairchild Aerial Surveys Collection. **Plate III.11:** Jerome De Perlinghi, Rumania, Bucarest, 1989, "A lonely Man walking down the street of Bucarest." **Plate III.14:** Photo Bianca Bosker. From *Original Copies: Architectural Mimicry in Contemporary China* (2013). **Plate III.15:** Splash News / Alamy Stock Photo. **Plate III.16:** China Photos / Getty Images News / Getty Images. **Plate III.17:** Photo Li Jilu, China Photographers Association. **Plate III.18:** f11photo / Shutterstock. **Plate IV.0; p. 209:** Getty Research Institute, Los Angeles (88-B10751). **Plate IV.1:** Fonds Pineau. SIAF / Cité de l'architecture et du patrimoine / Archives d'architecture du XXe siècle. **Plate IV.2:** Getty Research Institute, Los Angeles (93.R.94). **Plate IV.3:** Tan Yeow Wooi. **Plate IV.4:** Photo by Alexander Synaptic (synapticism.com). **Plate IV.5:** *Palladio*, Fasciolo III-IV, Lugio-Dicembre 1959 , Roma, De Luca Editore, p. 182–83. **Plate IV.6a:** Special Collections, J. Willard Marriott Library, The University of Utah. Sanborn Map Company. (1911). Salt Lake City, Utah. **Plate IV.6b:** Georeferenced Salt Lake City Sanborn, 1911: sheet 125. Created by Justin Bruce Sorensen, J. Willard Marriott Library, University of Utah. Map data © 2018 Google. **Plate IV.7:** © OMA. Digital Image © The Museum of Modern Art / Licensed by Scala / Art Resource, NY. **Plate IV.8:** David Rumsey Map Collection, www.davidrumsey.com, CC BY-NC-SA 3.0. **Plate IV.10:** Courtesy of Tokyo Metropolitan Library Special Collections Room. **Plate V.0; p. 400:** © 2019 Artists Rights Society (ARS), New York / Bildrecht, Vienna. ©The Bernard Rudofsky Estate Vienna / Bildrecht.at. **Plates V.3–4:** © Anna Maria Bozzola Insolera, 2013. **Plate V.5:** Roberta Brandes Gratz. **Plate V.7:** richardjohnson.ca. **Plate V.8:** Tom Harris © Hedrich Blessing, Courtesy of Rebuild Foundation. **Plate V.9:** AJ LaTrace. **Plate V.11:** © Michael Moran / OTTO Archive, LLC. **Plate VI.1:** Courtesy of the West Kowloon Cultural District Authority. **Plate VI.6:** Ben Bryant / Shutterstock.com. **Plate VI.7:** Sekondi Beachfront, Sekondi-Takoradi, Ghana.

© 2011 Christiane Badgley. **Plate VI.9:** Chintung Lee / Shutterstock.com. **Plate VII.0; p. 532:** Library of Congress, Prints and Photographs Division, LC-DIG-ppmsca-31363. **Plate VII.1:** Yu Yuan Chia. **Plate VII.2b:** © Rui Pinheiro. **Plates VII.5a–b:** © James and Karla Murray. **Plate VIII.0; p. 578:** Photo © Navjot Singh, British Writer and Photographer. **Plate VIII.2:** Karol Kozlowski Premium RM Collection / Alamy Stock Photo. **Plate VIII.4:** LOOK Die Bildagentur der Fotografen GmbH / Alamy Stock Photo. **Plate VIII.5:** © 2019 Chris Burden / licensed by The Chris Burden Estate and Artists Rights Society (ARS), New York. Digital Image © 2019 Museum Associates / LACMA. Licensed by Art Resource, NY. **Reading 5 fig. 1:** Fotocielo, Rome. **Reading 10 fig. 1:** España. Ministerio de Defensa. Instituto de Historia y Cultura Militar. Archivo General Militar de Madrid. **Reading 11 figs. 1–3:** Stefano Bianca, "Urban Form in the Arab World—Past and Present." **Reading 14 figs. 1–3:** © Barrie Shelton. Reproduced by permission of Taylor & Francis Books UK. **Reading 26 fig. 1:** Bibliothèque nationale de France. **Reading 29 fig. 1:** "Building the City: 1975–95," in *Urban Forms: The Death and Life of the Urban Block*, by Philippe Panerai, Jean Castex, and Jean-Charles Depaule; English edition and additional material by Ivor Samuels; translated by Olga Vitale Samuels (Oxford: Architectural Press, 2004), 158–64, 166–67. Figure 60, p. 160. **Reading 29 fig. 2:** "Building the City: 1975–95," in *Urban Forms: The Death and Life of the Urban Block*, by Philippe Panerai, Jean Castex, and Jean-Charles Depaule; English edition and additional material by Ivor Samuels; translated by Olga Vitale Samuels (Oxford: Architectural Press, 2004), 158–64, 166–67. Figure 61, p. 161. **Reading 29 fig. 3:** "Building the City: 1975–95," in *Urban Forms: The Death and Life of the Urban Block*, by Philippe Panerai, Jean Castex, and Jean-Charles Depaule; English edition and additional material by Ivor Samuels; translated by Olga Vitale Samuels (Oxford: Architectural Press, 2004), 158–64, 166–67. Figure 62, p. 163. **Reading 30 fig. 1:** © Gordon Cullen Estate. **Reading 32 fig. 2:** Archiv Volkmar Eidloth. **Reading 34 fig. 1:** Published with permission of the Strategic Information and Research Development Centre. **Reading 39 figs. 1–3:** Image courtesy Università Iuav di Venezia, Archivio Progetti, Astengo Archive. **Reading 40 fig. 1:** Photo courtesy Donald Insall Associates, Architects. **Reading 40 fig. 2:** Aerial Drawing courtesy Donald Insall Associates, Architects. **Reading 43 figs. 1–9, 13–16:** Courtesy Pier Luigi Cervellati, Studio Cervellati. **Reading 46 figs. 1–3:** © Rafael Moneo Office. **Reading 53 figs. 1–3:** © Sue Anne Tay. **Reading 54 figs. 1–2:** Courtesy Dr. Carmen C. M. Tsui. **Reading 58 fig. 1:** Donovan Rypkema, President, Heritage Strategies International. **Reading 59 figs. 1–2:** Drawings by Julian Smith. **Reading 67 fig. 1:** © Daniel Gonçalves.

Index

Note: *Italicized* page numbers refer to illustrations.

C

D

E

F

G

H

T

U